**United Nations Library on Transnational Corporations**

Volume 2

# TRANSNATIONAL CORPORATIONS: A HISTORICAL PERSPECTIVE

## Edited by Geoffrey Jones

General editor: John H. Dunning

London and New York
published for and on behalf of the United Nations,
Transnational Corporations and Management Division,
Department of Economic and Social Development

First published 1993
by Routledge
11 New Fetter Lane, London EC4P 4EE

Simultaneously published in the USA and Canada
by Routledge
a division of Routledge, Chapman and Hall, Inc.
29 West 35th Street, New York, NY 10001

Typeset by Leaper & Gard Ltd, Bristol, England
Printed and bound in Great Britain by
Mackays of Chatham PLC, Chatham, Kent

*British Library Cataloguing in Publication Data*

*A catalogue reference for this book is available from the British Library.*

ISBN 0-415-08535-7 (Vol. 2)
ISBN 0-415-08554-3 (Set A)
ISBN 0-415-08559-4 (All 20 volumes)

*Library of Congress Cataloging in Publication Data
has been applied for.*

ISBN 0-415-08535-7
ISBN 0-415-08554-3 (Set A)
ISBN 0-415-08559-4 (All 20 volumes)

# Contents

**Part Two:  Concepts**

**Part Three:  Impact and responses**

# Preface

The importance of transnational corporations and the globalization of production are now well recognized. Transnational corporations have become central actors of the world economy and, in linking foreign direct investment, trade, technology and finance, they are a driving force of economic growth. Their impact on the economic and social welfare of developed and developing countries is both widespread and critical.

It is one of the functions of the Transnational Corporations and Management Division (formerly the United Nations Centre on Transnational Corporations) – the focal point in the United Nations for all issues relating to transnational corporations – to undertake and promote research on transnational corporations to contribute to a better understanding of those firms and their impact. Over the past thirty years, research on this phenomenon has mushroomed, and hundreds of books and reports, as well as thousands of papers, have been published. It is the principal purpose of this twenty-volume *United Nations Library of Transnational Corporations* to distil, summarize and comment on some of the more influential of those writings on the role of transnational corporations in the world economy. In particular, the contributions in the *United Nations Library* deal with four main issues: the determinants of the global activities of transnational corporations, their organizational structures and strategies, their interactions with the economies and legal systems of the countries in which they operate and the policies that governments pursue towards those corporations. The twenty volumes are intended to cover a wide range of topics that embrace economic, organizational and legal issues.

To accomplish that task, the Centre assembled a distinguished group of editors, who were commissioned to select the seminal contributions to their subject areas published over the past 20 to 30 years. They were also asked to prepare comprehensive bibliographies of writings on their subjects for inclusion in the volumes, and state-of-the-art introductions that summarize the development of their subjects, review the most important current issues and speculate about future work. We hope that the result in each case is a volume that provides a succinct, yet comprehensive, overview of the subject to which it is devoted.

It is entirely appropriate that the second volume of this series should be devoted to the historical development of the activities of transnational corporations, and particularly to some of its consequences for the economic development and restructuring of countries in the late nineteenth and early twentieth centuries. To most international business scholars, that is a neglected area of research. Yet, in recent years, it has become a major fascination of business historians and applied economists. As the contributions in the present volume show, many of today's most topical and contentious issues involving transnational corporations were no less debated by previous generations of researchers and practitioners; modern analysts and policy-makers neglect their findings and experiences at their peril.

Geoffrey Jones, the editor of the present volume, is Professor of Business History in the Department of Economics of the University of Reading, United Kingdom; he has written and researched extensively on the history of the activities of transnational corporations. In the introduction, he surveys the very considerable research on this subject, and describes how it is helping to shed new light on previously unknown aspects of the activities of transnational corporations. It is a volume which is to be highly commended to scholars, business persons and policy-makers, not least because it takes a historical perspective of many of the issues with which other writers deal in later volumes of this series.

New York, May 1992

Karl P. Sauvant
Chief, Research and
Policy Analysis Branch
Transnational Corporations and
Management Division

John H. Dunning
General Editor of
United Nations Library on
Transnational Corporations

# Acknowledgements

The editors and publishers would like to thank the following publishers and other organisations for permission to reprint copyright material: Avebury, Gower Publishing Group; *Business and Economic History*, College of William and Mary; *Business History Review*, Harvard University; Frank Cass Publishers; *Harvard Business Review*, Harvard Business School; *Japanese Yearbook on Business History*, Tohoku University; *Journal of Economic History*, Cambridge University Press.

Acknowledgement is also due to: Basil Blackwell Inc.; and Basil Blackwell Publishers.

# Introduction: Transnational Corporations – A Historical Perspective

Geoffrey Jones

Over the past decades, research into the history of transnational corporations (TNC) has emerged as one of the most exciting and dynamic areas of the study of international business. When TNCs were first identified by economists in the 1960s, it was assumed (with a few notable exceptions) that they were a post-1945 phenomenon originating in the United States. Historical research has shown this not to be the case. Even in the late nineteenth century there were hundreds of TNCs in the manufacturing sector, while international business activity involving foreign direct investment can be traced back to the Middle Ages in Europe. However, establishing the chronology of TNC development has been the least important aspect of historical research on the phenomenon. More important has been the contribution of scholars to identifying the diversity of institutional and contractual forms that have and do exist in international business; to bringing a wealth of empirical data into debates on the role of TNCs which, so often, are clouded by prejudice and ignorance; and to providing a testing ground whereby theoretical models developed by economists and others can be judged against in-depth research on actual events.

Two main academic disciplines have made a distinctive contribution to historical research on TNCs. The initial pioneering work, and much subsequent analysis especially of aggregate data, was undertaken by economists with an interest in change over time. In the United States, government agencies and academics began to distinguish between portfolio and foreign direct investment in the interwar years; as a result, studies of direct investment by United States corporations appeared.[1] During the 1950s and 1960s, concern over the consequences of inward direct investment on host economies led to studies of the subject in the United Kingdom, Canada and elsewhere. The work of the British economist John Dunning deserves special mention in this respect. In 1958, Dunning published a monograph on United States direct investment in British manufacturing industry. Although that study did not use the term "transnational corporations" or "multinational corporations", which had yet to be coined, it carefully documented the origins and impact of United States investment in the United Kingdom back to the mid-nineteenth century.[2] Much of Dunning's subsequent work has shed light on TNC history, but particular mention should be made of his estimates, in 1971, of the foreign direct capital stock in the United States, and of his 1983 estimates of changes in the level and structure of the world capital stock over the past 100 years.[3] Among other things, those latter estimates confirmed the view of P. Svedberg[4] and others that a high percentage of international investment in the nineteenth century was direct, rather than portfolio.

Dunning suggested that the stock of accumulated foreign direct investment in 1914 amounted to $14,302 million, or over a third of total world foreign investment. He estimated that the stock had risen to $26,350 million by 1938, before soaring in the 1950s to reach $66 billion in 1960. Before the Second World War, at least 60 per cent of this foreign direct investment had gone to developing countries, mainly in Latin America and Asia, and was largely located in the extractive sector. By contrast, after the Second World War, the proportion of foreign direct investment located in the developing world fell sharply to around 32 per cent by 1960. Possibly the most interesting aspect of Dunning's estimates was his data on countries of origin. Dunning showed that, before the Second World War, the United Kingdom had been the world's largest foreign direct investor, accounting for 45 per cent of the stock in 1914 and 40 per cent in 1938. The era of American predominance came only after the Second World War. By 1960, the United States accounted for 49 per cent of the stock, and the United Kingdom 16 per cent. However, the United Kingdom continued through the 1960s and 1970s to be the world's second largest foreign direct investor, despite the relative decline of its economy.

**Early Research**

*The History of United States-based Transnational Corporations*

The estimates of the overall size of foreign direct investment raise the issue of what corporate form it took. Much of the initial research on the historical evolution of the TNC was undertaken by applied economists. The work of Raymond Vernon at Harvard Business School, who in the 1960s, undertook a major project to study United States TNCs, was critical. In the early 1970s, two of his students, John Stopford and Lawrence Franko, published the first surveys of the historical evolution of British and Continental European TNCs.[5] The problem for these early studies was an acute shortage of accurate historical data. Stopford could locate only 14 British manufacturing TNCs active before 1914, and therefore focused his analysis on why British manufacturers had apparently been slower than their American equivalents to become TNCs. That, in fact, proved not to be the case.

Franko discovered a more dynamic picture in Continental Europe. He established that at least 37 Continental companies had created foreign manufacturing affiliates before 1914. The most extensive transnational operations were by such German electrical and chemical companies as Siemens, Bosch, Hoechst, Bayer and Agfa; but Swiss (Ciba, Geigy, Nestlé), French (St. Gobain), Belgian (Solvay) and Swedish (SKF) firms were also included in his lists of pioneering TNCs before 1914. Subsequently, doubts were raised on the methodology of this research. Stopford and Franko selected their enterprises on the basis of the largest firms active in 1971, and then traced their histories backwards. That meant that many early TNCs were missed, because they were no longer active in 1971. Nevertheless, that research had opened up a new and exciting world in the history of business enterprise.

During the 1970s, the challenge of tracing the origins of TNCs was taken up by business historians. The study of the historical evolution of business was well established by the interwar years, especially at Harvard Business School. The subject originated with studies of single firms, and the case study approach based on in-depth research into confidential corporate archives has remained the most characteristic feature of business history. From the 1960s onward, however, a series of books by the United States scholar Alfred D. Chandler on the rise of modern corporations pushed the subject more towards generalizations and concepts. Chandler related the rise of large corporations in the United States from the late nineteenth century to changes in markets and technologies. He argued that the development of professional managerial hierarchies within a multi-divisional corporate structure was critical to the success of the mass production and science-based industries which began to appear in the decades before the First World War. More recently, Chandler has applied his model beyond the United States, suggesting, for example, that many of the problems of British business in the twentieth century stemmed from its failure to develop appropriate managerial structures. Chandler's work has had a profound impact on the methodology of business historians, including those working on TNCs. He also explicitly addressed the question of the managerial factors influencing the growth of TNCs, especially in his latest book, *Scale and Scope.*[6]

However, it was another business historian from the United States, Mira Wilkins, who has perhaps made the most significant contribution to our knowledge and understanding of the history of TNCs. In 1970 and 1974, she published two seminal books which traced the evolution of United States TNCs from their beginnings to the present day. These books exploded any view that the TNC was a post-1945 phenomenon. Wilkins discovered that, as early as the 1850s, Colt, the United States gun manufacturer, had built a factory in Britain, but it had failed. The first sustained United States transnational investment had come in the following decade, when Singer Sewing Machines built a factory in Glasgow in 1867. During the following decades, many more United States companies, especially in the machinery and food sectors, built foreign factories. By 1914, Wilkins showed that over 40 United States companies, including such well-known names as Coca-Cola, Gillette, Heinz, Quaker Oats and Ford, had factories overseas, often in Canada or the United Kingdom.

In her second volume, Wilkins traced the growth of United States transnational corporations from the First World War until the early 1970s. The 1920s saw the three leading United States car companies – Ford, General Motors and Chrysler – become large-scale TNCs. In 1929, Ford began construction of the largest car factory in the world at Dagenham, near London, United Kingdom, while in 1929 General Motors purchased Opel of Germany, one of that country's 10 largest industrial enterprises. In addition to surveying extractive TNCs, Wilkins also examined early United States direct investment in utilities and services, a pioneering aspect of her research which has yet to receive adequate recognition. In the 1920s, ITT began operating telephone systems in a number of Latin American countries, such as Mexico, Uruguay and Argentina, and in 1924 it took over the entire Spanish telephone system and, in the process, became the largest United States investor in Spain. By 1929, the company was employing 95,000 people outside the United States. The airline, Pan American, also began transnational activities during that decade. In 1928, it purchased a Mexican airline, followed by a Colombian airline in 1929.

In the 1930s and 1940s, economic depression, exchange controls and war dramatically slowed the growth of United States TNCs. However, there was some "enforced" investment. Because profits were trapped by exchange controls, United States direct investment in manufacturing in Germany increased by nearly 50 per cent between 1929 and 1940, while it fell by the same amount in France and was stagnant in the United Kingdom. After the Second World War, Wilkins showed the resumption of United States transnational activity, followed by its rapid growth beginning in the 1950s.

Wilkins's volumes are distinguished by their comprehensive range and by the depth of their material. She traced the motives and experiences of individual companies, showing the diversity of international business activity. The books were written in a period when there was much criticism of TNCs in general, and United States TNCs in particular. By examining individual cases, she de-mythologized the subject, showing, for example, that the risks of international business could lead to failure and disinvest-ment, and that TNCs were rarely powerful enough to challenge national sovereignty.[7]

*The European and Japanese Dimension*

The one problem with the Wilkins volumes was that, by providing such rich data on the historical experience of the United States, they reinforced the conventional view that the origin of TNCs was in the United States. Wilkins, however, perceived that this was a distortion of reality and, in 1977, she published a *cri de coeur* calling for European business historians to investigate the history of European-based TNCs.[8]

In the 1980s, a flood of publications answered her call. The United Kingdom, which it soon became apparent was the world's biggest TNC investor before 1945, received most attention. A series of articles and books by Geoffrey Jones and Stephen Nicholas mapped out the general outlines of the history of British TNC investment in the manufacturing sector before the Second World War.[9] The Stopford view that the United Kingdom was a belated transnational investor was overturned. That research established that the first manufacturing British-based TNCs had developed in the 1880s, and that, by 1914, there were probably hundreds of British-owned TNCs operating factories in other countries of Europe, the United States and the settler countries of the Empire.

The pioneer British manufacturing TNCs included some of that country's largest companies, such as Lever Brothers (soap), J & P Coats (cotton thread) and Dunlop (tyres). Some of these firms had widespread foreign manufacturing networks. J & P Coats and Lever Brothers, for example, owned and managed factories in the United States, Canada, South Africa, Australia, Russia, Switzerland, France and Germany. Subsidiaries of British firms monopolized the United States artificial silk industry, as well as the United States and Russian cotton-thread industries before 1914. Nor was transnational activity confined to the United Kingdom's largest manufacturing companies. In the United Kingdom, unlike the United States, but as in Sweden and some other European countries, small and medium-sized enterprises made foreign direct investments. For example, the Gramophone Company, manufacturers of records and gramophones, had factories in India, Russia, France, Spain and Austria by 1914.

In the interwar years, British transnational manufacturing expanded further. A new generation of companies made their first foreign direct investments. Prominent among these were the United Kingdom's largest chocolate and confectionery manufacturers, Cadbury and Rowntree, which erected overseas factories in Australia, Canada, New Zealand, Ireland, South Africa and Germany between the wars. Jones and Nicholas have both suggested that, by the interwar years, there was a distinct bias towards investment within the British Empire, and this trend was maintained in the early post-Second World War period. By 1960, British TNCs were very heavily clustered in Australia, New Zealand, South Africa and Canada, while there was remarkably little investment in the rest of Europe. In 1960,

British TNCs had more assets in Ghana than in the Federal Republic of Germany. From the 1960s onward, however, there was a re-orientation towards the United States and Europe.

Germany was the third most active home economy for TNCs before the First World War, and beginning in the late 1970s a series of articles and books by Peter Hertner established the main outline of German TNC activity, which was heavily clustered in the chemical and electrical sectors. The Siemens electrical enterprise established a factory in St. Petersburg (Leningrad) as early as 1855, followed by a manufacturing subsidiary in the United Kingdom in 1863. A complicated network of wholly-owned subsidiaries, partnerships and joint ventures developed.[10] Research on individual industries has revealed the extensive nature of this early German foreign direct investment. Schröter, for example, has established that German chemical companies had at least 153 production subsidiaries abroad in 1913.[11]

The early German TNCs, however, were devastated by the First World War, which resulted in the sequestration of many subsidiaries. In the United Kingdom, for example, the Siemens subsidiary was sequestrated and given to competing British interests. The same happened to Bayer's subsidiary in the United States, which had pioneered the production of aspirin in the United States in the 1900s. This venture was seized by the United States authorities and sold to Sterling Products. In the interwar years, capital-short German companies resorted to international business strategies other than foreign direct investment, including exporting, participation in international cartels and alliances with other companies.

Subsequent research has established that early TNC activity was by no means confined to the United States, the United Kingdom and Germany. The pre-1939 history of Swedish[12] and Japanese[13] TNCs has been traced, as well as those of many other countries.[14] An outstanding feature of this research has been the unusual degree of international contact and collaboration between scholars. One result is that much of the substantive research in this area has been published in volumes originating at international conferences.[15]

Transnational activity by certain small European economies, such as Switzerland and Sweden, was particularly noteworthy. The first Swedish firm to start manufacturing abroad was a cork company, Wicander, which established factories in Finland and Germany in the 1870s and 1880s. The predecessor to Alfa Laval, today one of the world's largest producers of dairy and barn equipment, established a factory in the United States in the 1890s which, by 1910, contributed almost three quarters of the Swedish parent company's profits. Other Swedish companies which had adopted a transnational strategy before 1930 included Electrolux (domestic electrical appliances), SKF (ball bearings), L.M. Ericsson (telephone equipment and operation) and Swedish Match (matches). The transnational activities of

Swedish Match were particularly extensive. By 1930, it controlled about 40 per cent of total world match production, with factories in numerous countries. During the 1920s, that group had an extremely aggressive acquisitions policy, which included the purchase of many Japanese match companies. This was combined with extensive market agreements and the negotiation of match monopoly agreements with various, mainly European, governments, often in return for loans to those governments. Swedish Matches' history in the interwar years provides an immensely valuable store of data about the use of strategic alliances and collusive agreements in international business.

By contrast, Japanese transnational manufacturing investment was modest until the 1970s, although Wilkins and others have shown it to be far from non-existent. As early as 1892, Kikkoman invested in soy sauce manufacturing in Denver, Colorado, to cater for the needs of Japanese emigrants. The main focus of Japanese interest before the Second World War was, however, in textile manufacture in China. This set a pattern for Japanese foreign direct investment, which continued to have a disproportionate bias both towards Asia and to the textile sector well into the 1970s.

Wilkins has recently greatly deepened our knowledge of the evolution of TNCs with the publication of a comprehensive study of foreign investment within the United States before 1914.[16] A second volume is planned on the post-1914 period. This industry-by-industry study has revealed the existence of hundreds of foreign manufacturing companies in the United States before 1914. However, she also examined foreign activity in extractives, utilities, services and banking, as well as portfolio investment. Wilkins's underlying theme, written at a time when United States public opinion was greatly worried at the scale of Japanese foreign direct investment in the United States, was the benefits that this foreign investment had brought. Foreign capital had opened up United States resources, introduced new technology and facilitated important substitution. The benefits derived by the United States economy from foreign investment, Wilkins argued, far surpassed the costs, and played a considerable role in making the United States the world's largest industrialized economy by 1914.

Coincidental with this research on TNCs and foreign direct investment, considerable historical work on overall foreign investment was conducted, including portfolio flows. The case of nineteenth-century United Kingdom, the world's largest creditor at that time, has attracted most attention. In recent years, the conventional estimate that British portfolio investment overseas in 1913 stood at around £3.7 billion has been challenged in a series of studies by D.C.M. Platt, who has sought to reduce the figure by as much as a third.[17] Platt's revisionism, however, has in turn been questioned by other prominent economic historians, such as Charles Feinstein.[18] There is much in this literature of interest to students of TNCs, but unfortunately the historical writers on portfolio investment have often neglected or been ignorant of the parallel literature on TNCs and direct investment. As late as 1987, for example, the London School of Economics economic historian W.P. Kennedy published a major study which sought to explain that the United Kingdom's relative decline in the decades before 1914 was, in part, due to capital market imperfections which diverted a high percentage of British savings into foreign investment. Kennedy's view that Victorian foreign investment was overwhelmingly portfolio, cautious and risk averse, simply ignored the work of Svedberg, Dunning, Wilkins and others.[19]

## Issues Emerging from Business History

### Corporate Forms

Many important issues have emerged from the research on the origins and growth of TNCs. It is apparent that there are considerable variations in the industrial distribution and management structures of TNCs from different countries, reflecting, in part, differences in the characteristics of their home economies.[20] Early German transnationals showed a tendency to invest in other Continental European economies. Early TNCs from the United States focused on Canada and the United Kingdom. German firms, as already noted, were prominent in the electrical and chemical sectors. The United States firms were often in food and machinery, and the British in consumer durables. At least before 1914, different countries differed in their propensity towards establishing multiplant operations. While the United States manufacturers often established a single plant in a foreign country, some European companies established multi-plant operations early in their transnational history.

It has become evident that early TNC activity took a variety of institutional forms, such as the "free-standing" companies observed by Wilkins in the case of pre-1914 British foreign direct investment,[21] and that direct investments, cartels and other forms of cross-border activity were seen by firms as alternative tactics in their overall international business strategies.[22] The "free-standing" concept has attracted particular attention. Wilkins demonstrated the existence of thousands of such firms in pre-1914 United Kingdom, which did not grow out of domestic operations, but were formed to manage a single investment. Typically, these ventures maintained a tiny office in the United Kingdom which supervised the overseas business. According to Wilkins, the small head offices and weak governance structures of these firms doomed them to extinction, at least in the United States, and most failed or were acquired by indigenous capital before the First World War. This interpretation and, in particular, the view that free-standing companies were a poor vehicle for international investment, has not found complete acceptance.[23]

The concept has, however, generated excitement from economists seeking to use transaction cost analysis to explain why alternative institutional and contractual arrangements are made in international business. Hennart has argued that free-standing companies were a means of internalizing the market for capital. Portfolio lending for certain activities, Hennart suggests, was subject to high transaction costs. It was almost useless to take simply the title to mines or agriculture investments as collateral, because they would have little value if things went wrong. Free-standing companies enabled lenders to monitor the use of their funds and exercise managerial control. They provided, Hennart suggests, a way to reduce the costs of transferring capital from Europe to the rest of the world for investments which had little collateral value. The proof, according to Hennart, is that this form of direct investment survived longer in countries with underdeveloped capital markets. By the 1920s, British free-standing companies had almost disappeared from the United States, but they survived in countries like Malaysia and Nigeria right up to the 1960s.[24]

In fact, much research is still needed on the demise of the free-standing company. Almost certainly, this form of international business activity continued beyond the First World War, even in the Americas. One example was Ultramar. This was a classic British free-standing company with a Board and little else in London, established to exploit oil fields in Venezuela. It was not, however, a product of the nineteenth century, but of the 1930s and, moreover, it did not fail or transmute into a more conventional TNC. During the 1950s and 1960s, Ultramar developed oil exploration and marketing activities in Canada, the United States, Indonesia and the North Sea. Operational management was exercised from offices in New York, while the Board in London continued in existence. This form of organization has been retained until the present day.[25]

Business historians have identified other unusual corporate forms. Jones identified "migrating" TNCs, which transferred their assets from their home countries over time, for example. This concept has been applied to the history of the giant British tobacco transnational corporation, BAT.[26] BAT was created in 1902 after the American Tobacco Company, the dominant United States firm in the industry at that time, attempted to enter the British cigarette market. British tobacco firms had amalgamated their interests to form the Imperial Tobacco Company in response to this threat. A truce was subsequently arranged, as part of which BAT was created to administer the two groups' export business. The new company became an extensive transnational investor, with large-scale manufacturing in China. Originally the majority of ownership was held by the American Tobacco Company, but by the end of the First World War ownership and control of BAT had fallen into the hands of the United States investors. It is unclear how common the phenomenon of the "migrating" TNC is, but at least one very large example can be identified in 1976. In that year ANZ, one of the United Kingdom's transnational banks, transferred its domicile from the

United Kingdom to Australia, where most of its business, but almost none of its equity, was located.[27]

## Performance

Business historians have also turned their attention to the question of the performance of direct investments. It has been suggested, for example, that although the United Kingdom was a prolific TNC investor before 1939, management and other problems made the subsequent performance of British-owned TNCs sub-optimal. Such research, however, raises complex problems of how to measure performance. Detailed accounting data on the financial performance of most TNC subsidiaries, at least before the 1960s, is unavailable. A full assessment of performance would, however, also have to include considerations of market share, non-financial benefits from foreign direct investment (such as technology transfer) and the counter-factual position of what would have happened if investments had not been undertaken.[28] Research on such matters has hardly begun.

## Explaining the Origin of the Activity of Transnational Corporations

Researchers have adopted two different approaches to explaining the origins of TNC activity. Most of the business historians active in the field, notably Wilkins, Hertner and Jones, began with the standard business history methodology of establishing the empirical "facts", often using corporate case studies, and then attempting to generalize from them. In particular, they emphasized the importance of trade protectionism in stimulating the emergence of TNCs. Few firms in the late nineteenth century wanted the risks of direct investment, but tariffs rendered an export strategy unviable. More generally, these business historians utilized a simple form of Dunning's eclectic paradigm, searching for the "advantages" held by TNCs which permitted their development. One of the most interesting developments of the 1980s was that, in a series of small working conferences on the "theory-and-history" theme (the results of which were published), these business historians came into direct contact with economists working on international business, notably those at the University of Reading, United Kingdom, such as Dunning and Mark Casson.[29] As a result of these contacts, by the 1990s, many business historians were making more use of such concepts as internalization in their work, and their writings were to some extent being integrated into mainstream international business research.

A second approach was to test existing models of TNC growth against historical evidence. Dunning himself ventured into this area.[30] Stephen Nicholas made explicit use of transactions-cost models which he tested against a large sample of British TNCs,[31] while Hennart, as already discussed, has been active in applying internalization models to the historical experience of foreign direct investment. That work has generally demonstrated the usefulness of theoretical models in real-time situations.

*An Historical Assessment of the Impact of the Activity of Transnational Corporations*

The nature of the impact of TNCs was initially neglected by business historians. That reflected their preoccupation with management structures and with the firm as a unit of analysis. In the 1970s, some pioneering historical work was undertaken on TNCs and technology transfer. That research has still not been developed to its full potential, although an interesting development came in 1986 when Casson published an article demonstrating how business history case studies could be used to test economic theories of the TNC in respect of technology transfer.[32]

Nevertheless, a historical literature has developed on the political and economic impact of TNCs on host economies in both the developing and developed world. A pioneering work was Fieldhouse's historical study of the role of the Anglo-Dutch TNC Unilever in a number of developing countries, published in 1978.[33] Subsequent studies have looked at the impact of foreign direct investment on the extractive industries of Spain in the late nineteenth century;[34] at TNCs in Chilean nitrates;[35] at the strategies, and their consequences, pursued by foreign oil companies in Latin America;[36] and at the impact of foreign banks on Iran.[37] The role of TNCs in Japan's early economic development has also been investigated.[38] In most cases, this research has pointed to the positive side of transnational investment, and it has certainly suggested that the rewards from such investment for the companies were not always as great as might have been imagined. A recent monograph about a British goldmining company active in Brazil from the mid-nineteenth century until 1960 has made a major contribution to this literature, explaining the impact of the company on the local Brazilian community where it operated, and its involvement – or rather lack of it – in the politics of its host economy.[39]

There has been a recent tendency for business historians to explore TNC activity in a particular country or region, and this is contributing significantly to the impact of the literature. German and Swiss investment in Italy, Belgian investment in Canada, and British investment in Asia are among the topics which have been studied.[40] There have also been industry studies, notably a special issue of the journal *Studi Storici* on TNCs in the electrical industry in Europe before 1946, which contains considerable new information on the impact of foreign TNCs on the electrical industries of southern Europe.[41] An interesting Australian study has also examined the impact of TNCs on the structure of the interwar Australian tyre industry.[42]

The impact of TNCs on developed host economies has attracted less attention. Wilkins, however, considered the issue in her study of foreign investment in the United States before 1914, and the impact of foreign TNCs on the United Kingdom before 1945 has been researched.[43] Foreign

TNCs in Germany during 1933–1945 have also been discussed.[44] Business historians have contributed nothing, however, to debates about the impact of TNCs on their home economies.

The history of host country regulation of TNCs has also attracted only modest attention. Recent research has, however, explored the long-term policies of the Government of the United Kingdom towards TNCs. In the United Kingdom, in contrast to France and many other European countries, governments assumed that inward investment brought net benefits, and adopted an open policy towards foreign TNCs. Industrial policies were ownership neutral, except in a very limited number of strategic sectors, such as domestic banking and defence.[45] Japan provided an obvious contrast, especially after 1945 when the Government of Japan strongly discouraged wholly-owned TNC investments, preferring foreign companies to license technology to Japanese companies, or else form joint ventures. Mark Mason has traced the evolution of Japanese government policies towards foreign TNCs before the Second World War.[46]

## An Agenda for Future Historical Research

There are a number of obvious candidates for any future agenda for historical research on TNCs. First, the existing literature is heavily biased towards manufacturing TNCs, and to a much lesser extent TNCs active in extractive industries. The historical development of services sector TNCs needs more research, although research in this area is now in progress. The historical evolution of transnational banks (TNBs), for example, has received some attention.[47] TNBs can be traced back to at least the 1830s, when the first British overseas banks were established to operate in Australia, Canada and the West Indies. By the end of the century, German, French, Belgian and other European banks also had branches in other countries. British banks, however, had the most extensive branch networks: they had almost 1,300 overseas branches in 1914. In contrast, regulatory restrictions meant that there were virtually no United States TNBs before 1914. The United Kingdom remained the world's leading TNB home economy until the 1960s, when the advent of global money and capital markets was accompanied by the rapid growth of United States, and later Continental European and Japanese TNBs.

Trading companies, especially the *sogo shosha* of Japan, have also been explored by business historians.[48] The first *sogo shosha* was Mitsui Bussan established in 1876. By 1900, this firm handled around one third of Japan's total foreign trade, and it had nearly 40 foreign branches in Asia and Europe. Subsequently *sogo shosha* continued to handle a high proportion of Japan's trade and to play a prominent role in the country's international business activities. Japanese business historians have produced a number of explanations for the growth of *sogo shosha*, which feature an unusual system of governance, sharing characteristics of both vertically-integrated firms and the market. Japan's peculiar history was a key factor in their emergence. Nearly 250 years of seclusion from the outside world before the 1850s left the country with a huge "information gap" about overseas markets. The *sogo shosha* provided the institutional means to overcome the scarcity of knowledge about the outside world. Strong government support was also critical for the early growth of Mitsui Bussan, although much less so for later *sogo shosha*, such as Mitsubishi Shoji founded in 1919.

There are other fine examples of studies of the evolution of non-manufacturing TNC activity. Douglas West, for example, has published pioneering studies of the history of transnational advertising agencies.[49] Canadian business historians have examined Canadian foreign direct investment in utility businesses in Latin America and the West Indies.[50] Canadians were in the vanguard of establishing foreign utility TNCs. These studies are also of interest for their focus on the relationship between these TNCs and governments and national elites in Brazil and elsewhere. Much work remains to be done, however, on the history of non-manufacturing TNCs.

More fundamentally, although business history has generated an enormous amount of data on TNCs, methodological weaknesses and excessive preoccupation with individual case studies have meant that much of this work has been neglected by mainstream students of international business. Yet, business history can reveal data in some of the most critical topics of concern to international business researchers. For example, current work on international coalitions between firms (including licensing agreements, joint ventures, supply and marketing agreements) can be enhanced by reference to historical data which, among other things, allow such coalitions to be studied over time. Work on the organization of TNCs by Christopher Bartlett and others has recently stressed that a company's organization is shaped not only by its external task environment, but also by the historical path by which the company's international activity developed – its "administrative heritage" in Bartlett's language.[51] The business history data have an enormous store of information on such administrative heritages, and also about how firms have changed their organizational structures in the past. The fields of comparative and cross-cultural management could, similarly, utilize historical data on the TNCs.

In recent years, many economists and management scholars working on international business have shown a new interest in the value of historical data. Initially, they regarded it as a magnificent, if elusive, databank on which to test models. In the late 1980s, however, there was a growing recognition that theory and history could enter a more dynamic partnership, which could unlock new ways of understanding issues such as competitiveness, organizational structures and entrepreneurship. For this dynamic dialogue to be fully effective, historians of international business need to refine and develop their research methodologies. They need to focus on specific themes, such as control, performance and coalitions within international business. Case studies should not be abandoned, but should be chosen on a more systematic basis. Alfred Chandler has shown how business history in general can achieve wider recognition through greater conceptualization combined with the highest standards of historical scholarship. Rich rewards await those who can explore the historical development of TNCs using the concepts and methodologies of modern international business analysts, for the history of the last hundred years provides rich material for those seeking to explain and understand the role of TNCs in the modern world.

## Notes

1. F.A. Southard, *American Industry in Europe* (Boston, Houghton-Mifflin, 1931).

2. J.H. Dunning, *American Investment in British Manufacturing Industry* (London, Allen and Unwin, 1958). For Canada, see A.E. Safarian, *Foreign Ownership of Canadian Industry* (New York, McGraw-Hill, 1966). For Australia, see D.T. Brash, *American Investment in Australian Industry* (Canberra, Australian National University Press, 1966).

3. J.H. Dunning, *Studies in International Investment* (London, Allen and Unwin, 1971), and "Changes in the level and structure of international production: the last one hundred years", in Mark Casson, ed., *The Growth of International Business* (London, Allen and Unwin, 1983), pp. 84–139.

4. P. Svedberg, "The portfolio – direct composition of private foreign investment in 1914 revisited", *Economic Journal,* LXXX (1978), pp. 763–777.

5. J.M. Stopford, "The origins of British-based multinational manufacturing enterprises", *Business History Review,* XLVIII (1974), pp. 303–345; L. Franko, "The origins of multinational manufacturing by continental European firms", *Business History Review,* XLVIII (1974), pp. 272–302; L. Franko, *The European Multinationals* (London, Harper and Row, 1976).

6. A.D. Chandler, *Strategy and Structure* (Cambridge, Mass., Harvard University Press, 1962); A.D. Chandler, *The Visible Hand* (Cambridge, Mass., Harvard University Press, 1977); A.D. Chandler, *Scale and Scope* (Cambridge, Mass., Harvard University Press, 1990).

7. M. Wilkins, *The Emergence of Multinational Enterprise* (Cambridge, Mass., Harvard University Press, 1970); M. Wilkins, *The Maturing of Multinational Enterprise* (Cambridge, Mass., Harvard University Press 1974).

8. M. Wilkins, "Modern European economic history and the multinationals", *Journal of European Economic History,* VI (1977), pp. 575–595.

9. S. Nicholas, "British multinational investment before 1939", *Journal of European Economic History,* II (1982), pp. 605–630; G. Jones, "The expansion of British multinational manufacturing, 1890–1939", in A. Okochi and T. Inoue, eds., *Overseas Business Activities* (Tokyo, University of Tokyo Press, 1984), pp. 125–153; G. Jones, "The growth and performance of British multinational firms before 1939: the case of Dunlop", *Economic History Review,* XXXVI (1984), pp. 35–53; G. Jones, "Multinational chocolate: Cadbury overseas 1918–1939", *Business*

*History*, XXVI (1984), pp. 59–76; G. Jones, ed., *British Multinationals: Origins, Management and Performance* (Aldershot, Gower, 1986).

10. Peter Hertner, "Fallstudien zu deutschen multinationalen Unternehmen vor dem Ersten Weltkrieg", in N. Horn and J. Kocka, eds., *Law and the Formation of the Big Enterprises in the 19th and early 20th Centuries* (Göttingen, Vandenhoeck and Ruprecht, 1979), pp. 388–419; P. Hertner, "German multinational enterprise before 1914: some case studies", in P. Hertner and G. Jones, eds., *Multinationals: Theory and History* (Aldershot, Gower, 1986), pp. 113–134, reprinted in this volume.

11. Harm G. Schröter, "Die Auslandsinvestitionen der deutschen chemischen Industrie 1870 bis 1930", *Zeitschrift für Unternehmensgeschichte*, 35 (1990), pp. 1–22.

12. Ragnhild Lundström, "Swedish multinational growth before 1930", in Hertner and Jones, eds., *Multinationals: Theory and History* (Aldershot, Gower, 1986), pp. 135–156.

13. T. Kuwahara, "The Japanese cotton spinners' direct investments into China before the Second World War", in A. Teichova, M. Levy-Leboyer and N. Nussbaum, eds., *Historical Studies in International Corporate Business* (Cambridge, Cambridge University Press, 1989), pp. 151–162; H. Yoshihara, "Multinational growth of Japanese manufacturing enterprises in the postwar period", in A. Okochi and T. Inoue, eds., *Overseas Business Activities* (Tokyo, University of Tokyo Press, 1984), pp. 95–120; M. Wilkins, "American–Japanese direct foreign investment relationships, 1930–1952", *Business History Review*, 56 (1982), pp. 497–518; *idem*, "Japanese multinational enterprise before 1914", *Business History Review*, 60 (1986), pp. 199–231.

14. Much of this work is reviewed in Mira Wilkins, "The history of European multinationals: a new look", *The Journal of European Economic History*, XV (1986), pp. 483–510.

15. Alice Teichova and P.L. Cottrell, eds., *International Business and Central Europe 1918–1939* (Leicester, Leicester University Press, 1983); A. Okochi and T. Inoue, eds., *Overseas Business Activities* (Tokyo, University of Tokyo Press, 1984); A. Teichova, M. Levy-Leboyer and H. Nussbaum, eds., *Multinational Enterprise in Historical Perspective* (Cambridge, Cambridge University Press, 1986); P. Hertner and G. Jones, eds., *Multinationals: Theory and History* (Aldershot, Gower, 1986); P. Hertner, ed., *Per la storia dell'imprese multinazionale in Europa* (Milan, Franco Angeli, 1987); A. Teichova, M. Levy-Leboyer and H. Nusbaum, eds., *Historical Studies in International Corporate Business* (Cambridge, Cambridge University Press, 1989).

16. M. Wilkins, *The History of Foreign Investment in the United States before 1914* (Cambridge, Mass., Harvard University Press, 1989).

17. D.C.M. Platt, "British portfolio investment before 1870: some doubts", *Economic History Review*, XXXIII (1980), pp. 1–16; D.C.M. Platt, *Britain's Investment Overseas on the Eve of the First World War* (London, Macmillan, 1986).

18. Charles Feinstein, "Britain's overseas investments in 1913", *Economic History Review*, XLIII (1990), pp. 280–295.

19. William P. Kennedy, *Industrial Structure, Capital Markets and the Origins of British Economic Decline* (Cambridge, Cambridge University Press, 1987).

20. M. Wilkins, "European and North American multinationals, 1870–1914: comparisons and contrasts", *Business History*, XXX (1988), pp. 8–45, reprinted in this volume, discusses this problem.

21. M. Wilkins, "Defining a firm: history and theory", in Hertner and Jones, eds., *Multinationals: Theory and History* (Aldershot, Gower, 1986), pp. 80–95,

reprinted in this volume; M. Wilkins, "The free-standing company, 1870–1914: an important type of British foreign direct investment", *Economic History Review*, XLI (1988), pp. 259–285.

22. Harm Schröter, "Risk and control in multinational enterprise: German businesses in Scandinavia, 1918–1939", *Business History Review*, 62 (1988), pp. 420–443, reprinted in this volume.

23. Charles Harvey and Jon Press, "The city and international mining, 1870–1914", *Business History*, XXXII (1990), pp. 98–119.

24. J.F. Hennart, "The transaction cost theory of the multinational enterprise", in C. Pitelis and R. Sugden, eds., *The Nature of the Transnational Firm* (London, Routledge, 1991), pp. 81–116.

25. Paul Atterbury and Julia MacKenzie, *A Golden Adventure* (Silversted, Hurtwood Press, 1985). Ultramar was taken over in 1991.

26. Geoffrey Jones, "The Gramophone Company: an Anglo-American multi-national, 1898–1931", *Business History Review*, 59 (1985), pp. 76–100; Howard Cox, "Growth and ownership in the international tobacco industry: BAT 1902–27", *Business History*, XXXI (1989), pp. 44–67.

27. David Merrett, *ANZ Bank* (Sydney, Allen and Unwin, 1985).

28. Geoffrey Jones, "The performance of British multinational enterprise, 1890–1945", in P. Hertner and G. Jones, eds., *Multinationals: Theory and History* (Aldershot, Gower, 1986), pp. 96–112; S. Nicholas, "Locational choice, performance and the growth of British multinational firms", *Business History*, XXXI (1989), pp. 122–141.

29. P. Hertner and G. Jones, eds., *Multinationals: Theory and History* (Aldershot, Gower, 1986) was the result of the initial conference held at Florence in 1983. G. Jones, ed., *Banks as Multinationals* (London, Routledge, 1990), reported the results of a similar conference held at Reading in 1989.

30. John H. Dunning and Howard Archer, "The eclectic paradigm and the growth of UK multinational enterprise 1870–1983", *Business and Economic History*, 16 (1987), pp. 19–49, reprinted in this volume.

31. S. Nicholas, "Agency contracts, institutional modes, and the transition to foreign direct investment by British manufacturing multinationals before 1939", *Journal of Economic History*, 43 (1983), pp. 675–686, reprinted in this volume.

32. M. Wilkins, "The role of private business in the international diffusion of technology", *Journal of Economic History*, 34 (1974), pp. 166–188, reprinted in this volume; S.R. Brown, "The transfer of technology to China in the nineteenth century: the role of foreign direct investment", *Journal of Economic History*, XXXIX (1979), pp. 181–197; M. Casson, "Contractual arrangements for technology transfer: new evidence from business history", *Business History*, XXVIII (1986), pp. 5–35.

33. D.K. Fieldhouse, *Unilever Overseas* (Beckenham, Croom Helm, 1978).

34. C. Harvey and P. Taylor, "Mineral wealth and economic development: foreign direct investment in Spain, 1851–1913", *Economic History Review*, XL (1987), pp. 185–208, reprinted in this volume.

35. Thomas F. O'Brien, "Rich beyond the dreams of avarice: the Guggenheims in Chile", *Business History Review*, 63 (1989), pp. 122–159, reprinted in this volume.

36. Jonathan C. Brown, "Domestic politics and foreign investment: British development of Mexican petroleum, 1899–1911", *Business History Review*, 61 (1987), pp. 387–416; J.C. Brown, "Why foreign oil companies shifted their production from Mexico to Venezuela during the 1920s", *American Historical Review*, 90 (1985), pp. 362–385.

37. G. Jones, "The Imperial Bank of Iran and Iranian economic development 1890–1952", *Business and Economic History*, 16 (1987), pp. 69–80.

38. M. Mason, "Foreign direct investment and Japanese economic development, 1899–1931", *Business and Economic History*, 16 (1987), pp. 93–107, reprinted in this volume; M. Wilkins, "The contributions of foreign enterprises to Japanese economic development", in T. Yuzawa and M. Ugadwa, eds., *Foreign Business in Japan before World War II* (Tokyo, University of Tokyo Press, 1990), pp. 35–57; M. Udagawa, "Business management and foreign-affiliated companies in Japan before World War II", in T. Yuzawa and M. Udagawa, eds., *Foreign Business in Japan before World War II* (Tokyo, University of Tokyo Press, 1990), pp. 1–30.

39. Marshall C. Eakin, *British Enterprise in Brazil* (Durham, Duke University Press, 1989).

40. Peter Hertner, *Il capitale tedesco in Italia dall unità alla prima guerra mondiale. Banche miste e sviluppo economico italiano* (Bologna, Il Mulino, 1984); G. Kurgen-van Hentenryk and J. Laureyssens, *Un siècle d'investissements belges au Canada* (Brussels, Editions de l'Université de Bruxelles, 1986); Pierre-Alain Wavre, "Swiss investments in Italy from the XVIIIth to the XXth century", *Journal of European Economic History*, 17 (1988), pp. 85–102; R.P.T. Davenport-Hines and G. Jones, eds., *British Business in Asia Since 1860* (Cambridge, Cambridge University Press, 1989).

41. "Industria elettrica e movimenti di capitale in Europa", *Studi Storici*, 28 (1987), pp. 815–1026 (special issue).

42. J. Stanton, "Protection, market structure and firm behaviour: inefficiency in the early Australian tyre industry", *Australian Economic History Review*, XXIV (1984) pp. 91–113.

43. M. Wilkins, *The History of Foreign Investment in the United States* (Cambridge, Mass., Harvard University Press, 1989); G. Jones, "Foreign multinationals and British industry before 1945", *Economic History Review*, XLI (1988), pp. 429–453, reprinted in this volume.

44. Charles Cheape, "Not politicians but sound businessmen: Norton company and the Third Reich", *Business History Review*, 62 (1988), pp. 444–466.

45. G. Jones, "The British Government and foreign multinationals before 1970", in M. Chick, ed., *Governments, Industries and Markets* (Aldershot, Edward Elgar, 1990), pp. 194–214.

46. Mark Mason, "With reservations: prewar Japan as host to Western Electric and ITT", in T. Yuzawa and M. Udgawa, eds., *Foreign Business in Japan before World War II* (Tokyo, University of Tokyo Press 1990), pp. 175–192.

47. G. Jones, "Lombard street on the Riveria: the British clearing banks and Europe, 1900–1960", *Business History*, XXIV (1982), pp. 186–210; G. Jones, *Banking and Empire in Iran* (Cambridge, Cambridge University Press, 1986); G. Jones, *Banking and Oil* (Cambridge, Cambridge University Press, 1987); G. Jones, ed., *Banks as Multinationals* (London, Routledge, 1990).

48. Shin'ichi Yonekawa, "The formation of general trading companies: a comparative study", *Japanese Yearbook on Business History*, 2 (1985), pp. 1–31, reprinted in this volume: N. Kawabe, "Development of overseas operations by general trading companies 1868–1945", S. Yonekawa and H. Yoshihara, eds., *Business History of General Trading Companies* (Tokyo, University of Tokyo Press, 1987), pp. 71–103; and H. Yamazaki, "The logic of the formation of general trading companies in Japan", in S. Yonekawa and H. Yoshihara, eds., *Business History of General Trading Companies* (Tokyo, University of Tokyo Press, 1987), pp. 21–64; W.R. Purcell, "The development of Japan's trading company network in Australia 1890–1941", *Australian Economic History Review*, XXI (1981),

pp. 114–132; Ann Carlos and Stephen Nicholas, "Giants of an earlier capitalism: the chartered trading companies as modern multinationals", *Business History Review*, 62 (1988), 398–419.

49. Douglas C. West, "From T-square to T-plan: the London office of the J. Walter Thompson advertising agency, 1919–70", *Business History*, 29 (1987), pp. 199–217; D.C. West, "Multinational competition in the British advertising agency business, 1936–1987", *Business History Review*, 62 (1988), pp. 467–501.

50. Duncan McDowall, *The Light: Brazilian Traction, Light and Power Company Limited, 1899–1945* (Toronto, University of Toronto Press, 1988); Christopher Armstrong and H.V. Nelles, *Southern Exposure: Canadian Promoters in Latin America and the Caribbean, 1896–1930* (Toronto, University of Toronto Press, 1988).

51. Christopher A. Bartlett, "Building and managing the transnational: the new organizational challenge", in Michael E. Porter, ed., *Competition in Global Industry* (Boston, Mass., Harvard Business School Press, 1986), pp. 367–401.

# Bibliography

Buckley, Peter J. and Brain Roberts, *European Direct Investment in the U.S.A. before World War I* (London, Macmillan, 1982).

Casson, M., ed., *The Growth of International Business* (London, Allen and Unwin, 1983).

Chandler, A.D., *Strategy and Structure* (Cambridge, Mass., Harvard University Press, 1962).

——, *The Visible Hand* (Cambridge, Mass., Harvard University Press, 1977).

——, *Scale and Scope* (Cambridge, Mass., Harvard University Press, 1990).

Dunning, J.H., *American Investment in British Manufacturing Industry* (London, Allen and Unwin, 1958).

——, "Changes in the level and structure of international production: the last one hundred years", in Mark Casson, ed., *The Growth of International Business* (London, Allen and Unwin, 1983), pp. 84–139.

Fieldhouse, D.K., *Unilever Overseas* (Beckenham, Croom Helm, 1978).

Franko, L., *The European Multinationals* (London, Harper and Row, 1976).

Fridenson, P., "The growth of multinational activities in the French motor industry, 1890–1979", in Peter Hertner and G. Jones, eds., *Multinationals: Theory and History* (Aldershot, Gower, 1986), pp. 157–168.

Hennart, J.F., "Internalisation in practice: early foreign direct investment in Malaysian tin mining", *Journal of International Business Studies*, 17 (1986), pp. 131–143.

Hertner, Peter, "Fallstudien zu deutschen multinationalen Unternehmen vor dem Ersten Weltkrieg", in N. Horn and J. Kocka, eds., *Law and the Formation of the Big Enterprises in the 19th and early 20th Centuries* (Göttingen, Vandenhoeck and Ruprecht, 1979), pp. 388–419.

——, *Il capitale tedesco in Italia dall' unità alla prima guerra mondiale. Banche miste dall'unita e sviluppo economico italiano* (Bologna, Il Mulino, 1984).

——, "German multinational enterprises before 1914: some case studies", in Peter Hertner and G. Jones, eds., *Multinationals: Theory and History* (Aldershot, Gower, 1986), pp. 113–134.

——, and G. Jones, eds., *Multinationals: Theory and History* (Aldershot, Gower, 1986).

Jones, Charles A., *International Business in the Nineteenth Century* (Brighton, Wheatsheaf, 1987).
Jones, G., *The State and the Emergence of the British Oil Industry* (London, Macmillan, 1981).
——, "The growth and performance of British multinational firms before 1939: the case of Dunlop", *Economic History Review*, XXXVI (1984), pp. 35–53.
——, "Multinational chocolate: Cadbury overseas 1918–1939", *Business History*, XXVI (1984), pp. 59–76.
——, "The Gramophone Company: an Anglo-American multinational, 1898–1931", *Business History Review*, 59 (1985), pp. 76–100.
——, ed., *British Multinationals: Origins, Management and Performance* (Aldershot, Gower, 1986).
——, *Banking and Empire in Iran* (Cambridge, Cambridge University Press, 1986).
——, *Banking and Oil* (Cambridge, Cambridge University Press, 1987).
——, "Foreign multinationals and British industry before 1945", *Economic History Review*, XLI (1988), pp. 429–453.
——, ed., *Banks as Multinationals* (London, Routledge, 1990).
Levy-Leboyer, M. and H. Nussbaum, eds., *Multinational Enterprise in Historical Perspective* (Cambridge, Cambridge University Press, 1986).
——, eds., *Historical Studies in International Corporate Business* (Cambridge, Cambridge University Press 1989).
Lundström, Ragnhild, "Swedish multinational growth before 1930", in P. Hertner and G. Jones, eds., *Multinationals: Theory and History* (Aldershot, Gower, 1986), pp. 135–156.
Nicholas, S., "British multinational investment before 1939", *Journal of European History*, II (1982), pp. 605–630.
——, "Agency contracts, institutional modes, and the transition to foreign direct investment by British manufacturing multinationals before 1939", *Journal of Economic History*, 43 (1983), pp. 675–686.
——, Okochi, A. and T. Inoue, eds., *Overseas Business Activities* (Tokyo, University of Tokyo Press, 1984).
Safarian, A.E., *Foreign Ownership of Canadian Industry* (New York, McGraw-Hill, 1966).
Schröter, Harm G. "Risk and control in multinational enterprise: German businesses in Scandinavia, 1918–1939", *Business History Review*, 62 (1988), pp. 420–443.
Southard, F.A., *American Industry in Europe* (Boston, Houghton-Mifflin, 1931).
Stopford, J.M., "The origins of British-based multinational manufacturing enterprises", *Business History Review*, XLVIII (1974), pp. 303–345.
Svedberg, P., "The portfolio-direct composition of private foreign investment in 1914 revisited", *Economic Journal*, LXXX (1978), pp. 763–777.
Teichova, Alice and P.L. Cottrell, eds., *International Business and Central Europe 1918–1939* (Leicester, Leicester University Press, 1983).
Transnational Corporations and Management Division, *World Investment Report 1992: Transnational Corporations as Engines of Growth* (New York, United Nations, 1992).
UNCTC, *World Investment Report 1991: The Triad in Foreign Direct Investment* (New York, United Nations, 1991).
Wilkins, M., *The Emergence of Multinational Enterprise* (Cambridge, Mass., Harvard University Press, 1970).
——, *The Maturing of Multinational Enterprise* (Cambridge, Mass., Harvard University Press, 1974).

——, *The History of Foreign Investment in the United States before 1914* (Cambridge, Mass., Harvard University Press, 1989).

Yuzawa, T. and M. Ugadawa, eds., *Foreign Business in Japan before World War II* (Tokyo, University of Tokyo Press, 1990).

# PART ONE: Emergence and Growth

It is hardly surprising that one of the major contributions of historical research on TNCs has been to show that TNCs have a history. The articles selected for this part demonstrate the nineteenth-century origins of modern TNCs. The survey article by M. Wilkins (1988) drew together two decades of research on TNCs. She demonstrated the extensive nature of transnational business activity before 1914, as she surveyed the thousands of TNCs active in manufacturing, services and extractive sectors. J. Dunning and H. Archer (1987) and P. Hertner (1986) provided more detailed information on early TNC investment by British and German firms, while Wilkins (1986) demonstrated that even Japan was the home of substantial transnational business activity before the First World War.

Two particularly important issues were raised in that literature. The first was that the TNCs of different countries show different characteristics. There were in the past, as today, considerable variations in the geographical and industrial distribution of the TNCs of different countries. Although it is hardly surprising that TNCs reflect home economy characteristics, early research assumed the "United States model" of TNC development was the normal pattern. However, the reality was often more complicated than at first it appeared. Whilst it was true that, in sharp contrast to the case of the United Kingdom, German TNCs before 1914 were particularly active in high technology products such as chemicals and electrical goods, Hertner (1986) pointed out that there was also German TNC investment in consumer goods. Wilkins (1986) showed that some of the special characteristics of contemporary Japanese-based TNCs had already surfaced before 1914, in particular, the importance of textiles, and of services sector companies, especially the trading companies *sogo shosha*. Yonekawa (1985) discussed the rise of *sogo shosha*, and makes an important contribution by putting their growth in a comparative context, asking why similar companies did not develop elsewhere.

The second important issue raised by that selection is that appropriate methodology is necessary for studying the evolution of TNCs. Dunning and Archer (1987) applied the eclectic paradigm of international production to the history of British TNCs between 1873 and 1983, examining the ownership-specific, location-specific and internalization incentive advantages of those TNCs. This is a good example of historical data being used to test models developed by economists. A. Chandler (1980) discussed the apparent divergency between United States and United Kingdom TNCs in terms of the corporate management structure of the two economies. In particular, he noted the slow growth of managerial hierarchies in the United Kingdom, which handicapped companies in the chemical, machinery and electrical equipment industries, but was less of an obstacle in branded and packaged consumer goods. Hertner (1986) exemplified the case study approach to TNC history. He examined the early development of German TNCs on a company-by-company basis. That approach permitted powerful insights into the process of transnationalization, but it was one that many conventional economists have found distressing because of the lack of representativeness in the case studies. Business historians have yet to agree on the problem of how many case studies make a case.

# 1

# European and North American Multinationals, 1870–1914: Comparisons and Contrasts*

## Mira Wilkins[†]

*Source: *Business History*, XXX (1988), pp. 8–45.

In the late nineteenth century and early twentieth centuries, the world shrank in its physical dimensions, as steamships, railroads, telegraph, and cables compressed distances. In Europe and North America, economic conditions changed. This was a time of substantial technological advance, with new products, processes, and forms of business organisation, challenging the older order. Because of improvements in transportation and communications, innovations spread rapidly throughout the industrialising world. One crucial conduit was business itself.

British businesses led in the process of multinational expansion. They were, however, not alone and companies headquartered in Continental Europe, the United States, and Canada also extended their activities over borders, making foreign direct investments, defined as those business investments that were or had the potential to be controlled or at least influenced in a significant manner from a headquarters in the United Kingdom, Germany, France, Belgium, Switzerland, Sweden, or other European countries or the United States or Canada.[1] Typically, the phrases 'multinational enterprise' and 'foreign direct investment' have been considered as synonymous, but it is more appropriate to see the relationship as follows: multinational enterprises make foreign direct investments – and carry on other tasks as well. The investments, the capital flows, are only part of the activities of multinational enterprise. These companies must have a business association with the foreign operations.

British business historians can learn from looking at the experiences of British multinational enterprise, but they learn even more through comparisons. Thus, this article will cover British business overseas, but it will also deal with continental European and North American enterprise. In the conclusion, I will stress the insights that British business historians can obtain by virtue of such comparisons.

Some companies that did business across borders in the pre-1914 years did so in only a single foreign country; others by 1914 already had operations in several or even numerous lands and were truly multinational. The late nineteenth and the early twentieth century was the first period in world history when, owing to the transportation and communications innovations, it became possible to have meaningful business coordination, control, and influence over distance and for our purposes over country frontiers. The new products, processes, and forms of business organisation were integral to this development. Higher per capita income was also critical, placing more individuals in a market economy and providing disposable income for the purchase of a myriad of goods and services. For these reasons, 1870–1914 was the initial era of the modern multinational enterprise.

Because the late nineteenth and early twentieth centuries witnessed great economic change and growth, in considering modern multinational enterprise I am not merely concerned with the beginnings, but with the subsequent course of the institution. In the years prior to 1914, a firm with business abroad in only one foreign country might be starting in the direction of expanding into other countries as well. Yet, no determinism, no inevitability, existed – and the process might be truncated. The business might fail (domestically and internationally), or alternatively a business might succeed but shed its multinational character, becoming a national enterprise in a host country or in the home country, or as a fourth possibility, a purely bi-national relationship might persist over a long period, with no broad multinational spread. The paths in multinational enterprise growth might start from different origins and involve diverse strategies. No simple, single, neat model fits every case. It is important, however, in studying the evolving institution to look at both beginnings and growth.

My definition of multinational enterprise, for purposes of this article, is comprehensive. I include any company that has a headquarters in one country (a home) and that operates in at least one foreign country (the host). 'Foreign' is defined as synonymous with abroad, that is, not in the home country; it could be within or outside an overseas Empire. A company that crossed a border and made business (operating) investments in only one foreign country was by this definition a multinational enterprise; so, too, I will include a firm with operating investments in many foreign lands. 'Operations' could be in the production of goods or services: a trading company, a bank, a public utility, and an owned sales outlet that produced services are included under the rubric 'operations'. In short, I do not limit myself to manufacturing firms – either at home or abroad.

Multinational enterprise involves *cross-border* control, or potential for control, or, at least, influence. An enterprise run by expatriates or immigrants frequently did not represent an ongoing foreign investment, much less a foreign *direct* investment. If there was no headquarters at home, there was *no* multinational enterprise. This is very important. A Britisher or German who migrated to the United States (for example) and set up business in this nation, if he had no obligation to any investor in the home country, there was no ongoing foreign investment, or foreign direct investment. (To call Andrew Carnegie's steel business in America a British investment is bizarre). Likewise, Swedes and Germans resident in Russia or Britishers resident in Argentina, who retained no headquarters abroad, are not foreign direct investors.[2]

Mark Casson in his latest book has argued that 'the modern theory of the MNE [multinational enterprise] has the potential to become a general theory of the enterprise in space, and as such, to embrace theories of the multi-regional and multi-plant firm'.[3] How can the comparative study of the history of multinational enterprise contribute to the efforts of the theoretician? I believe that the way to do so is to present our findings as we inquire into the development of such companies.

The rise of multinational enterprise is receiving substantial attention. Scholars know a great deal about the history of American, British, German, and Swedish multinationals.[4] We know far less about the history of French, Belgian, and Swiss business abroad.[5] In this essay, I seek synthesis. What is known, what is absent? What can the British business historian learn from the comparisons? What appear to be the common features in the historical experiences? If not neat nor simple, is there none the less an 'ideal type' – a model? Does the evidence fit into the emerging theory of multinational enterprise? What is distinctive to multinationals of Great Britain and of other particular home countries; can the special features be ordered in any discernible pattern? How was the rise of multinational enterprise associated with the changing national and world economies, 1870–1914? Or, is generalisation impossible, and regional (or host country) differences so vast as to nullify attempts to find patterns?[6] What are the new frontiers for research? How will they help the British business historian in furthering his search for an understanding of British business overseas?

I am not considering the years after 1914, because of space constraints, but also because I am convinced that 1914–18 (the period of the First World War) forms a watershed[7] and that a post-First World War analysis requires a greatly expanded treatment. Yet, as indicated earlier, it is possible to study entries and growth, as well as retreats and frustration in the pre-1914 years. In short, what follows is a look at an institution, the multinational enterprise, that seeks private profit through managed business abroad (in 1870–1914 there were few government-owned multinational enterprises).[8]

**Influences at Home on Multinational Enterprise**

All companies with business investments abroad are and have been shaped by economic and other conditions in their homeland, and only subsequently, by economic and other conditions in the countries abroad in which they did business. In each home country circumstances differed from one another, and in addition there were regional differences *within* home countries (in a short article it is impossible to inquire whether there were systematic differences between London and Glasgow-headquartered companies as they operated abroad, or between New York and Chicago ones, or more obviously Vevey and Basle ones – yet we accept the proposition that such differences existed).[9] In each headquarters nation unique national characteristics had an impact on the nature and extent of firms' foreign direct investments. The galaxy of influences include factor costs, level and pace of industrialisation, areas of technological expertise, size and nature of the domestic market, relationships between banking and industrial units at home, national endowments of and requirements for natural resources, the availability of professional education, national status as exporter or importer of capital, government policies, geographical position, trade patterns (exports and imports), emigration, and undoubtedly such vague imponderables as culture and taste.[10]

Factor costs are helpful in explaining what advantage a company might have *vis-à-vis* companies with head offices in other nations. For a company to venture abroad, it had to have some expected (anticipated) advantage – for otherwise there was no rationale for the expansion and no hope of persistence.[11] It has often been pointed out that American costs of labour were high; thus, Americans substituted machines for labour; American business tended to have advantages abroad in businesses that were capital intensive, in mass production industries.[12] An analysis of British multinationals in 1870–1914 in terms of factor costs would stress the relative cheapness of capital. A recent study suggests that British firms had a comparative disadvantage in goods that were intensive in the use of human capital.[13] Factor costs by themselves, however, seem inadequate as a complete explanation of differences between and among multinationals from different nations. Relatively high labour costs in Canada did not make Canadian development similar to that of the United States. Canadian business abroad varied in numerous ways from its south of the border counterpart. Likewise, I find it very difficult to explain the huge differences between German and French multinational enterprise solely or even fundamentally in terms of factor costs.

The more industrialised, the more economically advanced the country, *ceteris paribus*, the more likely for it to be a headquarters for business abroad. While the match is imperfect, we would predict more German enterprise abroad than Spanish headquartered business over borders and our prediction would in fact be fulfilled. So, too, the large number (in relative terms) of British multinationals fits well under this explanatory rubric. Britain was after all the 'first industrial nation'.

Often technological advantage has been behind specific business enterprise expansion into foreign lands. The explanation is especially helpful *vis-à-vis* many US and German multinationals, but it is by no means adequate as an all-encompassing rationale. Moreover, there have been identified a number of Swedish cases of business abroad based on technology obtained in Germany (a third country) and British cases of business overseas to obtain (to pull in) technology from abroad. Technological advantage is also often inadequate in explaining an enterprise's backward integration into resource development.

The size and nature of the domestic market (including the number of customers, disposable income, and geographical dispersion) shaped business at home and became a significant influence on the characteristics of both domestic business and business abroad.[14] It had impact on the shift from family firm to managerial enterprise.[15] Yet, the size-of- and nature-of-market impacts were not always consistent. Swedish and Swiss firms with geographically and demographically small domestic markets, but relatively high income ones, made substantial foreign direct investments, while Danish and Norwegian companies did not. The 'heterogeneous' American market (with consumers from different cultural backgrounds, with extremes in climate, and with other substantial regional variations) offered an excellent learning experience for American managers abroad; the more homogeneous British domestic market had a limiting effect on operating companies' managerial training.[16] Business abroad required managing enterprises over distance. This was in no way a given. Coping with the problems of a long span of managerial control often made the difference between success and failure of the ventures.

In most European and North American countries, banks seem not to have been of major importance *vis-à-vis* the vast quantity of their nationals' foreign business operations,[17] but in Germany and Sweden, banks were highly instrumental.[18] And, the foreign direct investments made by British and to a lesser extent, Canadian banks were a significant type of pre-1914 multinational enterprise.[19]

Lack of natural resources at home – when there was a domestic demand for such resources – stimulated some businesses to extend their operations abroad, although the absence of (or alternatively high cost of) a particular raw material did not by definition mean a foreign direct investment in obtaining it (French business invested abroad in phosphate production; I have no evidence that Swiss companies did).

British professional education came later than that in America and Germany; educational systems seem to have had influence on the multinationals of the respective nations.

Operations in foreign countries were embarked on by companies in home countries that were net importers of capital (Russian insurance companies had multinational business) as well as by firms in countries such as Great Britain that were net capital exporters; creditor versus debtor nation status had an impact in shaping business abroad.

Home government policies had a complex collection of effects on business abroad, from those associated with imperial policies, antitrust policies, to tax policies, for instance. Empire created a familiar political infrastructure overseas that in general served to encourage nationals to invest in these countries, for uncertainty was reduced. Thus, British investment in Malaya and India exceeded that from continental Europe or the United States; Dutch companies had a relatively greater significance than any others in the Dutch East Indies. Antitrust policies (or their absence) altered the strategies of foreign investors: that restraint of trade agreements were illegal in the United States had substantial effects on American business abroad. Tax policies began to affect companies' investment tactics (if not strategies) by the early twentieth century; this is a subject about which we know very little; my own research, however, suggested that in the first decade of the twentieth century British taxes may well have influenced the path of British business abroad.[20] It has long been accepted that French taxes redirected French portfolio investment (much of which was done through Switzerland to avoid taxes); yet, whether taxation had a similar impact on French foreign *direct* investment is a subject that as far as I know has never been explored.

The geographical position of the home country seems crucial to an understanding of where a nation's companies invested abroad, when they went abroad, as well as important in understanding their relationships with firms in neighbouring lands. Yet, sometimes, being 'politically', 'culturally', or 'linguistically' nearby was more important that geographical proximity. Directions of trade gave enterprises greater familiarity with certain areas – and a clear connection exists between the extension of business investment abroad and a nation's commerce, albeit there was never a perfect correlation (and, at any particular time, thwarted trade – because of tariffs – might be an incentive to raise foreign direct investment). So, too, often (but not always) there existed a positive relationship between emigration and the locales for foreign direct investment. Once, again, migration served to provide information flows and lower uncertainty costs.

I included the impact of culture, with reluctance, since it seems an amorphous concept. I am not sure that there was one American or German 'culture' that has shaped foreign direct investments, although it is easy to note proto-typical national characteristics and attribute them to culture. The 'American frontier spirit' and 'German aggressiveness' are examples. As a Frenchman explained (in 1915), 'the German is industrious, a remarkably hard worker, who sets about his task with diligence and energy

... Germany is disciplined'.[21] 'Taste' must sometimes be resorted to as a sole explanatory factor. How else is it possible to understand the sizeable British foreign direct investments in tea and German multinationals' involvements in coffee. (Is perhaps taste a sub-set of culture?).

In sum, we can itemise crucial variables in a home country that have impact, but such a roster is merely a start. It is the combinations of these economic, demographic, political, social and cultural impacts that form the basis for our discussion and for the marked differences country-by-country in the development of European and North American multinationals.

## British Business Abroad

Of all nations, the one with the greatest foreign direct investment and the greatest number of overseas operations (1870–1914) was clearly Great Britain.[22] Vying for second place in this period were Germany and the United States, both of which nations headquartered numerous companies with business abroad.[23] After these three leaders, it is difficult to establish which country would rank fourth. Candidates include France and Sweden. Belgium is also a possibility for fourth place. Switzerland ranks high on the list, as does Holland.[24] Lower down on the tabulation are Canada, Austria-Hungary, Italy, Russia, and Bulgaria.

British business in 1870–1914 spanned the globe. Britain had in these years slower growth rates at home than did the United States and Germany. Its enterprises were, however (or as a consequence in some cases), very active abroad. The extent of British *business* overseas is just becoming known; many ventures were shortlived. For this article, I made a very rough count of British headquartered enterprises that I could document as having built or acquired manufacturing plants *in the United States* before 1914. The number of parent companies ran in excess of 100. Many had multiplant businesses in America. They owned roughly 255 manufacturing plants. But, approximately a third of these factories had shut down, or were no longer British-owned by 1914.[25]

British firms that operated overseas were of two basic varieties. First, and foremost, there were what I have called 'free-standing' companies.[26] Second, there were companies that did business in Britain and then expanded overseas, extending their existing operations.[27] There were many more free-standing companies than any other type of British foreign direct investment. The companies were registered in the United Kingdom and were established to do business typically in a single country abroad. Thus, there were Anglo-Argentine, Anglo-Australian, Anglo-Russian firms. Each usually operated in a single economic activity overseas, but together they covered the economic spectrum; they were in agriculture, manufacturing, and services (including public utilities, transportation, and banking services). The enterprises were both 'market-oriented' (to serve the host country markets) and 'supply-oriented' (to provide for British, or less often, third country needs). Their founders hoped to unite the abundant capital in Great Britain with the potentially or actually profitable opportunity abroad. Each had a board of directors in Britain, charged with managing the overseas business. The British headquarters was, however, at least at origin usually limited to the part-time board of directors and possibly one full-time secretary. In short, the head office did not amount to very much.

There were literally thousands of British free-standing companies. They attracted British capital, but also French, German, Belgian, and other foreign investors. The firms, however, were the investors abroad. The free-standing companies were frequently grouped in loose clusters – clusters that were often overlapping. A single firm might be classified in a handful of different clusters. The principals in the clusters provided a range of services to the free-standing companies.[28].

There were British free-standing companies in many different activities from rubber in Malaya to copper mining in Russia, from cattle ranches in the United States to nitrate mines in Chile, from railroads in Brazil to hotels in Egypt, from mortgage companies in Australia to meat-packing in Argentina. The variety was extraordinary.

In addition, there were in Britain many companies that first developed their business operations with the home market preeminent and then invested abroad to pursue added markets and to obtain sources of supply. Such businesses included 'industrials', but also numerous British producers of services (trade, shipping, insurance, accounting, engineering, and so forth). The British producers of goods that invested abroad in the years before 1914 appear to have been heavily concentrated in the consumer products sector (soap, thread, and patent medicines are excellent examples).[29] All were trademarked. If the companies made producer goods, the home industries were often related to textiles (Bradford Dyers, United Alkali, H & G Bullock). There seems to have been very little British overseas business based on advanced technology. The crucible steel makers – which had major technical advantages – appear to have had their advantage in long experience rather than especially new developments.[30] Four examples of British 'high-technology' companies that did invest abroad in this era are: (1) Courtaulds (rayon); (2) Burroughs & Wellcome (drugs); (3) Brunner, Mond (alkalis); and (4) Marconi (radio installations). The first case was in synthetic textiles (and the technology here was developed in part outside Britain or with the aid of foreign ideas); the second was of a company founded by Americans, which sold patent medicines as well as ethical drugs; the third was a firm that was part of a Belgian multinational enterprise (and it was the latter rather than the British one that was at the centre of the multinational business behaviour);

and the fourth was a company founded by a man with an Italian father and a British mother (it was not a 'purely' British enterprise), and moreover, although radio was new, economic historian Hugh Aitken could write of the 'technological conservatism' of the Marconi organisation and that the technological leadership Marconi once held was already 'shaky' by 1914; 'confident in its technical supremacy, it [the Marconi organisation] had failed to mount a sustained research program'.[31]

It has often been assumed by American students of multinational enterprise that textile companies did not become multinationals. Yet, the largest British textile enterprises were engaged in overseas direct investments. By 1914 J. & P. Coats had mills in the United States, Canada, and Russia.[32] English Sewing Cotton Co. produced through affiliated companies in the United States, France, and Russia. Linen Thread Co., Ltd., had factories in the United States and France.[33] The Fine Cotton Spinners' & Doublers' Association acquired around the turn of the century 'a dominant interest' in its most prominent French competitor, La Société Anonyme des Filatures Delebart Mallet Fils.[34] Bradford Dyers had a major plant in the United States and one in Germany. Nairn Linoleum (linoleum is made of jute or burlap – and thus can be classified as a textile) had factories in the United States, France, and Germany.[35] This is only a small sample of the British textile plants abroad. The host country list – the United States, Canada, France, Germany, Russia – is, however, worth noting.

British businesses also integrated backward to obtain needed raw materials, from cotton seed and palm oil (by Lever) to crude oil (by the 'Shell' Transport and Trading Co.), to iron ore (by Consett and Dowlais).[36] It was apparently even more common for British enterprises to use the free-standing firm for investments in basic inputs and other agricultural products.

Prominent among the 'service' sector multinationals were trading companies.[37] Often trading houses set up free-standing companies (combining the two forms). Likewise, men involved in overseas shipping frequently were associated with free-standing units.[38] So, too consulting and managing engineers had responsibility for managing free-standing mining companies.[39] As yet we know little about the role of the British overseas banks in assisting the expansion of British business abroad.[40] We do know that British banks abroad were a significant aspect of British business overseas.[41] We also know that many of the British international and imperial banks began as free-standing companies.[42]

In my *Economic History Review* article, I outline ten cluster sets that united British free-standing companies. These clusters and others need more attention. While most, as indicated, involved a very tenuous coupling of companies – joined by a functional service provided to the enterprise (promotion, engineering, accounting, services) – some cluster sets could be tighter and then we move to a description of the pivotal service firm as a multinational enterprise.[43] We need to think about the nature of influence and control, influence that is specific to particular functions (finance, construction, engineering, purchasing, marketing) and control (which determines or has the potential to establish overall administrative direction).[44] Faithful and effective performance in a single function might be simpler for a British business to achieve than full internalisation.

While the two basic forms of British overseas business before 1914 appear to have been the free-standing company and the enterprise that evolved from a home base, two other variants in origin have been identified. The first is what Geoffrey Jones has called the migrating multinational.[45] This is a company that began with a headquarters in one country, invested in Britain, and then became over time a British-headquartered multinational. The second variant is more difficult for me to incorporate in my frame of reference. This is a firm established abroad (with no UK registration) that attracted both British capital and British management. It is not, by my definition, a free-standing firm, since it did not have a legal headquarters in Britain; it was not a *company* investing over borders. Yet, some have felt this type of activity should be included under the category of British business abroad.[46] Frequently, companies set up abroad became free-standing ones with British registration and then the free-standing company was dissolved, to be again replaced by a local firm. Sometimes, a free-standing company was set up anew and then the place of incorporation migrated abroad. My research suggests (tentatively) that when the last step occurred, the administrative control from Britain either weakened substantially, or terminated; what was once a direct investment became a portfolio one.[47] The 'British' management was by immigrants or expatriates – if it persisted. Some overseas-registered companies seem to have been established by British trading houses that provided their management and arranged their financing. Can it be said that such companies are part of a multinational enterprise in which the trading house provides the administrative guidance? The trading house, in turn, had the UK head office.

If we were able to identify a company *registered* abroad, with a concentrated ownership in the United Kingdom that provided a British 'head office' and assumed a 'managerial role' but had no 'operations' by the unincorporated head office – I would be prepared to call this a 'free-standing firm – variant I'.[48] More research needs to be done on the distinctions between British- and locally-registered firms and the management of the business institution.[49]

One significant British multinational captured aspects of three of the four categories, but, none the less, could be classified in one of them. Borax Consolidated, Ltd., by 1914 was a major British multinational – with a headquarters in London and operations in Britain, North and South

America, and Europe. It was a vertically and horizontally integrated international enterprise with a legal and administrative headquarters in the United Kingdom.

Its genesis was when an American went to England – seeking markets and monies. He met a Britisher. What evolved was a merger of the British Redwood and Sons and the American's far more extensive operation. A headquarters was established in the United Kingdom, as was a British holding company. For Redwood this was backward vertical integration. I am prepared to call the new holding company, a *British* multinational enterprise. Yet, even though the legal and administrative head office was in Britain, the largest stockholding in the parent company was by the American. The parent was to integrate operations (uniting the British and American businesses), but also to raise capital in Britain for the entire business. While the new British enterprise was clearly not a free-standing one, it bore resemblances to many such companies. It had a prestigious chairman of the board – brought in to encourage Britishers to invest. And, when another British 'free-standing company' shifted its headquarters from London to New York, the principal American stockholder in the borax company suggested that it follow suit. It did not. London remained the headquarters for not only the British and American, but the firm's newly-acquired worldwide business operations. Eventually, in 1913, the American was forced out of the business (and sold his shareholdings).[50] It could be argued (although I do not want to do so) that this was a migrating multinational; clearly, however, the insights and recognition of the existence of migrating multinationals helps us understand this British business abroad.

The idea of the migrating multinational provides even more insights into the activities of another giant British multinational enterprise (albeit I would argue that this firm did not become a *British* multinational until the 1920s). The British–American Tobacco Co. (BAT) came into being in 1902, as a part of a division of market agreement that followed American Tobacco's aggressive attempt to penetrate the British market. BAT at origin was owned two-thirds by American Tobacco and one-third by Imperial Tobacco, and had operations worldwide; it could not sell in the United States nor in the United Kingdom, but had export-related activities in both countries, and most important, it had a London headquarters. At the start, its top management seems to have been American. In 1902, it was an American business abroad. In time, the American stock ownership was reduced, the American management cut back, the home office well established in London, and this company became a British multinational (a migrating multinational enterprise).[51]

I am less sure that when a free-standing registered company shifted to foreign registration (as was often the case) that there was retained British direct investment characteristics. Thus, Otis Steel, an American company, was acquired by a British free-standing company. For years it was a British direct investment in the United States. In time, however, the British headquarters had seemed superfluous. The British-registered company was dissolved. A British accountant joined the US board of directors, presumably representing British investors. When the British registered company was dissolved, I would suggest that the *company* that had made the direct investment was also out-of-the-picture; now the individual British investors had portfolio rather than direct investment stakes (despite the accountant who represented their interests).[52]

In considering British business abroad, we must have a flexibility in evaluating what we find. We need to inquire why was the British free-standing company more common than the British enterprise that developed its operations abroad out of an existing business in Britain? What happened to the free-standing companies through time? How did they deal with the problems of managing business overseas? Why did consumer goods industries predominate in those British businesses that went abroad? Why was the textile industry so visible in British business abroad? To what extent was there foreign direct investment in raw materials and foodstuff production? Why did the trading company take such a key role in diffusing British business abroad? What exactly was the role of banking institutions? What insights does the paradigm of the cluster set provide? What do the discoveries of migrating multinationals tell us about British business activities? Is the transfer of registration overseas an aspect of the migration of business headquarters? What insights are cast on British managerial performance overseas?

The home country influences outlined earlier in this paper help us to start to answer some of these questions. Factor costs: British capital was abundant; the relative cheapness of capital meant that the British had the opportunity (the incentive) to invest it elsewhere around the world where the returns were higher than at home. Free-standing companies were the institutional device to maintain control. Britain was industrialised; it had been the first industrial nation. Britain used its technological advantage in textiles abroad – and on occasion British multinationals borrowed abroad to overcome technological deficiencies. There was a high income domestic market in which consumer goods had been sold; the textile industry had grown first and foremost in that market. Many British investments abroad were designed to provide for the domestic market. But, the geographically small British domestic market was inadequate as a training ground for managers. The family firm without a well-developed managerial structure persisted in Britain. British companies had problems operating abroad. The free-standing firm was a compromise and may in many cases have substituted for British firms that apparently found the extension of management internationally a difficult proposition.[53]

Since Britain did not have 'universal' banks, it was often 'the investment group', with a trading company at the centre that assisted British business abroad.[54] Britain was a small island, dependent on international trade, which meant the emergence of well-developed and numerous trading companies with important roles in developing British business abroad.

Lack of certain basic natural resources (plus demand for them) encouraged not only trade, but also British business investment abroad. The investment, however, was highly selective and more needs to be done on the institutional structure and management of British mining and agricultural investments abroad and especially on the management of the marketing of the output.[55] Many British direct investments in railroads were associated with primary product procurement.

Scots abroad often ran British overseas investments with Burma to Canada to Chile. The overseas Scot provided the British company with a familiar dependable representative abroad. Culturally, Britain is frequently perceived as 'insular', and smug. A number of years ago, however, Charles Wilson pointed out that Unilever and Imperial Chemical Industries in the 1920s had involved a merging of multinational founders.[56] So did Royal Dutch-Shell much earlier. The more one deals with the British international business community, the more cosmopolitan it seems.[57] It is a paradox that contrasts with the stereotype – although it has long been recognised that British business innovation was promoted by 'outsiders' rather than by those in the mainstream of British life.[58] None the less, the insularity does appear to have created in many instances constraints on British management abroad,[59] constraints that the many Scots abroad could only partially rectify.

## German and American Multinationals

The differences between British and German multinationals were vivid, yet, as we will see, there were similarities. There was not the same mix of the two (or four) varieties of German and British business abroad. There seem to have been few (or certainly far fewer than the British, in relative terms) German free-standing companies that operated in foreign countries – at least this is my present view – though the subject needs more investigation, especially as relates to public utilities, transportation, and raw material procurement (some of the German investments in US phosphate mining, for example, seem to have been by free-standing companies). Migrating multinationals do not appear to have been a particularly important feature in the origins of German multinationals (albeit could the Rheinische Stahlwerke AG be seen in these terms – it was established in 1869 by Frenchmen and Belgians and headquartered in Paris;[60] and what about Allgemeine Elektrizitäts Gesellschaft? could it be considered a migrating multi-national? its predecessor was part of an American business

abroad).[61] I have not been able to identify *independent* German companies
registered in the host country, with German capital *and* management
direction *from* Germany (there were, however, numerous firms established
by German immigrants and registered in the host country, but these either
fit into the category of German multinational enterprise – where the
immigrant represented a parent firm abroad – or were separate businesses
of the immigrant and *not* part of a German business abroad, not a foreign
direct investment). We need more study, however, of third-country
registrations – London-registered companies that operated in Argentina
(for example) – that were German-owned and probably (in the host
country) German-managed. The London-registration seems to have been
to aggregate capital, to have a convenient operating framework, but where
was the real 'headquarters'? In a German city? I do not know, but that
would be my hypothesis. If so, this might well be part of a German
multinational enterprise expansion.

There were many German companies that began to do business in
Germany and then based on their advantage at home, extended their
business abroad, typically to reach foreign markets and to obtain raw
materials.[62] Such investments included many in public utilities, designed to
*sell* German electrical equipment. There were also numerous German
trading companies – mercantile houses – that had outlets throughout
Europe and in addition appear in locales from Guatemala to Turkey.[63]
Especially important were the German metal traders.[64] And then there
were the German banks active in Europe, North and South America, Asia,
and Africa, encouraging and representing German business abroad.[65]

The extent of German-managed enterprise in foreign countries in the
pre-First World War years is just being deciphered; there are studies of
German foreign direct investment in the United States, in Great Britain,
and elsewhere.[66] What seems evident is that unlike the British ones,
German multinationals were particularly active abroad in 'high technology'
products – especially in the chemical and in the electrical industries.[67]
German companies also operated abroad in iron and steel manufactures.[68]
They were involved in capital goods industries. German industrial enterprise took the initiative in world markets – exporting, setting up marketing
organisations abroad, and establishing foreign manufacture, and foreign
companies that would buy German output.

The British – as we have seen – excelled in trademarked consumer
products. The Germans also used the trademark as an important property
right in their business abroad. Yet, the use may have been different. In the
United States Bayer, for example, sold aspirins, which it would claim was
its trademarked product. The drug was sold through prescriptions;
however, increasingly *before 1914*, consumers bought it over-the-counter
and decided on 'self-medication'. Bayer advertised widely, *but* to physi-
cians and to the trade, rather than to the final consumer. Ultimately (in

1921), Bayer would lose the trademark Aspirin in America; the reason the court gave was that before 1915, the company had let the retail druggist (or the manufacturing chemist, who bottled or transformed powder into tablets) sell to the consumer *without* the Bayer name on the product. Thus, in the trademark case, the court ruled that for the consumer the word had passed into the public domain.[69] Germans invested abroad in chocolates – a consumer product. Here again, the product was trademarked, but once again, Stollwerck in many instances sold not to the ultimate buyer, but as a cooking chocolate to other producers.[70]

Actually, there were a surprising number of trademarked German consumer products.[71] The A.W. Faber pencil was one. The German Faber firm by the 1870s was a multinational enterprise, with its main factory in Stein (near Nürnberg); a large slate facility at Geroldsgrun, Bavaria; branches in Paris and London; an agency in Vienna; and a pencil factory in Brooklyn, New York. In the early twentieth century, the American subsidiary, A.W. Faber, was advertising that the German company had manufactories in Germany, France, and the United States. The idea that there were no (or few) German consumer goods manufactured by German multinationals abroad is false.[72]

Like the British, there were some important German textile investments in foreign countries – in woollens and silk (not the textiles most typically associated with British overseas business) – albeit some scholars have found that German textile producers were not active abroad.[73]

Certain German industrial firms integrated backward to obtain raw materials. This was true of German iron and steel manufacturers.[74] Trading companies also appear to have made investments in producing activities abroad. Metallgesellschaft is an excellent example.[75]

German banks were ubiquitous abroad, aiding industrial enterprises in numerous manners. They were active, for example, in relation to the German search abroad for oil – in Romania and in the Middle East.[76]

Like the German multinationals, US multinationals often invested abroad to sell and to make goods, based on new technology and typically trademarked products (whether sold to producer or consumer).[77] In some of the same industries, American and German business both expanded abroad, but, in the main, the industries were different. The US-registered free-standing company existed (in Cuban sugar, for example), although it was of little significance in American business abroad in the pre-1914 years. Again, while I can identify some migrating multinationals (W.R. Grace started in Peru, and then became a US-headquartered business), that pattern was atypical. In both the American and German cases, the prototype multinational was a firm that started at home and then expanded over borders – either to reach markets or to obtain sources of supply. Yet, in the German evolution of multinational enterprise, the role of the giant banks was key, whereas in the United States, to be sure private banks had

London and Paris outlets (principally to encourage the flow of European monies to America), but US national banks could not branch abroad until after the passage of the Federal Reserve Act (1913). Thus, not only did the United States have virtually nothing comparable to the numerous British overseas banks (the International Banking Corporation established in 1902 is the one possible exception), it had nothing that was anywhere near equivalent to the Deutsche Bank or the other great German banks.[78]

Here again, home country characteristics help explain why the German and American multinational enterprise pattern differed from that of the British. Clearly, in each case, factor costs were different. German enterprise could draw on an abundance of skilled workers and professionals; in products that were skill- and research-intensive, German business excelled and expanded at home and abroad. This was especially relevant in the dyestuff sector of the German chemical industry, where literally thousands of products were produced in small batches by large companies, heavily manned with skilled and often university educated personnel. Americans found labour costs high and substituted capital for labour. Mass production techniques used unskilled labour. American companies expanded abroad in sewing machines, harvesters, and mass produced automobiles. America had abundant oil; new refineries had large throughput; the country became a large exporter of refined oil, and Standard Oil became a major multinational enterprise.[79] Differences in factor costs in part accounted for the differing German and American advantages. In Alfred Chandler's terms, economies of scope and economies of scale created differences in cost advantages.[80] By 1914, Germany ranked second and the United States ranked first in world manufacturing (Britain was third). The growth of industrialisation spurred new enterprises that quickly expanded over national frontiers. It was often in the newest and most technologically advanced products that German and US businesses invested abroad. Technologically innovative enterprises abounded, and it was these companies that introduced the new processes and products abroad (through foreign direct investments).

German and US firms sold first at home and then abroad. In both Germany and the United States, administrative hierarchies in business organisation emerged more rapidly than in Britain. In Germany, however, the family firm seems to have lingered longer in sizeable enterprise (and in business abroad) than was the case in the United States. If family members went abroad, they often supported German business expansion (George Merck in America, for example). The Germans, like the British, and far more than Americans, found business over borders very difficult. The German electrical companies' problems in controlling their business investments in the United States are a case in point.[81] In the United States, where scale economies were key, the huge and heterogeneous US market offered a superb training arena for business managers who would move abroad. The ever-present German bank in domestic business reflected itself in the international scene.

US and American states' banking laws sharply restricted American banks in their expansion at home (and abroad). We need more information on German business abroad and natural resource procurement; there were many German foreign direct investments in production of primary products. The Germans had little oil – and German companies, accordingly, desired to fill domestic needs. By contrast, the US international oil industry began based on abundant oil and refined oil exports. The evolution of the German and US (and for that matter the British) international oil companies was entirely different. By 1914, one American tyre company (US Rubber) had begun to invest in rubber plantations in Sumatra; the British, Dunlop had invested in rubber estates in Malaya; did the leading German tyre company have similar investments? Many of the products required for the German economy – but not produced there – were obtained through German importing firms.

German professional education – the scientific training – had immense impact on German advantage in world markets. American education was more practical, more engineering-oriented. This seems to have had an influence on the firms in America that had advantages and that moved abroad. The connections in the German case are very specific; in the American one more general.

Germany was a net exporter of capital, but its growth at home absorbed substantial investment. None the less, that it was a net capital exporter may help explain the important role of banks in its international expansion. The United States before 1914 was a net importer of capital. Its portfolio investments abroad (1870–1914) were very small compared with its foreign direct investments. US companies moved abroad not to locate better financial returns, but to reach markets and to obtain sources of supply. When we compare American and British business abroad, this difference is vivid. In Britain, there was substantial surplus capital and rates of return were higher overseas. The evidence in the British case indicates that foreign portfolio investments were larger than foreign direct investments. The free-standing company served to direct and to monitor the use of passive investors' capital abroad. Since America was a net importer of capital, there was generally little need for the free-standing company form. Business abroad grew out of the requirements of business at home.

In Germany, because cartels were perfectly acceptable, there existed some foreign direct investments by cartel representatives to encourage exports.[82] Cartels may have also deterred some foreign direct investment. The restraint of trade rules in America encouraged mergers; domestic conditions required integration of operations; integrated business abroad was a natural extension.

German business crossed over into neighbouring countries; Austria–

Hungary – especially the Austrian part, where the language was German – was especially attractive. In some ways, Austria–Hungary may have been to German enterprise rather like Canada to US business, with German business 'spilling over' the border. Likewise, there were sizeable German investments in other nearby countries; transportation and communication links within Europe had by 1870–1914 become very easy – and enterprising German businessmen often made their presence felt – from France to Switzerland, and in many other European countries. But German businesses made their greatest direct investment in the United States (in part because that was where there was the major German immigration). American business abroad went first and foremost to nearby countries (geographically nearby such as Canada, Mexico, and the Caribbean) and culturally nearby (such as Canada and the United Kingdom). German emigrants were very significant in developing German business abroad. There were German settlers from China to Russia. (Odessa in 1910, for example, had a German community of 12,000).[83] There was nothing at all similar with American emigrants; the United States was a country of immigrants not emigrants. Germans abroad created familiar conditions for German business in foreign lands and helped overcome some of the difficulties of doing business in strange lands. (As noted earlier, American businessmen learned at home how to deal with 'foreigners' in the domestic markets, since American business was already selling at home to a nationally diverse population.)

Clearly, 'the culture' of economic growth influenced German and American businesses in their expansion over borders. There was a vitality in the German and American people that reflected itself in the spread of business abroad. Whereas in Britain at least some of the business activities overseas (particularly those of the free-standing companies) involved a conscious reallocation of resources – at least capital resources – from domestic to international use; in the German and US cases, business abroad was more typically complementary to that at home.

### French, Swedish, Belgian, Swiss, and Dutch Business Investments Abroad

French business abroad was extensive in the years 1870 to 1914; while substantial work has been done on French finance, we are slowly learning about the institutional mechanisms by which French industry extended itself over borders.[84] The St. Gobain glassworks as early as the 1850s had built a branch plant in Germany; by 1900 it was a multi-plant enterprise in that country.[85] Before the First World War, St. Gobain was also manufacturing in Italy, Belgium, Holland, Spain, and Austria–Hungary.[86] (How aggressive it seems compared with Pilkington; that British firm had manufacturing abroad in only one country – Canada).[87] The French family firm, Michelin, had by 1914 factories in the United States, Italy, and Great Britain (its rival, Dunlop, in 1914 manufactured in Germany, France, and Japan; no German nor US tyre company had three foreign manufacturing plants in 1914).[88] French car companies also had a collection of business investments abroad.[89]

Most extensive, however, were the international operations of Société Schneider et Cie. Claude Ph. Beaud has done remarkably well in deciphering its business aborad – from Italy to Chile to England (all disappointing ventures). Often the firm's participations were minority ones, but they were designed for business purposes – that is, to obtain orders for Schneider. In Morocco, Schneider set up a diversified group of companies, associated with Moroccan development – from mining companies to gas and electric ones. In Argentina, it made major investments, with the hope of obtaining orders from the newly-established firms. It invested in iron-mines in Lorraine and collieries in Belgium. In 1911 it participated in developing the Russian armaments industry.[90]

I have found a surprising number of French businesses that operated in the United States;[91] more operated in Russia; Spain was attractive to French businessmen (often operating through London-registered companies).[92] French free-standing companies seem to have existed, albeit the extent of them is unknown.[93] French trading companies need investigation,[94] as do French banks.[95] John McKay's 'The House of Rothschild (Paris) as a Multinational Industrial Enterprise, 1875–1914', breaks new ground in the study of French business abroad.[96] Wherever there was gold, French businessmen were interested; thus, students of British business in South Africa have encountered French (and German) involvements.

The French always complained that German business had grabbed, in international business, what was French technology (in silk, for example). The French were the innovators in rayon – but initially the prominent multinational in rayon was the British-headquartered Courtaulds. The Héroult process in aluminium was a French one – and yet, American, German-Swiss, and to a far lesser extent British companies took precedence over French business abroad in this new industry. In a number of different industries where the French excelled, we know little about why or how French business enterprises took, or failed to take, the initiative in business abroad. Often, in the French case we are talking about family firms, not publicly-owned companies. Yet, France was a large capital exporter in the years before 1914 (second only to Great Britain) and it does seem that some (and perhaps much) of this foreign investment was in the form of direct investment (business investment), probably more than is generally assumed.[97]

Ragnhild Lundström has documented the remarkable expansion of

Swedish business abroad. Swedish companies (often based on German technology) spread internationally – seeking new markets, setting up plants abroad. Banks played a crucial role, in assisting Swedish international business and Swedish entrepreneurs who went abroad. Swedes established operations in Russia; they financed these ventures in European capital markets; often, the Swedes settled in Russia. Can this be called 'Swedish' business abroad, or Swedish direct investment? Once the migration took place, should this not be described as a Russian business, financed by European (portfolio) investment? Such activities bear resemblance to the Britisher, who went abroad, set up business in a country overseas, and then called on home capital for financing. It appears frequently that in neither case was there a real European head office administering operations. The investment from Europe seems to have been pure finance. Here, again, family associations must be traced.[98]

Lundström identified a hybrid-type operation. A man went abroad to do business, set up a manufacturing company, and got full equity financing from the Enskilda Bank. Is this a foreign direct investment by the Bank? The bank had control. Yet, the initiative came from the trusted entrepreneur, who was in a business abroad that had nothing to do with banking. How common was such a pattern?[99]

There were numerous Belgian businesses in foreign lands that are very well known – from Leopold's extensive activities in the Congo to Solvay & Cie.'s international business.[100] Belgium had heavy industry. Société Générale de Belgique made direct investments in Spain, Italy, France, Austria, Russia, China, Mexico, Brazil, Argentina, and of course, the Congo, in railroad construction, to help secure markets for Belgian industry. The Société Générale also invested in an extensive chain of banks that did business outside of Belgium.[101] There were formidable Belgian foreign direct investments in tramways, especially those of the Empain group.[102] Individual Belgian entrepreneurs had many direct investments abroad.[103] The complex Belgian direct investments in the Russian iron and steel industry have been well documented by Ulrich Wengenroth.[104] More modest investments were those of Gevaert, an Antwerp maker of photographic paper. His production began in 1892 and by the eve of the First World War, Lieven Gevaert had opened branch distribution depots in Paris, Vienna, Berlin, Milan, Moscow, London, Buenos Aires, and Rio.[105] If Solvay & Cie.'s and Gevaert's business abroad seem comfortable in the conventional model of multinational enterprise, many of the other Belgian businesses outside the country do not conform as neatly. Robert Liefmann, many years ago, concluded that the big banks in Belgium 'have had a greater influence upon the initiation and financing of enterprises [at home and abroad] than in any other country'.[106] By all accounts, Belgian-managed business over borders was extensive. How and where did banks find managers that were appropriate to the task to be performed abroad?

We need more studies on how the managerial structure emerged. Likewise, we require more evidence on where Belgian business went; from all appearances, Belgian enterprise was truly multinational; yet Solvay & Cie. excepted, it was conspicuously absent in the United States before the First World War.[107] Is the reason, that Belgian industrial advantages were not advantages in the United States?

Swiss multinational enterprise, likewise, requires far more attention. Many Swiss businesses invested abroad – in silk, cotton, wool and embroidery, canned goods, chocolates, pharmaceuticals, electro-technical and electrochemical industries, machinery, and so forth.[108] By 1914, there were five Swiss hotel companies that ran hotels in Italy, France, and North Africa.[109] The common feature of all Swiss investments was always quality goods and services.[110] If Ernest Himmel's figures on 77 Swiss companies are to be trusted, in 1913 they had the most invested in France, followed by 'North America' (principally the United States), Germany, and then Italy.[111]

According to an obituary of Robert Schwarzenbach (1839–1904), this Swiss pioneer in silk power looms had by 1904 established silk manufacturing plants not only in Switzerland, but in the United States, Italy, France, and Germany.[112] When in 1900, Nestlé built its American factory in Fulton, New York, a local town directory announced that 'The milk received at the Fulton factory is subjected to the same high test as has been observed for 30 years and more at the Swiss factories of Henri Nestlé at Vevey, Bercher and Payerne, as well as at the Norwegian factory at Christiania, and those at Edlitz, Austria, and Tutbury, England'.[113] Brown, Boveri & Co. – one of the largest manufacturers in Switzerland – had by 1914 'branches' in Italy, France, and Norway.[114] This is merely a small sample of Swiss multinational enterprises, in different industries. Where did the Swiss find management for all these businesses abroad? How often were family connections significant? How were these plants administered over borders? What role did Swiss banks play? There are many unanswered questions. Throughout the period Himmel studied (1898–1919), the Swiss businesses he monitored had greater investments *outside* Switzerland than at home.[115]

Whereas in the case of Switzerland, I identified very few 'free-standing companies', by contrast, this form is prevalent in the case of Dutch foreign direct investment.[116] Dutch finance has captured substantial attention, as have certain Dutch businesses abroad. (The Royal Dutch Company and its successor, Royal Dutch-Shell, for example). Yet, we require more information on the nature of Dutch business abroad (1870–1914).[117] In Holland, private banks set up administrative trusts to hold American railroad securities, which securities were, in turn, owned by Dutch small investors. The effect was concentrated ownership that gave the banks a say in the conduct of the business abroad, at least *vis-à-vis* the financial function.

Was this, therefore, foreign direct investment? The railroads in the United States were American-incorporated, American-administered, but the Dutch bankers often had more influence (at least on financial matters) than a typical 'portfolio' investor.[118] How does the student of multinational enterprise view such investments? This brings us to the matter of influence and control, and 'functional' relationships to which I will return in the conclusion.

In short, France exempted, all these contestants for fourth rank as homes to foreign direct investors were geographically small, relatively high income countries. In each case the nature of domestic business operations shaped business abroad. There seem to have been identifiable business elites (sometimes cosmopolitan in nature) that can be tracked in connection with the business abroad; some, but certainly not by any means all, of these business elites had banking connections. All of these countries except Holland and Switzerland appear to have looked more east than west in their investments and had larger direct investments in Russia than in the United States. Beyond this, it is difficult to generalize about this very diverse group of home countries, and I will leave that for future researchers. How many – aside from the Swiss – had greater investments abroad than at home?

**The Other Multinationals**

Canadian business abroad went typically across the border into the United States, albeit it did extend further into the Caribbean and Latin America. In public utilities particularly there was a marked expansion of Canadian business abroad.[119]

Austro-Hungarian businesses across Empire borders were few and isolated, but there were some important ones. The Austrian Hermann Schmidtmann, with his direct investments in Germany and the United States, provides a good case in point.[120] Often, multi-plant Austro-Hungarian enterprises became 'international', after the break-up of the Empire! Fiat was exceptional among the modern Italian businesses in this period to invest abroad; it had manufacturing branches in Austria, the United States, and Russia by 1913.[121] Russian and Bulgarian fire insurance companies were before 1914 multinational enterprises. 'Bulgaria', First Bulgarian Insurance Co. of Routschouk, Bulgaria, in 1913 operated in England, Germany, Belgium, Bulgaria, France, Holland, Spain, Turkey, and the United States.[122]

In sum, such debtor countries and Empires as Canada, the Austro-Hungarian Empire, Italy, Russia, and Bulgaria were homes to multinational enterprise.[123] The business abroad that was headquartered in these places tended, in the case of Canada, to be very limited as to where it went abroad, and in all these 'homes' tended to be quite restricted in terms of the economic sectors represented.

## The Host Countries

Of all the hosts to foreign direct investment, the United States was in 1914 by far the most important. It was a high income market, surrounded by a high tariff wall; it was rich in natural resources; and the opportunities for profit seemed immense. I will not give rankings beyond this, for I believe that any attempt to try to give the standing of host countries is at this stage premature.[124] Part of the problem in ranking hosts to foreign multinational enterprise is the lack of consensus on what is to be included as 'foreign direct investment'. In this article, I have tried to indicate what I believe should and should not be included. Until there is consensus in definition, however, country ranking will lead to nothing but frustration. This, however, is only part of the problem: each region or country has been studied separately, without comparative evaluations (scholars are trained as experts in European history, Chinese history, South African history, and so forth).

Without question, wherever a European or North American multi-national enterprise invested, circumstances in the host country influenced its behaviour. It is, however, doubtful that each host country was so distinctive as to transform or to homogenise the foreign business, though over time, host country consumers might not be aware they were buying products of a foreign-owned firm.[125]

The evidence suggests that since a foreign direct investment by definition has a headquarters in the home country, the strategies of the firm (at least initially) can be said to be more shaped by home rather than host country considerations, albeit clearly both play an important role and it goes almost without saying that the characteristics of the host country – from size of market to resources available, to political conditions (including tariff policies) – determine at the start whether a company will invest, in what sectors it will invest, and the legal forms of the investment. These matters also shaped the pace and the course of the expansion (or contraction, in some cases) of the business. A number of business investments of this era were 'joint-ventures' of one type or another – and the joint-venture relationships varied substantially, based on host country considerations.

Such comments accepted as a given, none the less, it seems to me that there are comparisons that can be made and that if one begins with the firm and its investments, there are patterns that transcend host country and regional impacts. One of the virgin territories for students of multinational enterprise relates to how companies of different nationalities performed differently in a host country.[126]

More is needed on the relationships between trade and emigration patterns in considering why particular investors chose to invest in particular host countries. As I study European-headquartered firms, I find myself asking many questions about 'partial' relationships – how these 'groupings', clusters, functional ties, reflected themselves in the management of business abroad in different countries; this seems to need more scrutiny.

## Conclusions

While substantial research has been done on the history of multinational enterprise, much more is clearly required. The general, comparative research is particularly important to the British business historian, for it poses new questions and presses the historian toward a recognition of what is and what is not distinctive about the British experience. Research has made it evident that it is useful to look at the behaviour of business over borders. Too often there have been two constraints. The first is the assumption that the findings on the history of American business abroad (the American model) can be rigidly applied to business headquartered in Great Britain, Continental Europe and Canada. The second is that multinational enterprise and foreign direct investment are identical.

Let us look at each in turn. The application of the American model has provoked exciting new research. British business historians have been particularly active in this respect. Often, there is congruence in the behaviour of multinationals from different countries. However, the newer research shows considerable differences in the development of multinational enterprise in the pre-1914 years from one country to the next. The British experience is not exactly coincident with the American one. The modes used (free-standing enterprise versus operating base for example; involvement of banks, as another example) were different.[127] Whereas in the American case, by 1870–1914, it was the large-scale enterprises with administrative organisations that were the innovators in business abroad,[128] in the case of many British and continental European companies we are often describing family firms and kinship rather than corporate linkages over borders. Even in the German instance, where certain of the electrical and chemical companies had huge domestic employment and hierarchical managerial organisations,[129] at the same time, there were many family firms with business both at home and abroad.

These differences reflected themselves in motives. Because America was a net importer of capital, because profitable opportunities were available at home, in 1870–1914, only in the rarest instance was the motive for foreign direct investment purely financial. In countries, particularly Great Britain, where there were 'free-standing' companies often the reason for a specific business investment abroad was purely and simply a higher return in the foreign country, albeit the investment was designed as a managed business abroad. Some free-standing companies were established by promoters that arranged the business investment abroad with the sole purpose of their own quick personal financial gain. Free-standing companies aside, the other rationales do not seem to vary. Thus, companies made foreign direct investment to obtain better representation abroad, to be closer to (and thus more responsive to) customers, to save on transportation costs, to get behind tariff walls (and on rare occasions other host government barriers to trade), to assure sales to an enterprise abroad, and to complement existing foreign direct investments. Some products do not travel well and must be made near the customer (for example, explosives, products that get stale, and beer in this period). Still other foreign direct investments were made to develop or to secure sources of supply. Some foreign direct investments were designed to obtain information. While these motives did not vary by home country, what varied was the relative importance of particular motives – and that needs further study.

One major difference between and among countries was the extent of the business abroad *vis-à-vis* domestic operations. American business at home was always larger than its firms' foreign direct investments. If Himmel is correct, by contrast, Swiss business investments abroad were greater than those at home; are there other geographically small countries that fit this pattern? British business historians need to ask of companies engaged in business abroad, what percentage of their assets, sales, and employment were at home and what percentage abroad?

America was a country receiving immigrants. While there were individual Americans who went abroad to establish businesses, by 1870–1914 this was not the principal pattern and the 'American model' of multinational enterprise correctly excludes such activity. In the case of Great Britain (and some continental European countries), there was a dispersion – a worldwide spread – of business entrepreneurs. This has posed major problems for students of British multinational enterprise. British-born individuals spanned the globe; they went to the United States, Canada, Argentina, to Sicily, India, Hong Kong – and so forth. Sometimes they brought capital with them; sometimes, they established businesses using monies they had earned abroad. Sometimes they used locally available capital; sometimes they tapped British capital markets for their overseas businesses. I have argued in the introduction to this article (and elsewhere as well) that to fit the definition of multinational enterprise there must be *cross-border* control, or potential for control. The problem lies in defining 'home', in deciding, was there a *cross-border* activity? The Britisher who went to the United States and, in many instances, Canada settled in these countries. There was no ongoing foreign direct investment. Likewise, the Britisher who went to Argentina typically settled, but he often thought of Britain 'as home'. Since he actually settled, and if there was no British home office or British legal registration, I cannot (as indicated in the introduction to this article) refer to his managed business in Argentina as a British foreign direct investment. The matter gets far more difficult with the expatriate rather than the emigrant – with businesses in Sicily, India, and Hong Kong. Take the case of Benjamin Ingham, who spent most of his life in Sicily, but who kept his bank account in the United Kingdom and saw the United Kingdom 'as home'. In real terms, the United Kingdom was home for Ingham, even though his trading business was managed from his base in Sicily. What of British 'expatriates' in India and Hong Kong? They were conspicuously 'British' – white men in a non-white world. 'Home' was Britain: their children were educated there. Hong Kong was frequently a base for business elsewhere in the Far East, especially in China. How should the businesses of these expatriates (as distinct from emigrants) be treated by students of multinational enterprise? This question is important for several reasons: (1) how we define such business affects our statistics on 'British' capital abroad and particularly on British foreign direct investment; (2) in many cases, the expatriates in India and Hong Kong did seek capital in the United Kingdom. It seems to me that if there was no UK home office, the 'British' capital (the cross-border capital) invested in these expatriate ventures must be referred to as British portfolio investments; (3) even more important, from an institutional standpoint, what happened to these enterprises through time? When the individual entrepreneur died or went back 'home' to Great Britain, how were these ventures sustained? If there was some means of replenishing management through time in the United Kingdom, perhaps that can define a 'real' head office. The discussion of multinational enterprise pushes us to look not merely at the individual entrepreneur, but at the continuing managerial structure through time. The answers to these fundamental questions may help us in determining whether the business can legitimately be classified as a 'British' multinational enterprise. In any case, the operating characteristics and the administration of such expatriate businesses – as distinct from ones clearly headquartered in the United Kingdom – need further investigation.

An additional difference that emerges from the comparisons is associated with the 'partial' or functional relationships. Frequently, I found British and Continental European firms (or individuals joined with those companies) participated in business investments abroad, designed not to control the foreign enterprise, but none the less to capture a business opportunity. The business motive could be general, such as obtaining insider knowledge on how the foreign firm performed and whether there would be security of supply of a raw material, or it could be highly specific, such as an arrangement to handle the company's financing (the sale of a service) or a contract to sell goods or other particular services to the firm, or one to market the firm's output. Do such 'partial' relationships fit into the category of foreign direct investments? And if so in what manner? The investor often exercised influence (or even control) over a key function, yet in no way sought to run or even had the potential to manage or to control the entire foreign business. Such business investments usually have been dealt with in the literature as foreign direct investments and put in the context of joint-ventures, which seems reasonable.[130] And, what of the trading company – especially the British trading company – with an investment in a particular productive activity (beyond trade) abroad? Its earnings often came from the management contract (a sale of an important service), assured by the investment. It did have the potential to control the overseas enterprise, through the management contract. It seems to this author that the management contract may well be different from the purely functional relationships; in this case, the entire business of the 'joint-venture' is controlled, though the 'owners' of the business presumably had the power to void a management contract.[131]

The industries of key importance from one home country to the next were different. British business historians must ask why British business abroad was concentrated in particular industries *and* why certain companies in those same industries showed little interest in overseas business. So, too, the locales where investments were made differed by home country. The 'American model' would hypothesise that the firm goes first to the 'nearby' – defined not merely in geographical, but in cultural, linguistic, and political terms. Dr Geoffrey Jones has suggested to me that whereas American business went abroad initially to geographically nearby regions: Canada, Mexico, and the Caribbean (it also went to 'culturally nearby' ones: Canada and the United Kingdom), the British business tended to favour the linguistically (the United States, but also Canada, Australia, and South Africa) and politically (imperial) 'nearby'. This needs more verification with added research on British business investments on the geographically nearby European continent.

The performance of management abroad also differed by home country, and in a way that may well be amenable to systematic treatment. Indeed, I believe that the distinctive British and other home country characteristics – an enquiry into the home environment – can be used to explain not only many of the differences in the way (including 'the why') firms moved abroad and how they behaved once there, which firms went abroad, but in addition how they performed in foreign lands.

On the second and related matter, multinational enterprise and foreign direct investments are not the same. To repeat what I wrote at the beginning of this article, multinational enterprises make foreign direct investments – and they also do other things as well *vis-à-vis* a business abroad. Management of such a business (just as at home) involved financial decisions; it also calls for operating ones: hiring workers, supervisors, and managers; making choices on technology; selecting appropriate machinery; finding suppliers and purchasing (as needed) raw materials, parts and components, and other supplies, as well as the capital goods; deciding what should be bought and what should be made; and developing relationships with suppliers.

None of these decisions on inputs is 'one-time': management consists (among other things) of training those who are hired, altering technology choices as appropriate and as the learning process goes forward, maintaining as well as buying machines, changing 'make-buy' decisions, and educating suppliers. It involves coordinating and administrating the inputs once acquired, organising work, assigning tasks. There is, thus, not only management of the purchasing functions, but of the labour relations, the engineering, and the production activities.

And then there are output decisions. Some of these relate to how much of a process will be done by the firm: does a mining company own a concentrator, a smelter, and a refinery as well? does a plantation company do any further processing? All of these new activities must be managed. And, then if the output is not used or further processed within the firm, how is the product to be marketed? does the company integrate forward into the marketing activity? the management of the marketing function is again not a given. All of these (and many more) management requirements accompany the establishment and development of business abroad. Financing the operation, the foreign direct *investment,* is but one facet (a single function) of what a business does abroad. Thus, students of the history of multinational enterprise must consider and ask questions about how a business abroad is managed, how managers perform; it must separate overall management from the 'partial' functional relationships. British business historians have only begun their task when they identify foreign direct investments.

A study of the history of multinational enterprise needs to look at firms extending a specific business over borders. We must ask of the origins, why, which, how, and where did a firm invest? What were its options? A firm grows over time, and I find myself fully in sympathy with Mark Casson and others who view the multinational enterprise in terms of the theory of the firm.[132] As the firm moves over borders, we must look not merely at the basis for the entry, but the subsequent choices and strategies pursued. The dynamics are critical. We have figures on numbers of British companies in particular regions (the materials are not as rich on other nationalities), but we have far less information on how the business abroad was pursued and managed over time. How and where was the output marketed? In the British case, the void is particularly evident in relation to the free-standing firm.[133]

A crucial subject is the relation between trade and foreign direct investment. British business historians need to ask the relationship between both British exports and imports and foreign direct investment. In many instances, foreign direct investment encouraged further exports of goods and services; in other instances it substituted for exports; and in still others it encouraged imports. The effects on trade need to be systematically studied by home country, through time; were there differences by home country?[134]

We need more discussion of performance and measures of success. Geoffrey Jones has suggested that British business abroad was often unsuccessful in its performance. Comparative studies help British business historians pinpoint some of the problems British enterprise had as it moved overseas.

We are by training comfortable in dealing with national behaviour and while it is now relatively easy to write about the international operations of national firms,[135] it is far harder to deal with some of the more complex multinational relationships. Regrettably, I do not have space here to discuss the cooperative ventures over borders that disclose the cosmopolitan nature of pre-1914 investment patterns – yet these must be analysed, particularly in relationship to the management of the cross-border participations.[136]

Comparative research on the pre-1914 years is probably simpler than for the post-1914 ones, because in the years 1880–1914 there was little fluctuation in foreign exchange values and also some of the greater complexities that developed later had not yet emerged. It ought to be possible to put together legitimate comparative figures, not significantly distorted by exchange variations. Before, however, the number game is played and the definitions are fixed in stone, the first step for British business historians is to establish the institutional dimensions of their nation's business over borders. This effort is greatly aided by the comparative approach that stimulates new questions. There seems no doubt that the business institution, controlling operations outside its home country, served as a key conduit of capital and also of production methods and new products, of personnel, technology, marketing arrangements and managerial expertise. How it carried forth all these functions within the firm – and using outside contractors – needs still to be charted. How it succeeded in its own terms (profits to the business) and in social terms (as an assister in economic growth and development at home and abroad) requires additional investigation. The research – while it explores home, and host country, circumstances – must concentrate on the business enterprise per se. A good start has been made, but the opportunities for further research are legion.

## Notes

† I owe a great debt to Alfred D. Chandler and Geoffrey Jones in the development of the ideas in this article. Likewise, I am grateful to Rondo Cameron

for including me in his 'Bellagio group', which has broadened my horizons.

1. For statistical purposes, the US Department of Commerce uses a ten per cent equity interest to qualify. A ten per cent interest is always adequate for 'influence'; it may not, in fact – as this article will indicate – be enough for 'control'.

2. Such settlers are often referred to as 'foreign' investors. I believe that it is inappropriate to refer to their activities as a foreign direct investment, if there was no financial obligation to a headquarters in Sweden, Germany, or Great Britain.

3. Mark Casson, *The Firm and the Market* (Cambridge, MA, 1987), p. 1.

4. Much of the huge 1977–84 literature on the history of European multinationals is summarised in Mira Wilkins, 'The History of European Multinationals: A New Look', *The Journal of European Economic History*, Vol. 15 (1986) pp. 483–510. An immense amount has been published subsequent to 1984. While Geoffrey Jones (ed.), *British Multinationals: Origins, Management and Performance* (Aldershot, 1986) greatly advances our knowledge of the history of British multinationals, there is still no comprehensive history. Stephen Nicholas has one in process, albeit it will be confined to industrial enterprises. Charles A. Jones, *International Business in the Nineteenth Century* (Brighton, 1987), provides an excellent introduction to the network of trading companies that evolved in nineteenth-century Britain. Likewise, S.D. Chapman's 'British-Based Investment Groups Before 1914', *Economic History Review*, 2nd series 38 (1985), pp. 230–51, has stimulated new perspectives on British business abroad. While the work of Peter Hertner and others has greatly enlarged what we know of German multinational enterprise, there is once again no overall history. Likewise, although Ragnhild Lundström, 'Swedish Multinational Growth before 1930', in Peter Hertner and Geoffrey Jones (eds.), *Multinationals: Theory and History* (Aldershot, 1986), pp. 135–56, covers the history of Swedish multinational enterprise, there is no book-length synthesis. Alfred D. Chandler's forthcoming history of modern managerial enterprise will be immensely helpful on the rise of the major British and German multinationals.

5. Harm Schröter is doing research on multinationals with headquarters in small European countries. There are also many firm-, industry-, and host-country-specific studies of French, Belgian and Swiss business abroad.

6. Robert Vicat Turrell and Jean Jacques Van-Helten, 'The Investment Group: The Missing Link in British Overseas Expansion before 1914?' *Economic History Review*, 2nd series 40 (1987), p. 269, scold Chapman for his generalisations and write 'In view of the historical specificity of economic developments in Africa and Asia ... it would have been more profitable to emphasise the different paths of development of business enterprise'.

7. Because of (1) the breakdown of the international gold standard; (2) the loss of the clear primacy of Great Britain as the great creditor nation in the world; (3) the defeat of Germany and its effect on German business abroad; and (4) the shift of the United States from debtor to creditor country in international accounts.

8. Albeit there were some: For the Russian government's business investments in China, see C.F. Remer, *Foreign Investments in China* (1933; reprint, New York, 1968), pp. 89, 558–9. The Russian bank in Persia was owned by the Russian state bank after 1894: Geoffrey Jones, *Banking and Empire in Iran* (Cambridge, 1986), p. 56.

9. There is a large literature on Scottish overseas investments, as distinct from the broader literature on 'British' overseas investments, which usually includes both Scottish and English business abroad. However, the *Dictionary of Business Biography* – now the standard work on businessmen in 'Britain' – omitted business

leaders based in Scotland, in deference to a project being carried out in Glasgow. The first volume of the *Dictionary of Scottish Business Biography*, edited by A. Slaven and S. Checkland, was published in 1987.

10. I began to identify crucial features of the home environment in Wilkins, 'The History of European Multinationals'. For some preliminary early testing, see Mira Wilkins, 'Japanese Multinational Enterprise before 1914', *Business History Review*, 60 (1986), pp. 199–231.

11. Until recently this has been universally accepted among students of multinational enterprise (MNE). Casson, however, suggests that the high benefits of internalisation (integrating operations) offset the costs of such integration over borders and thus the theorist does not have to find an additional advantage. Casson, *The Firm and the Market*, pp. 32, 34. He recognised, however, that the success (persistence) of MNEs does depend on some advantage, but stresses that this advantage may lie in internalisation, that is, in managing resources within the firm. Casson wants to separate choice (entry decisions) and performance. Ibid., pp. 35–6. My problem with this analysis is that it does not explain which firms make the choice to go abroad; some do and some do not. The choice, it seems to me, must entail at least a perception of advantage.

12. This view is the accepted one. Professors Raymond Vernon, John Dunning, Lawrence Franko, and others have all made this point.

13. N.F.R. Crafts and Mark Thomas, 'Comparative Advantage in UK Manufacturing Trade 1910–1935', *Economic Journal* 96 (1986), pp. 629–45.

14. I found this particularly true of American business abroad. Mira Wilkins, *The Emérgence of Multinational Enterprise* (Cambridge, MA, 1970). See also Alfred D. Chandler, *The Visible Hand* (Cambridge, MA. 1977).

15. Professor Chandler has made this point in a number of places.

16. Wilkins, 'The History of European Multinationals'.

17. A forthcoming book edited by Rondo Cameron and V.I. Bovykin, *International Banking, Investment, and Industrial Finance, 1870–1914*, explores some of these relationships.

18. Ibid. See also J. Riesser, *The German Great Banks and Their Concentration* (1911; reprint, New York, 1977).

19. A.S.J. Baster, *The Imperial Banks* (1929; reprint, New York, 1977) and idem., *The International Banks* (1935; reprint, New York, 1977). Geoffrey Jones is in the process of preparing the basic work on British overseas banks since 1890. See also his two volumes on The British Bank of the Middle East: Jones, *Banking and Empire in Iran* and idem., *Banking and Oil* (Cambridge, 1987). F.H.H. King, *The History of the Hongkong and Shanghai Banking Corporation* (Cambridge, 1987), Vol. 1, covers 1864–1902. (Volumes 2–4 are forthcoming, scheduled for 1988). For Canadian banks' extension into the United States, see Mira Wilkins, *The History of Foreign Investment in the United States to 1914*, forthcoming.

20. For example, because of new taxes imposed during the Boer War, Eastman Kodak, Ltd. changed from a legal British to an American headquarters. Carl W. Ackerman, *George Eastman* (Boston, MA, 1930), pp. 173–4. Other examples of tax motivated decisions are provided in Wilkins, *The History of Foreign Investment in the United States.*

21. Carl N. Degler's presidential address to the American Historical Association was entitled 'In Pursuit of an American History'. *American Historical Review*, 92 (1987), pp. 1–12. Degler argues that there were significant national attributes, some of which he seems to define in terms of 'culture'. The quotation is from a chapter, entitled 'Qualities of the Germans', in Henri Hauser, *Germany's Commercial Grip on the World* (New York, 1918), p. 9. This is a translation from

the French. Hauser was a professor at Dijon University; the first edition of this work, in French, appeared in 1915.

22. I agree with Geoffrey Jones in this conclusion. Lawrence Franko, *The European Multinationals* (Stamford, CT, 1976), p. 10, put the United States in first place as a home country, based on data collected by James Vaupel and Joan Curhan. These statistics – which are constantly reprinted – have been superseded by more recent research. They were, moreover, based on companies *still in existence* when the research was undertaken, which created a bias on the low side.

23. This is my own conclusion, based on my own research and my reading of the work of other students of the history of multinational enterprise. John H. Dunning, 'Changes in the Level and Structure of International Production: The Last One Hundred Years', in Mark Casson, *The Growth of International Business* (London, 1983), p. 87, presents estimates on the level of foreign direct investment by country of origin in 1914. He ranked the United Kingdom first, and far out front, followed by the United States in clear second place, and then came France; he put Germany in fourth place. I think he has greatly underestimated the activities of German business abroad.

24. Franko, *European Multinationals*, the first book that dealt with the history of European multinationals – and one that holds up very well over time – never makes an attempt to rank continental European home countries.

25. Based on data provided in Wilkins, *The History of Foreign Investment in the United States*. Franko, in *The European Multinationals*, p. 10, using the Vaupel and Curhan data, was able to identify only 60 UK 'manufacturing subsidiaries established or acquired' by UK parents before 1914 *worldwide*! Only nine were in the United States. See breakdown in Dunning, 'Changes in the Level and Structure', p. 90. But, Dunning elsewhere in the same article did recognise that the UK was 'far and away' the largest source of foreign direct investment in 1914. See ibid., pp. 86–7, and note 23 above.

26. Wilkins, 'The Free-Standing Company, 870–1914: An Important Type of British Foreign Direct Investment', *Economic History Review*, 2nd series 41 (1988). I first used the term 'free-standing' firm at a conference in Florence in 1983. Wilkins, 'Defining a Firm', in Hertner and Jones (eds.), *Multinationals*, pp. 84–7.

27. On these companies, see Jones (ed.), *British Multinationals, passim.*

28. I give more details on the clusters in 'The Free-Standing Company'. The theoretical literature on multinational enterprise has dealt with 'modes' of operations – direct investment, licensing, and market – or direct investment, contract, and market. The loosely-coupled groupings of the free-standing companies represent a mode of handling business abroad that the theoretical literature has failed to consider (because this institutional path is just coming to be understood). The British free-standing company could invest abroad directly or serve as a holding company, owning the securities of a locally-incorporated company. It made a difference.

29. On patent medicines, see the work of T.A.B. Corley, for example, 'Interactions between British and American Patent Medicine Industries', *Business and Economic History*, forthcoming.

30. The authority on crucible steel is Geoffrey Tweedale, *Sheffield Steel and America* (Cambridge, 1987).

31. Hugh G.J. Aitken, *The Continuous Wave* (Princeton, NJ, 1985), pp. 317, 357–8.

32. Wilkins, *The History of Foreign Investment in the United States.*

33. US Federal Trade Commission, *Report on Cooperation in American Export Trade*, 2 vols. (Washington, 1916). I, pp. 252, 254.

34. Ibid., I, p. 250.
35. Wilkins, *The History of Foreign Investment in the United States.*
36. Consett and Dowlais were joint-venture partners with Krupp in Orconera Iron Ore Co., Ltd., that carried on mining in Spain. Ulrich Wengenroth, 'Iron and Steel', in Cameron and Bovykin (eds.), *International Banking.*
37. See Shin'ichi Yonekawa and Hideki Yoshihara (eds.), *Business History of General Trading Companies* (Tokyo, 1987), for fascinating material on British trading companies. See also, Stephanie Jones, *Two Centuries of Overseas Trading. The Origins and Growth of the Inchcape Group* (London, 1986); Charles Jones, *International Business*; and Chapman, 'British-Based Investment Groups'.
38. See, for example, Andrew Porter, *Victorian Shipping, Business and Imperial Policy: Donald Currie, the Castle Line and Southern Africa* (Woodbridge and New York, 1986).
39. John Taylor & Sons, for instance, were in 1907 managers of 45 companies around the world. Charles Harvey and Peter Taylor, 'Mineral Wealth and Economic Development: Foreign Direct Investment in Spain, 1851–1913', *Economic History Review*, 2nd series 40 (1987), p. 189 n. 22. See also Wilkins, *History of Foreign Investment in the United States.*
40. Geoffrey Jones's new research will rectify that.
41. Baster, *International Banks*, p. 248, indicated that in 1910 24 British international banks had 308 foreign branches, while Baster, *Imperial Banks*, p. 269, states that in 1915, 18 imperial banks had 1,169 branches and sub-branches overseas. According to Oliver Pastré and Anthony Rowley (in 'The Multi-nationalisation of British and American Banks', in Alice Teichova, *et al.*, *Multinational Enterprise in Historical Perspective* (Cambridge, 1986), p. 233), who cite no source, in 1914, 36 banking companies in Britain had 2,091 branches 'in the world', and in addition, there were 3,538 colonial banks (surely, colonial bank branches and agencies?) It is hard to reconcile Pastré and Rowley's numbers with those of Baster.
42. The Imperial Bank of Persia, for example. See Jones, *Banking and Empire in Iran.*
43. Some of the trading companies at the centre of cluster sets were clearly multinational enterprises.
44. Questions about control are, for example, posed in Turrell and Van-Helten, 'The Investment Group'.
45. Jones (ed.), *Multinationals*, p. 7.
46. Discussions with Geoffrey Jones and Charles Jones.
47. In the case of British investment in America, this appears to have happened immediately. See text of this article. But take the case of the New Gellivara Co. Ltd. with mines in Sweden. In 1882, it was transformed into a Swedish Company (Gellivara Aktiebolog), which was 100 per cent owned by Sir Giles Loder, London. When the latter died, in 1889, his heirs lost all of their concessions. Wengenroth, 'Iron and Steel'. The suggestion was that control could no longer be maintained.
48. The description is theoretical. At present, I have no candidates that fit this model.
49. In this connection, host country policies were often crucial. In 1908, a Court in Alexandria ruled that a company formed to do business in Egypt, must be considered Egyptian, and a Khedival decree was required before it could be legally constituted. The Court ruling, however, specifically stated that no restriction was placed on the operations in Egypt of a bona-fide branch of a foreign company with headquarters abroad. The Court's decision 'referred only to companies whose operations, headquarters and sole "raison d'être" were in Egypt'. A.E. Crouchley,

*The Investment of Foreign Capital in Egyptian Companies and Public Debt* (Cairo, 1936), p. 63.

50. The best history of Borax Consolidated is Norman J. Travis and E.J. Cocks, *The Tincal Trail* (London, 1984). See also Wilkins, *History of Foreign Investment in the United States.*

51. Wilkins, *The Emergence*, pp. 91–3; Jones (ed.), *British Multinationals*, p. 7.

52. Had the ownership been concentrated, perhaps control might have been maintained.

53. I make this last point in 'The Free-Standing Company'.

54. On investment groups, see Chapman, 'British-Based Investment Groups'. On the absence of 'universal' banks, see P.L. Cottrell's forthcoming paper on British banking in Cameron and Bovykin (eds.), *International Banking.*

55. Harvey and Taylor, 'Mineral Wealth', provide rich information on British companies producing lead, iron ore and pyrites (sulphur and copper) in Spain. The article, however, tells us little about the extent to which these mining operations were part of integrated enterprises – in the United Kingdom, France, or Germany. Were the spectacular profits of the Orconera Co., for example, related to the intra-company pricing arrangements made by its three parent companies? On its parents, see note 36 above.

56. Charles Wilson, 'Multinationals, Management, and World Markets: A Historical View', in Harold F. Williamson (ed.), *Evolution of International Management Structures* (Newark, DE, 1975), p. 193.

57. In this connection, see the fascinating Editor's Introduction (by Maryna Fraser) of Lionel Phillips, *Some Reminiscences* (Johannesburg, 1986), pp. 11–30, on 'British' business in South Africa. See also D.C.M. Platt, *Britain's Investment Overseas on the Eve of the First World War* (New York, 1986), pp. 31–6.

58. In this connection, see Everett E. Hagen, *On the Theory of Social Change* (Homewood, IL, 1962), pp. 294–309.

59. Geoffrey Jones has found many cases where British management had severe difficulties in operating abroad.

60. Rondo Cameron, *France and the Economic Development of Europe* (Princeton, NJ, 1961), p. 396; on the important Belgian role, see Wengenroth, 'Iron and Steel'.

61. Wilkins, *The Emergence*, pp. 52–9.

62. Peter Hertner has written extensively on German business abroad. For a start, see his excellent 'German Multinational Enterprise before 1914: Some Case Studies', in Hertner and Jones (eds.), *Multinationals*, pp. 113–34. See also W. Feldenkirchen, 'The Export Organisation of the German Economy', in Yonekawa and Yoshihara (ed.), *Business History*. Chandler's new book will consider the international extension of German business.

63. The German trading house, Schuchardt and Schutte, for example, was probably 'the most prestigious distributor of machine tools in Europe'; it had 'outlets' in Germany, Austria, Belgium, and Russia. Charles W. Cheape, *Family Firm to Modern Multinational: Norton Company, a New England Enterprise* (Cambridge, 1985), p. 50. See also, Feldenkirchen, 'The Export Organisation' on export houses. The firms in Guatemala and Turkey were more active in providing imports into Germany than in selling exports from Germany. Schuchardt and Schutte handled some American exports as well as German ones.

64. See Wilkins, *History of Foreign Investment in the United States.*

65. Richard Tilly, 'International Aspects of the Development of German Banking, 1870–1914', in Cameron and Bovykin (eds.), *International Banking.*

66. My *History of Foreign Investments in the United States* has a sizeable amount on German business investments in the United States. Geoffrey Jones, 'Foreign Multinationals in Britain before 1945', *Economic History Review*, forthcoming, has much on German business in the United Kingdom. It has long been known that there were large German investments in Latin America – from railroads in Colombia to nitrate mines in Chile, but the nature of the management of such investments is still ambiguous. The reviews of Walther Kirchner, *Die Deutsch Industrie und die Industrialisierung Russlands 1815–1914* (St. Katharinen, F.R.G. 1986), indicate that it covers the activities of German multinationals in Russia.

67. Every basic history of the chemical industry, covering 1870–1914, deals with the German direct investments abroad (as well as at home). On the electrical industry, see, for example, Peter Hertner, 'Financial Strategies and Adaptation to Foreign Markets: The German Electro-Technical Industry and Its Multinational Activities'. Teichova, *et al., Multinational Enterprise*, pp. 145–59, and Albert Broder, 'The Multinationalisation of the French Electrical Industry 1880–1914; Dependence and its Causes', in Hertner and Jones (eds.), *Multinationals*, pp. 178–80, 184–5. According to Feldenkirchen, 'The Export Organisation', p. 325 n. 91, Siemens had in 1913, 17 plants in nine European countries.

68. On the foreign marketing organisation of the principal German iron and steel companies, see Feldenkirchen, 'The Export Organisation', pp. 310–11. On Bochumer Verein, Mannesmann, and Rheinische Stahlwerke's major foreign investments, see ibid., pp. 318–19, and Wengenroth, 'Iron and Steel', on the last two.

69. Bayer Co., Inc. v. United Drug Co., 272 Fed. 505 (SDNY, 1921).

70. Wilkins, *History of Foreign Investment in the United States.*

71. Here my conclusions depart from Franko, *European Multinationals*, p. 22, who was struck by the fact that 'continental European' enterprises rarely had advantages in marketing and advertising.

72. Data on the Faber firm in the 1870s are based on an undated (probably 1872–73) newspaper article, provided to me by Eberhard Faber, Wilkes-Barre, Pennsylvania. See also A.W. Faber's US colour advertisement (in English), reprinted in L. Fritz Gruber, 'Das Bleistift Schloss', *Frankfurter Allgemeine Zeitung*, 13 Feb. 1987. My thanks go to Richard Tilly for directing my attention to this. The parent company became Faber-Castell in 1900. Peter Hertner describes Kathreiner's Malzkaffee-Fabriken, as having direct investments in manufacturing plants in Austria–Hungary, Sweden, Russia, and Spain by 1914. It marketed and advertised a consumer product, malt coffee. Hertner, 'German Multinational Enterprise', 118–19.

73. Compare Wilkins, *History of Foreign Investment in the United States*, with Feldenkirchen, 'The Export Organisation', p. 317.

74. Franko, *European Multinationals*, p. 50, and Wengenroth, 'Iron and Steel'.

75. On its interests in American Metal Company, see Wilkins, *The History of Foreign Investment in the United States*. Franko, *European Multinationals*, p. 50, on other of its foreign direct investments.

76. For the involvements in Romania, see M. Pearton, *Oil and the Rumanian State* (Oxford, 1971) and Fritz Seidenzahl, *100 Jahre Deutsche Bank, 1870–1970* (Frankfurt, 1970), pp. 205–24. For German oil activities in the middle east, see ibid., pp. 224–7, and Marian Kent, *Oil & Empire* (London, 1976).

77. My *The Emergence of Multinational Enterprise*, published in 1970, provided a history of American business abroad in the years before 1914. Subsequently, there have been many studies of the history of US businesses abroad. Among the recent contributions are Fred V. Carstensen, *American Enterprise in*

*Foreign Markets. Studies of Singer and International Harvester in Imperial Russia* (Chapel Hill, NC, 1984); Lawrence A. Clayton, *Grace. W.R. Grace & Co. The Formative Years 1850–1930* (Ottawa, IL, 1985); and Cheape, *Family Firm to Modern Multinational.*

78. On I.B.C., see Wilkins, *The Emergence*, p. 107.

79. See Alfred D. Chandler, *The Visible Hand*; his 'Technological and Organisational Underpinnings of Modern Industrial Multinational Enterprise: The Dynamics of Competitive Advantage', in Teichova, *et al., Multinational Enterprise*, pp. 30–54; and his forthcoming book.

80. Ibid. Sometimes economies of scale and scope are viewed as part of an advantage – based on factor costs. More recently, new developments in trade theory have looked at economies of scale (and scope) as separate from traditionally-defined comparative advantages; trade (and, in turn, investments) arise directly from such economies. See Paul R. Krugman, 'Is Free Trade Passé?', *Economic Perspectives*, Vol. 1 (1987), p. 133. The distinction is between what is endogenous to the firm and exogenous. Yet, the achievements of economies of scope and scale (albeit endogenous) were based, I firmly believe, on conditions in the home country.

81. Wilkins, *History of Foreign Investment in the United States.*

82. The Potash Cartel, for example, had a sales company in the United States. See ibid.

83. P. Chalmin, 'The Rise of International Commodity Trading Companies in Europe in the Nineteenth Century', in Yonekawa and Yoshihara (ed.), *Business History*, p. 290.

84. Some of the best work on this subject remains that in Rondo Cameron's 1960 book, *France and the Economic Development.*

85. Ibid., pp. 397–400. On St. Gobain's German factories, see Jean-Pierre Daviet, 'Un Processus de Multinationalisation de Longue Durée: L'Exemple de Saint-Gobain (1853–1939)', unpublished paper (1984). This paper has been published (in Italian) in Peter Hertner, *Per La Storia delli'impresa multinazionale in Europa* (Milan, 1987). Daviet completed a 1793-page doctoral dissertation at the Sorbonne in 1983.

86. Daviet, 'Un Processus'.

87. Theo Barker, 'Pilkington', in Jones (ed.), *Multinationals*, p. 185.

88. Wilkins, *History of Foreign Investment in the United States*, on Michelin. On Dunlop, Geoffrey Jones, 'The Growth and Performance of British Multinational Firms before 1939: The Case of Dunlop', *Economic History Review*, 2nd series 37 (Feb. 1984), p. 36. In addition, Dunlop had licensing agreements with companies in Canada, Australia, and Russia. Ibid., p. 39.

89. Patrick Fridenson, 'The Growth of Multinational Activities in the French Motor Industry, 1890–1979', in Hertner and Jones (eds.), *Multinationals*, pp. 157–9.

90. Claude Ph. Beaud, 'Investments and Profits of the Multinational Schneider Group: 1894–1943', in Teichova, *et al., Multinational Enterprise*, pp. 87–102. See also idem., 'La Schneider in Russia (1896–1914)', in Hertner, *Per La Storia*, pp. 101–48.

91. Wilkins, *History of Foreign Investment in the United States.*

92. French investors often appear to have used British-registered companies for investments abroad – not only in Spain. I found this to be true of some French investments in the United States, principally in mining. Beaud found that Schneider (and other French investors) used the Bolivian Rubber and General Enterprise, Ltd., registered in London, for its investments in Bolivia. Beaud, 'Investments and Profits', p. 90.

93. Robert L. Tignor, *State, Private Enterprise and Economic Change in Egypt, 1918–1952* (Princeton, NJ, 1984), pp. 19–20, found that in the pre-First World War years 'French businessmen experienced great difficulty in maintaining managerial control over French firms in Egypt. French investment was widely dispersed, and small French shareholders took little interest in the management of companies so long as dividend payments continued to arrive. Hence, small groups of organised shareholders on the ground could gain control of companies, even though holding only a fraction of the shares.' This sounds like some of the problems faced by British free-standing companies. I suppose one could call the Suez company a free-standing firm. See Hubert Bonin, *Suez* (Paris, 1987).

94. On French trading companies (and French banks), see Chalmin, 'The Rise', especially pp. 289–91. Chalmin argues that 'the first disease of French trade [was] the determination of the [French] industry to do its marketing itself' – and it was always a job badly done. The 'second disease' was that the French concentrated on quality and luxury products – perfumes, cognac, champagne, and fashion, which sold themselves. Thus there was no need to bother to have representatives abroad. He believes, however, that French trading houses were more efficient on the import than on the export side. On the large French West African chartered company, see Hubert Bonin, *La Compagnie Française d'Afrique Occidentale* (Paris, 1987).

95. Geoffrey Jones is planning a conference on 'banks as multinationals'. It will be extremely useful to compare the role of French banks with those of other nationalities. For one recent contribution on French banking abroad, which despite its title does cover the pre-1914 years, see Yasuo Gonjo, 'La banque de l'Indochine devant l'interventionisme (1917–1931)', *Le Mouvement Social*, 142 (Jan.–March, 1988), pp. 45–74.

96. John McKay, 'The House of Rothschild (Paris)', in Teichova, *et.al*, *Multinational Enterprise*, pp. 74–86.

97. Cameron found this to be true. See *France and the Economic Development*. Maurice Lévy-Leboyer's work also suggests this.

98. The footnotes in Lundström, 'Swedish Multinational Growth', bear witness to the large literature on Swedish multinationals. Since her article was written, the synthesis volume on Swedish Match and its predecessors has been published, Karl-Gustaf Hildebrand, *Expansion Crisis Reconstruction, 1917–1939* (Stockholm, 1985). Lundström's contributions to Cameron and Bovykin's forthcoming book add further material on Swedish business abroad.

99. Data from Lundström on Empire Cream Separator Co. See also Wilkins, *History of Foreign Investment in the United States* on this company.

100. There is a history of Solvay & Cie. J. Bolle, *Solvay, L'Invention, L'homme, L'entreprise Industrielle* (Brussels, 1963).

101. This is all from Herman Van der Wee and Martine Goosen's splendid contribution, 'International Factors in the Formation of Banking Systems – Belgium', forthcoming in the Cameron and Bovykin volume.

102. Ibid. and John McKay, *Tramways and Trolleys* (Princeton, NJ, 1976), pp. 149, 244 (on the Belgian role).

103. Van der Wee and Goosen, 'International Factors'.

104. Wengenroth, 'Iron and Steel'; see also John P. McKay, *Pioneers for Profit* (Chicago, 1970).

105. Lutz Alt, 'The Photochemical Industry' (Ph.D. dissertation MIT, 1986), pp. 71–9.

106. Robert Liefmann, *Cartels, Concerns, and Trusts* (London, 1932), p. 269.

107. Wilkins, *History of Foreign Investment in the United States*, and Van der Wee and Goosen, 'International Factors'.

108. For a list of Swiss companies engaged in international business, see Ernst Himmel, *Industrielle Kapitalanlagen der Schweiz im Auslande* (Langensalza, 1922), pp. 116–37.

109. Ibid., pp. 132–3.

110. Every Swiss company history – and they are numerous – attests to this.

111. Himmel, *Industrielle Kapitalanlagen*, Recapitulation, no page number. But see also Urs Rauber, *Schweizer Industrie in Russland* (Zurich, 1985). Rauber believes Himmel underestimated Swiss industrial investments in Russia. (Rauber's book sent me to Himmel, albeit I have had difficulty matching Rauber's numbers with Himmel's. The data in my text are from Himmel).

112. Silk Association of America, *Annual Report 1905*, pp. 60–61.

113. *Fulton, New York 1901*, p. 65.

114. Federal Trade Commission, *Cooperation*, I, p. 145.

115. Himmel, *Industrielle Kapitalanlagen*, Recapitulation.

116. Based on my own research.

117. See F.C. Gerretson, *History of the Royal Dutch Company*, 4 vols. (Leiden: E.J. Brill, 1953–57). K.D. Bosch, *Nederlandse Beleggingen in De Verenigde Staten* (Amsterdam, 1948), is invaluable on Dutch investment in the United States.

118. See Wilkins, *History of Foreign Investment in the United States*, and Augustus J. Veenendaal, Jr. 'The Kansas City Southern Railway and the Dutch Connection', *Business History Review*, Vol. 61 (1987), pp. 291–316. Often, the Dutch delegated their authority to Americans; such delegation, however, would not by definition bar such stakes from the category of foreign direct investment.

119. Wilkins, *History of Foreign Investment in the United States*; Christopher Armstrong and H.V. Nelles, 'A Curious Capital Flow: Canadian Investment in Mexico, 1902–1910', *Business History Review*, Vol. 58 (1984), pp. 178–203.

120. Wilkins, *History of Foreign Investment in the United States*. Geoffrey Jones has directed my attention to the Hungarian Bank for Commerce and Industry of Pest's controlling interest in the Romanian oil company, Steaua Romana, from 1892–1902. See Pearton *Oil and the Rumanian State*, pp. 23–31. Three large Hungarian banks were owners of the Transatlantic Trust Co., New York, founded in 1912. Wilkins, *History of Foreign Investment in the United States*.

121. Fridenson, 'The Growth', p. 157.

122. *Best's Insurance Report – Fire and Marine, 1914*.

123. There were, in addition, some non-European, non-North American headquartered multinational enterprises. See, for example, Wilkins, 'Japanese Multinational Enterprise before 1914'.

124. It is my own conclusion that the United States ranked first. For my forthcoming *History of Foreign Investment in the United States*, I prepared a ranking of debtor nations in 1914; this included, however, both foreign portfolio and direct investments and does not offer a legitimate ranking for direct investment alone. Dunning, 'Changes in the Level and Structure', p. 88, made estimates and provided a 1914 ranking that is not broken down by country in Latin America (32 per cent of the world's foreign direct investment), but which, excluding Latin America, suggests the following leading recipients: the United States (10.3 per cent), China (7.8 per cent), Russia (7.1 per cent), Canada (5.7 per cent). These were, as Dunning recognizes, 'estimates'. In Latin America, Argentina, Brazil, Mexico, Chile, Peru, and Cuba would figure as the most important recipients of foreign direct investment in 1914. All of Europe – excluding Russia, the UK (a mere 1.4 per cent), and 'Southern Europe' (2.8 per cent) – had by Dunning's reckoning 9.2 per cent of the total.

125. This was true of aspirins in the United States (made by Bayer) and sewing

machines in Germany (made by Singer) in this period.

126. For some thoughts on this matter, see Mira Wilkins, 'Efficiency and Management: A Comment on Gregory Clark's "Why Isn't the Whole World Developed?"' *Journal of Economic History*, Vol. 47 (Dec. 1987), pp. 981–3.

127. Since this article has space constraints, I have not discussed the pre-1914 licensing activities of multinationals as a separate 'mode'. However, the comparative evidence on the amount of licensing done by companies headquartered in different home countries seems too lean – at present – for anything but the most superficial conclusions. If joint-ventures are to be considered a 'mode', there were a large number of such by multinationals of all nationalities – although the exact nature of the shared relationships is still ill-defined and it would be impossible to choose say 1914 and to rank the prevalence of joint ventures by home country of the multinationals.

128. America had lots of small companies that had nothing but local business.

129. Professor Alfred D. Chandler, has been important in pointing out to me how very large employers some of the pre-1914 German enterprises actually were, when compared with their American counterparts.

130. I found in my research on *American* business abroad a number of such 'partial' relationships, but they seem far more conspicuous in the European context – especially in connection with primary product production – agriculture, or mineral extraction.

131. Porter, *Victorian Shipping*, noted that the dividends paid by the Castle Line were not impressive; yet, Donald Currie, who had a management contract to run the line, emerged as a very wealthy man. He obviously obtained his returns from the management contract, *assured* by his equity holdings. Whenever management contracts exist, the scholar must check the account books carefully. Sometimes, a British agency house abroad could have a negligible (or even no) investment and still have a management contract that provided it good returns – whether there were or were not profits.

132. See Mira Wilkins, *The Maturing of the Multinational Enterprise* (Cambridge, MA, 1974), pp. 414, 565 ns. 8–9; Chandler, *The Visible Hand*; O.E. Williamson, 'The Modern Corporation: Origins, Evolution, Attributes', *Journal of Economic Literature*, Vol. 19 (1981), pp. 1537–68; Wilkins, 'Defining a Firm', and most recently, Casson, *The Firm and the Market*, p. 1. There has been some dispute as to who first applied the ideas of R.H. Coase to the theory of multinational enterprise. The first two published applications were in 1970 by Stephen Hymer, 'The Efficiency (Contradictions) of Multinational Corporations', *American Economic Review*, Vol. 60 (1970), pp. 441–8, and Robert Z. Aliber, 'A Theory of Direct Foreign Investment', in Charles Kindleberger (ed.), *The International Corporation* (Cambridge, MA, 1970), p. 20. In 1974 I picked up on the idea (in a footnote which no one ever read). Wilkins, *The Maturing*, p. 565 n. 9.

133. I consider that my *Economic History Review* article poses more questions than it answers. For some of the applications, see Wilkins, 'Efficiency and Management'.

134. Kiyoshi Kojima has described US multinationals as trade-destroying, while Japanese ones were trade-creating. Kojima, *Japanese Direct Foreign Investment* (Tokyo, 1978) and idem., *Japan and a New World Economic Order* (Tokyo, 1977). I do not think that in 1870–1914, American multinationals were trade-destroying; in fact, I believe that all the multinationals of 1870–1914 were trade creating – albeit to different extents. It is very important to study exports and imports separately in this context.

135. Note that this was the title of Stephen Hymer's seminal Ph.D. dissertation (1960).

136. For example, when parent entrepreneurs have 'homes' in three countries and operate in a host nation, say South Africa, how does one decipher a 'home' or headquarters? I believe one must close one's eyes to 'nationality' and look at administrative and legal institutional relationships. Was Alusuisse, for instance, a German or a Swiss aluminium company – or a truly co-operative venture?

# 2

# The Eclectic Paradigm and the Growth of UK Multinational Enterprise 1870–1983*

John H. Dunning and Howard Archer

*Source: *Business and Economic History*, 16 (1987), pp. 19–49.

## Introduction and Background

UK multinational activity, as we understand it today, started to evolve in the 1860s and 1870s, strongly influenced by the rapid growth of international trade, and the technological, organizational and institutional developments of the second half of the century. Yet, even at that time, UK enterprises were no strangers to overseas investment; indeed exports of portfolio, migratory, merchant and financial capital date back to the late 16th century [16, p. 28]. These early overseas interests were primarily directed towards (a) the primary sector, i.e., mines, plantations, etc., (b) services such as railways, utilities and banking; and (c) trade and commerce. Although, in several cases, they involved some degree of managerial control, they could not be regarded as foreign direct investment in the sense that is accepted now. Foreign market-seeking and resource-seeking productive activities by UK companies already producing in their home economy only began to emerge in the 1860s; while it was not until nearly a century later that multinational enterprises seeking to pursue a globalized market and production strategy came on the scene.

It is generally accepted that, prior to World War I, the UK was the world's leading outward direct investor. Estimates in Table 1 show that in 1914, the UK accounted for 45.5 percent ($6.5 billion) of the estimated stock of accumulated foreign direct investment by country of origin, well ahead of the US which was in second place with 18.5 percent ($2.652 billion). In 1938, the UK still retained its position as the leading foreign capital stakeholder, with 39.8 percent ($10.5 billion) of the total but the US was significantly closer with 27.7 percent ($7.3 billion). The UK was forced to sell out a large proportion of its overseas assets in World War II; since when, although there has been a continuous increase in the value of

*Table 1* Estimated stock of accumulated foreign direct investment by selected country of origin 1914–1983

|  | 1914[a] | | 1938[a] | | 1960[a] | | 1971[a] | | 1978[b] | | 1980[b] | | 1983[c] | |
|---|---|---|---|---|---|---|---|---|---|---|---|---|---|---|
|  | $b | % | $b | % | $b | % | $b | % | $b | % | $b | % | $b | % |
| Total | 14.3 | 100 | 26.4 | 100 | 66.7 | 100 | 172.1 | 100 | 392.8 | 100 | 511.5 | 100 | 591.5 | 100 |
| Developed | 14.3 | 100 | 26.4 | 100 | 66.0 | 99.0 | 168.1 | 97.7 | 380.3 | 96.8 | 497.5 | 97.3 | 575.6 | 97.3 |
| of which: | | | | | | | | | | | | | | |
| UK | 6.5 | 45.5 | 10.5 | 39.8 | 10.8 | 16.2 | 23.7 | 13.8 | 50.7 | 12.9 | 74.2 | 14.5 | 88.5 | 15.0 |
| US | 2.7 | 18.5 | 7.3 | 27.7 | 32.8 | 49.2 | 82.8 | 48.1 | 162.7 | 41.4 | 215.6 | 42.2 | 227.0 | 38.4 |
| Canada | 0.2 | 1.0 | 0.7 | 2.7 | 2.5 | 3.8 | 6.5 | 3.8 | 13.6 | 3.5 | 13.6 | 3.7 | 28.8 | 4.9 |
| FDR | 1.5 | 10.5 | 0.4 | 1.3 | 0.8 | 1.2 | 7.3 | 4.2 | 28.6 | 7.3 | 37.6 | 7.4 | 38.9 | 6.6 |
| Japan | 0.0 | 0.1 | 0.8 | 2.8 | 0.5 | 0.7 | 4.4 | 2.6 | 26.8 | 6.8 | 37.1 | 7.3 | 61.2 | 10.4 |

*Sources:* [a] Dunning [12] Tables 5.1 & 5.2. [b] Stopford and Dunning [29] Tables 1.2, 1.3 & 1.7. [c] Estimated by authors.

its overseas investments, its share of the world capital stake has steadily fallen.

The UK is also an important recipient of foreign direct investment. The first flurry of foreign multinational enterprise activity in the UK occurred in the 1880s, and in the following quarter of a century, US multinational enterprises such as Ford, Eastman Kodak, and Heinz established bridge-heads in most of the newer industrial sectors, including those in which the UK later built up a strong comparative advantage. By 1914, however, as Table 2 reveals, the UK still only accounted for 1.4 percent ($200 million) of the estimated world stock of accumulated inward foreign direct investment, and in 1938 its share was 2.9 percent ($700 million). Table 2 also shows that, among the largest inward investors since World War II, the UK has consistently ranked third behind the US, with a share remaining relatively constant between 8.1 percent (1971) and 10.2 percent (1980).

Taken together, these data show that the UK has been, and remains, a major net outward investor. Not as immediately apparent, is the extent to which the ratio of its outward to inward direct capital stake has declined since 1914. Table 3 shows that this ratio fell from 33:1 in 1914 to 15:1 in 1938; and then to 1.6:1 in 1978, since when it has increased again. This contrasts strongly with the experiences of US, Japan and Germany. *Inter alia* it reflects the changing entrepreneurial, innovatory, production, managerial and marketing advantages of UK firms relative to those of their overseas competitors, the role of the UK government in affecting these, and the general economic climate.

Historically, the structure of UK outward and inward direct investment has been very different from that of its major competitors. Inward investment has always been oriented towards the high- and medium-technology sectors; while outward investment has been concentrated in the relatively low technology and consumer good industries. The Reddaway Report [26] showed that, in 1964, 71 percent of the net foreign assets owned by the leading UK manufacturing multinational enterprises were in the less technology-intensive sectors of food, drink and tobacco, household products, paper, metal products, building materials and textiles, while 29 percent were in the more technology-intensive sectors of chemicals, engineering, electronics and vehicles. This contrasted strongly with the pattern of inward investment. In 1964, 67 percent of the net assets of foreign firms in UK manufacturing were in the more technology-intensive sector, and only 33 percent in less technology-intensive sectors.

The reasons why UK inward and outward direct investment has followed the pattern just described, are well documented in the literature [14, 30]. While the UK led the way in the Industrial Revolution and gained an early technological lead in a wide range of industries, it was the US which largely pioneered the second generation of industrial discoveries in the last quarter of the 19th century. New sources of energy, production

*Table 2* Estimated stock of accumulated foreign direct investment by selected recipient country 1914–1983

| | 1914ᵃ | | 1938ᵃ | | 1960ᵃ | | 1971ᵃ | | 1978ᵇ | | 1980ᵇ | | 1983ᶜ | |
|---|---|---|---|---|---|---|---|---|---|---|---|---|---|---|
| | $b | % | $b | % | $b | % | $b | % | $b | % | $b | % | $b | % |
| Total | 14.1 | 100 | 24.3 | 100 | 54.5 | 100 | 166.3 | 100 | 361.7 | 100 | 440.9 | 100 | 540.5 | 100 |
| Developed | 5.2 | 37.2 | 8.4 | 34.3 | 36.7 | 67.3 | 108.4 | 65.2 | 251.8 | 69.6 | 313.7 | 71.7 | — | — |
| of which: | | | | | | | | | | | | | | |
| UK | 0.2 | 1.4 | 0.7 | 2.9 | 5.0 | 9.2 | 13.4 | 8.1 | 32.5 | 9.0 | 44.8 | 10.2 | 52.7 | 9.7 |
| US | 1.5 | 10.3 | 1.8 | 7.4 | 7.6 | 13.9 | 13.9 | 8.4 | 42.5 | 11.8 | 68.4 | 15.5 | 137.1 | 25.4 |
| Canada | 0.8 | 5.7 | 2.3 | 9.4 | 12.9 | 23.7 | 27.9 | 16.8 | 43.2 | 11.9 | 45.5 | 10.3 | 59.9 | 11.1 |
| Germany | na | na | na | na | na | na | na | na | na | na | na | na | 29.6 | 5.5 |
| Japan | 0.0 | 0.2 | 0.1 | 0.4 | 0.1 | 0.2 | 2.5 | 1.5 | 6.0 | 1.5 | 6.6 | 1.7 | na | na |

*Sources*: see Table 1.

*Table 3* Ratio of outward/inward direct capital stake for selected countries
1914–1983

|           | 1914    | 1938    | 1960   | 1971   | 1978   | 1980   | 1983   |
|-----------|---------|---------|--------|--------|--------|--------|--------|
| Developed | 2.73:1  | 3.16:1  | 1.80:1 | 1.55:1 | 1.51:1 | 1.59:1 | na     |
| UK        | 32.50:1 | 15.00:1 | 2.16:1 | 1.76:1 | 1.56:1 | 1.66:1 | 1.68:1 |
| US        | 1.83:1  | 4.06:1  | 4.32:1 | 5.96:1 | 3.83:1 | 3.15:1 | 1.66:1 |
| Canada    | 0.19:1  | 0.30:1  | 0.19:1 | 0.23:1 | 0.32:1 | 0.30:1 | 0.52:1 |
| Germany   | na      | na      | na     | na     | na     | na     | 1.31:1 |
| Japan     | 0.57:1  | 7.50:1  | 5.00:1 | 1.76:1 | 4.47:1 | 5.62:1 | na     |

*Source:* Tables 1 and 2.

techniques and organizational forms, and dramatic improvements in transport, communication and distribution facilities, helped create many of today's mass production industries, e.g., automobiles, office machinery, electrical goods, and synthetic chemicals, etc.; and the UK missed out on many of these developments. As a result, these sectors were heavily influenced by American, and to a lesser extent, German innovations and practices. When examining the industrial distribution of the 200 largest manufacturing firms in selected countries at the time of World War I, Chandler [4] found that 49.5 percent of the US firms were in the newer or mainly producer good industries compared with only 28.0 percent of the UK firms. The respective percentages for firms in the older or mainly consumer good industries were 50.0 percent and 70.5 percent.

This emerging industrial retardation left many gaps in the UK economy to be filled. As a consequence, it became the recipient of these new product and process innovations, initially by imports, but later, by inward direct investment. Although this paper is primarily concerned with the activities of UK multinational enterprises, the role of inward investment must be acknowledged, as it had a significant influence on the organization and pattern of resource allocation in the UK. In some cases, the presence of foreign firms introduced new market structures [10], and provided a much needed competitive stimulus; in the inter-war years, for example, a good deal of rationalization occurred in sectors such as motor vehicles and electrical equipment in which foreign firms were especially well represented. The analysis of Chandler [4] also suggests that the UK subsidiaries of US parents were the first, in the UK, to adopt new organizational structures (e.g., the M-form) and management techniques, which helped facilitate diversification and international growth. Overall, the balance of evidence suggests that inward direct investment has consistently steered the UK's economic structure towards the technologically more advanced, and internationally oriented sectors [10].

The rest of this paper concentrates on UK outward investment, examining, within the framework of the eclectic paradigm of international production, the emergence and development of UK manufacturing multinational enterprises since 1870; and the changing nature and interaction between the competitive advantages of firms, the comparative advantages of countries and the organizational form of cross-border transactions. The data for the paper have been obtained from company archives, business records, industrial histories and published documents of some 187 British industrial multinational enterprises, which, in 1983, accounted for about four-fifths of all outward UK direct investment in manufacturing industry. In addition, questionnaires were completed and/or interviews conducted with a sample of these companies. A fuller account of the results of the study is set out in Archer [1].

## The Eclectic Paradigm and the Need for a General Explanation for the Historical Examination of UK Multinational Enterprises

The examination of the emergence and development of UK multinational enterprises over the last century is a vast subject to study. Not only has the underlying international economic, political and technological environment changed significantly over time, but also very different motives prompt firms to undertake market-seeing (import substituting), resource-seeking (supply orientated) and efficiency seeking (rationalized) foreign direct investment. Moreover, it is not only the determinants of foreign direct investment by large multinational enterprises such as ICI and Unilever that has to be explained, but also those of the many smaller specialized companies such as Hallite and Vinten.

The framework required to study the history of UK multinational enterprises must therefore be of a widespread, general and integrated nature. This is precisely the advantage claimed by Dunning [11; 12; 13] for the eclectic paradigm of international production. According to this paradigm there are three conditions that must be satisfied if a firm is to engage in foreign direct investment. These are:

1.  It must possess net competitive or ownership specific (O) advantages vis-a-vis firms of other nationalities in serving particular markets. These ownership advantages may take two forms (a) the exclusive or privileged access to specific intangible assets, e.g., technology, management skills, markets, and (b) the ability to govern, i.e., coordinate, the use of these and other assets, particularly where the enterprise is multi-activity and geographically dispersed.
2.  Assuming condition (1) is satisfied, it must be more beneficial to the enterprise possessing these advantages to use them itself rather than to

sell or lease them or their rights to foreign firms, that is, for it to internalize the markets for its advantages, through an extension of its activities, rather than externalize the sale of them or their rights to independent foreign firms.

3.   Assuming conditions (1) and (2) are satisfied, it must be profitable for the enterprise to utilize these advantages in conjunction with at least some factor inputs (including natural resources) outside its home country; otherwise, foreign markets would be served entirely by exports and domestic markets by domestic production.

Two points must be noted immediately. Firstly, the three conditions are intimately related: for example, Dunning [13] distinguished between the asset $(O_a)$ and transaction $(O_t)$ ownership advantages of multinational enterprises and observed that while the former arise from the favored possession of individual assets by multinational enterprises vis-a-vis other enterprises, the latter

mirror the capacity of multinational enterprise [multinational enterprise] hierarchies, vis-a-vis external markets, to recoup the transactional benefits (or lessen the transactional costs) of the common ownership of separate but interrelated activities located in different countries. [13, p. 13]

The second point to be noted is that the OLI variables are not static and may change over time. The fact that a UK company might have had strong O advantage pre-1914 does not necessarily mean that its competitive position was as strong in subsequent periods; and, if it was, this may have been due to different combination of asset $(O_a)$ and transactional $(O_t)$ advantages than those possessed in the earlier period. Similarly, in many industries, as knowledge has become more idiosyncratic, tacit and non-codifiable, the market has proved an increasingly inappropriate modality for the organization of cross-border transactions [32]. Finally, the merits of particular countries as locations for productive activities are constantly shifting as the value and importance of such variables as wage rates, material prices, market size, tariffs, transport costs and government policies and attitudes towards foreign direct investment change.

Although several criticisms have been leveled against the eclectic paradigm of international production [13], it is our belief that this approach offers a robust and powerful framework for analyzing and explaining the international transactions of firms and the international economic involvement of countries. The purpose of the remainder of this paper is to identify and evaluate the specific OLI variables which have affected the different types of foreign direct investment by UK multi-national enterprises, and to examine how these variables have changed over time.

## Ownership-Specific Advantages of UK Multinational Enterprises 1870–1983

In examining these advantages, a distinction must be made between firm-specific, industry-specific and country-specific factors. Firm-specific factors relate to O advantages that enable firms to compete successfully with other firms within their own industry both in the UK and in foreign markets: these include both structural and strategic related advantages. Industry-specific factors relate to O advantages that may accrue to all firms within a given industry, and include those concerned with market structure and the economics of production. Country-specific factors relate to O advantages that may accrue to all firms of one nationality over those of other nationalities. These advantages may be generated by the size of a country's market, its level of income, its resource endowments, its educational system, its government's policy towards R & D, patent and trade mark legislation, and so on. Countries are not homogeneous in their factor endowments; in consequence, firms originating from different countries are likely to possess different O advantages. In the context of this paper, at least some of the competitive advantages of UK multinational enterprises may be expected to reflect the country-specific factors of the UK that generated and sustained them.

This paper identifies 15 major UK multinational enterprises which had emerged by 1914,[1] although it must be acknowledged that they were by no means the only UK overseas investors of the period. Consistent with our primary concern, 14 of the 15 were manufacturing companies (the exception being Royal Dutch Shell). To a large extent, their foreign activities mirrored the comparative trading advantages of the UK, which, in 1914, was most pronounced in the products that it had pioneered 50 years earlier. UK multinational manufacturing activity was then oriented towards the production of branded consumer goods and heavy engineering equipment, rather than towards products generated by the technological developments of the 1870s, e.g., automobiles, chemicals and electrical machinery. The reasons for this have been widely discussed by economic historians; basically, while the UK provided a large, standardized, high-income market which encouraged the development and marketing of consumer goods, it failed to encourage the development of new technologies.[2]

All the major UK multinational enterprises that emerged pre-1914 held strong oligopolistic positions in their domestic markets, with the majority being among the largest and older established UK companies. An examination of their advantages reveals access, not only innovatory strength (e.g., Babcock, Gramophone, Pilkington and Dunlop), but also the ability to supply differentiated and high quality products, and the control of selling outlets (e.g., Imperial (in tobacco), Bryant and May (in matches), Lever Bros. (in soap and margarine), and Reckitt (in household products)). Moreover, several of the UK multinational enterprises, whose competitiveness was based on the more recently developed products and/ or processes, relied heavily on technology and knowledge acquired from overseas (usually US) sources (e.g., Babcock (industrial machinery) Gramophone (records), Nobel Explosives (chemicals) and Wellcome (pharmaceuticals)).

Several of the early UK multinational enterprises were members of international cartels or market-sharing agreements (examples included BAT, Babcocks, Bryant and May, Gramophone and Nobel). These agreements were important in that they both allowed the participants favored access to certain markets; and also protected them from competition from other firms. The UK companies were generally allocated the Empire markets. A further advantage of some UK manufacturing multinational enterprises was their privileged access to essential inputs. A guaranteed and constant supply of raw materials at a reasonable and steady price was seen as being fundamental to future development and growth in the case of such firms as Dunlop, Imperial, Lever, Cadbury's and Reckitts. Ownership of their primary inputs was no less important to the strength of such UK resource-based multinational enterprises such as RTZ and Shell.

Perhaps the most outstanding feature to emerge from the examination of the O advantages of these major pioneering UK multinational enterprises, however, was the importance of individual entrepreneurship in their overseas (and domestic) growth. Foreign direct investment was a new and risky phenomenon, and men such as William Lever (Lever), Henry Tetley (Courtaulds), T. R. Ferens (Reckitt), Marcus Samuel and Henri Deterding (Shell), and Henry Wellcome (Wellcome) were fundamental in controlling or influencing the pattern of their companies' growth. In fact, it is possible to identify such entrepreneurs for all 15 companies; by contrast, Corley [7] has suggested that Huntley and Palmer experienced poor entrepreneurship and lost out in several overseas markets through lack of foresight.[3]

Examination of the competitive advantages of UK multinational enterprises during the inter-war years and early post-World War II period yields very similar results to that of the pre-1914 era, although the underlying economic and political environment in which foreign direct investment was undertaken changed significantly between 1919 and the 1960s.[4] UK manufacturing multinational activity remained oriented towards the mature, relatively low-technology sectors and the O advantages of UK multinational enterprises were predominantly of an $O_a$ nature.[5]

The continuing domination of UK foreign direct investment by companies from the mature, relatively low-technology industries again mainly reflected the particular characteristics of the UK economy. These included a host of institutional barriers to industrial restructuring, and an inability of the UK economic machine to redirect resources to the growth-oriented sectors. The high income, large and standardized UK market continued to foster large firms, product differentiation and marketing skills—all characteristics favoring the consumer goods multinational enterprises which emerged both during the inter-war years, e.g., Cadbury and Rowntree (confectionery), Distillers (drink); and in the early post-World War II period, Beechams (pharmaceuticals), Chubb (locks and keys) and Clarks (boots and shoes).

By contrast, the UK continued to be generally uncompetitive in the technologically advanced and vertically integrated engineering and chemical industries. Several reasons have been adduced for this. For example, Murphy [22] stated that, in the 1900s, at the more advanced educational levels, technical and scientific instruction and inquiry remained "poor cousins in the family of higher learning" in the UK. A similar point was made by Ashworth [2], who also referred to "the lack of provision for commercial studies and for any kind of technical education for managers and senior industrial staff." In comparing the growth of multinational enterprises in the US and UK until 1939, Chandler [4] noted that, whereas in the US the need for trained production and marketing specialists in the technologically advanced machinery, electrical and chemical sectors had been quickly recognized and catered for by universities and business schools; this was not the case in the UK, where top managers continued to come from the owning family and middle managers from the company's ranks. It was in the newer, higher technology industries that the need for organizational and financial control systems and management techniques was the greatest; and the UK's failure to adapt to this need contributed greatly to the lack of competitiveness of UK companies in the newer, high-technology industries. It was not until 1947 that the British Institute of Management was formed, and, only in the 1960s, that the London and Manchester Business Schools were founded.

It is true that, during the inter-war years, the traditional industries declined and the newer sectors expanded in the UK, but generally, the latter proved ineffective in international markets. Too often, UK companies failed to invest in the kind of innovatory activities which were the foundation of the success of their international competitors. Indeed, even after 1945, the preference of UK firms for reinvesting in old industries and the continued commitments to traditional and safe markets, continued to persist. Products designed for home consumption found ready markets in the Commonwealth, and as long as these were growing and profitable, there was little incentive to change or invest heavily in new technology and production processes.

The examination of the competitive advantages of UK multinational enterprises between 1919 and 1960, therefore, yields very similar results to those for the pre-1914 era, but several points need to be highlighted. Given the industrial structure of UK international production, and the fact that most companies were in the later stages of their product cycles, the importance of product differentiation and quality, together with marketing and managerial skills and experience, as competitive advantages, is only to be expected. The success of such UK multinational enterprises as Beecham, Cadbury, Clarks, Chubb, Distillers, etc. are ample testimony to this. Moreover, the major UK multinational enterprises tended to hold a strong position in their domestic market and to have been established for a long time. Technological strength, including the ability to offer after sales and maintenance service, was clearly an important factor for most of them; and several UK multinational enterprises—particularly those in the higher technology industries—still relied greatly on help from the US, e.g., Coates Bros., Metal Box, Plessey and Thorn. Technological strength in niche markets was also an important source of competitive advantage to many of the relatively small, specialized UK multinational enterprises that emerged after World War II: examples include APV, Acros, Brockhouse, A. Cohen, Creda, and McKechinie Bros.

We have already noted that a Commonwealth preference for UK foreign direct investment emerged during the inter-war years and peaked during the immediate post-World War II period. This was not only due to the fact that UK multinational enterprises were generally more competitive than indigenous firms in these regions, but also to the more favorable access that many of them enjoyed through a combination of (i) psychic proximity and indirect enforcement, and (ii) international producers in which such companies as EMI, ICI, and Metal Box, etc., were actively involved.

The general absence of managerial hierarchies among UK companies during the inter-war period—even by 1950 only a small proportion of UK companies investigated by Channon [5] had established a multidivisional structure—meant that there remained scope for the owner-entrepreneur to play a dominant role in the internationalization of production. The importance of such entrepreneurs before 1914 was stressed earlier in this section; but the vast majority of leading UK multinational enterprises which emerged during the inter-war and immediate post-war periods were also dominated by individuals with similar drive and vision. Examples include Maurice Coates (of Coates Bros.), Louis Stirling (of Columbia, EMI), Sir H. Sephcott (of Glaxo), Sir R. Barlow (of Metal Box), Lord McFadzean (of BICC), H. G. Lazell (of Beecham), Eric Bowater (of Bowater), Sir O. Aisker (of Marley), and Sir J. Thorn (of Thorn).

The risk aversion strategy of UK firms in continuing to invest in sectors in which they had achieved success in the past, rather than in the industries of the future, a protected home market, and a preferential access to Commonwealth markets during the 1940s and 1950s, meant that the UK was slow in adjusting to new conditions and opportunities. Even in the 1980s, British outward investment remains "heavily skewed" towards the mature, relatively low-technology industries, e.g., food, drink, tobacco, household products, textiles, paper and building materials. Consistent with this fact, of our sample of 187 UK multinational enterprises which have been significant overseas investors since 1960, 97 had origins going back to the 19th century (or earlier) and at least 150 had been established by 1930. Even over half of the increasing number of relatively small, specialized UK multinational enterprises had origins going back to before World War I. Clearly, then, prior to venturing abroad, the vast majority of UK multinational enterprises held established strong positions in their domestic markets, and were very experienced in their respective fields. This, of course, may have contributed to the complacency and lack of "controlled commercial aggression" among UK multinational enterprises abroad, observed by Stopford and Turner [30].

The asset advantages ($O_a$) of the 187 UK multinational enterprises investigated in the early 1980s [1] are summarized in Table 4.[6] It must be stressed that, as in previous periods, the competitive strength of UK multinational enterprises was generally the result of a combination of factors which varied from market to market. In addition to the $O_a$ advantages identified in the table, a number of companies such as BP, ICI, Imperial, RMC, Shell and Unilever, emphasized the advantages that directly resulted from their size and diversification, e.g., the ability to gain inputs on favorable terms, generate scale economies, etc. It is not absolute size, but relative size *vis-a-vis* the major competitors that is the often crucial factor and it is generally considered that too many of the major UK multinational enterprises are small in this respect.

Table 4 shows that approximately three-quarters of the companies perceived that "superior technology" was a crucial factor in their inter-

*Table 4* Major asset ownership advantages of 18 significant UK multinational enterprises 1960–1983

| Source of advantage | % |
| --- | --- |
| Superior technology | 73.2 |
| Managerial capacity and skill | 70.1 |
| Brand names, trademarks | 61.0 |
| Marketing skills | 49.2 |
| Research and development | 43.9 |
| Reputation for quality | 19.8 |
| Service provided | 14.4 |
| Ownership of raw materials | 8.0 |

*Source:* [1, p. 442].
Data obtained by interview or by questionnaire completed by the chief executive officer, or company secretary of the company in question.

national competitiveness; the exceptions being resource-based companies and several companies in industries where technology was mature or played a minor role, e.g., Allied-Lyons (bread and bakery products), BAT, Rothmans (cigarettes and tobacco), Distillers (drink), Tarmac (road surfacing materials). Obviously, technological strength was considered to be most important by the UK multinational enterprises in the more dynamic and research intensive industries, e.g., electronic companies such as GEC and Plessey, but a wide range of companies in other industries regarded it as central to their competitiveness; Clarks (boots and shoes) and Whitbread (drink) are examples. R & D activities were regarded as crucial to many companies not just in the development of products and processes, but also in modernizing existing technology, adapting it for different purposes, and customizing products and processes to specific local requirements. Technological strength in niche markets was perceived to be the most important intangible asset by the majority of the small, specialized UK multinational enterprises, e.g., Allied Colloids, Bowthorpe, British Vita, Tace, Unitech and Vinten.

The importance of brand names or trademarks and marketing skills among the $O_a$ advantages of UK multinational enterprises is again consistent with the industrial orientation of UK outward direct investment and the fact that most UK multinational enterprises were supplying products at a later stage of their product cycles. These intangible assets, for example, were perceived as being particularly important by consumer good companies such as Allied-Lyons, Beecham, Bass, DRG, Guinness, Rank Xerox, Cadbury, Schweppes, Imperial Tobacco and Unilever.

Although Stopford and Turner [30] have criticized the general managerial performance of the UK multinational enterprises, 70 percent of those in our sample considered that managerial capacity, skills and experience was an integral part of their competitive strength. Stopford and Turner suggest, however, that the relatively stronger performance of the smaller, specialized UK multinational enterprises was largely the result of superior managerial capabilities, and our findings certainly support this contention. In addition, it would seem that entrepreneurs with international vision and drive generally played a greater role in the international expansion of the smaller specialized UK multinational enterprises than of the larger ones during 1960–84.[7] However, in spite of the fact that, during this period, the large UK multinational enterprises adopted new organizational forms [5], entrepreneurs still played a crucial role in the domestic and multinational development of several of them, e.g., Allied-Lyons, Beecham, Blue Circle, Pilkington, Redland and Thorn.

At the beginning of this section, it was stated that, during the 1970s and 1980s, several UK multinational enterprises became increasingly aware of a whole set of transaction cost reducing advantages $(O_t)$ arising from their geographical diversification. Among those identified from our reading of company histories and documents are the ability to (i) offer customers the security of multiple sources of supply—as exampled by Automative, De La Rue, Lucas; (ii) keep more fully abreast of the major international developments in their industries, e.g., Beecham, De La Rue, Vinten; (iii) circumvent institutional constraints, e.g., tax codes, antitrust provisions, financial limitations, etc.; (iv) exploit imperfections in the capital exchange rate markets; (v) engage more effectively in competitive strategies such as cross-subsidization and predatory pricing (e.g., vis-a-vis uninational competitors); and (vi) enjoy greater strength and stability through the geographical spread of assets, e.g., by being in a better position to withstand cyclical profits, economic downturns, exchange rate volatility and political pressures of individual governments, e.g., Babcock, Beecham, Blue Circle, Foseco, ICI, Lonrho, Pilkington, Reckitt and Coleman, Unilever.

However, although reference to Doz [9] and Kogut [18; 19; 20] highlights these and other advantages which arise from the linking and specialization of production and markets across national frontiers, the number of UK companies actually pursuing such strategies in the 1970s remained small. In part, this may be because most of the products supplied by UK foreign subsidiaries are for local markets. There are suggestions, however, that over the last decade, there has been an increasing amount of intra-firm trade taking place within UK multinational enterprises, which implies the practice of some product and process specialization. Examples of such companies engaging in such trade include Courtaulds, Glaxo, GKN, ICI, Lucas, Plessey, Pilkington, Racal and Unilever.

**Internalization Incentive Advantages of UK Multinational Enterprises, 1870–1983**

The first condition of the eclectic paradigm determines how firms are able to compete with indigenous companies (and other foreign companies) in foreign markets, but it does not explain *why* firms which possess O advantages choose to exploit themselves in these markets rather than to sell or lease them to indigenous firms. If a firm is to engage in foreign direct investment, therefore, a second condition must be satisfied, i.e., it must be more beneficial to the firm possessing O advantages to use them through an extension of its own value adding activities rather than externalize them through licensing and similar contracts with independent firms. The fact that multinational enterprises prefer to internalize markets for their O advantages immediately implies that market failure exists; otherwise, firms would be able to earn the full economic rent on these advantages by selling or licensing them to independent buyers. Similarly, under perfect market conditions, there would be no incentive to integrate backwards or forwards.

Internalization theory, therefore, concerns itself with the conditions under which firms seek to replace external markets with administered decision taking. In this connection, economists have distinguished between *structural* market imperfections (which affect $O_a$ and L advantages) and *transactional* market imperfections (which affect $O_t$, L and I advantages). The desire to internalize markets arises because of the presence of the latter type of imperfections; thus the greater the perception of transactional market failure by firms, the more they are likely to exploit their O advantages through international production than through licensing and other contractual arrangements with indigenous firms.

The literature usually identifies three main kinds of transactional market failure: (i) those which arise from risk and uncertainty; (ii) those associated with the presence of plant economies of scale and imperfect product markets; and (iii) those which occur wherever individual transactions create costs and/or benefits external to those transactions but internal to the enterprise undertaking them. Although the reasons given by firms for internalizing their operations in an overseas market may be expressed rather differently, e.g., to safeguard supplies of inputs, to protect product quality and guarantee markets, to lessen the risk of the dissipation of proprietary rights through patent infringement, etc.—the desire to vertically integrate production, or to engage in horizontal or lateral foreign direct investment stems from the presence of one or other of the above three forms of transactional market failure. Although this paper is primarily concerned with UK manufacturing multinational enterprises, UK multinational activity was initially strongly oriented towards the primary product sector (especially in developing countries). For example, in 1960 about 35 percent of the UK and US accumulated investment was in manufacturing, compared with about 25 percent in 1938 and 25 percent in 1914 [12]. Vernon [33] stresses the importance to resource-based companies, such as BP and Shell, of being fully integrated, noting that unintegrated companies were particularly vulnerable to sudden price increases and/or supply interruptions. This can be seen as the rationale behind the numerous resource-seeking overseas investments made by BP, Shell, Burmah, RTZ, and Charter Consolidated, over the last century. At the same time, the increasing imperfection of primary product markets in the nineteenth and early twentieth centuries prompted several UK manufacturing companies to internalize the markets for their required resources through investing in foreign facilities, e.g., Dunlop in Malaysian rubber plantations, Lever in palm oil plantations in the Solomon Isles, Belgian Congo and Nigeria; Turner and Newall in asbestos mines in Rhodesia and South Africa, etc. The decline of supply-oriented foreign direct investment by UK multinational enterprises in the later 20th century can be seen as a combination of the growing efficiency of commodity and futures markets, and—more significantly—the increasingly hostile stance taken by host governments in the resource-rich developing countries to the foreign ownership and exploitation of their strategic resources.

A notable feature of UK multinational activity throughout the past century has been the internalization of downstream production and marketing and distributing operations, in overseas markets. Nicholas [23, 24], for example, has argued that the importance of vertical selling of UK multinational enterprises before 1939 reflected their bias towards selling consumer goods in high per capita markets. Moreover, in large part, they were able to set up successful selling networks abroad due to the advantages of a differentiated product and the marketing expertise developed in the home market. By contrast, overseas selling agencies found it more difficult to commit, or even acquire, the resources and motivation necessary to successfully develop the UK company's product in the local market; or to have the capability and incentive to provide the necessary quality of after-sales service and maintenance.

Through replacing these agents by their own selling outlets, the companies were able to gain total control over their distribution outlets and could employ the expertise that they had developed in the UK and other foreign markets. Governance over marketing activities was important in all periods covered by this paper not only for consumer goods companies, but also, for producer goods firms, which typically incur large sunk costs, and need to ensure and stabilize the demand for their products. In their analysis of global competition, Stopford and Turner [29] stress the value of having "greater control of access to the market place," and observed that "selling a good product in a distributional vacuum is a recipe for disaster." It is then not surprising that there are numerous examples of UK companies which internalize the markets for their foreign sales activities, and, significantly, during the 1960–84 period, to capture the benefits of regional integration or free trade areas. The justification given in Annual Reports for strengthening investments in the EEC in the 1970s was usually expressed by the companies in terms of "controlling," "strengthening," "coordinating," "reinforcing," "consolidating," and "increasing the penetration of" their European operations.

In the case of manufacturing overseas investments made before World War II, data relating to the reasons why UK multinational enterprises chose to internalize the markets for their O advantages is difficult to find. The majority of relevant company histories and archive material fail to mention the contractual, e.g., licensing, option; and give the impression that when exporting from the home country became difficult or impossible, foreign direct investment was the only alternative route of servicing the market considered by the company. Stopford and Turner [30] assert that few UK companies seem to have chosen the licensing option during this period, due, perhaps, to the lack of enforceable patent legislation, or to difficulties of monitoring the licensee's business.

Such scattered evidence as does exist, suggests that several UK companies were concerned lest a licensee might become a future competitor, e.g., Glaxo's problems with Bachus Marsh in Australia around 1914; or of being unable to maintain proper quality control, e.g., Dunlop's experiences in France and Germany, foreign direct investment was also undertaken where patent disputes and difficulties arose, e.g., in the case of Albright and Wilson in Canada (1901) and Courtaulds in Germany (1925). Since, too, several of the markets in which the British companies invested were in their early stages of development, many companies were keen to establish total control over their operations from the start, and avoid the drawbacks of licensing and other contractual arrangements.

There were other features that influenced the decision of UK multinational enterprises to engage in foreign direct investment rather than to license foreign firms. First, in several cases—notably those involving the production of high quality consumer goods—there did not exist a licensee with the necessary capabilities, and who was sufficiently trustworthy to manufacture (and service) the product to the licensor's satisfaction. Second, UK—like other multinational—enterprises in some high technology sectors found it appropriate to use the market for the transfer of knowledge, e.g., when it was noncodifiable, idiosyncratic or tacit. Third, it was often relatively easy and inexpensive to set up overseas operations, e.g., as in the case of Gramophone's local record pressing plants. Fourth, foreign direct investment enabled UK companies to take advantage of incentives offered for indigenous manufacture by local governments, e.g., Lever in South Africa (1910). Fifth, the ownership of foreign subsidiaries afforded UK companies more freedom to react to the strategies, or anticipated strategies, of their major competitors, than would have been possible with licensing agreements.

With respect to this last point, it is abundantly clear that, in their foreign direct investment decisions, many UK companies before World War II were influenced by the actions or anticipated actions of their major international competitors. This was particularly so during the inter-war years which were characterized by a growth in industrial concentration, rationalization and cartelization: indeed Jones [17] has stated that, during the 1920s, the operating decisions of most large UK multinational enterprises were taken against a background of intense international oligopolistic rivalry. Major examples of foreign direct investment by UK multinational enterprises that responded to the oligopolistic pressures and strategies included Shell's actual (1911) and Imperial Tobacco's threatened (1901) investments in the US; Pilkington's investments in France (1892), Canada (1913) and a threatened one in Belgium (1928); Courtauld's investments in France (1925), Germany (1925) and Italy (1927) etc. Other UK companies behaving in a similar fashion were APOC, Bowater, Cadbury, Dunlop, George Kent and Rowntree. For example, in spite of making losses of £750,000 during 1909–24, Dunlop's French subsidiary was kept going to combat the competition from Michelin.

Since, as the previous section noted, the predominant source of competitive strength for UK multinational enterprises until the 1970s was their privileged possession of, or access to, intangible assets, the motivation for these companies to internalize the foreign market for these advantages in the immediate post-World War II period was essentially the same as that which existed before 1939. UK companies remained keen to exploit their most important markets on a permanent basis, with full control over their operations, when exporting became difficult or no longer practicable. These companies perceived that foreign direct investment would better enable them to appropriate the economic rent on their technological, marketing and managerial capabilities, and more effectively protect their proprietary rights and product quality.

Taking account of the dominant Commonwealth preference for UK foreign direct investment which existed until the early 1960s, the attitude of many UK companies towards foreign direct investment, in preference to licensing, was typified by McKechinie Brothers who stated:

> With a licensing agreement one only has a certain percentage of turnover or profits or other criteria as a return to the company and in certain circumstances this may be considered adequate. However, when you are in a position to enter into a market in its infancy as McKechinie were undoubtedly in the mid-1940s in South Africa and in the mid-1950s in New Zealand, then it is clearly better to establish a manufacturing operation under your total and complete control ... you are in a position to control your manufacturing operation, the sale of your product and to obtain the full benefit of your investment by retaining all the post taxation profit.

A further relevant point was made by Delta who, in stating why foreign direct investment was preferred to licensing in Australia, South Africa, Rhodesia, and Kenya during the 1950s remarked that it was

> because the territories concerned were in the early stages of industrial development so that there was no indigenous industry for which licensing agreements might be considered.

Even where licensees did exist, records of companies such as BICC, Bridon, and Hawker-Siddeley suggest a reluctance to enter into agreements for fear of creating or assisting a potential competitor. In view of the increasing desire of UK companies during the 1950s and 1960s to diversify their foreign portfolios, the acquisition of overseas companies was often seen as a quick and efficient way of achieving this objective. It appears, however, that, during the 1940s and 1950s, UK companies were not generally influenced by the behavior of their competitors' foreign investment decisions; exceptions include Pilkingtons, Unilever, BP and Shell Oil. Too few UK companies had the resources or competitive strength to engage in widespread foreign direct investment as part of an international oligopolistic strategy; for most, the Commonwealth continued to be their main outlet for manufacturing.

For the UK multinational enterprises that neither engaged in rationalized production and investment, nor sought to benefit from transaction cost advantages, the incentives to internalize markets that existed during the intermediate post-war period remained no less relevant in the 1970s and early 1980s. The analysis of Stopford and Turner [30], for example, suggests that, to be successful in an environment of global competition, UK companies must both exploit the full economic rent from their individual $O_a$ advantages and efficiently coordinate these advantages. Numerous companies have recognized this fact and perceived foreign direct investment as the best way to achieve this aim, given the inadequacies of using the market to transfer and control resources. Additionally, foreign direct investment, by way of acquisition, has been increasingly preferred to greenfield ventures as a means of gaining access to markets; or as part of a wider diversification strategy. Imperfections in Anglo–US capital and exchange markets also resulted in a flood of UK takeovers of US firms in the late 1970s and early 1980s. Although very few UK companies appear to have been in a position to engage in oligopolistic strategies on a global scale during the 1970s and early 1980s, in certain important markets, at least, several companies were influenced in establishing local subsidiaries by the actions of their major competitors. "Exchange of threats" and "follow the leader" considerations, for example, figure frequently in the Chairman's reports of BP, ICI, Unilever, Redland, Allied Colloids, and Tace, over this period.

Since 1970, some rationalized (efficiency-seeking) investment has been undertaken by UK multinational enterprises; and, with it, as revealed by an increasing amount of intra-firm trade between parent companies and subsidiaries, a growing degree of product and process specialization. The motivation for such integration has been threefold; first, to secure a presence in the major growth markets of the world and thus be better able to maintain an international competitive stance; second, to take advantage of differences in international factor endowments and costs; and third, to capture the gains from the economies of specialization and integration. In addition, as the previous section observed, there is some reason to suppose that UK multinational enterprises are becoming increasingly apprised of the gains that can accrue to them through multinationality per se. Awareness of these advantages and the desire to fully exploit them has, therefore, provided an important added incentive in the foreign direct investment strategy of UK multinational enterprises such as Beecham, ICI, Pilkington and Unilever.

## Location-Specific Determinants of UK Multinational Enterprises 1870–1983

Location (L) factors are relevant to the theory of the multinational enterprise both insofar as they influence the "where" of value added activities, and also as they interact with O and I factors to generate advantages (and costs) for multinational enterprises, that arise specifically from the geographical diversification of their activities.

The first way in which location factors enter the eclectic paradigm relates to structural market distortions (which may be "natural," e.g., transport costs, or "artificial," e.g., import quotas, export subsidies). By their affect on production costs and revenues in different locations, they may encourage or discourage foreign direct investment [15]. The second way relates to transactional and market failure, for even in the absence of structural market distortions, multinational enterprise activity might still occur wherever there are benefits, e.g., operational flexibility, likely to result from the common ownership of activities sited in different locations.

The locational parameters influencing the investment decisions by UK multinational enterprises have changed markedly over the last 100 years as a result, *inter alia*, of technological advances, economic development and shifts in home and host country Government policies. To give one or two examples: labor and many material costs are now generally a much less important ingredient of manufacturing costs than they used to be; intra-firm communication costs have dramatically fallen; technology-related variables have become increasingly decisive; within the industrialized world, at least, there has been a convergence of the structure of factor endowments, and consumer spending patterns; and Governments have become highly sensitive to inward investment in key strategic sectors.

In the case of resource-seeking multinational enterprises, the presence of the required resources was, and still is, the main "pull" factor making for a foreign location; other variables identified by UK multinational enterprises include exploration and extraction costs, land rents, transport costs, and host governments' attitudes towards the foreign ownership of natural resources. This latter variable, for example, explains why Lever developed plantations in the Belgian Congo rather than the Gold Coast pre-1914; why Booker McConnell was forced to divest its sugar plantations in Guyana in the 1970s; and why very little resource-seeking foreign direct investment has been undertaken by UK multinational enterprises since 1960. Numerous developing and newly-industrialized countries gained independence during the 1960s and 1970s;[8] during which years an increasingly hostile stance was taken by their governments to the foreign ownership and exploitations of their natural resources.

Although several UK manufacturing multinational enterprises undertook foreign direct investment in the 1950s (e.g., Courtaulds, Unilever and Wellcome) and the 1960s (e.g., Babcock and Guinness) as part of diversification policies aimed at improving their overall competitiveness; until the 1970s, UK manufacturing foreign direct investment remained almost entirely of an import-substitution kind rather than an efficiency-seeking one; and the locational determinants were primarily those associated with the production and transfer costs of a limited range of activities.[9] However, these locational determinants changed significantly over time, strongly influencing the distinctive location patterns that UK foreign direct investment has followed since 1870.

Prior to World War I, UK manufacturing multinational enterprises displayed a preference for high-income markets, with a slight Empire bias due to political and other psychic ties. Some companies, e.g., Babcock, Bryant and May, Gramophone and Nobel entered into international market-sharing agreements which allocated the Empire and/or European markets to them. It was the high-income markets which offered the best prospects for the kind of consumer goods supplied by UK multinational enterprises while other locational variables such as technological infrastructure, market size and growth, and government policies and attitudes towards foreign direct investment and the remittance of profits were generally favorable.

Although there is little reason to suppose that UK companies were influenced by lower production costs in undertaking foreign direct investment before 1914 (noticeable exceptions include those by Lever and Courtaulds in the 1900s[10]) there can be no little doubt that they were strongly influenced by transfer costs; indeed, the imposition of tariffs by governments in Continental Europe and the US on important manufactured goods in the late second half of the 19th century was frequently the single most important factor behind the decision by many UK companies to begin foreign manufacture. Company histories and internal documents of such multinational enterprises as Babcock, J and P Coats, English Sewing Cotton, Courtaulds, Dunlop, Gramophone, Lever and Reckitts all testify to this. Tariffs also induced several investments in Commonwealth markets, e.g., those by Lever and Reckitts in Australia, Nobel in Australia, Canada and South Africa, etc. Transport costs encouraged foreign production by companies such as Babcocks, Gramophone and Nobel, whose products were high volume/low value or, in the case of Nobel, dangerous to export over long distances. Tariffs and transport costs often combined to prompt UK companies to establish overseas subsidiaries, particularly in countries where there was strong or emerging indigenous competition; examples include J and P Coats, and English Sewing Cotton in the US.

Host governments also influenced the foreign direct investment decisions of UK companies in other ways before 1914. These included the offering of incentives for local manufacture, e.g., Lever's investment in South Africa; direct requests for participation in local venture, e.g., Vickers investment in Italy, Japan, Canada, Russia and Turkey; patent legislation requiring the local working of a patent, e.g., Dunlop's investments in France and Germany; and, through the encouragement and fostering of nationalism (a particularly important factor in Europe and some during Commonwealth controls during the inter-war period).

During the inter-war years, an Empire–Commonwealth preference for UK foreign direct investment emerged and grew in strength. The locational factors which contributed to this are clear. Firstly, due to psychic proximity, traditional ties and indirect enforcement [31], many UK companies regarded the Empire markets—particularly the White Dominions and India—as a natural extension of their domestic markets. Most, indeed, had already developed important trading links with them; examples include Coates Bros., George Kent and Metal Box, Chubb, Glaxo and Ransom and Marles. Host-country pulls such as political stability, large and/or growing markets, transportation and communications infrastructure were also generally favorable, especially when compared with Europe where the political situation was volatile, and innovative local firms were buttressed by cartels and government policy [27].

A further stimulus for foreign direct investment at this time was the transportation difficulty that UK firms had faced in exporting to foreign markets during 1914–1918. This reason was cited by companies such as Babcocks, Baker, Perkins, GKN with respect to their markets in Australia, Ferranti in Canada, and Gramophone in Italy. However, most commentators [e.g., 4; 8; 17; 23; 27] cite import restrictions as the main pull of multinational expansion during this period.[11] The economic and political climate, as the inter-war period progressed, increased and strengthened the protectionist stance of governments. Faced with these problems and the consequent loss of important export markets, a growing number of UK companies engaged in foreign direct investment, even though the economic rationale for it was less congenial than it had been prior to the War.

After World War II, the international economic and political scenario became increasingly favorable for foreign direct investment. In the first decade after 1945, the outstanding feature of UK multinational expansion was its almost exclusive orientation towards Commonwealth markets, and especially to Australia, Canada and South Africa.[12] As was the case during the inter-war years, the principal Commonwealth markets were attractive not only because of psychic proximity and traditional ties, but because they offered expanding markets, high incomes, a relaxed attitude to foreign direct investment, and, perhaps most important of all, less intensive competitive pressures than in Europe and US. In addition, UK government exchange control policy favored outward investment directed to the Commonwealth, on account of large sterling credits accumulated by Commonwealth countries during 1939–45.

While these factors explain the attractiveness of the Commonwealth as an overseas production base for UK multinational enterprises, they do not fully explain why the companies chose to invest in them rather than export from the UK. Evidence suggests, however, that in many less developed countries, UK companies frequently came under the most intensive economic and political pressure to start local manufacture [1]. As in the inter-war years, governments were keen to develop their economies and local competition was growing under their protection. Nationalism was an important contributory factor to decisions of UK multinational enterprises to establish overseas manufacturing subsidiaries. Barker [3] for example, notes that after 1945, pressures—sometimes political, sometimes economic—were brought to bear on Pilkington to start sheet glass manufacture in South Africa, Canada and India; while the experience of Pilkington in South Africa suggests that UK companies were often forced to manufacture in an overseas market, even when cost considerations determined that UK production was preferable. Reference to Turner and Newall's company history suggests that their Canadian involvements in the 1950s were largely in response to the host Government's desire to become more economically independent in asbestos and related products.

Apart from imposing tariffs, import controls and encouraging economic nationalism, Commonwealth governments influenced UK companies foreign direct investment decisions in other ways. Courtaulds for example, was prompted by government industrialization policies to invest in Australia; Glaxo was approached by the Indian authorities to invest in India; Unilever was asked by the Colonial Development Corporation to assist in the development of the Kenya economy. Conversely, many UK companies were discouraged from investing in India and Pakistan by restrictions on ownership, imports of intermediate products and profit remittances.

After 1960, there was a marked shift of interest by UK multinational enterprises in their choice of investment outlets. The earlier preference for a Commonwealth location fell sharply, and an increasing proportion of UK investment was directed to the original six members of the EEC, and to the USA. While conditions in the principal Commonwealth markets became less attractive for many UK companies during the 1960s,[13] recovery followed by expansion in Europe, together with the moves towards economic integration, increased the attraction of markets nearer home. The accession of the UK to the EEC in 1973 underlined new opportunities for UK companies, while the US was clearly a vitally important market throughout the period, although competitive pressures were intense.

Stopford [28] suggests that there was a growing propensity for UK companies to invest in countries with per capita incomes higher than in the UK. There is certainly strong evidence to support this, and it could be argued that some UK companies invested in the EEC not because of the existence of the Community *per se* but because of the high income and large markets of the individual member countries in which the investment was made. More recently, the desire of several UK companies to establish a presence in the major centers of technological excellence, has been prompted by the growing phenomenon of global competition.

There were, of course, other factors influencing the location of UK multinational enterprise activity. Government pressure and xenophobia prompted import substitution investment be made in the developing countries (especially when the products were considered strategically sensitive) in the EEC (where "economic nationalism remains a potent force and a major barrier to the free trade of assets within the community" [30, p. 85], and in the US (e.g., investments made by Johnson Matthey, GEC, George Kent and Tube Investments). Transfer costs were also influential; tariffs and nontariff barriers caused UK companies, e.g., Bowater, ICI, Tube, Turner and Newall, Vickers to establish subsidiaries in the EEC well before the UK's accession. Transport costs continued to exert a strong influence on the siting decisions of companies producing low value/high volume products, e.g., BOC, British Vita, Hepworth Ceramic, Foseco, Redland, and products that needed to be consumed quickly after manu-facture, e.g., United Biscuits short-life cakes.

At the beginning of this section, it was stated that until the 1970s, UK foreign manufacturing subsidiaries largely consisted of a federated group of operations, each of which was designed to produce and sell products for the particular national markets in which it operated. Such affiliates were largely truncated replicas of their parent companies; and the "where" of their location was mainly determined by comparative production costs of their value adding activities and the international transfer costs of inter-mediate and/or final products. It is also clear from our analysis of the competitive advantages of UK multinational enterprises, that the majority perceived that foreign direct investment was the best way of exploiting these advantages; and that only a few engaged in overseas production as part of a strategy of geographical diversification, aimed to advance their international competitive position.[14] However, we also suggested that there was evidence to suggest that in the 1960s UK multinational enterprises were becoming more aware of the advantages that multinationality bestowed upon them; and that, during the following two decades, several of them sought to establish integrated operations (especially in the EEC), e.g., ICI, Pilkington and Unilever.

Finally, although it has been observed [16, 30] that, in the 1970s, UK multinational enterprises were slower to take advantage of low labor cost locations than their US, other European or Japanese counterparts, there were some noticeable exceptions. BICC (Hong Kong), Clarks (Cyprus), Courtaulds (Tunisia and Morocco), Lucas (Malaysia), Pilkington (Taiwan and Brazil) and Unitech (Mexico) are all examples of UK multinational enterprises which engaged in foreign direct investment in the 1970s so as to take advantage of cheap, plentiful and well motivated labor to produce their labor-intensive products and processes for export markets.

**Conclusions**

In this paper, we have used the eclectic paradigm as a theoretical framework for examining the growth of UK manufacturing multinational enterprises since their initial emergence around 1870. The types of multinational enterprises that have dominated UK multinational activity, the sources of their competitive strengths and weaknesses, the geographical orientation of their foreign direct investment, and how these have changed over the last century, has been explained in terms of the changing nature of the OLI variables and the interaction between them.

At the same time, the competitive position of UK firms, particularly in oligopolistic industries, their growth strategies, their attitudes to risk, innovation and diversification, and their perception of, and reactions to, their rivals' actions, have also been shown to be important behavioral variables influencing the investment decisions of UK multinational enterprises when confronted with any particular OLI configuration. Archer [1], for example, has shown that it is not unusual for a UK multinational enterprise to invest in a market which it had previously been servicing quite satisfactorily through exports, largely because of a change—or anticipated change—in the behavior of a major competitor rather than a change in the value of the OLI parameters facing it. Noticeable examples include Shell in US (1912); Pilkington in Canada (1913), Dunlop in Eire, India and South Africa (1930); Allied Colloids in South Africa (1970s) and BP, ICI, and Plessey in the US during the 1960s and 1970s.

Finally, the growing emphasis that is being placed on a product and process specialization and integration across national boundaries, and on new forms of collaborative arrangements among the leading multinational enterprises, suggests that more attention should be given to the dynamics of the competitive advantages of multinational enterprises; and to the ways in which the interaction between these and the organization and location of their exploitation affect their international competitive position.

## Notes

1. These pioneering UK multinational enterprises were: BAT, Babcock & Wilcox, Bryant and May, J&P Coats, Courtaulds, Dunlop, English Sewing Cotton, Gramophone, Lever Brothers, Nobel Explosives, Pilkington Brothers, Reckitt & Sons, Royal Dutch Shell, Vickers and Wellcome.

2. The reasons for the UKs emerging industrial retardation has been the subject of great debate in numerous books and papers, e.g., Hobsbawm (1968). There is insufficient scope to go into all the suggested reasons in this paper.

3. In his history of Bryant and May, Lucas [21] stated that, a major effect of the 1901 amalgamation was the managerial association of Gilbert Bartholomew and George W. Paton as together they became the architects of the rapid growth of the company and its widening outlook. Corley [8] referred to the poor entrepreneurship of the company prior to amalgamation. Wellcome's failure to continue its multinational growth after World War I can be largely attributed to Henry Wellcome's loss of much of his former commercial drive (Courtenay History pp. 29–30).

4. The inter-war years saw the collapse of international capital markets in the late 1920s and the early 1930s, were characterized by political instability, depressed and fragmented markets, etc. and where characterized by industrial concentration, rationalization and cartelization. During 1945–60, the international and economic and political environment became increasingly favorable for foreign direct investment as countries recovered from the effects of war. A 1984 OECD report referred to the first 20 years of the post-war period as the "golden age of stability and growth."

5. Among the new major UK multinational enterprises to emerge were (a) 1915–39: Aspro, BBA, BOC, Baker Perkins, Cadbury, Coates Bros., Columbia (EMI), Distillers, Glaxo, GKN, G. Kent, Metal Box, Rowntree, Turner & Newall (and commodity-based: APOC, Brooke Bond, Tate & Lyle), (b) 1940–59: APU, Acrow, BICC, BPB, Beecham, Bowater, Brideon, Brockhouse, Chubb Clarks, A. Cohen, Creda, Delta Metal, Dexicon-Comino, Foseco, Hawker-Siddeley, Johnson Matthey, Lucas, Marley, McKechinie Brothers, Plessey, Ransome Marles & Co., Simon Engineering, Smith & Nephew, Thorn, Tube Investments.

6. These results obtained from a questionnaire survey must be treated with a certain amount of caution as (i) they are determined largely by how the companies perceived their own sources of strength; and (ii) many of the factors included are interdependent, and (iii) companies, on occasion, referred only to the most important ones, regarding the others as implicit, e.g., superior technology, marketing skills, etc., are relevant on R&D activity, service and quality are central to the strength of brand/company names, etc.

7. It appears that during 1960–84 an individual—or a small group of individuals—played a dominant role in the multinational expansion of two-thirds of the smaller, specialized UK multinational enterprises. The corresponding ratio for the large UK multinational enterprises was between one-quarter and one-third.

8. These included: Nigeria (1960), Tanzania (1961), Jamaica (1962), Kenya (1963), Malawi (1964), Zambia (1964), Singapore (1965) and Guyana (1966).

9. It should also be noted that even during the period 1870–1939 one aspect of transaction power was beginning to show itself [12]. As we have seen, the market structure of many of the new industries was oligopolistic, and the foreign strategy of the constituent firms was designed often to protect their overall position. In such cases, the motive for foreign direct investment was primarily to preclude rivals from gaining a foothold in a foreign market or in response to their penetration of one's own markets rather than to make additional profits.

10. See C. Wilson, *The History of Unilever,* Vol. 1, p. 99, and D. C. Coleman, *Courtaulds: An Economic and Social History,* Vol. 2, p. 277.

11. See: W. J. Reader: *Imperial Chemical Industries: A History,* Vol. 2, p. 198.

12. Figures contained in Houston and Dunning [16], for example, suggested that the cumulative net flow of direct investment into all Commonwealth countries 1946–60 amounted to 80 percent of recorded UK direct investment during this 15-year period; and that by 1960 about 71 percent of the total stock, excluding oil, banking and insurance was situated in Commonwealth countries.

13. For example, South Africa left the Commonwealth in 1969; UDI was declared in Southern Rhodesia in 1965; there was increasing US competitive pressure in Australia, stagflation in India, losses were being made in Canada, etc.

14. Numerous UK companies followed such diversification policies during the 1960s, and particularly the 1970s and early 1980s. These policies were followed to reduce the cyclical nature of profits of their products and/or markets; compensate for poor prospects in the UK and their traditional markets; offset mature products and markets, etc. Diversification was seen as giving "flexibility," "stability," "resilience," "strength," etc. and reducing vulnerability.

# References

1. H. J. Archer, "An Eclectic Approach to the Historical Study of UK Multinational Enterprises," (Doctoral Dissertation, University of Reading 1986).

2. W. Ashworth, *An Economic History of England, 1870–1939* (London: Methuen, 1960).

3. T. C. Barker, "Pilkington, the reluctant multinational," London Business History Unit mimeo (1986).

4. A. D. Chandler, Jr. "The growth of the transnational industrial firm in the United States and the United Kingdom," *Economic History Review,* Series 2, 33, (1980) pp. 396–410.

5. D. F. Channon, *The Strategy and Structure of British Enterprise* (London, Macmillan, 1973).

6. D. C. Coleman, *Courtaulds: An Economic and Social History,* 3 volumes (Oxford, Clarendon Press: 1969, 1980).

7. T. A. B. Corley, *Quaker Enterprise in Biscuits: Huntley and Palmers of Reading, 1822–1972* (London, Hutchinson, 1972)

8. ——,"The nature of multinationals 1870–1939," University of Reading, mimeo, 1985.

9. Y. Doz, *Strategic Management in Multinational Companies* (Oxford, Pergamon Press, 1986).

10. J. H. Dunning, *American Investment in British Manufacturing Industry,* (London: Allen and Unwin, 1958).

11. ——, *International Production and the Multinational Enterprise* (London, George Allen and Unwin, 1981).

12. ——,"Changes in the level and structure of international production: the last one hundred years" in Casson, M. C. (ed), *The Growth of International Business* (London, George Allen and Unwin, 1983).

13. ——, "The eclectic paradigm of international production: a restatement and some possible extensions" *Journal of International Business Studies,* XIX Spring 1988.

14. ——,*Multinational Enterprises, Economic Structure and International Competitiveness* (Chichester, John Wiley, 1985).

15. S. Guisinger, (ed.) *Investment Incentives and Performance Requirements,* (New York: Praeger, 1985).

16. T. Houston and J. H. Dunning, *UK Industry Abroad* (London, Financial Times, 1976).

17. G. Jones, "The expansion of British multinational manufacturing 1890–1939" in Inoue, T. and Okochi, A. (eds.), *Overseas Business Activities: Proceedings of the Ninth Fuji Conference* (Tokyo, 1984).

18. B. Kogut, "Foreign direct investment as a sequential process," in C. P. Kindleberger and D. B. Audretsch (ed), *The Multinational Corporation in the 1980's* (Cambridge, Mass., MIT Press, 1983).

19. ———,"Normative observations on the international value-added chain and strategic groups," *Journal of International Business Studies,* 16 (Fall 1984), pp. 151–67.

20. ———,"Designing global strategies: profiting from operational flexibility," *Sloan Management Review,* 27, No. 1, (Fall 1985), pp. 27–39.

21. W. Lucas, *A Hundred Years of Match Making, Bryant & May 1861–1961* (London, Newman Neame Ltd., 1959).

22. B. Murphy, *A History of the British Economy 1086–1970* (London, Longman, 1973).

23. S. J. Nicholas, "British Multinational Investment before 1939," *Journal of European Economic History,* 11, (Winter 1982), pp. 605–30.

24. ———,"Agency Contracts, Institutional Modes, and the transition to foreign direct investment by British manufacturing multinationals before 1939," *Journal of Economic History,* 43, (September 1983), pp. 675–686.

25. W. J. Reader, *Imperial Chemical Industries: A History,* 2 volumes (London, Oxford University Press, 1970 and 1975).

26. W. Readdaway, S. J. Potter, and C. T. Taylor, *The Effects of UK Direct Investment Overseas: Final Report* (Cambridge University Press, 1968).

27. J. M. Stopford "The origins of British-based multinational manufacturing enterprises," *Business History Review,* 48, No. 3, (Autumn 1974), pp. 303–345.

28.———,"Changing perspectives on investment by British manufacturing multinationals," *Journal of International Business,* 7, No. 2, (Fall/Winter 1976), pp. 15–27.

29. J. M. Stopford and J. H. Dunning *Multinationals: Company Performance and Global Trends* (London, Macmillan, 1983).

30. J. M. Stopford and L. Turner, *Britain and the Multinationals* (Chichester, John Wiley, 1985).

31. P. Svedberg, "Colonial enforcement of foreign direct investment," *Manchester School of Economic and Social Studies,* 50 (1981) pp. 21–38.

32. D. J. Teece, "Technological and organizational factors in the theory of the multinational enterprise," in Casson, M. C. (ed), *The Growth of International Business* (London, George Allen and Unwin, 1983).

33. R. Vernon, "Organizational and Institutional Responses to International Risk," in Herring, R. (ed.), *Managing International Risk* (Cambridge, University Press, 1983).

34. C. Wilson, *The History of Unilever,* 3 volumes (London, Cassell & Co., 1954 and 1968).

# 3

## The Growth of the Transnational Industrial Firm in the United States and the United Kingdom: A Comparative Analysis*[1]

Alfred D. Chandler

*Source: *Economic History Review*, XXXIII (1980), pp. 396–410.

This article is an exercise in comparative institutional history. It examines the beginnings and continuing growth of a powerful economic institution, the modern transnational industrial corporation, in two quite different economies. Such a comparative analysis has the advantage of pointing to basic institutional similarities and, at the same time, suggesting how institutions are affected by differing economic needs and opportunities as well as by differing culture attitudes and values. And, although the similarities in the history of the large industrial firm in the two countries are significant, it is the differences that are particularly striking.

This analysis is based on a comparative study that I have been carrying out with Prof. Herman Daems on the rise of large-scale industrial enterprise in the United States, Britain, and the Continent. Our plan has been to make use of lists of over 100 of the largest industrial firms (ranked either by assets or market value of securities outstanding) in the United States, the United Kingdom, Germany, and France for three sets of years: those immediately after World War I, those just prior to the onslaught of the great depression, and those immediately following World War II.[2]

These lists document what I found to be the case for the United States.[3] The largest firms clustered in a few capital-intensive and energy-intensive groups of industries whose products are distributed in volume in national and international markets. In all four countries the largest enterprises were found primarily in the chemical, machinery, and metal-making industries. In Britain, as might be expected from its industrial history, there were more large textile firms. In the United States there were more large petroleum enterprises. In both the United States and the United Kingdom there were many large companies in the food industries, but in Germany and France there were almost none. In no country, however, were there more than one or two large firms in the apparel, furniture, lumber, leather, and printing and publishing industries.

Because of the nature of this clustering we decided to focus our research efforts on the individual histories of the largest firms in three industries: chemicals (including soap and allied industries, paint, pharmaceuticals, explosives, and fertilizers as well as industrial chemicals); machinery (including electrical machinery and transportation equipment), where the large firm clusters in all major economies; and food (including drink and tobacco), where many large enterprises appeared in the United States and the United Kingdom. These industries provide a spread in production from simple to the most complex technologies and in distribution from mass consumer to highly specialized industrial markets. The companies in these industrial groups plus those in petroleum, rubber, and glass, whose experience parallel closely that of the chemical firms, accounted in the 1970s for 81.3 per cent of the 256 companies in the world employing more than 30,000 workers in 1973, and for approximately 80 per cent of the world's 800 largest industrial companies in the same year. Of this 80 per cent nearly all were transnationals.[4] A review of their history from their beginnings until World War II can, therefore, tell us much about the institutional development of today's market economies.

The composite history of the largest firms in these industries in the United States and the United Kingdom makes it absolutely clear that modern industrial enterprise did not become large merely by expanding the company's industrial plant or factory.[5] Instead, these enterprises grew by adding new units of production and distribution, by adding sales and purchasing offices, by adding facilities for producing raw and semi-finished materials, by obtaining shipping lines, railroad cars, pipelines, and other transportation units, and even by building research laboratories. Growth through the addition of new units came in two ways: either the enterprise itself built new offices, plants, and opened mines, all of which were normally paid for out of retained earnings, or it obtained them through the acquisition of or merger with other enterprises. (And nearly all of these acquisitions and mergers were financed by the exchange of stock.)

Either route to growth meant the hiring of managers. Managers were needed not only to administer the activities of the new units but also to co-ordinate and monitor these units and to allocate resources to them for the firm's future production and distribution. Thus the growth of the firm led to the creation of multi-unit enterprises administered through managerial hierarchies. Such growth also meant that in many industries the productive assets became concentrated in a few large business enterprises.

One of the most striking differences between the history of big business in the two countries is that these managerial hierarchies became larger and appeared much more quickly in the United States than they did in the United Kingdom. In neither case did large multi-unit industrial firms appear before the 1880s. They came only after new forms of transportation and communication—the railroads, steamships, telegraph and cable—had been improved enough to make possible high-volume production and distribution, the basic characteristic of the modern industrial firm. From the 1880s such enterprises appeared in the United States with unprecedented speed and took their place in the economy in a revolutionary way. In Britain they came in a slower, more evolutionary manner. Let us review these differing processes of growth in the two countries.

# I

In the United States the first to grow large in the 1880s did so by integrating forward into wholesaling and backward into direct purchasing and then into the control of raw and semi-finished materials. They explicitly carried out a strategy of vertical integration. They did so, however, only in four subsets of industries, each of which had somewhat similar characteristics. The large multi-unit firm appeared in the production of low-priced, branded, packaged products where manufacturers adopted large batch and continuous-process technologies of mass production; in the processing of perishable products for the national market; in the making of new mass-produced machines that required specialized marketing services to be sold in volume; and, finally, in the manufacturing of volume-produced machinery and chemicals which were standardized, but technologically complex, and which called for somewhat different specialized marketing services.

During the 1880s pioneering enterprises of the first of these four groups included American Tobacco producing cigarettes; Washburn and Pillsbury both making flour; Quaker Oats in breakfast cereals; Heinz, Campbell Soup, Borden's Milk, and Libby, McNeil & Libby in canned goods; Procter & Gamble in soap; Sherwin-Williams in paints; and Parke Davis, Colgate, and Squibb in proprietary drugs. The managers of these enterprises continued to use the wholesaler to handle the physical distribution of goods, but they took over branding, advertising, and they scheduled the flows of the goods from the factories to the new mass markets.

In the same decade, meat packers, including Armour, Swift, Morris, Hammond, Cudahy, and Swartschild & Sulzberger, and brewers, including Pabst, Miller, Schlitz, and Anheuser-Busch, began to build national, and often international, networks of branch houses with refrigerated warehouses and distribution facilities, as well as to obtain fleets of temperature-controlled railroad cars and ships. Similar networks were formed in the 1890s by the precursors of United Fruit to produce and sell bananas on a mass scale. These firms often by-passed the wholesalers completely, for the latter were unable to provide extensive refrigerated facilities or to schedule with the necessary precision the flow of these perishable products over thousands of miles from the initial processing to thousands indeed tens of thousands of local butchers, grocers, and other retailers. At the same time, like the producers of semi-perishable products, they created extensive purchasing organizations to ensure a continuous flow of raw materials into their mass-producing facilities.

The third group, the makers of newly invented machinery produced by assembling interchangeable parts, also by-passed the wholesalers. To sell their relatively complex and costly products in the volume at which they could be produced, these manufacturers had to provide demonstrations, continuing service and repair on machines sold, and credit to consumers. Moreover, the weekly delivery of thousands of machines on schedule required careful co-ordination, as did ensuring a high-volume flow of a wide variety of materials through the factory. Nearly all these firms quickly built world-wide marketing organizations. The pioneers were the makers of sewing machines. The most successful of these, the Singer Sewing Machine Co., was the innovator in direct canvassing of consumers, that is, it moved into retailing as well as into wholesaling. Others, particularly the makers of agricultural implements, such as McCormick Harvester, Deering Harvester, John Deere, and J. I. Case, preferred the less expensive alternative of using franchise dealers supported by a strong, well-organized wholesale organization that permitted dealers to market aggressively and to provide necessary services. The manufacturers of new machines, including Fairbanks Scales, Remington Typewriter, National Cash Register, A. B. Dick Mimeograph Machines, Burroughs Adding Machine, and Computer-Tabulator-Recorder (the predecessor of I.B.M.), also came to rely on the franchise dealer. Nearly all of these enterprises either built or perfected their sales departments in the 1880s.

During the same decade, makers of standardized heavy machinery created comparable world-wide organizations. Normally, they staffed these with college-trained engineers because of the technological complexity of their products and the uses to which they were put. These firms included the forerunners of General Electric and Allis Chalmers, as well as Westinghouse Electric, Westinghouse Air Brake, Western Electric, Otis Elevator, Worthington Pump, Babcock & Wilcox, and Mergenthaler Linotype. The fast-moving technology of the machinery-makers, particularly that of the manufacturers of electrical equipment, required close co-ordination among salesmen, product designers, and manufacturing managers. Early in the twentieth century, this kind of co-ordination became significant in the growth of the American Solvay Process Co., Union Carbide, and other new large chemical producers.

As they were building these organizations at home, the large American firms often moved overseas. They first set up branch offices and ware-houses on foreign shores. Then, as demand grew and as local tariffs appeared or as shipping costs increased and scheduling of flows across oceans became complex, the enterprise built plants abroad which it soon began to supply from near-by sources. By 1914 at least 41 American companies, clustered in machinery and in food industries, had built two or more operating facilities abroad.[6] The largest number of these were in Canada; but by 1914 23 had factories in Britain and 21 in Germany, with a small number scattered in other countries. That the largest number of factories outside of Canada was built in Britain, still a free-trade country, indicates that transportation costs and scheduling problems were as important considerations for direct investment abroad as was the desire to get within the tariff barriers. In this way, then, American entrepreneurs had created, within less than a generation, giant multinational enterprises whose names are all well known today.

All these integrated enterprises developed much the same type of organizational structure to administer their operating units. At some, the new structure came quickly in a planned manner; at others more slowly and in an *ad hoc* way. All had large central offices, housed in multi-storeyed buildings, where salaried middle managers supervised, through functionally defined departments, the work of the many lower-level operating managers. The Production or Operating Department adminis-tered the operations of a number of factories, works or plants. The Sales Department managed the branch offices in the United States and abroad. The Purchasing or Essential Materials Department watched over the buying or production of raw and semi-finished materials. The Financial Department had its accounting, auditing, and treasurer's offices. A smaller Traffic Department handled shipments to, from, and through the enter-prise. Often an Experimental or Research Department worked on improving products and processes. In addition, Legal, Personnel, and Real Estate Departments were formed. Finally, where the companies had factories or other direct investments abroad, they had begun to set up their international departments by World War I.

The top management consisted of the Vice-Presidents in charge of the major functional departments, the President, and the Chairman of the Board. Legally constituted as the Executive Committee of the Board, the senior executives monitored the performance of the functional depart-ments, defined policies for the enterprise as a whole (of these the policies to determine the co-ordination of flows of materials through the enterprise were of particular importance), and allocated the resources, both capital and personnel, needed to maintain and expand the activities of the firm. Because most of these enterprises had financed their expansion from retained earnings, the founders and their families normally continued to own the controlling shares of stock. So they continued to sit on the Board and often to take an active part in top management. No family, however, could provide the lower and middle level managers required to administer one of these business giants, whose managerial staff by World War I numbered often over 100 and in some cases even 300 or 400.

As I have suggested, the British story is different. In the United Kingdom large integrated enterprises first appeared about the same time and in some but not all of the same industries as in the United States, but they grew more slowly. They flourished in the consumer sectors of the chemical and food industries where low-priced, packaged products were sold in Britain's rapidly growing urban markets. They came, too, in the processing and distribution of perishable goods—meat, dairy products, and beer—but on a smaller scale than in the United States. They were fewer, however, in the machinery industries, where in general firms still produced relatively uncomplicated machines for the older industries—such as textiles, mining, metal-making, and food. Until the expansion of the automobile and the appliance industries in the 1920s, almost no British-owned firm mass-produced consumer durables. The leading producers of standardized machines in Great Britain remained the subsidiaries of such American companies as Singer Sewing Machine, International Harvester, Ford, United Shoe Machinery, General Electric, Westinghouse, and Western Electric.

In Britain nearly all the producers of low-priced, packaged, and brand products followed the same strategy of growth. These included the makers of chocolates (Cadbury, Rowntree, and Fry), biscuits and confectionery (Peek Frean, Huntley & Palmers, and Barratts), jams and sauces (Crosse & Blackwell, Lea & Perrins, and H.P. Sauce), condiments (J & J Colman and Cerebos), meat products (Bovril and Liebig's Extract), soft drinks (Schweppes), soap, starch, and toilet articles (Gossage, Reckitt, and Yardley), paints (Pinchin Johnson, Lewis Berger, and Goodlass, Wall), and pharmaceuticals (Beecham and Sangers). Nearly all were small family partnerships that were well established before the new transportation and communication facilities opened national and overseas markets. As more distant markets began to be reached, firms branded their products, started to advertise nationally, and, most important of all, sent out an army of salaried salesmen, or "travellers", to obtain orders from wholesalers and the larger retailers and to be responsible for the delivery of the orders on schedule. These family firms, however, rarely set up a network of branch offices, as did their American counterparts. The sales force continued to be supervised from the factory. Only in the 1920s did Cadbury, Crosse & Blackwell, and others begin to build a network of warehouses and depots and to own and operate their own lorries and other transportation facilities.

Most of these firms had branch offices staffed by salaried managers overseas before they had them at home. Nearly all began to sell overseas first in what were to become the white Commonwealth nations—Australia, New Zealand, Canada, and South Africa. Only a few looked to the Indian subcontinent. In the twentieth century more ventured into the United States and continental Europe. Occasionally, before World War I and more often in the 1920s, overseas sales grew to a size that warranted building factories abroad. The reason for building overseas plants appears to have been tariffs in the United States and on the Continent, and also in some Commonwealth nations, rather than the need to reduce shipping costs or to improve the scheduling of flows.

Growing demand at home and abroad brought a gradual enlargement of the firm's main factory and with it an expansion of its buying organization. Unless materials were needed in quantity and on relatively precise schedules, the firms continued to rely on existing middlemen to obtain raw and semi-finished materials from overseas. However, early in the twentieth century some makers of chocolate, soap, margarine, and meat products did consider it necessary to acquire plantations, agencies, and trading companies in distant lands in order to have assured sources of supplies.

The histories of these individual firms varied of course. Some moved overseas earlier than others; some entered the American and continental markets with more energy and enthusiasm than their competitors. In nearly all cases, however, the growth of the enterprise came gradually over a period of two or even three generations.

Such evolutionary growth permitted a family to continue to own and to manage the firm it had founded. The travellers and buyers continued to be supervised from small offices usually housed in or next to the factory. Before the coming of the aeroplane, the managers of overseas sales branches, purchasing offices, and plantations were too far away to make practical the close supervision and scheduling which American firms had developed for their branches within the continental United States. After all, San Francisco was only three days from Chicago, and New York one; while South Africa was three weeks from London, and Australia six. So British enterprise-builders were under less pressure than their American colleagues to hire middle and top managers. As late as the 1930s, the great majority of the leading firms making packaged, branded goods continued to be run by one or two families. The Cadburys, Frys, Rowntrees, Colmans, Reckitts, Ranks, Lyles, Barratts, Beechams, Sangers, Courtaulds, Albrights, and Wilsons, and the families who owned Crosse & Blackwell, Peek Frean, Huntley & Palmers, Gilbeys Gin, Cerebos, Liebig, Bovril, Carreras, Yardley, Pinchin Johnson, and Goodlass, Wall, and Borax Consolidated continued to manage their firms into the third and even fourth generations. Thus, in the 1930s the Chairman of Barratts, long owned by the Barratt and Sennett families, had quite properly the name of J. Barratt Sennett. When a line ran out, the succession usually went to a collateral branch. Until the 1930s, close to 80 per cent of the companies studied in the food and chemical industries had family members on the Board and in active positions of top and middle management.

Thus, the continuance of the family firm in Britain was encouraged by the existence of a well-established distribution network both at home and in the long-distance trades serving small but fast-growing overseas markets and sources of supply. The invisible hand of the market worked more effectively in the United Kingdom than in the United States. Nevertheless, these factors cannot alone account for its longevity. The career of William Lever, a driving entrepreneur, and the success of American machinery companies such as Singer, General Electric, Westinghouse, and United Shoe Machinery suggest that there was in Britain a potential for the more tightly controlled, integrated firm with its own sales branches, buying offices, and transportation facilities—that is for the visible hand of administrative coordination. By building such organizations, Lever in soap and the American firms in machinery quickly became the leading enterprises in their industries in Britain.[7] Surely, many of the family firms could have created comparable powerful enterprises, if they had wanted to invest in the facilities and personnel.

## II

Differences in the second route to size—that by merger and acquisition—were as significant as in the first route—that by direct investment in marketing and purchasing facilities. And the differences in the second route suggest a more fundamental cause for the continuation of the family firm in the United Kingdom. That was simply that the family wanted to retain and manage its birthright. In the United States mergers brought administrative centralization and industrial rationalization. In Britain they remained federations of autonomous family enterprises. Until the 1930s, British mergers rarely brought economies of scale or other advantages of administrative co-ordination and control.

In the United States a successful merger went through the following steps. First came legal consolidation, which gave a central office complete legal power over the activities of the constituent companies. Initially this took the form of creating a trust, and after the 1890s a holding company. Then came administrative centralization and industrial rationalization. Some of the manufacturing facilities of the constituent companies were enlarged, more were eliminated, and a few new ones built. Then the administration of these facilities was placed under control of a single production or operating department. Next the consolidated centralized enterprise normally embarked on a strategy of vertical integration by moving forward into marketing by setting up a branch office and distribution network, and backward by obtaining its own purchasing offices and sources of raw and semi-finished materials.

The first modern mergers came in the United States in the 1880s, when existing trade associations—loose federations of small, single-function firms—created during the economically depressed years of the 1870s, realized that they were not able to control price competition within an industry. The first of these associations to turn to legal consolidation and administrative centralization were those in the refining and distilling industries, where new continuous-process techniques of mass production were first introduced and where, therefore, pressure for rationalization first appeared. Thus the earliest national merger came, not surprisingly, in the oil industry. As soon as John D. Rockefeller and his associates formed the Standard Oil Trust in 1882, the American petroleum-refining industry was rationalized with the concentration of two-fifths of the world's production of refined oil in only three refineries. As a result, the unit cost of producing a gallon of kerosene was reduced from $1\frac{1}{2}$c to $\frac{1}{2}$c.[8] Next, Standard Oil built a national and indeed an international marketing network, and in the late 1880s it began to produce crude oil for the first time. In the 1880s the Cotton Seed Oil, Linseed Oil, and National Lead Trust (the last was a producer of white lead for paint) followed Standard Oil's example, with the Sugar and Whisky Trusts taking a little longer than the others to centralize and to integrate. In the 1890s mergers using the holding-company form became increasingly popular, and culminated during the years 1898 to 1903 in the nation's largest and still most significant merger movement. Among the best known examples of consolidated centralized mergers of this period in the three sets of industries studied were National Biscuit, Corn Products, and Standard Milling in food; DuPont and General Chemical in chemicals; and General Electric and International Harvester in machinery.

Again, the organizational response was quite similar. The pioneering firm, Rockefeller's Standard Oil Trust, devised a complex system of committees, and staff officers operating out of the massive headquarters at 26 Broadway in New York City. Nearly all the other successful mergers, however, moved to a functional organization similar to that used by the firms that had grown large through building their own marketing and purchasing networks from retained earnings. In addition to their primary departments of production, sales, purchasing or essential materials, and finance, each with its own staff and often with its own advisory committees, these consolidations formed departments for traffic, research and development, personnel, and legal matters. Because the organizers of the merged firm usually were, at least initially, involved in rationalizing what was often a large part of a major American industry, because they drew their managerial personnel from a number of companies, and because they had to institute industry-wide accounting, auditing, and other control systems, they created larger central or corporate offices than those firms which had attained their size by reinvesting retained earnings. For these reasons nearly all of the techniques of modern top management—those developed to co-ordinate, to monitor, and to allocate resources to the operating units—were devised in the corporate offices of these integrated consolidations. It was there that present-day procedures of budgeting, forecasting, and control had their beginnings.

Whatever the initial route to size—by merger or by reinvesting retained earnings—most large industrials continued to grow through acquisitions. Normally the personnel and facilities acquired were melded into the existing functional core organization of the acquiring firm. This was true even where, as in the case of International Harvester, the trade names and dealer organizations of the constituent companies were for a time retained. Only after the invention of the multi-divisional form with its autonomous operating divisions administered by a large, general corporate office[9] were acquired companies permitted to continue to operate as autonomous administrative units with their internal organizations relatively unchanged.

Therefore, mergers in the United States, although at first considered as a means of control competition, in most cases became instruments to improve industrial productivity through rationalization and centralization. In Britain, on the other hand, the goal of mergers remained primarily to restrain competition. The internal organizations of constituent companies were little changed; their autonomy was not challenged, so little rationalization occurred. In the late nineteenth century, mergers which normally used the legal form of a holding company were mostly large horizontal combinations including as many as 30 to 50 firms.[10] In these mergers price and output of the group were determined by the representatives of the constituent firms sitting on the Board of Directors or by a smaller management committee. Such mergers occurred largely in the older textile and iron and steel industries. In the food, chemical, and machinery industries the most common type of merger was that of two or three of the industry's leaders who joined to co-operate with each other in purchasing materials, especially materials coming from abroad; to divide overseas markets; and, to a lesser extent, to stabilize prices at home. Such were the motives for the mergers between Cadbury and Fry that formed British Chocolate & Cocoa in 1918; Peek Frean and Huntley & Palmers that formed Associated Biscuits in 1921, and those forming Crosse & Blackwell, Reckitt & Colman, and Tate & Lyle. In none of these mergers was the independence of the constituent companies impaired. The same was true for a number of brewery mergers such as Watney, Combe, Reid in London; Bass, Ratcliffe & Gretton in Burton-on-Trent, and Scottish Breweries in Edinburgh, and also true for the merger of Dewar and Buchanan that formed Scottish Whisky Brands.

The largest and certainly the best known of this type of merger was Imperial Tobacco. This company, formed as a direct response to an attack from James B. Duke's American Tobacco Company, was a combination of one large firm, W.D. & H.O. Wills and 12 smaller ones.[11] Its formation, however, brought little rationalization to the British tobacco industry. Imperial's subsidiaries did lose their legal identity in becoming "branches", but they remained administratively autonomous. They did co-operate in purchasing their tobacco—largely from the United States and Turkey—and in obtaining cigarette paper and other supplies. The "branches", however, continued to produce, sell, and advertise their own products and, indeed, to compete with one another. An Executive Committee of the Board, consisting of representatives of the families of the four largest members of the federation, set pricing policies, controlled advertising expenditures, and reviewed the capital expenditures of the constituent enterprises. The central office remained small; in fact it was housed in rooms attached to Wills's largest factory, a striking contrast to American Tobacco's multi-storey office building at 111 Fifth Avenue, New York. This organization, which lasted relatively unchanged until the 1960s, permitted generations of Wills, Players, Butlers, and Mitchells to compete decorously with one another in the British market.

If mergers did not bring administrative centralization, nor did more gradual growth by acquisition. The companies acquired were not incorporated into the central organization of the acquiring company, as was the case in the United States, but were left to operate quite autonomously. This was true of Ranks Ltd. the largest flour millers in Britain, which acquired an impressive number of mills in the second and third decades of the century. As the company's official history explained: "As each mill consolidated its position and strengthened its hold on a particular trade so it tended to be self-contained, each branch (of the company) naturally striving to do the best for itself."[12] Pinchin Johnson in paints expanded in much the same way in the 1920s, as did the Distillers Co. Ltd. and Lever Brothers somewhat earlier.

Lever Brothers provides a useful example of the process of growth through acquisition in Great Britain. Between 1910 and 1921 William Lever carried out the consolidation of the soap industry in a piecemeal fashion by acquiring nearly all of his competitors by means of exchange of stock.[13] Lever did not attempt, however, to administer these companies through a single centralized administrative hierarchy. All he did was to assign one of the directors of his enterprise to supervise a number of the new "associated companies", as they came to be called.[14]

As a result, acquisition brought little rationalization. The Lever purchasing organization did begin to buy for the associated companies at home and abroad, but there was no systematizing of production or distribution. During the 1920s the Lever combine included 49 different soap-making sub-companies with 48 different sales organizations.[15] This condition remained, even though one executive pointed out that administrative centralization could bring a saving of £2 per ton in distribution costs alone. Lever and his salaried directors favoured, in Lever's words, "healthy" but not "frenzied" competition between the associated companies.[16] Committees were formed to set pricing policies and to control advertising expenditures. Nevertheless, relatively unrestricted competition continued between Lever Brothers and the other large subsidiaries.

Rationalization and centralization did not become effective until the early 1930s after the formation of Unilever, a combination of Lever and Dutch margarine-makers in 1929.[17] The failure to centralize and rationalize may account for the drop in Lever's share of the British soap market from 67 to 60 per cent between 1920 and 1929 (and to 51.5 per cent in 1935), and for the entry into the British market in strength of the American giants, Procter & Gamble and Palmolive-Peet.[18] At Lever, as in nearly all other acquisitions and mergers in Britain until the 1930s, the result was federation rather than centralization.

In Britain, the historical record makes clear that mergers were specifically arranged to maintain family control. In most cases the constituent firms remained legally and administratively autonomous entities managed by descendants of the founder's family. Sons took over from fathers. The consolidated company permitted its members to co-operate in the purchasing of raw materials and in overseas marketing, and it stabilized the domestic market by preventing uncomfortable price competition and high advertising costs. Representatives of the family on the Board worked out policies by negotiation.

Only severe financial and competitive pressures caused federations of British firms to move towards a centralized management structure before the 1930s. The mergers and acquisitions that resulted in United Alkali in the 1890s and Spiller's and Union Cold Storage in the 1920s provide the relatively rare examples in the industries studied. United Alkali was a merger of 40 producers of alkali by the Le Blanc process which had become obsolete with the development of the new far more efficient Solvay process.[19] In attempting to meet the overwhelming competition of the new technology, United Alkali centralized control, rationalized its production, set up a research laboratory, and diversified into new products. However, because it remained saddled with an obsolete process, it never was able to acquire sufficient funds or personnel to exploit its improved managerial controls or the findings of its research laboratory. Spillers, the second largest processor of wheat, began to centralize and rationalize its domestic production and its overseas marketing in 1927 after substantial losses and passing of dividends had frightened the families whose firms dominated the federation into calling on the well-known accounting firm of Price, Waterhouse to reorganize their enterprise.[20] The resulting changes in middle management were not, however, accompanied by major ones at the top, where the same families continued to dominate. Finally, in the meat-packing trade, where retailers rather than manufacturers played a major role in developing the early integrated enterprises, and where American competition, particularly in Argentine imports, drove down sharply the share of the British market held by British firms, merger was followed by centralization and rationalization.[21] Even so, the Vestey family, the architects of the final consolidation, The Union Cold Storage Company, has

continued to dominate the top management of Britain's one large integrated meat-packing enterprise until today.

This review of the processes of merger and acquisition in Britain makes
clear the importance of the merger that formed Nobel Industries, for it was
the first to be followed quickly by rationalization and administrative
centralization.[22] The merger brought together in 1918 four makers of
dynamite and other explosives—two family firms (Kynoch and Bickford
Smith), a federation of such firms (Curtis's & Harvey), and Nobel
Explosives, Britain's largest explosive company which had acquired in the
fashion of Lever Brothers a number of subsidiaries and which, as was so
rare in Britain, had been long run by salaried managers instead of owners.
The members of its Organization Committee first looked at the experience
of comparable firms in Britain—the Calico Printers, Bradford Dyers, J. &
P. Coates, Metropolitan Carriage, United Steel, and others. They found
that, although the majority of these firms had centralized their purchasing
and were moving towards centralizing other activities, each still remained,
in the committee's words, "an aggregation of a number of companies".[23]
The organizers turned instead to the United States. There, as the
committee's report pointed out, "the policy of large American amalgamations, after passing through a phase of some sort of loose agreement: a
pool, a trust, a holding company, has crystallized into the complete merger
in which the separate management and personnel of the individual units
disappear, even if the units themselves retain their nominal existence, a
single executive and operating staff is created in which the entire control is
centralized." The committee's specific model was an old Nobel ally, the E.
I. DuPont de Nemours & Company. The organizing committee travelled to
the DuPont headquarters in Delaware, studied the company's lengthy
reports on organization, discussed structure and accounting with senior
DuPont executives, and came home impressed—at least the salaried
managers of the old Nobel Explosives Company returned impressed.
Arthur Chamberlain, the chairman of Kynoch, the second largest firm
coming into the merger and a member of one of Britain's best known
industrial families, had doubts. He urged his colleagues to "go slowly in
altering the inherited and accepted notions of British Industrial Management and instead of jumping to complete control at once, only adopt it if
and when distinctive trades' control has shown a weakness."[24] However,
the managers had their way. The centralized structure was adopted. In the
resulting rationalization of production and distribution the names of several
old and respected family firms disappeared. Within a short time Arthur
Chamberlain retired. The new organization at Nobel Industries provided
the model for that of Imperial Chemical Industries, the much larger merger
which it helped to instigate in 1926. It was a model, too, for a number of
other British mergers during the depressed economic years of the early
1930s, when continuing financial and competitive pressures forced

federations to centralize and rationalize. It was only in the 1930s, therefore, that mergers in Britain began to create extensive managerial hierarchies, and then only in a relatively few, though important, cases.

## III

This comparative analysis of the growth of the large industrial firm in the two countries emphasizes how much more quickly managerial enterprise appeared in the United States than it did in the United Kingdom. Normally, it took a British firm three generations to reach the size and managerial strength that a comparable American enterprise achieved in one. Certainly the continuance of the family firm helps to account for differences in the processes of growth. But did the continuance of the family firm and the slower appearance of the managerial enterprise make any real difference? Did the continuance and the delay have an appreciable effect on the performance of the large industrial firm in Britain and of the British economy as a whole?

I think that it did. In the first place, the failure to build up managerial hierarchies may have deprived British industrialists of some of the cost advantages and therefore market power of large-scale enterprise. Although sophisticated in merchandising consumer goods, British manufacturers moved slowly into their mass production, for that required new methods of organizing distribution as well as production. Their delay in adopting the new methods made it possible for American firms to obtain a significant share not only of international markets but also of the British market itself in canned goods, frozen meat, proprietary articles such as toothpaste and pills, as well as in such durables as sewing machines, typewriters, cash registers, and other office machinery. The failure of the local heavy-machinery firms to develop marketing organizations within Britain also made it easier for the Americans to take over the British market for volume-produced standardized producers' goods, such as harvesters, electrical equipment, elevators, shoe machinery, and printing presses.

Second, delays in building managerial hierarchies meant that the British were slow in adopting modern management methods. The American managers in the first years of the twentieth century and even earlier, as they were perfecting the basic techniques of mass production and mass distribution, were also devising new methods of inventory and quality control. In addition they worked out cost-accounting procedures based on standard volume and capacity that permitted middle managers to monitor systematically and continuously the work of the operating units under their command. They also perfected scheduling procedures necessary to maintain a high and steady flow of material through an enterprise's plants and departments. Such accounting and control methods, so important in improving a firm's competitive ability by reducing unit costs, only began to be adopted in Britain extensively in the 1930s. In many cases such methods were borrowed directly from the United States.[25]

More serious was the longer delay in adopting top-management procedures—procedures so essential for the continuing efficient use of an enterprise's resources. In the United States such procedures had been initially devised in the large corporate office of the consolidated mergers— offices that were so rare in Britain. There, senior executives drew up organizational plans that defined the functions of managerial positions, drew the lines of authority, responsibility and communication, and differentiated between a line and staff activities. They developed accounting and budgetary procedures to permit top management to monitor systematically the performance of their middle managers and to allocate resources for future activities of the enterprise. These men also devised short-term forecasting of financial and market conditions necessary for co-ordinating flows of goods through the enterprise, and long-term forecasting necessary in the evaluation of capital appropriations for facilities that would not come into production for two or three years. To aid in this monitoring and planning, they also invented sophisticated formulas for determining the rate of return on total investment. I have run across little evidence of the systematic use of such basic top-level organizational and control procedures even in the largest British multinational firms until after World War II. Such methods were imported into Britain, largely by American consultants, only in the 1950s and 1960s.

Finally, the differing processes of the growth of the firm affected the recruitment and training of managers in both countries. In the United States during the 1880s and 1890s the need for trained production and marketing specialists, particularly in the technologically advanced machinery, electrical, and chemical firms, quickly brought state and private universities and the new technical schools, like the Massachusetts Institute of Technology, into offering a variety of courses in mechanical, electrical and chemical engineering. A decade later the continuing demand for functional specialists in the consumer as well as in the producer goods industries led the nation's most prestigious universities—Harvard, California, Chicago, Dartmouth, and Pennsylvania, to name a few—to create new courses and even schools of business where professional training was given in finance, production, marketing, and even policy-making. In Britain, however, there was little such training. Top managers came from the owners. The few middle managers could be recruited from the company's ranks, from its travellers, buyers, or production supervisors. So there was little demand for engineering courses—particularly for those in chemical or electrical engineering—and even less for business schools.

This lack of engineering and business training can hardly be blamed on the supposed bias of British universities and British undergraduates against trade. When large firms, such as I.C.I. and Unilever, first began to recruit college graduates, they had little difficulty in getting the men they wanted from Oxford, Cambridge, and other universities.[26] Until there was a significant demand for managers, however, the British could hardly be expected to provide facilities to train them. After World War II, when managerial hierarchies became larger and more numerous in Britain, the educational system responded by expanding engineering and inaugurating business schools.

This lack of contact between the industrial enterprise and the university had a particularly debilitating effect on technologically advanced industries. In the United States, and also in Germany, managers on both the production and distribution sides of these industries kept their ties with the universities and institutions in which they had been trained.[27] They looked to their former professors not only to supply them with a steady flow of new recruits but also for a flow of technological advice about process and product. Their contacts were often with the scientists as well as with the engineers in the educational departments involved. This close relationship between theoretical and applied science permitted the Americans and the Germans to develop a commanding lead in many of the most important new technological processes and products of what has come to be called the Second Industrial Revolution.

The lack of engineers and managers and of sophisticated technological skills and management techniques may have made little difference in the production and distribution of branded, packaged consumer goods, except possibly perishable products. It did, however, make a vital difference in the chemical, machinery, and electrical equipment industries. These were precisely the industries which became organized through managerial enterprise; for in these industries trained managers and engineers and carefully defined organizational and control systems have been essential to reducing the cost of production, to providing delivery to specification and on schedule, and to assuring continuing specialized marketing services. And it was in just these industries that the Americans and the Germans successfully invaded the markets of the world and of Britain itself.

The British failure to participate fully in the growth of the new industries and to meet the competition from the United States and the Continent has often been explained as entrepreneurial failure. A better term may be managerial failure: that is, the continuing existence of the family firm helped to deprive Britain of a class of trained managers and sets of technological and managerial skills that became increasingly essential, not only to technically advanced industries but also to the operation of modern urban, industrial economies. Possibly, Britain is still paying for that deprivation.

# Notes

1. The Tawney Memorial Lecture for 1979.
2. I wish to acknowledge with gratitude the valuable assistance received from Margaret Ackrill, who compiled the three lists of the 200 largest firms in Britain; from Peter Grant, who categorized these lists into S.I.C. categories and provided data on ownership, sales branches, and factories; and from other scholars, who compiled comparable lists for Germany and France. I am also indebted to the Alfred P. Sloan Foundation, the German Marshall Fund, and the Research Division of the Harvard Business School for the financial support they provided for this research.
3. For the United States, see my *Visible Hand: The Managerial Revolution in American Business* (Cambridge, Mass. 1977), pp. 370, 503–12. The findings for Britain, Germany, and France are presented in Alfred D. Chandler, Jr. 'The Place of the Modern Industrial Enterprise in Three Economies', a paper presented at International Symposium in Economic History held at the University of East Anglia, 19–22 Sept. 1979.
4. Based on an analysis of *Fortune*'s large 800 industrials in the United States and abroad in 1973.
5. The information on the growth of the large American firm comes from Chandler, op. cit. particularly chs. 7–11. That on Britain comes from a wide variety of business histories and biographies, company-sponsored commemorative volumes, memoirs, annual and other corporate reports, and financial news in specialized and daily newspapers. As Prof. Daems and I have not yet completed the review of the machinery industries, the examples used in this article will be taken primarily from the food and chemical industries.
6. Mira Wilkins, *Emergence of Multinational Enterprise* (Cambridge, Mass. 1970), pp. 212–16, and Chandler, op.cit. p. 368.
7. Charles Wilson, *History of Unilever*, 2 vols. (1954), 1, chs. 3–4, esp. pp. 42–3, 50–2. On p. 52 Wilson refers to the Newcastle, Leeds, and Port Sunlight Branches. For Singer see Robert B. Davies, 'Peacefully Working to Conquer the World: The Singer Manufacturing Company in Foreign Markets, 1858–89', *Business History Review*, XLIII (1960), 299–346. United Shoe Machinery, Westinghouse, and General Electric, including its subsidiary British Thomson Houston, are mentioned in F. A. McKenzie, *The American Invaders* (1902), pp. 49–51, 81–5, 157–64.
8. Ralph W. Hidy and Muriel E. Hidy, *Pioneering in Big Business* (New York, 1955), pp. 108–21.
9. This structure was invented in the early 1920s primarily to administer firms that carried out a new strategy of diversifying into different product lines.
10. Peter Mathias, 'Conflicts of Function in the Rise of Big Business: The British Experience', in Harold F. Williamson, ed. *Evolution of International Management Structures* (Newark, Del. 1975), pp. 40–3.
11. B. W. E. Alford, *W.D. & H.O. Wills and the Development of the U.K. Tobacco Industry* (1973), pp. 309–14, 330–3.
12. Hurford James, *The Master Millers: The Story of the House of Rank* (1956), pp. 64–8.
13. Wilson, op. cit. 1, chs. 8–9, 18.
14. In 1917, in answer to a request from Lever, each of his directors defined their duties. Their replies are summarized in a file in the Unilever archives entitled 'Management and Labour'. The letters are in the LC 6391 file.
15. Wilson, op. cit. 11, 302, 345,

16. W. Lever to F. A. Cooper, 14 Oct and 11, 24 Nov. on the subject of competition within the firm in file LC 1482.

17. Wilson, op. cit. I, 299–304; II, 354–7.

18. H. R. Edwards, *Competition and Monopoly in the British Soap Industry* (Oxford, 1962), pp. 183–6.

19. I am greatly indebted to Yuichi Kudo for information on United Alkali.

20. *The Times*, 25 Jan., 5 Feb., 9 May 1927.

21. The meat-packing story can be pieced together from James T. Critchell and James Raymond, *A History of the Frozen Meat Trade* (1912), [U.S.] Federal Trade Commission, *Food Investigation: Meat Packing Industry*, summary and pt. 1 (Washington, 1919), *The Times*, 17 June 1913, 30 March 1917, and stock-exchange year books.

22. W. J. Reader, *Imperial Chemical Industries, A History, Vol. I The Forerunners, 1870–1926* (1970), pp. 254–6, ch. 17.

23. This and the following quotation are from the 'Report of the Committee on Organization to the Chairman and Directors of Explosives Trades, Limited', 21 April 1919, in the I.C.I. archives. The report further stated that "the keynote of the American system appears to be: (1) Complete centralization of control. (2) Reliance on individuals and not upon committees. (3) Full authority and responsibility for each individual within his own sphere. (4) The employment of younger men in positions of importance."

24. Quoted in Reader, op. cit. 1, 393.

25. A good example of such borrowing is that done by Boots. See Stanley Chapman, *Jesse Boots of Boots the Chemist* (1974), pp. 144–54.

26. Both Wilson and Reader make this point.

27. As indicated in David Noble, *America By Design* (New York, 1977), chs. 7–9.

# 4

# German Multinational Enterprise before 1914: Some Case Studies*

## Peter Hertner

*Source: P. Hertner and G. Jones, eds., *Multinationals: Theory and History* (Aldershot, Gower, 1986), pp. 113–134.

After 20 years of growing interest and research in the field of multinational enterprise (MNE), the business historian does not suffer from a shortage of definitions of what constitutes the structure and the behaviour of the firms concerned. If he had to evaluate, in a very pragmatic way, the theories that best fit his sources on the historical development of direct investment, he would probably start with what Dunning calls the 'monopolistic competitive theories' presented by Hymer, Kindleberger and Caves.[1] If he then considered more recent contributions, he would quickly become aware that they try to combine the results of international trade theory, location theory, theories of the firm, and theories of imperfect competition.[2]

From the historian's point of view there can be no doubt that the internalisation paradigm, first presented by R.H. Coase[3] and further developed by O.E. Williamson in the framework of a 'new institutional economics' approach,[4] gives important insight particularly for empirical research. It is more than evident that industry has been organised in quite different ways as one follows the line of historical evolution from medieval craft to modern trusts, cartels, and giant corporations. Nevertheless, the historian's conceptual framework can only profit from those seemingly obvious statements which are at the origin of the internalisation process, namely that economic 'co-ordination can be effected in three ways: by *direction*, by *co-operation*, or through *market transactions*'.[5] On the other hand, the historian would find it somewhat difficult to accept the flat statement by A.M. Rugman that 'internalization is the modern theory of the multinational enterprise'.[6] He would rather take sides with M. Casson who accepts internalisation 'as a key element in the theory of the multinational enterprise' but stresses at the same time that

> Internalization is in fact a general theory of why firms exist, and without additional assumptions it is almost tautological. To make the theory

operational, it is necessary to specify assumptions about transactions costs for particular products and for trade between particular locations.[7]

It has been accepted that the multinational type of internalisation takes place when (a) there is a strong incentive to control raw material resources via backward integration; (b) research-and-development-intensive industries want to exploit their knowledge advantage; and (c) tariffs, international tax differentials and foreign exchange controls favour transfer pricing. Casson, however, pleads for an extension to cases when buyer uncertainty can be reduced by internalisation, the MNE thus guaranteeing quality control by international marketing through its established brand names.[8] Without any doubt this attempt to extend the practical validity of the internalisation concept to the specific needs of consumer industries can, as will be shown later, be most useful to historical research.

Empirical investigations into the long-term development of MNEs will, however, inevitably have to start with the causes that motivate individual firms to go abroad, switching eventually from exporting to licensing or to direct investment. Particularly for these initial phases one can agree with Dunning that 'the internalisation paradigm may be more helpful in explaining degrees of multinationality than discrete acts of foreign investment.'[9] The business historian might therefore choose Dunning's eclectic approach which, taking into account R. Vernon's stage concept of the 'product cycle', stresses the essential relationship between trade and international production and sees the engagement in foreign production by a firm as dependent on its 'comparative ownership advantages *vis-à-vis* host country firms and the comparative location endowments of home and foreign countries'. If these ownership advantages are obtained and if the advantages of location speak in favour of direct investment then there must be, as a third condition, 'the possibility of internalising the firm's activities and thus substituting in part functions of the market.'[10]

There remains the problem, already mentioned in the introduction to this volume, of how a MNE should be defined. Should it be the 'broad definition' adopted by Dunning that MNEs are 'firms that engage in foreign direct investment',[11] or should the MNE be seen, following R.E. Caves, as 'an enterprise that controls and manages production establishments—plants—located in at least two countries'?[12] Should we, in the end, agree with L.G. Franko who considers that 'the word "multinational" ... only denotes the existence of manufacturing operations, owned to significant extent by the parent firm, in numerous countries'?[13] In any case, it will be quite a difficult task to find a definition based on purely structural aspects (equity quotas, number of foreign subsidiaries) which at the same time satisfies the needs of a majority of economists and business historians.[14] The growing importance assumed by the internalisation concept in recent studies seems, however, to facilitate the problems of historical analysis of the MNE which is now being considered as 'any firm which owns outputs of goods *or services* originating in more than one country'.[15] Since this definition presupposes only a minimal threshold level of multi-nationality and includes firms which merely operate foreign sales sub-sidiaries,[16] it seems to be ideally suited to historical research concentrating on the origins and early phase of development of the MNE and, in fact, it has already been accepted by business historians.[17].

We still lack a comprehensive study of German MNE before World War I,[18] and in this chapter only a few cases of German multinational invest-ment can be presented. Nevertheless, an attempt will be made to respond to some of the questions put forward in the introduction to this volume, notably: the transfer of technology via direct investment as an example of a typical 'ownership advantage'; the effects of visible and invisible trade barriers—'location-specific advantages'—on multinational investment; the influence of the size of the firm on multinational investment; some effects of the MNE on the economy of the host countries.

Finally, to a greater degree than has been done so far in empirical studies which cover only the contemporary period, it will be shown how advantages–firm-specific or country-specific—can change over time,[19] thus demonstrating that the process of internalisation can either continue its course, or in certain circumstances, owing to internal or external causes, revert. We should in any case agree with Thomas Horst who wrote over a decade ago '... if we are ever to unravel the complexity of the foreign investment process, a systematic study of the dynamic behaviour of firms must be undertaken'.[20]

## Multinational Activity in the Consumer Goods Sector: Merck and Kathreiner's

The pharmaceutical firm of E. Merck grew out of an apothecary shop founded in 1654 in Darmstadt, then a small residential town south of Frankfurt. It started to produce pharmaceuticals on a large scale in the 1820s. In 1900 it employed 800 workers, 50 chemists, pharmacists, engineers and doctors and an administrative staff of 150. By 1913, employment had risen to 1629 workers, while the scientific and administra-tive staff numbered 440. At that time, the firm specialised 'in alkaloids and organo-therapeutical compounds'.[21] Measured in employment figures, Merck was the largest of the 'purely' pharmaceutical companies existing in Germany before 1914, followed by Schering of Berlin which in 1913 employed 935 workers and an administrative staff of about 300. Some of these firms were incorporated by that time, but Merck remained a partner-ship owned by the same family since 1668.[22] In addition to these relatively small firms many of the large chemical companies, among them especially

Bayer and Hoechst, dedicated part of their activities to the manufacture of pharmaceuticals. This renders the delimitation of the market particularly complicated since it meant a high degree of potential competition due to the technical capacity and the financial power of these very large chemical firms. Bayer's total turnover in 1913, for instance, was about six times as high as Merck's, and Hoechst employed in 1913 more than five times as many workers and staff—10360 to be exact—as Merck.[23]

The Darmstadt firm was an extremely active exporter. In 1900–1 only 23 per cent of its sales went to Germany, 49 per cent to other European countries and 28 per cent to the rest of the world. Germany's share in Merck's sales gradually rose, and by 1912 had reached 33 per cent, while Europe took 43 per cent and the rest of the world 24 per cent.[24] The most important foreign markets in 1900–1 were Russia (17.6 per cent of total sales), followed by Latin America (11.4 per cent) and New York which evidently served the US market (11 per cent). Then came Britain (5.5 per cent), Austria-Hungary (5.3 per cent), Spain and Portugal (5.1 per cent), and Italy (4 per cent). These proportions did not change dramatically until 1912. The growth in importance of the German market was accompanied by a shrinking quota of exports to Russia (12 per cent in 1912) and to the United States and Canada (7.5 per cent in 1912).

This latter trend was probably caused by an internal factor. George Merck, a member of the Darmstadt family, had emigrated to the US, where in 1887 he founded a sales affiliate in New York. A contract concluded in 1890 between George Merck and the Merck firm of Darmstadt shows that the former received $200000 which constituted his entire participation in a partnership he was establishing together with a certain Theodor Weicker of New York, probably another German emigrant. In 1894 the Darmstadt firm gave another $50000 and, in return, George Merck had to deliver his entire profit share to the parent company.[25] In 1899 the firm of Merck & Co was founded, and started production of pharmaceuticals in Rahway, NY. When in 1917 it was taken into custody under the Trading with the Enemy Act, its capital amounted to $1 million. During the last years before the War it had built up an integrated production which no longer depended exclusively on the imports of German intermediates.[26] The relatively high American import duties on pharmaceuticals, and the fast growth as well as the dimension of the American market must have been the principal reasons for this direct investment in manufacturing.[27] A further motive might have been supplied by the particular structure of American demand where the ordinary drugstores selling pharmaceuticals were not supervised by scientifically trained pharmacists which meant that preference was given to ready-made and packed drugs.[28] The diminishing exports of Merck to the United States were thus probably a consequence of direct investment by the same firm.

If we follow Merck through particular foreign markets, Italy and France might serve as good examples of attempts to increase gradually the degree of internalisation. The Italian market was never a principal one for Merck, but it grew slowly from 1899–1900, when its share in total sales amounted to 3 per cent, until 1912, when it reached 4.3 per cent. Merck had established a number of small sale agencies all over the peninsula (in Genoa, Florence, Rome, Livorno, Naples, Palermo and Catania) whilst Milan was the main bridgehead for the conquest of the Italian market. Around 1900—the exact date could not be determined—the Milan agency was enlarged by the addition of a depot, and from then on the Italian customers were increasingly being served from there. Whereas in 1900–1, 87 per cent of Merck's exports to Italy were delivered directly by the Darmstadt factory, in 1913 this proportion had diminished to a mere 34 per cent.[29] Clients increasingly preferred being served from the Milan depot because it released them from the nuisance of getting their orders through the complicated formalities of the Italian customs service.[30] Discussions took place on bottling and packing in the Milan depot the products for which there was greatest demand, thereby economising on freight and customs duties. This was finally realised in 1910, and Milan served as example for a corresponding initiative in London in the following year. The entire size of the Milan affiliate remained rather limited. The deposit and its packing and bottling department employed only eight persons; all machines came from Germany; the commercial staff of the agency consisted of seven 'gentlemen', three of them Germans who occupied the leading positions.[31]

In France, where the same problems of passing goods through customs existed, a depot had already been set up in Paris in 1902.[32] A limited joint venture with a Paris firm (Bousquet) was started. Merck authorised its French partner to use its brand names for certain so-called 'specialities' which were then bottled and packed in France, a measure certainly provoked by the French prohibition against the import of pharmaceuticals in tablet or capsule form.[33] Moreover, the French patent law of 1844 did not allow the patenting of any type of medicine. This certainly did not favour the growth of a vigorous national industry and, as a result, according to contemporary sources, shortly before the outbreak of World War I 90 per cent of the fine chemicals needed for French pharmaceutical production came from Germany or passed through French affiliates of German industry.[34]

The problem of establishing a direct manufacturing investment in France was pondered over and over again by Merck, especially as the joint venture with Bousquet did not prosper as planned. Furthermore, the existing tariff was, if one is to believe the Merck officials, continuously changed whenever a new French 'infant' pharmaceutical competitor entered the scene.[35] Finally, in 1910, a small chemical factory at Montereau near Paris was bought and, after considerable investment exceeding all previous calculations, production of some pharmaceutical chemicals, such as glycerophosphate and theobromine, started two years later. The initial difficulties were immense, and in the spring of 1913 Merck almost decided to give up the Montereau plant. Up to that point 574 000 marks had been invested and over the same period a total loss of 128 000 marks had accumulated, including depreciation. Nevertheless, prestige considerations encouraged Merck to keep the Montereau factory open, although the outbreak of World War I prevented its capacity to survive being clearly demonstrated. When the works were seized by the French authorities in 1914, their value was calculated at 671 000 marks (839 000 francs).[36]

The already mentioned structure of Merck's exports reflects fairly well the overall export figure of the German pharmaceutical industry, which in 1913 held a dominant 30.3 per cent share of world exports, followed by Britain (21.3 per cent), the USA (13 per cent) and France (11.9 per cent). 21.4 per cent of these German exports went to Russia, 13.7 per cent to Austria-Hungary, 11.3 per cent to Britain, 10.7 per cent to the USA, 4.8 per cent to Italy, and 3.4 per cent to France.[37] Russia, the principal export market, was a notoriously high-tariff country, and Merck considered direct investment there as almost inevitable in the long run. However, the German firm preferred to establish only a bottling and packing department at its Moscow agency in 1906,[38] and when war broke out, it had not yet started manufacturing. Schering of Berlin, one of its major competitors, did, on the other hand, take this step and established in 1905 a pharmaceutical factory in Moscow which imported the chemical raw materials and intermediates from Germany. In addition, a charcoal plant using the immense resources of Russian timber was built at Wydriza in the Mogilev province.[39]

Another typical example of a producer of a consumer good is the case of Kathreiner's Malzkaffee-Fabriken, founded in 1892 in order to produce malt coffee, a substitute made from barley with odorous substances added to give it at least a certain coffee flavour.[40] It was a typical low-income product but, with the help of intensive publicity, the firm tried to persuade the public that its malt coffee, being free of caffeine, was also an extremely 'healthy' product and not only a second-best solution. Special emphasis was laid on the diffusion of the brand name and, particularly in the US, marketing efforts were directed at German immigrants.[41]

Up to 1914, the company had built seven factories in Germany. Sales increased from 17 718 quintals in 1891–2 to 57 812 quintals in 1901–2 and to 496 582 in 1913–14, doubtless pushed up after 1910 by the rapid rise in the price of coffee. In 1914 the firm was established in nine different foreign countries. It had given licences to a French, a Swiss, and a US firm, whereas it had undertaken direct investment in manufacturing companies in Austria-Hungary, Sweden, Russia, and, in 1912, in Spain after a sevenfold increase there in customs duties on malt coffee. The tariff situation in Argentina, where sales developed in a very satisfactory way, suggested a similar move but this was then prevented by the outbreak of the First World War. The Belgian and Dutch markets were supplied by a Rotterdam sales affiliate, and in Italy a sales depot was established in 1893 in Milan. One year later, a manufacturing company was created together with Italian partners in Genoa but it had to be closed down very soon afterwards because of internal differences with the Italian co-entrepreneurs and because of a newly established tax on production. There was probably also a misapprehension as to the taste of the Italian consumer who seemingly preferred if not 'real' coffee, at least the substitutes made from chicory with their stronger flavour. Kathreiner's Italian sales showed, in any case, a very slow development between 1900 and 1914.

Both cases of consumer goods producers examined here illustrate in detail the process and different modes of internalisation. Moreover, the Italian experience of Kathreiner's suggests that it was not a one-way process. In certain circumstances plans had to be rapidly revised, which meant that the dynamics were not limited to expansion only. Finally, the example of Merck shows that it was not necessarily the large oligopolistic firm which went for direct investment.[42] Particularly in the early phases of development of a specific market, ownership advantages were to be found also with smaller companies and could, if the market subsequently became more differentiated, as was certainly the case with the pharmaceutical industry, eventually be maintained.

**Multinationalisation and the Transfer of Technology: Bosch and Mannesmann**

In the middle of 1914, the Stuttgart firm of Robert Bosch employed 4726 workers and staff. Its production consisted almost entirely of magneto ignitions for automobiles and, to a much lesser degree, for aeroplanes. Shortly before the war a diversification into other electrical equipment for the car industry, such as starters and headlights, was undertaken. In the first half of 1914 Bosch had agencies and factories in 25 countries and 88 per cent of its production was exported.[43] The firm had grown out of a small mechanical and electrotechnical workshop founded by Robert Bosch in Stuttgart in 1886. Its growth gained in momentum when Bosch started to produce magneto ignitions for automobiles in 1898. In 1901 his firm employed a work-force of 45, but thereafter it expanded very rapidly in parallel with the rapid growth of the car industry, to 506 employees in 1906 and to more than 4000 in 1914.[44] Bosch, a self-made man who never gave up control of his company during his lifetime, founded in 1899 the 'Automatic Magneto Electric Ignition Company Ltd', which was made responsible for sales in France and Belgium and later changed its name to

Compagnie des Magnétos Simms-Bosch. His British partner Frederic R. Simms represented the Stuttgart firm in Britain[45] but sold his share in the French affiliate to Bosch in 1906.[46] The fact that in 1908 the French firm changed its name to Société des Magnétos Bosch reflected the new ownership situation. In 1907 it started to produce magneto ignitions for trucks since subsidies given by the French state to producers of these vehicles depended on the condition that all parts had to be French made.[47] The French automobile industry, the most important in pre-1914 Europe, was an extremely important customer, and it seems that Bosch had 'un quasi monopole sur le marché français' with annual sales that amounted to 10 million francs just before the outbreak of the war.[48] In Britain Bosch separated from Simms in 1907 and founded a new affiliate in London called The Bosch Magneto Company Ltd.[49] When it was required that racing cars and all their components had to be made in Britain if they wanted to participate in certain events, production, which seems, however, to have been largely assembly, was started in London. During the first half of 1914 Bosch satisfied approximately 85 to 95 per cent of British demand for magnetos and spark plugs.[50]

When the collaboration with Simms, who was also a general agent for the US came to an end in 1906, Bosch immediately founded an American affiliate in New York.[51] Soon agencies in Chicago (1908), San Francisco (1909), and Detroit (1910) followed.[52] The US market was of the greatest importance but exports suffered from the cost of freight and especially from a tariff which in the case of magnetos amounted to not less than 45 per cent of their value.[53] There were certainly enough ownership advantages due to the firm's technology to induce Bosch to start direct investment in manufacturing. Consequently, in 1910 construction of a magneto factory was undertaken in Springfield, Massachussets.

Production started in 1912. Two years later, the plant employed 2000 workers and staff and was considered a 'model factory' by American observers.[54] The US Alien Property Custodian who seized the American Bosch properties in 1918 gave an impressive report on the company's achievements.[55]

> The Bosch Magneto Co. was a tremendously powerful organization. Its combined capital and surplus exceeded $6,500,000. It owned and operated a modern factory at Springfield, Mass., with branches at Detroit, Chicago, and San Francisco. Its main office and sales department was in New York City, but it had agencies and supply depots in over one hundred American cities. Its product had obtained first place in the minds of the American purchasing public and was indeed regarded as the standard with which all other similar products were compared.

In 1912 Bosch acquired 45 per cent of the equity capital of the Eisemann Magneto Company, an American affiliate of its principal German competitor. In the same year, there followed the purchase of the Boonton Rubber Manufacturing Company of Boonton, NY, 'the largest producer of molded insulation, a product which was essential to the magneto industry. Again, in May 1914, it acquired outright, at a price of $750,000 in cash, the plant, business and goodwill of ... the Rushmore Dynamo Works at Plainfield, N.J. ... This factory was shortly thereafter shut down and dismantled.'[56] This latter fact speaks for itself and indicates clearly an oligopolistic market structure; as a matter of fact, according to the Alien Property Custodian, Bosch and Eisemann together produced 'at least half' of all the magnetos sold in the USA before war broke out in Europe.[57]

Turning now to Mannesmann, the company showed great technological originality, but for almost two decades its growth was much more hesitant and never led to a dominant position in its sector. Based on the highly original invention, patented in 1886, for producing seamless rolled tubes, the firm seemed to become a MNE right from the outset.[58] In practice however, in addition to the original plant owned by the two inventors Reinhard and Max Mannesmann, between 1887 and 1889 three other companies were created, each of them formally independent: one at Bous near Saarbrücken, one at Komotau in the then Austro-Hungarian Bohemia and one in Britain, where the Siemens family had an interest and took a licence for a plant which was to be installed at Llandore. The German and Austrian works were amalgamated in 1890 as the Deutsch-Österreichische Mannesmannröhren-Werke, with a capital of 35 million marks and under the financial guidance of the Deutsche Bank, the two inventor brothers receiving half of the new shares for bringing in their patents. Since the tube rolling process was at the beginning scarcely ripe for continuous production, the first years of the new firm were overshadowed by considerable technical and, consequently, financial difficulties. The two Mannesmann brothers left the firm quite soon and sold out their shares in 1900, the Deutsche Bank becoming the uncontested 'entrepreneur' and financier of the company. No dividend could be distributed until 1906; by then several rationalisation measures and the generally favourable economic climate guaranteed solid further growth.

Around the turn of the century the process of multinationalisation was resumed. In 1899 the Landore Mannesmann Tube Company, which otherwise would have had to be closed down and which was completely independent from the German firm, was taken over. This move into direct investment was motivated by the attempt to get control of the British market for seamless tubes. Moreover, being based in Britain, Landore was able to profit from Empire preferences which were increasingly built up by the dominions.[59] As a 'national' firm Landore became also one of the main suppliers of boiler pipes for the British navy. In 1913 the construction of a second and larger rolling mill at Newport near Cardiff was decided, its future production intended as a replacement for imports from the German parent firm, notably large-diameter tubes so far not produced in Britain. The Newport works had not yet gone into operation when the war broke out.[60]

In 1906, when, as we have seen, the Mannesmann firm started to distribute its profits, the establishment of a rolling mill in Italy was decided; up to that moment, the peninsula had been an export market of growing significance.[61] The investment was made not so much because of the Italian tariff, but in the hope that it could profit from State orders for the railways, the navy or for the new programme of municipal aqueducts in southern Italy. In practice, State orders went increasingly to national businesses even if its tenders were up to 5 per cent higher than the average tender from abroad. Accordingly a company was founded under Italian law and with an Italian metallurgical firm as a minority partner. The works were built at Dalmine near Bergamo where two electric furnaces were also installed in order to be able to produce the special type of steel needed for rolling seamless tubes. Production started in 1909 but the technical difficulties were considerable, and after two rather unsuccessful years the Italian partner withdrew its participation. A real improvement as far as output and profitability were concerned came only in 1912. Still, technically and financially the Società Tubi Mannesmann depended entirely on the parent company at Düsseldorf. As an example, the parent company waived its right to the licence fees fixed by contract in order to 'improve' the balance sheet of the Italian affiliate. Credit lines opened by Italian banks were used only at the end of 1913; up to that point all financial means were provided from Germany. When Italy entered the war in May 1915, the firm was seized. Nevertheless, Mannesmann succeeded in selling the Dalmine works in 1916 to a group of Italian banks, a transaction made with the agreement of the Italian government via neutral Switzerland.[62]

The most important foreign asset of Mannesmann remained, however, the Austrian affiliate, 'which reached about one third of the Mannesmann combine's total turnover in the last pre-war year' when all non-German subsidiaries accounted for 45 per cent of the overall volume.[63] The Komotau works certainly profited from high Austro-Hungarian tariffs and soon succeeded in attaining a share of 35 per cent in the tube cartel of the country.[64]

In brief, one could say that both firms, Bosch and Mannesmann possessed strong ownership advantages through their patented technology. Foreign direct investment in manufacturing was, however, only induced when additional country-specific factors such as tariffs or non-tariff trade measures became effective in the particular foreign country. In the case of Bosch, its nearness to important customers such as the French and the American automobile industry certainly also played an important role.

**Patent Legislation, Tariffs and Multinationalisation: the Case of the German Chemical Industry**

The dominant position of the German chemical industry up to World War I is common knowledge among economic historians. If one excludes petroleum refining, which was particularly important in the US chemical sector, the German chemical industry retained a clear lead in world chemical production. Its exports 'accounted for an estimated 28 per cent of world exports in chemicals'.[65] The German superiority in the artifical dyestuffs sector was crushing. The total value produced by eight firms and their foreign subsidiaries in 1913 amounted to 75–80 per cent of world production, and some 85 per cent of German production was exported.[66] It is commonly accepted that the rapid rise of the German chemical industry which started in the 1860s was due to country-specific advantages like the German university system which favoured the training of chemists and chemical engineers. There were industry-specific advantages like the oligopolistic market structure and the access to fuel and raw materials. In some sectors enterprise-specific advantages shrank after 1900 and in the dyestuffs sector this resulted in the formation of two *Interessengemeins-chaften*, the so-called Dreibund (BASF, Bayer and AGFA), and Hoechst, which controlled Casella and Kalle on the other hand. The largest of these firms had gone abroad fairly early. In Russia, BASF, Bayer and Hoeschst founded or participated in producing affiliates in 1877, 1883 and 1885 in response, as is generally asserted, to growing Russian protectionism after the tariff moves of 1877.[67] The smaller chemical firms (Cassella, Kalle, and AGFA) came to Russia in the following years. Especially in the dyestuffs sector, production by these affiliates comprised only the final stages; intermediate products on which the duties were much lower were imported from the parent firms; in this specific case they contributed up to 80 per cent of the value added.[68] Tariff problems, but even more the French patent law which required an immediate start of production in the country by patent holders, were responsible for the foundation by Hoechst in 1881 of the Compagnie Parisienne de Couleurs d'Aniline which started production of aniline dyes and pharmaceutical products at Creil (Oise) in 1884.[69] BASF had started a plant in 1878 at Neuville-sur-Saône near Lyon.[70] A change in British patent legislation occurred in 1907 which prescribed that a foreign patent, after its transfer to Britain, had to be exploited there or else it would be revoked. As a result Hoechst, repre-senting also Cassella and Kalle, established a plant in Ellesmere Port near Liverpool and BASF, acting for the Dreibund, founded the Mersey Chemical Works not far from there and transferred nearly one-fifth of its patents to this new affiliate. In the following years Hoechst produced practically the whole volume of domestic production of indigo, amounting to about 50 per cent of domestic demand, at Ellesmere Port, whereas the

BASF subsidiary concentrated on other aniline dyes. Patent transfers from Germany decreased, however, very soon after it became clear that British jurisdiction had, in practice watered down the enforcement of the 1907 Patent and Designs Act.[71] Looking to the situation of British producers, Haber is probably right when he states that apart from the virtual failure of the new patent legislation, another possible measure, 'a tariff, would not have helped the British producers because they lacked patents, know-how and, above all, research and enterprise'.[72]

The impact of patent legislation is also shown in the case of the United States where there was no legal obligation to use patents given by the US administration in the country itself. For this reason the BASF thought it useless to establish a factory there. It registered, however, up to 1914 about 1000 patents. Roughly the same number were registered to Bayer, which owned, however, a factory at Albany, NY and another company, the Synthetic Patents Company, Inc., which held all the Bayer patents registered in the US and gave licences to the American Bayer Company; the latter was thus able to reduce its tax burden because gains from licences paid lower taxes than gains from production.[73] All the other German dye makers had little in the way of manufacturing in the United States; they did have, however, very extensive commercial organisations.

A final illustration could be given by the Italian case where there was, up to the First World War, no artificial dyestuffs production at all; in 1913, Germany provided 77 per cent of Italian dyestuffs imports. By making concessions to agricultural imports from Italy, the German negotiators succeeded after 1878 in all tariff discussions in keeping dyestuffs and related chemical imports totally free of all duties. Consequently there was not one German chemical plant of any importance in Italy.[74]

The dominant position of the German chemical industry before 1914 was certainly due to patented technology and intangible know-how based on significant outlay on research and development. If at the same time foreign states were not willing to respect the simple registration of patents but demanded that they be actually implemented within the national frontiers, if they constructed tariff walls or if they fell back on non-tariff trade measures, then direct investment was the logical consequence if a specific market was to be conserved.

**Technology and Finance: the German Electrical Industry**

The last sector that will be considered here is electrotechnical production where German industry shared world-wide leadership with US trusts. According to one estimate, Germany in 1913 had a share of about 35 per cent of world production as compared to a United States share of 29 per cent,[75] whereas another estimate gives a figure of 31 per cent for Germany and 35 per cent for the United States.[76] There is agreement, however, that German industry dominated world exports of electrotechnical material with its share of 46 per cent, followed by the British with 22 per cent and their American competitors with 16 per cent.[77]

This is not the place to discuss the rise of the German electrotechnical industry as such.[78] I should only mention that Siemens & Halske started as early as 1847 and owed its success during the first three decades of its existence mainly to business in the telegraph and later in the slowly developing telephone sector. Its main competitor, the Allgemeine Elektricitäts-Gesellschaft (AEG), only started in 1883 as the German licenseholder of Edison. During its first decade it depended, apart from its technical ties with the American Edison companies, quite heavily on the Deutsche Bank and Siemens itself, both of which took equity participations. The rise of the AEG took place in the high-voltage sector right from the beginning and still more so when it had finally gained complete independence from Edison and Siemens in 1894. Siemens, the older firm and more conservative in its outlook, fell back comparatively because it did not involve itself so much in the high-voltage business during the late 1880s and the early 1890s. However, at the turn of the century, it began to expand again in this sector too, when it had been transformed into a limited liability company and its liquidity problems had been solved. Like a considerable number of smaller companies, the third competitor, Schuckert, founded in 1873, could hardly survive the crisis of 1901 which hit the German economy particularly hard and above all its too rapidly growing electrical industry. In 1903 Schuckert merged its plant with Siemens which combined it with its own high-voltage activities in the new firm of Siemens-Schuckert, although Schuckert remained independent as a holding company retaining participation in a considerable number of domestic and foreign power, tram and lighting companies. In any case, after 1903 the German electrotechnical industry was characterised by a virtual duopoly of Siemens and AEG which dominated the market, leaving space however to a host of smaller so-called 'specialised' firms.

What interests us in this context is the international dimension of this sector, and there can be no doubt that it was important right from the beginning. It started at a very early stage in the case of Siemens, which, as a consequence of considerable orders from the Russian government for the construction and maintenance of a telegraph network, established a plant at St Petersburg as early as 1855, where parts sent from Berlin were assembled. The Russian business was directed on the spot by Carl Siemens, brother of Werner, the firm's founder, and it was another brother, William, who represented the Siemens interests in Britain from 1850 and directed the British Siemens subsidiary (founded in 1858), which started with the production of sea cables in 1863.[79] In order to settle disputes about responsibility and profit distribution which had arisen between the brothers, the whole firm was reorganised in 1867 under the roof of a common business (*Gesamtgeschäft*) with its seat at Berlin; it split up into two companies, Siemens & Halske in Berlin and Siemens Brothers in London; the Russian branch was assigned as an affiliate to Siemens & Halske.[80] One could talk, of course, at first sight of a multinational group, which had been formed with a centre in Berlin and direct investments in Britain and Russia. But if one looks more closely, one sees that at least in the British case William Siemens operated quite independently, relying financially on his brother Werner in Berlin on occasions. The whole family enterprise structurally was more similar to more traditional models, for instance to the business of Huguenot bankers and merchants in the Refuge operating contemporaneously in Geneva, Amsterdam and London, if not in Paris.[81] Even after the turn of the century 'the great principle of international family unity' characterised the different Siemens branches,[82] and this meant that when there were problems a member of the family was called in to manage the various foreign affiliates. Expansion abroad continued in the sense that in 1903, for instance, there were 30 so-called technical bureaux installed, eight of them in European countries.[83] Some of these started production, normally at first by assembling parts sent from the mother firm, as for instance in 1879 in Vienna and in 1903 in Bratislava, in the Hungarian part of the Habsburg Empire, where after the merger with Schuckert its plant was incorporated.

In some countries, as for instance France, where anti-German feelings after 1871 certainly did not favour sales and autonomous direct investment, joint ventures proved to be a viable solution. Thus in 1889 Siemens & Halske, Siemens Brothers (London) and the Société Alsacienne de Constructions Mécaniques (Mulhouse) founded a jointly-owned company which was supposed to produce high-voltage material in Belfort, just on the French side of the border. The Mulhouse firm which held a share of 37.5 per cent was to provide all the non-electrical mechanical equipment, and Siemens the electrical parts. In the longer run the Belfort company proved to be quite successful but Siemens had to withdraw from it in 1904 since the merger with Schuckert the year before had left Schuckert's French subsidiary, the Compagnie Générale d'Electricité de Creil, founded in 1897, practically at Siemens' disposal. Consequently, Siemens rented the Creil works from the Schuckert holding which formally was still independent. With the Société Alsacienne a jointly-owned cable factory at Belfort was nevertheless continued.[84]

In Russia production for low- and high-voltage material started in 1880–2. The reason must be seen not so much in the increasing Tsarist tariff duties as in the growing pressure from the Russian administration which insisted on domestic production for continuing State orders.[85] The AEG for its part resisted such pressures for quite a long time and tried to look after its Russian business through local agents. In 1898 it founded an affiliate for Russia which was simply a sales company based in Berlin and had to transfer its legal seat in 1902 to St Petersburg so as to avoid being thrown out of business. Only in 1905, after its merger with the Union Elektricitäts-Gesellschaft, previously controlled by General Electric, could the AEG get hold of the Union's electrotechnical factory at Riga.[86]

We could go on listing other examples of direct investment by the German electrotechnical industry, but looking at the motives we would find in most cases State intervention in the form of tariffs or non-tariff trade measures, especially if the State was an important customer, as in the case of Russia. However, there must have been still other factors at stake if, for instance, in 1913, 87 per cent of all electrotechnical imports to Russia came from Germany,[87] if in the same year in the Italian case the quota of imports from Germany reached 70 per cent[88] and if the German electro-technical industry succeeded in taking up regularly about half of Argentinian imports in this field between 1903 and 1913.[89] The reason must be found in the so-called *Unternehmergeschäft*, which meant that the large German trusts created their own market by founding local and regional power, tramway and lighting companies in those countries (for example Russia, Italy, Spain, Latin America) and for those customers (particularly local public authorities) which suffered from chronic lack of capital, and because these new companies were forced by statute to buy their electro-technical material from their big industrial founders.[90] No doubt these operations were further steps in internalisation bound to reduce the risks of selling in a foreign market. On the other hand, the risk was created of accumulating a growing volume of equity capital and bonds in the portfolio of the electrotechnical producers and a dangerous reduction of their liquidity. The solution lay in founding financial holdings together with the great banks. These financial holding companies took over the shares and bonds of the newly created public utility companies, held them in their portfolio during the period of construction and initial development and sold most of their holdings to the general public as soon as they had 'matured' and yielded a profit, afterwards in general only retaining controlling minority holdings.[91] Each of the German producers possessed such an intermediate financial holding. AEG had the Bank für elektrische Unternehmunger, founded in 1895 in Zürich by itself and a number of German and Swiss and, to a minor extent, Italian and French banks. The same holds for Siemens with its Basel-based Schweizerische Gesellschaft für elektrische Industrie, created in 1896, and its Elektrische Licht- und Kraftanlagen AG, founded at Berlin in the same year. Schuckert and the minor electrotechnical producers possessed, of course, their own *Finan-zierungsgesellschaften.* The fact that part of these financial holdings were based in Switzerland or Belgium (in the latter country, for instance, was the AEG-controlled SOFINA) arose mainly from the very liberal company law and stock exchange regulations of these countries. In part, it probably owed something to the participation of the influential Swiss and Belgian banks in these holdings.[92] One can further observe an increasing regional specialisation by the creation of national or regional subholdings controlled directly by the electrotechnical producer and its banks or by one of its financial holdings such as, for instance, the Società per lo sviluppo delle imprese elettriche in Italia and the Deutsche Überseeische Elektricitäts-Gesellschaft, the one 'responsible' for Italy, the other for Argentina, Chile and Uruguay, both of them emanations of AEG.[93] As a result, in 1913 about 50 per cent of the capital of the Italian and about 40 per cent of the Russian companies producing electrical energy were controlled by German capital.[94]

Even if one can agree that the German *Elektrokonzerne* enjoyed substantial ownership advantages because of their superior quality of management, their advanced technology in electrotechnical mass production, their thorough marketing techniques and their after-sales service, the high-voltage material itself was by the mid-1890s technically 'mature' and in the medium term few observers expected radical innovations. For German industry this meant probably slowly shrinking advantages and growing competition on the world market, especially from its US rivals. It could, up to a certain degree, meet this challenge—particularly in countries where investment capital was relatively difficult to obtain—through the extraordinary process of internalisation described above, which was made possible by the advantage of easy access to factor markets, that is, in this case to international capital via its financial holdings and ultimately via its close ties to the German type of mixed banks.

When the First World War ended this access to the international capital markets and led to the loss of the major part of German direct investment, the high-voltage business of the type described above found itself in considerable difficulties. But—and the Italian example shows this quite well—the then technologically faster advancing low-voltage sector (above all the telephone installation business) survived much more easily and its exports performed comparatively better in the inter-war period.

Summing up, it must be emphasised that the examples and brief case studies offered in this chapter do not provide a comprehensive study of German MNE before 1914. What is needed in the future are studies that concentrate on the historical development of a specific German multinational as well as the type of synthetic overview that Mira Wilkins has done for US MNE. At the same time the point must be made that the astonishing vitality of the pre-1914 German economy and its rapid international expansion cannot be described in a convincing way without reference to the MNE, its concepts and its gradual evolution.

## Notes

1. S.H. Hymer, *The International Operations of National Firms: A Study of Direct Foreign Investment* (Cambridge, Mass., 1976); C.P. Kindleberger, *American Business Abroad, Six Lectures on Direct Investment* (London, 1969); R.E. Caves, 'International Corporations: The Industrial Economics of Foreign Investment', *Economica* (1971), pp. 1–27.

2. B. Swedenborg, *The Multinational Operations of Swedish Firms. An Analysis of Determinants and Effects* (Stockholm, 1979), p. 39.

3. R.H. Coase, 'The Nature of the Firm', *Economica* (1937), pp. 386–405.

4. O.E. Williamson, *Markets and Hierarchies: Analysis and Anti-trust Implications* (New York, 1975), especially chapter 1; O.E. Williamson, 'The Modern Corporation: Origins, Evolution, Attributes', *Journal of Economic Literature* (1981), pp. 1537–68.

5. G.B. Richardson, 'The Organisation of Industry', *The Economic Journal* (1972), p. 890 (italics in original).

6. A.M. Rugman, 'Internalization and non-equity forms of international involvement' in A.M. Rugman (ed.), *New Theories of the Multinational Enterprise* (London, 1982), p. 11.

7. M. Casson, 'Transaction Costs and the Theory of the Multinational Enterprise' in A.M. Rugman (ed.), *New Theories of the Multinational Enterprise*, p. 24.

8. Ibid., p. 36.ff.

9. J.H. Dunning, 'Explaining the International Direct Investment Position of Countries: Towards a Dynamic or Developmental Approach', *Weltwirtschaftliches Archiv* (1981), p. 33.

10. J.H. Dunning, *International Production and the Multinational Enterprise* (London, 1981), p. 27.

11. Ibid., p. 3.

12. R.E. Caves, *Multinational Enterprise and Economic Analysis* (Cambridge, 1982), p. 1.

13. L. Franko, 'The Origins of Multinational Manufacturing by Continental European Firms', *Business History Review* (1974), p. 279, note 10.

14. Y. Aharoni, 'On the Definition of a Multinational Corporation' in A. Kapoor and P.D. Grub (eds), *The Multinational Enterprise in Transition* (Princeton, NJ, 1973), pp. 4ff; F. Grünärml, 'Kritische Anmerkungen zu einer merkmalspezifischen Typologie multinationaler Unternehmen', *Jahrbuch für Sozialwissenschaft* (1975), pp. 228–43.

15. M. Casson, op. cit., p. 36 (emphasis added).

16. Ibid.

17. See, for example, M. Wilkins, 'Modern European Economic History and the Multinationals', *Journal of European Economic History* (1977), pp. 575–95, particularly p. 578, note 11.

18. See, however, the various contributions mentioned in notes 28–30 of the introduction to this volume. [*Multinationals: Theory and History.*]

19. See, for instance, P.J. Buckley, 'New Theories of International Business: Some Unresolved Issues' in M. Casson (ed.), *The Growth of International Business* (London, 1983), pp. 34–50, particularly p. 42.

20. T. Horst, 'Firm and Industry Determinants of the Decision to Invest Abroad: An Empirical Study', *Review of Economics and Statistics* (1972), p. 265.

21. Cited in L.F. Haber, *The Chemical Industry 1900–1930. International Growth and Technological Change* (Oxford, 1971), p. 133; see also J.H. Merck,

*Entwicklung und Stand der pharmazeutischen Grossindustrie Deutschlands* (Berlin, 1923), p. 12; W. Vershofen, *Wirtschaftsgeschichte der chemisch-pharmazeutischen Industrie*, vol. 3 (Aulendorf, Württ, 1958), p. 39ff.

22. L.F. Haber, op. cit., p. 133ff; J.H. Merck, op. cit., p. 14.

23. L.F. Haber, op. cit., p. 121, 131; Merck archives, Darmstadt, F3 Nr. 17.

24. Merck archives, F3 Nr. 5 and Nr. 16.

25. Ibid., H 1 Nr. 45/46.

26. T.R. Kabisch, *Deutsches Kapital in den USA. Von der Reichsgründung bis zur Sequestrierung (1917) und Freigabe* (Stuttgart, 1982), p. 234; 65th Congress 3rd Session, Senate Documents, vol. 8 (Washington, D.C., 1919), p. 59 (hereafter referred to as *Alien Property Custodian Report*).

27. See T.R. Kabisch, op. cit.

28. R. Schmitt, 'Die pharmazeutische Industrie und ihre Stellung in der Weltwirtschaft' (unpublished thesis, Frankfurt am Main, 1932), p. 124.

29. Merck archives, F3 Nr. 5–17.

30. Ibid., F3 Nr. 9.

31. Ibid., F3 Nr. 14, H1 Nr. 9.

32. Ibid., F3, Nr. 5/6.

33. Ibid., F3 Nr. 6.

34. R. Schmitt, op cit, p. 123; E. Grandmougin, *L'essor des industries chimiques en France*, (Paris, 1917), p. 173ff.

35. Merck archives, F3 Nr. 6, 9.

36. Ibid., H1, Nr. 22, 23, 24, 25, 29; see also R. Poidevin, *Les relations économiques et financières entre la France et l'Allemagne de 1898 à 1914* (Paris, 1969), p. 740.

37. R. Schmitt, op cit, pp. 218, 164.

38. Merck archives, F3 Nr. 10.

39. H. Holländer, *Geschichte der Schering Aktiengesellschaft* (Berlin, 1955), p. 36ff.; Schering, or at least a member of the Schering family, participated in the New York firm of Schering & Glatz in the late 1870s and took in 1897 a short-lived participation in a borax mine in Chile, a typical raw-material venture (ibid., p. 15, 19).

40. For the following see above all *Denkschrift anlässlich des 25-jährigen Bestehens von Kathreiners Malzkaffee-Fabriken, 1892–1917* (München, 1917); H. Aust, *Organisation eines Markenartikel-Grossunternehmens der Nahrungs- und Genussmittelindustrie* (undated typewritten manuscript in the library of the Institut für Weltwirtschaft at Kiel, Germany), particularly p. 35ff., 167ff.

41. For an analogous strategy in the same market but with another type of coffee surrogate see the case of the Heinrich Franck firm of Ludwigsburg mentioned by T.R. Kabisch, op. cit., p. 280ff.

42. R.E. Caves, 'International Corporations' and T. Horst, 'The Multinational Corporation and Direct Investment. A comment' in P.B. Kenen (ed.), *International Trade and Finance. Frontiers for Research* (Cambridge, 1975), pp. 368–9 see the typical MNE as a large oligopolistic firm whereas B. Swedenborg, op. cit., pp. xiv, 153ff., looking at the historical development of Swedish multinationals, comes to the conclusion that 'large firms do not have a higher propensity to produce abroad than small firms do' (ibid., p. 188).

43. O. Debatin, *Sie haben mitgeholfen Lebensbilder verdienter Mitarbeiter des Hauses Bosch* (Stuttgart, Robert Bosch GmbH, 1963), p. 37ff; *Fünfzig Jahre Bosch 1886–1936* (Stuttgart, 1936), pp. 27, 290.

44. O. Debatin, op. cit., p. 46; see also T. Heuss, *Robert Bosch: Leben und Leistung* (München, 1975; 1st edn Tübingen 1946); *75 Jahre Bosch 1886–1961*.

*Ein geschichtlicher Rückblick* (Stuttgart, Robert Bosch GmbH, 1961).

45. *Der Bosch-Zünder. Eine Zeitschrift für alle Angehörigen der Robert-Bosch-AG und der Bosch-Metallwerk AG, Stuttgart und Feuerbach,* vol. 1, no. 4. (1919), p. 59.

46. Ibid., p. 60; O. Debatin, op. cit., p. 23.

47. O. Debatin, op. cit., p. 20.

48. R. Poidevin, op. cit., p. 20.

49. *Fünfzig Jahre Bosch.,* p. 25.

50. O. Debatin, op. cit., p. 32ff.

51. *Der Bosch-Zünder,* p. 60; *75 Jahre Bosch,* p. 31, T. Heuss, op. cit., p. 121.

52. *Der Bosch-Zünder,* p. 61ff; *75 Jahre Bosch,* p. 34.

53. O. Debatin, op. cit., p. 68ff.; T. Heuss, op. cit., p. 122; T.R. Kabisch, op. cit., p. 32.

54. O. Debatin, op. cit., p. 55ff.; T. Heuss, op. cit., p. 150ff.

55. *Alien Property Custodian Report,* p. 109.

56. Ibid.

57. Ibid., p. 108.

58. See especially *75 Jahre Mannesmann. Geschichte einer Erfindung und eines Unternehmens, 1890–1965* (Düsseldorf, Mannesmann Aktiengesellschaft, 1965), p. 27ff.; P. Hertner, 'Fallstudien zu deutschen multinationalen Unternehmen vor dem Ersten Weltkrieg' in N. Horn und J. Kocka, *Recht und Entwicklung der Grossunternehmen im 19. und im frühen 20. Jahrhundert* (Göttingen, 1979), pp. 388–419, particularly p. 400 ff; H. Pogge von Strandmann, *Unternehmens-politik und Unternehmensführung. Der Dialog zwischen Aufsichtsrat und Vorstand bei Mannesmann 1900 bis 1919* (Düsseldorf, 1978); A. Teichova, 'The Mannesmann Concern in East Central Europe in the inter-war period' in A. Teichova and P.L. Cottrell, *International Business and Central Europe, 1918–1939* (Leicester, 1983), pp. 103–37, particularly pp. 103–6.

59. *75 Jahre Mannesmann,* p. 82; for the problem of Empire preferences see, for instance, F. Capie, *Depression and Protectionism: Britain between the Wars* (London, 1983), pp. 23, 42.

60. R. Bungeroth, *50 Jahre Mannesmannröhren 1884/1934* (Berlin, 1934), p. 135.

61. See P. Hertner, 'Fallstudien', p. 403ff; P. Hertner, 'Deutsches Kapital in Italien; Die "Società Tubi Mannesmann" in Dalmine bei Bergamo, 1906–1916', *Zeitschrift für Unternehmensgeschichte* (1977), pp. 183–204, (1978), pp. 54–76.

62. P. Hertner, 'Deutsches Kapital in Italien', p. 66ff.

63. A. Teichova, op. cit., p. 105.

64. Ibid.

65. L.F. Haber, op. cit., p. 108.

66. Ibid., p. 121.

67. P.A. Zimmermann, *Patentwesen in der Chemie* (Ludwigshafen am Rhein, 1965), p. 113; C. Schuster, *Vom Farbenhandel zur Farbenindustrie. Die erste Fusion der BASF* (Ludwigshafen am Rhein, 1973), p. 71ff; N. Kirchner, 'Die Bayer-Werke in Russland, 1883–1974. Ein deutscher Beitrag zur Industrialisierung Russlands', H. Lemberg *et al., Osteuropa in Geschichte und Gegenwart. Festschrift für Günther Stökl zum 60. Geburtstag* (Köln 1977), pp. 153–70; *Dokumente aus Hoechst-Archiven,* 43 (Frankfurt am Main, 1970), p. 7, 11ff.

68. F. Redlich, *Die volkswirtschaftliche Bedeutung der deutschen Teerfarben-industrie* (doctoral thesis, Berlin, 1914), p. 83; L.F. Haber, op. cit., p. 173; L.F. Haber, *The Chemical Industry during the Nineteenth Century* (Oxford, 1958), p. 142.

128     *United Nations Library on Transnational Corporations*

69. *Dokumente aus Hoechst-Archiven,* 44 (Frankfurt am Main, 1970), p. 7.
70. P.A. Zimmermann, op. cit., p. 113; *Die Badische Anilin- & Soda-Fabrik* (1921), p. 17; for these subsidiaries and others founded in France by Casella and AGFA see also R. Poidevin, op. cit., p. 29.
71. L.F. Haber, *The Chemical Industry 1900–1930,* p. 146ff.; P.A. Zimmermann, op. cit., p. 121ff; F. Redlich, op. cit., p. 81; *Dokumente aus Hoechst-Archiven,* 45 (Frankfurt/Main, 1971), p. 7ff, 14ff; it was for the same reasons that Schering, the above mentioned pharmaceutical firm, decided after 1908 to establish a manufacturing subsidiary near London which was to cover the markets of Britain and its Empire (H. Holländer, op. cit., p. 37).
72. L.F. Haber, *The Chemical Industry 1900–1930,* p. 148.
73. T.R. Kabisch, op. cit., p. 164ff., 225ff.
74. P. Hertner, 'Das Auslandskapital in der italienischen Wirtschaft 1883–1914. Probleme seiner Quantifizierung und Auswertung' in H. Kellenbenz (ed.), *Weltwirtschaftliche und währungspolitische Probleme seit dem Ausgang des Mittelalters* (Stuttgart, 1981), pp. 93–121, particularly p. 105.
75. P. Czada, *Die Berliner Elektroindustrie in der Weimarer Zeit* (Berlin, 1969), p. 48ff.
76. G. Jacob-Wendler, *Deutsche Elektroindustrie in Lateinamerika. Siemens und AEG (1890–1914)* (Stuttgart, 1982), p. 11.
77. Ibid.; P. Czada, op. cit., p. 48ff.; see also the statistical tables in the Siemens Museum, München, Firmenarchiv (hereafter referred to as Siemens archives), SAA 11/Lb 581 (Liedtke).
78. See, among others, G. Siemens, *Geschichte des Hauses Siemens,* 3 vols. (Munich, 1947/1952); '50 Jahre AEG' (printed manuscript, Berlin, Allgemeine Elektricitätsgesellschaft, 1956); J. *Kocka,* 'Siemens und der aufhaltsame Aufstieg der AEG', *Tradition* (1972), pp. 125–42; G. Eibert, *Unternehmenspolitik Nürnberger Maschinenbauer (1835–1914),* (Stuttgart, 1979), pp. 182–281, 311–404 (on Schuckert).
79. S. von Weiher and H. Goetzeler, *Weg und Wirken der Siemens-Werke im Fortschritt der Elektrotechnik 1847–1972, Tradition,* Beiheft 8, (1972), p. 15; J.D. Scott, *Siemens Brothers 1858–1958* (London, 1958), pp. 31, 52.
80. G. Siemens, op. cit., vol. 1 (Munich, 1947), p. 87.
81. See the monumental work by H. Lüthy, *La banque protestante en France de la révocation de l'édit de Nantes à la Révolution,* 2 vols. (Paris, 1959).
82. J.D. Scott, op. cit., p. 79.
83. G. Siemens, op. cit., vol. 2, p. 206.
84. Siemens archives, SAA 68/Li 177.
85. I. Mai, *Das deutsche Kapital in Russland 1850–1894* (Berlin, DDR, 1970), p. 99ff., 197; G.S. Holzer, 'The German electrical industry in Russia: from economic entrepreneurship to political activism, 1890–1918' (PhD thesis, University of Nebraska, 1970), pp. 29ff., 41; W. Kirchner, 'The Industrialization of Russia and the Siemens firm 1853–1890', *Jahrbücher für Geschichte Osteuropas,* new series, 22 (1974), pp. 321–57, particularly p. 330; S. von Weiher, 'Carl von Siemens 1829–1906. Ein deutscher Unternehmer in Russland und England', *Tradition* (1956), pp. 13–25, particularly p. 23.
86. *50 Jahre AEG,* 94ff., 132, 158; G.S. Holzer, op cit, p. 34, 41ff.; 83; J. Mai, 'Deutscher Kapitalexport nach Russland 1898–1907' in H. Lemke and B. Widera (eds), *Russisch-deutsche Beziehungen von der Kiever Rus' bis zur Oktoberrevolution* (Berlin, DDR, 1976), pp. 207ff.; V. Djakin, 'Zur Stellung des deutschen Kapitals in der Elektroindustrie Russlands', *Jahrbuch für Geschichte der UdSSR und der volksdemokratischen Länder Europas* (1966), p. 122ff.

87. V. Djakin, op. cit., p. 142ff.

88. P. Lanino, *La nuova Italia industriale,* vol. 2 (Rome, 1916), p. XXVIII.

89. G. Jacob-Wendler, op. cit., p. 69.

90. See the fundamental contribution by R. Liefmann, *Beteiligungs-und Finanzierungsgesellschaften. Eine Studie über den modernen Kapitalismus und das Effektenwesen* (Jena, 1913), in particular p. 103ff.

91. F. Fasolt, *Die sieben grössten deutschen Elektrizitätsgesellschaften. Ihre Entwicklung und Unternehmertätigkeit,* doctoral thesis, Heidelberg (Borna-Leipzig, 1904), p. 31ff.; M. Jürgens, *Finanzielle Trustgesellschaften,* doctoral thesis (Stuttgart, 1902), p. 117ff.

92. A. Strobel, 'Die Gründung des Züricher Elektrotrusts. Ein Beitrag zum Unternehmergeschäft der deutschen Elektroindustrie' in H. Hassinger (ed.), *Geschichte-Wirtschaft-Gesellschaft. Festschrift für Clemens Bauer zum 75. Geburtstag* (Berlin, 1974), pp. 303–32; H. Grossmann, *Die Finanzierungen der Bank für elektrische Unternehmungen in Zürich,* Staatswiss. Diss. Zürich (Zürich, 1918); K. Hafner, *Die schweizerischen Finanzierungsgesellschaften für elektrische Unternehmungen,* Jur. Diss. Fribourg (Genève, 1912), p. 32ff.; P. Hertner, 'Banken und Kapitalbildung in der Giolitti-Ära'; *Quellen und Forschungen aus italienischen Archiven und Bibliotheken* (1978), pp. 466–565, particularly p. 508ff.

93. P. Hertner, *Banken und Kapitalbildung,* p. 526f.; G. Jacob-Wendler, op. cit., p. 71ff.

94. P. Hertner, *Das Auslandskapital,* p. 104; V. Djakin, op. cit., p. 142f.

# 5

# Japanese Multinational Enterprise before 1914*

Mira Wilkins[†]

*Source: *Business History Review*, 60 (1986) pp. 199–231.

The current scholarly interest in contemporary Japanese businesses has somewhat obscured their equally fascinating early historical development. In this article, Professor Wilkins emphasizes both the extent and the variety of Japanese multinational enterprise before the First World War, and offers a basis for comparing its differences and similarities with the conventional American model.

Just as American and European multinational enterprises have a history preceding recent times, so Japanese multinational enterprises have existed since well before the Second World War—indeed, since the late nineteenth century.[1] Yet, although a substantial literature has grown up on the current remarkable expansion of Japanese business abroad, considerably less attention has been paid to the historical developments.[2] This article explores some of the early (pre-1914) activities of Japanese multinationals.

## Views of Multinational Enterprise

The ensuing discussion adopts the now-common practice of including not only those multinationals that manufacture, but also all business enterprises that extend over borders and have regular employees overseas. This definition is broad enough to include trading companies and other "service-sector" investments, such as banking and shipping. Alfred D. Chandler, Jr., has questioned whether the seventeenth-century English, Dutch, and other East India companies—trading companies—should be termed multinational enterprises.[3] These firms did possess many attributes of contemporary multinationals: they operated over borders, they co-ordinated operations within a single enterprise, and they participated in activities beyond trade, since they had representatives stationed outside their homelands. Chandler argued that they were nonetheless substantially different from modern multinational corporations in one fundamental respect—the quantity of their transactions. In the seventeenth century, when these giant Western trading firms came of age, months were required to send messages and receive replies. The slowness and uncertainty of communications precluded development of the coordination and control of large numbers of transactions—the administrative organizations—that are the characteristics of the modern multinational enterprise. The literature has therefore come to reflect the view that the modern multinational firm developed only in the late nineteenth century when steam-ships, cables, railroads, and telegraphs united distant areas.

This discussion needs refinement in the Japanese context. Much of the early international business of the Japanese trading companies clearly was constrained by distance and delays in the transmission of messages. Yet, a very important distinction exists between the East India companies of the seventeenth century and the Japanese trading firms: the Japanese enterprises have survived into the twentieth century as viable and important economic units, taking advantage of the modern innovations in transportation and communication. Because these businesses bridge the gap between historical and contemporary study, no treatment of Japanese multinational enterprise should exclude them.

One of the most fascinating topics in the history of Japanese multinationals is the "layering" of the Japanese trading company and the Japanese manufacturing enterprise, as the two types of firms both expanded overseas. The large Japanese trading companies with general experience in international trade could not develop specialized knowledge of the varied products that constituted parts of their business; on the other hand, an individual manufacturing company knew its particular goods thoroughly, but did not have international business experience. As a response to this difficulty, the producer came to replace the trader in some international investments, while in others joint ventures between trading company and manufacturer were organized. These relationships need systematic analysis, for which the historical record provides fruitful data. The timing and nature of the shifts relate to the volume and importance of the activity; the extent to which they were also a function of the type of product requires further investigation.[4]

Much of the research on multinational enterprise has been based on an American model, which views the company (usually an industrial one) as expanding abroad out of domestic growth and particularly out of experiences in its own domestic market. Students of multinational enterprise have been impressed by the general applicability, in both contemporary and historical terms, of that paradigm, in which the advantages of manufacturing firms at home (in their home activities) become advantages in foreign countries. Firms internalized—that is, handled within the single enterprise—added operations abroad. Sometimes the American model has been carried further; scholars have argued that certain industries in which American business excelled worldwide were by their very nature amenable to multinational-type behavior.[5]

Students of contemporary multinational enterprise have not been content to look only at investment, but have also examined the institutional nature of corporate expansion. The path American companies took internationally seemed to represent a universal one. Studies of contemporary European, and, to a large extent, Japanese, multinational enterprises therefore followed the same pattern of analysis. The outstanding work of Raymond Vernon, John Dunning, Charles Kindleberger, Richard Caves, and Mark Casson—to mention a few leading scholars—makes the assumption that a general model of multinational enterprise is broadly applicable.[6]

Just as contemporary studies of multinational enterprise multiplied when American business was triumphant around the world, so historical scholarship on multinational enterprise blossomed then. The history of American companies abroad accordingly formed the basis for the initial research on the history of multinational enterprise. In the 1970s and early 1980s new and substantial attention turned to the growth of European multinational enterprise, and many students of this development assumed that the historical course of European business abroad was fundamentally the same as that of its American counterpart. Systematic variations were usually explained by reference to differences in comparative advantage in the home countries, while the similarities seemed remarkable. Reflecting this view, a leading student of multinational enterprise who has dealt with both the contemporary and historical aspects of the subject, Raymond Vernon, has written, "By the early 1980s ... the multinationalizing trend was widely recognized as similar in nature irrespective of the nationality of the parent firm."[7]

While striking similarities unquestionably exist, some scholars have had doubts. Kiyoshi Kojima described Japanese multinational enterprises as trade-creating, American ones as trade-destroying. Keiichiro Nakagawa stated at a business history conference in 1982, "I do not think Japanese and Western firms developed their overseas activities in the same way."[8] This article looks at the early history of Japanese business overseas, and asks whether it resembled or differed from the pattern familiar to students of either contemporary multinationals or multinationals in historical perspective. A critic of a preliminary draft of this article asked, rhetorically, "Why wouldn't one assume that cultural and situational factors led to different business practices [by Japanese enterprises] prior to 1914, especially when it is evident that they still do today?" Obviously, this historian is correct, yet this assumption has frequently not been made, because of the acceptance of the more general model by students of multinational enterprise.[9] It is inadequate, moreover, to allude to vague cultural differences or to special historical traditions. Patterns might exist in the similarities and differences, patterns that this essay seeks to decipher.

The present article is not meant to be definitive. Its uniqueness lies in its attempt to understand the course of pre-1914 Japanese multinational enterprise based on available statistics and evidence, and to suggest some of the reasons for the similarities and, more important, for the differences, between the beginnings of modern Japanese and modern American multinational enterprise. This article applies general insights developed through research on the history of multinational enterprise specifically to the history of Japanese developments. It demonstrates the extent of Japanese multinational enterprise before the First World War (which may surprise some readers) and endeavors to explain the breadth of the involvement. Hopefully, it will stimulate additional inquiries.[10]

## Bases for Comparison

In the late nineteenth and early twentieth century, when American and Japanese modern multinational enterprises first took form, Japan was far behind the United States in the industrialization process. As noted, others have pointed out that multinationals in various home countries develop differently based on different comparative advantages. America was a nation were labor costs were high; land was available and raw material costs were relatively cheap. Thus, American technology emphasized labor-saving devices (substituting captial for labor) and was wasteful of raw materials. In terms of inputs for a modern industrial economy, Japan's development was characterized by the need for imported raw materials and for the exports to pay for those imports. To be sure, in the late nineteenth century Japan was an exporter of raw materials—of coal and raw silk; and while silk exports retained their importance, Japan became aware of its requirements for basic raw material imports far faster than the United States did. The United States after all had cotton, iron, and coal—all the key items of the early Industrial Revolution. Japan soon became an importer of raw cotton and of iron, and even its coal eventually became inadequate for its needs.

Other significant features of the American and Japanese home environments can be compared: 1) the size of the home market; 2) heterogeneity or homogeneity at home; 3) national status as importer or exporter of capital; 4) geographical position vis-à-vis other economic leaders; and 5) antitrust attitudes. Why select these particular aspects through which to study Japanese multinationals? I have already used these items to define differences between American and European firms; it is valuable, for comparative purposes, to employ the same framework in considering

American and Japanese business. Moreover, using these aspects as a handle for discussion brings out key elements in the history of Japanese multinationals.[11] The five points utilized in this inquiry (which are by no means all-inclusive) provide help in understanding some significant similarities in the evolution of U.S. and Japanese multinationals, important differences, and in addition the nature and extent of pre-1914 Japanese multinational enterprise.

**The Home Market**

By the beginning of the twentieth century the United States constituted the world's largest market, while Japan did not yet rank as an important market, based on international comparisons. Put simply, Japan was a far less developed country than the United States. In 1913 the United States had the world's greatest manufacturing output, representing some 35.8 percent of world production; Japan's represented a mere 1.2 percent. By every criteria, Japan's national market was smaller than that of the United States: in geographical size, per capita income, and population size. (Japan's average annual population [1905–9] was 47.5 million, compared to the U.S. population at the time of 87.1 million.) These differences in the size of the home market would almost by definition lead one to anticipate a separate pattern of multinational enterprise development.[12]

When one views Japanese industrialization in the late nineteenth and early twentieth century, what stands out? Not the mass production, not the beginnings of mass consumption that were characteristic of the American economy and that presented the managerial challenges in the United States. Rather, in Japan the important circumstances were the rapid coming of age of the Japanese domestic textile industry; economic growth and military triumphs (in the Sino-Japanese War and the Russo-Japanese War); and a recognition that because of its resource limitations and the smallness of the country—as defined earlier—Japan would by its very nature be highly dependent on trade, on imports of raw materials. Exports were required, in turn, to pay for these imports, creating a fundamental need for an infrastructure in support of trade—banking facilities, shipping companies, shipbuilding, insurance, and, most of all, enterprises familiar with the complexities of doing business abroad—that is, trading companies. Without such activities, Japanese economic development could not occur.[13]

All of these functions, however, could be carried on by foreigners. Indeed, in many countries around the world, foreign-headquartered multinational enterprise did control international trade. Why was Japan different? Why did its nationals come to handle and to control all these important functions? Perhaps Japanese companies undertook these activities, on a broad scale, because foreign business was not prepared to do so, and because the trade was more important to Japan than to her trading partners.[14] The relatively limited Japanese home market, resulting in small domestic firms incapable of handling extensive international trade by themselves, was an even more significant influence on the development of a Japanese-run infrastructure for overseas trade: specialized companies were required to carry forth operations abroad. The Japanese management challenge was, accordingly, different from that facing U.S. business.

Interestingly, in late nineteenth- and early twentieth-century Britain, also a small country by geographical size, constant problems of management over distance also existed, and the response to them was often the establishment of specialized institutions; trading companies, managing agencies, consulting engineers and, of course, shipping companies—in short, a service apparatus. The Japanese use of trading companies and development of service-sector companies in general seem closer to the British than to the American experience.[15] Also, like the British, the Japanese made some large foreign direct investments in railroads, specifically designed to meet Japanese domestic requirements.

## Heterogeneity and Homogeneity

If one assumes that multinational enterprises arise out of domestic conditions, one must look to other specific circumstances as well. Japan, unlike the United States, was not a country of immigrants. The American market was characterized by domestic diversity. In contrast, a visitor to Japan is impressed by the homogeneous nature of the population. Years of isolation produced a separate development, a distinctive ethic, that must be taken into account in any discussion of the evolution of Japanese multinational enterprise. Two pertinent consequences were inexperience at home in working closely with outsiders (creating a larger sphere of what was alien and unfamiliar) and a less varied demand for goods (resulting in a rigidity in taste). Here again, the parallels between the Japanese and British situations seem far closer than those between the Japanese and American experiences.

Comparison of American and European multinationals suggests that business enterprises investing abroad use three methods in coping with the unfamiliar: they seek out the most familiar within the unfamiliar; they try to create the familiar within the unfamiliar; and they adapt. It is easier to adapt in relatively familiar circumstances than in unfamiliar ones. In the American case, early foreign investment went disproportionately to geographically nearby areas—Canada, Mexico, and the Caribbean—and to culturally nearby ones—Great Britain.[16] The earliest Japanese foreign investments were, likewise, in geographically close and relatively familiar regions.

**Japanese Investment in China**

In 1931, the Bank of Japan prepared statistics on Japanese foreign investments in 1914 at the special request of American economist Harold Moulton (see Table 1). Moulton added estimates for other investments not covered and concluded that the total for 1913–14 amounted to 600 million yen (or $295.5 million at 100 yen = $49.25). A recent Japanese source provides similar figures (see Table 2), based on estimates of Japanese investment in China prepared for C.F. Remer for his 1933 study and the Moulton 1931 figures from the Bank of Japan on the United States and Hawaii. All of the Moulton-Bank of Japan "elsewhere" figures are attributed in this rendition to the Philippines and the South Sea Islands. The estimates indicate Japanese investments abroad in 1914 of between $227 and $296 million.[17] To provide a sense of the dimension of such foreign investments, they can be calculated as a percentage of 1914 Japanese gross national product, amounting to 9.9 percent and 12.8 percent, respectively—surprisingly high percentages; the figures include both portfolio and direct investments.[18]

The estimates show that Japanese foreign investments in 1914 were largest in China (including Manchuria), and consisted overwhelmingly of foreign direct investments that carried management and control. All the foreign direct investments seem to be closely related to Japanese development, including the Japanese government's sizable investment in the South Manchurian Railway (1906). They need to be studied within the framework provided by current knowledge on the nature of multinational enterprise.[19]

The Shimonoseki Treaty between Japan and China was signed in 1895, for the first time permitting foreigners to manufacture in Chinese treaty ports. Almost at once a British trading firm, Jardine, Matheson & Company, established the Ewo Cotton Spinning and Weaving Company in Shanghai, and three other foreign textile firms quickly followed (another British, one American, and one German).[20]

Japanese spinners saw their export markets in China threatened by these foreign-owned manufacturing facilities. Accordingly, two Japanese spinners established plants in Shanghai, but, as Tetsuya Kuwahara found, these initial ventures failed because of inadequate evaluation of the market and ineffective management. The Japanese retreated to a more familiar activity—exporting from Japan.[21]

Then, in 1902, Jōtarō Yamamoto, the Shanghai branch manager of Mitsui & Co., purchased a Chinese cotton mill and reestablished it under the name Shanghai Cotton Spinning Company, Ltd. Four years later, Mitsui & Co. acquired the Santai Cotton Spinning Company, Ltd., another Chinese cotton mill, extended its capacity, and placed Yamamoto in charge. On 5 December 1908, Mitsui organized a new local subsidiary,

*Table 1* Japanese foreign investment, July 1914 (based on unpublished Bank of Japan figures)

| | Value in millions of | |
| --- | --- | --- |
| Location and type | Yen | Dollars |
| China: | | |
| Loans to | 54.70 | 26.9 |
| Foreign securities purchased | 6.45 | 3.2 |
| Business enterprises: | 400.00 | 197.0 |
| In China | (310.00) | (152.7) |
| In the United States and Hawaii | ( 50.00) | ( 24.6) |
| Elsewhere | ( 40.00) | ( 19.7) |
| Totals | 461.15 | 227.1 |

*Source:* Harold Moulton, *Japan* (Washington, D.C., 1931), 391–92. Rate of exchange used: 100 yen = $49.25.

*Table 2* Japanese foreign investment, in 1914 (Ippei Yamazawa and Yuzou Yamamoto estimates)

| | Value in millions of | |
| --- | --- | --- |
| Location and type | Yen | Dollars |
| China | 439 | 216.2 |
| comprising | | |
| Loans to government | ( 19) | ( 9.4) |
| Loans to private enterprise | ( 35) | ( 17.2) |
| Direct investments | (385) | (189.6) |
| The United States and Hawaii | 50 | 24.6 |
| The Philippines and the South Seas | 40 | 19.7 |
| Totals | 529 | 260.5 |

*Source:* Ken-ichi Yasumuro, "The Contribution of the Sogo Shosha to the Multi-nationalization of Japanese Industrial Enterprise," in *Overseas Business Activities*, ed. Akio Okochi and Tadakatsu Inoue (Tokyo, 1984), 84. Professor Yasumuro's source was a 1979 Japanese volume on foreign trade and the balance of payments by Ippei Yamazawa and Yuzou Yamamoto. Rate of exchange used: 100 yen = $49.25.

Shanghai Cotton Manufacturing Company, which owned the two spinning mills. Yamamoto managed this affiliate separately from Mitsui & Co., because Takashi Masuda, the risk-averse head of Mitsui, did not want the trading company itself to become directly involved. Ken-ichi Yasumuro noted that Masuda "preferred to earn commissions by acting as an intermediary between buyers and sellers"; should the Chinese mills fail, Yamamoto would take the blame. In fact, Shanghai Cotton proved very profitable. By 1914, the firm had also installed 886 looms, and thus participated in weaving as well as spinning.[22]

The Japan Cotton Trading Company, a major firm in the raw cotton trade, had a cotton spinning mill in Shanghai by that time. In 1909 the Naigaiwata Company, a Japanese spinner, built what has been described by Yasumuro as "a new and powerful spinning mill in Shanghai." Equipped with the most advanced machinery and managed by a Japanese staff sent from the parent company, its labor-management relations replicated Japanese practice—for example, by providing dormitories for Chinese girls working at the mill. It was extremely successful. The Naigaiwata Company had been a trading firm, but it had bought out two Japanese spinners and established itself as a spinner in Japan before entering China.[23] Naigaiwata was the first Japanese spinner (as distinct from trading company) to be a success in manufacturing in China. Whereas the Japanese trading companies had bought existing Chinese mills, it constructed its own mill, following its own designs. While the Naigaiwata Company was not one of the largest spinning establishments in Japan, it gained experience from its Japanese mills before it began to manufacture abroad; by 1914, based on its Japanese and Chinese assets, it ranked nineteenth among the one hundred largest Japanese mining and manufacturing companies.[24]

By 1913, the Shanghai mill of the Naigaiwata Company was far more efficient than any Chinese-owned mill. Kuwahara explains that when the other, larger Japanese spinners made plans for mills in China, one important factor encouraging their subsequent entry was their recognition of the capability of Naigaiwata's Shanghai mill to compete in the Chinese market, a competitiveness that Kuwahara attributes to management knowledge. The Japanese mill owners also had the advantage of experience in buying raw cotton. Hiroaki Yamazaki suggests that a third advantage lay in their practice of blending raw cotton from different sources to obtain low-cost raw materials.[25]

Recently Stephen C. Thomas has argued that "the initiation of the Chinese-owned cotton industry was one of the most promising achievements of the pre-1897 period." He maintains that the foreign investments in China were a consequence of the profits being made by Chinese-owned mills. Then, severe competition from foreign-owned mills reduced profits. "By the early 1900s, three of [Chinese enterpreneur] Sheng [Hsuan-huai]'s mills had to be sold to Japanese interests...."[26] What does Thomas mean by "had to be sold"? It seems likely that they were not competitive with imports and the European-owned mills.

All the Japanese textile investments in manufacturing in China served the Chinese market. They appear to have been established in response to the presence of both Western and Chinese investments in Chinese spinning mills, as well as to the sale in China of cheap Indian yarn. They all grew out of existing business operations. The Japan Cotton Trading Company and the Naigaiwata Company's initial interest in China seems to have been in the export of raw cotton from China to Japan. As the Japanese cotton textile industry developed, interest in export markets grew, and Japanese businessmen, whether trader or spinner, needed to know conditions in China.[27] The early twentieth-century Japanese investments in Chinese manufacturing may initially have been made to discover Chinese costs, test out Chinese raw cotton, and keep close to the Chinese textile market. Tariffs were not a consideration in these early investments.

Thomas maintains that "unlike sovereign countries ... China could not control ownership of this [cotton textile] technology after 1895, regulate imports with a protective tariff, or tax foreign-owned mills in China."[28] None of Thomas's commentary, however, explains Japanese competitiveness. The technology was not proprietary; and China's inability to regulate the import of products is irrelevant to foreign investment in manufacturing. The influx of Indian yarn, for example, may have stimulated Japanese investment, but Chinese businessmen could have responded in a comparable manner. Presumably tax policy could have been framed to void any advantages of the Japanese mills. Japanese superiority was not a consequence of suppression of Chinese sovereignty, but of experience and entrepreneurial ability. A Chinese-American historian, Kang Chao, writes:

> ... the cotton textile industry in Japan ... [by the early twentieth century] had developed some excellent management systems, marketing organizations, and raw material procurement organizations. It did not take long for the Japanese to apply these organization principles to their plants in China. Furthermore, managers of Japanese mills in China quickly learned to adapt to local conditions, probably because of the high degree of cultural and linguistic similarities between the two countries. All these factors contributed to the quick establishment of an overall superiority of Japanese mills over both Chinese and British mills.[29]

The Japanese investments were overwhelmingly in spinning, although, as noted, the Shanghai Cotton Manufacturing Company owned looms. In 1913, Japanese spinning mills in China had 111,900 spindles (compared to British-owned mills in China with 138,000 spindles); that year in China there were 886 Japanese-owned power looms (and 800 British-owned ones). Whereas 63 percent of the spindles in China in 1897 were Chinese-owned and 37 percent Western-owned (with no Japanese ownership), by 1913 the ratios were 60 percent Chinese, 27 percent Western, and 13 percent Japanese. For power looms, in 1897 the ratios were 70 percent Chinese-owned and 30 percent Western-owned (none Japanese-owned); in 1913, 56 percent were Chinese-owned, 25 percent Western-owned, and 19 percent Japanese-owned.[30]

The pre-First World War Japanese investments in Chinese spinning and weaving were harbingers of far larger and more important ones to follow. They are, however, of particular interest in that they offer a preview of some of the dilemmas of trading (as opposed to manufacturing) companies as manufacturers abroad. The management of Mitsui & Co. in Tokyo was prepared to delegate decision making and management at the Shanghai spinning mills to its branch manager on the scene; the home company had little interest in the venture. The Naigaiwata Company, which used its direct experiences with its Japanese spinning operations as a basis for its Chinese mill, was the most successful of these early Japanese investors in China.[31] This was a case of creating the familiar abroad—creating the familiar within the unfamiliar. It was their transfer of familiar experience to China that contributed to the Japanese success. And, as Chao points out the Japanese were also prepared to adapt to Chinese conditions; it was easier for them than for westerners to do so.

What else do we know of the pioneer Japanese business in China? Albert Feuerwerker, using materials published in Peking in 1957, found that of the 136 foreign and Sino-foreign manufacturing and mining firms established in China, 1895–1913, forty-nine of them, or 36 percent of the total, were Japanese. The Japanese were the largest investors in terms of number of firms, followed by the British with thirty-seven firms and 27 percent of the total. In value, however, based on initial capitalization, the British investments represented 48 percent, the Japanese 25 percent. While Remer's 1933 book and Hou's 1965 study give details, we need to know much more about these ventures. They included the manufacture of bean oil in Manchuria (Nisshin founded a mill in Dairen in 1907 with a capital of 3.75 million yen), and the making of flour in Shanghai and Manchuria (Mitsui & Co., for example, had a flour mill in Shanghai).[32]

The Japanese exported matches in large quantities in the early twentieth century. In 1900–1914, the Chinese match market "was entirely in Japanese hands," and the Japanese were also making inroads into India and the Dutch East Indies. According to Remer, Japanese investors had five match manufacturing "plants or firms" in Manchuria and in north, central, and south China in 1914, though the sums invested were not large. The Japanese—with their highly competitive "cottage" match industry at home, using Japanese wood and chemicals imported from Europe—could compete through exports.[33]

The Hanyehping Coal and Iron Company, located just south of Hankow, represented one of the most important Japanese investments in China. From this firm's mines came the bulk of iron ore needed for the Japanese government-owned Yawata iron and steel works in Kyushu. The Japanese investments appear to have been in the form of loans, although by agreements the Japanese were given a "considerable degree of control, which was exercised through the Yokohama Specie Bank." The Japanese-controlled South Manchurian Railway (SMR) took part in developing the Fushin coal mines—the richest ones in Manchuria. In 1907 sales of Fushin coal were a mere 202,320 long tons; by 1913–14, they were 2.5 million long tons, roughly half of which was consumed in Manchuria (mainly meeting the SMR's requirements and those of the Chinese Eastern Railway) and half of which was exported to Japan.[34]

The government-supported Yokohama Specie Bank, founded in 1880, was international from its origin. It developed an extensive network of branches, facilitating trade through its participation in foreign exchange activities, trade financing, and even long-term financing of the raw material procurement needs of Japanese industry, as in its loans to the Hanyehping Coal and Iron Company in China. The Yokohama Specie Bank set up its first representative office in Shanghai in 1893, associated with the growing triangular cotton trade among Japan, India, and China. It did so at the request of Japanese businessmen, who—when India ended free coinage of silver that year—had major difficulties with foreign exchange transactions.[35]

The Industrial Bank of Japan, organized in 1900, and in operation by 1902, was used by the Japanese government to attract foreign capital and to help finance government-sponsored ventures. It provided early loans, for example, to the Tayeh mines that became part of the Hanyehping Company complex, and it raised monies for the South Manchurian Railway and for other investments in China. Hugh Patrick calculated that "of the 294.4 million yen in foreign portfolio capital underwritten by the Industrial Bank [1902–13] 46 percent was exported as semigovernmental direct investment," primarily to China and Korea. By 1902 a private bank, the Yasuda Bank, apparently also had important Chinese interests.[36]

Japanese companies assumed importance in Chinese shipping, as well as in other international shipping routes. Japan's first overseas shipping line was a weekly service from Yokohama to Shanghai, started by Mitsubishi as early as February 1875. Less than nine months later, in October, Mitsubishi acquired four ships from the Pacific Mail Steamship Company, an American firm, which relinquished its Yokohama-Shanghai service to its new Japanese rival.[37]

Mitsui & Co.'s first shipments to China (of coal) were on Mitsubishi ships. In 1880, Mitsui started its own Tokyo Fūhansen Kaisha (sailing ship company) for freight between domestic ports and China and Korea; it also continued to use Mitsubishi vessels. In 1885, Nippon Yūsen Kaisha (NYK) was established, replacing the old Mitsubishi shipping lines. Mitsubishi retained an interest in NYK; the latter became a "national policy company," with a large government interest. NYK, at origin, was in domestic, coastal shipping, but it had three overseas lines to nearby areas: to Shanghai, Vladivostok, and Inch'on. Of the foreign routes, only the Shanghai line was of any significance. Later in the nineteenth century and in the early twentieth century, NYK developed close ties with the Japanese cotton spinners, which added to its cargo in the China trade. Its Chinese shipping activities expanded.[38]

The Osaka Shōsen Kaisha (OSK), organized in 1884, also played a significant role in Chinese shipping. OSK was the first major Japanese shipping company to operate on the Yangtze River. With a subsidy from the Japanese government, it opened a Shanghai-Hankow line in January 1898, penetrating deep into the Chinese interior. NYK soon followed, further augmenting its Chinese routes. In 1906, Nisshin Kisen Kaisha (NKK) was formed for Yangtze river shipping (the dominating influences in NKK were OSK and NYK); by 1911, NKK carried almost 47 percent of the traffic of the main carriers on the Yangtze. By 1913 almost 32 percent—measured by tonnage—of the foreign ships calling at Chinese ports were Japanese.[39] The shipping interests involved branch offices, wharves, and warehouse facilities.

Trading companies, especially Mitsui & Co., developed a sizable business in China. Mitsui & Co. opened it first overseas branch in Shanghai in 1877—just a year after its founding—for the purpose of selling Japanese coal in China. Its principal customers were the British trading companies, Jardine, Matheson & Company and Butterfield & Swire. By 1886 this branch of Mitsui was being used to buy Chinese raw cotton for the Osaka Spinning Mills, which was closely associated with Mitsui, and then to sell Japanese cotton yarn and fabrics in China. As noted above, Mitsui's Shanghai branch manager was responsible for an early Japanese investment in Chinese spinning, and the company also had a flour mill in Shanghai. Indeed, Mitsui & Co. opened branches throughout China, and as an adjunct to its Chinese business had a branch in Hong Kong. By 1910, its Shanghai office had forty-eight employees, its Hong Kong office forty-one.[40] China was without doubt the major locale for pre-1914 Japanese foreign investment.

Japanese business did invest elsewhere in Asia, however. Well before Korea became a Japanese colony in 1910, business involvements had developed.[41] Japanese banking, shipping, and trading companies also established branches in India. Yokohama Specie Bank opened a branch in Bombay in November 1894; Nippon Yūsen Kaisha had begun regular shipping service to India the year before. About the same time, Mitsui & Co. opened a Bombay office for direct purchase of Indian cotton. The Naigaiwata Company and Japan Cotton Trading Company also had agents in Bombay to buy cotton. The Gosho Company sent procurement agents into the Indian interior to deal with cotton farmers and local cotton merchants.[42]

## Japanese Investment in the United States

Though Japanese business interests in Asia outside China were not insignificant, second place (in monetary value) for Japanese foreign investments in 1914 was held by the United States. The sums invested were small relative to those placed in China, but not minuscule or unimportant. By 1914, according to Bank of Japan figures (see Table 1), they constituted a little over 10 percent of Japanese overseas investment.

How can one explain the extent of Japanese investment in the United States in terms of the categories of "familiar" and "unfamiliar"? Clearly, the United States was not familiar. A tentative hypothesis is that Japan found the United States to be an important trading partner. The trade was lopsided, however, with Japan relatively more dependent on it than the United States. The pursuit of trade in this unfamiliar land required a familiar infrastructure. Thus, the Japanese faced the management challenge of recreating in the United States institutions for conducting business that were familiar to them.[43]

As early as 1881, fourteen Japanese trading companies had branches in New York, and thirty-one Japanese employees lived in the city as representatives of these firms.[44] They used the Yokohama Specie Bank for trade financing, foreign exchange transactions, and as a source of general information. The bank was an active member of the Silk Association of America in the early twentieth century. It established its New York office in 1880, the same year that it was incorporated in Japan; its San Francisco "branch" opened in 1899, and a sub-branch was established in Los Angeles in 1913. It also inaugurated a branch in Hawaii in 1899. Other Japanese banks operated in San Francisco and Los Angeles in the early twentieth century, but these may have been banks set up by Japanese emigrants to the United States rather than foreign direct investments.[45]

Japanese shipping companies were well established in the trans-Pacific trade by 1914. As early as 1876, Yatarō Iwasaki had contemplated a trans-Pacific line for the Mitsubishi Company, which did not materialize at that point; but when the Japanese government approved emigration of its citizens to Hawaii in 1884, a new demand for passenger shipping was established. In the next decade (1885–94) Nippon Yūsen Kaisha ships made twenty-four trips, delivering twenty-seven thousand immigrants to Hawaii. In May 1886, NYK entered into a through-freight agreement with the Pacific Mail Steamship Company and the Occidental & Oriental Steamship Company (based on an earlier contract between Mitsubishi and the two shipping firms); NYK covered Shanghai-Yokohama, while the two American firms handled the Yokohama-San Francisco route. This agreement was canceled a decade later, in 1896, when NYK initiated its own American line. It originated with a July 1896 contract between NYK and the Great Northern Railroad; the combined transportation network allowed NYK to quote through-freight rates for trade between Asia and the U.S. Midwest to the American east coast. In 1899, Shanghai was made the departure port for that line, and Seattle became the terminus. In 1898, Tōyō Kisen Kaisha (established in 1896 by Sōichirō Asano) opened a route to San Francisco. In 1909, the Osaka Shōsen Kaisha started a line to Tacoma.[46] Thus by 1914 Japanese shipping was providing regular service to Seattle, San Francisco, and Tacoma. By 1913, 51 percent of the ships entering Japanese ports were Japanese, 52 percent of Japanese exports were carried on Japanese ships, and 47 percent of Japanese imports arrived on Japanese ships; the presence of Japanese shipping lines in the trans-Pacific trade is therefore not surprising. On 15 August 1914, the Panama Canal opened, providing new possibilities for Japanese shipping.[47]

The trading companies, again led by Mitsui & Co., were also active in the United States. Mitsui had opened a branch in New York as early as 1879 and then closed it at the start of the 1880s, when the Japanese government changed its policy of direct export subsidies. Then, in 1895, Kenzo Iwahara of Mitsui & Co. left Tokyo to reopen the New York office. Mitsui & Co., New York, handled imports into the United States of Japanese raw silk and exports of U.S. railroad equipment, machinery, and most important, raw cotton.[48]

Japan's raw cotton requirements were met, in the main, by imports from India, the United States, and China. In 1911, Mitsui & Co. founded the wholly owned Southern Products Company in Houston, Texas, to facilitate its American raw cotton export trade. Mitsui came to handle more than 30 percent of the raw cotton imported into Japan from the United States, and by 1914 was also responsible for 33.6 percent of all Japanese silk imports into the United States, Mitsui & Co. had its own fleet and, in addition, chartered ships from Nippon Yūsen Kaisha.[49]

The number of Japanese trading firms present in the United States in 1914 is uncertain. The fourteen in New York in 1881 did not survive the change in Japanese government policy. A one- to three-person office was easy to close, and when the Japanese government stopped direct subsidies of exports in the early 1880s, many shut down. A sample of the annual reports and directories of the Silk Association of America reveals a changing pattern of Japanese involvement. The 1882 directory, for example, listed Oria Kai (a Japanese weaving association) as "agent" for the Yamato Trading Company, which advertised that its home office was in Tokyo and that it had branches in Yokohama, London, and Vladivostock, as well as a corresponding house in Lyons, France. The same directory included R. Arai as "New York General Representative of the Doshin Silk Company (Doshin Kaisha), Yokohama." Doshin Kaisha, an export company made up of Japanese silk manufacturers, was also reported to have a branch office in Lyons. By the early twentieth century, the Yokohama Silk Trading Company was important in silk imports into the United States.[50]

Nobuo Kawabe found that the Japan Cotton Trading Company had established a subsidiary in Fort Worth in 1910 for the export of raw cotton, and that the Gosho Company had opened an office in San Antonio in 1913. Thus, all three of the major Japanese trading firms participating in the raw cotton trade—Mitsui & Co., Japan Cotton Trading Company, and the Gosho Company—had Texas-based offices before the First World War. A historian of the American chemical industry recorded that Mitsui, Suzuki, Iwai, Miura Shozo, and Kuhara—all Japanese trading firms— brought camphor, menthol, pyrethrum (a flower used in making insect repellant), rhubarb root, and other medicinal and aromatic products into New York from Japan and China. Yamanaka and Company, Osaka, in about 1900 established a New York Fifth Avenue retail showroom, selling antique Chinese paintings, furniture, brocades, and porcelain to wealthy Americans.[51] The more one looks, the more evidence of Japanese business activity in the United States one finds.

At least one Japanese insurance company invested in the United States. Tokio Marine Insurance Company, Ltd. was included in the American publication *Best's Insurance Reports*; its Japanese parent had a worldwide business. In the United States in 1913, Tokio Marine collected $135,000 in net premiums—not much compared with other insurers in America; and its so-called admitted assets were a modest $347,000. Nonetheless, Tokio Marine operated in the United States and formed part of the network of investments associated with Japanese-American trade.[52]

Yosuke Kinugasa has written about Kikkoman's 1892 direct investment in Denver, Colorado, in a factory to make soy sauce for Japanese emigrants—a perfect example of creating the familiar in the unfamiliar (from the standpoint of the plant) and finding the familiar in the unfamiliar (from the standpoint of the market).[53]

A picture emerges from all these activities of an investment infra-structure tailored to Japanese requirements that had arisen in the United States before 1914. Because Japan was a highly homogeneous society, both its citizens and its emigrants had difficulty adapting to conditions outside the country; thus Japanese businessmen before the First World War—and later as well—established abroad their own familiar environment, where Japanese could be spoken and communication breakdowns avoided. Ease of communication resulted in substantial savings of time and energy.[54] In terms of transaction cost economics, the results were lower information, bargaining, and negotiating costs. If the Japanese were to enlarge their trade, they had to create their own international infrastructure to do so.

Thus, it was not solely in Asia that Japanese business expanded. The network of interconnections, not only in China, the rest of Asia, and the United States, but also in London, Hamburg, Paris, and particularly Lyons (the center of the French silk industry), remains a fruitful area for research. The Yokohama Specie Bank had an important London office. In shipping, William Wray found that NYK's European line was more significant than its American one. In 1899, NYK received special annual government subsidies of 2,673,894 yen for its European line, compared to a mere 654,030 yen for its American route. In 1903, NYK had twelve ships on its European line and only six on the American one. By contrast, if number of employees is a guide, Mitsui & Co.'s New York office with twenty-eight employees was more significant than its London one, which had eighteen employees in 1910.[55]

As one studies the early Japanese businesses abroad, several questions—based on other nationalities' experiences—arise: How often were Japanese businesses abroad "transplanted enterprises," that is, set up by Japanese entrepreneurs without any Japanese company as parent? These would not be considered foreign direct investments by students of multinational enterprise. What different types of joint ventures grew up, and what factors influenced the choice? Most important, how was foreign investment joined with trade, and when was a company (as distinct from an arm's-length relationship or a contract) required to organize transactions?

**Capital Importer Versus Exporter**

When American business abroad began, the United States was a net importer of capital; when Japanese multinational enterprise started, the same was true of Japan. This circumstance was extremely relevant to the nature of the investments: it is clearly inappropriate to explain Japanese business abroad before 1914 in terms of capital surpluses: they did not exist. There was also no need for "flight capital"—capital that escapes from insecurity; the Japanese had ample opportunities to invest at home. So, like U.S. investments abroad before the First World War (and for the same reasons), Japanese foreign investments were predominantly business investments (direct investments), those carrying management and control and related specifically to Japanese business growth.[56] The 1914 figures (see Tables 1 and 2) show clearly that there was far more Japanese direct than portfolio investment abroad.

Even though the Japanese were net importers of capital when multi-national enterprise began, one Japanese bank—the Yokohama Specie Bank—appears to have played a far more strategic role in extending Japanese foreign direct investment than any single U.S. bank played in

American foreign enterprise. America's largest banks, its national banks, were not permitted to establish overseas branches until the Federal Reserve System was established in 1914. Some U.S. trust companies had one or two branches abroad, private banks had houses in London and Paris, and America's national banks had foreign correspondents, but no real American counterpart to the Japanese international banking story exists.

The history of the Yokohama Specie Bank was intimately associated with the rise of Japanese worldwide business. Historians of Mitsui & Co. wrote that "the relationship between the company" and that bank became so close that "almost every time Mitsui & Co. opened a new branch overseas a new Yokohama Specie Bank branch opened in the same city." In 1893, Kōkichi Sonoda, president of the Yokohama Specie Bank, joined the board of directors of Japan's largest shipping enterprise, Nippon Yūsen Kaisha.[57] The Yokohama Specie Bank was ubiquitous in Japanese multinational business activities in a manner totally unlike the role of any single American bank. Can it be that Americans could rely on London for trade financing in a manner that the Japanese could not? Anglo-American financial connections were long-standing, and a whole coterie of London Facilities were available to Americans. By contrast, Japan was a new entry into the international trading arena. London as a source for trade financing was probably not as accessible to the Japanese as to Americans. Accordingly, the Japanese may well have had more need to develop their own specialized institution for that purpose, whereas Americans could be more reliant on existing intermediaries.[58] The Yokohama Specie Bank in London and New York also served to pay interest on the Japanese debt. Its presence and reliability made it possible for the Japanese government to raise monies abroad.

The role of other Japanese banks in early international business requires further research. The Industrial Bank of Japan (Nippon Kogyo Ginko) was, as noted, a conduit for foreign investment into Japan. It sold its own debentures abroad to obtain monies for other Japanese domestic and foreign undertakings. Though it was listed in the London *Stock Exchange Official Intelligence, 1914*, it had no London office. The principal and interest on its sterling bonds were "unconditionally guaranteed by the Japanese government"; payments of interest were made at the London office of the Yokohama Specie Bank. The Industrial Bank recycled monies it raised abroad into enterprises outside Japan.[59]

The first Japanese bank to branch abroad had been the Dai Ichi Ginko— the First National Bank in Japan—which opened a branch in Korea in 1878, before the Yokohama Specie Bank was formed, and long before Korea was annexed to Japan. After Formosa (Taiwan) became a Japanese possession in 1895, an Osaka bank opened a branch there and, in 1896, so did the Bank of Japan. Three years later, the Bank of Taiwan came into being; one-fifth of its five million yen capital was subscribed by the

Japanese government; the rest appears to have been Japanese private capital. It issued notes and became the government's fiscal agency. It also functioned as an ordinary commercial bank. According to *Palgrave's Banking Almanac, 1914*, the Bank of Taiwan by that year had branches in San Francisco, Manila, Singapore, Calcutta, Bombay, seven points in China, and about fourteen in Japan and its dependencies.[60]

Meanwhile, in Korea after 1905 the Dai Ichi Ginko served as a note-issuing central bank. It was replaced in this function by the Bank of Korea in 1909, which in turn was transformed into the Bank of Chosen after the Japanese colonization of Korea was completed. Like the Bank of Taiwan, the Bank of Chosen was a note-issuing bank, engaged in financing development, and it was in part Japanese government-owned. In time, it too developed foreign branches, but probably not before 1914.[61]

In short, because Japan was before 1914 a net debtor nation (and there was no reason for flight capital), multinational enterprise investment was a far larger component of total foreign investment than portfolio investment, as in the case of the United States in the pre-First World War years. But while in the United States banks were relatively unimportant vis-à-vis U.S. business abroad, in Japan banks—in particular the government-sponsored Yokohama Specie Bank—engaged in banking abroad and played a major role in aiding the expansion of Japanese international business and intermediating the flow of foreign capital into Japan for use there and for recycling for Japanese use abroad. Before 1914 British banks to a great extent performed these functions for Americans; the Japanese, in large part, provided at least a bridge for their requirements.

**Geographical Position**

Although America was a net importer of capital in the formative years of U.S. multinationals, it was still the key economic power within its region. This was equally true of Japan, for by the end of the first decade of the twentieth century, no Asian nation was as economically advanced as Japan. Like the United States, Japan solved many problems itself because of its geographical isolation. Note, however, how asymmetrical a discussion of the isolation of the two countries must be. America was not isolated in terms of trade financing, but Japan was; America was more isolated than Japan in terms of some technological transfers, because of the special characteristics of the huge U.S. market and the relatively high cost of American labor that required major modifications in imported technology. Japanese industry, for example, apparently could more readily adopt British textile technology than the United States.[62]

British technicians, technology, and machinery played a crucial role in the development of Japan's textile industry, and when the Japanese invested in spinning mills in China, they entered using the same British technology and equipment. Likewise, the looms installed in Chinese mills by the Japanese were made by Platt Brothers in Britain. This technology was also available to Chinese-owned mills. The Japanese, however, came to have the advantage over *both* Chinese and British mills, and the question is, why? Experts on the Japanese spinning companies in China have asserted that the advantages Japanese business had in China—which increased over time—were not related to production technology, but to other factors: management (Japanese *spinners* proved to be better managers of foreign spinning mills than the British *trading* companies); raw cotton procurement techniques (the Japanese developed means of buying raw cotton direct from the growers that resulted in cheaper supplies than the British could procure); and the blending of raw cotton from different locales (that improved input quality and lowered cost). Geographical proximity reduced the costs of management over distance. Alfred Chandler suggests that the Japanese may also have had a marketing advantage, based on their earlier trading company experiences.[63]

## Antitrust Attitudes

In a study of Japanese business abroad, it is more essential than in the American case to look at cooperative efforts. In Japan the whole issue of antitrust was irrelevant. The industrial structure of Japanese foreign investment in these early years appears unified and holistic, with a cooperative effort among the manufacturer, the trading company, and the shipping enterprise. In the more general coterie of trade-related investments, community of interest typified activities among the banks and shipping, insurance, and trading companies in pursuing trade and investment. William Wray has correctly identified the "big four" in Japanese international business before 1914 as the Yokohama Specie Bank, Nippon Yūsen Kaisha, Tokio Marine Insurance, and Mitsui Bussan.[64] The quartet were joined in numerous transactions. The absence of antitrust obstacles gave the Japanese more options in their international expansion. As influential, an antitrust policy reflects an adversarial relationship between government and business, which never developed in Japan. Cooperation existed not only among companies, but also between the government and companies. The Japanese government had sizable investments in two of the largest international businesses—NYK and Yokohama Specie Bank. It also had major stakes in the important South Manchurian Railway. What stands out in Japanese history is not business-government conflict (that occasionally arose), but rather the typically supportive role the Japanese government played for its business enterprises.

**Conclusions**

Some of the more significant pre-1914 Japanese foreign direct investments have now been surveyed. Five basic points—1) size of domestic market; 2) heterogeneity or homogeneity at home; 3) national status as exporter or importer of capital; 4) geographical position in the region; and 5) antitrust attitudes—have been used as a basis of analysis and have served to bring out key characteristics of the pioneer Japanese multinational enterprises. First, because domestic markets were limited and because crucial natural resources to provide for home markets were not available, foreign trade became very important to Japan. American companies learned about business management at home, and then used that knowledge in their expansion abroad. Most Japanese manufacturers were too small to do that effectively. To develop international trade, the Japanese needed an international business infrastructure, with personnel stationed abroad; the service network came to be separately managed from the producing companies in Japan. An exception was in textiles, where Naigaiwata— which had spinning mills at home—developed its own cotton spinning in China.[65] Also, because of raw material shortages, large investments were made in the South Manchurian Railway (for access to raw materials).

Second, because of the homogeneity of the population within Japan, Japanese businessmen had little experience with different customs, languages, or cultural norms. Like American and European companies they went initially to nearby, relatively familiar areas. In order to do business in alien lands—nearby and afar—Japanese businessmen very often replicated familiar infrastructures, providing channels where the Japanese language could be spoken, and where they could deal with men of their own nationality in the foreign land. The process created a core of businessmen with experience in international transactions. Third, because Japan was a net importer of capital and because it had political stability at home, its foreign investments were made overwhelmingly with operating purpose, rather than with purely financial goals. There was no surplus capital. Here it is the similarity with the United States, rather than the difference, that stands out. The difference lies, however, in the role of banks (especially the Yokohama Specie Bank), which was important in Japan's international business and not significant in American business abroad before 1914.

Fourth, just as the United States was the leader in its region, so too Japan was by 1914 far more developed than other countries in Asia. The sizable Japanese investments in nearby China reflect that leadership. Both America and Japan had advantages over other foreign investors in nearby regions. Each fended for itself to assert its own prominence. Fifth, because of an absence of antitrust policy, in creating an international business infrastructure Japanese businesses could cooperate with one another in a manner very dissimilar from that of American enterprises. Moreover, Japanese international business was at crucial times supported by the government to a significant extent, much more so than American international investment. Japanese managers were highly entrepreneurial; nonetheless, a supportive government certainly assisted multinational expansion.

This survey of some of the more important pre-1914 Japanese overseas direct investments makes it evident that Japanese multinational enterprise did not begin in the 1950s, or even in the 1920s or 1930s, as has often been assumed.[66] There were many Japanese foreign direct investments in service activities. Large ones existed in the South Manchurian Railway. Trading, banking, and industrial companies also made some overseas direct investments in manufacturing and mining before the First World War. Japanese gross overseas investments in 1914 (the bulk of which were direct investments) represented between 9.9 and 12.8 percent of the nation's 1914 gross national product.

A number of the special characteristics of contemporary Japanese multinational enterprise had already surfaced before 1914. The first emerging pattern was the important role of textiles in Japanese foreign investment. Even today, Japan has, relative to other home nations involved in international business, a disproportionate amount of its multinational investments in textiles. A second feature was the significant role of service-sector companies, especially the trading company. A 1983 *Annual Report* of Mitsui & Co. described how crucial Japan's general trading companies were, "with their unmatched combination of capabilities in collecting and analyzing information, providing and arranging for finance for trade and projects, and their extensive know-how in organizing major projects."[67] The scale has obviously altered, but clearly the skill that the Japanese now display in raw material procurement is not newly acquired.[68]

A third feature, already apparent before the First World War, was what I have called the layering effect of foreign investments by trading companies and those by manufacturers. In later years, trading companies often acted for Japanese manufacturers abroad, setting up small plants, or they went into joint ventures abroad with Japanese producers and with nationals in the host countries. Then, in time, Japanese manufacturers acted on their own—bypassing the trading company. This pattern too was present between Japanese textile manufacturers and trading companies before 1914.

When one compares the history of Japanese and American business abroad, there were, to be sure, similarities. In each case, conditions in the home country influenced the evolution of international business. In each case it was the new, dynamic industries that led the move into foreign direct investment (textiles in Japan, mass production industries in the United States). In each case, specialists have found that an advantage of the U.S. and Japanese companies abroad lay in managerial abilities. In each case, the U.S. and Japanese foreign direct investors went initially, to a disproportionate extent, to areas either geographically or culturally "nearby." Before the First World War, when in each nation the evolution of modern multinational enterprise began, both the United States and Japan were net debtors in world accounts. Both countries, however, had investments in foreign lands, and each had a far higher proportion of its gross investments abroad in direct than in portfolio stakes. In its own region, by 1914, the United States and Japan each held economic leadership that provided a setting for the expansion of entrepreneurial enterprise abroad. Both the United States and Japan in 1914 had firms that engaged—relative to the domestic economy of each—in substantial foreign direct investments.

These shared attributes notwithstanding, when compared with American business abroad before 1914, Japanese practices show significant differences. Japanese multinational enterprise had a far greater role in providing services—in trade, banking, shipping, and marine insurance. The textile industry was important in early Japanese overseas development, while there were no early American multinational enterprises in this industry. The cooperation of separate Japanese firms in international business operations was commonplace, while similar cooperative behavior among American enterprises was uncharacteristic. And, the Japanese government role seems different from that of the U.S. government; the former was more directly supportive of international business activities.[69]

Although Japanese business overseas expanded far more dramatically during the First World War and in the 1920s than in the period with which this article deals, nonetheless the very early Japanese foreign direct investments are important and require further attention.[70] They set the stage for much of what followed. They need to be studied in the context of the growth of the Japanese firm, using the work that has been done on the history of multinationals as a guide. What has been presented here is merely an initial, exploratory effort, meant to be suggestive rather than conclusive. A model based on the evolution of U.S. multinational enterprise is useful in asking questions about Japanese multinational business, but one must bear in mind that departures from the model are at least as significant as the congruencies.

**Notes**

    † This many-times revised paper had its genesis in a lecture delivered in Japan in the summer of 1984. I am deeply indebted to Professor Tetsuo Abo of the Institute of Social Science, University of Tokyo, and to that university for the invitation to Japan; Professor Abo was immensely helpful in the development of the

ideas presented herein. I have also benefited from comments on earlier versions made by Professors Alfred D. Chandler, Jr., Richard Tedlow, Nobuo Kawabe, Hiroaki Yamazaki, Ken-ichi Yasumuro, Tetsuya Kuwahara, Frank H.H. King, Hafiz Mirza, William D. Wray, Simon Pak, Amitava Dutt, Ali M. Parhizgari, Panos Liossatos, and Maria Willumsen, as well as two anonymous critics. My thanks go to the John Simon Guggenheim Foundation, which provided funding for a year's sabbatical, as well as to the Florida International University Foundation.

1. Mira Wilkins, *The Emergence of Multinational Enterprise: American Business Abroad from the Colonial Era to 1914* (Cambridge, Mass., 1970), and Wilkins, *The Maturing of Multinational Enterprise: American Business Abroad from 1914 to 1970* (Cambridge, Mass., 1974) John M. Stopford, "The Origins of British-Based Multinational Manufacturing Enterprise," *Business History Review* 48 (Autumn 1974): 303–56; Lawrence G. Franko, *The European Multinationals* (Stamford, Conn., 1976); Mira Wilkins, "Modern European Economic History and the Multinationals," *Journal of European Economic History* 6 (Winter 1977): 575–95. Raymond Vernon's Harvard project on foreign multinationals paid special attention to the history of European business abroad. Recently, there has been a proliferation of interest in the history of European multinational enterprise. Much of the newer work has been surveyed in Mira Wilkins, "The History of European Multinationals—A New Look," *Journal of European Economic History*, forthcoming. Alfred D. Chandler, Jr., has in process a major work that will encompass the history of both American and European multinational enterprise.

2. Included among the best works on post-Second World War Japanese multinationals are M.Y. Yoshino, *Japan's Multinational Enterprises* (Cambridge, Mass., 1976); Yoshi Tsurumi, *The Japanese Are Coming* (Cambridge, England, 1976); Kiyoshi Kojima, *Japanese Direct Foreign Investment* (Tokyo, 1978); and Terutomo Ozawa, *Multinationalism, Japanese Style* (Princeton, N.J., 1979). Nobuo Kawabe's work on the history of Japanese multinationals was unique. His Ph.D. dissertation at Ohio State (1980) was on Mitsubishi Shoji Kaisha's pre-Second World War history in the United States; he has published a revision in Japanese.He continues to pursue research on the history of Japanese multinationals. More recently, there have been the innovative articles in *Overseas Business Activities*, ed. Akio Okochi and Tadakatsu Inoue (Tokyo, 1984). See also Mira Wilkins, "American-Japanese Direct Foreign Investment Relationships, 1930–1952," *Business History Review* 56 (Winter 1982): 497–518. Unquestionably, however, the most outstanding contribution in recent years relevant to the history of early Japanese multinational enterprise is William D. Wray, *Mitsubishi and the N.Y.K., 1870–1914: Business Strategy in the Japanese Shipping Industry* (Cambridge, Mass., 1984). At the University of Bradford in England, Hafiz Mirza is preparing a Ph.D. dissertation on pre-Second World War Japanese overseas investments.

3. Most current discussions of multinational enterprise include more than manufacturing. Thus, for example, *The Growth of International Business*, ed. Mark Casson (London, 1983) has a chapter on the growth of transnational banking. The issue of the status of early European trading companies first arose, I believe, at a conference held in Delaware in May 1972 on the evolution of international management structures. Wilkins, *The Emergence of Multinational Enterprise*, 3, begins with a discussion of early trading companies. Some of the first textbooks on multinational enterprise began with brief historical reviews, including materials on these European enterprises. See, for example, Richard D. Robinson, *International Business Policy* (New York, 1964).

4. Ozawa, *Multinationalism*, 31, noted that in 1976, the first five of Japan's top fifty overseas investors were trading companies: Mitsui, Mitsubishi, Marubeni,

C. Itoh, and Sumitomo. I have borrowed the concept of layering from Fernand Braudel, *Afterthoughts on Material Civilization and Capitalism* (Baltimore, 1977). Lest one think in a parochial manner that the Japanese trading company is *sui generis* in the modern world, the reader should consult Philippe Chalmin, *Negoçiants et Chargeurs*, 2d ed. (Paris, 1985).

5. Beginning with Stephen Hymer's 1960 MIT dissertation, published as *The International Operations of National Firms* (Cambridge, Mass., 1976), many economists have studied the theory of multinational enterprise in the context of industrial organization theory and oligopolistic behavior. Since most of the industries in which American multinational enterprises were active seemed characterized by a market structure that involved relatively few large firms, it came to be assumed that this was true of multinational enterprises in general. The very influential "product cycle" theory of multinationals, developed by Raymond Vernon and Louis Wells, in its early renditions began with advantages (principally technological advantages) held by American manufacturing firms. For the current state of multinational enterprise theory, see, for example, Richard Caves, *Multinational Enterprise and Economic Analysis* (New York, 1983) and the charming essay by Charles Kindleberger, "Plus çà change—A Look at the New Literature," in his *Multinational Excursions* (Cambridge, Mass., 1984), 180–88. Even the British scholars, including John Dunning, assumed the applicability of an "American model." I have barely touched on the exciting work that is being done on the theory of multinational enterprise.

6. Raymond Vernon's large-scale study of multinational enterprise began at Harvard in the 1960s with American business abroad; by the 1970s he was asking identical questions of European and Japanese enterprises, and then his students were discussing the same issues in terms of the Third World multinationals.

7. For example, on the history of American international business, see Mira Wilkins and Frank Ernest Hill, *American Business Abroad: Ford on Six Continents* (Detroit, 1964); Wilkins, *Emergence of Multinational Enterprise*; Wilkins, *Maturing of Multinational Enterprise*; Alfred D. Chandler, Jr., *The Visible Hand: The Managerial Revolution in American Business* (Cambridge, Mass., 1977). On European international business, see Stopford's and Franko's work, cited in note 1 above. The influence of the American experience was evident at a conference on "European Multinational Enterprise: Theory and History," held in Florence in 1983; some of the papers given there have been published as *Multinationals: Theory and History*, ed. Peter Hertner and Geoffrey Jones (Aldershot, 1986). See Franko, *European Multinationals*, on variations; other variations have been suggested—for example, that European investors were more prone to joint ventures—but systematic historical analysis of the differences does not exist. Raymond Vernon, *Two Hungry Giants* (Cambridge, Mass., 1983), 12 (the quottation).

8. Kojima, *Japanese Direct Foreign Investment*, and his *Japan and a New World Economic Order* (Tokyo, 1977). From a historical standpoint, I do not see evidence to substantiate Kojima's differentiation; early U.S. multinationals were clearly trade-creating. Nakagawa's statement is in Okochi and Inoue, *Overseas Business Activities*, 62. In a forthcoming article in the *Journal of European Economic History*. I question whether an identical model—without modifications—can be used to study the history of American multinational enterprises and those headquartered in various different Western European countries. That article seeks to delineate some of the differences (other than those based on comparative advantage) in the evolution of American and European multinational enterprise and to clarify what seemed distinctive about the American environment that in a special

manner had shaped U.S. multinational enterprise growth. Wilkins, "History of European Multinationals."

9. Anonymous critic. Almost a decade ago, I gave a paper at a business history conference on asymmetry in foreign direct investment. Wilkins, "Crosscurrents: American Investments in Europe, European Investments in the United States," in Paul Uselding, ed., *Business and Economic History*, 2d ser. 6 (1977): 22–35. Historians there made the same comment; why should one assume symmetry? But the literature on multinational enterprise, beginning with Hymer, *International Operations of National Firms*, has assumed just that; the theory of the oligopolistic behavior of multinationals assumes that, irrespective of home countries, firms in particular industries will be prone to make foreign investments.

10. I was surprised at the extent of Japanese business abroad before 1914 when I started to write this, but became less surprised as I delved deeper. Students of Japanese business history will be less surprised than students of the history of multinational enterprise.

11. Wilkins, "History of European Multinationals." I could have chosen to discuss in isolation the role of government (more in the Japanese case than in the American) or the role of educational systems (important in both countries). To add these separate categories seemed unnecessary, since they would not alter the basic analysis that follows. Professor Frank H.H. King (historian of the HongKong and Shanghai Banking Corporation), on reading the penultimate draft of this article, presented the stimulating notion that specific Japanese government-inspired national goals should be considered with "special reference to the replication of foreign-type institutions as an end in itself." (Letter to the author, 4 Oct. 1985) To incorporate (or to refute) this contention would involve a major revision of this paper. Ultimately, I believe that the Japanese (through imitation and innovation) developed appropriate institutions and that the development of multinationals per se was not in its essence a government-inspired replication of foreign behavior, albeit in some instances—for example, the Yokohama Specie Bank compared with the Hong-Kong and Shanghai Banking Corporation—this may have been a relevant consideration.

12. League of Nations, *Industrialization and Foreign Trade* (Geneva, 1945), 13; W.W. Lockwood, *The Economic Development of Japan* (Princeton, N.J., 1954), 89 (1905–9 Japanese figures). U.S. figures (1905–9 average) from U.S. Bureau of the Census, *Historical Statistics of the United States* (Washington, D.C., 1960), 7.

13. In studying the history of Japanese business, I have found extremely useful Johannes Hirschmeier and Tsunehiko Yui, *The Development of Japanese Business 1600–1973* (Cambridge, Mass., 1975).

14. As Angus Maddison, *Economic Growth in Japan and the USSR* (New York, 1969), 28, points out, as late as 1887, nine-tenths of Japan's external trade was handled by foreigners—mainly British houses. Yet, the Japanese replaced them and as trade expanded, Japanese firms handled the bulok of it. Wray, *Mitsubishi and N.Y.K.*, 20, suggests that foreign shipping companies in the early 1870s were a threat to Japan's economic security because they exacerbated Japan's balance of payments difficulties by carrying all its foreign trade; but this was true of many countries that failed to make the transition from foreign to domestic control.

15. The British problems with management over distance will be discussed in my forthcoming history of foreign investment in the United States. Large British trading companies of the late nineteenth and early twentieth century included firms such as Jardine, Matheson & Company, Butterfield & Swire, and Balfour, Williamson. Some American companies of this sort, such as the American Trading Company, existed in this era, but they seemed dwarfed by their British counterparts.

16. Wilkins, "History of European Multinationals"; Wilkins, *The Emergence of Multinational Enterprise.*

17. See Harold Moulton, *Japan* (Washington, D.C., 1931), 391–92; on my Japanese trip in July 1984, I tried to obtain the originals of the Moulton figures. Professor Hiroaki Yamazaki of the Institute of Social Science, University of Tokyo, discovered that the Bank of Japan had prepared these figures at Moulton's special request and hand-delivered them to him in the United States. The figures in Ken-ichi Yasumuro, "The Contribution of Sogo Shosha to the Multinationalization of Japanese Industrial Enterprises in Historical Perspective," in Okochi and Inoue, *Overseas Business Activities,* 84, should be compared with C. F. Remer, *Foreign Investments in China* (New York, 1933), 446 (a different rate of exchange altered these numbers slightly), and Moulton, *Japan,* 391.

18. I used the gross national product figure in current prices (4,665 million yen) as given in Kazushi Ohkawa and Henry Rosovsky, *Japanese Economic Growth* (Stanford, 1973), 278. At the rate of exchange used in the tables, that equals about $2.3 billion. By way of comparison, U.S. investment abroad (direct *and* portfolio investment) in 1914 was 3.5 billion; as a percentage of the American GNP of $36.4 billion in 1914, it equaled 9.6 percent. Based on data in Wilkins, *Emergence of Multinational Enterprise,* 201. Thus, in 1914, even using the lowest Japanese figure, the Japanese foreign investment was relatively larger than that of the United States. Japanese GNP was smaller in 1914 than in 1913. In 1913 it was 5,212 million yen (or about $2.57 billion). Ibid. When I calculated the Japanese foreign investment estimates as a percentage of the higher 1913 GNP, the figures still came out surprisingly big: 8.8 to 11.5 percent of the GNP.

19. Remer, *Foreign Investments in China,* and Chi-ming Hou, *Foreign Investment and Economic Development in China 1840–1937* (Cambridge, Mass., 1965) are the basic works on foreign investment in China. See also Tien-yi Yang, "Foreign Business Activities and the Chinese Response, 1842–1937," in Okochi and Inoue, *Overseas Business Activities,* 215–25. On Japanese investments in China everyone has to start with Remer, *Foreign Investments in China,* 414–46, 474–92, and passim. Hou, *Foreign Investment,* 19, calculated that 36 percent of the total Japanese direct investment in China in 1914 was in transportation, chiefly in the South Manchurian Railway. Remer did not differentiate between investments made by Japanese firms headquartered in Japan and by Japanese residents in China; a student of multinational enterprise would do so.

20. Kang Chao, *The Development of Cotton Textile Production in China* (Cambridge, Mass., 1977), 115–16, notes that the second British-owned mill was called Laou Kung Mow Cotton Spinning Company; the American one was that of the International Cotton Manufacturing Company; and the German-owned one was built by Soy Chee Spinning Company. See an interesting article on the cotton-spinning industry in Shanghai, in *The Times* (London), 11 Feb. 1896.

21. Tetsuya Kuwahara, "The Business Strategy of Japanese Cotton Spinners: Overseas Operations 1890 to 1931," in Akio Okochi and Shin-ichi Yonekawa, *The Textile Industry and its Business Climate* (Tokyo, 1982), 140; interestingly, S.D. Chapman, "British-Based Investment Groups before 1914," *Economic History Review,* 2d ser. 38 (May 1985): 234, writes that Jardine, Matheson had built its cotton spinning mill in Shanghai "to meet incipient Japanese competition." The article in the London *Times,* 11 Feb. 1896, evaluates the Japanese entry plans and suggests an added reason why a Japanese firm in China might *not* succeed: inland taxes on raw cotton.

22. Yasumuro, "The Contribution," 67, and Albert Feuerwerker, *China's Early Industrialization* (Cambridge, Mass., 1958), 224, Chao, *Development of Cotton*

*Textile Production*, 116, appears to mix up Mitsui and Mitsubishi. Data from Professor Kuwahara, 16 Jan. 1986, and from Professor Yasumuro, Osaka, 24 July 1984; Chao, *Development of Cotton Textile Production*, 138, shows Shanghai Cotton's profitable performance.

23. Kuwahara, "The Business Strategy," 140; the Japan Cotton Trading Company had established its first branch in China in Shanghai in 1903; Mitsui & Co., *The 100 Year History of Mitsui & Co., Ltd. 1876–1976* (Tokyo, 1977), 64, Yasumuro, "The Contribution," 68; Tetsuya Kuwahara, "The Formation of Oligopolistic Structures of the Cotton Spinning Industry in Japan and the Growth Strategies of the Latecomers: Case of Naigaiwata Company," *Japan Business History Review* 18 (Jan. 1984): iii–iv; Kuwahara, "The Business Strategy," 158; and data from Professors Yasumuro and Kuwahara, Osaka, 24 July 1984, on the Naigaiwata Company.

24. Mitsui & Co., of course, had close connections with the Osaka Spinning Mills. Takashi Masuda of Mitsui & Co. in 1879 had prompted the plans for this modern establishment; Masuda became a chief shareholder of the Osaka Spinning Mills; and Mitsui & Co. had the responsibility for importing spinning machines. See Mitsui & Co., *100 Year History*, 44–47. Mitsui & Co.'s relations with other spinners appear to have related to raw cotton sales. Nonetheless, Mitsui & Co. connot be called "a spinning company" in the same manner as the Naigaiwata Company. For the ten largest cotton spinners in Japan in 1913 see S. Yonekawa, "The Growth of Cotton Spinning Firms," in Okochi and Yonekawa, *The Textile Industry*, 8. The Naigaiwata Company is not included. I am indebted to Professor Yamazaki (22 July 1984) for finding the Naigaiwata ranking for me. Ranked by total assets, only three other Japanese cotton spinners were larger. None of the latter, in 1914, had investments in Chinese spinning.

25. Kuwahara, "The Business Strategy," 158, 165; M. Miyamoto, "Comments," in Okochi and Inoue, *Overseas Business Activities*, 172; Yamazaki in Conversation with the author, Tokyo, 19 July 1984.

26. Stephen C. Thomas, *Foreign Intervention and China's Industrial Development, 1870–1911* (Boulder, Colo., 1984), 150–51.

27. Mitsui & Co., *100 Year History*, 47. China had been an importer of raw cotton, but from roughly 1888 to the time of the First World War it was a net exporter of raw cotton; coincidentally, it was an importer of cotton yarn and cotton cloth. Bruce L. Reynolds, "The East Asian 'Textile Cluster' Trade, 1868–1973: A Comparative Advantage Interpretation," in *America's China Trade in Historical Perspective*, ed. Ernest R. May and John K. Fairbank (Cambridge, Mass., 1986), 137. The Japanese trade in cotton manufactures came to be very important. In 1913 exports of cotton manufactured goods and yarn totaled 33.9 percent of Japanese exports to China and 11.7 percent of total Japanese exports. Remer, *Foreign Investments in China*, 462.

28. Thomas, *Foreign Intervention*, 151.

29. Chao, *Development of Cotton Textile Production*, 140; Chao, p. 157, presents production cost data for Chinese and Japanese mills in China for 1935. Japanese management had obtained remarkably lower costs than the Chinese. Regrettably, similar comparative data are not available for 1913–14, but see Kuwahara, "The Business Strategy," 165, which indicates that in 1913 Naigaiwata's Shanghai Mills produced 1.24–1.32 pounds of 16–count yarn per spindle each 24–hour day, while the Chinese mills produced 0.87–1.00 pound.

30. Hou, *Foreign Investment*, 88; Chao, *Development of Cotton Textile Production*, 117, 301, 305. Hou's breakdowns are by spindles and looms rather than by company. Chao (p. 301) shows the rapid rise of Japanese-owned spindles, 1902–

13. He notes that the looms were "power looms" (p. 305), but not whether they were of Western or Japanese design. Ibid. ("Western" includes British, German, and American). Kuwahara—using Minejiro Yoshida, *Zaishi Hojin Boseki no Shōrai ni tsuite* (1927) as a source—has established that the 886 Japanese-owned looms in Shanghai Cotton Manufacturing Company's mill no. 1 and mill no. 2 were of British manufacture—by Platt Bros.

31. All the sources stress that these early Japanese investments in manufacturing were small compared with what followed. For the first time, in 1919 Japanese-owned cotton spindles in China exceeded those in *all* Western-owned mills. By 1936, roughly 44 percent of the cotton spindles in China were in Japanese-owned mills. See Chao, *Development of Cotton Textile Production*, 125–29, 301–2. On looms, ibid., 125–29, 305–7. Remer, *Foreign Investments in China*, 497, gives slightly different figures for 1909–31 but documents the same formidable expansion in Japanese involvement in spinning. See also Kuwahara, "The Business Strategy," 141–60. Profit figures provided in Chao, *Development of Cotton Textile Production*, 138, seem to show larger profits for Shanghai Cotton than for Naigaiwata, but none of the years monitored coincide and the 1908 results for Naigaiwata were *before* its mill was built.

32. Albert Feuerwerker, "The Chinese Economy, ca. 1870–1911," Papers in Chinese Studies (Ann Arbor, Mich., 1969), 34. These figures should be compared with data in Remer, *Foreign Investments in China*, 431. Remer identified 63 "Japanese" manufacturing "plants or firms" in China in 1914, all of which appear to have been inaugurated after 1900; see ibid., 419. It is not clear how Feuerwerker defined "foreign." Does he include resident Japanese investors in China? As noted, Remer did. Economists would predict that British enterprises in China would employ relatively more capital than the Japanese ones; after all, Britain was in these years a capital-rich economy, relative to Japan. Remer, *Foreign Investments in China*, 431, is a good starting point for further study, even though he did not differentiate nonresident and resident foreign investment. See Hou, *Foreign Investment*, 11, for a good discussion of Remer's methodology; ibid., 89, 246, and Remer, *Foreign Investments in China*, 500, on the flour mills. Remer wrote that the oldest flour mill in China was probably the Mitsui mill at Shanghai. He does not give a date of origin, but obviously it preceded the Japanese-owned South Manchuria Milling Company at Tiehlin in Manchuria, which was founded in 1906; ibid.

33. Håkan Lindgren, *Corporate Growth: The Swedish Match Industry in Its Global Setting* (Stockholm, 1979), 53–54 and Hans Modig, *Swedish Match Interests in British India during the Interwar Years* (Stockholm, 1979), 41–45. Remer, *Foreign Investments in China*, 431. Since Remer did not differentiate between nonresident and resident foreign investments, these may have been small plants run by Japanese businessmen who lived in China. It was not all "cottage" industry in Japan. Modig, *Swedish Match Interests*, 41–42, cites an "eye-witness" report of 1910 on the Japanese match industry, which indicated that the Japanese had to a large degree adopted the German system of match making; the Japanese built machinery

> which imitate the German but with some small alterations, in order that the patent law is not infringed. The appearance of the machines and the manu-factures does not completely come up to the German standard but they only cost from a third to a quarter as much as the German machines. As far as possible wood is used in the Japanese machines instead of iron.... A Japanese factory works as far as possible without expensive and continuous machines but uses instead homemade machines often constructed by the factory manager.

Japanese matches before the First World War were "a good third cheaper wholesale than the Swedish"; ibid., 43. One wonders whether Mitsui had match factories in China. Mitsui Bussan made volume purchases from domestic producers and well before 1914 had established a trademarked Japanese match export business. Wray, *Mitsubishi and the N.Y.K.*, 450. In the mid-1920s Mitsui Bussan controlled the greater part of Japanese match exports. Lindgren, *Corporate Growth*, 338. By 1922, in response to Indian tariffs, unspecified "Japanese interests" in partnership with Indian wholesalers had started to manufacture matches in India; the splints and boxes were imported. See Modig, *Swedish Match Interests*, 76, 66. On the expansion of Japanese-owned match factories in the Bombay area in 1923, see ibid., 79.

34. Wray, *Mitsubishi and the N.Y.K., 395; Remer, Foreign Investments in China*, 104, 507–8. Particularly useful on Japanese interests in the Hanyehping Company is William D. Wray, "Japan's Big Three in China: International Business and Changing Industrial Structure," unpub. paper (Feb. 1986), 23–26. See Kungtu C. Sun, *The Economic Development of Manchuria* (Cambridge, Mass., 1969), 65, on the Fushun coal mines.

35. Yang, "Foreign Business," 222–23. Hirschmeier and Yui, *Development of Japanese Business*, 183, call the Yokohama Specie Bank a "special bank established under government auspices." G.C. Allen, *A Short Economic History of Modern Japan* (London, 1962), 53, describes the Yokohama Specie Bank's operations as "from the beginning closely supervised by the government. The state provided one-third of its initial capital and the appointment of its President and Vice-President required the authorization of the Ministry of Finance. The Yokohama Specie Bank was entrusted with funds from the Treasury Reserve Fund to enable it to deal in foreign bills of exchange...." As of June 1913, the "Imperial Household" owned 121,000 shares of the 480,000 shares issued. *Stock Exchange Official Intelligence, 1914* (London), 419. Hugh Patrick, "Japan 1868–1914," in *Banking in the Early Stages of Industrialization*, ed. Rondo Cameron (New York, 1967), 267–68, writes that while the Yokohama Specie Bank was at the start of private origin, within a decade it became in effect a government bank. "The government initially provided one-third of the capital and up to three-quarters of the deposits. The bank suffered major losses in its early operations, and in the process of repeatedly bailing it out the government assumed complete control." He writes that in the late 1880s the Ministry of Finance arranged that the Bank of Japan would "not engage in foreign exchange business, would provide cheap deposits to the Yokohama Specie Bank, and would rediscount its foreign exchange bills at preferentially low interest rates." Thus, the specialized bank not only came to dominate foreign trade financing, but could subsidize export industries by making them low interest-rate loans. See also Phra Sarasas, *Money and Banking in Japan* (London, 1940), 158–61. There are several histories of the Yokohama Specie Bank in Japanese: one was published by the bank, in Tokyo, in 1920; another is a recent multivolume work by Shinji Arai, *History of the Yokohama Specie Bank* (this is partly a documentary collection, mixed with historical summaries; Shinji Arai was the project editor; Japanese scholars cite it as *YSG zenshi*). Very useful is Japan, Ministry of Finance, *Business Report of Banking and Trust Business* (Tokyo, 1916). The Bank's *Annual Reports* are located at the University of Tokyo. I am indebted to Professor Yamazaki for his gracious and splendid help with the Japanese-language literature. His insights were invaluable. On YSB's first branch office in Shanghai, see Wray, "Japan's Big Three in China," 17, and Wray to Wilkins, 25 June 1986.

36. Sarasas, *Money and Banking in Japan*, 258; Wray, *Mitsubishi and the N.Y.K.*, 395 (loans to the Tayeh mines); Patrick, "Japan," 271; Allen, *Short*

*Economic History*, 54, writes that the Industrial Bank of Japan raised monies in London, guaranteeing and selling several issues of South Manchurian Railway sterling debentures between 1907 and 1911. The South Manchurian Railway Company, Ltd., registered in Tokyo, 7 Dec. 1906, was listed in the *Stock Exchange Official Intelligence, 1914* (London), 379, but with no mention of the Industrial Bank of Japan. Employees of the Yokohama Specie Bank, Ltd., 7 Bishopsgate, London, were "The London Agents for the Sterling Bonds" of this railway. Principal and interest on the sterling bonds were guaranteed by the Japanese government and payable at the Yokohama Specie Bank office in London. I think Allen is wrong, and that the Industrial Bank raised money on its *own* debentures in London and then (as Hugh Patrick suggests) channeled it through Japan to the South Manchurian Railway and other ventures. According to Sarasas, the Industrial Bank's first overseas investments were in 1906 in public utilities and loans to private enterprises in Korea. *Money and Banking in Japan*, 258. Sarasas seems to have neglected the earlier loan to the Tayeh mines in China in 1903 that preceded the Korean loans. Wray, *Mitsubishi and the N.Y.K.*, 349 (on the Yasuda Bank).

37. Ibid., 60, 85–86.

38. Ibid., 2, 61, 133–36, 219ff., 342, 355–56. At first Mitsubishi was the largest single stockholder in NYK, but by the mid–1890s, the Imperial Household was in first place; ibid., 239, 258. By the early 1880s, the connections between Yokohama and Shanghai had become very easy with almost daily steamers plying the route. See J. Whitie, London, to E.M. Sang, Brussels, 6 March 1883, acq. 2, box 7, Singer Manuscripts, State Historical Society of Wisconsin.

39. Wray, *Mitsubishi and the N.Y.K.*, 186, 342, 346, 348ff., 388–89, 391; Hou, *Foreign Investment*, 61. The British, with 52 percent, were in first place among the shipping companies calling at Chinese ports.

40. Mitsui & Co., Ltd., *100 Year History*, 27, 31, 44–46. For its early activity importing raw cotton into Japan, see Kazuo Sugiyama. "Trade Credit and the Development of the Cotton Spinning Industry," in *Marketing and Finance in the Course of Development* (Proceedings of the Third Fuji Conference), ed. Keiichiro Nakagawa (Tokyo, 1978), 69, Mitsui & Co., *100 Year History*, 63; data on employment from unpublished material in the Japanese Business History Institute, Tokyo.

41. Note that neither Table 1 nor 2 includes Korea, undoubtedly because Korea was annexed to Japan in 1910 and thus in 1914 was a Japanese colony. Before 1910, Korea had attracted sizable Japanese investments in banking, trade, and shipping facilities, as well as in railroads and certain agricultural ventures; investments grew after colonization. The Japanese interests were not nearly as large as those in China, but their precise extent is not clear. See the extremely useful article by Peter Duus, "Economic Dimensions of Meiji Imperialism: The Case of Korea, 1895–1910," in *The Japanese Colonial Empire 1895–1945*, ed. Raymond H. Myers and Mark R. Peatti (Princeton, N.J., 1984), 128–63.

42. Data on India are also missing in Tables 1 and 2. Wray, *Mitsubishi and the N.Y.K.*, 229, 289, 293–302, and 400–408 (on the Bombay and Calcutta lines of NYK, 1896–1914). Mitsui & Co. began importing Indian raw cotton into Japan in 1892–93, buying it from Ralli Brothers, a British trading house. Soon, Mitsui & Co. bypassed Ralli Brothers and purchased cotton directly at the cotton exchange in Bombay. By 1897, the Bombay office of Mitsui & Co. was purchasing all its cotton directly, independently of the Bombay cotton exchange. Mitsui & Co., *100 Year History*, 48. On Ralli Brothers, see Chalmin, *Negoçiants et Chargeurs*, 25–26; Ralli Brothers had established itself in Calcutta in 1850 and then in Bombay. On Naigaiwata, see Mitsui & Co., *100 Year History*, 48–49; on Gosho, Chao,

*Development of Cotton Textile Production*, 99, though this information may refer to a period after 1914 (Chao is not explicit).

43. In 1913, the share of Japan's trade with China (22.9 percent) roughly equaled its share with the United States (22.5 percent). In subsequent years, the United States became far more important than China in Japan's foreign trade. Remer, *Foreign Investments in China*, 460.

44. Mitsui & Co., *100 Year History*, 27.

45. Silk Association of America, *Annual Reports*; Shinji Arai, *History of the Yokohama Specie Bank* (Tokyo, 1981), 2: 36, 38 (in Japnese; I am indebted to William Johnston for the translation), and U.S. Alien Property Custodian, *Annual Report 1943–1944*, 87–88. Actually, as early as 1880, the Japanese Finance Ministry gave permission to the Yokohama Specie Bank to set up "branches, agencies or representative offices in London, Paris, New York, San Francisco, and Shanghai." Arai, *History of the Yokohama Specie Bank*, 2: 38. As noted, the bank did not open a Shanghai office until 1893. But a small representative office (or "agency") appears to have opened in San Francisco in 1886, supplementing the one opened in New York in 1880. See Yokohama Specie Bank, *The History of the Yokohama Specie Bank* (Tokyo, 1920), in Japanese (Professor Yamazaki referred me to the 1886 date in this reference). Arai, *History of the Yokohama Specie Bank*, 2: 91, notes that in 1899, according to a decision of the bank's directors, the offices in Tokyo, Nagasaki, Lyons, San Francisco, Hawaii, Bombay, Hong Kong, Shanghai, and Tientsin were made branches, but because of U.S. law (actually because of New York state law), the New York "agency" remained as it was, as an agency. See Ira Cross, *Financing an Empire: History of Banking in California* (Chicago, 1927), 2: 641, on the San Francisco branch of the Yokohama Specie Bank from 1899 onward; ibid., 3: 517, on the branch in Los Angeles. The Yokohama Specie Bank appears to have had some kind of representation in Hawaii in 1892 (before U.S. annexation). See Japan, Ministry of Finance, *Business Report*, 66. On the Hawaiian "branch," Arai, *History of the Yokohama Specie Bank*, 2: 91. Undoubtedly, the latter was a facility to cope with the needs of Japanese emigrants to Hawaii. See Wilkins, *History of Foreign Investment in the United States*, forthcoming. Cross, *Financing an Empire*, is very good on the "Japanese" banks in California, but says nothing on the place of the owners' residence.

46. Wray, *Mitsubishi and the N.Y.K.*, 91 (initial plans), 264 (Hawaii); 264–66, 277, 344, 400, 408–9, 421.

47. U.S. House of Representatives, Committee on Merchant Marine and Fisheries, *Steamship Agreements and Affiliations in the American Foreign and Domestic Trade*, 63d Cong. (1914), 131; Allen, *Short Economic History*, 92; before the opening, NYK was already making plans to take advantage of the canal; Wray, *Mitsubishi and the N.Y.K.*, 400, 409.

48. Mitsui & Co., *100 Year History*, 32, 34, 69; *Report of Business Conditions of Mitsui Bussan*, Nov. 1913–April 1914, in Mitsui & Co., Ltd., Archives, Tokyo. Professor Yamazaki was most helpful with the translation of this Japanese-language report.

49. *Report of Business Conditions*. Prior to 1911, Chinese raw cotton imports into Japan had exceeded American raw cotton imports. After 1912, U.S. raw cotton imports grew rapidly. In first place, throughout, were imports into Japan of Indian raw cotton. See *A Yearbook of the Cotton Industry of the World and Japan* (1935), pt. 2, p. 7 (in Japanese). My thanks go to Professor Yamazaki for this reference. As noted earlier in this paper, the Japanese trading companies were buying cotton directly in India; Mitsui & Co., *100 Year History*, 50, and Kazuo Yamaguchi, et al., "100 Year History of Mitsui & Co.," unpub. MS (1978), 1: 357 (in Japanese);

Mitsui & Co., *100 Year History*, 50, 71–72; 77–78.

50. Details are in Wilkins, *History of Foreign Investment in the United States*, forthcoming. I am grateful to Professor Kawabe for the identification of "Oria Kai." On the Yokohama Silk Trading Company, Mitsui & Co., *100 Year History*, 70. "R. Arai" was Rioichiro Arai, the grandfather of Haru Matsukata Reischauer. He came to the United States in 1876 and at once began to handle Japanese silk imports into America. Haru Reischauer's new book documents this Japanese immigrant's experiences—as representative of Japanese silk exporters. *Samurai and Silk* (Cambridge, Mass., 1986), 190–257, 223 (Doshin Kaisha).

51. Nobuo Kawabe, "Japanese Business in the United States before World War II: the Case of Mitsubishi Shoji Kaisha, the San Francisco and Seattle Branches," (Ph.D. diss., Ohio State University, 1980), 18. In addition, Rioichiro Arai in 1903 established a separate cotton department in his silk trading company. Reischauer, *Samurai and Silk*, 237. Williams Haynes, *American Chemical Industry* (New York, 1954), 2: 274 Wilkins, "American-Japanese Direct Foreign Investment," 510.

52. *Best's Insurance Report, 1914*, 360, which describes the firm as operating all over the world. Professor Tsunehiko Yui has been very helpful in discussing with me the international character of this particular Japanese insurance firm.

53. Yosuke Kinugasa, "Japanese Firms' Foreign Direct Investment in the United States—the Case of Matsushita and Others," in Okochi and Inoue, *Overseas Business Activities*, 57. W. Mark Fruin, *Kikkoman: Company, Clan, and Community* (Cambridge, Mass., 1983), regrettably does not mention this early foreign direct investment.

54. As Ozawa, *Multinationalism*, 83, points out, the Japanese "in general are notoriously poor linguists."

55. I can document the pre-1914 presence of Japanese business in all these places and other cities as well; Wray, *Mitsubishi and the N.Y.K.*, 14–15, 306, 414 (on NYK). NYK also had an Australian line, which had three ships in 1903; ibid., 414; data on Mitsui employment from Japanese Business History Institute, Tokyo. In 1908, Japanese immigrants began arriving in Brazil as wage workers. In time, a thriving Japanese community developed and Japanese multinational enterprise invested. Ozawa, *Multinationalism*, 127; I have found no evidence, however, of multinational enterprise involvements before 1914.

56. For U.S. figures, see Wilkins, *Emergence of Multinational Enterprise*, 201.

57. Mitsui & Co., *100 Year History*, 55; Wray, *Mitsubishi and the N.Y.K.*, 270.

58. The Japanese did use British and Continental banks. See the fascinating table in *Report of Business Conditions of Mitsui Bussan*, Nov. 1913–April 1914, on the lines of credit from foreign (principally British) financial houses. Clearly, however, the Japanese could not expect the same kind of regular steady financing from Britain as Americans could; the difference in degree is crucial. There was also the "Mitsui Bank," founded in 1876, but in these years Mitsui & Co. appears to have used it at home and the specialized Yokohama Specie Bank for its international business transactions.

59. Allen, *Short Economic History*. 54; Patrick, "Japan," 271; *Stock Exchange Official Intelligence, 1914*, 404.

60. Sarasas, *Money and Banking in Japan*, 271, and Duus, "Economic Dimensions," 154–55. Also on the Dai Ichi Ginko, see Patrick, "Japan," which says nothing about its role in Korea. On Taiwan banking, see Sarasas, *Money and Banking in Japan*, 269–371 and *Palgrave's* as cited in U.S. Federal Trade Commission, *Report on Cooperation in American Export Trade* (Washington, D.C., 1916), 1: 64.

61. The Bank of Korea had an original paid up capital of ten million yen, of

which three million came from the Japanese government. By 1940 the Bank of Chosen had branches in Korea, Japan, China (especially in Manchuria), and a "branch" in New York, Sarasas, *Money and Banking in Japan*, 271, 274–76. See also Allen, *Short Economic History*, 55.

62. I am arguing here that Americans *altered* British textile technology to meet U.S. conditions, while the Japanese appear to have adopted the technology—at least in spinning—in a more exact manner. On this see Gary Saxonhouse, "A Tale of Japanese Technological Diffusion in the Meiji Period," *Journal of Economic History* 34 (March 1974): 150–55. In weaving, the Toyoda Automatic Loom was an important Japanese innovation. Mitsui & Co., *100 Year History*, 74–77. Yet, it was not until after our period that it was widely adopted in Japan and in Japanese mills abroad. Data from Professor Kuwahara, 16 Jan. 1986.

63. These conclusions have been developed out of lengthy discussions I had in Japan in July 1984 with Professors Yamazaki, Yasumuro, and Kuwahara. As noted in my introduction, students of multinational enterprise emphasize that for a company to succeed abroad it must have some kind of advantage. Substantial attention had been paid specifically to "technological advantages." Thus, in attempting to explain the Japanese success in China, my first search was for a technological advantage. Obviously, I found none, since Chinese firms as well as Japanese ones could adopt the British technology. Then I asked, why did the Japanese do better than the British with the same British technology? I found Japanese advantages, but not in production technology. These advantages contributed to Japan's economic superiority in the region.

64. Wray, *Mitsubishi and the N.Y.K.*, passim, makes it very clear how tied shipping was to the textile industry. In this context. Wray writes, "If we take, for example, the 1893 Bombay line alliance of the cotton spinners, the Japanese government, the Yokohama Specie Bank, Tata's Indian raw cotton-exporting firm, Japanese importers like Mitsui Bussan, and N.Y.K., it is hard to imagine this organized entrepreneurial system working for several decades with a foreign shipping company in place of N.Y.K." Ibid., 453. The only alien element in this cooperative scheme was the Tata group, which eventually withdrew from the coalition; ibid., 509. Mitsui Bussan and Mitsui & Co. were the same firm. Ibid., 6 (on the big four).

65. Kikkoman's soy sauce plant in Denver was another exception.

66. Most authors on Japanese multinational enterprise have assumed that the phenomenon is new. Kojima, *Japanese Direct Foreign Investment*, 7, for example, writes that "the activities of multinational corporations are *new* dynamic elements in the international economy" (my italics); Ozawa, *Multinationalism*, 3, notes that before the Second World War, Japanese companies set up production facilities abroad, but only in Japanese colonies—Manchukuo, Korea, and Formosa. Tsurumi, *The Japanese Are Coming*, 2, gives a chronology of Japanese foreign direct investments with the first one in the 1920s. He lists nothing during or before the First World War, and only four manufacturing subsidiaries worldwide before the Second World War. He looked at manufacturing subsidiaries of trading as well as manufacturing companies. Until very recently historians of Japan have neglected the history of Japanese multinational enterprise. When they have dealt with corporate histories, they have not taken into account the extensive literature on multinational enterprise. Wray, *Mitsubishi and the N.Y.K.*, who does look at business managers' international strategies, found a dearth of comparable studies (see his comments on Japanese business historiography on p. 11). A partial exception is the research on Mitsui & Co.

67. In 1975, 22.2 percent of Japanese worldwide investments were in textiles—

the largest single sector for its foreign direct investment. Ozawa, *Multinationalism*, 29. More recent figures show a lesser role for textiles, but still one of importance. United Nations Centre on Transnational Corporations, *Transnational Corporations in World Development, Third Survey* (New York, 1983), 296. In its *Annual Report 1983*, 13, Mitsui & Co. pointed out that it had the highest level of overseas investment of any Japanese company. "In recent years, Mitsui & Co. has had more than U.S. $1 billion investments and loans committed to more than 280 ventures, located in diverse parts of the globe." Together, these ventures and Mitsui & Co. itself employed 129,900 persons; ibid., 16.

68. Ozawa, *Multinationalism*, 166, recounts how the Japanese responded to the aftermath of the 1973–74 oil crisis, by buying oil directly from nationalized companies and saving costs in the process. The student of Japanese direct raw cotton purchasing techniques has a sense of *déjà vu*.

69. The U.S.-owned textile mill in China, noted earlier in this paper, was *not* owned by an American textile manufacturer. While clearly there was more Japanese government ownership participation in its nationals' pre-1914 international business—in shipping and banking—than in the U.S. case (U.S. government ownership of pre-1914 multinational enterprises was nonexistent), I do not see how this served to change—or to determine—Japanese entrepreneurial strategy in a significant manner. My finding in this regard seems to coincide with that of other researchers, including Kozo Yamamura, *A Study of Samurai Income and Entrepreneurship* (Cambridge, Mass., 1974), 187. Duus, "Economic Dimensions," 147, writes of Japanese businessmen in the early twentieth century that, while they "supported political expansion [in Korea], they did not regard the acquisition of new territory as necessary for the expansion of private business interests abroad. The prevailing view among business leaders [at this time] was that the most promising business opportunities in East Asia lay not in Korea but in China, where there was no possibility of extending political control." The large Japanese government direct investments in the South Manchurian Railway suggest, however, a highly supportive role.

70. On subsequent expansion, for a start see data in Kuwahara, "The Business Strategy," and Remer, *Foreign Investments in China*, 446–50, 469–553. Lockwood, *Economic Development in Japan*, asserts that the war years, 1914–18, brought a "sudden reversal" in Japan's debtor nation position, and that Japan in the post-First World War years became a creditor nation. In any study of early Japanese multinationals, it is important that students deal with the companies' worldwide investments, not simply those in East Asia.

# 6

# The Formation of General Trading Companies: A Comparative Study*

Shin'ichi Yonekawa

*Source: *Japanese Yearbook on Business History* (Tokyo, Japan Business History Institute, 1985), pp. 1–31.

## Introduction

Japanese general trading companies have contributed significantly to the economic development of Japan. From the mid-1890s, roughly speaking, approximately half of Japan's total exports were generated by her general trading companies, despite changes in their fortunes. In the pre-war period, Mitsui Bussan was the most prominent of four companies, followed by Mitsubishi Shoji, Iwai Shoten and Kanematsu Shoten. Suzuki Shoten and Takada Shoten were the second and third largest general trading companies during the First World War, but they were dissolved during the depressed 1920s. Meanwhile, Mitsubishi Shoji separated from Mitsubishi Goshi in 1918, taking the first step to becoming a fully-developed general trading company. By far the greater part of its turnover, however, was through dealing with firms affiliated to the Mitsubishi group, and furthermore its sales amounted to only half of Mitsui Bussan, even in the period immediately before the Second World War. Kanematsu Shoten, however, became a small general trading company when it diversified from dealing only in the import business from Australia to other localities and commodities by the 1930s.

The greatest opportunity for development of general trading companies, however, came after the Second World War when Mitsui Bussan and Mitsubishi Shoji were forced to dissolve, groups of their ex-employees forming a large number of small trading companies. Meanwhile, several trading firms grew into general trading companies. They were mainly associated with the textile industry, as cotton importers and textile merchants. Toyo Menka (now Tomen), Nippon Menka (now Nichimen) and Gosho (now Kanematsu Gosho) each specialized in the business of importing raw cotton in the pre-war period. Itochu Shoji and Marubeni, which originally stemmed from one family, were also principally engaged in the textile business, the former in the export trade, while the latter was the largest firm in the domestic cloth market. The ex-employees of the trading department of dissolved Sumitomo Goshi were to found a company which became the present Sumitomo Shoji. Nisho and Ataka, which dealt mainly with steel before the Second World War, also became interested in diversifying their trading business.

In the decade after the Korean War, the structure of the Japanese economy again underwent considerable change. One feature of this was that the export of textile goods decreased dramatically as a proportion of total exports. Thus further diversification became an urgent necessity for trading companies which had originally concentrated on textiles. The restoration of Mitsubishi Shoji and Mitsui Bussan in the 1950s marked a new era for post-war general trading companies in Japan. Small-scale general trading firms were forced into amalgamations by the tough competition then prevalent. In 1955 Marubeni absorbed Takashimaya Iida Shoten, which had originated in the cloth trade and had slowly grown into a general trading company in the 1930s. Kanematsu Shoten and Gosho were amalgamated to form Kanematsu Gosho in 1967. Ataka Sangyo, which had failed to make a success of oil-refining in the U.S.A., was absorbed into Itochu. Thus, general trading companies in Japan are now struggling for their existence by seeking new areas of business throughout the world.

**Framework**

A great number of articles have been published discussing the formation and development of general trading companies in Japan.[1] This article aims to focus on the logic and reality of the formation of the general trading company – which has often been regarded as a type of business peculiar to Japan – with special attention to the comparative standpoint. According to the author too much emphasis has been placed on the Japanese aspects of this type of enterprise.[2] The development and transformation of a specialized trading company into a general trading company is, however, perfectly logical and possible.[3] If this is correct, the next step is to inquire why general trading companies are not to be observed in the West to the same extent as in Japan, and what historical circumstances have prevented their growth. At the same time we should investigate the reasons why this phenomenon has reached such heights of prosperity in Japan.

Firstly, the definition of a general trading company needs to be clarified. It is basically a company which deals in a variety of commodities on a global scale, in the import and export trades. As a logical consequence of this activity, such a company may open a number of overseas branches with their own staff. The late N.S.B. Gras has brought attention to a class of 'sedentary merchants' who were engaged in dealing in a number of commodities in the late eighteenth and the nineteenth centuries.[4] But these merchants did not employ staff abroad, preferring to receive orders through commercial travelers, with the result that their business activities were necessarily limited. This is the crucial difference between the 'sedentary merchant' and the general trading company, in addition to the different legal forms of their businesses. Modern-day general trading companies are often primarily seen in terms of their functions – of financing, informing and organizing their customers. This is not incorrect, but these should be considered as ways in which their trading activities may be more fully developed. Moreover, it should not be forgotten that the degree of significance of these functions is subject to change in the course of time.

Secondly, after defining the general trading company, this paper now aims to briefly consider the historical logic of the emergence of the general trading company, and to examine such examples as may be found in the field of western business. Finally, an attempt will be made to answer the question of why the general trading company has achieved greater prominence in Japan compared with other countries.

It is not easy to define the changes in the degree of difficulty of entering the business of foreign trade over the centuries. However, in the period of private merchants and partnerships, it is reasonable to assume that starting a foreign trading business was not difficult in the West. Due to the large number of such businesses, though, successfully contriving an enterprise was another matter altogether.

Thanks to the technological revolution of the nineteenth century, manufacturing industries required increased amounts of capital to start new lines of business. As a result, the legal form of the limited company became predominant at the turn of the century, thus enabling a clear line to be drawn between pre-modern and modern businesses. However, as regards mercantile and trading enterprises, such a distinction cannot readily be made. The availability of steamships and cable networks made a great impact on the conduct of foreign trade but merchants could use these facilities without owning or investing in them. All they needed was working capital – the initial fixed investment of capital en bloc was not essential in this business. This all simply means that mercantile firms could maintain their traditional forms – without becoming limited liability companies – up to this century.

The ease of entry of firms into foreign trading inevitably meant keen competition and a high failure rate. Accordingly, to maintain and expand their business activities, foreign traders were obliged to make innovations, even if not technological which were undertaken step by step. Logically, there were two ways in which they could deepen and widen their overseas activities. Firstly, foreign trading firms could appoint buying and selling agents for given areas who worked on a commission basis. However, the expansion in this form of business was limited by the fact that these agents remained independent and were not subject to the particular foreign trading firm. Secondly, an overseas trading company could start to open offices abroad with a few employees, which often developed into branches, and then into subsidiary companies with their own separate staff. In the last century, these branch offices frequently took the form of another partnership, whose constituents differed from those of the mother company, and often included one or more natives as partners. In such cases, the growth of an overseas trading firm could result in a federation of partnerships all over the world.[5]

It is possible for mercantile businesses to diversify into handling a greater magnitude of goods by means of increasing the number of its overseas agents. But to use management resources to the best advantage, it is preferable to establish offices or branches abroad, which are more likely to aid in the creation of further general trading business, in both trading areas and commodities. For these branches to be maintained in business, they have to continually seek new trading commodities to replace those which experience a fall in demand, especially through the discovery of substitutes. The transition to general trading company is often accompanied by investment in a number of manufacturing businesses, so that it can monopolize their buying and selling functions.[6] As such, the foreign trading firm can become a holding company as well as an operating concern. In any case, if trading companies work to maintain and extend their business, their activities inevitably develop into general trading.

It should also be mentioned that the activities of mercantile businesses can be directed in other ways. Instead of diversifying the wholesale business, it would be possible for specialized merchants to integrate production processes in the domestic market. Otherwise it would be possible for them to integrate their retailing functions through organizing a greater number of retail outlets. Examples of the former are the textile business in the U.S.A.[7] Such a case was even observed in Japan; Naigai-wata Co. - a specialized cotton importer - integrated backwards, building spinning and weaving mills in China, and becoming fully integrated by exporting its products itself. The latter case is shown in conformity with domestic wholesalers in the U.S.A.[8] In general terms, the extending of their business activities has not been directed to importing and exporting - but rather to organizing more domestic retail outlets throughout the country. This suggests that the extent of dependence on foreign markets within a national economy is very important to the development of the general trading company - if it is acknowledged that to be engaged in foreign trading is an essential aspect of a general trading company.

Of importance but not yet considered here is the integration of industrial sectors in each country. General trading companies have to be created in a given business setting, which is usually favorable to the integration strategy of an industrial enterprise.[9] The timing of the emergence of the general trading company is vital in this context. It was relatively easy for specialized trading companies to diversify in developing countries in the nineteenth century, because they did not meet with such powerful competitors in their chosen fields. Thus many British companies, once engaged in colonial trade, could grow into general trading companies. In this sense they became like a 'Jack of all trades' engaged not only in the handling of a variety of commodities, but also in acting as shipping, banking and insurance agents.

The last, but not least important problem is the legal form of the foreign trade business. Typical industrial concerns, equipped with machinery, tend to develop into multi-unit firms which are successfully developed by salaried managers. These firms are usually limited companies, and often become public limited companies in the course of time. The conversion to this form of business is often connected with the need to raise capital for fixed investment, which the family business is unable to supply. In the case of mercantile business, however, there is no such pressure to become a public company. Needless to say, a number of entrepreneurs lost their initial vigor after their early successes and turned into rentiers, as many business histories have shown. This is especially applicable to many merchant houses of the last century.[10] Starting as family businesses, partners tended to be satisfied by limited success when their firms were managed by members of their family. As often emphasized, the most strategic resource for a trading business is human capital. Family-managed businesses, therefore, suffer from severe limitations to their growth. As long as a specialized trading firm relies upon management controlled by the owners, it is unlikely to develop into a general trading company. Only exceptional companies have grown into a general trading company by means of a group partnership – cases will be further discussed below. At any rate, the appearance of energetic and able salaried managers is essential to the development and growth of a general trading company. Thus their recruitment and promotion is vital: many such managers emerge due to the change of legal form of a company, but also they may achieve promotion within a partnership and develop their company into a general trading firm and recruit other salaried officers. Then, as a result of its growth, the firm may be converted into a limited company. In general terms the legal form applicable to a full-fledged general trading company may be a public limited company.

## General Trading Companies in the West

Many international merchant businesses may be observed in the *Times 1000: The World's Top Companies* – these could possibly become general trading companies. Often, they are still private limited companies, and information concerning their business activities does not come easily to hand. The amalgamation movement of the 1960s seems to have been of importance in the growth of these large trading companies – but whether or not they will develop into mature general trading companies remains to be seen.

The British economy of the last century depended largely upon foreign trade. A great many international merchant businesses, therefore, came into being during this time. They were generally specialized merchant houses dealing in cotton and cloth. European merchant bankers often originated from such businesses which concentrated on trading in primary goods. However, they often withdrew from their original business. Alexander Brown, for example, made an important figure as a cotton importer, but his firm was later to specialize in international banking.[11] Warburg and Co., a merchant banker, also started out as a cotton importer.[12] Shipping companies sometimes were known to diversify into mercantile business which will be mentioned below.[13] Yet almost all of these companies did not grow into fully-developed general trading companies in Britain, except for a number of colonial merchant businesses. Why did they not grow in this way? Largely because to be an expert in dealing in a commodity, they needed to acquire long experience and thus they were hesitant in dealing in unfamiliar goods. Limited human resources were a serious barrier in this context. A basic reason was, however, that as family businesses they were more interested in the status quo rather than the future growth of their businesses. Consequently the vigorous growth of mercantile businesses dating from the last century is rare. Antony Gibbs and Co., a firm engaged in foreign trading on a world scale is a remarkable exception in the period before the Second World War.[14]

### Antony Gibbs and Co.

Antony Gibbs was originally engaged in the export of English woolen cloth to Spain in the eighteenth century, but this trade was seriously interrupted by the Napoleonic Wars. As a partnership, Antony Gibbs and Co. was founded in London in 1808. Its business as a merchant banker is well-known, but that is to look at only one side of the coin. To a considerable extent, the business of international banking was closely linked to foreign trading. The company's involvement in overseas trade began in South America, importing bark, cotton and alpaca, and in turn exporting industrial goods made in Great Britain. In the course of time, offices or branches were established in a number of countries where partnerships including native merchants were founded. Thus a group of firms, headed by Antony Gibbs and Co. of London, was formed. The firms in South America were deeply involved in the industrialization of the countries in which they were located. For example, the company in Chile obtained the sole rights to exploit guano and nitrate ores, while it built mills for manufacturing woolen cloth and nitric soda.[15] They were also very active in the running of agency businesses in connection with railway construction. These activities made it possible for Antony Gibbs and Co. of London to enter the issuing business in 1887. Thus trade and banking were complementary to each other. In addition to South America, the group extended its business to North America,[16] Africa and Australia: of these, the latter is of the greatest interest and deserves detailed examination later.

In the years prior to the Second World War, the group was composed of a number of partnerships, including the London head office. Four years after the war, Antony Gibbs and Co. was organized into a private limited company. Notably, in 1946 a salaried officer was promoted to director. Until that time, Antony Gibbs and Co. was an entrepreneurial firm whose business vitality was presumably supported by such salaried officers. During the 1950s, various departments of Antony Gibbs and Co. were separated and made into subsidiaries.[17] The parent company itself was converted into a public company in 1972 when it came under the control of the Hongkong and Shanghai Banking Corporation Ltd. Since then, it has been running down its interest in foreign trade, but why this is so is not clear. It has been inferred that the business climate in many host countries has so changed that it is no longer profitable to continue such diverse trading activities. In many cases, the economic policy of host countries was not benevolent to the firm. Also, the tendency worldwide since the war to favor an open economy has made competition keener than ever.

The group's mercantile business and overall strategy bears a strong resemblance to that of many general trading companies in Japan. This is especially true of its activities in Australia. The group's business in this country originated in a shipping agency linked with Gibbs, Bright and Co. of Liverpool. The Melbourne office, which opened in 1853, formed the principal base for the Australian business, which concentrated on providing shipping agency services for vessels trading between England and Australia. The rapid increase in immigration into that country resulted in a demand for the import of all sorts of industrial goods. Besides Melbourne several overseas offices were established in Australia and New Zealand. Brisbane in 1862, Dunedin in 1864, Sydney in 1875, Adelaide in 1883, Newcastle in 1885, Kalgoorlie in 1908, Fremantle in 1908, and Perth in 1922.[18] As far as foreign trading was concerned, the business was originally concerned with the import of goods only.

During the economic depression of the 1880s the firm's business was dull, with the head office in London cautious about the locking-up of capital. The Melbourne office, however was keen to extend its business into the export of local wool and wheat. This export would not only help to balance the foreign trade of the country, but would mean further opportunities for the firm's local employees. In spite of the overseas branch's proposal, the London head office was slow in entering this trade: 'what is most essential is that we should *know* the business. – I know how the wool business is managed, but as to wheat, I think a somewhat hazardous experiment is being made.'[19] However, through taking over depressed sheep farming firms and milling plants, a number of subsidiaries were formed. At the turn of the century, the firm played an important part in the exploitation of mineral ores, including tin, copper and sulfur. Large amounts of capital were invested in the mining companies, some of whom were run by managers provided by the company. Their business activities in Australia became so widespread that by 1916, the list of agencies held by Gibbs Bright and Co. included thirteen insurance, one mining, three shipping, five financial, one pastoral, and sixty-two manufacturing companies.[20]

During the First World War, the commission business of the Australian branches reached its zenith. In the two years 1915 and 1916, the average cash capital employed by them amounted to £312,395 and £265,223 respectively, the Melbourne office showing the largest share with £186,044 and £138,771. The Sydney and Brisbane branches used £88,286 and £22,433 in 1915, and £84,586 and £23,784 in 1916. The Adelaide and Fremantle offices combined used £15,662 and £18,082, in 1915 and 1916. In addition to this, the current account of Antony Gibbs and Sons at their Australian branches amounted to on average £55,700 for 1915 and £105,000 for 1916. The profits of these firms – after providing interest at 6 percent on cash capital – totalled £88,680-15-9 for 1915 and £82,492-19-6 in 1916. The largest part of the profit was derived from commissions and allowances. According to their classification, of six departments, Shipping and Mining gained the most, followed by Sales, but the criterion of these classifications cannot always be clarified, as business records were not fully explained.[21]

With the industrialization of Australia after the First World War, the business climate of the country changed considerably, and Antony Gibbs and Sons had to adapt to it. The manufacturing companies for whom the firm acted as agents requested more services and market information than before. It had to respond to the growing need for new products. One of the most promising export commmodities appeared in this period: that of timber. Meanwhile jute goods were treated with great circumspection: 'the market risks involved in trading in jute goods, *unless a system of simultaneous purchases and sales is practicable,* are often so considerable that we should doubt whether the business is really deserving of your attention.'[22] The company's survival had been obviously due to avoiding speculation in the commodities with which it dealt. However, as far as the profit on commission business in Australia was concerned, the company found it fairly difficult to surpass its war time level during the interwar period. It reached £60,960 in 1924, but declined to £34,476 and £21,790 in the following two years.[23]

In observing the business activities of this company, its strategy may be seen as similar to that of a typical general trading company in Japan. The overseas branches each dealt in a major commodity, and when it experienced a fall in demand, they had to aggressively develop new ones.[24] In order to maintain close connections with manufacturing firms, the company provided financial aid, or owned them as subsidiaries. The head office in the home country initially founded a business base in a host country, to be followed by a number of offices in various parts of the country. When a project was not realized it was quick to retreat from it, and sometimes speculative dealings in overseas branches caused serious damage to the group.[25]

## (ii) Harrison & Crossfield Co. and Guthrie Corporation

The development of colonial mercantile business into a general trading company may be seen in the examples of two present-day firms, Harrisons and Crossfield Ltd. and the Guthrie Corporation Ltd. Both companies became general trading firms just after the First World War. Harrison, Crossfield and Co., with a capital of £8,000, originated as a partnership dealing in tea and coffee.[26] Its remarkable development was achieved through the efforts of two able managers, Heath Clark and Arthur Lampard, who entered the business as salaried managers in the 1880s and were promoted to the status of partners in 1894.[27] The following year, the firm of Crossfield and Lampard was founded in Colombo with Lampard, Clark and Co. in Calcutta, and Crossfield, Lampard, Clark and Co in New York. Offices in Shanghai and Kobe were opened during the First World War. Their vigorous business activities led the way to their expansion into a general trading company by the beginning of this century.

The company's major concern, however, was in dealing in primary commodities in Malaysia and Ceylon, originally in coffee and rubber estates in the late nineteenth century. During this time, the company stood at the crossroads of the business; one way was obviously to diversify as a general trading company, while another was to attempt further forward integration in Great Britain. The latter course was also tried, with the extending and mechanization of its blending department and the creation of its own brand. This strategy, however, led to friction with the domestic retailers, with the result that the business began to diversify abroad.[28] Furthermore, the rapid changes in the business climate of the postwar period turned the company to expand into unknown fields of business; into manufacturing activities. With the object of keeping closer links with

industrial firms than before, the company sponsored a number of manufacturing enterprises associated with rubber, glass and heavy chemicals in
several countries. As a result, it became a holding as well as an operating
company. Before long, however, in 1977–8, a number of its subsidiaries
were internalized to achieve management consolidation.[29]

Alexander Guthrie, the founder of Guthrie and Co., was engaged early
in the last century in foreign trading based in Singapore, in the export of
woolen cloth, yarn, and smallwares and in the import of pepper, tin and
gold plate.[30] By the mid-nineteenth century, the firm had diversified into
acting as an agent for certain finance, insurance and shipping business.
They afterward diversified by financing coffee growing through establishing
themselves as selling agents, as well as running coffee, rubber and palm oil
estates as managing agents. Although in 1905 it was registered as a private
limited company in Singapore, the business was heavily concentrated in
Malaya, Borneo and Sumatra. The reorganization of the firm resulted in
the appointment of J. Hay, an able manager, as head of the managing
agency department, who took an active part in the growth of the company
when he became general manager in 1924.[31] This strategy lay in the
integration of the rubber business. The company was, however, required to
change its policy once more after the Second World War. Diversification in
terms of location and commodity was necessary for it to survive.[32] The
process of later development of the firm was similar to that of Harrisons
and Crossfield. The Guthrie Corporation Ltd. was created as a public, and
a holding company in 1968, its subsidiaries comprising a large number of
both manufacturing and estate management companies. The concentration
of the firm on the southeast Asian region and the estate business then
diminished, accounting for only 30.6 percent and 24.9 percent respectively
of the company's total turnover in 1977.[33]

### Inchcape Group[34]

As far as the British colonial trade is concerned, however, two well-known
enterprises are yet to be discussed – the Inchcape Group and Jardine,
Matheson & Co., although the latter's business activities have generally
concentrated on the Far Eastern trade. A brief description of these two
companies is given below.

The Inchcape Group is composed of a great number of companies
whose activities cover a variety of service sectors including trading,
shipping and insurance.[35] A number of subsidiaries are involved in
manufacturing processes, the products of which are sold through the parent
companies. The Group's business activities are global, including Africa, the
Gulf, India, Australia and the Far East, to say nothing of the U.K. and the
U.S.A. Several firms, which are members of the Group, date back to
before the First World War. Their activities differed according to their
territories and fields of business. The whole history of the Group has yet to

be written. Here, we are only concerned with treating the history of the major constituents.

Mackinnon Mackenzie & Co., one of the founding firms of the group, was started in 1847. Under the favorable circumstances of expanding Asian trade, the firm was initially engaged in general mercantile business, which was conducted from Ghazipur, Cossipore and Calcutta. The partners were not slow to realize that they could successfully charter ships to carry their own goods and those of others as well. The gold rush in Australia gave the firm the opportunity of importing tea, sugar, rice and other consumer goods into that country. In 1862 Mackinnon and his associates floated the British India Steam Navigation Co., which appointed the firm as its agents. Step by step, the company grew into a great eastern agency house. J.L. Mackay, later the first Lord Inchcape, was originally connected with the firm as a salaried employee, rather than as a partner.[36] As the ablest and longest serving partner, however, his family were eventually to gain a controlling interest by 1950, and the next year it was converted into a private limited company.

The group's interest in North India originated in the businesses of three partnerships, Barry & Co., Macneill & Co., and Kilburn & Co. From the middle of the last century, they dealt in a number of commodities, especially tea, jute and indigo. They acted as managing agent for a number of manufacturing companies, in terms of selling their products and providing financial support. They also had a hand in the shipping business through their personal links with local shipping firms. The Mackinnon and Macneill families were closely related, but it is not clear how Lord Inchcape was connected to Barry & Co. At any rate, Inchcape acquired the entire U.K. and India interests of both Barry & Co. and Macneill & Co. Furthermore, after the Second World War, these firms acquired a minority holding in Kilburn & Co. and outright ownership by 1956.

Binny's, on the other hand, represented the group's interest in South India. Similar to the above three families, the founder came from Scotland, but the firm originally acted as a banking house, dating back to the end of the eighteenth century. They soon set about dealing in commodities, sometimes venturing to Java and the Malay Peninsula and diversified by the mid-nineteenth century into estate management and acting as agents for textile mills.[37] When Binny's was hit by the failure of their sugar business, Sir James Mackay, then managing director of the B.I.S.N. Co., bought up the shares in the old firm and helped form Binny & Co. Ltd., registered in London.

The group's activities in Australia also show its business strategy. Its major interest, from the beginning, was in the shipping industry, as part of the worldwide network of P. & O. and B.I. services. Inchcape sponsored the formation of Macdonald, Hamilton & Co., a partner of whom, B.W. Macdonald, was another Scot who had risen from the ranks in the shipping world. Similar to Antony Gibbs, its business in Australia before long diversified into the management of mining and pastoral activities. When the firm was converted into a private company owned by the Inchcape family in 1959–60, 'those of its activities not associated, with P. & O. agencies were hived off.'[38] In the rapid progress of economic development in Australia, the group's interest in mining and engineering, however, has been brought back to life, whilst its traditional trade in marine services was declining.

The group's activities in London were based on Gray, Dawes & Co., which has been seen as the catalytic agent in the formation of the Inchcape Group. Archbald Gray, one of its founders, was a nephew of Mackinnon. Starting off as a shipping agency, its activities were in decline when the B.I. and the P. & O. were amalgamated in 1914. Meanwhile, at the end of the last century, the future Earl of Inchcape became a partner. Looking for a means of survival, the firm found its way into the banking business. Converted into a private company in 1951, it relinquished its other activities to became a full-fledged merchant bank and issuing house in the 1970s.

The name of the Inchcape group is well known to the Japanese through Dodwell & Co. Ltd., a subsidiary whose area of activity was mainly concentrated in the Far East. Before long, after the Treaty of Nanking of 1842, a group of Macclesfield silk manufacturers sent W.R. Adamson to Shanghai to secure a supply of raw silk. G. Benjamin Dodwell arrived in Shanghai in 1872 and joined his firm. After steady growth through two decades the firm met with difficulties, as G.B. Dodwell then formed a new partnership which took over the previous firm's shipping agencies. The company also dealt in exporting tea, porcelain and silk with other Chinese products from their branches at Yokohama, Shanghai, Hong Kong and Kobe. Sales of brick tea to Moscow made the firm the leading tea buyer in Hankow. In 1891 the head office was transferred from Hong Kong to London, and was converted into a private limited company – named Dodwell & Company Ltd. – in 1899. Up to the First World War, the firm made remarkable progress on the merchandizing side. The tea trade was initially the most profitable, but the firm soon diversified into handling a variety of commodities as a 'Jack of all trades'. In the interwar period record profits were made, and the company was operating sixteen branches throughout the world. After the Second World War, its business activities achieved a remarkable expansion, under the favorable circumstances of the successful economic development of Japan and Hong Kong.[39] It was only in 1972 that the whole of issued shares were acquired by the Group.

*Jardine, Matheson and Co.*

This firm was founded by two men: William Jardine, a Scot, who had gained considerable knowledge of ships and their management through service with the East India Company, and a fellow Scot, James Matheson, who was twelve years younger than his partner and had been educated at the University of Edinburgh. The Mathesons were also well represented in the East India Company. Jardine, Matheson & Co. was founded in 1832, several years after they first met. Before long, Jardine left the company to become a member of the House of Commons. The firm continued, however, and succeeding generations of these two families were to join the company, with the result that the sixteen original shares, called 'Annos,' were increased to thirty-two in order to provide for additional partners.

The 1850s and early 1860s were very prosperous times for Jardine's and their competitors. The company's income was mainly derived from commission business in the tea and silk trades. By 1870 the traditional pattern of trade between India and China began to change, with native merchants entering the trade in primary goods and causing a demand for manufactured products. The elder partners were not entirely receptive to this new business, but the younger generations, which were eventually promoted to the management of the company, took a different view. William Keswick, the first of five generations of his family in the firm, took a leading role in the global diversification of the company.[40] The management of cotton mills and land was undertaken in the late nineteenth century, and the firm began trading with Japan, by exporting tea, silk, and 'habutae' silk to the U.S.A.

Under these circumstances Jardine, Matheson & Co. was converted into a private company in 1906, followed by the formation of Matheson & Co. as the London office in 1908. The former purchased the Matheson family's remaining interest in the London House in 1912. By 1920, the firm had probably more branch offices in China, Japan, Manchuria and Formosa than it was to have at any other time. In 1923 its engineering department was separately incorporated as the Jardine Engineering Corporation, involved in railways, marine and general engineering, electrical engineering and the manufacture of textile machinery. After the Second World War, Jardine's made phenomenal progress, obtaining a listing of its shares on the Hong Kong Stock Exchange in 1961.[41] With the retreat from China, its areas of business have changed considerably, with ventures in Southeast Asia, Australia and Hawaii. Expansion in the late 1960s and early 1970s took Jardine's not only into new geographical areas but into many new activities, including merchant banking, offshore oil services, and the manufacture of agricultural machinery.

## W.R. Grace & Co. and Anderson, Clayton Inc.

The economy of the U.S.A., by the latter half of the last century, differed from that of Great Britain, insofar that the domestic market of the former was enormous, providing businessmen with ample opportunities for investment. Early in the nineteenth century, American merchants had the chance of making their fortunes in the Atlantic trade. However, investment in domestic markets became more attractive, largely because of high customs duties imposed by the government, and the completion of national railway networks. As is widely known, a great number of spinning and weaving mills in Lowell and Lawrence were built by Boston merchants whose fortunes had originally been made in foreign trading. Accordingly, only a few large merchant houses continued in business up to this century. As far as the domestic market was concerned, the process of integration of industrial firms was such that domestic wholesale companies found difficulty in maintaining their businesses. The policy of the former included operating a large number of retail outlets. Many examples of this type of big business appeared in the U.S.A. from the late nineteenth century. Thus, the growth of general trading companies in the U.S.A. has occurred but rarely.

W.R. Grace & Co. may be seen as a rare example of an American general trading company. It originated as Bryce & Co., an English company in Peru which R.C. Grace joined in 1859. Bryce, Grace & Co. was then formed, engaged in trading with the U.S.A., opening an office in New York in the mid-1860s. They exported manufacturing goods and lumber to Peru, and their triangular trade between Peru, Europe and the U.S.A. set the pattern for the Grace commercial business for years to come.[42] R.C. Grace then founded Grace Brothers & Co., with a number of branches in the U.S.A., the U.K., and in the South American countries. Michael Grace, his brother, entered the trade with the U.K., and was also deeply involved in various financial businesses as a merchant banker. They gradually established a group of businesses on a worldwide scale, headed by the group's head office located in New York, and thus it became primarily an American business.

In the depressed years of the 1880s, W.R. Grace put his hand to the management of cotton spinning and sugar refining in Peru. He also entered the woolen manufacturing business. Further opportunities in Chile and Colombia were discovered in a variety of industrial fields, including the production of vegetable oil and paper. At the end of the Second World War, the company's gross fixed assets were about $62 million, with approximately $29 million in South America and the remainder in the U.S.A.[43] In the former the major businesses were integrated sugar production in Peru and seven cotton mills in Peru, Chile and Colombia. By the 1950s its assets had grown to $167 million, of which two-thirds was invested in domestic companies, especially in the chemical industry. However, as soon as W.R. Grace & Co. was converted into a public company in 1950 its strategy changed remarkably. In addition to the creation of Grace Chemical Co., three other chemical companies, Davidson's, Thurston's and Deway's, were acquired by the group in 1953–4. This resulted from 'studies directed toward investment opportunities in profitable growth industries.'[44] The metamorphosis of the company was rapid; when J.P. Grace, the president of the company from 1945, reviewed the past in 1971 he said 'We have totally changed our emphasis. After World War II, Grace's earnings came entirely from steamship operations and Latin American investments. Shipping started declining in the mid-Fifties, and Latin America became a problem area in the Sixties'.[45]

Anderson, Clayton Inc. also may be seen as one of the few exceptions. Cotton was the most important of exports from the U.S.A. throughout the nineteenth century.[46] William Lockhard Clayton established himself as a cotton exporter in 1904. He was later able to expand his business by running cotton ginning mills, and by the manufacture of cotton seed oil. It was his enterprise that first reduced the leading role of European traders in this field.[47]

The partnership was organized into a corporation after the First World War, and was registered in Delaware as a public company in 1929. Its business activities then branched out to a number of countries in South America, and into the field of insurance against loss. Probably because cotton was such a speculative commodity, it was natural that as one of the largest traders in this item, the company became deeply involved in the insurance business. The firm continued to diversify during the interwar period. A remarkable change in policy came in the 1950s, when the government, by maintaining a stable price for domestic cotton, made it unprofitable for the company to continue dealing in cotton.[48] Their subsequent diversification was directed in three ways: firstly, by developing their holdings in the insurance business by the acquisition of many insurance firms; secondly, by extending its interests in manufacturing, making margarine and sauces with cotton seed oil; and thirdly, by making the most of its experience as a land developer in South America, and by buying out S.A. Medina Co, in 1955, a large firm engaged in importing coffee and cocoa. It then became obvious that this policy of diversification had to proceed further, because extensive investment in landed estates proved to be risky in post-war South America. Since then, they have increased their activities in the development of the domestic market, including warehousing and dealing in machines.[49]

The cases above suggest that in the West, mercantile trading firms grew into general trading companies by pursuing such services as shipping and insurance as side lines. Otherwise, this type of company developed from shipping companies which supplemented their business with mercantile activities. Both formed businesses which included general merchandising, shipping and banking. The growth of these functions together is a condition unknown to general trading in Japan, as will be mentioned later. The strategy of growth in the wholesale business has differed country by country, with differences in the business setting in each region. Another crucial element in the emergence of the general trading company is the recruitment of salaried managers. Thus, the shortage of human capital resources could be a serious limiting factor in the development of a partnership into a general trading company. This is also true in the case of industrial enterprises. In contrast with those of British companies, the two cases of American companies seem to suggest that it is not easy for general trading companies based in the U.S.A. to grow in the postwar period.

**General Trading Companies in Japan**

Business historians in Japan have largely concentrated on the emergence of Japanese general trading companies in the prewar period. Although as far as present-day general trading companies are concerned the majority of them have appeared since the Second World War, this does not deny the significance of the pre-war forerunners, especially of Mitsui Bussan Co., on which many subsequent companies have been modeled. In a sense, the destruction of the Japanese economy during the Second World War seems to have helped in the later proliferation of the general trading company. A similarity may be seen in the economic circumstances existing in the Meiji and in the postwar periods: the postwar economy had to be built up from the beginning as in the case of the Meiji era. The postwar economic conditions were therefore favorable to the development of general trading companies. Scholars have often implicitly considered that the general trading company is to be associated with the zaibatsu business group. According to their assertions, the appearance of general trading companies in only understandable in the context of the zaibatsu group. This is not necessarily true, despite its appropriateness to the growth of the Mitsubishi and Sumitomo trading companies, which have developed from each group's selling department. The Mitsui Bussan Co. became the sole selling agent for Miike coal before the mines were disposed of by the government, and similarly concluded an exclusive agency agreement with the Onoda Cement Co. These events helped in the formation of the Mitsui group, rather than vice-versa. As a matter of fact a considerable part of Mitsui Bussan's turnover came from dealing with companies outside the group. In this respect the Mitsui group is typical of many other general trading companies of the present time – when business groups have functioned through a core and then formed affiliated companies. This leads to the conclusion that it is possible for us to argue that a general trading company may be formed without associating it with zaibatsu.

The economic circumstances in the Meiji era were favorable to the growth of the general trading company, because there had been no native foreign traders previously. The business of foreign trading was then almost entirely new to Japanese people, as was industrialization. It is an astonishing fact that in the Japanese economy, the business of foreign trading experienced a number of innovations, but the domestic mercantile business remained as it was up to the post-war era. Foreign trade in Japan saw the advent of an entirely new type of business – the general trading company.

In this analysis, the emphasis has been put on the legal form and the human resources of companies. Organization is also important in the favorable development of general trading companies. Now we turn to the previously unexplored aspects of pre-war general trading companies, especially of Mitsui Bussan.

Since 1858, with the opening of Japanese ports to foreign trade, this activity was entirely confined to foreign merchants residing in the foreign settlements, because it was entirely new to native merchants after the long period of national isolation. Anxious about this situation, the government began a scheme to persuade the most prominent businessmen to initiate trading companies which aimed to become directly engaged in foreign trade. The Mitsui business's venture into foreign trading was initially cautious, with a capital of only 50,000 yen borrowed from the Mitsui Bank.[50] This was natural, as up to this time 'the Mitsui company' was one of the most traditional merchant firms, having originated in cloth-dealing in the late seventeenth century. The expressed policy of Mitsui Bussan was to stick to the commission business, because it was then considered that this did not require a great deal of capital. At any rate this resulted in the development of Mitsui Bussan, which had been formed in 1876, without strong family managerial influence.[51]

It was made clear in the company's memorandum of association that the original object of the firm was to concentrate on foreign trading by means of handling a wide variety of commodities. Despite its original intentions, the activities of the firm were also based in the domestic market, to the extent of nearly half of their dealings. Its foreign trade was exclusively confined to China. It experienced great difficulty in entering foreign trade, through a lack of experience in dealing with foreign merchants abroad. Takashi Masuda, the de facto president of Mitsui Bussan, was an exception, as he had been apprenticed with Walsh Hall and Co., an American merchant house in Yokohama, where he became acquainted with R.W. Irwin, an American merchant. In the early years of Mitsui Bussan, Irwin was responsible for all the foreign correspondence, visiting the firm twice a week.

Under these circumstances, the firm was able to enter foreign trading, if only by a process of trial and error. The year following its foundation, a branch of the firm was opened in Shanghai, followed by offices in Hong Kong and Paris. The London branch was opened in 1880, and continued mainly through the help of Irwin. The branches in Milan, Paris and New York were less successful, having to be closed within a few years. Masuda acutely felt that the lack of human capital was a crucial barrier against the firm's growth in overseas business. Foreign trade know-how is now seen as a form of self technology, like bookkeeping, which had to be transferred from the West. This created a need for appropriate educational establishments, such as the Tokyo Commercial School.[52] The students had scarely left the School when Masuda began to recruit them each year. The development of the firm into a general trading company in the mid-1890s would not have been possible without a large salaried staff who were being quickly promoted to managerial posts. In 1880, none of the general managers of its five overseas branches were university graduates. By 1893, graduates had been appointed to all these general manager's posts except the Shanghai office. Graduates in the field of natural sciences began to be regularly recruited about the time that the firm grew into a general trading company in the mid–1890s.[53] Masuda also sent employees to China to learn Chinese and the country's business customs, from 1898, with the effect that the comprador system was undermined, and eventually abolished.

These policies were due to Masuda's deep insight into the management of overseas business. Mitsui Bussan's growth, however, was more due to the fact that as a newly-created firm, it enjoyed freedom from the restraints of more traditional mercantile business. From the beginning, it was a managerial enterprise, becoming a Gomei Kaisha in 1893. Under the old Shoho (Commercial Law), this was a type of partnership with a corporate identity. In 1909 the firm was further reorganized into a limited company. A person from the original Mitsui was kept on as president, but this was a formality.[54] Masuda later said that the success of the Mitsui businesses was due not only to their credit in business circles but also to abundant human resources. On the other hand, an insight into the firm is seen in the visit of Yukio Ozaki, a member of parliament in Japan, to London in 1933. He asked a British gentleman if there was such a thing as a general trading company like Mitsui Bussan in Great Britain, and received the answer 'no', and that he considered that the success of the firm was due to its business organization.[55]

The company's marvelous growth has been undoubtedly due not only to abundant human resources but to the careful development of its organizational structure. In general terms a workable organization is not easily built in the case of general trading companies. The organization of Mitsui Bussan has seen many changes since its foundation, but it remained largely departmentalized in terms of the lines of commodities it handled. At the same time each overseas branch accumulated its own profits independently, which functioned as a driving force to the rapid expansion of their businesses. This has also been aided by speculative dealings, although the top management often warned against speculation in commodities. Innumerable trading firms throughout the world went bankrupt as a result of dabbling in speculation. A system of internal inspection was essential, but only the building of an overall organization could make the firm workable.

Despite its active graduate recruitment policy, university graduates working for Suzuki numbered only 72 in 1914,[56] while those in Mitsui Bussan amounted to 731, which was the largest number among all Japanese companies. Although Mitsui by far exceeded Suzuki in terms of both human capital and organization, it became increasingly cautious about speculative dealings in the course of the war.[57] Suzuki, on the contrary, continued speculating. The company became the sole agent for camphor in Taiwan and then entered the sugar trade. Naokichi Kaneko, Suzuki's managing director, sent a letter to the general manager of its London office in 1917 informing him that Suzuki's goal was to pass Mitsui and Mitsubishi in turnover; and that if this turned out to be impossible, they aimed at least to share Japan's foreign trade on an equal footing with their rivals.[58] In fact Suzuki's turnover surpassed that of Mitsui in the same year. Kaneko himself, towards the end of the war, became increasingly anxious about speculative dealings, but was surprised to find that his staff did not share his views.[59] Thus the rapid expansion of the business was not followed by the development of the organizational structure as was intended. Furthermore, the abrupt large-scale recruitment of university graduates from the early 1900s had created friction between them and the 'traditional people' in the firm.[60] The postwar depression led to Suzuki's bankruptcy in 1927. Possibly an underlying reason for the dissolution of the company lay in its excessive involvement in speculative dealings after and during the temporary boom of wartime.

Among the hundred largest firms which employed university graduates in 1914, only six were trading firms.[61] Takada Shokai, which followed Mitsui Bussan in terms of graduates employed, had also been wound up largely because of its heavy involvement in the mining business during and after the First World War.[62] Likewise Yokohama Kiito, which specialized in the export of raw silk, also disappeared. The Mitsubishi business operated a divisional system at the time, with the trading division functioning only for the group. Meanwhile, despite its small scale, Iwai and Co. had been gradually diversifying as a general trading company. Since the beginning of the century, the staff of newly created import departments were mainly university graduates.[63] The policy of Iwai, however, was to place emphasis on the development of industrial companies for the domestic market, relying on agencies abroad for its foreign business. As a result their growth into a general trading company was steady but slow.

In addition to these companies, a number of small business groups tried to enter foreign trading in the booming years of the First World War, but failed. Furukawa and Kuhara, zaibatsu-like businesses, separated their trading divisions from their head offices. Involved in speculative dealings during the booming years of the war, they both failed before long. Nippon Menka (now Nichimen), founded by a number of cotton dealers in 1892, was a traditional mercantile company when Matazo Kita, a graduate from

Osaka Commercial School, joined it in 1891. Promoted to the post of general manager at the head office in 1903, he began to recruit graduates 'with the object of becoming the leading company in the Kansai area.' This ambition, however, suffered a severe setback when the Shanghai office sustained a heavy loss due to speculation in foreign exchange in 1908.[64] Itochu and Co., on the other hand, was so conservative in its way of business that it believed that apprenticeship and the mercantile business were unfit for graduates.[65] Starting from a family business engaged in dealing in cloth in the domestic market, the firm quickly expanded during the First World War and created a separate foreign trade department. The post-war depression, however, was such that this department had to be separated from the parent company. After the Second World War, it moved to form the Marubeni Company. Mitsui Bussan also separated its cotton department, as the Toyo Menka Company (now Tomen), just after the First World War, because they considered that it was such a risky business that it should be formed into another company.[66]

The examples described above suggest a number of conclusions. Ample human resources and a long experience of commodity handling is necessary to the growth of firms into large trading companies. Deviation from the commission business was so common and attractive that almost all these trading firms were more or less involved in speculative dealings. We can thus understand why Mitsui Bussan repeatedly made their employees pay attention to the firm's original principle that it should stick to the commission business. The overwhelming majority of the hundred largest companies grew through a process of amalgamations and absorptions. Mercantile businesses, however, were exceptions – as even if they grew up into large firms, they were often on the verge of bankruptcy – a characteristic of this particular sector of world business.

## Concluding Remarks

The growth of this form of business enterprise was much more conspicuous in Japan than in other countries. Thus, historically, a number of general trading companies emerged in Japan before the Second World War, whilst almost all of the existing general trading companies of the West postdate this period. In terms of number, present-day Japanese general trading companies overwhelmingly surpass those of the West.

It has been shown that the pattern of national economy which formed the background to the business setting in each country was the most momentous force in determining the emergence of a general trading company. Often important factors were the tendency towards integration of manufacturing enterprises, and the extent of the economic development of the countries where mercantile businesses were active. These may be regarded as objective factors in the formation of these enterprises. Subjective factors may also be seen as important, although scholars often overlook them, or play down their significance. Without a strong intention and enthusiasm for business growth, it would be impossible for merchant houses to become general trading companies especially in the case of British firms. The problem of the legal form of the business may also be considered in this context.

The stage of economic development and the intention of the management of firms to expand, has encouraged the appearance of general trading companies in Japan. On the other hand, the early growth of specialized and general trading companies engaged in foreign trades seems to have been a limiting factor in the realization of fully-integrated industrial companies in this country. This was because these trading businesses rendered good service to manufacturing companies for low commission charges.

Do Japanese general trading companies differ from those of the West? Western general trading companies, as a rule, began their business activities in developing areas, such as South America, Asia, Australia, and Africa. Of significance in this context is that their emergence was reinforced by their shipping and insurance businesses. However, in Japanese companies, these activities were seen as auxiliary only. Mitsui and Mitsubishi both had shipping departments, but mainly for the purpose of handling their own cargoes. In the 1930s, forty percent of the cargoes handled by Mitsui's Shipping Department were their own goods. Thus, shipping activities were seen as no more than an appendage to Japanese companies and they did not take a positive part in the growth of general trading companies in Japan.

In this article, a great deal has intentionally been left unexplored, especially in reference to the managerial aspects of general trading companies. For example, it has often been said that only certain groups of commodities are suitable for handling by general trading firms: that recent sophisticated industrial products are not appropriate for these enterprises. Their role as suppliers of information and project organizing has been referred to: this is outside the scope of this article.

*       *       *

This paper is an enlarged version of the paper on the same subject, the research of which was sponsored by the United Nations University. Some sections were entirely rewritten with the addition of some case studies.

## Notes

1. Whereas an overwhelming number of works have been written on this subject in Japanese, works written in English are rather limited, for example, G.J.

Robert, *Mitsui: Three Centuries of Japanese Business*, New York, 1973; Y.M. Yoshino, *Japan's Multinational Enterprise*, Cambridge, 1976; A.K. Yound, *The Sogo Shosha: Japan's Multinational Trading Companies*, Boulder, 1979. Among the works dealing with the topic, H. Morikawa's is the first that has put emphasis on human resources as an important driving force for the growth of modern enterprises, H. Morikawa, 'Sogoshosha no Seiritsu to Ronri', in M. Miyamoto et al. eds., *Sogoshosha no Keiei Shi* (Business History of Japan's General Trading Companies), Toyo Keizai Shimpo-sha, 1976.

2. Refer to the following two representative papers: K. Nakagawa 'Nippon no Kogyoka Katei ni okeru Soshiki sareta Kigyosha Katsudo' [Organized Entrepreneurship in the Course of Industrialization], *Keiei Shigaku* (Japan Business History Review), Vol. 2, No. 3, 1967; K. Yamamura, 'General Trading Companies in Japan – Their Origins and Growth,' in *Japanese Industrialization and its Social Consequences*, ed. by H. Patrick, Berkeley, 1976.

3. Therefore, it would also be insufficient to explain the theoretical basis of the establishment of general trading companies solely from the various conditions which accompanied Japanese industrialization after the Meiji era.

4. N.S.B. Gras, *Business and Capitalism*, 1939, p. 168. According to his stage theory, mercantile capitalism was completed by the end of the eighteenth century. Sedentary merchants, its central figures, however, are occasionally observed until later.

5. Refer to the case of Antony Gibbs mentioned below.

6. Indian managing houses could be said to be a deviation from this type of business.

7. In the U.S.A., generally speaking, present-day large textile businesses are produced through backward integration by cloth merchants.

8. A.D. Chandler, Jr., *The Visible Hand*, Cambridge, 1977.

9. Refer to works by A.D. Chandler, Jr.

10. In England, merchants who had succeeded in East India trade became politicians and advanced into the Parliament as early as the eighteenth century. Among famous politicians, the Gladstone family, for example, made its fortune from the slave trade.

11. A. Ellis, *Heir of Adventure: The Story of Brown, Shipley & Co.*, London, 1960; J. Killick, 'Risk, Specialization and Profit in the Mercantile Sector of the Nineteenth Century Cotton Trade: Alexander Brown and Sons', *Business History*, Vol. 16, No. 1, 1974.

12. E. Rosenbaum and A.I. Sherman, *M.M. Warburg & Co., 1798–1938*, London, 1976; B.E. Supple, 'A Business Elite: German–Jewish Financiers in Nineteenth Century New York', *Business History Review*, Vol. 31, No. 2, 1957.

13. F.E. Hyde, Blue Funnel: *A History of Alfred Holt & Company of Liverpool from 1865 to 1914*, Liverpool, 1956; A.H. John. *A Liverpool Merchant House: Alfred Booth and Company, 1863–1958*, London, 1959; S. Marriner and F.E. Hyde, *The Senior: John Samuel Swire, 1825–98*, Liverpool, 1967; S. Marriner, *Rathbones of Liverpool, 1845–73*, Liverpool, 1961.

14. Regarding this company, the detailed history is worth referring to: The Company, *Anthony Gibbs and Sons Limited: Merchants and Bankers, 1808–1958*, London, 1958. Business records of the company are available at the Guildhall Library in London.

15. W.A. Mathew, *The House of Gibbs and the Peruvian Guano Monopoly*, 1981.

16. The firm established a New York office in 1912. The activities in New York, however, were limited to trade and the agency business, and it was prohibited from

venturing into financing. This was most likely due to an agreement with the London headquarters. It can thus be surmised that there was a restriction on growth, resulting from their dissimilarities.

17. The Company, *op. cit.*, p. 72.

18. *Ibid.*, pp. 125–6.

19. Papers of Antony Gibbs & Sons, Letters of H.H. Gibbs to Vicary Gibbs; 9, 18 and 25 January 1884.

20. Papers of Antony Gibbs & Sons, Report on the Melbourne Accounts, 25 May 1917.

21. *Ibid.*

22. Papers of Antony Gibbs & Sons, Private Accounts (Adelaide), 1926.

23. Papers of Antony Gibbs & Sons, Private Accounts (Melbourne), 1927.

24. The company, *op cit.*, p. 115 'Overseas manufacturers on their part began to send salesmen, or establish their own agencies ... Thus, as has happened elsewhere, the Firm has had to adapt itself to the times and employ its resources in local developments.'

25. The New York branch failed in speculation on hessian, and its business in Canada was not successful due to its low reputation in the country.

26. Regarding histories of both firms the author is indebted to articles (written in Japanese) by Miss Keiko Saruwatari who has been studying British merchant houses.

27. Harrison 'Crossfield,' *One Hundred Years as East India Merchants, 1844–1943*, 1944, pp. 3–4.

28. *Ibid*, pp. 31–4, 54–5.

29. *Stock Exchange Official Yearbook*, 1978–9, p. 819.

30. S. Cunyngham-Brown, *The Trader: A Story of Britain's South-East Asian Commercial Adventure*, London, 1971, pp. 184, 229; Gow, Wilson & Stanton, Ltd., *Rubber Producing Companies*, London, 1909, p. 60.

31. *Ibid.*, pp. 251–2.

32. *Economist*, 15 June 1963, p. 1177; 22 June 1963, pp. 1287–8; 30 July 1966, p. 483. *Stock Exchange Year Book*, 1966, p. 1330.

33. The Guthrie Corporation registered in Malaysia has been controlled by the Malaysian government since 1981 when the government bought 50.41 percent of the total shares.

34. The author expresses his deep sense of gratitude to Dr. Stephanie Jones, who has been working on the history of Inchcape, particularly to her comments on this paper. S. Jones, 'The Decline of British Maritime Enterprise in Australia', *Business History*, Vol. 26, No. 1, 1985.

35. The Group is composed of a number of firms which have grown out of historically different origins. Six major group members are sketched here.

36. P. Griffiths, *A History of the Inchcape Group*, London, 1977, pp. 10–11. The following description came from the above work.

37. *Ibid.*, pp. 42–6.

38. *Ibid.*, p. 90.

39. *Ibid.*, p. 156ff.

40. M. Keswick, ed., *The Thistle and The Jade*, Hong Kong, 1982, pp. 180–208.

41. *Ibid.*, pp. 228–36.

42. J.P. Grace, Jr., *W.R. Grace and The Enterprises He Created*, 1953, p. 13.

43. *Ibid.*, p. 18.

44. W.R. Grace & Co., *Annual Report for 1952*, p. 17.

45. Ibid., *Annual Report for 1971*, pp. 7–10.

46. J.R. Killick, 'The Transformation of Cotton Marketing in the Late Nineteenth

Century: Alexander Sprunt and Son of Wilmington,' *Business History Review*, Vol. 55, No. 2, 1981.

47. E.C. Greenwood, *Will Clayton: A Short Bibliography*, Austin, 1958, pp. 100–1.

48. In 1955–6 sixty percent of the total turnover was composed of cotton, but the proportion decreased to twenty-four percent in 1965–6, then to twelve percent in 1973. *Annual Report*, 1966 and 1973.

49. Regarding Anderson, Clayton & Co. Inc., the proportion of the turnover from foreign trade to total turnover decreased to around half in the early 1980s. *Annual Report*, 1980, pp. 26–7

50. Mitsui Bussan started as a Shimei-gaisha (a 'private corporation') without any capital, and the business had to be managed with a loan of 50,000 yen. Although this fact is quite well-known, the nature of 'private corporation' is not necessarily clear. What is evident is the fact that it did not take the form of a proper company – with an authorized capital – but it lacked its own capital. This was a reflection of Takashi Masuda's opinion that Mitsui Trading did not need any capital, because of its engagement in the commission business. He considered a loan of 50,000 yen from the Mitsui Bank would suffice for working funds. At the same time, the Mitsui view was that 'capital is not handed to the said company in order for both parties to avoid any losses in the future.' Consequently, Mitsui at its outset was not in a financially comfortable state. Nevertheless, the company's fundamental constitution was formed during this period when it was without capital, and because the company held fast to being non-capital, it could pursue venturesome business strategies without being restricted by the Mitsui family. Mitsui Bussan's liberal and open-minded tradition was formulated during this period.

51. A perusal of its history, particularly its burgeoning period, is indispensable for an understanding of its brilliant achievements. Concurrently with the opening of Yokohama Port, Mitsui, a traditional big merchant, opened a Yokohama office and advanced into overseas trading on the recommendation of the Tokugawa Government. Its Edo office also ventured into raw silk export. In addition, Mitsui's affiliated stores Mitsukoshi (especially its Yokohama branch) at one time were heavily involved in the sales of silkworm larvae, paper and tea.

Upon entering the Meiji period, leading merchants in Tokyo established the Tokyo Boeki Shosha (Tokyo Trading Company) under the forceful guidance of the Government. The prospectus for its founding states: 'Now that foreign trade is pursued briskly, the outlook of foreign merchants has become increasingly egotistic and they insist on various difficult propositions. . . .' The prospectus goes on to assert that merchants should unite their capital and establish a trading company in order to counteract foreign trading houses.

Mitsui subsequently opened domestic-products offices at various places in 1874 which were aimed at the pursuit of cash payment for land taxes as well as exchange transactions and the sales and transportation of rice. Of these offices, the Export Department was established at the Tokyo Domestic Products office in March 1876 and began to export rice. However, because the sales were very disadvantageous to the selling party and because there was insufficient overseas business knowledge and information regarding direct exports, these operations were far from profitable.

Compared to these efforts, the Senshu Trading Company, one of the parent bodies of the Mitsui Trading Company, was far more successful. The Senshu Trading Company originated with Okada and Co. which was established at the beginning of 1874. An American trading firm called Edwin Fisher and Co. joined Okada and Co. Owing to the participation of this trading firm, rice was exported to London. Although it seemed as if the business would expand smoothly, the operation came to a standstill due to the sudden death of Heizo Okada, who was the key figure. At the time Kaoru Inoue, president of Okada and Co., reorganized it into the Senshu Trading Company. The rules of this company stated: 'This trading company inaugurates a great business with worldwide transactions and devotes itself to the distribution of products made in the Empire to foreign countries.'

52. Incidentally, it is interesting to find Takashi Masuda's name in 1879 as a member of the school committee to establish school rules. Masuda happened to be a brother-in-law of Jiro Yano, director of the training school. The educational objective of the Tokyo Commercial School, which succeeded this training school, was to master new knowledge pertaining to trade practices and trade finances. Even after the change of this training school into the government-run Tokyo Commercial School in 1884, Masuda maintained a close tie with the school as a member of the School Affairs Consultation Committee. At that time, Masuda, who was the president of Mitsui Bussan, was paying keen attention to the graduates of the training school.

53. One of the cardinal contrasts between enterprise management in Japan and that in the West is the fact that in Japan the separation of owners from managers was traditionally established from before the modern period. As this is a commonly accepted theory, this paper will not delve into this topic further.

Traditionally Japanese business was operated by managers or controllers chosen from long-term servants who were competent in managerial capabilities. On the other hand, because there was a tradition in the West that proprietors alone had the qualification to manage, the separation of ownership from management did not take place for a long time. It became possible only after the public offering of stocks became prevalent. When stocks were opened to the public, stockholding was diffused and ownership came to have only a relative meaning. This process, in one sense, would be extremely natural.

Absolute loyalty on the part of managers to owners was indispensable when owners entrusted the actual power of management to someone who did not own the enterprise. However, loyalty is something which could not be easily guaranteed in any country. In the West, therefore, managers were given some part of the profit even though they were not investors so that their loyalty to owners could be enhanced.

Why was it possible for Mitsui (which had as many as one thousand employees already at the end of the Tokugawa period) to have separated its management from ownership? The existing theory is persuasive. First of all, a family business ought to be continued from its ancestor to descendants. In other words, there is a tradition that it is a growing concern. There is no room for loyalty from employees to the employer to take root in such a business as the one based on partnerships whereby most of the contracts are not renewed after five years, and it is natural that partners come to opt for independence themselves. Second, in addition to the above, such systems as the branch family and the establishment of the same line of business for competent senior employees played a role in reinforcing the tradition. Employees' loyalty was maintained because they had the prospect of being promoted and being set up in the same line of business or even further being granted the honor of treatment as a branch family, should they work hard and serve the employer. To put it differently, dedication to the owner family brought about 'pseudo-family consciousness' in the entire family business.

It has been asserted that merchant families in the Tokugawa period generally followed this ideology. However, if such a unique mechanism that guaranteed the perpetuity of family businesses functioned easily in every merchant family, there would have been many Mitsuis. The fact that only a very small number of families were able to achieve the aim seems to suggest that, despite its remarkable ingenuity, the attainment of long-term prosperity of family business was a thorny path full of difficulties. At any rate, getting back to the Meiji period, the relation of employees of Mitsui Bussaning at that time to salaried managers should be discussed here.

54. At the beginning of the 20th Century, as many as 55 employees were graduates of Tokyo Commercial School, of whom more than 19 were working at such overseas branch offices as the ones in London, Shanghai, Hong Kong, Singapore, San Francisco, Taipei, and Tienchin. From this time onward, ten to twenty graduates entered Mitsui Trading every year, and thus the school was truly a training school for Mitsui employees.

55. T. Masuda, *Jijyo Masuda Takashi-O Den (An Autobiography)*, 1939, pp. 175–80.

56. S. Yonekawa, 'University Graduates in Large Japanese Enterprises before the Second World War,' *Business History*, vol. 26, No. 2, 1984, pp. 196–7.

57. It should be noted that ever since the birth of Mitsui Bussan, one of the principles of foreign trade was to pursue the sales operations on a commission basis. Any speculative transaction required approval of the headquarters. During the period of Gomei Kaisha when the company finalized its strategies to develop primarily on the basis of foreign trade, this point was again validated severely. When the postwar boom was coming to an end, the issuance of instructions that stated: 'pay special attention to the selection of commodities and do not rush recklessly into the pursuit of a large profit in vain,' reveals the confirmation of this principle. Mitsui Bussan, *Kohon Mitsui Bussan Kabushiki Kaisha Hyaku Nen Shi (A 100-Year History of Mitsui Bussan)*, 1978, p. 66, 184; H. Yamasaki, '1920-nendai no Mitsui Bussan,' *Senkanki no Nippon Keizai Bunseki (Analysis of Japanese Economy during the Inter-War Period)*, ed. by T. Nakamura, 1981, pp. 309–10.

58. Nissho Company, Nissho Yonju Nen no Ayumi (A 40-Year History *of Nissho*), 1968, pp. 18–21.

59. *Ibid.*, pp. 28–9.

60. *Ibid.*, p. 42. 'Employees who came fresh out of schools did not last long because the senior clerk tormented them regarding business correspondence,' *Ibid.*, p. 35. This occurred at about the end of the Meiji era when Suzuki and Co. started to employ school graduates.

61. S. Yonekawa, *op. cit.*, pp. 196–7.

62. Virtually no literature touches upon the bankruptcy of Takada and Co., but this company had invested in mining and spinning from the end of the Meiji era. The immediate causes for the bankruptcy were the Great Kanto Earthquake, the decline of the exchange rate, and the stagnation of affiliated companies. Among the bank credits, the Industrial Bank of Japan was the largest creditor, and the Eiraku Bank, which was the company's main bank, was also hit by a run. See *Chugai Shogyo Shimpo*, 20–23 February 1925.

63. Iwai Sangyo Kabushiki Kaisha, *Iwai Hyakunen Shi (A 100-Year History of Iwai)*, 1964, p. 127.

64. Nippon Menka Kabushiki Kaisha, *Kita Matazo Den (A Biography of Matazo Kita)*, 1933, pp. 86–7, 121.

65. Ito Chu Shoji, *Ito Chu Shoji Hyaku Nen (A 100-Year History of Ito Chu Shoji)*, 1969, p. 32. Although the number of Ito Chu's employees around 1912 is recorded to be 325, the number of school graduates employees was still small at the time.

66. Toyo Menka Kabushiki Kaisha, *Tomen Yonju Nen Shi (A 40-Year History of Tomen)*, 1960, pp. 75–6.

# PART TWO: Concepts

Although the Chronological and institutional history of TNCs has been well mapped out over the last two decades, business historians have been less successful in placing their research in rigorous conceptual frameworks. Nevertheless, progress has been made, as the articles selected for inclusion in this part indicate. Although most work has consisted of business historians applying economic concepts, M. Wilkins (1986) illustrated how the business historian can devise his or her own concepts. In that article, she discussed the nature of the "firm", and introduced her concept of "free-standing" companies, which she was to explore in later work.

S.J. Nicholas has been prominent in applying transactions costs and other theoretical insights to the growth of British TNCs before the Second World War. In Nicholas (1983), he discussed the transition from agencies to sales subsidiaries in British companies, using the agent-principal theory. J. Hennart (1987) and C. Schmitz (1986) explored the use of the transactions costs approach to explain TNC activity in tin and copper respectively. Hennart found the theory of use in understanding both vertical and horizontal integration in the tin industry. The article is particularly interesting in showing how differences in lode and alluvial tin mining translated into different levels of transactions costs, which, in turn, led to differences in vertical integration between the two sub-industries. By contrast, Schmitz (1986), was less convinced that transactions costs could explain all aspects of the growth of vertical integration in the international copper industry, and he emphasized the impact of technological change, particularly on the mining and smelting sectors.

H. Schröter (1988) takes up the theme that foreign direct investment is only one of several potential international business strategies. He investigated German TNCs in Scandinavia between the First and Second World Wars, and examined the factors that led them to choose between foreign direct investment, cartels and long-term contracts. Schröter argued that security was the overriding aim of German enterprises in the interwar years, and that given their scarcity of capital after 1918, that often led them to opt for participation in cartels. The discussion of the foreign direct investment versus cartel choice is particularly interesting, and merits more research given the prominence of international cartels in the interwar years. By the 1930s, between 30 per cent and 50 per cent of world trade was controlled by international cartels. After 1945, that form of transnational activity declined, but remained strong in certain sectors, particularly extractive industries and certain services, such as airlines.

# 7

# Agency Contracts, Institutional Modes, and the Transition to Foreign Direct Investment by British Manufacturing Multinationals before 1939*

Stephen Nicholas[†]

*Source: *Journal of Economic History*, 43 (1983), pp. 675–686.

This paper analyzes the transition from agents to branch selling as alternative institutional modes for transacting abroad by pre-1939 British manufacturing multinationals. A model to explain the shift between alternative modes is specified in terms of transaction costs. Agent opportunism and contract monitoring costs are the major transaction costs. Besides transaction costs, the frequency of transactions and the accumulation of market-specific knowledge by the principal were found to be important variables.

Economic historians have only recently become interested in multinational enterprise.[1] The interest was stimulated by the literature on the evolution of the large corporation and by new estimates of aggregate foreign direct investment, which found that over 40 percent of British overseas investment in the Third World and South America by 1914 was direct.[2] According to John Dunning, by 1914 company investment abroad reached £14 billion, representing as much as 35 percent of the long-term capital stake and by 1939 there were well over 350 British manufacturing multinational enterprises.[3] The studies reveal that British multinational enterprises acted as an important but neglected mechanism for transferring technology, products, management skill, and know-how abroad.

The analysis of British multinational enterprises has been largely directed to explaining the reasons firms transact abroad. Utilizing a sample of British multinational enterprises, I discovered that 50 percent had technology advantages and 45 percent selling advantages; 32 percent integrated abroad to secure raw materials and 31 percent to avoid tariffs.[4] From eight case studies of European investment in the United States, Buckley and Roberts found that the three dominant motives for making a foreign direct investment were the desire to avoid American tariffs, the opportunity to exploit "patents," and the need for local production to satisfy local demand.[5] To explain pre-1939 foreign direct investment, Dunning emphasized the technological capacity of international firms.[6] Patented technology and special skills in selling are knowledge created inside a firm but nonappropriable because of transaction costs in the international market.[7] By nonappropriable I mean that the firm is unable to capture the value to society of the knowledge. All the studies argue that the internalization of the functions of the market within the firm was the point of direct investment.[8] The firm economized on transaction costs by providing an institution for appropriating technology and selling knowledge and transferring property rights in goods.

The uniformity of approach by economic historians reflects the consensus by economists that internalization explains foreign direct investment.[9] The roots of the notion are found in Coase's work on the nature of the firm.[10] Coase derived the dictum that the firm will "tend to expand until the cost of organizing an extra transaction within the firm becomes equal to the cost of carrying out the same transaction by means of exchange in the open market."[11] Recent theoretical work has replaced the Coasian firm-market dichotomy by a "comparative institutional analysis" distinguishing institutions (such as markets, intermediate cooperative modes—agents, licensing, franchising, and other long-term contracts—and the hierarchical firm) all of which economize on transaction costs.[12] The comparative institutional analysis recognizes that nonmarket organizations do not simply duplicate the allocative results of a price system. They are chosen because they lead to a different allocation of resources.[13]

But the comparative institutional analysis is static. The transition between alternative institutions remains unexplained. The historical evidence shows British and American multinational enterprises passing through stages of overseas involvement from exporting with merchants and the firm's salesmen to the so-called agency system, thence to the foreign direct investment as a sales subsidiary, and finally to direct investment in foreign production.[14] For example, in a study of British multinational enterprises, 88 percent of the firms entered into agency agreements before making an initial direct investment in a sales branch abroad, and few British multinational enterprises began overseas production without first establishing sales subsidiaries.[15] In part, the static analysis of the comparative institutional approach arises from the failure to distinguish between the reasons firms transact abroad and the reasons they choose a particular form. The same arguments used to explain the decision to transact with foreign countries have been used to explain the choice of the mode of transacting.[16] I offer here a dynamic model to explain the transition from selling through an agency system to selling through a hierarchical sales subsidiary between 1870 and 1939. Using agent-principal theory, a transaction cost model is developed to explain the choice of mode.

## The Principal's Problem

The theory of the agent and the principal concerns long-term contracts for repeat sales. The repeat sales are between the producer (the principal) and the seller of the product (the agent). The principal will often have exported through his salesmen or merchant houses, but the appointment of an agent indicates that the principal's knowledge of the market is limited. The agent knows the language, local customs, and laws, and lives in the country where the product is sold. The principal has knowledge of the product, which is imperfectly transferred to the agent.[17] Conflicts tend to develop between agent and principal over holding stocks in the good, promotional effort, discretionary pricing, and "reasonable" levels of service.[18]

Contractual arrangements between agent and principal are essentially decision problems under uncertainty.[19] The principal tells the agent what to do. The more accurate the principal's knowledge of the agent and the lower the costs of monitoring his behavior, the lower the risks. The risks in the agent-principal problem are that the agent will make a bad decision, hurting the principal. Even if he promises not to, the agent may have incentives to cheat the principal.[20] The contract will be drawn to attenuate such opportunism. Nevertheless, there are costs of monitoring the agent, especially when he provides a service dependent on the energy he devotes to the task and when he is distant from the principal.

A commission on sales is both a control and incentive system. As a control system, commissions meter the agent's performance, allowing the principal to identify and punish bad performers. As an incentive system, commissions discourage opportunism. Having made a promise to sell vigorously, the salesman has less incentive to renege if he is on commission. The posting of a bond by the agent is another control device. Bonding includes investments by the agent in physical capital such as warehouses, or human capital such as knowledge of the product, which locks the agent into the contractual relationship.[21] The more idiosyncratic to the principal's products is the agent's specialized capital investment the greater the lock in effect of bonding. Government or legal enforcement is a third control device, used sparingly because of its great cost. Overwhelmingly, principals rely on the threat of dismissal or the withdrawal of future business for contract enforcement.[22] The model predicts a transition to branch selling when monitoring costs incurred by the principal outweigh the agency's benefits relative to branch selling. The transition from agency agreements to foreign direct investment in a selling branch by pre-1939 British multinational enterprises provides a testing ground for the model.

## Testing the Model

A nonrandom sample of 21 British multinationals was selected on the basis of archival availability and access.[23] All the sample firms met the United Nations definition of multinationals, as enterprises that control assets, either factories, mines, or sales facilities, in two or more countries.[24] The sample included a range of firm sizes. The four agricultural machinery firms were among the ten best known and largest in the 1870–1939 period, and Huntley & Palmer, Reading, and Peek Frean, London, were the two largest biscuit firms in the pre-1939 period. Other firms (for example, Harvey & Co. and Blackie & Sons Ltd.) were medium-sized firms. The basic agency contract was fairly standard across sizes of firms, specifying exclusive sales areas, sole agency requirements, and specific arrangements for performance, holding stocks of the good, and promotional effort. As far as it is possible to determine, the agency contracts for the firms in the sample correspond to agency agreements for nonsample firms.[25]

Agency contracts focused on the selling of goods and the payment for them. In every agency contract, vague (and unenforceable) provisions required the agents to "push the sale" of the principal's products.[26] Such promises to behave nonopportunistically involved monitoring by the principal. Agents could sit back and wait for orders. The demand for the principal's products, coming from investments in brand names, good will, product differentiation, and advertising, created an appropriable rent that the agent could capture at the cost of rudimentary paperwork. The scope for opportunistic behavior obviously increased when agents received some payment irrespective of the level of sales. By replacing the salary or guaranteed income with a commission the principal reduced the possibility of opportunistic behavior.[27]

One attempt to strengthen vague performance clauses and to ensure service quality was to write into the contract specific input requirements covering the amount of traveling, advertising, and showing the agent was required to do. The requirements were a form of bonding, involving investments by the agent, which locked the agent into the contractual relationship. To ensure a competent sales staff, principals required agents to invest in engineers or special salesmen with specific technical knowledge of the principal's product. For example, the 1898 agreement between Platt Bros. and N. Wadia & Sons, Bombay, stated "The Agents should at their own cost employ and retain the services of duly qualified representatives."[28] Even with such requirements, however, principals could not be sure that sales performance was adequate. One common practice was to share the expense of a technical representative or salesman, particularly when knowledge of the product was concentrated in the principal. The sugar mill machinery firm, A.W. Smith, shared the £300 salary plus expenses of a technician with their Indian agents, Martin & Co.[29] Many firms, particularly in engineering, provided a technical salesman or mechanic who lived with the agent. By 1920 five textile machinery firms, Asa Lees, Tweedale & Smalley, Platts, Dobson and Barlow, and Howard and Bullough, had one technical man at their expense based at the office of their Indian agents.[30] Having one of the principal's employees inside the agency reporting back to the principal was an effective if costly monitoring mechanism.

Perhaps the most important bonding and monitoring arrangement was the requirement that agents carry stock of the good to be sold. Stocks were vital to ensure prompt delivery, and also served as advertising when displayed in offices and showrooms. Idiosyncratic investment in machines, offices, warehouses, and showrooms effectively locked the agent into the contract. Stocks for sale purchased by the agent, however, tended to be carried at less than the optimum level, while consignment goods, which earned the agent commission but remained the principal's property, tended to be overstocked. Nearly all firms accepted that their agents would hold mainly consignment stock, since most agents lacked the capital resources to purchase stock.[31] Moreover, consignment stock allowed the principal to advance credit to customers and assured prompt delivery.

Provisions for consignments in the contract were supplemented by a range of monitoring mechanisms. Stocks were monitored by weekly, monthly, or half-yearly stocklists provided by the agents.[32] Alternatively, agents might be required to send terms of each sale to the principal.[33] The arrangements were given teeth by rights to inspect the stock, to inspect the agent's books on demand, and to appoint the agent's bookkeeper or storekeeper.[34] Nevertheless, stocks were a source of principal-agent conflict. For example, when Marshall's found that Johannes Donalsen, their Swedish agents, kept consignment stocks above the four engines and three thrashers stipulated in their 1883 agreement, a new 1889 contract specified that three engines and two thrashers could be stocked.[35] The contract encouraged vigorous selling by moving consignment stock to the sales account after 12 months and making it immediately payable to the agents.[36] Spear and Jackson's contract with Aktu Mokuzai Kaisha, Tokyo, although allowing the agent to keep consignment stock, required the agent to purchase stock valued at £1,000 per year.[37]

A large part of the costs of agency agreements involved regulating sales behavior and stock levels. The most effective monitoring mechanism was to send directors or the firm's traveling representatives to check agents. For example, after accumulating high stocks with little evidence of increasing sales activity, directors of Osborn Steel visited B.M. Jones in the United States, replacing the consignment stock agency with a purchasing or sales agency in 1909.[38] In 1911 Osborn's decided that stockholding of their Warsaw agents was not justified and sent a salesman to Warsaw to review the agency and report to the Board.[39] Frequent trips by directors and traveling representatives were undertaken by every firm with an agency network. William Mackie, a director with A.W. Smith, traveled to monitor agents in India in 1920, 1935, 1937, South Africa in 1927, South America in 1931, 1932, and the West Indies in 1933 and 1937, in addition to yearly visits by their American and European salesmen.[40] One of Ransomes's representatives made 81 trips abroad between 1890 and 1900 including 5 to France, 18 to Germany, and 8 to Russia, while directors traveled regularly to Europe and the Americas.[41]

The second major area open to opportunism was the payments system. Of course, stock monitoring and the right to inspect the books also allowed the principal to monitor payments. Such methods were superfluous when the principal insisted on direct execution of orders to customers. Spear & Jackson and Gourock Rope Company, for example, specified that the principal would bill directly.[42] But the agent, by misinforming the principal, could collect a commission by passing orders of noncreditworthy customers. As a result, contracts specified that the agent should take every precaution to pass orders only of creditworthy customers, or to advise the principal whether credit should be given.[43] Peek Frean, the London biscuit firm, required the agent to share the loss from customers' bad debts.[44] Contracts explicitly allowed principals to refuse orders or to make the final approval of orders.[45] Despite such safeguards bad debts were common under the agency system. There were also risks in receiving payment for stock on consignment when customers paid agents for goods that were the property of the principal. A common arrangement was the requirement that agents pay by bill of exchange or letters of credit drawn on a London or European merchant house.[46] In these cases the draft or credit letter guaranteed the principal payment but involved the agent in the expense of a commission to the financial house.[47] Principals also encouraged payment through charging interest on outstanding payments and offering a discount—usually $2^{1}/_{2}$ or 3 percent—for cash within one to three months of the sale. The provisions, however, did not always work. Osborn's in 1905 demanded that their American agents, B.M. Jones, reduce their outstanding credit of £23,000. When the next six months witnessed the dispatch of goods valued at £11,000 but payment of only £9,600, a director's investigation of the agency resulted.[48] Sales representatives or directors also were used as a monitoring and enforcement mechanism to encourage payment. When Ransomes's agent in Rumania in 1882, F. Freund, "never completed payments within specified times," Ransomes's director visited Freund in 1883 to sort out discounts, payment, and the size of the trade.[49] Ransomes's found that Freund was "perfectly honest."[50] A Fowler's director sent to sort out a similar problem at the Societa Anonime La Penetrazione Roma concluded that "the main trouble is that Fowler's are completely in the hands of the Italians who are as cute as can be."[51]

The ultimate enforcement device was the termination of the contract.

The standard nonrenewal clause required three to twelve months notice after the contract had run a specific duration, usually two years but on occasion as many as ten. Additional termination conditions including "failure to carry out provisions," "termination at any time," or "termination at the pleasure of the principal" favored the principal.[52] Many principals followed Spear and Jackson's contracts, which provided for termination due to "misconduct or incapacity," and in fact, most terminations were for fraud or concealment by the agents.[53] The option of termination in midcourse was, however, rarely used. Most agency agreements ended by nonrenewal. For example, Burn & Co. were appointed by A.W. Smith as their Indian agents in 1932 and immediately ran into trouble over nonfulfillment of the agency contract. Rather than terminating the agency, Smith's decided in June 1935 to await payment by Burn before ending the agreement. By September a further recommendation saw nonrenewal replace termination "due to the threat of a lawsuit which would freeze money in India."[54]

### Frequency and Nature of Transacting and Learning

A solution to costs resulting from monitoring and opportunism is vertical integration. There is evidence that shifts from an agency system to a selling subsidiary occurred in order to economize on such costs. The shifts seem commonly to occur as direct investment in response to a crisis, where the collapse of the agency triggers investment in a selling branch by the principal. For example, John Dickinson, papermakers, Cape Asbestos, Harvey & Co., engineers, Thomas Fenner, makers of leather belts for machinery, all established sales branches as a response to crisis.[55] Nevertheless, it would be misleading to see crisis investment as the typical case of the transition between agency and branch selling. Most firms who made a foreign direct investment in branch selling were not reacting to an immediate contractual breakdown, but were investing abroad after an agency nonrenewal. To construct the theory of foreign direct investment solely on the basis of transaction costs disregards the cooperative nature of contracts. What really happened is that the principal gradually gained information about the market, including the name of customers through direct sales data, regular stocklist, and sales reports by the agent. The monitoring of the agency relationship, by which directors and travelers visited the agents, inspected books and stock, and provided skilled mechanics and representatives, meant an accumulation of knowledge within the firm on the servicing of a particular overseas market. Learning by the principal made the agent unnecessary, even occasionally when sales were few.

There was, however, a minimum sales volume or transaction frequency before a foreign direct investment could be undertaken. For example, Ransomes calculated that a £10,000-a-year trade would be required before a Paris depot could economically compete with an agency trading on less than £2,000 per year.[56] The costs of running branch sales offices were not insignificant, as the 1929 cost of Fowler's Budapest branch of £11,593 and George Wostenholm's New York City branch of £15,700 per year show.[57] The wholly-owned sales subsidiary incurred higher fixed transaction costs but a lower marginal cost of extending sales relative to employing an agent.[58] Furthermore, the larger the number of sales the greater were the monitoring costs of the agency system. Thus, the propensity to establish branch sales was greater the larger were the number of sales, the more complex the product, the greater the idiosyncratic investment in specialized capital and brand name by the principal, and the greater the appropriable rents from opportunism by agents. In part, this explains the sophisticated sales and stock level monitoring arrangements utilized by the agricultural and engineering firms.

Clearly, then, the timing of the transition between modes depended on the frequency and nature of sales, the size of the opportunities for cheating, and the extent of the firm's knowledge of the market. Knowledge of markets was most easily gained by taking over the agent. Fowler's asked their South Africa agent W.A. McLaren in March 1904 to investigate the establishment of branch selling.[59] "The only advantageous way to work our business in South Africa is to work it ourselves," McLaren argued, since there was a "business to work up which needed a lot of energy and special knowledge of machines."[60] McLaren argued that a branch would give people confidence that the firm was not composed of "itinerant bagmen who may never be seen again."[61] In 1905 a South African branch managed by McLaren was opened. Similarly, in 1939 Cowan's took the advice of Conmon Thompson and Thomas Steed, their Argentinian agents, to establish a warehouse, and the agents became full-time company employees.[62] When Cowan's took over their Brisbane agents the staff, including five salesmen, some motormen, warehousemen, office boys, clerks, and typists, were all continued.[63] The establishment of most selling branches did not involve the take-over of former agents, but it did require learning about the market.

## Conclusion

The agency system was a unique institution, in which information on markets and products was exchanged between agent and principal. For the principal the exchange of information was a learning experience about servicing a distant market. Market-specific knowledge shifted down the costs functions for branch selling relative to the agency. The greater the frequency of transactions and the more complex the nature of transactions the higher the costs of agency contracting and the relatively cheaper was branch selling. The accumulation of country-specific knowledge of markets, and some minimum transaction frequency were key variables in the timing of the transition to a foreign direct investment in a selling organization by British pre-1939 multinational enterprises. Of course, opportunism and monitoring costs were not totally eliminated: they occurred within the firm-owned selling branch itself. Within the firm however, the organization could be more effectively audited and the machinery of resolving disputes within the firm replaced termination and nonrenewal as enforcement mechanisms. The firm-owned selling branch reflected the growing institutional and organizational maturity of British multinational enterprise in the years before World War II. The shift from one institution to another was dynamic and historical, a matter of learning by doing.

## Notes

† The author would like to thank Mark Casson, Diane Mort, Donald N. McCloskey, and two referees for assistance. The usual disclaimer on errors applies.

1. John Stopford, "The origins of British Based Multinational Manufacturing Enterprises," *Business History Review*, 48 (Autumn 1974), 303–45; D. Paterson, *British Direct Investment in Canada, 1870–1914* (Toronto, 1976); S.J. Nicholas, "British Multinational Investment Before 1939," *Journal of European Economic History*, 11 (Winter 1982), 605–30; Peter J. Buckley and Brian Roberts, *European Direct Investment in the U.S.A. Before World War I* (London, 1982).

2. Peter Svedberg, "The Portfolio: Direct Composition of Private Foreign Investment in 1914 Revisited," *Economic Journal*, 88 (Dec. 1978), 690–722.

3. John Dunning, "Changes in the Level and Structure of International Production: The Last 100 Years," mimeographed (1982), pp. 4, 31.

4. Nicholas, "Multinational Investment," p. 10.

5. Buckley and Roberts, *European Direct Investment*, p. 119.

6. Dunning, "International Production," pp. 4.26–4.65.

7. See Peter J. Buckley and Mark Casson, *The Future of the Multinational Enterprise* (London, 1976), pp. 10–30; Mark C. Casson, *Alternative to the Multinational Enterprise* (London, 1979), pp. 31–43; Harry G. Johnson, "The Efficiency and Welfare Implications of the International Corporation" in *The International Corporation*, ed. Charles P. Kindleberger (Cambridge, Massachusetts, 1970), pp. 35–39; Steven P. Magee, "Technology and the Appropriability Theory of the Multinational Corporation" in *The New International Economic Order*, ed. J. Bhajwati (Cambridge, Massachusetts, 1976), pp. 319–21.

8. See Buckley and Roberts, *European Direct Investment*, pp. 8–9; Nicholas, "Multinational Investment," pp. 9–10; Dunning, "International Production," pp. 4–24, 4–34.

9. For a review of the literature see A.K. Calvet, "A Synthesis of Foreign Direct Investment Theories and Theories of the Multinational Firm," *Journal of International Business Studies*, 12 (Spring/Summer 1981), 43–57.

10. R.H. Coase, "The Nature of the Firm," *Economica*, n.s. 4 (1937), 381–405.

11. Ibid., p. 397.

12. A. Alchian and H. Demsetz, "Production, Information Costs and Economic Organization," *American Economic Review*, 62 (Dec. 1972), 777–95; C.J. Dahlman, "The Problem of Externality," *Journal of Law and Economics*, 22 (April 1979), 141–62; O. Williamson, "The Modern Corporation: Origins, Evolution, Attributes," *Journal of Economic Literature*, 19 (Dec. 1981), 1545–50.

13. John C. McManus, "The Costs of Alternative Economic Organizations," *Canadian Journal of Economics*, 8 (Nov. 1975), 335–50.

14. Nicholas, "Multinational Investment," pp. 14–16. See also Mira Wilkins, *The Emergence of Multinational Enterprise* (Cambridge, Massachusetts, 1970), pp. 207–13; Mira Wilkins, *The Maturing of Multinational Business* (Cambridge, Massachusetts, 1979), pp. 417–22, 432–37; Buckley and Roberts, *European Direct Investment*, pp. 44, 65, 87, 91–92.

15. Nicholas, "Multinational Investment," p. 15.

16. For a similar point see Calvet, "Synthesis," p. 56.

17. Magee, "Technology," p. 316.

18. This problem has been examined by the marketing channel literature. See L.W. Stern, B. Sternthal, and C.S. Craig, "Managing Conflict in Distribution Channels: A Laboratory Study," *Journal of Marketing Research*, 10 (May 1973), 169–79; M. Pearson and J. Monoly, "The Role of Conflict and Co-operation in Channel Performance," in *Marketing: 1776–1976 and Beyond*, ed. K.L. Bernhardt (Chicago, 1976), pp. 240–44; L.J. Rosenberg and L.W. Stern, "Conflict Measurement in the Distribution Channel," *Journal of Marketing Research*, 8 (Nov. 1971), 437–42.

19. M.C. Jensen and W.H. Meckling, "Theory of the Firm: Managerial Behaviour, Agency Costs and Ownership Structure," *Journal of Financial Economics*, 3 (Nov. 1976), 305–11; Stephen Ross, "The Economic Theory of Agency: The Principal's Problem," *American Economic Review*, 63 (May 1973), 134–49; Stephen Ross, "On the Economic Theory of Agency and the Principal of Similarity," in *Essays on Economic Behaviour Under Uncertainty*, ed. M. Balch, D. McFadden, and S. Wu (Amsterdam, 1974), pp. 215–20.

20. Oliver Williamson, *Markets and Hierarchies: Analysis and Antitrust Implications* (New York, 1975), pp. 26–37; David J. Teece, *Vertical Integration and Divestiture in the U.S. Oil Industry* (Stanford, 1976), p. 31; Oliver Williamson, "Transaction-Cost Economics: The Governance of Contractual Relations," *Journal of Law and Economics*, 22 (Oct. 1979), p. 233. Of course, the principal could also act opportunistically. The paper, however, is concerned with the principal establishing branch selling rather than the agent's contractual problems with the principal.

21. B. Klein, R. Crawford, and A. Alchian, "Vertical Integration, Appropriable Rents, and the Competitive Contracting Process," *Journal of Law and Economics*, 11 (Oct. 1978), 297–326; B. Klein, "Transaction Cost Determinants of 'Unfair' Contractual Arrangements," *American Economic Review*, 70 (May 1980), 356–62; B. Klein and K. Leffler, "The Role of Market Forces in Assuring Contractual Performances," *Journal of Political Economy*, 89 (Aug. 1981), 615–41; Williamson, "Transaction Cost Economics," p. 234, 238–45; Klein, "'Unfair' Contractual Arrangements," pp. 358–59; Klein, Crawford, and Alchian, "Competitive Contracting Process," pp. 302–7; Klein and Leffler, "Role of Market Forces," pp. 618–25.

22. Klein, Crawford, and Alchian, "Competitive Contracting Process," p. 303; Klein and Leffler, "Role of Market Forces," pp. 616–20.

23. The firms, by industrial groups, were Huntley & Palmer and Peek Frean in food; Bentall, Ransomes, Marshall and Fowler in agricultural machinery; A.W.

Smith and Mirrlees Watson in sugar-crushing machinery; Alexander Cowan and Blackie & Sons Ltd. in paper and publishing; in steel products and cutlery, Osborn Steel, Spear and Jackson, and George Wostenholm & Sons; in engineering, the pump makers, Weir, and Harvey & Co.; Gourock Rope Company in rope; Morton (Sundour) and Linen Thread Company Ltd. in textiles; and Beardmore in shipbuilding and iron and steel. The merchant houses, Anthony Gibb, London, and John Finlay, Scotland, acted as agents when they signed exclusive agreements to represent British firms abroad.

24. United Nations, *Transactional Corporations in World Development: A Re-Examination*, E.78 II A5 (New York, 1978). This definition is also used by the Group of Eminent Persons in their report, United Nations, *The Impact of Multinational Corporations on Development and on International Relations*, E.74 II A5 (New York, 1974), p. 25; and by John Dunning, *International Production and the Multinational Enterprise* (London, 1981), p. 3. Further, 13 of the firms subsequently made an investment in assembly and manufacturing in the period.

25. D. Coleman, *Courtaulds: An Economic and Social History* (Oxford, 1969), vol. 1, p. 193. I would like to thank Robert Kirk for information on Platt Bros. agency contracts.

26. For example, Spear and Jackson's agent promised to "diligently and faithfully service the market to the best of his ability and judgment" (Spear and Jackson, Agreements, SJ65 3/7/29, Sheffield Public Libraries Archives). Gourock's agent agreed "to take steps to introduce and sell to local customers" (Gourock, Agency Agreements, UGD42/163/3, 22/1/31, University of Glasgow Archives [where page numbers are not available the date of the reference is given]).

27. Spear and Jackson, Agency Correspondence, Alex Vox, Paris, SJC65, 26/4/27, 1/6/27, 3/7/29, Sheffield Public Libraries Archives.

28. Platt, Agreement, DDPSL 1/109/1, Lancashire Record Office, Preston. Also Fowler, Toepffer Agreement, CO1/9, Institute for Agricultural History, University of Reading; and Bentall, Agreements, DFI/16 1924, Essex Record Office.

29. A.W.Smith, Directors' Minute Book, UGD118/13/1, 19/2/69, p. 5, University of Glasgow Archives.

30. S.M. Rutnager, *Bombay Industries: The Cotton Mills* (Bombay, 1927), pp. 643–46. I would also like to thank Robert Kirk for information on this point.

31. In 1929 Fowler's stocked machinery valued at £15,297 with their Italian agents and £16,956 with their German agents. Fowler, Memorandum on Branches, AC9/63, 31/12/29, Institute for Agricultural History.

32. Marshall, Agency Term Book No. 1, pp. 238–40, Institute for Agricultural History; Gourock, Agency Agreements, UGD42/103/3, 22/10, 31, University of Glasgow Archives; Smith, Minute Book, UGD118/13/1, 17/8/14, p. 114, University of Glasgow Archives.

33. Ransomes, Agency Book, AD7/48, p. 7, Institute for Agricultural History.

34. Ibid., pp. 36–42; Marshall, Agency Term Book No. 1, pp. 238–40, Institute for Agricultural History; Fowler, Toepffer Agreement, CO1/9, Institute for Agricultural History.

35. Marshall, Agency Term Book No. 1, pp. 165–68, 183, Institute for Agricultural History.

36. Ibid., p. 274.

37. Spear and Jackson, Agreements, SJC65 10/2/20, Sheffield Public Libraries Archives.

38. Osborn, Letter Book, Osb. 17, pp. 220, 230, 397, 421, Sheffield Public Libraries Archives.

39. Osborn, Works Meeting Minutes 1907–24, Osb. 142 9/10/11, 11/12/11. Sheffield Public Libraries Archives.

40. A.W. Smith, Directors' Minutes No. 1, UGD118/17/2a, pp. 11, 149; Directors' Minutes No. 2, UGD118/17/2b, pp. 102, 104, 127, 232–34, 275, University of Glasgow Archives.

41. G. Palmer, "The History of the Orwell Works," p. SPI/IHS, Institute for Agricultural History.

42. Spear and Jackson, Agreements, SJC65 3/7/29, Sheffield Public Libraries Archives; Gourock, Agency Agreements, UGD42/103/3 1/12/27, University of Glasgow Archives.

43. Gourock, Agency Agreements, UGD42/103/3 1/8/14; 1/12/27.

44. Peek Frean, *Carr Agency Records*, PK13/4 1/7/01, University of Reading Library Archives.

45. Spear and Jackson, Agreements, SJC65 12/3/19, 3/7/29, Sheffield Public Libraries Archives.

46. Ransomes, Agency Book, AD7/49, pp. 68–79, Institute for Agricultural History; Gourock, Agency Agreement, UGD42/103/3 1/6/26, 4/22, University of Glasgow Archives.

47. Gibb, General Records: Macfarlaine Strong Co. 1889, Ms 11,668/1, London Guildhall Archives; E.J. Perkins, *Financing Anglo-American Trade: The House of Brown, 1800–1880* (Cambridge, Massachusetts, 1978), pp. 5–8; P. Cottrell, "Commercial Enterprise," in *The Dynamics of Victorian Business*, ed. Roy Church (London, 1980), p. 240.

48. Osborn, Letter Book, Osb. 17, pp. 222–30, 397, 421, Sheffield Public Libraries Archives.

49. Ransomes, Agency Book, AD7/48, p. 8, Institute for Agricultural History.

50. Ibid.

51. Fowler, Packet: Societa Anonime La Penetrazione Roma, AD6/8, Institute for Agricultural History.

52. Marshall, Agency Term Book No. 1, pp. 47–48, 235–37, Institute for Agricultural History; Peek Frean, Special Agencies, PF14/2, University of Reading Library Archives.

53. Spear and Jackson, Agreements, SJC65 3/7/29, Sheffield Public Libraries Archives.

54. A.W. Smith, Directors' Minute Book, UGD118/13/2, pp. 213–14, 221–27, 275, University of Glasgow Archives.

55. J. Evans, *The Endless Web: John Dickinson & Co. 1804–1954* (London, 1955), pp. 138–41; *Cape Asbestos: The Story of Cape Asbestos Co. Ltd., 1894–1953* (private, 1953); Harvey, Johannesburg Branch: Hosken's Account, DDH/85, Cornwall County Record Office, Truro; E. Vale, *The Harvey's of Hayle* (private, 1960), p. 44; R. Davies, *Twenty One and a Half Bishops Lane: A History of J.H. Fenner & Co. Ltd.* (private, 1961).

56. Palmer, "Orwell Works," p. SPA/1F54C, Institute for Agricultural History.

57. Fowler, Branch Reports, AC7/63, Institute for Agricultural History; Wostenholm, New York Office, WosR12(b), Sheffield Public Libraries Archives.

58. Peter Buckley and M. Casson, "The Optimal Timing of a Foreign Investment," *Economic Journal*, 91 (March 1981), 75–87; M. Casson, "Forward," in *Inside the Multinationals: The Economics of Internal Markets*, A. Rugman (London, 1981), pp. 15–21; Buckley, "New Theories of International Business," pp. 2.12–15.

59. Fowler, South African Branch Correspondence, AD6/11 3/04, Institute for Agricultural History.

60. Ibid.
61. Ibid.
62. Cowan, Reports: Argentina 1938, UGD311/7/34, University of Glasgow Archives.
63. Cowan, Reports: Australia, UGD311/7/34, University of Glasgow Archives.

# 8

# Defining a Firm: History and Theory*

## Mira Wilkins

*Source: P. Hertner and G. Jones, eds., *Multinationals: Theory and History* (Aldershot, Gower, 1986), pp. 80–95.

## Introduction

As a business historian, I thought I knew what a firm was. If I started with the records of a company, I could see its growth and boundaries. Business history records defined for me an emerging operating entity, which had relationships with many otherwise independent firms. On occasion, when I studied the history of American business in its international dimensions, I puzzled over the limits of the firm. Most of the time, it seemed clear to me that I began with a US-headquartered company and could see it spreading its operations across borders—seeking new markets and new sources of supply and accordingly making foreign investments. I viewed the evolution of the multinational enterprise (MNE) as part of a process, whereby a domestic firm expanded into foreign investments. Theory helped in defining the advantages held by those enterprises that moved internationally, explaining why a firm in electrical equipment did and one in furniture did not invest in other countries. Recently, however, my research on foreign investment in the United States has plunged me into thinking about different theoretical considerations and into facing an immense and confusing secondary literature. Suddenly, I had a new problem, which was how to define the 'firm'.

## The Problem

First, the theoretical issues. I have become interested in the transaction-cost and the market-hierarchy approach to business history.[1] This stimulating approach of Oliver Williamson has excited the attention of Alfred Chandler and others.[2] The theoretical questions posed are: When does a firm extend itself, and when does this extension stop? Why does one firm integrate vertically and another sell to agents or buy from independent suppliers?[3] What shapes the growth of and particularly the direction of the growth of a firm? When is the firm more efficient than the market? As I studied the history of multinational enterprise and considered such issues, obviously I had to define the limits of the firm. I had to decide what a firm is.

Second, the secondary literature issues. The more research I did on European investment in the United States, the more I faced works by economists on capital flows that ignored the firm, put it into a peripheral role, or took it for granted. Since I wanted to understand European investment in the United States and sought to do so in terms of what I already knew about the growth of multinational enterprise, I found that I was in trouble. Thus I was back to the question of deciding what a firm is.[4]

## Definition

I have no problem with a definition of the firm as a producer of goods and services, or as an allocator of resources.[5] Likewise, the firm as a nexus of implicit or explicit contracts or contracting relationships[6] seems legitimate. A domestic firm operates within one nation; a multinational firm extends over national borders to operate (to do more than export) under more than one national sovereign. The definitions of the firm by economists and historians are not confined to any single legal form. A firm can be a proprietorship, partnership, company, corporation, branch, 'enterprise', or a commonly controlled or administered cluster of any or all of the above. My difficulties related to the boundaries of the firm, the limits of what constitutes a firm, and particularly a multinational firm.[7]

## Ownership and Control: The General Issues

As every business historian knows, the 'typical' pre-1850s firm combined ownership and control. The firm was one with its founder, owner, and manager. As business enterprise developed in the late nineteenth and twentieth centuries, there came to be a separation of ownership and control. Owners delegated to managers. An administrative organisation emerged. Overtime, relatively more people came to participate in administration, selling, research and development, and other such activities than in production per se.[8] There came to be not only top management, but middle management. The firm—in modern terms—has to be defined as separate from its owners.[9]

As a firm expanded over borders, over distance, there came very early to be a need for specialisation, delegation, and thus the separation of ownership and management. Indeed, unlike the typical domestic firm, already in the giant trading companies of the seventeenth century, the normal pattern was for the owners (shareholders) to remain in England, Holland or Sweden, and men were stationed overseas representing the owners.

Distance almost by definition meant delegation, since the individual owner could not be in two places at once.[10] In multinational enterprise, there came to be hierarchy not only in administrative, but in ownership delegation. The modern multinational 'enterprise' is in fact usually a cluster of owned firms (subsidiaries or affiliates) set up in foreign lands. In dealing with American multinational enterprise, I had had few problems. The firm was the owner; it controlled its overseas operations. Ownership and control was joined within the firm. I bypassed entirely the top ownership tier—that of the shareholders in the enterprise.

When I started to consider nineteenth and early-twentieth century European multinational enterprise, I needed to ask, when was ownership distinct from the firm and when was it one with the firm? What emerged was that 'owners' (individuals or firms) could be portfolio or direct investors or both, depending on *intention* and, more important, on the size of the investment relative to other investors in the same venture. If they were portfolio investors, ownership was separate from the firm. If they were 'direct' investors, it was one with the firm. Thus, individual owners had investments at home and abroad; some investments were large enough to exercise control or influence; these were direct investments. Likewise, firms had portfolio (purely financial) holdings *and* direct investments.[11] Domestic concepts of ownership and control were replicated internationally.

### Ownership and Control: The Family

This brought me back to the family firm. The giant international trading companies of the seventeenth century were in a sense anomalies. Some (the Hudson's Bay Company, for example) persisted and changed their character. Modern MNEs, companies connected by rapid transmission of information between and among the associated companies in a grouping, are quite distinct from the early chartered companies.[12] Accordingly, as we look at the history of multinational enterprise, we must ask: did the family firm, which clearly was so important in European enterprise, extend itself abroad, and if so, how? By definition, a family firm joins ownership and control. In the late nineteenth and early twentieth century as the modern MNE began to take form, internationally brothers, sons, and relatives served to extend the family firm internationally—in trade, banking, *and* manufacturing.

The family was the binder, the 'cement' of an enterprise. Trust between members of the family linked separate businesses into one and lowered internal transaction costs. Families in trade shared confidences. The Lazard brothers, for example, in trade and banking set up distinct houses, but they acted in concert. Eberhard Faber, who made pencils in the United States from 1861, was in the same industry as his father had been, and his brothers were, in Germany. George Merck in the United States in the late nineteenth and early twentieth century established a manufacturing facility in the United States essentially separate from E. Merck in Germany, but the two businesses pooled profits, technology, product information, and marketing knowledge. Family loyalty unified these enterprises, making the actual legal, commercial, and financial structures (that varied from case to case) less relevant to our definition of the firm than the mode of carrying on business (the *implicit* internal contracts). We have to ask, were these family affairs a 'firm' or more than one? We have a cluster, at times a very loose cluster, but certainly a unity of behaviour. What are the boundaries of a firm?

As I tried to define the MNE in the context of the family, it seemed legitimate to see ownership and management as joined across borders through the extended family and appropriate to call these multinational enterprises. Only after the divorce between ownership and management has occurred does the firm become equated with the *operating* entity separate from the ownership tier.[13] Thus, the family that sent its sons and brothers around the world acted as a firm, providing an implicit unity of management—and we can, I believe, talk legitimately of the Lazard house, or the Speyers, Rothschilds, Fabers, Mercks or Barbours as firms, to cite some pre-World War I examples. The scale of business and the ties between the houses in different nations varied substantially; there was delegation; but in each case the association was real. The implicit internal contracts were present.

Now, I want to add a complication. The Coats family in Scotland was active in J. & P. Coats Ltd which had thread factories in many parts of the world, including the United States. No scholar would deny J. & P. Coats Ltd the designation of multinational enterprise. Individual members of the Coats family also controlled (or had controlling interests in) mining and timber companies in the United States. Was the Coats 'family' a firm? Could a family, as one of my colleagues (Jean-François Hennart) suggested, act as a modern-day conglomerate, allocating financial resources? How do we define the firm? We are back to the issues of separating ownership and control. Owners can be involved in various investments (linked only by financial planning); unlike the family that plans its financial interests, the modern-day conglomerate sets up a structure for coordination (however small the central office may be); ownership of the conglomerate (the unifier) is distinct from the institutional entity, which in turn has its network of owned and coordinated units that *are* part of the firm. In the case of the Coats family's multitude of investment projects, no institutional unity separate from the individual family members emerged to coalesce the mining and sewing thread investments. In short, to understand the firm, we have to see it as sometimes one with the family or individual investor (the owner), but the unity of action must have some semblance of a separate 'operating' life. It did in the cases of the Faber and Merck families in Germany and the United States, and the Barbour family in Northern Ireland and the United States. It did not in the case of the Coats family in sewing thread and mining. Thus, we can see each of the personal Coats investments in the United States as a separate interest and define J. & P. Coats Ltd's investments in thread mills and marketing as that of *the* multinational firm.

**Ownership and Control: Other International Investments**

In the late nineteenth century, European capital flowed into US railroads. Investments were made by both individuals and non-railroad firms. The railroads were incorporated in the United States, had operating managements in the United States, and ownership was in the main divorced from management. To be sure, at times owners (domestic or foreign) had interests large enough to exercise control. When they could do so on a regular basis, there was a clear direct investment (the Erlangers in the Alabama Southern, for example). Normally, the firm (the railroad) and the ownership (foreign shareholders) were distinct.

Lord Strathcona had, for instance, giant investments in the Great Northern Railroad and in the Anglo-Persian Oil Company. As in an individual investor, nothing in his role *per se* united the American railroad with the British oil company. Thus, Lord Strathcona (like the Coats family in mining and sewing thread) did not act as a firm, much less a multinational one. Strathcona is, however, a foreign investor *in firms.* As an investor in the Great Northern Railroad (albeit a large one), he was separate and distinct from the Great Northern, which was the 'firm'.

**The Free-standing Firm**

My next problem involved the 'free-standing firm', incorporated in the United Kingdom, with a small head office there, but which did business in the United States.[14] S.J. Nicholas labelled such enterprises as 'little more than a brass nameplate someplace in the City'.[15] Were these 'multinational' firms? This form was not confined to business in the United States. The US Federal Trade Commission published a formidable list of British-organised or -controlled companies whose properties in 1914 were located outside the United Kingdom, United States, and Canada.[16] Students of British and continental European multinational enterprise must understand these ventures.[17] I am only going to discuss those that did business in the United States, since these are the ones I know something about, but the ideas I am presenting here should have broader applications.

Typically, especially in the years 1865–1900, a promoter (American or British) would discover an 'opportunity' in the United States, a mine, a cattle ranch, or manufacturing plant. The promoter would establish a company incorporated in the United Kingdom to raise money in that country to buy the properties. The 'vendors' would be paid in cash raised in the United Kingdom and in the stock of the new British company. The sellers would sometimes be retained to manage the new venture; sometimes new management was installed. A board of directors was established in Britain, with a roster of important names (members of parliament, members of the nobility). Often on the board of directors there would be someone who knew something about mining, cattle raising, breweries, etc. The promoter of a brewery company, for example, would select important brewers in Britain to investigate the US facilities and sit on the board. This would reassure prospective investors. Sometimes (but not always) there was an American 'board' of management, or if a US subsidiary existed, even a US board of directors. The pinnacle board of directors was in Great Britain.[18]

After the initial flotation, the firm maintained a UK address; the British Board of directors met (sometimes often: in one case, bi-weekly; sometimes seldom); a company secretary was appointed to monitor what was happening. In short, a home office in the United Kingdom existed, however minimal its functions. While the British home office did not market the output of the US mines, cattle ranches, flour mills, or breweries, it did intervene to varying degrees in financial and other decision-making. I asked whether I should treat such companies as multinational firms. They were not existing UK domestic businesses that extended themselves, nor were they family firms that became international. None the less, they were firms. They were the means by which capital was mobilised, *managed*, exported, and allocated. They had an ongoing institutionalised relationship with the capital that was transferred and provided a means of avoiding sending abroad 'disembodied' capital; by the latter, I mean exported capital not encased in any ongoing institutional 'hierarchy'. These firms are not the same as the capital flow from individuals or from firms into American railroads, where the railroad was distinct from its owners and where the capital input was not linked with any continuing operating relationship that extended beyond intermittent attempts to safeguard the investment.[19] These free-standing firms did cross borders; they did have ownership and the potential for control.

As theory pushed me to ask why a multinational firm is successful, I gained insights into why these free-standing multinational firms (at least in the United States) were notoriously unsuccessful: They did not grow out of the needs of existing enterprises to become multinational. They did not build on existing UK operating entities that had knowledge, experience, technology, and goodwill; thus, they did not benefit from the economies of international management.

Their rationale for existence in the United Kingdom was to tap British capital markets. That was their 'advantage'. While some of the American mines may have gained from UK expertise, while some of the US cattle ranches certainly imported British quality cattle into the United States, while some of these firms had very knowledgeable part-time directors, in most instances (at least as far as the American case was concerned), the presence of a British suprastructure brought only additional cost. These free-standing firms were separate from their promoters (that was their origin, but not the rationale for their sustained existence)[20] and separate from their stockholders. I view them as a form of foreign direct investment (a type of MNE) that in the US setting often floundered because the firm was unable to capture the very advantages (experience, technology, goodwill) that provide the basis for effective and efficient multinational enterprise.

In this paper, I have been cautious to confine my generalised findings on the free-standing firm to the US case; yet, as noted, this type of firm was not simply an Anglo-American phenomenon. Did it function better in South Africa, Australia, India, Argentina, Persia? Was it identical in those contexts? More study is required. In less-developed countries, the extension of a known corporate and administrative structure to a locale where political uncertainty was high may well have provided benefits to offset the costs of such a form, whereas for the United States the introduction of a British legal corporate entity was usually redundant, that is, unnecessary for securing property rights and inadequate in and of itself for securing effective control. There is also evidence that in at least some of the non-US cases the British 'home office' rose to the opportunity, developed or acquired the needed expertise, bought the technology (and 'internalised' it within the firm), set up research and development establishments, and came to acquire an administrative organisation that was far more than one or a handful of individuals occupying an 'office.' In these cases, the firm succeeded, benefiting from the economies of international management.[21]

## Why the Large Number of Free-standing Firms?

Why in Britain did all these free-standing firms exist while relatively fewer evolutions similar to those of the US multinational enterprise took place?

Firstly, in the late nineteenth century, when this form began to proliferate, Britain was a major capital exporter. Available captial was an important British advantage. These firms captured, that is, institutionalised, the capital export process in a manner not unlike the other institutional forms that contemporaneously served that function (those typically associated with Lombard Street).

My second insight was similar. When I studied American business abroad, I found it emerged in the context of its special environment. The United States was the world's largest domestic market. Enterprises gained experience at home with business over distance. This was then reflected abroad. But what of Britain? In the late nineteenth century firms merged;[22] firms grew domestically; yet the experience in the domestic market with multi-plant interactions over long distance was, because of the geographical facts of life, less than that of US business. Perhaps the ubiquitous free-standing firms in international investment that appeared in Great Britain were an outcome of conditions at home. In the American case, firms were familiar with extending themselves domestically and they went over borders in a comparable fashion; in the British case, there was not the same experience with domestic extension and so the crossing over borders 'within an existing firm' was less of a natural process.

In passing, I might note the other side of the coin: as I have studied foreign business within the United States, I have been impressed with how many established multiplant operations and how rapidly. This was true of 'free-standing' companies (with their numerous breweries) as well as of the more typical British MNEs (English Sewing Cotton's American Thread Company, for instance, had from origin many plants in the United States). When I studied US business abroad, it was always, initially anyway, one plant per country; multiplant establishments in individual nations abroad came later in the sequence. The point is one with my discussion. American business was familiar with a large-scale market; markets in foreign countries were, relatively speaking, segmented. Foreign businesses in the United States knew (were prepared to cope with) a relatively limited domestic market and the geographical dimensions of the American market meant the requirement for many branches and several plants.

**The Firm and its Special Relationships**

A number of European companies developed in the United States special relationships that are hard to classify. Thus, for example, the Rothschilds sent August Belmont to the United States in 1837; he replaced two bankrupt former 'agents'. Belmont was not a member of the Rothschild family. Initially (but only initially), he appears to have been paid a salary. Yet he came to be 'the Rothschilds' in the United States and after his death in 1890 his son continued as the Rothschilds' American representative. Was Belmont part of the firm? August Belmont & Co. had regular correspondence with N.M. Rothschild & Sons, London, and represented their interests. Yet the literature talks of no Rothschild house in the United States. How do we make the distinction?

Let us take the case of Pears' soap in America before World War I. The British soap company (before it was acquired by Lever Brothers) had for many years exported to the United States; it had an independent agent acting on its behalf. The agent proved extremely effective; Pears' soap was brilliantly advertised in the United States. The success of the agent seems to have militated against this company's integrating forward into direct investment in selling in the United States, although it seems to have owned a warehouse.

When I started to look at the market-hierarchy approach, I faced a problem. Belmont and Pears' agent would not have been part of 'hierarchy'—part of the Rothschild house or the Pears' firm—but the connections could hardly be described as arm's-length or market ones. Soon, however, I discovered that the market-hierarchy literature did not simply deal with the dichotomy between firm and market, but that Oliver Williamson had in 1979 specified an intermediate mode, which I found extremely helpful in looking at the nature of a firm in its foreign (as well as domestic) expansion.[23] I would like to argue that there are three *discrete* modes. The first mode is the firm that has limits, although they may be difficult to define. The second is the contract, by which I mean a whole range of special relationships that are not hierarchy, but are far from market. The third mode is the market, where there are arm's-length exchanges between parties to a transaction, that is, no special association can be identified between buyer and seller.[24]

What has long been evident is that firms as they expand internationally can simply export or purchase goods abroad; they can develop alliances or, alternatively, they can extend themselves, that is, make direct investments. We have long known that a firm often sells through an independent agent abroad, then in its largest markets replaces that agent with direct investment in marketing, and later makes further direct investments. The literature has discussed international licensing arrangements, managing agencies, management contracts. What theory has helped me to recognise is that most firms have all kinds of *regular, recurrent* involvements with 'outsiders' that are not part of the firm. This is true both domestically and internationally. I began to think about the nature of these close ties. There is the 'agent' who acts for the firm in specific capacities, who is not an employee. The Ford dealer uses the company name, has a recurring relationship, is dependent on the firm, but he is an 'independent dealer'. Many suppliers of giant enterprises rely for sales on their major (or only) customer; yet they are not part of that firm. Firms that are licensed to use a company's know-how, technology, patents, are often both distinct yet dependent. Division-of-market agreements between *otherwise independent entities* regularise connections without creating a firm.[25]

Hierarchical unity of administration (however loose) seems to define the firm.[26] This is what I see when I study business records. In the early years, the owner-manager is one; later there is dispersion of ownership and the divorce between ownership and control. The MNE owns firms abroad that are part and parcel of one business. The divorce occurs only at the top tier. A second mode must be the contract, which defines the rough edges of the firm, the special associations that most firms have that are not part of the firm, but are by no stretch of the imagination arm's-length. In this context, I am not using the word contract in legal terms of a written document. I see the contract as identifying a unique connection. Such a mode would cover the Rothschild dealings with August Belmont & Co. and those between Pears' and its agent. It encompasses franchising, licensing, long-term supply contracts, long-term leases, managing agency agreements, and cooperation within a cartel. None of these interactions involves an arm's-length relationship; all are recurrent; all reduce uncertainty by regularising arrangements; all lower transaction costs in this process; all imply a minimal control; none, in and of itself, requires ownership, although small minority ownership or financing frequently accompany 'contracts'.[27]

Some of these special interconnections that I have studied were over time transformed into internalisation (operations within the firm) and direct investment. Some direct investments have been abandoned for contract. The contract is an alternative to the firm. The market is not the only choice. In short, the contract defines the interactions of two or more otherwise independent firms.

This excursus helps in clarifying some of the dynamics of multinational enterprise. It aids in explaining the limits of a multinational firm as it expands over borders; there are alternatives; are they more or less efficient than internalisation? It helps to define activities that I never understood. For example, when I studied American business abroad, I found that American Sugar Refining Company had minority interests in Cuban sugar plantations, which were enough to keep the firm informed, to exercise some influence, but there was no evidence that control was imposed, nor that these plantations were managed by the sugar refining company. It would seem hard to call these plantation companies part of the sugar refining firm. The second mode, the 'contract', would seem appropriate. Likewise, when Rothschild interests acquired one-quarter of the stock of Anaconda, America's largest copper mine, and took over its European marketing, is it equally erroneous to call Anaconda part of the Rothschild multinational enterprise? In a sense it was, just as the sugar plantations were part of American Sugar Refining. In the case of Anaconda, the interest was sizeable, and operating responsibility (at least in European sales) was assumed. Business interests as distinct from purely financial considerations were at stake. Yet the records seem to indicate that Americans handled management and production decisions.[28] And what of Rio Tinto in Spain, to use a non-American example? Charles Harvey's history describes Rio Tinto as a firm.[29] Yet in this case the Rothschilds were large owners, concerned with the copper business, and represented on the management board. Should Rio Tinto be seen as part of the Rothschild firm?

When one deals with multinational enterprise, one often views firms within firms. There are, for example, separate business histories of Shell in the United States, Ford in England, Firestone in Liberia, and Sears, Roebuck in Mexico.[30] A multinational firm is a cluster, an administrative ordering, a hierarchy imposed in terms of decision-making. There is nothing in the definition of a firm that precludes delegation, or of the quasi-independence of affiliates. Accordingly, to understand the extent to which we can call Anaconda or Rio Tinto part of the Rothschild firm, we would have to examine the French and British Rothschild internal records. How did the Rothschilds as a firm see themselves in relation to Anaconda or Rio Tinto? Similar questions arise when we try to define the firm when considering, for instance, the connection between Burmah Oil and the Anglo-Persian Oil Company. R.W. Ferrier, the historian of Anglo-Persian Oil Company, would probably argue that APOC is the firm (and his history shows a unity of action). Yet T.A.B. Corley, a student of Burmah Oil, suggests—at least in the early years—the importance of the parent.[31]

Theory pushes us to try to define the MNE and its special relationships with outsiders. At the edge of the firm, the boundaries are at times hard to set. When does the firm expand by itself abroad? When does it join with others in its international business? What are its special links with others? Are they rooted in distinct transactions, such as marketing Anaconda's copper, or more intricate ones, such as those involving numerous types of joint venture, technology transfer, or agency interactions? Defining the firm becomes more difficult as we move to the perimeters of the firm and look at the firm's associations with other ones that are neither part of the MNE nor totally separate.

As we deal with the 'ragged edge of the firm', as we consider the intermediate mode, the contract, we obtain, I would like to suggest, a better sense of how a firm grows and its choices. Thus, we can take the case of the Dunlop tyre company in the United States. Its initial entry into the US market was export; its next stage was licensing; then apparently direct investment; it next sold its property rights to outsiders (and retained no interest). When it tried to resume its own corporate activity, when it saw the market potential, it sought once again to extend the firm.[32] The firm itself and its relationships with outsiders change over time.

Looking at the 'edges' of the firm helps us understand the connections between the MNE and the cartel. When does a firm absorb its rival? When does it divide world markets with an associated company, a competitor, a potential competitor? The concept of contract as a second mode helps answer those questions. Internalisation involves cost. As a firm expands, its internal transaction costs (its organisation costs) rise. Thus, the firm does not expand without limits. Yet, at least in a world that does not rigorously enforce anti-trust restrictions, the firm is not faced solely with the alternative of meeting competition. Returns on asset-specific investments can be increased through market divisions.[33] The cartel, 'the contract', regularises and stabilises relationships, eliminates uncertainty, and for the firm that finds the cost of extension of management too high a division-of-market agreement can simplify the task of internal management by imposing exogenous limits—that is, a firm's management need not worry about a competitor from abroad at home nor about expending resources to penetrate a market allocated to another firm.[34] The firm creates, through its accord, a high barrier to entry into its own market. Long-term supply contracts that at various periods of history have characterised purchases of raw materials and have substituted for backward integration are similarly amenable to this kind of analysis.[35]

In my study of foreign investment in the United States, as I consider direct investors I find many that fit comfortably into a model of multi-national enterprise that views the firm expanding internationally (from a home base) with units producing goods and services. At the same time, I have pushed myself to define the limits of the expansion and the nature of the firm.

## Conclusion

In conclusion, this paper has had three goals. First, I wanted to present some of the definitional problems I have faced in my studies of foreign investment in the United States. Secondly, I have sought to show how a theory pressed me to think about the limits of the firm—about hierarchy, contract, and market—and how this has served to clarify hitherto confusing data. And thirdly, I have shared with you some of the results I have reached in deciphering what is and what is not a multinational firm and, in the process, introduced my finding that there is a need to look at not only the firm itself, but the many special relationships that the firm enters into while doing business at home and abroad. I do not find a continuum between firm and market.[36] There is an institutional entity we can call a firm. It is conditioned by its home environment that affects how it operates abroad; likewise, circumstances in the host country shape its behaviour. This is true whether its foreign business is in the form of hierarchy, contract, or market. In 'contract', we see the limits of the firm. In this paper, I have not considered the easy cases of European multinational enterprise, for example, Courtaulds, Nestlé or Unilever.[37] Fundamentally, these can be analysed in the same manner I have considered the history of US multinational enterprise.[38] In this presentation, the difficult cases stimulated my interest and attention,[39] but in dealing with these, I find new light is cast on the timing, the contracts, and the degree of integration of the more familiar multinational corporations.[40] Clearly, many transactions of individual firms are neither intra-firm nor market ones. These are on the 'ragged edge' of the firm. The firm itself has to be, and can be, defined in administrative terms.

## Notes

1. Although I treat them as one approach, clearly they can be considered as distinct and separate.
2. See O.E. Williamson, 'The Modern Corporation: Origins, Evolution, Attributes', *Journal of Economic Literature*, 19 (December 1981), pp. 1537–68; O.E. Williamson, 'Transaction Cost Economics: The Governance of Contractual Relations,' *Journal of Law and Economics*, 20 (October 1979), pp. 233–61; *Markets and Hierarchies* (New York, 1979); and O.E. Williamson, *Corporate Control and Business Behavior* (Englewood Cliffs, N.J, 1970). See also, O.E. Williamson, 'Microanalytic Business History' and A.D. Chandler, 'Evolution of the Large Industrial Corporation: An Evolution of the Transaction-Cost Approach', both in J. Atack (ed.), *Business and Economic History*, 2nd ser., vol XI (1982), pp. 106–34.
3. S. Nicholas, 'Agency Contracts, Institutional Modes, and the Transition to Foreign Direct Investment by British Manufacturing Multinationals before 1939', *Journal of Economic History*, 43 (September 1983), pp. 675–86, has an interesting discussion of firm and agency relationships, looking at transaction costs.
4. This had not been a matter of concern to me when I began to look at European business abroad, see, for example, M. Wilkins 'Multinational Enterprise', in H. Daems and H. van der Wee, *The Rise of Managerial Capitalism* (Louvain, 1974), pp. 213–35, and M. Wilkins, 'Modern European Economic History and the Multinationals', *Journal of European Economic History*, 6 (Winter 1977), pp. 575–95. The concern arose from my careful and full reading of the literature. Everything on European multinational enterprise did not fit neatly with what I knew about American business abroad.
5. Such standard definitions appear in introductory economics textbooks, for example, R.G. Lipsey and P.O. Steiner, *Economics*, 6th edn (New York, 1981).
6. A. Alchian and J. Demsetz, 'Production, Information Costs and Economic Organization', *American Economic Review*, 62 (December 1972), pp. 777–95.
7. I have benefited particularly and immensely from the theoretical work of economists especially R. Vernon, O.E. Williamson, R.E. Caves, K. Arrow, M. Casson, J. Dunning, C. Kindleberger, J.-F. Hennart and many others, some of whom are specifically cited in the footnotes of this article. To this list, I should add the useful N. Hood and S. Young, *The Economics of Multinational Enterprise* (London, 1979). I have gained rich insights from the research of historians too numerous to mention, but particularly A.D. Chandler.

8. This point is made explicitly in A.D. Chandler, 'Global Enterprises: Economic and National Characteristics', unpublished paper (1982). Chandler has made the point elsewhere as well.

9. M. Casson, 'Introduction' in M. Casson (ed.), *The Growth of International Business* (London, 1983), p. 21, makes the valid point that separation of ownership and control and the growth of modern management must be linked.

10. In some of the early trading operations, however, the merchant owned the ship and travelled on it to carry out transactions—so even with distance, ownership and control for a time were united. See J.G.B. Hutchins, *American Maritime Industries and Public Policy 1789–1914* (Cambridge, Mass 1941), p. 241.

11. R. Gilpin, *U.S. Power and the Multinational Corporation* (New York, 1975), p. 11, made the point that British investments in the nineteenth century were by individuals, banks, and through bond markets; American ones in the twentieth century were by corporations. The distinction is too simple. Corporations in the nineteenth century made foreign investments, both portfolio and direct investments.

12. See A.D. Chandler, *The Visible Hand* (Cambridge, Mass., 1977) on the importance of economies of speed to modern business organisation.

13. A.A. Berle and G.C. Means, *The Modern Corporation and Private Property* (New York, 1968).

14. T.C. Coram, 'The Role of British Capital in the Development of the United States c.1600–1914', unpublished Master's thesis (University of Southampton, 1967), called them 'syndicates'. J. Stopford, 'The Origins of British-based Multinational Manufacturing Enterprises', *Business History Review*, 48 (Autumn 1974), pp. 303–45, saw them as 'expatriate' firms, a special type of portfolio investment.

15. S.J. Nicholas, 'British Multinational Investment Before 1939', *Journal of European Economic History*, 11 (Winter 1982), p. 606. He tells me that this designation was suggested to him by Leslie Hannah.

16. US Federal Trade Commission, *Report on Cooperation in American Export Trade* (Washington, 1916), II, pp. 537–74. Other sources for such firms are *Burdett's Official Stock Exchange Intelligence* and the *Stock Exchange Year Books*. G.H. Nash, *The Life of Herbert Hoover 1874–1914* (New York, 1983) shows the proliferation of 'free-standing' British companies world-wide that were linked through 'service sector' multinationals—e.g. a mining engineering firm.

17. Historians of French, German, Dutch, and possibly Swiss multinational enterprise need to look at this very same phenonemon—companies incorporated in France, Germany, Holland, Switzerland that carried on business in a single country abroad. A very interesting discussion of free-standing firms in the United Kingdom is in E.T. Powell, *The Mechanism of the City* (London, 1910), pp. 144–5.

18. On 'double' boards of directors, see C. Wilson, 'The Multinational in Historical Perspective', in K. Nakagawa (ed.), *Strategy and Structure of Big Business* (Tokyo, n.d. [1976?]), p. 269, and Powell, *The Mechanism of the City.* p. 145.

19. When there were railroad bond defaults, protective committees of shareholders (and bondholders) were established; they were shortlived and did not constitute ongoing relationships.

20. Thus I do not like to call these 'syndicate' investments.

21. A good example of this is provided in R.W. Ferrier, *The History of the British Petroleum Company* (Cambridge, 1982). In this context, we also need more study of the managing agent and the mining-engineering firm as multinational enterprises, providing initially at least economies of international management to the free-standing firm.

22. See L. Hannah, 'Visible and Invisible Hands in Great Britain', in A.D.

Chandler and H. Daems, *Managerial Hierarchies* (Cambridge, Mass, 1980), and other splendid works of Leslie Hannah, conveniently cited in *Managerial Hierarchies*, p. 72.

23. Williamson, 'Transaction Cost Economics'. When my article was virtually completed, I read G.B. Richardson, 'The Organization of Industry', *Economic Journal* 82 (September 1972), pp. 883–96, and discovered that over a decade ago, Richardson had been troubled by similar problems—that is the oversimplification involved in the dichotomy between the firm and market.

24. I have discussed these ideas at length with Jean-François Hennart. Likewise, much of my discussion is along the same lines suggested in Stephen Nicholas's paper in this volume. I wrote this before I had read his contribution. Richardson in 'Organization of Industry', p. 890, talks of direction (or consolidation), cooperation, and market, which is similar to what I refer to as hierarchy, contract, and market.

25. Geoffrey Jones's forthcoming case study (in *Business History Review*) of the history of the Gramophone Co. provides a splendid illustration of the special relationships between this British company and an American one.

26. I am using here—as before—the word 'hierarchy' as one with the concept of associations that exist within a firm. Within the firm there are people who report to others—that is, a hierarchy. My colleague Jean-François Hennart takes exception to this unified usage, and so, I suspect, would Mark Casson (see his 'Introduction' to Casson (ed.), *Growth of International Business*). Nonetheless, I am at present still convinced of the legitimacy of the usage.

27. Richardson, 'The Organization of Industry', specified four different types of inter-firm cooperation; while his categories differ from mine, he was arguing the identical point. His four were (1) backward vertical associations, long-term contracts and minority shareholdings; (2) subcontracting; (3) backward vertical associations that involve a retailer with its regular suppliers, but without formal contract; and (4) arrangements to pool or transfer technology.

28. My forthcoming study of foreign investment in the United States will give details and documentation.

29. C.E. Harvey, *The Rio Tinto Company* (Penzance, Cornwall, 1981).

30. K. Beaton, *Enterprise in Oil: A History of Shell in the United States* (New York, 1957); there are two unpublished histories of Ford in England, one by Norman St. John Stevas (1954) and one by C. Fawcett (1961); W.C. Taylor, *Firestone in Liberia* (Washington, DC, 1956); R. Wood and V. Keyser, *Sears Roebuck de México, S.A.* (Washington, DC, 1953).

31. T.A.B. Corley, 'Strategic Factors in the Growth of Multinational Enterprise: the Burmah Oil Company, 1886–1928', in Casson, *The Growth of International Business*, pp. 214–35.

32. Geoffrey Jones has been very helpful on Dunlop history. See G. Jones, 'The Growth and Performance of British Multinational Firms before 1939: The Case of Dunlop', *Economic History Review*, 2nd ser., 37 (Feb. 1984), pp. 35–53.

33. 'Asset-specificity' involves the degree of specialisation of physical or human assets. The term is Williamson's (see O.E. Williamson, 'The Modern Corporation'.). As John H. Dunning and many other students of multinational enterprise have long accepted, the firm must have some advantage in its move abroad. Dunning calls this advantage 'ownership specific advantage'. See, for example, J.H. Dunning, 'International Business in a Changing World Environment', *Banca Nazionale de Lavoro Quarterly Review* (December 1982), 351–2.

34. A superb discussion of various kinds of market division agreements is in W.J. Reader, *Imperial Chemical Industries* (London; 1970). The problem with a cartel, however, is that it often pays for individual participants to cheat; thus, the

cartel may not create the needed stability.

35. Jean-François Hennart has work in progress on this. See also D.J. Teece, 'Technological and Organizational Factors in the Theory of Multinational Enterprise', in Casson, *The Growth of International Business*, pp. 56–7, 60–61.

36. Richardson, 'Organization of Industry', p. 887, suggests the notion of continuum, but then backs away from this suggestion, p. 896.

37. Three excellent studies of multinational enterprise provide data on these particular firms, D.C. Coleman, *Courtaulds* (Oxford, 1969, 1982), II and III; J. Heer, *World Events, 1866–1966, The First Hundred Years of Nestlé* (Rivac, Switzerland, 1966); and C.Wilson, *Unilever*, 3 vols. (New York, 1968).

38. See M. Wilkins, *The Emergence of Multinational Enterprise: American Business Abroad from the Colonial Era to 1914* (Cambridge, Mass, 1970) and M. Wilkins, *The Maturing of Multinational Enterprise: American Business Abroad from 1914 to 1970* (Cambridge, Mass, 1974).

39. Thus, the companies considered by Stopford, 'The Origins' and L. Franko, *The European Multinationals* (Stamford, Conn., 1976) have not captured my attention in this paper, although I devote substantial attention to them in my forthcoming book on foreign investment in the United States.

40. For example, the timing of Samuel Courtauld & Co.'s entry into US business, Nestlé's relations with Borden, and Lever's association with Lamont, Corliss, all of which I will deal with in my forthcoming book.

# 9

# The Rise of Big Business in the World Copper Industry 1870–1930*[1]

Christopher Schmitz

*Source: *Economic History Review*, XXXIX (1986), pp. 392–410.

By any measure, the world copper industry between the 1870s and the 1920s was characterized by the growth of large corporations Assessed in terms of market share, the extent of vertical integration, or the accumulation of capital, the leading producers appear to have increasingly dominated the industry. By 1929, the capital assets of the leading United States copper firms alone stood in the region of $1.5 billion, which the leading four firms in the industry (also American) controlled more than 50 per cent of world production. This, coupled with the growing presence of multinationals like Anaconda, Kennecott, and Rio Tinto in Latin America and Africa, led to continuing fears being expressed about the monopoly position of these enterprises.

Recent research on the rise of the large-scale business corporation has reorientated analysis away from monopoly profit motives and more in the direction of responses to market imperfections, coupled with technological imperatives. In particular the work of Alfred Chandler and Oliver Williamson has emphasized the role of the large firm as an efficiency instrument, internalizing functions previously performed by the market.[2] Increasingly, from this viewpoint, resource allocation and intermediate product exchange would be conducted within firms in order to minimize the transaction costs of using the market price mechanism.[3]

Chandler and Williamson in large measure derive their generalizations from the experience of manufacturing industry. Consequently, the growth of big business in the copper industry provides a valuable opportunity to assess recent theories of corporate growth in relation to extractive industry. It is the contention of this paper that technological pressures, rather than transactional considerations, have been more significant in the mining and smelting sectors than Williamson might allow, even though the refining and fabricating sectors of the copper industry probably conform more closely to his views.[4] It is possible to show that in the mining industry the rise of big business resulted from the logic implied by a series of geological and technological considerations.

# I

The extent of business concentration in the copper industry after 1870 can be assessed at a number of levels. First of all, the size of firms as represented by their capital assets suggests a strong momentum towards large-scale activity. Allowing for data deficiencies which make it difficult to construct comparable long-term indicators of asset growth, it is possible to contrast the size of leading firms in the mid-nineteenth century with those of later periods. The leading copper firm in Cornwall and Devon (the world's main producing area until 1857) was Devon Great Consols. In January 1866, when it stood just before a long period of decline, this mine had a market valuation equivalent to $2.98 million.[5] In contrast, the market valuation of the issued stock of Calumet & Hecla, the leading U.S. (and at times leading world) producer to 1883, grew from a median point of $4.9 million in 1870, to $10.6 million in 1874 and $23 million in 1880.[6] Thereafter the growth of industry capital can be measured in broad terms by reference to Table 1.

The trend towards the growth of large firms accelerated after 1869, when a new tariff in the United States heavily increased duties on imported copper.[7] Behind the shelter of this legislation, the Lake Michigan producers, particularly Calumet & Hecla, rapidly increased their market share, while maintaining domestic prices by dumping copper overseas.[8] During the 1870s Calumet & Hecla accounted for around 52 per cent of United States output, and dominated the domestic American market until the early 1880s, when mining at Butte, Montana commenced on a large scale. A savage price war through the 1880s led to the emergence of the Butte producers, led by the Anaconda and Boston & Montana firms, as market leaders.[9] Outside the rapidly growing and protected American market, few copper firms grew to substantial size before the 1930s. In Spain, the Rio Tinto and Tharsis companies, working large low-grade ore-bodies, commanded nominal assets which, together, stood in the region of about $22 million in the late 1880s.[10] Until 1900, the other major producing regions, Chile, Germany, Australia, and Japan were characterized by firms with far smaller capital assets than the leading firms in the United States. Even with the spread of investment capital into large-scale mining prospects in Russia, Chile, Katanga, and Northern Rhodesia, between 1900 and 1939, the scale of capitalization of non-U.S. copper firms still lagged far behind that of firms like Anaconda.[11] Apart from any question of capital markets or institutional factors favouring a higher degree of business concentration in the United States than elsewhere, from the early

*Table 1* Leading corporations in the copper industry, 1898–1929

| | 1898 | 1909 | 1919 | 1929 |
|---|---|---|---|---|
| **United States (assets in $m)*** | | | | |
| Anaconda | 52.5 | 170.2 | 254.2 | 680.6 |
| United Copper | | 50.0 | | |
| Greene Cananea | | 15.0 | 61.1 | |
| Chile Copper | | | 155.5 | |
| ASARCO | | 118.6 | 215.3 | 241.0 |
| Calumet & Hecla | 57.0 | 57.8 | 100.0 | 87.0 |
| Copper Range | | 40.9 | 19.9 | 9.3 |
| Phelps Dodge | | 49.4 | 247.3 | 124.7 |
| Greenwater Copper | | 34.0 | | |
| Kennecott Copper | | | 135.6 | 337.8 |
| Guggenheim Exploration | | 36.9 | | |
| Utah Copper | | 25.0 | 83.8 | |
| **United Kingdom ($m equivalent)** | | | | |
| Rio Tinto | 19.1 | 22.5 | 23.1 | 39.9 |
| Caucasus Copper | | 11.1 | | |
| Great Cobar | | 8.5 | 9.0 | |
| Rhodesian Anglo-American | | | | 17.0 |
| Roan Antelope | | | | 6.1 |
| **Japan ($m equivalent)** | | | | |
| Sumitomo | | | 75.4 | 69.6 |
| Mitsubishi Mining | 7.5 | 7.5 | 15.1 | 46.4 |
| Furukawa | | 2.5 | 10.0 | 10.4 |
| **Belgium ($m equivalent)** | | | | |
| Union Minière du Haut Katanga | | 1.9 | 1.5 | 24.5 |
| **Australia ($m equivalent)** | | | | |
| Mount Lyell | 4.4 | 7.0 | 6.3 | 12.1 |
| Chillagoe | 7.3 | 5.3 | 5.7 | |
| Mount Elliott | | 3.6 | 6.1 | 8.5 |

*Assets equal nominal capitalization plus debenture issues. Anaconda 1898 includes assets of wholly owned subsidiaries; 1909 includes assets of Amalgamated Copper Co. Calumet & Hecla 1898 represents median marketing valuation of issued stock; on the same basis 1909 is $64m. Chillagoe 1898 represents assets of Chillagoe Mining & Railway Co. Ltd.
*Sources: Stock Exchange Year Book* (1895–1948); W. G. Skinner, *Mining Manual* (1887–1930); R. L. Nash, *Australasian Joint-Stock Companies Yearbook* (Sydney, 1899–1913); A. D. H. Kaplan, *Big Business in a Competitive System* (Washington, 1954), pp. 145–9.

1880s onwards the United States was both the world's leading producer and consumer of copper.[12] The high degree to which United States copper producers operated within a domestic market, at times relatively unaffected by world market forces, undoubtedly aided their growth.

The increasing size of the leading firms was paralleled by the growth in their market shares. On trend, from the 1880s to the late 1920s the leading four firms increased their share of world mine output from around a third to over a half (Table 2). After 1930, when the United States leadership of the industry faced a growing challenge from the African copperbelt, the extent of market control by the top firms declined. In the sphere of smelting and refining, where capital costs and economies of scale were greater than in mining, the control of the leading firms was even more pronounced. In 1911, the United Metals Selling Co. group (including Anaconda-Amalgamated, the Lake mines, the Arizona Copper Co. and Greene-Cananea) controlled 31 per cent of United States and 22 per cent of world refinery output. The American Smelting and Refining Co. (ASARCO) group (including Utah, Nevada Consols, Ray, and Cerro de Pasco) controlled 24 and 17 per cent respectively, while Phelps Dodge (with its Arizona mines) controlled 13 and 9 per cent.[13] With these three United States groups controlling some 48 per cent of world capacity, two German groups, the American Metal Co. (Metallgesellschaft) and Aron Hirsch und Sohn, between them controlled a further 13 per cent. In 1921, after rapid war-time expansion, the leading three United States firms controlled 74 per cent of world refining capacity, while the American Metal Co. (transferred from German to United States control in 1917) controlled another 8 per cent, and Japanese refineries a further 8 per cent.[14] By 1926 total United States capacity had contracted to around 50 per cent of the world level and following major refinery construction in Europe, Africa, and Canada, to 36 per cent in 1932.[15]

*Table 2* Mine production of the eight leading world copper firms as a percentage of world output, 1890–1935

| Rank of firm: | 1890 | 1900 | 1912 | 1923 | 1928 | 1935 |
|---|---|---|---|---|---|---|
| First | 11.0 | 15.9 | 15.5 | 21.2 | 21.1 | 16.9 |
| Second | 10.5 | 7.4 | 11.3 | 19.0 | 19.5 | 13.4 |
| Third | 9.8 | 7.1 | 8.0 | 6.2 | 6.5 | 7.7 |
| Fourth | 8.2 | 3.8 | 4.0 | 4.4 | 5.9 | 7.5 |
| Fifth | 5.8 | 3.7 | 3.1 | 3.5 | 3.5 | 6.6 |
| Sixth | 3.8 | 3.2 | 2.4 | 3.3 | 3.4 | 5.6 |
| Seventh | 2.2 | 2.3 | 2.1 | 3.2 | 3.1 | 4.3 |
| Eighth | 1.8 | 2.2 | 2.0 | 2.9 | 2.6 | 2.7 |
| Firms 1–4 | 39.5 | 34.2 | 38.8 | 50.8 | 53.0 | 45.5 |
| Firms 5–8 | 13.6 | 11.4 | 9.6 | 12.9 | 12.6 | 19.2 |
| Firms 1–8 | 53.1 | 45.6 | 48.4 | 63.7 | 65.6 | 64.7 |
| Coeff. C* | 0.045 | 0.041 | 0.047 | 0.091 | 0.094 | 0.068 |

*Coeff. C = Herfindahl's coefficient of industry concentration, calculated from the shares of the top eight firms.
*Sources*: *1890*, R. P. Rothwell, ed. *Mineral Industry, 1893* (New York, 1894), pp. 236–48; *Mineral Resources of the United States, 1894* (Washington, 1895), pp. 33–58.
     *1900*, T. R. Navin, *Copper Mining and Management* (Tucson, 1978) p. 396.
     *1912–35*, O. C. Herfindahl, *Copper Costs and Prices, 1870–1957* (Baltimore, 1959), pp. 165–7.

The increased size and growing market share of the leading copper firms arose partly through internal growth, but largely through merger activity. In the United States the three leading groups in the industry, Anaconda, ASAR-CO-Kennecott, and Phelps Dodge, all grew rapidly from the late 1890s by an active process of horizontal and vertical integration. Indeed, particularly during the great merger movement of 1898–1902,[16] at a time of rapid expansion in electrical technology and demand for copper, these giant firms increasingly seemed to epitomize the leading edge of the trust movement.

ASARCO was incorporated in April 1899 with a capital of $115 million, bringing together a number of trans-Mississippi lead smelters. Promoted by interests which included the copper-broking Lewisohn brothers of New York and Henry H. Rogers of the Standard Oil Co., by 1901 it had come largely under the influence of the Guggenheim family. With the construction of a plant at Garfield, Utah, in 1907 ASARCO entered copper smelting, in competition with Anaconda. Thereafter its interests in copper mining and smelting grew steadily. In 1904 the Guggenheims staked a claim in the development of the first of a new generation of giant, low-grade (porphyry) copper mines, with the incorporation of the Utah Copper Co. The Guggenheim Exploration Co. (1899) also pioneered the development of two large Chilean porphyry deposits, at Braden (El Teniente) and Chuquicamata (the latter being sold to Anaconda 1923–29). In 1907 the Guggenheims sold most of their ASARCO stock and in 1915 the main part of the Guggenheims' own copper interests were consolidated into the Kennecott Copper Co. (including Utah, Nevada, Ray, Chino, and Braden). Vertical integration continued with the acquisition of firms like the Alaska Steamship Co. and in 1929 the Chase Co., a leading fabricator. By 1937 Kennecott was the largest United States copper producer, with around 36 per cent of domestic mine production.[17]

From its origins at Butte, Montana in the mid-1870s, the Anaconda Company came to represent the prime example of large-scale, integrated enterprise in the world copper industry by 1929 (Figure 1). Through the 1890s it integrated horizontally into adjacent claims at Butte and vertically into timber, water, transportation, smelting and refining concerns. Its greatest spurt of corporate growth occurred during the great merger boom at the turn of the century, when the giant Amalgamated Copper Co. was floated, in April 1899, with an initial capital of $75 million (increased in 1901 to $155 million), in order to consolidate a large number of mining, smelting and refining interests.[18] The Amalgamated Copper Co., promoted by a powerful combination of Standard Oil interests (H.H. Rogers, J.D. Ryan and William G. Rockefeller) allied with the Lewisohn-Bigelow group and the National City Bank, at once dominated the United States and world copper markets through a complex corporate network. Throughout the life of the Amalgamated Co., Anaconda remained at the heart of the structure. On the liquidation of the former, in June 1915, Anaconda (having already absorbed many of the Amalgamated enterprises in 1910–15) assumed full control. Thereafter, through the 1920s, with capital assets passing half a billion dollars, the corporation made major acquisitions overseas, for instance obtaining in 1923 a majority stake in Chuquicamata, Chile, the world's largest copper mine. It also consolidated its integration into fabrication in 1922, with the purchase for $45 million of the American Brass Co.

Outside the United States, the network of control between copper firms generally occurred through less obvious channels. The London and Paris Rothschilds, for instance, held a large interest in Rio Tinto and other Iberian producers from the late 1880s, effectively owned the Boleo mine in Mexico from 1885, and in 1895 exercised an option to buy 25 per cent of the Anaconda stock for $7.5 million (although this interest was soon sold).[19] A number of German firms, including Metallgesellschaft, Aron Hirsch und Sohn, and Beer Sondheimer, also commanded diffuse networks of control through many areas of the world's mining and metal-trading businesses before 1914. The most prominent of these, Metallgesellschaft, operated through a number of major subsidiaries such as the American Metal Co. (1887) and the Australian Metal Co. (1898).

Whilst subject to variation, the profits of the major copper corporations were generally large up to 1930. By the end of that year total accumulated dividends from United States copper companies stood at $2,317 million.[20] Despite the impressive growth and profitability of big business in the world copper industry in the 60 years to 1930, it can be argued that that growth cannot be fully understood simply in terms of attempts to control the market. It is vital to set against the appearance of market domination the fact that the leading companies seem to have been increasingly unable to set prices and control supply for more than a few short-lived periods. Amongst primary commodity prices, those for copper are particularly unstable and through the period 1870 to 1939 were becoming more volatile on trend.[21] The question of price stability and the nature of the price system itself will be considered below. Meanwhile, business concentration in the copper industry, if not following directly from market control, should be approached in the context of the technological and resource-base complex within which this industry was set.

## II

The economic exploitation of copper minerals over at least the past two centuries has followed a broad pattern of mining progressively leaner ores from increasingly large individual deposits. This has arisen through a

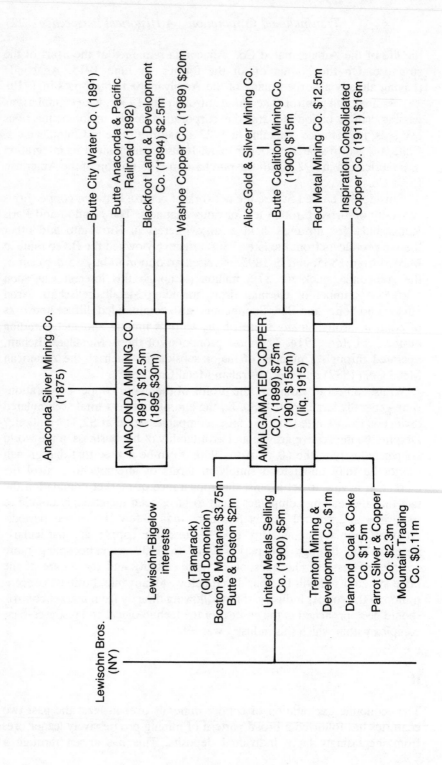

Lewisohn Bros. (NY)

Lewisohn-Bigelow interests

(Tamarack)
(Old Domonion)
Boston & Montana $3.75m
Butte & Boston $2m

United Metals Selling Co. (1900) $5m

Trenton Mining & Development Co. $1m

Diamond Coal & Coke Co. $1.5m
Parrot Silver & Copper Co. $2.3m
Mountain Trading Co. $0.11m

Anaconda Silver Mining Co. (1875)

ANACONDA MINING CO. (1891) $12.5m (1895 $30m)

Butte City Water Co. (1891)

Butte Anaconda & Pacific Railroad (1892)

Blackfoot Land & Development Co. (1894) $2.5m

Washoe Copper Co. (1989) $20m

AMALGAMATED COPPER CO. (1899) $75m (1901 $155m) (liq. 1915)

Alice Gold & Silver Mining Co.

Butte Coalition Mining Co. (1906) $15m

Red Metal Mining Co. $12.5m

Inspiration Consolidated Copper Co. (1911) $16m

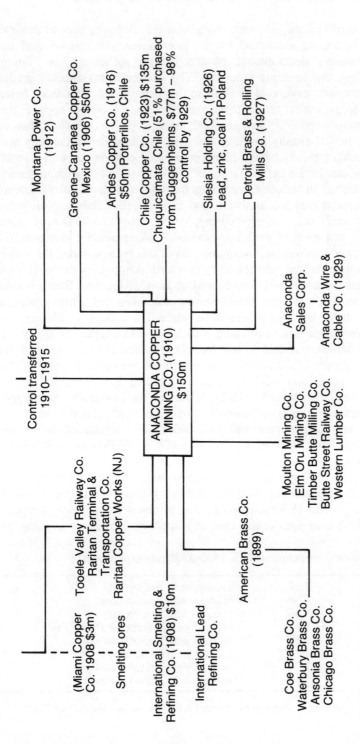

*Figure 1*  Anaconda: corporate growth, 1875–1929

*Sources: Stock Exchange Year Book* (1913–48); W. G. Skinner, *Mining Manual* (1896–1949); I. F. Marcosson, *Anaconda* (New York, 1957); F. E. Richter, 'The Amalgamated Copper Company: A Closed Episode in Corporation Finance', *Qu. J. Econ.*, xxx (1915–16), pp. 387–407. Tamarack was absorbed by Calumet & Hecla in 1917 and Old Dominion was increasingly associated with Phelps Dodge after 1918.

combination of shallow, relatively easily won vein deposits, such as those in Cornwall, becoming exhausted by the later nineteenth century and the contemporaneous development of cost-cutting technology in mining, concentrating, and smelting processes. The decline in average ore grades (Table 3) has been paralleled by shifts in the major types of ore-body being exploited. In geological terms, there are three main forms of copper ore-body: massive sulphide,[22] strata-bound, and porphyry deposits. Massive sulphide deposits, usually found in veins or infillings in sedimentary and volcanic rocks, typically have a high-grade metal content (around 4 to 20 per cent copper in the period up to 1939), but with a few exceptions are relatively limited in extent (containing from several thousand to several million tonnes of ore) and almost always have a well defined cut-off point where they meet the non-ore-bearing, or "country" rock. Due to their accessibility and ease of working, especially where subject to secondary enrichment and oxidization,[23] vein deposits of this type provided the major source of copper mined until the early twentieth century, for example from the mines of Cornwall and Devon, and of Butte, Montana. Strata-bound deposits are less common than massive sulphides but form generally medium to large bodies (ranging from around a million to 250 million tonnes of ore, commonly averaging 3 to 6 per cent copper, up to 1939). The Kupferscheifer worked in the Mansfield mines of Germany and the stratiform deposits of the African copperbelt are the best examples of this type which, like massive sulphides, tend to have a fairly well defined cut-off against barren country rock. Finally, there are the low-grade "porphyry" deposits (typically running at about 0.45 to 2.5 per cent copper), which are commonly very large (from 100 to 2,000 million tonnes of ore in the 1930s). These huge, low-grade, disseminated ore-bodies are not usually distinguished by a sharp cut-off between payable ore and barren rock, but rather large tracts of ground in which there is a gradation from relatively high-grade mineralization to material well below the economic definition of payable ore (in the 1930s a cut-off point of about 0.7 per cent copper). This gradation is of significance both in respect of theories concerning the

*Table 3* Declining copper ore grades, 1800–1930 (per cent copper)

| 1800 | 9.27 | average yield English ores |
|---|---|---|
| 1850 | 7.84 | average yield English ores |
| 1870–85 | 6.56 | average yield English ores |
| 1886–1905 | 2.96 | average yield Calumet & Helca ores |
| 1906 | 2.50 | average yield United States ores |
| 1915 | 1.66 | average yield United States ores |
| 1925 | 1.54 | average yield United States ores |
| 1930 | 1.43 | average yield United States ores |

*Source*: W. Y. Elliott et al. *International Control in the Non-ferrous Metals* (New York, 1937), p. 374.

relationship between ore grade and size of ore-bodies and in the tech-nology required to exploit these deposits.

In general terms it is apparent that there is a fairly strong negative correlation between ore grade and size of deposit. Data relating to 87 leading copper mines/prospects up to 1930–1 have been assembled and the average grade plotted against total copper content (defined as past production plus, in the case of mines/prospects in operation 1930–1, projected reserves).[24] This indicates (Figure 2) that certain broad groupings of mines/ore-bodies were exploited between the early nineteenth century and the 1930s. First, the Cornwall and Devon group consisted of relatively small but high grade mines, working principally between about 1800 and 1870, within the overall limits of about 4.5 to 12 per cent copper in ore-bodies containing up to 50 thousand tonnes of copper. The next group is a high-grade Australian group, including mines in South Australia and Queensland, worked mainly between the 1840s and 1870s, at about 17 to 22 per cent copper and containing 13,000 to 52,000 tonnes of copper. A scattering of points with a trend towards lower grades and higher volume deposits then represents mines working into the early twentieth century. Two major groupings complete the picture; the stratiform African copper-belt deposits, being opened up between 1907 and 1930, with grades of from 3.3 to 7.5 per cent and reserves of around 2.3 to 14 million tonnes of copper, and the important porphyry group, represented by 12 mines in 1931 (nine in the United States and three in Chile). These ranged in grade from 0.95 per cent (Miami, Arizona) to 2.18 per cent (El Teniente, Chile) and in terms of deposit size at 1931, from 450 thousand tonnes (Copper Queen, Arizona) to 22.5 million tonnes (Chuquicamata, Chile). Also plotted is a pyritic sub-group, represented by large, low-grade deposits in Iberia and at Mount Lyell in Tasmania, which are not porphyries but which contained on average less than three per cent copper.

Although there are localized exceptions to this model, such as the copper district of northern Michigan, where the larger deposits tended to exhibit higher grades,[25] in general, as mining companies have moved towards exploiting lower grade ores (as they increasingly must), then they have encountered disproportionately larger scale ore-bodies. This is particularly true of the porphyry coppers where a geological proposition known as Lasky's Law suggests that where there is a gradation from relatively rich to relatively low grade material in a deposit, the tonnage of ore increases geometrically as grade decreases arithmetically.[26] This is illustrated (Figure 2) by the example of Bingham mine in Utah, which moves through time (1899 to 1970) towards a lower grade and higher tonnage. Amongst non-porphyries, where there is a sharper cut-off from ore to barren rock, the relationship appears to be less clear although in general it would appear to hold true, for example with the Anaconda mine at Butte from 1907 to 1964.

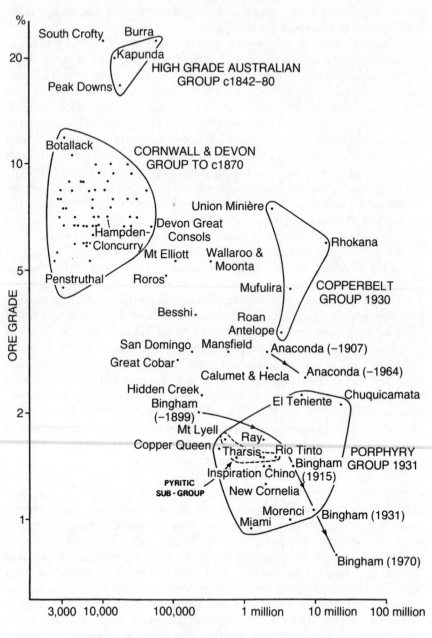

*Figure 2* Major copper deposits, 1800–1931: grade and tonnage

**III**

The implications of this relationship during the last century have been profound. Not only has more of the world's supply of new copper had to come from lower grade and larger bodies of ore, but also mining companies have had to finance larger-scale and more capital-intensive projects, each of which has tended to yield its return over longer periods of time, thus further increasing the true cost of finance. This trend was clearly emerging even in the second half of the nineteenth century, as larger-scale ore-bodies were encountered in the mines of the western United States and the pyritic deposits of Iberia and Tasmania. However, the trend was sharply accelerated by the growing prominence of the huge porphyry deposits, opened up after 1904 (by 1928 these contributed around 40 per cent of annual world mine production[27]), and by the development of the Northern Rhodesian stratiform deposits in the late 1920s.

As early as the 1870s, the opening up of a larger ore-bodies required a new scale of finance. In Spain, the Rio Tinto mines with their estimated 200 million tonnes of ore were purchased in 1873 by a consortium of British and German investors for £3.85 million, with further initial investment required (for example on a railway) to the extent of around £2 million. To cover this outlay the company had to commence working on a large scale and by 1884 was the leading copper producer in the world, processing over a million tonnes of ore a year.[28] Capital investment in Spain was, however, limited (compared with the United States) by the generally labour-intensive nature of the operations. In Tasmania in the early 1890s, the Mount Lyell Co. was opening up a huge pyritic orebody, which prompted the normally flamboyant chairman, Bowes Kelly, to counsel the 1894 A.G.M. that while production of rich silver ores had produced high returns "it is necessary that shareholders should always remember that the enduring and lasting value of the mine, from which we expect regular dividends in the future to come, exists in the enormous mass of low grade ore".[29] A similar sentiment, that the working of large-scale ore-bodies must go hand in hand with long-term and large-scale capitalization, was expressed in 1895 by Marcus Daly, chairman of the Anaconda Mining Co, on the occasion of increasing its capital from $12.5 million to $30 million:[30]

> The policy of the Company from the beginning has been not so much to realize immediate returns as it has been to try to lay the foundation for a long life of activity and usefulness. For this purpose, the profits of the Company have been expended in the enlargement and betterment of the plant until today, in its remodelled, reconstructed, and completed state, it stands without a peer among the copper producers of the world. It can

be truthfully said that in all the history of copper mining, no enterprise on so large a scale was ever before projected.

When Daly had first become interested in Anaconda in 1880, he quickly appreciated the need for heavy capital investment, in order to compete with the Michigan mines which were nearer the markets of the eastern seaboard and which dominated the United States copper market. Only a large throughput would ensure sufficiently low unit production costs and to achieve this he had to convince his backers, J.B.A. Haggin, G. Hearst and L. Tevis, to provide an initial personal investment of $4 million. At first "the magnitude of Daly's plan took Hearst's breath away",[31] but within a decade the scale was justified as Anaconda took the leadership of the domestic industry from Calumet & Hecla.

The background to rising capital costs in mining in general, lay with the continual need for technological change. As mines worked deeper and tackled larger and lower-grade ore deposits, the traditional skills of miners had to be supplemented by rock-drills, explosives, ventilation, and improved underground haulage, whilst at the surface better milling techniques, capable of handling larger volumes of ore, had to be implemented.[32] In addition, as the world's mining frontier passed to new regions in the late nineteenth century, mines came to be established in increasingly remote areas, with high costs of labour, power, and materials. The cost of shipping the product to an increasingly distant market, as well as necessitating higher investment on transport infrastructure, also encouraged more mines to integrate vertically into smelting capacity, since this effectively reduced the cost of shipping each unit of metal. With the development of the porphyry copper deposits after 1904, the trend towards higher levels of capital investment and the impetus to large-scale business activity was accelerated, not only because of the huge initial investments required but also the lengthened time scale over which those investments would be realized. In addition, longer lead times were often necessary before projects would start making a return. At Chuquicamata, the Guggenheims spent a reported $50 million between 1912 and 1922, opening up the world's largest copper deposit.[33] A comparison of two groups of porphyry and non-porphyry mines around 1911–16 (Table 4) suggests the nature of the difference between their expected life spans, as well as highlighting some differences in their cost structures.

Lower costs in exploiting porphyries resulted from the economies of scale arising through developments in both mining and milling techniques. The majority of porphyries were worked as open-cuts, borrowing blasting and steam-shovel stripping techniques from Michigan iron-ore mining. Where underground mining of porphyries were made necessary by the nature of the ore-body, such as at Miami and El Teniente, block caving techniques were employed. The net effect of both these was to replace

*Table 4* Porphyry and non-porphyry copper producers, 1912-16

|  | Ore Reserves, million tonnes | Ore grade, per cent | Ore costs per ton ($) | Years' life |
|---|---|---|---|---|
| **1. *Non-porphyries*** | | | | |
| Cape Copper (S)[13] | 0.162 | 4.6 | | 2 |
| Namaqua Copper (S)[16] | 0.051 | 7.1 | 4.47 | 3 |
| Hampden-Cloncurry (A)[16] | 0.299 | 6.9 | 21.54 | 3 |
| Great Cobar (A)[12] | 2.74 | 2.5 | | 8 |
| Mount Lyell (A)[14] | 3.12 | 2.4 | 7.00 | 10 |
| Mount Morgan (A)[14] | 3.13 | 4.2 | 11.94 | 10 |
| Mount Elliott (A)[12] | 0.455 | 12.3 | 27.70 | 12 |
| **2. *Porphyries*** | | | | |
| Nevada Cons. (U)[15] | 50.5 | 1.48 | 1.67 | 17 |
| Miami (U)[14] | 35.1 | 0.95 | 1.88 | 32 |
| Ray (U)[13] | 78.4 | 1.65 | 2.38 | 33 |
| Utah (U)[13] | 268.0 | 1.07 | 1.60 | 35 |
| Chino (U)[15] | 90.0 | 1.40 | 1.84 | 38 |
| El Teniente (C)[16] | 113.7 | 2.50 | | 78 |
| Chuquicamata (C)[16] | 700.0 | 2.12 | 2.11 | 87 |
| Inspiration (U)[15] | 97.1 | 1.40 | 1.98 | 125 |

*Notes*: Superscript = year data refer to. Years' life = current rate of output/ore reserves. Differences in computing ore costs in original sources suggest caution in their interpretation. *Location*: A, Australia; C, Chile; S, South Africa; U, United States.
*Sources*: *Mineral Industry* (1911-18); R. Allen, *Copper Ores* (1923); A. B. Parsons, *The Porphyry Coppers* (New York, 1933); J. E. Carne, *The Copper-mining Industry....in New South Wales* (Sydney, 2nd. ed. 1908); Queensland Mines Dept. *Annual Report* (Brisbane, 1912-17); Mount Lyell Mining & Railway Co. papers (University of Melbourne Archives).

selective by non-selective methods of mining, in which all material in the mineralized area was removed, waste as well as metallic ore. In the vein mines of Cornwall, Australia, and the United States the skilled "hard-rock" miner had a central role in the ore-winning process and much of the work-culture of mining revolved around his skills in following a tortuous and often deceptive lode. Excavator and truck drivers displaced the skilled miner and through the 1920s further economies were achieved through using increasingly large earth movers. As early as 1915 some marked differences existed in the costs of working copper ores by non-selective (open-cut and caving) methods, compared with traditional stoping methods (Table 5).

Complementing the move to non-selective mining was a revolution in milling techniques principally brought about by the application of flotation to copper ores. This process was first tried with these ores at Butte in 1912 and by 1915 had been introduced at Inspiration and El Teniente. Its success there soon led to its being generally adopted by porphyry producers and moved one mining engineer to comment in 1932 that "the

*Table 5* Estimated mining costs and labour productivity for selective and non-selective mining methods, 1915

|  | Average cost per ton ore ($) | Tons ore per man-shift |
|---|---|---|
| Open-cut mines | 0.31 | 24.69 |
| Caving | 0.52 | 12.74 |
| Open stopes | 1.25 | 6.84 |
| Shrinkage stopes | 2.68 | 6.02 |
| Square-set timbering | 4.83 | 1.55 |

*Source*: C. W. Wright, *Mining Methods and Costs at Metal Mines in the United States,* United States Bureau of Mines Information Circular 6503 (Washington, 1931), cited by T. J. Hoover, *The Economics of Mining Non-ferrous Metals* (Stanford, 1933), pp. 138–9.

oil flotation process ... has meant more to the copper industry, in so far as increased recoveries and reduced costs are concerned, than any other single factor in the past twenty years".[34] Downstream in the production process, advances in smelting and refining moved this part of the industry nearer continuous operation (for instance by the growing practice after 1890 of leaving the semi-finished copper matte in the furnace while it was recharged), at the same time reducing costs by larger scale working.[35] The net effect of all these technological changes, and one which reflected the impetus to big business in the United States industry, was its capital-output ratio, which increased markedly on trend from 0.76:1 in 1870 to 2.46:1 in 1919 (in 1929 prices).[36] The opportunity cost of not having adopted these technologies is suggested by one calculation that all the copper produced in the United States in 1929–30, by the methods known in 1912–15, would have cost an average 12.7 cents a pound rather than the actual cost of 6.06 cents.[37]

The opening up of porphyry and large stratiform deposits also increased the impetus to longer term planning and larger scale capitalization in the industry, inasmuch as they could be fairly accurately delineated with a minimum of exploration activity. With just a few exploratory drill holes, deposits such as Inspiration, Ray, or Roan Antelope, could be fully assessed in advance of any mining activity. This is in sharp contrast to vein mining where great uncertainty attached to any forward planning. Indeed, it could be argued that "permanent" mining corporations, that have become so prominent in the world mineral industry since the end of the nineteenth century, have largely grown out of particular mining areas where a high degree of forward planning was possible. The Rand banket reef, the massive lodes at Anaconda, or the low-grade ores of Spain and Chile, provided a more stable long-term environment for their respective companies and led to the steady growth of houses like Consolidated Goldfields, Rio Tinto Zinc, Anaconda, and Kennecott. For the first time, capitalist enterprise in metal mining could compete with manufacturing industry in terms of financial planning and long-term growth. The longer-term strategy of such mining corporations would also be encouraged, according to Chandler, by the formation of a managerial hierarchy that itself became "a source of permanence, power, and continued growth".[38] In this way, firms such as Anaconda were induced to maintain continuous exploration programmes, to ensure future mining projects of sufficient scale to match their asset growth.

## IV

Whilst economies of scale have propelled successful copper companies towards a larger scale of operations, they have also been prompted towards vertical integration, particularly downstream into refining and then into fabricating, by the desire to instil a degree of control into unstable markets for their products. As Chandler and Williamson have indicated, the internalization of intermediate product exchange within one firm can provide great advantages over the use of competitive market modes of contracting. Contractual uncertainties are avoided and transactions costs minimized, and in the words of Williamson, "the parties to an internal exchange are less able to appropriate subgroup gains, at the expense of the overall organization".[39]

The move into fabrication owes much to the greater value-added that accrues there compared with the earlier stages of production and with the lesser degree of volatility in prices for semi-manufactured products. For example, in the period 1912–13, the mean monthly New York price for ingot electrolytic copper was 15.88 cents a pound compared with a price of 21.88 cents for sheet copper (the latter thus enjoying a premium of 38 per cent over the raw metal). At the same time, the price of electrolytic copper fluctuated more widely than for sheet.[40] These facts no doubt helped prompt Anaconda to move into fabrication in 1922 with the acquisition of the American Brass Co, the leading United States fabricator. On the occasion of the merger, the Anaconda chairman J.D. Ryan commented:[41]

> The time has come when we cannot compete in the industry if we control only one stage of the business. Anaconda is not now able to operate its mines at a steady and economical rate. We have had high prices during periods of scarcity and low prices during periods of depression.... We believe that great benefits will arise by reason of the proposed merger. The raw material supply will be assured at steady prices.... In this way, from the mine to consumer, there can be one just and fair profit, and the industry will be stabilized.

One consequence of moving into refining was an immense increase in capital requirements, not only to equip the plants but for financing the stock of copper necessarily tied up in the process. Because of their high set-up and running costs, only ten electrolytic refineries were built in the United States up to 1911.[42] One report in 1908 suggested that the value of copper tied up in the electrolytic vats (representing a capacity of 400 thousand tonnes per annum) was around 50 thousand tonnes, valued at about $14.5 million.[43] Only firms the size of Anaconda or ASARCO could afford to finance this order of fixed capital.

The impression therefore emerges that the growth of big business in the copper industry owes much to a combination of geological and technological factors, in conjuction with market pressures, all of which have conspired to impel large mining and smelting companies to become even larger. This was in order to be able to finance, in a stable planning environment, the scale of operations necessary to sustain the growth in the world's demand for this raw material.

## V

In recent years, the work of Chandler and Williamson has transformed the approach to the study of big business and the relationships between markets and firms.[44] In particular, the concept of transactions costs has allowed a fundamental re-evaluation of the process of vertical integration. Assuming that the market mechanism of neo-classical economics is only used by firms at a cost (in essence the transactional costs of gathering market information, of advertising and contracting), the pressure will be to internalize these functions within the firm, where it is economical to do so.[45] This in turn has only been permitted by, and has encouraged, the development of new forms of managerial organization as detailed by Chandler.[46]

The transactions costs incurred by the copper industry in using the market mechanism have always been high. In common with other primary commodity markets, that for copper is subject to a high degree of instability, due in large measure to short-run inelasticities of demand and supply.[47] This resulted in pressure towards oligopolistic business forms and market controls even before 1870, as copper producers sought to reduce the uncertainties and costs attendant on contracting in ever fluctuating market conditions.[48] However, market control before 1870 rarely, if ever, entailed attempts at vertical integration. Not only, as Chandler has pointed out, did the slow growth of managerial divisionalization outside railway enterprises hinder this development before the 1870s, but also, it is argued here, in the case of the copper industry, vertical integration was promoted strongly by the move towards larger scale ore deposits, often increasingly remote from major markets. Once integration from mining to smelting was effected by such firms as Anaconda, then the transactions costs motive to integrate into refining and fabrication could assume larger proportions.

If big business in the copper industry has arisen mainly through the trend towards larger ore deposits, coupled with the pressures of an inherently unstable market, there still remains the question of whether these large corporations have had any significant effect in reducing price competition. There is a well established body of literature which credits such companies as Anaconda and Kennecott with having exercised some considerable degree of oligopoly power through the present century.[49] It can be argued, however, that there have been effective limits to such power. These arise from a combination of the short-run inelasticity of demand and supply (and hence the volatility of prices), the relatively weak barriers to industry entry, and the high propensity to substitution in the medium term, and the international nature of the market for copper coupled with the dual pricing system that prevails.

There is a considerable weight of evidence in recent studies that in anything but the short term, competitive price models provide the best explanation of the functioning of the world copper market.[50] The dual pricing system itself assumes great significance in these models. That is, whilst the majority of copper traded since the late nineteenth century has been sold under contract by the major producers (particularly in the United States), there remains a vigorous and influential free market, primarily centred on the London Metal Exchange. Since 1877 the LME has offered a forum for trading in physical copper (and more importantly in copper futures), which enables daily prices to be generated which are widely held to reflect the current balance of supply and demand in the world market, even though it only handles a fraction of world supply.[51] Studies such as those of Felgran show that not only have producer prices tended to follow those of the free market but that the former have not shown any particular tendency towards greater stability, except where they have been held considerably below market prices.[52]

In past periods of high prices brought about through market manipulation by leading producer groups, most notably the Secretan corner of 1887–9 and the Amalgamated pool of 1899–1900, the evidence suggests that alternative sources of supply from scrap copper and small, independent mines soon helped undermine their control. During 1929–30, when the American producers' combine, Copper Exporters' Inc. tried to hold the price at nearly 18 cents a pound in the face of world depression, the main result appears to have been the rapid development of the Northern Rhodesian copperbelt.[53] Also, by the 1930s, aluminium was becoming a viable substitute for copper in many areas of consumption. Despite the high costs of establishing large-scale mining and smelting/refining capacity, it is clear that the barriers to entry in the industry are weak. Even in the short run there is evidence that high prices will stimulate large numbers of small mines to commence production (reinforcing flows of scrap on to the market).[54] In the longer term, even high-cost operations like those of the Rhodesian copperbelt mines can be stimulated to undertake development.

As far as predatory price-cutting aimed at restricting competition is concerned, there is little evidence that this was practised to any significant degree before the 1950s, unless one excepts the vicious price war of the mid-1880s between Calumet & Hecla and Anaconda, which had the more specific aim of bringing down the new Butte producer. Indeed, during the 1920s the eventually disastrous build-up of excess capacity in the world copper industry was largely brought about because the leading producers failed to restrict the entry of new capacity by price cutting. The scope that large mining corporations has for cutting prices is also severely limited due to their continually moving towards larger-scale and more capital-intensive operations. With the marked trend to higher volume, lower grade ore-bodies and by integration into smelting and refining, the capital charge to each unit of production is increased, and with less elastic capital costs, supply becomes less elastic.[55] In certain circumstances such producers may even be tempted to increase output against falling prices, to maintain revenue, suggesting the possibility of a backward-sloping supply curve.

In the late 1950s Orris Herfindahl undertook a study of past price and market behaviour in the copper industry, in order to answer questions about the long-term cost and depletion of non-renewable resources. He concluded that, with a few exceptions, such was the long-run competitive nature of the world (and United States) copper market, that prices could be taken as a proxy for costs. He argued that "since the turn of the century, there have been no periods of collusion that produced price increases as large as those brought about by Secretan and Amalgamated".[56] In fact, since 1913 the copper industry has been dominated by a secular downturn in deflated prices. A comparison of current and deflated prices (Table 6) suggests that, as far as copper is concerned, the supposed price depression of the last quarter of the nineteenth century is largely a myth, but that a pronounced price fall, in real terms, began during the First World War and continued up to the Second. It is against this background that attempts to control the market by successive American-led producers' groups after 1919 must be measured.

Significantly, comparison between the deflated prices which successive market corners achieved shows a similar steady downward trend. In terms of 1913 prices, the Secretan corner topped out at around £93.67 a tonne (on the London market), while the Amalgamated pool reached £86.75, and the 1929 price plateau of the Copper Exporters' Inc. only represented the equivalent of £61.80.[57] Thus were all attempts at market control and price fixing trapped within the long-term dynamic of technological and

*Table 6* London metal exchange copper prices, 1870–1939 standard grades, £ per metric tonne, in current and at 1913 prices

|  | current prices | 1913 prices |
|---|---|---|
| 1870–9 | 78.06 | 67.88 |
| 1880–9 | 60.25 | 66.21 |
| 1890–9 | 53.42 | 68.49 |
| 1900–9 | 70.86 | 82.40 |
| 1910–14 | 66.36 | 68.41 |
| 1915–19 | 115.60 | 59.28 |
| 1920–9 | 73.40 | 43.69 |
| 1930–9 | 43.77 | 42.09 |

*Source*: C. J. Schmitz, *World Non-ferrous Metal Production and Prices, 1700–1976* (1979), pp. 270–2.

organizational change which inexorably reduced costs and prices. Increasing economies of scale in conjunction with the transactional economies enjoyed by vertically integrated firms, as emphasized by the Chandler and Williamson models, resulted in declining real costs. These were, in turn, largely translated into declining real prices, with little evidence of sustained super-normal profits being made by the leading producers. In all, Herfindahl concluded that "there is a body of opinion that tends to credit the copper industry with a degree of monopoly power that it does not have".[58] The continued instability of copper markets from 1870 to 1930 and beyond was at one and the same time a sign that market control was not readily attainable and signalled a strong incentive to further vertical integration for producers.

# Notes

1. Earlier versions of this paper were delivered at La Trobe University, the University of Leeds and the International Mining History Conference, University of Melbourne, 1985. I am grateful for numerous comments from participants at these meetings; also for advice from Roger Burt over a longer period of time.
2. A.D. Chandler, *The Visible Hand: The Managerial Revolution in American Business* (Cambridge, Mass. 1977); O.E. Williamson, *Markets and Hierarchies: Analysis and Antitrust Implications* (New York, 1975); O.E. Williamson "The Modern Corporation: Origins, Evolution, Attributes", *Journal of Economic Literature*, XIX (1981), pp. 1537–68.
3. L. Hannah, *The Rise of the Corporate Economy* (2nd edn. 1983), p. 3.
4. Williamson, *Markets and Hierarchies*, pp. 2–4, 60–1, 82–6.
5. G.C. Goodridge, "Devon Great Consols", *Transactions of the Devonshire Association*, XCVI (1964), pp. 228–68.
6. W.B. Gates, *Michigan Copper and Boston Dollars* (Harvard, 1951) pp. 224–7.

7. F.W. Taussig, *Tariff History of the United States* (New York, 8th edn. 1931), pp. 219–21.

8. O.C. Herfindahl, *Copper Costs and Prices, 1870–1957* (Baltimore, 1959), pp. 70–2, 246; Gates, *Michigan Copper*, pp. 39–63.

9. K.R. Toole, "The Anaconda Copper Mining Company: A Price War and a Copper Corner", *Pacific Northwestern Quarterly*, XL (1949), pp. 312–29.

10. W.R. Skinner, *Mining Manual for 1887* (1887), pp. 376, 435.

11. By 1937, the largest non-U.S. copper firm was the Rhodesian Anglo American-Nchanga Consolidated-Rhokana group, with combined assets of $87.4 million.

12. In 1883 the U.S. overtook Chile as the world's leading mine producer of copper, a position it maintained until the late 1970s. During the period 1892–1929 the U.S. accounted for 50–65 per cent of world output and some 35–45 per cent of total consumption; Metallgesellschaft A-G, *Metal Statistics* (Frankfurt-am-Main, 1894–1937).

13. *Mining Magazine*, V (1911), p. 464.

14. R. Allen, *Copper Ores* (1923), pp. 18–19

15. W.Y. Elliott et al. *International Control in the Non-Ferrous Metals* (New York, 1937), p. 479.

16. N. Lamoreaux, *The Great Merger Movement in American Business, 1895–1904* (Cambridge, 1985), pp. 1–5, 155; R.L. Nelson, *Merger Movements in American Industry, 1895–1956* (Princeton, 1959), pp. 71–105, 129–38, 144–53.

17. D. Lynch, *The Concentration of Economic Power* (New York, 1946), p. 135.

18. F.E. Richter, "The Copper Mining Industry in the United States, 1845–1925", *Quarterly Journal of Economics*, XLI (1927), pp. 236–91, 684–717; "The Amalgamated Copper Company: A Closed Episode in Corporation Finance", *Qu. J. Econ.* XXX (1915–16), pp. 387–407.

19. *Engineering & Mining Journal* (Sept. 1895), p. 294; (Oct. 1895), p. 389; (June 1896), p. 561. The British and French Rothschilds together held 30.8 per cent of the issued ordinary capital of Rio Tinto in 1905, rising to 36.2 per cent in 1929; C. Harvey, *The Rio Tinto Company, 1873–1954* (Penzance, 1981), p. 110; B.W.E. Alford and C.E. Harvey "Copper Merger: The Formation of the Rhokana Corporation, 1930–32", *Business History Review*, LIV (1980), p. 338.

20. Annual returns of North American mining company dividends, in *Eng. & Min. J.* (1908–31).

21. From the early nineteenth century, the coefficient of variation for the London price of standard grade copper (electrolytic wirebars from 1915) shows a clear trend of increasing instability; 1840–9 the C.V. was 5–7, 1870–9 it was 13.3, 1900–9 17.1, 1930–9 22.5, and by the 1960s was 36.6. For the period 1870–99, J.R. Hanson II. "Export Instability in Historical Perspective: Further Results", *Journal of Economic History*, XL (1980), pp. 17–23, suggests that in a group of 18 primary commodities only beef and coffee prices were, overall, more volatile than copper prices.

22. Massive, not in the sense of large scale, but in the strict geological sense of discrete mineral aggregations.

23. Weathering of original (sulphide) ores, by atmospheric action and percolating groundwater, can concentrate the copper content in an enriched zone, and render them easier to smelt.

24. Regression analysis of the data (where G = average percentage grade and T = copper tonnage in orebody) yields the following results:

$$\log. T = 3.73937 \quad - \quad 2.8948 \quad \log. G \quad r^2 = 0.5943$$
$$(0.19252) \qquad (0.25074)$$

Full details of the data set may be obtained from the author.

25. W.S. White, "The Native-Copper Deposits of Northern Michigan", in J.D. Ridge, ed. *Ore Deposits in the United States, 1933–1967* (New York, 1968), I, pp. 306–7.

26. S.G. Lasky, "How Tonnage and Grade Relations Help Predict Ore Reserves", *Eng. & Min. J.* (April 1950), pp. 81–5.

27. A.B. Parsons, *The Porphyry Coppers* (New York, 1933), p. 6.

28. Harvey, *Rio Tinto*, pp. 18–35; S.G. Checkland, *The Mines of Tharsis* (1967), pp. 113–5.

29. University of Melbourne Archives, Mount Lyell Mining & Railway Co. Papers, 2/5/1, minutes of A.G.M. 29 Nov. 1894.

30. I.F. Marcosson, *Anaconda* (New York, 1957), pp. 88–9.

31. Toole, "Anaconda Copper", p. 315; M.P. Malone, *The Battle for Butte: Mining and Politics on the Northern Frontier, 1864–1906* (Seattle, 1981), pp. 22–53.

32. For detailed discussion of improvements in mining, milling, and smelting techniques see, A.B. Parsons, ed. *Seventy-five Years of Progress in the Mineral Industry, 1871–1946* (New York, 1947), pp. 1–161, 199–222; H. Barger and S.H. Schurr, *The Mining Industries, 1899–1939: Output, Employment and Productivity* (New York, 1944), pp. 105–41, 222–39.

33. Parsons, *Porphyry Coppers*, p. 93; Elliot et al. *International Control*, p. 404.

34. P. Yeatman, *Choice of Methods in Mining and Metallurgy* (New York, 1932), cited in D.W. Fuerstenau, ed. *Froth Flotation: Fiftieth Anniversary Volume* (New York, 1962), p. 21.

35. Between 1890 and 1906 the smelting furnaces at Anaconda were expanded from 50 feet in length (capacity 122 tons/24 hrs) to 116 feet (270 tons/24 hrs), whilst fuel/ore ratios improved from 1:2.75 to 1:4.19; W.H. Dennis, *A Hundred Years of Metallurgy* (1963), p. 135.

36. I. Borenstein, *Capital and Output Trends in Mining Industries, 1870–1948* (New York, 1954), p. 36.

37. Parsons, *Porphyry Coppers*, pp. 13–16; in 1929, equivalent to a gross saving of $132 million on U.S. domestic copper production.

38. Chandler, *Visible Hand*, p. 8.

39. Ibid., pp. 6–7; Williamson, *Markets and Hierarchies*, p. 29.

40. The coefficients of variation of monthly prices 1912–13 for electrolytic and sheet copper were, respectively, 7.92 and 5.59.

41. Marcosson, *Anaconda*, pp. 175–6.

42. T.R. Navin, *Copper Mining and Management* (Tucson, 1978), pp. 65–6.

43. *Australian Mining Standard*, 23 Sept. 1908, pp. 357–8.

44. See, for example, S.J. Nicholas, "Agency Contracts, Institutional Modes, and the Transition to Foreign Direct Investment by British Multinationals before 1939", *J. Econ. Hist.* XLIII (1983), pp. 675–86; Y. Suzuki, "The Formation of Management Structure in Japanese Industrials, 1920–40", *Business History*, XXVII (1985), pp. 259–82; D.C. North, "Transaction Costs in History", *Journal of European Economic History*, 14 (1985), pp. 557–76.

45. Williamson, *Markets and Hierarchies*, pp. 29–51.

46. Chandler, *Visible Hand*, pp. 1–6, 9–10, 240 ff.

47. R.F. Mikesell, *The World Copper Industry: Structure and Economic Analysis* (Baltimore, 1979), pp. 154–7.

48. R.R. Toomey, *Vivian and Sons, 1809–1924: A Study of the Firm in the Copper and Related Industries* (1985), pp. 312–46. An alternative response from the 1870s was the increasing use of hedging contracts on the London Metal Exchange, to reduce contractual uncertainties within a competitive market context; Economist Intelligence Unit, *The London Metal Exchange* (1958), pp. 21–2, 26–48, 65–9.

49. D. Mezger, *Copper in the World Economy* (1980), p. 44, argues "the price of copper on the world market cannot be derived from usual notions of the relationship of supply and demand", while up to 1934 another source contends that "the years 1923 to 1926 make up the only period which we can class as 'normal' (competitive) in the history of copper since 1913"; Elliott et al. *International Control*, p. 427.

50. B.R. Stewardson, "The Nature of Competition in the World Market for Refined Copper", *Economic Record*, 46 (1970), pp. 169–81; S.D. Felgran. "Producer Prices Versus Market Prices in the World Copper Industry" (unpublished Ph.D. thesis, Yale University, 1982), pp. 35–6, 58–61; E.C. Hwa, "Price Determination in Several International Primary Commodity Markets: A Structural Analysis", *International Monetary Fund Staff Papers*, XXVI (1979), pp. 157–88.

51. Mikesell, *World Copper Industry*, pp. 81–93; R. Gibson-Jarvie, *The London Metal Exchange* (1976).

52. Felgran, thesis, pp. 35–6, 58–61.

53. Elliott et al. *International Control*, p. 67.

54. C.J. Schmitz, "Small is Sometimes Beautiful: Advantages of the Micro-project in the Australian Copper Industry, 1953–81", *Camborne School of Mines Journal*, 83 (1983), pp. 29–33. The growing role of scrap in the U.S. market is clear; in 1910–24 this was 22.8 per cent of consumption, rising to 33.3 per cent 1925–39; C.J. Schmitz, *World Non-ferrous Metal and Prices, 1700–1976* (1979), p. 34.

55. Elliott et al. *International Control*, pp. 430–2

56. Herfindahl, *Copper Costs*, p. 154

57. This despite Copper Exporters' Inc. controlling some 63.5 per cent of world output 1926–9; ibid. p. 124.

58. Ibid., p. 10.

# 10

## Transaction Costs and the Multinational Enterprise: The Case of Tin*†

Jean-François Hennart

*Source: *Business and Economic History*, 16 (1987), pp. 147–159.

Until the development of transaction-cost theory, economics did not have a theory of why firms exist and grow. Transaction costs theory seeks to explain which activities are organized within the firm and which ones are performed by independent agents. It is a theory of the role and size of firms. Since multinational enterprises are firms that extend their hierarchies across national boundaries, transaction costs theory can throw considerable light on the reasons behind the existence and the growth of such firms [4; 17; 9; 15].

With a few notable exceptions [5: 9; 15], most applications of the transaction costs approach to the multinational enterprise have focused on the internalization of knowledge. This reflects the postwar predominance of horizontal investments in manufacturing by knowledge-intensive firms. This emphasis on the internalization of knowledge as a cause of multinational expansion may have given the erroneous impression that the applicability of transaction costs theory is restricted to post-World War II multinational enterprises.

This paper argues that this is not the case. It seeks to explain the existence and growth of multinational enterprises in the tin industry, and, in the process, shows that transaction costs can be used to account for a very wide range of multinational enterprises, including those that do not fit the traditional mold. Recent research in business history has shown that the growth of European multinational enterprises differed in many ways from that of their European counterparts, and that British foreign direct investment often took unfamiliar forms [24; 25]. This paper suggests that transaction costs theory may prove useful in explaining these forms as well.

**Application of Transaction Cost Analysis to the Tin Industry**

A firm's expansion overseas can take four forms; horizontal expansion producing abroad the same products as at home); vertical integration (into an adjacent stage of the value-added chain); related diversification; and conglomerate diversification. Most foreign direct investments fall into the first two categories.

Horizontal investments result from the internalization by the firm of the international trade in factors of production. Many horizontal investments are made whenever firms find it more efficient to transfer know-how internally than across markets. Technological know-how is not, however, the only factor susceptible to be internalized by firms. High market transaction costs in goodwill explain many investments in services [9]. As we will see, imperfections in international capital markets can also lead to the development of multinational firms.

Vertical investments arise from the internalization of the international market for intermediate inputs. Forward vertical integration is typically motivated by the high cost of using independent wholesalers or retailers whenever distribution involves specific assets, as in the case of products requiring specialized handling or service [15]. Backward vertical integration arises when the international market for the supply of intermediate products is inefficient due to information impactedness, high measurement costs, or small-number conditions.

Historically, the development of multinational enterprises in the tin industry has arisen from two main factors: the internalization of inefficient markets for technology and long-term capital led to the establishment of a large number of "free-standing" firms during the first half of the twentieth century. The desire to internalize inefficient markets in tin concentrates led to the development of vertically-integrated multinational enterprises in the lode sector of the industry.

*Horizontal Investments*

The incentive for horizontal foreign direct investments in tin came in the late 1800s from the rapid expansion of British tin consumption and the gradual exhaustion of Cornish mines, then the main tin producers. Although a few French and British firms were established in Malaya and in Bolivia in the 1890s, horizontal FDI took off in the first decade of the twentieth century with a gradual increase in British foreign direct investments in Malaya and a speculative wave of flotations of Nigerian tin mining companies. Investments by British firms in Nigeria and Malaya, and to a lesser extent in Burma and Siam, continued until the 1950s, and, in the late 1960s, foreign companies, almost all U.K.-registered, were producing 70 percent of Nigeria's output, and 60 percent of that of Malaysia [3, p. 35].

Those tin mining companies were what Mira Wilkins [24] has called "free-standing" firms. Most of them were incorporated in the U.K., but did all of their business overseas. In the case of Malaya and Siam, they were usually small: each company managed a single deposit. Even contiguous deposits were incorporated as separate firms. To achieve economies of scale, free standing firms resorted to subcontracting: secretarial services in the U.K. were contracted to specialist firms, who held share registers and provided other secretarial services to more than one firm. Arrangements for local management varied: sometimes it was subcontracted to consulting engineers, sometimes to a local mine manager, with technical assistance from mining engineers, sometimes to friends and relatives of some of the London promoters, and, rarely in the case of tin, to agency houses. Consulting engineers, such as Osborne and Chappell of Ipoh, Malaya, helped manage a large number of foreign-based mining companies. This arrangement allowed relatively small firms to access the limited pool of experienced local personnel.

The historical record of tin mining in Malaya and Siam suggests that horizontal multinational enterprises in the tin industry were caused by inefficiencies in the international market for technology and capital. A privileged access to capital, in the absence of a clear technological advantage, was insufficient to overcome the additional costs of adapting to a foreign environment. Foreign firms gained a foothold when they developed new techniques which offset their initial handicaps. Because these innovative techniques were mainly developed outside the industry, they could be bought by their local competitors. Privileged access to capital appears to have been the crucial factor which gave foreign direct investors a clear advantage, at least until the development of international capital markets in the 1960s.

That technological advantage was a requirement for the development of multinational enterprises in the industry appears clearly from the early history of Western investments in Malaya and Siam. Up until the 1890s, the development of tin mining in Malaya was a purely Chinese endeavor. Chinese immigrants used primitive, labor intensive methods to mine and concentrate the tin ore. Between 1882 and 1897, 35 companies were registered in the U.K. to mine tin in Malaya. There were also an unknown number of Australian and French ventures. By 1897, only four Western companies were still actively mining tin in Malaya, all the others having folded [28, pp. 97–99; 26, p. 143].

The British and French firms which invested in Malaya were experienced in mining lode tin. Tin deposits in Malaya, with the exception of one deposit in the state of Pahang, are alluvial. Many of the mining and prospecting techniques with which foreigners were familiar were therefore not suited to Malayan conditions: given the difficulty of assessing alluvial deposits, the high fixed-investment Western mining methods were a handicap, for it meant that it was costly to discontinue mining once started.

Chinese miners, on the other hand, mined with labor intensive methods. They could easily abandon a disappointing deposit for a profitable one [28, pp. 102–3].

European firms had also disadvantages vis-a-vis Chinese miners. The best workers were immigrant Chinese. European firms found it difficult to obtain Chinese mine workers because the immigration system was tightly controlled by Chinese mine owners. European mine managers had to hire Chinese interpreters and overseers to supervise Chinese labor, a source of additional cost. The Chinese, having come first, controlled the best mining land. The superior efficiency of the Chinese during the period is confirmed by the fact that they often successfully took over the land abandoned by bankrupt Western companies [21, p. 341]. Western firms did better in lode mining, where they had a technological advantage. The Pahang Corporation, floated in London in 1887 to exploit the largest of Malaya's tin lodes, was one of the four surviving firms by 1897.

Western dominance in Malaya (and Siam) was achieved by the introduction of two new mining techniques, first gravel pumping, and then dredging. Both these methods were borrowed from another mineral industry, gold mining. Both allowed Western foreign direct investors to overcome the handicaps they had vis-a-vis the Chinese. Gravel pumping, which used jets of water to break the ore, had two main advantages: (1) it saved on skilled (Chinese) labor; (2) it could treat very poor deposits, which could not be profitably mined by the Chinese.

Tin dredging was introduced in Siam in 1907. Dredging intensified the advantages of gravel pumping. It was labor saving: by World War I a typical dredge, employing 90 Chinese under European supervision, could extract and treat in one day as much tin-bearing ground as 2,000 Chinese in a traditional mine [28, p. 134]. Dredges could efficiently operate on swampy ground, where Chinese could not mine. They could also profitably work very low grade deposits, including ground which had been already mined by the Chinese [28, p. 133].

In contrast to tin smelting, the technology of both gravel pumping and dredging was not developed by the mining firms themselves, but by subcontractors. Gravel pumps were manufactured by Western engineering firms supplying the gold mining industry. They were initially imported into Malaya by Malaya-based European mining engineering firms, who taught Chinese mine owners how to use them. By 1925, nearly all Chinese mines used gravel pumps, which by then were locally manufactured [27, pp. 210–11; 1, p. 153]. Dredges were designed and set up by specialist firms and built by independent shipyards. The skills needed to operate dredges were quickly picked up by the Chinese: as early as 1917 they were employed as winchmen on European dredges "with great satisfaction" [7, p. 79].

Yet, in contrast to the gravel pump sector, where Western enterprise was soon displaced by the Chinese, dredging remained the safe preserve of

Western firms, and the development of this technique between 1920 and 1927 gave them the control of the industry. By 1940, dredging companies, all Western controlled, accounted for 52 percent of Malaya's tin output, where the overall share of Western firms was 71.5 percent, and 60 percent of Siam's production [28, pp. 400, 402; 23, p. 62]. The first Chinese-owned dredging company did not start operations until 1965.

The difference in the speed of Chinese adoption of dredges and gravel pump points out to an important advantage which led to the long-term survival of Western firms. The advantage was privileged access to the London equity market. While the capital cost to equip a mine with gravel pumps is relatively modest, dredges are much more expensive (the cost of a relatively large gravel pump mine was estimated in 1977 at around half a million US$, vs. 15 million for an onshore, and 25 million for an offshore dredge) [2, pp. 71–74, 145]. Financing such investments posed problems for the Chinese. Domestic sources of finance were limited, as the Malayan Chinese remitted a large part of their savings to their relatives in China, or invested them in mortgages or real estate [19, p. 116]. The British banks which had branches in Malaya followed the British banking tradition of specializing in short-term credit to finance foreign trade and commercial activities, leaving the provision of long-term financing to the London stock exchange [1, p. 203; 11, p. 232; 12, p. 150]. The flotation of joint stock companies in London or in Cornwall was an efficient way to accumulate the long-term sources of finance necessary to enter dredging. Because shares in such companies could be easily sold, the risk to the investor was lower. The Chinese, whose familiar forms of organization were individual ownerships or partnerships, and whose capital came from relatives and friends, were unfamiliar with joint stock companies, and unwilling to adopt this new form of organization [28, p. 347]. Furthermore, they lacked the European connections that would have made a London (or Redruth) flotation possible.

To understand why British-based firms may have had an advantage in this respect, one must focus on the characteristics of capital markets. Because of the non-simultaneity of both sides of the transaction, lending involves the risk that the borrower may be unable to meet his obligations, either because he has willfully spent the funds with no intentions to repay, or because he has been unsuccessful in his investments. The easiest way for the lender to protect himself is to obtain some collateral, the value of which is greater to the lender than the value of the loan. Another possibility is to lend only to borrowers who are personally known to the lender as having both the intention and the ability to honor their obligations. These considerations suggest that raising capital will be easier the greater the personal contacts between savers and borrowers, the larger the borrower's assets, and the longer he has been profitably in business. Foreign entrepreneurs, especially if they are proposing new, unproved ventures, are at a special disadvantage, since it is difficult for them to establish personal contacts with savers. Conversely, domestic savers are unlikely to be aware of foreign investment opportunities.

A look at early British free-standing firms active in Malaya shows clearly how such firms could reduce transaction costs in the international transfer of capital from the U.K. Many of the first successful ones were floated in Redruth, then the center of Cornish tin mining—this was the case, for example, for the Gopeng Tin Mining Co., established in 1892, the first company to successfully operate gravel pumps in Malaya. The story of the company starts with a concession to mine tin being granted to F. D. Osborne, an Irish mining engineer then in Malaya, and to the former Warden of Mines of the State of Perak, E. R. Pike. Pike was the son of a well-known Cornish mine purser, and he enlisted the help of his father to contact a local share broker, James Wickett, who, in turn, persuaded 10 of his friends to put 700 pounds each into the company. All of these 10 initial subscribers were major investors in Cornish mines. Later, James Wickett's son, a mining engineer, went to Malaya to report and prospect on mines which, in some cases, were subsequently floated by his father. The story, which is representative of the experience of at least three of the major U.K. promoters of foreign tin ventures, illustrates the personal links which facilitated these early investments. Promoters became aware of profitable opportunities through direct personal contacts with friends or family members who were, or had been, in the foreign country. Stock in the companies they floated was initially sold to friends and associates in the U.K. Later, as the success of these early companies became known, stock was subscribed by the general public. Given the speculative nature of tin mining and the general ignorance of Malaya by the British public, appeal to the London equity market by Chinese-owned companies would not have had the slightest chance of success.

Because of the importance of personal links in the establishment of free-standing companies, their distribution across tin mining countries was uneven. We would, for example, expect more companies to be set up in countries where Britishers were residing than in those where there were fewer British expatriates. Consider, for example, the contrast between Siam, then an independent country, and Malaya, where the British exercised a strong political and economic influence. Both countries have similar tin deposits, and in recent years Siam's (now Thailand) production of tin concentrates has been about half of Malaysia's. Yet, by 1914, British investments in Siam were much smaller than in Malaya: there were only 9 foreign companies active in Siam, 6 Australian and 3 British, compared to 48 in Malaya, 35 of them registered in the United Kingdom [14].

If free-standing firms internalize imperfect capital markets, then they may result from firms in capital-rich countries undertaking operations in capital-poor locales, or from operating companies in capital-poor countries floating concerns in capital-rich countries. Perhaps because Britishers were reluctant to establish operations in Bolivia, a number of Bolivian entrepreneurs floated tin mining companies in London. Such was the case, for example, of Aramayo Francke and Co., a company registered in London in 1906 by the Aramayo family to tap the British capital market. Similarly, Vilaque Bolivian Tin Mines was floated in London in 1913 by the French owners of Bolivian tin and gold mining properties. In both cases, the appeal to the British public does not seem to have been successful. By 1916, the Avelinos and the Franckes still held most of the stock of Aramayo Francke, while the vendors of Vilaque, the Berthin brothers, still held most of the shares in the company.[1] Later, Patino was to register his firm in Delaware to tap the U.S. capital market, with much greater success.

The decline of Western free-standing firms can be explained by the same causes which led to their emergence. Two factors combined in the postwar period to reduce the comparative advantage that these firms enjoyed relative to their domestic competitors. First, the independence of host countries increased the costs experienced by free-standing firms in channeling funds from capital-rich countries. Unsettled political conditions in the host countries, adverse changes in the U.K. tax treatment of dividends earned overseas, as well as an increasingly hostile Malaysian view towards foreign investments, led to a disinvestment by foreigners in Malaysian tin companies. At the same time there was a development of alternative sources of finance. Between 1954 and 1964, the percentage of shares held by Malaysians in Western-controlled companies registered in Malaysia increased from 22 to 64 percent [28, p. 359]. This increased investment by locals in tin mining firms, as well as the growth of development assistance and of international bank lending, removed the only tangible advantage enjoyed by Western free-standing firms. If capital could be obtained by local firms from local sources or from international banks, the British-based free-standing company had no longer any raison d'etre. By 1986, such firms had just about disappeared from Malaysia, replaced by locally-incorporated companies and by a growing state sector. By contrast, the greater backwardness of local tin miners in Nigeria, their greater lack of managerial expertise, and the absence of a local stock market meant that British free-standing firms met little competition. Were it not for "Nigerianization" policies followed by the local government, those firms might still be profitably active today.

*Vertical Investments*

Transaction costs theory can also help explain the pattern of vertical investments in tin. Markets work well when there are many buyers and sellers. They suffer from high transactions costs when the number of buyers and sellers falls. In that case, it is possible for a trader to opportunistically renegotiate the terms of trade. His trading partner will have no other alternative than accepting the new terms if he experiences significant switching costs. In small-number conditions, traders can thus be "held up" by their partners. The level of transaction costs in markets, and therefore the likelihood of vertical integration, will hinge on the factors that determine the number of potential buyers and sellers, i.e., scale economies, transportation costs, and the degree to which parties make investments which are dedicated to their partner's inputs or outputs.

The tin industry is singular in that it can be partitioned into two distinctive sub-industries, lode deposits and alluvial deposits, which require different mining and smelting methods. These differences have led to different levels of transaction costs in the case of lode than in that of alluvial concentrates.

Alluvial deposits are found mostly in Southeast Asia. They are low grade, but close to the surface, and can be mined by low-scale methods. They are easily concentrated through gravity to 70–77 percent tin. These concentrates contain few impurities, and can be smelted through simple methods. Lode deposits are of higher grade, but are usually found underground, mainly in Bolivia. The ores are more complex, containing many troublesome impurities. Elimination of these impurities involves a loss of tin, and lode concentrates only grade 20 to 60 percent tin. Smelting such concentrates is tricky, as the process must be tailored to the particular characteristics of the ore [10].

Those technological differences have had profound influences on industry structure. Because mining of alluvial ores is a relatively low-scale operation, the mining sector of Malaysia and Thailand has been relatively atomistic. Smelting alluvial ores is also competitive, with low barriers to entry. Alluvial concentrates are of high grade and value and are homogeneous: they can be smelted anywhere and transported over long distances. Alluvial miners thus face a potentially large number of buyers for their concentrates. As a result, and until recently, the traditional industrial pattern in alluvial tin has been one of vertical disintegration: the miners and the smelters have organized their interdependence through spot prices set on the Penang market. The two Malaysian smelters have matched the supply of concentrates received from independent miners with bids for tin metal from independent traders and processors, and paid the miners the clearing price minus a smelting fee. Mining firms have not been integrated into smelting, while investments by the two Malaysian smelters into mining have been minimal.

Lode tin is mined and smelted under very different conditions. The lode mining sector has always been more concentrated. In contrast to Malaysia and Thailand, where tin is mined close to the coast, Bolivian mines are located in relatively inaccessible parts of the Andes. Because of the need to build extensive infrastructure, operation at high scale has conveyed significant advantages. Concentration of Bolivian ore also requires expensive equipment. Lastly, the size of lode deposits is larger than that of alluvial deposits: the Uncia lode, which launched Patino as a major tin producer, is the largest tin deposit ever found.

Smelting lode ores requires greater skill and investment. Smelters able to smelt Bolivian concentrates have always been few in number. As with mining, the smelting of lode ores have been concentrated. The market for lode concentrates has therefore been narrower than that for alluvial concentrates. These considerations explain why the main instances of vertical integration between mining and smelting (excluding the more recent politically-motivated ones) have taken place in the lode sector of the industry.

The best known example of a vertically integrated multinational in tin is Patino Mines and Enterprises. Simon Patin's tin fortunes started with his discovery in 1899 of an extremely rich tin vein in a small mine he had purchased. By 1910, he was the largest Bolivian producer of tin con- centrates, with close to 10 percent of world production. Patino's output was first sold on commission by the British trading firm of Penny and Duncan to smelters in Liverpool and Germany. One of them was Williams, Harvey, initially built to process Cornish ores, but by now dependent on Bolivian concentrates. As his production increased, Patino took increasing control over the marketing of his ores, bypassing Penny and Duncan and setting up an office in Hamburg in 1911 to place his own concentrates and to receive in consignment the concentrates of other producers [6, p. 123]. The blockade of Germany that followed the outbreak of World War I closed to Patino the Goldschmidt smelter that was smelting his ores, and they were all sent to Williams, Harvey in Liverpool. That smelter, then the largest in Europe, had developed a proprietary technique to process complex Bolivian ores.

German submarines soon made transportation to England difficult, and with the opening of the Panama canal, it became apparent that Bolivian ores could be advantageously smelted in the U.S., the main consumer of the metal. In 1915, Asarco decided to build a smelter near New York to treat Bolivian ores. The opening of that smelter in 1916 persuaded Williams, Harvey and Asarco's main competitor, National Lead, that they should join forces and do the same. In 1916, National Lead took a half share in Williams, Harvey in exchange for cash and a half share in the new U.S. smelter. Before proceeding, Williams, Harvey attempted to enlist the support of the Exploration Company to take over Patino's properties. Unsuccessfully, it then asked Patino for a five year contract for the production of his mines, then about 10,000 tons a year, enough to support an efficiently-sized smelter. Patino proposed instead to purchase a one- third share in both smelters, a proposition which was readily accepted.[2] Patino's vertically integrated empire was broken up in 1952 with the nationalization of his Bolivian tin properties, but the vertical links were reconstituted with the establishment of state-owned smelters in Bolivia in 1970. There are other historical examples of the tendency for the market for Bolivian concentrates to be vertically integrated, such as Asarco's development of a captive Bolivian property in the 1920s and Goldschmidt's interest in a Bolivian mine before 1914 [18; 13, p. 675].

## Conclusion

Taking the example of the tin industry, this paper has attempted to show that transaction costs theory can provide a useful framework for understanding the growth and development of multinational firms. The bulk of horizontal investments in tin were made by British-based free-standing firms. These firms, which differ considerably from present day multinationals, can be explained within the context of transaction costs theory as institutions devised to facilitate the international transfer of capital from capital-rich to capital-poor countries.[3] They evolved as a solution to a paradox: because of significant communication costs due to cultural and geographic distance, local businessmen, who knew best of local opportunities, had difficulties obtaining finance, while those individuals who had investible funds were unaware of these profitable investments. In Malaya, the local offices of British Imperial banks, who had both the funds and the knowledge, would not lend long-term to local miners. Tapping the London capital market was difficult for foreigners, as they did not have in London the reputation necessary to instill confidence. Instead, the initiative of internalization often proceeded from the other side: Britishers who had learned about opportunities in Malaya through personal contacts, and who were well connected and reputable, floated companies in the U.K. to operate in Malaya. Case studies of the development of free standing firms seem to support this view: they show promoters to be individuals active in tin (engineers, solicitors, or share brokers) and with personal links to the places of investment.

Although the transfer of capital through free-standing firms was often characterized by high transaction costs, and a large number of such firms were swindles, the history of these firms in tin shows that, in contrast to their record in the United States [20; 24], Canada [16], and Australia [8], many were efficient, profitable, and long lived. They survived as long as they filled their original role, and the political and tax environments were not too unfavorable.

The development of vertically integrated multinational enterprises in tin also supports the view that vertically integrated multinational enterprises arise in specific circumstances, i.e., whenever intermediate markets are subject to high transaction costs. Miners in Malaya and Siam never took control of the Malaysian firms that smelted their ores because they could sell their concentrates on competitive markets. Because of economies of scale at both stages, and because the number of smelters able to handle Bolivian concentrates has always been limited, the market for such concentrates is much narrower. Consequently, and in contrast to Malaya and Siam, miners and smelters of lode concentrates have sought to organize their interdependence through common ownership, and one uncovers many instances of vertical integration in that segment of the tin industry.

Naturally, not all features of multinational expansion can be explained by transaction costs. Transaction cost theory posits that the boundaries of firms are determined by the minimization of such costs. The applicability of the model is thus restricted to situations where individuals are both free to choose the most efficient institutional forms and forced to do so through competitive pressures. The theory also focuses on the internalization of non-pecuniary externalities, and ignores institutional changes that result from market power. This paper has attempted to show that, these limitations notwithstanding, transaction costs theory can provide a useful framework to understand a wide range of multinational firms.

## Notes

† This paper has benefited from frequent discussions with Mira Wilkins and from Steve Nicholas' comments. Financial support from the Wharton Center for International Management Studies is gratefully acknowledged.

1. Public Record Office, Kew, BT 31 17888/90459 and 21352/128143.

2. This information is derived from the records of Frank Harvey, one of the partners in Williams, Harvey, kept at the Cornwall County Records Office, Truro, Cornwall.

3. The argument is similar to that put forth in a recent piece by Wilkins [25]. I differ from her, however, in my assessment of the reasons behind the decline of free-standing companies.

## References

1. G. C. Allen and A. G. Donnithorne, *Western Enterprise in Indonesia and Malaya* (London: George Allen and Unwin, 1957).

2. H. W. Allen and B. Engel, *Tin Production and Investments* (London: International Tin Council, 1979).

3. W. Baldwin, *The World Tin Market* (Durham, N.C.: Duke University Press, 1983).

4. P. Buckley and M. Casson, *The Future of Multinational Enterprise* (London: Macmillan, 1976).

5. M. Casson, "Transaction Costs and the Theory of the Multinational Enterprise," in P. Buckley and M. Casson, *The Economic Theory of the Multinational Enterprise* (New York: St. Martin's Press, 1985).

6. C. Geddes, *Patino: The Tin King* (London: Robert Hale, 1972).

7. H. D. Griffiths, "Bucket Dredging for Tin in the Federated Malay States," *Mining Magazine* (December 1916–March 1917).

8. A. R. Hall, *The London Capital Market and Australia, 1879–1914* (Canberra: ANU, 1963).

9. J. F. Hennart, *A Theory of Multinational Enterprise* (Ann Arbor: University of Michigan Press, 1982).

10. ——, "The Tin Industry," In M. Casson and Associates, *Multinationals and World Trade* (London: Allen and Unwin, 1986).

11. Lim Chong-Ya, *Economic Development of Modern Malaya* (Kuala Lumpur: Oxford University Press, 1967).

12. C. Mackenzie, *Realms of Silver: One Hundred Years of Banking in the East* (London: Routledge and Kegan Paul, 1954).

13. *Mining Journal,* August 16, 1924.

14. *Mining Manual* (London, 1914).

15. S. Nicholas, "Agency Contracts, Institutional Modes, and the Transition to Foreign Direct Investment in British Manufacturing before 1939," *Journal of Economic History,* 43, 1983.

16. D. G. Paterson, *British Direct Investment in Canada, 1890–1914* (Toronto: University of Toronto Press, 1976).

17. A. Rugman, *Inside the Multinationals* (New York, Columbia University Press, 1981).

18. W. L. Schurz, *Bolivia: A Commercial and Industrial Handbook* (Washington, D.C.: U.S. Department of Commerce, Special Agents Series, No. 208, 1921).

19. Song Ong Siang, *One Hundred Years' History of the Chinese in Singapore* (London, 1923).

20. C. Spence, *British Investments and the American Mining Frontier, 1860–1901* (Ithaca: Cornell University Press, 1958).

21. F. A. Swettenham, *About Perak* (Singapore: Straits Times Press, 1893).

22. J. T. Thoburn, *Primary Commodity Exports and Economic Development* (London: John Wiley and Sons, 1977).

23. ——, *Multinationals, Mining, and Development: A Study of the Tin Industry* (Farnborough, U.K.: Gower, 1981).

24. M. Wilkins, "Defining the Firm: Theory and History," in P. Hertner and G. Jones, eds. *Multinationals: Theory and History* (Gower, 1985).

25. ——, "The Free Standing Company, 1870–1914," unpublished manuscript, 1987.

26. Wong Lin Ken, "Western Enterprise and the Development of the Malaysian Tin Industry to 1914," in C. D. Cowan, ed., *The Economic Development of Southeast Asia* (New York: Praeger, 1964).

27. ——, *The Malaysian Tin Industry to 1914* (Tucson: University of Arizona Press, 1965).

28. Yip Yat Hoong, *The Development of the Tin Industry of Malaya* (Kuala Lumpur: University of Malaya Press, 1969).

# 11

## Risk and Control in Multinational Enterprise: German Businesses in Scandinavia, 1918–1939*

Harm Schröter[†]

*Source: *Business History Review*, 62 (1988), pp. 420–443.

In the following essay, Dr. Schröter examines a specific case, German multinational activity in Scandinavia between the wars, and uses that information to raise more general questions about the nature of multinational enterprise. Before 1914, patterns of German foreign direct investment resembled those of the nation's competitors. After the First World War, however, having lost almost all their overseas holdings and suffering from a severe shortage of capital, German industries tried to replace foreign direct investment with other financial tools, principally cartels and long-term contracts. Using extensive German archival materials, Dr. Schröter describes the forces motivating these businesses.

A great deal of work has already been done on the nature of multinational enterprise.[1] The concept of internalization, which describes the process of enterprises' bringing outside factors under control through ownership, has been widely used in an effort to explain companies' expansion beyond national borders.[2] Some scholars have attempted to revise the theoretical definition of internalization in order better to accommodate it to reality, but others have become skeptical about the usefulness of the concept to economic historians.[3] They argue that so many cases are not covered by the theory that the theory itself ought to be reviewed and changed.[4] Others suggest that the theory should be put aside while the varieties of special cases are studied; then the theory could be reconsidered to determine whether some common ground emerges from the empirical evidence collected.[5]

Although it shares some of this skepticism, this contribution ultimately focuses on internalization theory, in that it asks why internalization—foreign direct investment—was bypassed in the cases examined in favor of other means of reducing transaction costs, notably cartels and long-term contracts. As Peter Hertner and Geoffrey Jones have noted, "business history can and should contribute empirical evidence that incorporates the dimensions of both space and time."[6] The time span of this study is the interwar period, and the space is German economic enterprise in Scandinavia (Denmark, Finland, Norway, and Sweden); the approach is analytical rather than chronological.

The information collected, gathered chiefly from the archives of German enterprises, reveals that these companies had one overriding goal: security. This goal is quite in accordance with certain economic theories in which foreign direct investment is seen as an attempt to diversify risks, a view suggested by Alfred Plummer as early as 1934.[7] Lawrence Franko's research on American enterprises showed that foreign direct investment was often used as security against the risks of losing a market, and Hans Merkle has found that the same motivation inspired German multinational enterprise.[8] According to Alan Rugman, risk diversification—which can be perceived conversely as security maximization—plays a large role in decision making about foreign investment, as does profit maximization.[9] The evidence of Alfred D. Chandler, Jr., shows that American managers were also interested in security, preferring long-term stability to quick profits.[10]

Most of these assumptions and the evidence behind them, however, assume as a model an international market composed of countries with free access to very large markets abroad, such as the British Empire.[11] In reality, nations often operate in smaller markets, and they almost always function under considerable political, cultural, or economic constraint. Although in certain political circumstances direct foreign investments in a free market provide risk diversification, an investment abroad is always a risk. Moreover, the current practice of assessing political risks by capital budgeting was not employed before the Second World War; the investor during the interwar period faced considerably more uncertainty than exists for enterprises in the 1980s.[12]

William Davidson has shown that decisions about foreign direct investment were made not only on the basis of empirical assessments of national or regional market developments, but also to a great extent because of a close relationship between the two countries involved, especially similarities in language and in economic and cultural conditions.[13] These criteria underline the importance of the general desire for security. In many cases companies chose for investment not the state for which they had the highest economic expectations, but rather the country in which they felt safest about their assets because of a better knowledge of vital noneconomic conditions, such as political stability or the legal system.

## Conditions of Interwar German Enterprise

This study attempts to show that German enterprises during the interwar period gave the highest priority in their long-term foreign economic policy to security.[14] Because they placed security first, businesses pursued their economic aims in foreign countries not primarily through direct investments, including joint ventures, but rather through cartels and long-term contracts (including licensing agreements)—tools with which German industry had experienced considerable success before the First World War. A decade ago Mira Wilkins pointed out the possible negative connection between investments and cartels: "There are cases where multinational behavior [direct foreign investment] did not occur because agreements between two, or more, otherwise independent enterprises precluded it."[15] Recently this discussion was expanded by Mark Casson, who suggested that theoretical approaches to both multinational enterprises and international cartels could be viewed as complements and substitutes for one another.[16] The historical evidence perhaps sheds some light on the connections between the two.

The findings of this study may not be unique to the special case of German business activities in Scandinavia during the interwar period. Interwar Germany is a particularly useful object for study in the context of alternatives to foreign direct investment. Having lost most of their foreign investments after the First World War, German multinational enterprises demonstrated a certain reluctance to reinvest abroad. As a result, alternatives such as international cartels and contracts were used more widely by German enterprises than by businesses in other nations.[17] It is therefore not the intent of this article to offer a comprehensive view of the goals and activities of the various industries discussed or to propose a new theoretical model. Much more work, especially at a comparative international level, remains to be done before such a project could be undertaken.[18] Nevertheless, the information gleaned from this study does, I believe, have implications for the more general study of multinational enterprise.

In the interwar period German industry operated under severe constraints, the most important of which was the desperate need for capital, especially foreign exchange. Furthermore, industry had to be reestablished in international markets at a time of serious internal disruption. It was commonly believed that these immense problems could be dealt with only if industrial strength was consolidated on a nationwide basis. This process was carried out in the mid-1920s, when large national cartels were formed and when major mergers created huge companies like Vereinigte Stahlwerke. After this domestic consolidation was accomplished, most German industries then sought international agreements in order to recapture their prewar share of the world market. Changing economic conditions in Germany—the great inflation in 1919–23, moderate growth in 1924–29, the crisis in 1929–33, and Nazi policies of armament and autarchy—caused variations in this behavior, but not a total revision.

German direct investments in Scandinavia had remained untouched throughout the First World War because those countries remained neutral, but some German assets in Scandinavia, such as those in chemicals and ores, had to be sold during the postwar inflation to meet the desperate need for foreign exchange. At the same time, German industries made major efforts to capture increased market shares in Scandinavia by a special export drive. During the late 1920s several direct investments were made, especially in the fields of chemicals, electrical technology, and raw materials, but during the entire interwar period, German industry tried to safeguard its scarcest production factor: capital. Whenever possible industry employed other financial tools, such as patents or cartels, in pursuit of its international aims. In many cases companies offset their lack of capital by offering access to high technology or by exchanging goods. These instruments were also used during the crisis and Nazi periods when foreign exchange became still more scarce. Capital was invested abroad only when no replacement could be found.

Scandinavia became increasingly important as a market for Germany during the interwar years. The region took 7.7 percent of all German exports in 1913 and 12.9 percent in 1938. The main competitors were British and American industries. Throughout the interwar period Great Britain remained the main recipient of Scandinavian exports, Germany the main exporter into Scandinavia. During the 1930s, when British-German competition in Northern Europe became fierce in both the economic and the political arena, each country succeeded in augmenting its influence at the expense of the United States. For Germany, Scandinavia represented not only a buoyant market with a high per capita income, but also, especially in the Nazi period, a source of wartime supply, particularly of food and raw materials. Geographically and psychologically proximate, with a modern network of communication and transport—and within the reach of German guns—Scandinavia was expected to be a major element in the German *Großraumwirtschaft* (expanded economic sphere) in the event of war. In this respect, long-standing German business aims in Scandinavia were reinforced after 1936 by Nazi political aims.

The primary foreign economic aims of German enterprises can be classified into four categories: 1) long-term security in the supply of raw materials; 2) access to markets, secure outlets for products, and a fair share of expected market growth; 3) strategic security against competition, ranging from the maintenance of a presence in a specific market merely to forestall national and international competitors to the establishment of an informal empire, based on intense economic involvement; and 4) influence in political decision making in either the home or the host country, or both, focusing mainly on customs duties, tariffs, and legal matters regarding ownership, but sometimes including attempts to influence national economic and even defense policy.

Enterprises operating in foreign markets used three means to achieve these long-term security goals: direct investment, cartels, and long-term contracts. The remainder of this article therefore considers each of the twelve possible combinations of goals and methods.

## Security in the Supply of Raw Materials

The continuity of raw material supply is of critical importance for a manufacturing or processing enterprise. If a steady flow of materials cannot be guaranteed, firms must either store and handle costly inventories or run the risk of losing customers and reputation by being unable to fill orders efficiently. This section discusses when and how direct investments, cartels, and contracts were employed by German industry in Scandinavia in order to forestall interruptions in the supply of raw materials.

### Foreign Direct Investment

The most important natural resources to be found in Northern Europe were iron and other ores, timber, and the potential to generate inexpensive hydroelectric power. Although the last item is not strictly a raw material, it deserves inclusion because the availability of water power attracted heavy foreign investment, especially in Norway. Germany had strong competition for the rich Scandinavian resources. British and American capital was deeply involved in the metallurgical industry, and French firms also had assets in Norway, primarily in the important Norsk Hydro Elektrisk Kvaelstofaktieselskap.[19] In the timber, pulp, and paper sector, indigenous enterprises had a strong presence, and foreign investments were even excluded from Finland shortly after the First World War. In the 1930s the important British firm, the Bowater Paper Company, Ltd., which already owned a minority holding in Risör Traemassefabriker, bought up several Swedish paper mills. The German Feldmühle Papier and Zellstoff AG had invested 300,000 Fmk in a Helsinki timber trading firm as early as 1925.[20] Its direct competitor, the German Waldhof AG, was even more heavily engaged in Scandinavia. In Norway it owned 100 percent of Stordö pyrites mine, and in 1929 it founded a subsidiary with a work force of eight hundred in Kexholmen, Finland.[21] In 1931, through a secret contract with IG Farben, the Kexholmen plant was to be exclusively provided with the chlorine necessary for its operation.[22] The purpose of all these investments was to have a secure supply of raw material from nearby sources.

Foreign direct investment in ore mining was hampered by Scandinavian laws. In 1906 the Norwegian parliament, the Storting, alarmed by the amount of foreign ownership in the country, passed a law limiting foreign investment in Norwegian natural resources.[23] Sweden and Finland soon followed with similar legislation. The German iron and steel industry, by far the largest buyer of Scandinavian ores, was very interested in direct ownership of ore fields and mines, particularly in Sweden, but despite numerous efforts to purchase ore fields, they had little success. Their failure resulted not so much from legal restrictions, which could often be circumvented by keeping foreign ownership secret, or "cloaked," but rather from the unwillingness of the owners of the ore fields to sell. The industry did acquire several mines, but their output represented only a small proportion of the total mined in Sweden.[24] When the industrialists realized that it would be impossible to purchase a substantial share of Swedish mining operations, they adopted a different strategy. They openly used their position as the biggest customers to influence prices.[25]

Foreign influence in the Norwegian iron ore mines was far more significant. Forty-three percent of the largest, AS Sydvaranger, was secretly owned by Vereinigte Stahlwerke in Düssdeldorf, which also held 50 percent of AS Rana Gruber; the Dunderland Iron Ore Company mine was under British control.[26] Although controlling a large number of shares did permit some influence, ownership of less than 51 percent of the capital of these concerns did not provide the German industries with the degree of control desired. To strengthen its position vis-à-vis Sydvaranger, Vereinigte Stahlwerke therefore used comprehensive, long-term delivery contracts to bind the Norwegian company to favorable terms. With these contracts, which ran for ten years, Vereinigte Stahlwerke took nearly the total output of the mines. When Sydvaranger attempted to export ore to the United States, for example, Vereinigte Stahlwerke intervened and prevented any significant shipping to America. Vereinigte Stahlwerke clearly acted to forestall Sydvaranger from diversifying its customer base so that the German conglomerate would remain Sydvaranger's biggest and most influential buyer.

In Finland, Germany tried to obtain control over the copper ore-producing Outokumpu mine, but failed in several attempts, first in 1922 and again in the late 1930s. German copper users already had long-standing delivery contracts with Outokumpu, but this arrangement did not provide a sufficiently secure access to the important ore field. Since the Outokumpu mine was one of the few European producers of copper ore, government officials as well as businessmen wanted the control that only outright ownership could offer. The German authorities became involved in the negotiations, but foreign investment was blocked by Finnish government intervention. In a similar case, the exploitation rights to the nickel ore deposits near Petsamo were handed over to the Mond Nickel Company, Ltd., London, despite vigorous German attempts to gain control of it.[27]

## Cartels

Before the First World War, cartels dealing with raw materials were generally arranged among suppliers, with customers organized only in a very few cases. There is one significant exception. In early January 1918 German steel producers agreed that they would negotiate with Scandinavian ore suppliers only as a group.[28] In this case, however, the contracts negotiated with the Scandinavian producers, not the inter-company understanding, were the important factors, and this agreement is therefore considered in the discussion of contracts.

## Contracts

Long-term contracts were the traditional means employed to obtain security in raw material supply. In Scandinavia the most important of these were to be found in the iron ore industry, the main partners being the Swedish firm Gränges and the German iron and steel enterprises.

Both sides were well aware that these contracts, which normally ran for five to twelve years, involved uncertainties, since over such a long period much could happen to market conditions, prices, or exchange rates. On the other hand, long-term contracts enabled companies to negotiate relatively secure terms and provided the stability of a known situation. Moreover, the parties involved developed clauses to deal with the hazards of unexpected fluctuations. In the long-term contracts between the German iron and steel companies and Gränges, two different quantities were listed for each year: a minimum amount to be delivered and an optional additional amount that could be purchased as needed. Since the option was nearly twice as large as the base amount, it offered the ore consumer a great deal of flexibility and security. Table 1 gives specific figures for the period 1933–42.

Orders for the foreseeable future were placed according to need, whereas orders for the more distant future were lower, with the understanding that they could be augmented if necessary up to the contracted option. The most valuable element, from the point of view of security, was the firm's ability to order, at short notice, a much greater amount of ore than initially contracted for. Rebates on higher consumption of ore were also included in the contracts; for example, the price per ton was lowered when more than 5 million tons were ordered within a year by the cartel.[29]

Exchange rates for the different currencies were also important. Some contracts, for instance those of Gutehoffnungshütte, were based on Swedish crowns (Skr), whereas others covering the same period were based on German marks.[30] Since there was a known tendency toward inflation of the mark, the German signatories had to guarantee a certain exchange rate for the two currencies. Exactly the same guarantee was incorporated in all contracts, even those based on Swedish crowns. This meant in practice that the German enterprises had to pay either in Swedish crowns or in another foreign currency during the subsequent inflation of the mark.[31] The

*Table 1* Iron Ore contracts between Swedish and German Enterprises (Contracts between Gränges and Various German Companies, 1933–1942) (in millions of metric tons)

| Enterprise | Annual contracted basis for 1933–37 | Annual contracted basis for 1938–42 | Annual option |
|---|---|---|---|
| Vereinigte Stahlwerke | 1.6 | 0.8 | 3.1 |
| Krupp | 0.7 | 0.3 | 1.2 |
| Gutehoffnungshütte | 0.4 | 0.2 | 0.7 |
| Hoechst | 0.5 | 0.5 | 0.8 |
| Klöckner | 0.3 | 0.3 | 0.6 |
| Mannesmann | 0.3 | 0.3 | 0.3 |
| Total | 3.8 | 2.4 | 6.7 |

*Sources:* Based on several contracts between each German company on the one hand and Gränges (Trafikaktiebolag Grängesberg-Öxelesund, Luossavara-Kirunavara AB) on the other, Archiv der Rohstoff GmbII, Düsseldorf (Thyssen). Schwedenerz 1933–42, compilation dated 1 July 1939.

contract signed on 20 January 1923 during the German hyperinflation, for example, explicitly incorporated the requirement that payment be in either Swedish crowns or a gold-standard currency.[32]

In the 1930s ore exports were a crucial element in all trade agreements between Germany, Great Britain, and Sweden, because Swedish iron ore was of strategic importance not only to Germany, but also to Britain and other countries. In order to safeguard its national interests, Sweden had enacted legislation that provided for a maximum amount to be shipped abroad annually, though this export quota was raised after 1937 following an official request by the British government. So significant was the Swedish role as a supplier of iron ore to the major powers that in the 1960s Alan Milward asked, "Could Sweden have stopped the Second World War?" by an embargo on ore exports.[33] The contracts between Gränges and the German firms therefore had to take into account the specifics of international trade treaties, leading to some remarkable clauses.[34] Additional charges beyond the cost of the ore, such as export or transit tariffs levied by Sweden and Norway, were to be paid by Gränges, whereas German customers had to pay those levied in the Netherlands and Germany. The contracts were thus based on neither a FOB (free on board) nor a CIF (cost, insurance, freight) system, but rather took into account possible actions of independent third parties, that is, of the national governments of the contracting firms, which were not directly involved in the agreements.

The most important security component of long-term contracts was not contained in any clause, but was rather the mutual goodwill of the trading partners. If differences arose, they were settled not by courts or by written contracts, but always through businesslike negotiations.[35] For example, in the early 1920s and again in the late 1930s all the German customers agreed to pay higher prices than had been laid down in the contracts with Gränges. On the other hand, during the slump German purchases were allowed to fall below the contracted minimum. In 1929 this relationship was enhanced by a secret exchange of letters in a "Gentlemen's Agreement."[36] Among other items, the price of iron ore was related to the price of iron in Brussels, which had been chosen by the international steel cartels of the interwar period as the basis for steel prices.

On the whole, the relations between the partners in these ore contracts were very good. But for the German businessmen contracts represented only a second-best solution, because they did not provide wholly secure access to vital raw materials. Before and during the First World War, the steel producers had made great efforts to acquire ore fields and mines in foreign countries, with some success. In 1913 Thyssen, for example, owned shares of mines operating in France, Russia, Norway, Morocco, Algeria, and India.[37] After the war, the German steel industry tried again to purchase foreign mines, primarily in Scandinavia (though plans were also made for investments in Africa and South America), because the risks of direct investment were outweighed in this case by the industry's urgent desire to control the supply of raw materials.

## The Security of Market Share

### Foreign Direct Investment

Foreign direct investments in production units to supply indigenous markets were not very widespread in Scandinavia. One of the best examples is the case of Osram. In 1919 three major German electrical firms, Siemens and Halske, Allgemeine Elektrizitäts (AEG), and Auer, merged the incandescent lamp sectors of their businesses to found Osram, which thus became the biggest light bulb supplier in Europe. It seems that this branch of industry had not been as severely affected as others by the First World War, for the Germans set up several foreign subsidiaries between 1914 and 1922.[38] These included Nordisk Glödelampe Industri AS, Copenhagen, which was founded in 1915 and was endowed with 0.5 million Danish crowns (Dkr), and Drammens Lampefabrik AS near Oslo, founded in 1920 with an investment totalling 0.5 million Norwegian crowns (Nkr). The AB Elektraverk in Stockholm followed in 1928.

These investments had a threefold aim. First, they were intended to supply the indigenous market. Second, they had the function of safeguarding this sphere of production against investment by another enterprise. Finally, they were important in negotiations for the revival of the worldwide bulb cartel. Talks about this understanding began in 1920, and the famous "Phoebus" agreement, covering all important light bulb producers in the world, including the United States, was signed in 1924.[39] In this agreement the home-market clause was very important, since Finland was the only Scandinavian country left open to all suppliers by the agreement. In the negotiations for the extension of the cartel in 1929, Scandinavia was placed in the territory belonging to Osram. Even Finland was included, but Dutch Philips, the second largest light bulb producer in Europe, strongly backed by General Electric, had to be given a small share in each of the four markets.[40] Still, the Osram investments in Scandinavia, which allowed the German companies to claim Scandinavia as a "home market,"[41] are an example of an investment that both met indigenous demand and served a broader strategic purpose.[42]

This diversity of aims and methods applied to most German enterprises engaged in Scandinavia. Companies used investments, cartels, and contracts, interlocked and supplementing each other, in their efforts to achieve the economic security that was the single focus of their long-term strategy.

*Cartels*

Two of the cartels operating in Scandinavia were particularly oriented toward issues of market share: the "International Coke Convention" and an association for certain electrical commodities.

Northern Europe was one of the most important markets for international coal and coke exports. Several attempts to set up an international coal cartel, either for Sweden alone as a testing ground or for Scandinavia as a whole, had failed, largely because of the lack of organization of the biggest supplier, the British coal industry.[43] This problem was remedied, however, by British government intervention, resulting in the Coal Mines Act of 1930, after which other national coal producers' associations looked on the British coal producers as reliable partners. In 1934 a coal agreement dealing with Scandinavia, which the British saw as a first step toward a comprehensive international agreement, was reached by Poland and Great Britain.[44] At one stage representatives of Germany, the second biggest exporter, also took part in the negotiations.[45] However, since the British-Polish agreement was based on quantities and did not include a definite price clause, the German Rheinische-Westfälische Kohlen-Syndikat, to whom prices were the most important issue, ultimately declined to participate in the understanding.[46]

The good results obtained by the British-Polish understanding nevertheless paved the way for the first major international coal agreement, the "International Coke Convention." One purpose of the convention—more favorable prices and other terms of sale—was quickly reached.[47] But all parties thought the convention should be more: the forerunner of a comprehensive European coal cartel, a plan that had been discussed since the early 1920s. Some months later Great Britain and Germany did sign such an agreement, but the Second World War intervened, and the larger coal cartel never went into operation. As in other cases, Scandinavia, and Sweden in particular, had been used as a testing ground for a much wider cartel.[48]

In the field of electrical power three enterprises, the Swedish ASEA and the German AEG and Siemens dominated Scandinavia. After a period of competition, these three firms formed a cartel, designed to guarantee the status quo, covering the Swedish market from 1925 onward. The degree of security acquired for their markets encouraged the cartel to raise prices in Sweden substantially (between 30 and 65 percent). The cartel established a new harmonious relationship among ASEA (the largest Swedish electrical firm), AEG, and Siemens, forming the basis for a cooperation in other markets that functioned without any additional written agreement.[49] In this case the influence of the cartel was much wider than the area of its original agreements; the spirit was far more important than the document.

*Contracts*

Firms could also obtain security of market share and opportunity for further growth by long-term delivery contracts if a partnership could be arranged with another enterprise that enjoyed a degree of influence in a particular market. Through the contract, one firm could benefit from the influence of the other.

In 1932 IG Farben signed such a contract with the Finnish "Valio" dairy cooperative, which had obtained patents for the AIV process used to conserve livestock fodder.[50] Contracts for its application were signed in Sweden, Norway, Denmark, and Iceland, and others were to follow.[51] The available data suggested a very fast growing market for the chemicals required in this process. Imperial Chemical Industries (ICI) of Great Britain had already signed a contract with Valio covering the Empire and Britain. Under IG Farben's contract, which ran from 1933 to 1940, the German chemical group was to supply the rest of the world, except the United States, with the chemicals needed for the AIV process. In an internal memorandum IG Farben officials listed several reasons for signing the contract.[52] The most important factor was the expected growth of sales in this particular market. Every year a certain increase in profits had to be obtained, aiming for a fivefold growth by 1940. Furthermore, Valio was to be responsible for the entire promotion costs of seminars and advertising. The contract was secret in order not to reveal Valio's link with IG Farben, since Valio would recommend the use of IG Farben chemicals. The benefits for IG Farben were clear, and Valio in return received secure outlets, guaranteed by a reliable partner operating worldwide, for its products.

## Security Through Strategic Market Presence

*Foreign Direct Investment*

Besides maintaining or increasing the market for their products and guaranteeing a supply of raw materials, enterprises had several other incentives to enter a particular market. For larger firms, mere presence in a market could be used to put pressure on competitors, even those in third markets, especially if the enterprise enjoyed a substantial share or domination of that market. Such a presence could prevent the entry of both indigenous and other foreign firms into a market, thereby avoiding the price-cutting and retaliation that the entry of another player could generate. A mixture of defensive and offensive motives therefore supported long-term strategies for security that went beyond immediate concerns about supplies and sales.

In 1944 IG Farben owned more than 50 percent of the shares of Norsk Hydro, one of the most important enterprises in Scandinavia and by far the largest company in Norway. It had attracted one-third of all foreign investments in the country. Why and how did IG Farben acquire control of it? Before the First World War a German chemical enterprise, Badische Anilin- und Sodafabrik (BASF), had had a 15 percent interest in Norsk Hydro. These shares were sold, but as early as 1923 BASF tried to regain its influence by proposing an agreement based on a share of its patents for a superior process for the manufacture of nitrogen. In 1927 Norsk Hydro accepted this offer from IG Farben (into which BASF and other German chemical companies had merged in 1925). The Norwegian company hoped to increase its production of nitrogen by nearly 200 percent without using more energy through access to AG Farben's patents and technical knowledge. The enterprises agreed to an exchange of shares by which Norsk Hydro obtained a minor holding in IG Farben, and IG Farben received 25 percent of Norsk Hydro's stock in return.[53] In addition, the Norwegian company had to dissolve most of its sales organization, because distribution was now to be carried out by the German "Stickstoff-Syndikat" (nitrogen syndicate). The German influence in Norsk Hydro, moreover, was much greater than the 25 percent share indicated. Major decisions could not be taken without German consent.[54] Consent to IG Farben's role had been obtained from the French majority shareholder, ETS Kuhlmann, via Banque de Paris et des Pays Bas, through the founding in the same year of a dyestuff cartel that supported major interests of both companies.[55]

IG Farben's control of Norsk Hydro was not, however, as tight as that provided by most direct investments, because the Norwegian enterprise had the backing of its national government when disputes arose. In 1929, when Norsk Hydro had just rebuilt its factories to use the German process, the market for nitrogen slumped, leading to some discontent on the part of the Norwegian company and its government with the terms of the agreement with IG Farben.[56] After some negotiations, the disputes were settled.

During this time IG Farben nevertheless discovered that Norsk Hydro's relatively independent standing, as opposed to the position of a direct subsidiary of IG Farben, held certain advantages. IG Farben—like ICI— pursued a policy of hampering the establishment of competitive industries in other countries in order to maintain its own exports. When IG Farben was consulted about the construction of a nitrogen factory in Denmark in 1936, for example, the company reported that such a step would be unprofitable.[57] Norsk Hydro, being of Scandinavian origin, was thought to be independent and reliable, especially in this case, and it was also asked for an opinion. It concurred with IG Farben's recommendation, and the plant was not constructed. There were several similar cases. IG Farben even suggested to firms requesting their advice that they should also consult Norsk Hydro.[58] Yet in a case of direct competition with IG Farben, Norsk Hydro was itself compelled to stop production; and IG Farben managed to obtain a majority holding when German troops invaded Norway.[59]

IG Farben had several good reasons for acquiring a foothold in Norsk Hydro in 1927. Managers were aware that the German enterprise, the biggest nitrogen producer in the world, would soon run into trouble because of huge overcapacity. The company could not stop Norsk Hydro from building up its own capacity, but the agreement enabled IG Farben to control Norsk Hydro's exports and to channel them through the German sales network. As a result IG Farben's power in international negotiations rose as much as its market share. IG Farben's policy of international cartelization achieved a major success in 1929, when it formed an export cartel with ICI that formed the nucleus of all international nitrogen agreements from that time onward. Thus IG Farben did not acquire its stake in Norsk Hydro primarily to increase its holdings, but rather for reasons of long-term market policy.[60]

As Peter Hertner has shown, the international policy of German electrotechnical enterprises before 1914 was focused on technology and finance.[61] After the experience of losing most of their foreign assets after the First World War, and because of the severe shortage of finance, the industry became very cautious about investing abroad. Nevertheless, the German electrotechnical industry was always very interested in the Swedish market, because it was one of relatively few rapidly growing markets in the interwar period. The Swedish enterprise ASEA also offered goods of high technical quality, so competition became quite fierce, although the intensity was reduced after 1925, when an agreement was signed. ASEA still remained a difficult partner from the German point of view: in regard to bids on contracts, Siemens did not always enjoy the protection from ASEA to which it felt entitled. In some cases only resort to "recklessness, threats, and rudeness" made ASEA move in the desired direction.[62] In 1930 the president of the Swedish enterprise Elektromekano suggested that Siemens should take over his firm.[63] Although Siemens was not interested in taking up production in Sweden, it considered the offer because it wished to use Elektromekano as a means of putting pressure on ASEA, especially because a cartel of ASEA, AEG, and Siemens was to be negotiated in the following year. This motive was discussed quite frankly in a special meeting of Siemens directors: "Today a purchase would perhaps be of interest in the perspective of our relationship with ASEA.... By acquiring Elektromekano, which produces high-voltage material, we could of course render ASEA's business in Sweden more difficult. This would move ASEA to adopt a more conciliatory attitude."[64]

In the end the takeover was not carried out for financial reasons; Elektromekano's liabilities were not fully known. Financial caution was forced on Siemens not by the incipient world economic crisis, but by the fight over the world's telephone market, in which Siemens was engaged with International Telephone and Telegraph (ITT). ITT, in its turn, carried out a direct investment in Denmark for exactly the same reasons that Siemens considered buying Elektromekano: to establish a market presence and to gain acceptance as an indigenous enterprise (though for ITT imports were important as well). ITT viewed its Danish investment primarily as a competitive move against Siemens.

*Cartels*

The basic motivation underlying a cartel is defense. It is meant to guarantee that no sudden movement will disturb the market conditions on which its members have agreed among themselves. In German industry during the interwar period, IG Farben specialized in taking the offensive within the framework of cartel policies.[65] In the following case, however, even IG Farben's cartel membership was a purely defensive strategy.

Ferrosilicon, used as a flux by the steel industry, required cheap energy for its production. The industry grew rapidly in Scandinavia because of the abundance of hydroelectric power. When an international ferrosilicon cartel was formed in 1927, the strength of Scandinavia's interests was reflected in the quotas: Norway with ten factories received 36.5 percent; Germany had 25.4 percent, Sweden 20.5 percent, Yugoslavia 14.1 percent, and Switzerland 3.5 percent. (Since the Yugoslavian enterprise Elektrobosna in Jajce was indirectly owned by IG Farben, the German-influenced share was about 39 percent).[66] The Norwegian share was also influenced to some extent by U.S. and British ownership. The cartel's main purpose of safeguarding markets was not adequately fulfilled, since the Norwegian enterprise AS Bjölvefossen withdrew in order to increase its production capacity only a few months after the cartel was founded. During the 1930s the Scandinavian producers continued to press for higher quotas in the various iron alloy cartels, and their share was gradually augmented.[67] Nevertheless, the cartel, which endured until 1939, was partially successful, and the members' experience led to the cartelization of other iron alloys as well. For IG Farben these cartels played a decisive role in avoiding heavy price competition, not only in export markets but also in its domestic market.

In 1938 IG Farben and its U.S. counterpart Du Pont divided between themselves the world market in synthetic fibers. Scandinavia was placed in IG Farben's area.[68] Since the production of synthetic fibers required the application of high technology, and as the market was thought to be extremely buoyant and attractive to other enterprises, a cross-licensing agreement was devised to prevent newcomers from entering. To reinforce this policy, the contract with Du Pont stipulated that IG Farben was to build a plant with a designated minimum output in Germany immediately.[69] Ensuring their own ability to meet all anticipated demand was thought to be the best means of safeguarding the market for Du Pont and IG Farben.

In some other industries a cartel was not considered sufficiently secure, but none of the cartel partners was ready to give up its independence through a merger. Accordingly, they chose a form of cooperation between trust and cartel. The European linoleum industry was almost entirely united in the "Continentale Linoleum Union," which had its headquarters in Zurich. The partners held shares according to their economic strength, and Germany therefore dominated.[70] The union had linoleum factories in Germany, the Netherlands, Switzerland, France, and Scandinavia. Among these was "a small factory in Copenhagen" with a share capital of 130,000 Danish crowns (Dkr) in 1926 that was wholly owned by the German branch of the union.[71] In Sweden there was the Linoleum AB, Forshaga, which also held 50 percent of AS Victoria Linoleum in Baerum, Norway.[72] These were not German or Swiss investments, however, but Union investments, made with pooled earnings and dividends, with the companies keeping their own management and decision-making powers.

## Contracts

Contracts concerning patents were often made with a view to strategic market presence. German firms licensed valuable patents to only a few reliable and well-known enterprises unless under political pressure, and even then the reputation of the recipient was taken into account. Swedish chemical enterprises received such licenses from IG Farben shortly before the Second World War.[73] Usually a license was not given on a worldwide basis, but only for a restricted geographical area, and the home market of the license-giver was always closed to licensees. A licensing agreement of this type excluded important German enterprises from the Swedish market for turbines. STAL (Svenska Turbinfabriks AB Ljungström), a subsidiary of ASEA, provided the patents for the "Internationale Ljungströmturbinen Union," Basle. Its shares were held equally by AEG, ASEA/STAL, MAN (an important German machine-building enterprise), and Siemens.[74]

In nearly all cases it was a far-reaching decision whether to give or take a license or to develop an alternative out of a company's own resources. Sometimes a license was the first step to closer cooperation among the enterprises involved.

## Security by Influencing Political Decisions

### Foreign Direct Investment

Political activities involving foreign direct investors, members of cartels, or the partners of a contract are difficult to trace. Most political actions undertaken by enterprises were aimed at their home governments.

Since IG Farben's overall policy was to expand its markets outside Germany in order to make full use of its existing production facilities, the company usually adopted a hostile attitude toward the industrialization of other countries.[75] But this policy was pursued quite flexibly, and IG Farben changed its position if the establishment of indigenous production could not be prevented. Then the company usually provided technical and economic expertise, machinery, and sometimes even capital. As a result its influence grew rather than diminished.

In Scandinavia IG Farben kept a network of different enterprises for different purposes. One of these firms was the AB Anilinkompani in Göteborg. In the late 1930s Sweden was about to raise duties on a variety of foreign chemical products to allow its own industry a better chance to develop. This put IG Farben's interests at risk, and the company pursued two strategies to halt the increase. The German government was asked to send a note of protest to Stockholm, which was done. Also, IG Farben advised its subsidiary, the Anilinkompani, to take steps as an indigenous Swedish company to resist the increase in import duties on a variety of special products that IG Farben wanted to export to Sweden.[76] The strategies were successful to the extent that some products were taken off the list and the duties for others were only slightly raised.

### Cartels

The influences of cartels on the decisions of foreign governments are not easy to trace. For obvious reasons it was useful, as a high-ranking IG Farben representative admitted, not to put agreements down in writing but to rely on oral negotiations instead.[77] Moreover, a cartel had to be very firmly based before being able to engage in such activities. However, some examples concerning Scandinavia do exist. In the context of structural overcapacity, established enterprises tried to hinder the development of newcomers through political action.[78]

From 1934 onward the Finnish government was determined to build a factory to produce chlorine. The importance of the project derived not only from the pursuit of a national industrialization policy, but also from the military usefulness of the proposed factory: the chlorine was intended for use in the event of war to neutralize poison gas. ICI and the German "Chlorstelle," later joined by the Belgian Solvay company, had formed a cartel for chlorine exports that had been running smoothly since 1931. The Finnish government asked the British ICI to build the new factory, but it was clear that other enterprises would share in the undertaking through the chlorine cartel.[79] As much on behalf of the cartel as on its own behalf, ICI at first tried to persuade the Finnish government to drop its plan for the factory entirely, but because of the military interest involved this attempt was unsuccessful.[80] ICI did succeed in delaying the construction of the plant for several years, however, and when it was finally completed it was not ICI, the official contractor of the Finnish government, that owned it, but the members of the chlorine cartel.[81]

This experience drew the cartel partners even more closely together. In November 1938, notwithstanding the worsening international political situation, Solvay, ICI, and IG Farben signed a secret and comprehensive "long-term agreement." A particularly important point was that the policy of preventing the development of new industries in nonmember countries should be pursued in common and, failing this (as in the case of Finland), investments were to be made jointly. "In any case," the agreement concluded, "a generous and friendly understanding [between ourselves] should be found."[82]

IG Farben also played the most active role in Scandinavia among the members of the worldwide nitrogen cartel.[83] There were plans in Denmark, supported by the royal government, to create an indigenous nitrogen industry to serve the needs of Danish agriculture. In a coordinated action directed by IG Farben and supported by ICI, Norsk Hydro, and the German diplomatic service, the construction of a nitrogen factory was averted.[84] In Finland, too, the government planned to build up the country's own nitrogen industry for political and economic reasons. Again IG Farben tried to persuade the "decisive circles" not to implement these plans, but it seemed clear that the best achievable result would be a considerable delay.[85] Various means were used to hinder construction. In summer 1936 IG Farben sent representatives to Helsinki to argue that the Finnish plans were uneconomical and to suggest alternatives, such as keeping large supplies within the country. In April 1937 IG Farben submitted drafts for the plant to the Finnish government, but these turned out to be remarkably incomplete, and they had to be reviewed, which required another eight months. The Finnish representatives were still not satisfied, and they asked the German firm Uhde for an alternative draft. Uhde, which had a great deal of experience in the construction of chemical plants, also maintained intimate links with its best customer, IG Farben, and it was therefore well informed about IG Farben's policy in general and about the Finnish project in particular. At an internal meeting of IG Farben representatives, it was stated that: "The firm of Uhde ... handed over a protective bid (*Schutzangebot*), which had been worked out together with our technical department."[86] Since the Uhde document was also submitted to the Finnish authorities after considerable delay, this maneuver gained time for further exports of nitrogen to Finland.[87] The plant was fully constructed, though there is no evidence that production started before the Finnish-Soviet War in the winter of 1939–40.

This case was by no means unique; it is, rather, a typical example of the policy of the nitrogen cartel, the Convention de l'industrie de l'Azote (CIA), directed by the Deutsch-Englisch-Norwegische-Gruppe (DEN Group).[88] As in the case of chlorine, the policy of preventing new entrants was secure only if all the enterprises able to build such plants stood together in trying to block construction. Since the nitrogen cartel did not cover the construction of plants owned by nonmembers, it was supplemented by an agreement among the most important firms, similar to the one organized by the chlorine cartel. ICI and IG Farben signed a contract "to the greatest extent possible, to avoid foreign investments, as long as possible...."[89] Shortly after the agreement had come into force on 1 January 1938, Norsk Hydro joined the pact.[90]

*Contracts*

Few examples of the final case, private contracts between enterprises to obtain influence on political decision making in third countries, can be found, because contracts were not the right tool for this purpose. The chemical cartel agreements aimed at slowing down industrialization that are described above were formally private contracts, but their real strength lay in the cartels that generated them and in the trust that arose from these understandings. However, contracts concluded to exert political influence indirectly can be found.

In the 1930s, in particular, well-known German enterprises were not prepared to leave their foreign propaganda solely to the Nazis. In a secret letter to its members, the Federation of German Industries (Reichsstand der Deutschen Industrie) warned them not to cooperate with certain propaganda organizations such as the "Nordische Gesellschaft." In Scandinavia, efforts were concentrated mainly on Sweden, which had the closest ties with Germany, but Denmark was also targeted for attention when Great Britain chose Copenhagen as the site for the first and second British Industrial Fair in Scandinavia.[91] In monitoring these British activities, German industry detected a lack of pro-German feeling in

Scandinavia.[92] To remedy this, a secret organization, the "Deutsch-Schwedische Ausschuß," was set up. It was founded and financed by major businesses that had their own representatives in Sweden, such as AEG, Seimens, IG Farben, and Vereinigte Stahlwerke. Though contact was established with reliable partners in the German state bureaucracy, it was agreed that the organization should be kept out of sight of Joseph Goebbel's Ministry of Propaganda. The efforts focused on Swedish journalists working for newspapers, radio stations, and other media, and they were reported to be very effective.[93]

## Conclusion

Security was the overriding aim of German enterprises involved in foreign markets, and this goal determined the strategies that the companies pursued. Each type of activity involved a trade-off between risk and control that firms weighed carefully in specific cases. Long-term contracts were not often used because their efficacy was largely dependent on the good faith of the host partner. If the partner was powerful and had the political and legal protection of its government, such a contract meant dependence for the German firm. The German steel industry did become dependent to some degree on its Swedish iron ore suppliers, but it did so only because important advantages were also secured: 1) long-term contracts gave more security than day-by-day purchases and locked in lower prices; 2) reliance on a neutral Swedish supply was preferred to reliance on the alternative—French ore—because the Swedish ores had a higher iron content, and because long-term steel policy toward France precluded this kind of cooperative agreement; and 3) the dependence was mutual.[94] Even so, the dependent status of the German industries under these contracts caused great unease, and companies made various efforts to reduce it by revitalizing indigenous German iron ore mines, seeking other sources of ore supply, investing in Swedish ore mines, and investing in other foreign mines and ore fields. Only when economic strength was clearly on the German firm's side, as in the case of the Valio—IG Farben agreement, were long-term contracts the preferred form of action.[95]

Given the overall shortage of financial resources from which German industry suffered so badly in the period, it is extremely significant that companies did not have greater recourse to long-term contracts, which caused the least financial strain, or to joint ventures. It appears that they tried these steps, but were dissatisfied with the degree of control—and therefore of security—that these lesser risks could provide. In most cases businesses worked toward 100 percent ownership of the foreign firm, as in the case of Norsk Hydro. It is clear that the most extensive influence on foreign markets—that is, on conditions of operation, appeal to consumers, government influence, security of resources—was gained by direct investment. In that sense, foreign direct investment was the safest of all strategies, for it allowed the highest level of control. But because it required long-term investment from a country suffering economic disruption and a severe shortage of capital, foreign direct investment also entailed an unacceptably high level of risk for many German interwar enterprises.

These constraints made cartels the most important foreign trade tool for Germany in this period. As Alice Teichova has shown, cartels are easily adaptable to new or changing situations in both economic and political spheres.[96] They also save financial resources that would otherwise have to be poured into various direct investments. Having just lost most of their foreign assets after the Versailles Treaty and possessing a substantial amount of surplus capacity, most of German industry resorted to international cartelization rather than direct investment in order to safeguard its foreign interests. Cartels, however, had the drawback that they worked well only when all the members were strong international companies able to influence economic activity.

This study has attempted to show that internalization—foreign direct investment—may be undertaken for reasons other than profit maximization, that is, as a long-term competitive strategy to secure a market presence. Further, if firms are driven, as were the German firms dealing in Scandinavian markets between the wars, by a desire for security, they face the paradox that higher degrees of control require higher risks, which they must attempt to balance by applying different strategies in different circumstances. Therefore, the question of whether an enterprise is a "multinational"—or on its way to becoming one—cannot be answered solely on the basis of its direct foreign investments. Instead, the whole interlocking network of long-term contracts, cartel agreements, and direct investments has to be considered.

## Notes

† A portion of the research for this article was funded by the Deutscher Akademischer Austauschdienst.

1. A multinational enterprise in this context is defined as "an enterprise that controls and manages production establishments—plants—located in at least two countries." Richard E. Caves, *Multinational Enterprise and Economic Analysis* (Cambridge, Mass., 1982), 1.

2. Alan M. Rugman, ed., *New Theories of Multinational Enterprise* (London, 1982); but see the critique of this concept by Mark Casson, "General Theories of the Multinational Enterprise: Their Relevance to Business History," in *Multinationals: Theory and History*, ed. Peter Hertner and Geoffrey Jones (Aldershot, 1986), 42–63.

3. Mark C. Casson, "Transaction Costs and the Theory of the Multinational Enterprise," in Rugman, *New Theories*, 24–43.

4. "The moral of our review of the literature is that there is no really satisfactory general theory of the MNE." Casson, "General Theories of the Multinational Enterprise," 53. See also John H. Dunning, "Changes in the Level and Structure of International Business," in *The Growth of International Business*, ed. Mark Casson (London, 1983).

5. David K. Fieldhouse, "The Multinational: A Critique of a Concept," in *Multinational Enterprise in Historical Perspective*, ed. Alice Teichova, Maurice Lévy-Leboyer, and Helga Nussbaum (New York, 1986), 9–29, 24.

6. Peter Hertner and Geoffrey Jones, "Multinationals: Theory and History," in their *Multinationals*, 1–18, 15.

7. Alfred Plummer, *International Combines in Modern History* (London, 1934), 54.

8. Lawrence C. Franko, "The Origins of Multinational Manufacturing by Continental European Firms," in *Business History Review* 48 (Autumn 1974): 277–302; Hans L Merkle, "Internationale Aufgaben des Unternehmers," in *Schwerpunkte unternehmerischen Ilandelns* (Frankfurt, 1971), 29–46, 35.

9. Alan M. Rugman, "Motives for Foreign Investment: The Market Imperfections and Risk Diversification Hypothesis," *Journal of World Trade Law* 9 (1975): 567–73, 568.

10. Alfred D. Chandler, Jr., *The Visible Hand: The Managerial Revolution in American Business* (Cambridge, Mass., 1977), 10.

11. Casson, "General Theories," 42.

12. Thomas C. Brewer, "Political Risk Assessment for Foreign Direct Investment Decisions: Better Methods for Better Results," *Columbia Journal of World Business* (Spring 1981): 5–11.

13. William H. Davidson, "The Location of Foreign Direct Investment Activity: Country Characteristics and Experience Effects," *Journal of International Business Studies* (Fall 1980): 9–22.

14. In Germany after the introduction of state regulation of the handling of foreign exchange (*Devisenbewirtschaftung*) in 1931, very few direct investments were made up to 1939. But in those rare cases usually not all the money was transferred from Germany; instead profits of the enterprises in third markets were used for this (for example, the cooperative investment of IG Farben and ICI in their dye factory in Trafford, England, in 1938).

15. Mira Wilkins, "Modern European Economic History and the Multinationals," *Journal of European Economic History* 6 (1977): 575–95, 592; Wilkins, "The History of European Multinationals: A New Look," ibid., 15 (1986): 483–510, 506.

16. Mark Casson, "Multinational Monopolies and International Cartels," in *The Economic Theory of the Multinational Enterprise*, ed. Peter Buckley and Mark Casson (London, 1985), 60–97.

17. In the interwar period German enterprises and their foreign performance differed at least as much from more general patterns as did the Swedish businesses investigated by Ragnhild Lundström. See Lundström, "Swedish Multinational Growth before 1930," in Hertner and Jones, *Multinationals*, 135–56.

18. Casson, "Multinational Monopolies," 96; Helga Nussbaum, "International Cartels and Multinational Enterprise," in Teichova, Lévy-Leboyer, and Nussbaum, *Multinationals in Historical Perspective*, 131–44; Alice Teichova, "Multinationals in Historical Perspective," in *Debates and Controversies: 9th International Economic History Congress, Bern, 1986* (Zurich, 1986), 112–23. I am working on a project comparing multinational enterprises based in small European countries (Belgium, the Netherlands, Sweden, and Switzerland).

19. For details see A. Stonehill, *Foreign Ownership in Norwegian Enterprises* (Oslo, 1965).

20. R. Hjerppe, and J. Ahvenainen "Foreign Enterprises and Nationalistic Control: The Case of Finland since the End of the 19th Century," in Teichova, Lévy-Leboyer, and Nussbaum, *Multinationals in Historical Perspective*, 9: Stonehill, *Foreign Ownership in Norwegian Enterprises*, 20; Political and Economic Planning and Industries Group, *Report on International Trade* (London, 1937), 116; Pohjolan Puutavarau Vienti OY.

21. The investment amounted to nKr 600,000 in 1926; Politisches Archiv des Auswärtigen Amtes, Bonn [hereafter, PA AA], Sonderreferat Wirtschaft, Industrie 20, Band 1, Kartelle.

22. The amount, 6,000 tons of chlorine per year, was quite significant. Any production of chlorine on its own was prohibited. Contract of 9 Jan. 1931, Bayer Werks Archiv, Leverkusen [hereafter, BWA] 19, Chlor 5.

23. E. Lange, "The Concession Laws of 1906–1909 and the Norwegian Industrial Development," *Scandinavian Journal of History* 2 (1977): 311–30.

24. The investments of the German iron and steel industry, both hidden and open ones, are listed in Harm G. Schröter, *Außenpolitik und Wirtschaftsinteresse: Skandinavien im außenwirtschaftlichen Kalkül Deutschlands und Großbritainniens, 1918–1939* (Frankfurt, 1983), 412–14.

25. "Some of [the German ore mines] are being developed under great sacrifices purely for the purpose to safeguard a minor influence upon the Swedish market...." Ausschuß zur Untersuchung der Erzeugungs-und Absatzbedingungen der deutschen Wirtschaft, *Die Rohstoffversorgung der deutschen eisenerzeugenden Industrie* (Berlin, 1928), 84.

26. For this problem, see also G. Aalders and C. Wiebes, "Stockholm's Enskilda Bank, German Bosch, and IG Farben: A Short History of Cloaking," *Scandinavian Economic History Review* (1985): 25–50; Schröter, *Außenpolitik*, 412; Alan S. Milward, *The Fascist Economy in Norway* (Oxford, 1972), 56. Milward's account of German investments in Fosdalens Bergverks AS and in Sovestad mines (p. 56) has not been substantiated by German sources until now.

27. The reason for this was twofold. These were the only nickel ores Germany would have access to in case of war, and the German navy longed for a submarine base at Petsamo. Carl-Axel Gemzell, *Raeder, Hitler und Skandinavien: Der Kampf für einen maritimen Operationsplan* (Lund, 1965), 45, and Gemzell, *Organization, Conflict and Innovation: A Study of German Naval Strategic Planning, 1888–1940* (Lund, 1973), 278.

28. Note of a meeting held on 1 January 1918, Historisches Archiv der Gutehoffnungshütte, Oberhausen [hereafter, GHH], 30006/11.

29. Contracts between each German company on the one hand and Gränges (Trafikaktiebolag Grängesberg-Öxelesund, Luossavara-Kirunavara AB) on the other, Archiv der Rohstoff GmbH, Düsseldorf (Thyssen), Schwedenerz 1933–42, compilation dated 1 July 1939.

30. The price of ore class "Kiruna D" was, up to 5 million tons: 17.5 Skr; 5 million tons and above, 16.5 Skr (contract of 11 Nov. 1938, Rohstoff GmbH, Schwedenerzverträge 1933–42). For the same class "Kiruna D" during the 1920s, GHH had to pay: from 400,000 tons onward, 13 Skr; up to 200,000 tons, 15 Skr; up to 100,000 tons, 17 Skr (all fob Narvik). Contracts, GHH-Gränges, 26 Nov. 1920, 16 Dec. 1920, Archiv of GHH, 30006/17. The contract of Gränges and Thyssen (August Thyssen Hütte; hereafter, ATH) dating from 28 May 1919 was based on the following conditions:

| Year | Purchase in 1,000 tons | Price per ton in marks | Surcharge per ton in marks | Actual price |
|------|------|------|------|------|
| 1920 | 850 | 18,000 | 2,000 | 20,000 |
| 1921–22 | 900 | 18,144 | 2,000 | 20,144 |
| 1923 | 900 | 18,144 | 1,500 | 19,644 |
| 1924–25 | 950 | 18,171 | 1,500 | 19,671 |
| 1926 | 950 | 18,171 | 1,000 | 19,171 |
| 1927–30 | 1,000 | 18,195 | 1,000 | 19,195 |
| 1931–32 | 1,000 | 18,650 | 1,000 | 19,650 |

Historical Archive of ATH, A/560/4.

31. For example, in the GHH contract of 26 Nov. 1920/16 Dec. 1920 the rates for 1920 were: 100 marks = 80 Skr, rising annually by 1 Skr up to 1927, when 100 marks = 87 Skr. See contract, 26–29 April 1919, GHH archive, 30006/11; corresponding ATH-archive A/560/4, dated 28 May 1919. Like other enterprises, ATH used Dutch credits and paid in Florins (contract of 5 Dec. 1922, ATH-archive A/597/1).

32. Rohstoff, GmbH, Schwedenerzverträge, 1933–42.

33. Title of Alan S. Milward's contribution in the *Scandinavian Economic History Review* 15 (1967): 127–38.

34. Swedish-German Trade Treaty of 1926, Bundesarchiv Koblenz, BA R 43 I/1114, see Ånhlander; British-Swedish Trade Treaty of 15 March 1933, Utrikes Departements Arkiv, Stockholm, HP 64 Ba XVII.

35. Telegram of Gränges to ATH of 28 June 1919. ATH archive A/560/4.

36. Exchange of letters of 20 June 1929, Rohstoff GmbH, Schwedenerzverträge 1933–42.

37. Wilhelm Treue, *Die Feuer verlöschen nie. August Thyssen Hütte, 1890–1926* (Düsseldorf, 1966), 156.

38. See also the following, W. Meinhardt, *Entwicklung und Aufbau der Glühlampenindustrie* (Berlin, 1932). The author was Generaldirektor of Osram in the interwar period.

39. Harm G. Schröter, "A Typical Factor of German International Market Strategy: Agreements between the U.S. and the German Electrotechnical Industries up to 1939," in Teichova, Lévy-Leboyer, and Nussbaum, *Multinational Enterprise in Historical Perspective.*

40. In some cases, small direct investments in a country were made in order to safeguard exports there. If high tariffs or other protectionist barriers were present, modest investment in a small enterprise to carry out finishing or the packing of small units was often sufficient to overcome these disadvantages.

41. Note dated 29 June 1929 about the talks between Osram and General Electric. Siemens Archiv Akte, Munich [hereafter, SAA], 4/Lt 398 VI.

42. The Osram investments were also based on ownership advantage, as Peter Hertner has shown was the case for Bosch and Mannesmann before 1914. See Peter Hertner, "German Multinational Enterprise before 1914: Some Case Studies," In Hertner and Jones, *Multinationals,* 113–34, 123.

43. League of Nations Economic Committee, *The Coal Problem* (Geneva, 1932), 18.

44. See Sven-Olof Olsson, *German Coal and Swedish Fuel, 1939–1945* (Göteborg, 1975).

45. Patrick Salmon, "Polish-British Competition in the Coal Markets of Northern Europe," *Studia Historiae Oeconomicae* 16 (1981): 217–43; 234.

Meynen's letter of the German legation in Stockholm to the German Auswärtige Amt, dated 18 May 1934, in which the German share was placed at 8 percent; PA AA, Wirtschaft, Rohstoffe + Waren, Kohle, Bd. 9.

46. Polish sea-bound coal exports were to be 21 percent of British exports. Letter of the German ambassador to London to the Auswärtige Amt, 13 Dec. 1934, ibid., Bd. 10. The Polish prices were to be oriented to the British "green list," letter of the Swedish legation in London to the Utrikes Departement, 31 May 1935, Riksarkiv, HD HA F II aa/153. The Germans viewed it as ". . . an unperfect bungle, which in the most important question, in that of prices, was totally without impact"—a remark that seems to be quite unfair; internal letter of the German syndicate, 10 Nov. 1936. Historiches Archiv der GHH, 400101320/88; my translation.

47. Signed on 11 June 1937, valid from 1 April 1947 to 31 March 1940, with automatic annual prolongation unless cancellation. Quotas: Germany, 48.43%; Great Britain, 20.88%; Holland, 17.8%; Belgium, 9.66%; Poland, 3.20%; Bundesarchiv Koblenz, R 7/622; Olsson, *German Coal and Swedish Fuel*, 31, 56, 70.

48. As in the case of the world covering potassium syndicate: Harm G. Schröter, *Die internationale Kaliwirtschaft 1918 bis 1939: Zum Verhältnis von industrieller Kartellpolitik und Staatsinterventionismus* (Kassel, 1985). The files in no case give a reason why Scandinavia was chosen as a testing ground. I presume cartel partners could agree on this area because during the 1930s it was one of the very few fairly liberal and growing markets in which no partner had a substantial noneconomic advantage.

49. Some other Swedish enterprises were included as well as junior partners. See in detail, Jan Glete, *ASEA under 100 År* (Västerås, 1983), 98; the main purposes for the cartel are summarized in Jan Glete, *Storföretag i starkström* (Västeras, 1984), 98; Schröter, *Außenpolitik*, 331.

50. Voivienti-osuusliike Valio r.l. Halsinki, a central dairy cooperative. Sitzung des Kaufmännischen Ausschusses der IG Farben, 6 Sept. 1932, BWA 13/9; AIV were the initials of the inventor of the process, Professor A. I. Virtanen of Helsinki University.

51. BWA Verträge 19, Grünfutterkonservierung 1.

52. Sitzung des Kaufmännischen Ausschusses der IG Farben, 6 Sept. 1932, BWA 13/9.

53. Exactly a 3.6 percent share of IG Basle, a subsidiary of IG Farben in Switzerland, set up for the handling of its financial strategies on an international scale; see BWA 91/2, "VoWi-Bericht" Nr. 2815, 30 May 1938.

54. In a private and confidential letter of the British Legation in Oslo to the chancery of the British Foreign Office, dated 24 May 1939, this point was stressed: "The French Legation in Oslo at any rate are very uncomfortable on the subject [Norsk Hydro-H.G.S.] and declare that, notwithstanding the French holding of shares in the company, they have no say in the management." Public Record Office, London [hereafter, PRO]. FO 371/23675.

55. The French side was represented by ETS Kuhlmann dominating the Centrale des Matières Colorantes. See Verena Schröter, *Die deutsche Industrie auf dem Weltmarkt* (Frankfurt, 1984), 295–313.

56. Harm G. Schröter, *Das internationale Stickstoffkartell, 1929–1933: Privatwirtschaftliche Marktregulierung und staatliche Interessenpolitik* (forthcoming, 1989).

57. Schröter, *Außenpolitik*, 296.

58. For example, in the Chinese projects of nitrogen factories in 1935,

Stickstoffbesprechung der IG Farben, 23 Oct. 1935, Hoechst Archiv, Frankfurt, 85.

59. Norsk Hydro's subsidiary Norsk Tjaereprodukter started to manufacture dyes, which was one of IG Farben's special fields. When this turned out to be profitable, the Norwegian plant was forced to close down in 1936, and the German company paid a minor sum as compensation. Schröter, *Außenpolitik*, 290; Milward, *Fascist Economy in Norway*, 189.

60. It cannot be traced, but perhaps IG Farben's later policy of establishing a dominant role in certain markets—in southeast Europe, for example—already was employed as early as 1927 in this case of Norsk Hydro or in Scandinavia as a whole.

61. Hertner, "German Multinational Enterprise," 125–29.

62. Note of Dr. Meinen, 23 Dec. 1930, SAA 4/Lt 398, Bd. 3; F. Werner, Mein Werdegang, 84, unpub. MS at SAA.

63. LaCour in vain wanted to avoid a takeover by his sworn competitor, ASEA; see Glete, *ASEA*, 115.

64. Note of the meeting, 23 Dec. 1930, SAA 4/Lt 398, Bd. 3.

65. For the case of Czechoslovakia, see Alice Teichova, *An Economic Background to Munich: International Business and Czechoslovakia, 1918–1938* (New York, 1974).

66. Protokoll des Chemikalien-Ausschusses, 13 April 1927, BWA 134/11; the complicated network is outlined by Verena Schröter, "The IG Farbenindustrie AG in Central and Southeast Europe, 1926–38," in *International Business and Central Europe, 1918–1939*, ed. Alice Teichova and Phillip Cottrell (Leicester, England, 1983), 139–72; see Peter Hayes, *Industry and Ideology: I. G. Farben in the Nazi Era* (New York, 1987), appendix.

67. Seventh session of IG Farben's "Metall-Unterkommission," 31 Jan. 1935, Hoechst Werks-Archiv, No. 32.

68. Contracts at BWA, Nr. 19, Polyamide 1 + 2.

69. The minimum was to be 200,000 pounds annually; ibid.

70. In 1929 the Deutsche Linoleum Werke AG, Berlin, stood for a profit of 90 million Reichsmark (RM) out of a total of 125 million RM for the whole trust. A. Benni, et al., *Internationale Industrie-Kartelle* (Berlin, 1930), 88.

71. Note of the Statistisches Reichsamt, PA AA, Sonderreferat, Wirtschaft, Industrie 20, Bd. 1 Kartelle.

72. Stonehill, *Foreign Ownership in Norwegian Enterprises*, 166.

73. Among these were the following: Elektrokemiska AB, Bohus: Liljeholms Stearinfabrik, Stöms Bruk AB, Svenska Cellulosa AB; Hoechst Werks Arhiv, Hö R V A/F 256; BWA 19 Chlor 18.

74. Letter of MAN to Reusch, GHH, GHH-Werksarchiv 4001012026/31; see also Glete, *ASEA*, 99.

75. For examples see V. Schröter, *Weltmarkt*, 442.

76. Exchange of letters between IG Farben and Arilinkompani between May and November, 1937, Hoechst Werks Archiv, R V A/F 256.

77. Internal statement of von Schnitzler, 18 Feb. 1937. Hoechst Werks-Archiv, Nr. 801.

78. For example, the development of the Finnish electrotechnical enterprise, F. Strömberg OY, which grew after the First World War. During 1919–25, together with AEG and Siemens, ASEA tried to hamper this development—even before the three firms agreed to their cartel.

79. See BWA Nr. 19 Chlor 6; note of the commercial secretary of the British legation in Helsinki to the Foreign Office and the Department of Overseas Trade, 1 Aug. 1936, PRO FO 371/20329.

80. "The policy of ICI has been directed towards preserving this trade as far as

possible, and in the pursuit of such aims they have endeavoured to negotiate longterm contracts with the Finnish mills.... Meanwhile the Chemical Department of the Ministry of Defence has been assiduous in its efforts to persuade ICI to manufacture chlorine locally instead of importing it from the UK and the company, though reluctant to do so, has finally yielded to persuasion in the fear that if they continued to resist it would only be a matter of time before they lose the Finnish market altogether." Note of the Foreign Office to the Department of Overseas Trade, PRO FO 371/20329.

81. ICI, Solvay, and IG Farben had a share of one-third each; BWA, Nr. 19 Chlor 17.

82. Dated from 28 Nov. 1938, valid from 1 Jan. 1939–31 Dec. 1951; BWA, Nr. 19 Chlor 19.

83. The core of this cartel, called the CIA (Convention de l'Industrie de l'Azote) was the DEN-Group (Deutsch-Englisch-Norwegische Gruppe); see Schröter, *Stickstoffkartell.*

84. Minutes of IG Farben's Stickstoffbesprechungen, 17 Dec. 1936, 22 Feb. 1937; 25 Feb. 1938, Hoescht Werks-Archiv, Nr. 86.

85. Ibid., 18 June 1935.

86. Ibid., 25 March 1938.

87. Ibid.

88. Ibid.

89. Ibid., 22 Dec. 1937.

90. BWA, Nr. 19 Stickstoff 4.

91. Because the first fair in 1930 was not very successful, the second one was very well prepared and conducted (24 Sept. 1932–9 Oct. 1932). Combined with the visit of the Prince of Wales, it left a deep impression, a considerable amount of goodwill, and a growing readiness to buy British products. Report of the British Legation in Copenhagen to the Foreign Office/Board of Trade, PRO, BT 60/30/2.

92. The Federation of German Industry (RDI) noticed in October 1932: "For much too long a period we looked upon the Northern states as our own backyard [*Domäne*] and neglected them in propaganda." RDI Wochenbericht 22/32. 31 Oct. 1932, Krupp, Historisches Archiv, FAH IV E 181.

93. Minute of the meeting, 23 June 1933, SAA 49/Ls 68; for further details, see Schröter, *Außenpolitik*, 82–84.

94. In the 1920s only Germany had the technical installations to consume great amounts of the highly phosphorous Swedish ore.

95. This attitude is notably different from that of American firms, as shown by Mira Wilkins in her major books, *The Emergence of Multinational Enterprise* (Cambridge, Mass., 1970), 77, and *The Maturing of Multinational Enterprise* (Cambridge, Mass., 1974), 51, 69.

96. Teichova, *Economic Background to Munich*, 61.

# PART THREE: Impact and Responses

The articles in this part look at the impact of TNCs and their complex interaction with host economies. The overall thrust of that research has been to suggest that TNC activity has a broadly favourable impact on host economies. Given the paucity of research in that area, however, it is too soon to say whether that is a valid generalization or a reflection of the case studies chosen up to date, or even the conservative inclinations of many business historians.

C. Harvey and P. Taylor (1987) examined foreign investment in Spanish mining before 1914, using a sample of 174 mining companies registered in the United Kingdom and a carefully crafted methodology. They found little evidence of imperialist exploitation, and generally pointed to the long-term advantages of that inward investment, and to the fact that the profits earned by foreign firms were much less than appeared at first sight. They also showed the importance of the indigenous response to TNCs. Foreign direct investment can particularly stimulate development, they argued, if there was a large enough indigenous business elite. M. Mason (1987) was also positive about the impact of TNCs on development in Japan before 1931. Most accounts of the economic success of Japan minimized the role played by foreigners, and indeed tended to emphasize the hostility to foreign business displayed by successive governments of Japan. Mason argued that although the amount of foreign direct investment in Japan was small, it had a great impact, by providing knowledge about Western technology and management practice, boosting employment and raising the level of exports. The United Kingdom TNC, Dunlop Rubber, for example, established the rubber tire industry in Japan in the early 1900s. G. Jones (1988) examined the impact of TNCs on the United Kingdom before 1945, an economy which has always welcomed foreign direct investment. He established a data base of 125 inward investments in manufacturing and utilities. Like Mason, he argued that although their overall size was not great, they had a considerable impact in the fastest growing/high technology industries of the period. TNCs introduced new technologies and products into the United Kingdom, and sometimes stimulated an entrepreneurial response, but contemporaries sometimes overestimated the superiority of the foreign companies in areas such as management.

Assessing the impact of TNCs on host economies is a complicated matter. In his case study, G. Taylor (1981) showed that the impact depended in part, at least, on the managerial autonomy of TNC sub-sidiaries. Canadian Industries Ltd. was a Canadian chemical company jointly owned by a United Kingdom and United States TNC. Despite the legal appearances, it exercised considerable autonomy and had a kind of bargaining relationship with its parents. Nationalistic fears about loss of sovereignty, Taylor concluded, need to be qualified by a more realistic view of the balance of power within companies. T. O'Brien (1989) suggested that economic theories of the TNC need to be supplemented by more serious consideration about business–government relationships. In Mexico and Chile, the Guggenheims and the host governments influenced and impacted on each other.

Finally, M. Wilkins (1974) considered technology transfer. While that subject has attracted enormous attention from economists, historical research has been minimal and Wilkins's pioneering piece was never followed up. Wilkins examined, using historical evidence, the various ways that a business can transfer technology across international borders. She also suggested that there was a difference between the transfer and absorption of technology within host countries, postulating the existence of an "absorption gap" consisting of the time between the introduction of a new technology and when that new technology is used by nationals of the country.

# 12

## The Role of Private Business in the International Diffusion of Technology*

Mira Wilkins[†]

*Source: *Journal of Economic History*, 34 (1974), pp. 166–188.

Clearly, private business is but one agent for the diffusion of technology. Yet it is an important one. In the normal pursuit of business, technological knowledge and skills pass over political boundaries and private enterprise takes part in the international diffusion of technology. In this paper I want to try to delineate the means by which private companies have shared in the international diffusion of technology in the nineteenth and twentieth centuries. I will note briefly the "imitation lag" and then what I want to call the "absorption gap." From generalizations, I will turn to some explicit examples and analyses. Finally, in conclusion, I want to return to my concept of the absorption gap and the role of private enterprise in bridging that gap.[1]

## I

In theory at least there appear to be eight distinct ways by which a private company can act to transfer technology across political borders. The eight methods are broad and each contains sub-categories. First, a private concern can export for sale or for exhibition a new or improved product. If the exports are capital goods, they transfer technology directly when used in modernizing production processes. But any export, whether of a producer or a consumer good, may be imitated in foreign lands and by this means move technology from one country to another. Thus, the first manner by which a company transfers technology involves simply the *export of products.* Second, a private enterprise can take out patents in a foreign country, patents that may be worked in that nation. In registering a patent, there is disclosure. There are opportunities for its sale or licensing, or for designing similar but not covered products. Thus, the second approach involves the *export of patents.* Third, a firm can make a range of different types of technical assistance agreements or provide technical aid to foreign companies or governments. Here there is the *export of technical knowledge and services.* And, fourth, a company can undertake direct foreign investments, that is, act as a multinational enterprise and transfer its technology abroad with its investment. This fourth approach involves an *export of, or rather an extension of, the firm itself abroad.* All these methods are those of enterprises that possess technology to transmit.[2] Note that a single company can participate in all four forms of transfer. The distinctions between these methods of transfer may be real or simply theoretical, depending on the particular circumstances.

The second four manners by which a company transfers technology are counterparts of the first group. These four are associated with the receipt of technology: One, a firm can *import* machines used in production processes new to its nation; an importer can sell or present any new product, which is then imitated within the recipient nation. Two, a company can commercialize the *patents* of a foreign enterprise in its domestic market. Three, it can make *technical assistance arrangements* from which it will benefit. Four, it can acquire technology from a *direct foreign investor.* All these last four approaches involve the utilization of foreign technology. Perhaps these four manners of receiving technology may be as much or more responsible for international technological diffusion as the four manners used by the holders of the technology.

Still, the second group of businessmen is often, although not always, reliant on the first group, since it is impossible to import if something is not exported; a patent must exist before any one can work or modify that particular patent; someone must have the technology before a technical assistance agreement can be made; for there to be technology derived from a direct foreign investor, there must be that investor. Note, however, that the holder of the technology—the exporter, the owner of the patent, the provider of technological assistance, or even the direct foreign investor—need not be a private company. In short, there need not be symmetry in the relationship between our two groups of private companies.[3] Note, too, the second group of businessmen may in certain instances be one and the same as the first group; exporter and importer may be part of one company; holder of the patent and exploiter of it abroad may be identical; and so forth.[4] Once again, the distinctions may be real or simply theoretical.

There are additional ways by which a technologically-advanced company participates in a passive manner in the transfer of technology.[5] The eight modes described above seem to be the *active* ways by which private companies take part in technological transfers.

## II

Before I elaborate on these eight modes of transfer, it is worth considering the difference between mere transfer and the absorption of technology within the host country. A company can export capital goods. In one country the machines installed might be allowed to break down and eventually fall into disrepair; in another country, the same machines might be used efficiently in modern industry, copied, adapted, and produced locally. A company can export consumer goods to two countries. In one the product might continue as an import; while in the second, host-nation businesses might manufacture the product. A company may register patents in countries abroad. In one nation the patents may not be worked, or be worked by foreigners; in a second, the patents may be commercialized by nationals of that land. A firm may transfer its technology through a technical assistance arrangement and in one country no one may be able or willing to utilize the advanced methods, whereas by contrast the technical assistance in another country might effectively train nationals of the host country. Similarly, a direct foreign investment carries with it technology but the technologies transmitted may be confined to the foreign corporation, or alternatively, may be absorbed by enterprises within the host nation. In each of these paired cases there is a transfer of technology, but only in the second situation in the pair does absorption or true international diffusion occur.

These comments distinguishing transfer and absorption are obviously too black and white, since they do not take into account time lags.[6] The poles are lack of absorption and rapid absorption; between the poles, absorption may take years or even decades. There seems to be not only an "imitation lag," but an "absorption gap." The literature on technological transfers says a great deal about the international imitation lag, defined by others as the lapsed time between when a product is first produced in the innovator country and in each subsequent nation.[7] The imitation lag is relatively uncomplicated to determine, yet it seems to me inadequate, because it says nothing about absorption (or true international diffusion). It does not differentiate whether the product was produced by nationals of the "imitating" country on their own, or by such nationals with extensive foreign assistance or by subsidiaries of multinational enterprises.[8] It would seem that only when nationals on their own (or virtually on their own) are able to produce the product does true diffusion—in contrast with mere geographical transfer—of the technology occur. Tentatively, I will define the absorption gap as the lapsed time between the introduction of a new technology, process or product, into a nation and the point when that technology is used in processes of comparable or near comparable efficiency and the manufacture of products of comparable or near comparable quality under ownership and control (defined here as technological ability) of nationals of that country. "Near comparable" is probably a better formulation than "comparable," for with effective absorption there will be modification when appropriate and also improvement to fit national requirements. Note that I am referring here to the initial—original— absorption of the new technology within a recipient nation. In going beyond international diffusion and dealing with economic development, obviously one must consider two absorption gaps, one defined, as above, to indicate simple *international* diffusion of the new technology, and the second defined to indicate infusion (or successful *national* diffusion), that is when the new technology is not only adopted and adapted by nationals but also becomes the dominant technology of the host nation industry.[9] In this paper, I am considering only the first absorption gap involving diffusion over international boundaries. In short, the international imitation lag (as defined by others) covers the transfer of technology to a foreign nation and does not take into account the nationality of the producer in the host country. The absorption gap stresses the absorption of the new technology by nationals of the recipient country. As I have defined these terms, international transfers are a necessary but not a sufficient condition for absorption or true international diffusion.[10]

With the concept of the absorption gap we are brought squarely to the need to analyze the conditions under which the international technology is received—that is, the institutional structure prepared to accept the technology, and for purposes of this paper, specifically private companies within the host country that can digest the technology. Our second group of four modes by which technology is transferred deals with this matter. Only if the companies in the second group (the receivers of technology) are nationals of the host country, I suggest, does effective international diffusion take place.

Since I am arguing that transfer does not necessarily mean diffusion, this brings me to the point that there are barriers to effective diffusion of new technology that directly relate to the receivers of technology. These often co-existent and sometimes overlapping barriers include: (1) demand barriers (there may not be sufficient demand to warrant national production); (2) capital barriers (local producers may not have or be able to obtain the capital to utilize the technology)[11]; (3) national resource barriers (a nation's commercially-developed natural resources may be inappropriate for the effective utilization of the technology)[12]; (4) labor-cost barriers (low labor costs relative to other costs may discourage the application of a particular technology); (5) technological barriers (local producers may not have the skills or education to absorb the incremental technological knowhow)[13]; (6) scale barriers (foreign producers may have economies of scale that cheapen costs vis-à-vis host nation producers; without government protection, national producers may have no possibility of meeting foreign competition); (7) infrastructure barriers (there may not be sufficient supporting services or complementary techniques to warrant diffusion); (8) cultural barriers (there must be values and norms of behaviour conducive to the absorption of technology); and (9) most easily overcome, language barriers, which may slow absorption. There may also be "priority barriers" within a particular economy.[14] Herein, I do not intend to elaborate on these barriers, which are obviously of vast importance. The barrier, however, that directly concerns me is one that should be (but is often not) included on the above list—that of "business organization." There must be effective business organization (private or governmental) to absorb the technology.[15]

## III

With these general comments, I am now ready to examine the actual process of technological transfer by private companies. Regrettably, my examples are unsystematic. The difficulty lies in the shortness of the paper. The examples should, however, demonstrate forms of transfer and their relation to diffusion, as well as provoke thought about methodology in dealing with international technological diffusion by private business. Whether the classification scheme proves useful in studying the success of the particular type of international diffusion has to be tested in subsequent research.

All the eight modes of transfer that I have outlined in the early part of this paper have existed in the nineteenth and twentieth centuries. First, exports: The British, fearing the diffusion of technology in the early nineteenth century, barred the sale abroad of certain textile machinery.[16] Britishers bypassed the law and established manufacturing enterprises on the continent and *exported* from there, directly transferring and diffusing British manufacturing methods.[17] In the late 1820's and 1830's, English builders sold their locomotives in the United States; these were copied and improved upon and "a locomotive-building industry sprang up in the United States almost at once."[18] In the 1840's, Stephen Moulton carried to (exported to) England samples of Charles Goodyear's vulcanized rubber, exhibiting the product to prospective manufacturers; these samples were seen by Englishman Thomas Hancock, who had worked on rubber manufacture for many years; not long after, Hancock took out his own patents that virtually duplicated Goodyear's process. He then proceeded to manufacture rubber goods.[19] The Singer records are full of data expressing concern about the imitation of Singer sewing machines in western Europe.[20] In the twentieth century, capital equipment exports were often a means of transferring technology abroad. Likewise, exported products of all sorts were imitated.

Second, registering of patents abroad served to transfer technology. In the nineteenth and twentieth centuries U.S. companies in Europe and European enterprises in the United States obtained patents. The patents were worked in the foreign country. Examples include manufacture of revolvers, aluminum, electrical equipment, and chemicals.[21]

Third, a range of technical assistance arrangements have been made by private firms to communicate technology. Often capital equipment exports were accompanied by a single mechanic or a group of technicians that installed the equipment and instructed the customer in its operation and maintenance.[22] When, for example, American elevators and electrical equipment were marketed abroad in the late nineteenth century, technicians frequently accompanied the export.[23] The German Von Kohorn Company sold machinery and technical aid for the establishment of the viscose rayon industry in Czechoslovakia (1919), Greece (1923), Turkey (1935), Rumania (1937) and then farther afield in Peru (1946) and Egypt (1948).[24] In more recent times, as well, this phenomenon of exporters sending technical knowhow with their exports has persisted.[25] Likewise, when patents were worked abroad, often the innovating firm would transfer technological information beyond what was in the patent registration. Thus, for instance, when in the 1850's, the Singer Company sold its French patent, it agreed to send to the purchaser an aide for his manufacturing department so that merchant could make "perfect machines."[26] Frequently, in the twentieth century, the licensing of patents and technical assistance accords went together.[27]

While associated with exports and patents, technical assistance arrangements may go far beyond the other two modes of transfer. There were patents included in the interchange of information between Standard Oil (N.J.) and I. G. Farben and between du Pont and the large European chemical companies before World War II, but the technological assistance transcended the mere licensing of patents.[28] In recent years, the many agreements between U.S. and Japanese enterprises for technological exchanges sometimes include patent exchanges yet they comprise far more than the licensing of such patents.[29] Some technical assistance accords may be entirely independent of patents. In 1908, Herbert Hoover organized an international mining consulting firm to sell U.S. technological services.[30] British Managing Agents in India transferred technological knowhow.[31] When management contracts are made between western companies and firms or governments in less developed countries there is a sale of organizational and technological skills.[32]

Private business enterprise has had experience with a particular technology that it has developed or used. It has trained individuals to work with the technology. It has knowledge of the problems and difficulties in commercializing the particular technology. It has organizational knowledge. It is in short in a unique position in the transfer of the specific technology. It seems clear that often the product, or the description in the patent, or mere drawings and instructions, are inadequate for transfers of technology; men are needed to carry, explain, and facilitate the introduction of the new processes or products. The private firm can provide the institutional framework whereby these men can transfer the technology.[33]

Four, technology also crosses boundaries through direct foreign investment. Closely associated with exporting, registering patents abroad, and technical assistance is direct foreign investment. Generally, the international business carries on all these functions and has done so since the nineteenth century, if not before.[34] As practically every writer on the subject has pointed out, direct investors communicate management, technology, and skills across national boundaries. Recent studies have indicated that the firm that invests abroad generally has an advantage, an advantage in technology, product design, marketing, or managerial expertise.[35] It has this advantage to communicate. Corporations that own foreign factories, mines, oil properties, and plantations transmit technology in various ways: (1) There is clearly a physical (geographical) transfer. Beyond that, the products made and the processes used abroad are there to be imitated within the host nation.[36] Also, there can be a shift of the technology of the direct investor to host country nationals should expropriation occur or should a national firm purchase the properties of the direct investor.[37] (2) Host nation workers and managers gain knowledge of products and processes. The training may be on the job, in the corporation's home operations, at local educational institutions supported by the company, or at foreign universities (subsidized by scholarships granted by the multinational business).[38] The training can range from that in simple skills to that in highly-sophisticated modern technology and business administration. (3) If the activity of the international enterprise is a joint-venture, foreign technology is brought under partial host nation ownership.[39] (4) Suppliers of the direct foreign investor frequently obtain significant technological assistance.[40] (5) If technology is broadly defined to encompass marketing experience (including the servicing of complex products), technology is often transferred to dealers and distributors. (6) In addition, indirectly, but of great significance, the multinational corporation acts to transfer technology by paying taxes and offering employment in the host nation, which actions create capital resources and demands there. The resources and demands often in turn become magnets that will result in the emergence of agencies for the subsequent transfer of technology not specifically required by the multinational corporation.[41] Examples of all these types of transfers of technology abound.[42]

The fact of transfer by export, by patent, by technical assistance, or by direct investment says nothing about the appropriateness of the technology transferred for the host country. Some argue that technology suitable in one country may be less suitable in a second nation that has different relative costs of factors of production and a different demand structure.

Indeed, in the main (although far from always) when a firm transfers technology, it does little to modify manufacturing methods; it transmits what it has developed at home. In many industries, the high engineering costs of designing plants "strongly militate against redesigning [them] to employ more labour and less capital" or to take advantage in other ways of different resource availability in the recipient nation.[43] Brazilian economist Celso Furtado insists that the introduction of new technology in manufacturing in less developed countries by giant technologically-advanced international business creates "structural imbalances."[44] On the other hand, many feel that not only in industrial nations, where there is more comparability in factor costs, but also in less developed countries, the advanced technology is appropriate.[45] More research needs to be done and better tests of appropriateness developed. Yet I would suggest—as I have earlier— that it is more the receiver than the communicator of the technology that is responsible for diffusion and the most stringent tests lie in that arena.

This brings me to the second group of transmitters of technology. First, the importer: Within the host country, private companies (the importer or other firms) may undertake to manufacture an import locally. Such import substitution is far from automatic. There must be a demand for the new product or processes and also an institutional structure to undertake the import substitution. While a great deal has been written about import substitution by less developed countries in recent times, there appears to be a paucity of analysis on the pace and character of import substitution in the nineteenth and early twentieth centuries and the extent to which import substitution has involved "mere transfer" or full absorption. For example, there are figures available on the number of power looms in France and Germany in the 1860's and 1870's,[46] but not the number actually manufactured within those countries; we have figures on the capacity of steam engines worldwide in the late nineteenth century,[47] but not the breakdown on the steam engines from abroad and those produced within a host nation. We have inadequate data on the extent to which power looms or steam engines that were made within a particular country were manufactured by nationals of that country and the extent to which they were produced by foreign companies operating within that country.

From available information, it is clear that one aspect of technological diffusion in the nineteenth century lay in the significant import substitution in the United States and western Europe. There is substantial evidence that in certain products, American firms, for example, rapidly substituted locally-produced goods for imports. Likewise, in the late nineteenth century, when British shoe manufacturers met American competition, *they* replicated U.S. methods to meet competition.[48] On the other hand, comparable import substitution did not occur when U.S. shoe manufacturers, for instance, sold in Latin America—at least in the nineteenth century. Americans and Britishers had companies capable of—and determined to—copy and adapt the methods of foreigners. In the twentieth century numerous cases exist of limitation of imports, resulting in the diffusion of technology.[49] On the other hand, not every nation has companies able or ready to imitate or adapt the technology. It may be foreign and not national business that provides for the import substitution, closing the imitation lag but not the absorption gap.[50]

Two: Firms operating on the basis of foreign patents sometimes merely transfer as distinct from diffuse technology. This may be the case when the manufacturer abroad is part of a multinational enterprise. It was the case when the revolvers produced by Europeans under Colt license never reached the high standards of the American product.[51] By contrast, often, the exchange of patents between private firms has proved highly effective in the diffusion of technology. Data available to business historians reveal substantial evidence of domestic-incorporated companies that have obtained licenses to work foreign patents at home.[52] The German General Electric Company (Allgemeine Elektrizitäts Gesellschaft) started its business on the basis of American patents and a minimum of technical aid. The assimilation of technology was highly successful, and A.E.G. was soon innovating.[53] Diffusion was not always so rapid; German chemical patents were registered in the United States in the nineteenth and early twentieth centuries. Some of these patents were worked by German subsidiaries in the United States. There was a transfer of the technology to this side of the Atlantic. Then, with World War I, these patents were confiscated and made available to American companies; only at this time was there absorption of the technology. In 1917–1918 there existed in the United States companies capable of working these patents and a domestic demand for the output under them.[54]

We turn next to item three in this group: the receivers of technical assistance. Technical assistance may be communicated to firms incapable of absorbing this aid. It may be communicated to foreign subsidiaries of the holder of the technology and thus kept within the holders' own family group—a geographical transfer. On the other hand, technical assistance from abroad may be *requested* by—sought out by—host nation companies, be effectively utilized, and serve as a highly viable means of both technological transfer and diffusion. Technical assistance obtained from abroad may be particular or general, informal or formal, short-term or long-term. A few examples will suffice. In the late 1860's or early 1870's, Henry Phipps, financial director of Union Iron Mills Company (one of the firms that would become part of Carnegie Steel Company) visited a mill in Germany and noticed that the piles made ready for the heating furnace, to be used for rolling "I" beams, contained more than double the amount of scrap iron rails employed in Pittsburgh. He sketched the pile and once home ordered a change in Union Mills' practice. We are told that "the cost of this trip to Europe was saved almost daily thereafter to his firm."[55] Here was a case of specific technological assistance, informally obtained, on the basis of one journey. Similarly, on a European trip in 1872, Andrew Carnegie studied Bessemer steel works, recognized the significance of the new technology, and on his return made plans based on what he saw in England.[56] Here, too, we have technical information, information obtained, on a single trip, but in this case general technological know-how transmitted by the chief executive of the recipient firm. Earlier in American history, when in 1801–1802, Irénée du Pont planned a powder mill in the United States, he drew on French technical aid. He sought out and arranged that French government draftsmen would draw the plans for his company's machinery, that the machines would be constructed in France, and that if needed, the French would send technical aid. Soon, however, Irénée du Pont's powder plant had absorbed the French technology and was on its own.[57] Here we have general technical assistance on a formal but short-term basis.

Sometimes technical assistance came from the men hired. Thus, British mining companies in South Africa sought out and employed American technicians.[56] When the Belgian firm SIDAC began producing cellophane in 1925, it did so with the aid of the chief engineer from La Cellophane (a French company that was the first producer of cellophane in 1917). The engineer brought to the Belgian company blueprints and complete data on the French firm's secret processes for cellophane manufacture.[59]

J. S. Fforde in his volume, *An International Trade in Managerial Skills*, tells of how Britishers "of the technical managerial type" went to the Indian sub-continent and Latin America for "career service" in one business and would be recruited by one enterprise after another (in jute manufacture, cotton spinning and weaving, paper manufacture, flour milling, and light engineering) as "a type of efficiency expert."[60] Unfortunately Fforde does not tell when this practice started; presumably it relates to the late nineteenth and early twentieth centuries. He also implies but does not state that these men were hired by local capitalists as well ad foreign enterprise. How effective this was in diffusion of technology still needs closer study.

On a more formal basis we have the technological assistance arrangements that existed between Standard Oil of New Jersey and I. G. Farben and between du Pont and the major European chemical companies. In the chemical industry in the first part of the twentieth century, European, especially German, technology greatly impressed Americans. "I was plunged into a world of research and development on a gigantic scale such as I had never seen," wrote Frank A. Howard of Standard Oil Development Company (a subsidiary of Jersey Standard) after a tour of the Badische Anilin und Soda research laboratories at Ludwigshaften in early 1926. What Howard saw was a pilot plant for the hydrogenation of oil. Badische was then being merged into the newly-formed I. G. Farben and Jersey Standard entered into arrangements with the giant German firm to obtain technological knowledge. Jersey Standard's historians have recorded that "with the help of I. G. Farben 'know-how'" engineers of Jersey Standard's affiliates "mastered a new, difficult, and promising process." The company's historians conclude that from I. G. Farben, Jersey Standard gained "research concepts and techniques" as well as "the stimulus that [in time] contributed to the building up of a large research staff soundly trained in chemistry and chemical engineering."[61] In a similar vein, an internal memo from du Pont's files, dated December 9, 1936, shows the impact of the international exchange of technical aid on that receiving company. "It should be borne in mind that a number of the du Pont Company's most important activities have originated from technical information derived from European sources, examples being rayon, 'Cellophane,' ammonia, hydrogen peroxide, titanium dioxide, to mention only a few." The memo noted that as a result of its technical agreements with European groups "the du Pont Company has been able to offer numerous products developed in Europe in the American market."[62]

Perhaps the most impressive (and successful) technical assistance accords have been between Japanese and Western firms in the post-World War II years. Here, too, in the main, Japanese companies seem to have taken the initiative in seeking out the technology. Over the years 1950 to 1970, the Japanese government approved 8,324 contracts made by Japanese concerns involving the purchase of technology from western enterprises.[63]

These are only a scattering of technical assistance arrangements prompted by actions (desires) of *recipient* private enterprises. Clearly, one needs more than assorted instances and a systematic treatment by industry, as well as by country and region, of the effectiveness of the various types of technical assistance in technological diffusion. My point here is simply that often domestic—receiving—firms took the initiative in obtaining technological assistance from abroad and that this type of initiative should be tested as possibly one of the most effective forms of international technological diffusion. I might suggest that the reason for its effectiveness was that when this occurred there was an existing private business structure, an agency, that could absorb the technology. The defined demand was determined by the recipient rather than by the donor. The selection of the technology to be received was by the recipient, who hoped to profit from its receipt.

The last of our four modes by which private companies obtain technology involves the receipt by companies of technology from direct foreign investors. As we have earlier noted, when a company invests abroad, in a geographical sense it transfers technology; yet, as we have also noted, it may not diffuse technology for the latter may be contained within the corporation. Yet there do exist imitators (absorbers) of the processes and products introduced by multinational corporations. In developed countries, it is commonplace that when a direct foreign investor undertakes operations, competitors using similar processes and making similar products emerge. (Sometimes the direct investment is made because the imitation of the export has taken place and the holder of the technology can not maintain its market unless it manufactures nearby; often imitation seems likely and occurs *after* the direct investment has been made.)[64] This type of absorption by private companies in the host country is, however, more difficult in less developed countries, where private companies have neither the organization nor the capital to replicate the methods of the foreign investor.[65] Sometimes technology is diffused when a direct investor sells out to a private domestic firm. In England, for example, before World War I Westinghouse set up a foreign manufacturing subsidiary; this subsidiary was sold to the British, Metropolitan-Vickers, which obtained Westinghouse's technology in the transaction.[66] U.S. direct investors dominated the Cuban sugar industry in the 1920's, introducing new technology; gradually, over time, a number of the properties were transferred to Cuban capital, and Cuban businessmen took the place of Americans.[67]

Employees and managers of foreign subsidiaries often have been hired by host nation enterprises and serve to transfer technology. In recent years, European companies have eagerly sought personnel who have worked for foreign subsidiaries of American firms.[68]

When the direct investor participates in a joint-venture with a host nation firm, that company obtains valuable technology. This has been the motive of a number of host-nation companies that have approached foreign firms, suggesting joint-venture relationships.[69]

Because a direct investor in a foreign country creates certain demands, there are linkage effects resulting from the direct investor's activities. Private companies in the host country often seek to fill the demands. Here the technological diffusion often will be *associative* rather than direct. For example, when a foreign company invests in an extractive industry in a less developed country, its employees probably need housing; local private companies often learned from the foreign company not the basic technology of the latter's industry but rather a new technology of home building.[70] So, too, when Sears, Roebuck opened a department store in Peru in 1955, it did not create other mass marketers in Peru. Rather, its technological diffusion was associative. Soon it was seeking local suppliers, and local suppliers started to seek out Sears. In 1959, the president of the Lima firm of Industrias Reunidas, S. A. asked Sears whether it would be interested in marketing a nationally-made refrigerator. Sears was interested; the Peruvian firm obtained with Sears' help a license from an American manufacturer. Two years later, using American technology, the first refrigerator was made in Peru. The demand created by the direct investor had been the stimulant for such production; Sears had been the catalyst for the transfer and diffusion of technology; the Peruvian firm, however, had initiated the suggestion.[71]

Sometimes the linkage effects are more general; thus, in Canada, employment offered by multinational corporations has contributed to a higher standard of living and the raising of the level of demand. Canadian firms have sought to attract new technology to meet the demands.[72]

These are but a few of the many instances wherein private companies in receiving countries have tried to obtain technology and have been successful in obtaining that technology from, through, or based on the presence of the direct foreign investor.

# IV

In conclusion, then, this paper has been a modest attempt to define various aspects of the role of private business as a vehicle for the diffusion of technology. It has been difficult to write because there are so many facets of this fascinating subject that seem to cry out for exploration. Because of space limitations, I have had to be highly selective. Among the numerous relevant topics not discussed or barely considered are: (1) the relations between the *motive* behind technological diffusion by private enterprise and the effectiveness of that diffusion; (2) the process whereby private enterprise changes its strategies through time and takes on over the years an altered role in the diffusion of technology; (3) the attributes of successful diffusers of technology (do such attributes exist in the abstract?); (4) the variation between and among industries and technologies in technological diffusion by private firms (are certain industries and technologies more amenable to technological transfers by private enterprise than others?); (5) the success of technological diffusion by private firms as compared with other agencies for diffusion (has this varied through time?); (6) a systematic look at differences in receptivity to international diffusion of technology by various nations; (7) a comparison of the demand structure and factor proportions within both the donor and recipient nations and the effects on international diffusion by private firms; (8), which is associated with point (7), the appropriateness of technology developed by private firms for international diffusion; (9) the distinctions between what is economically sound for the private enterprise and for the nations receiving the technology; and (10) an exploration of the types of measures that might be employed as indices of the effectiveness of private enterprise in technological diffusion (how much, for example, can productivity data be used as a measure of technological diffusion?). On each of these topics, and many others as well, there is a vast amount to be learned. Because of space constraints, I have, however, limited my content.

I have herein presented eight ways by which private enterprise in technologically advanced and in receiving countries acts to transfer technology. Clearly, private enterprise transfers technology in a variety of manners within these eight categories. I have tried to emphasize that for true international diffusion there must be more than simple geographical transfer of technology; there must be absorption of technology by national enterprises within the host country. While there are a number of factors affecting absorption by the host nation, ranking high among them is the existence or non-existence of agencies to receive the technology. One of the most significant of such agencies has, in the past, been private business. Thus, I have argued in this paper that one must not only study the holders of technology as vehicles of diffusion but also the receivers of technology. I have suggested that with the existence of international business, the concept of the "imitation lag" may cover more transfers and not diffusion per se. A more fruitful concept might be that of an "absorption gap," a notion that considers the time that true international diffusion takes, the time between the introduction of a new technology into a nation and that point when the innovation is utilized in processes of near comparable efficiency and in the production of products of near comparable quality under the ownership and control of nationals of that land. Using such a concept may offer a more meaningful guide to questions of international diffusion. I hope the distinctions made in this paper will provoke further research on the agencies for technological diffusion, particularly the role of private business.

## Notes

† This paper has been revised since its delivery on September 14, 1973, in light of comments made at the Economic History Association meeting by Professors Kozo Yamamura, Ralph Hidy, Stuart Bruchey, David Felix, and others.

1. Technology has been defined in narrow terms to comprise simply tools and machines. I prefer a more comprehensive definition, including in addition to tools and machines, product design, knowhow, and organizational ability, that is, concept along with technique. I am well aware that technological diffusion often takes place in "bits and pieces." Indeed, technology itself evolves in a complex fashion. While these points are not elaborated on herein, there is nothing in my paper to imply otherwise.

2. If the exporter of the product is independent of the producer of the product, it can be argued that the export firm does not have the technology of production; yet it is still the holder of (owner of or agent for) the product that contains within it the technology.

3. The holder of the technology may be, for example, a national or international public agency, or an individual or individuals, a periodical, or a scholarly text. Technology obviously does not have to be received by private companies from other private companies, or alternatively, transmitted by private companies to other private companies.

4. By identical I mean within the same corporate group—company and branch

or foreign subsidiary of that company. I am in this case piercing the corporate arrangements to determine the actuality.

5. An employee of the technologically-advanced firm may leave it and travel abroad, taking with him technological information or proficiency. Nathan Rosenberg, "Economic Development and the Transfer of Technology: Some Historical Perspectives," *Technology and Culture*, XI (July 1970), 553ff., points out that in the nineteenth century it was common for technological transfers to be made by the migration of trained personnel. See also William Woodruff, *The Impact of Western Man* (New York: St. Martin's Press, 1967), Chap. 5. A technologically-advanced company may open its plants to visiting foreign technicians, who see processes they can imitate in their homelands. A firm may sell or exhibit its products domestically, which products may be seen by foreigners who may reproduce the innovations in their own countries. A man may conduct industrial espionage in a plant of a technologically-advanced company and then transmit the secrets across the border. In each of these cases, technological transfer occurs, but the technologically-advanced private firm is essentially passive. It does not send goods, patents, technology, capital, or men across borders; instead, the agency for the transfer is an individual, an ex-employee, or a visitor who may or may not be associated with a private business *abroad.*

6. Everett Rogers, *Diffusion of Innovations* (New York: The Free Press, 1962), pp. 18–19, 79–120, and his second edition of the same book, *Communication of Innovations* (New York: The Free Press, 1971), pp. 128–132, are excellent on time lags between awareness of the innovation and adoption.

7. To my knowledge, the term "international imitation lag" was first used by Michael Posner, "International Trade and Technical Change," *Oxford Economic Papers*, XIII (October 1961), 323–341. See also G. C. Hufbauer, *Synthetic Materials and the Theory of International Trade* (Cambridge, Mass.: Harvard University Press, 1966), chaps. 1 and 5, and Louis T. Wells, Jr., ed., *The Product Life Cycle and International Trade* (Boston, Mass.: Division of Research, Graduate School of Business Administration, Harvard University, 1972), pp. 23–25.

8. John R. Tilton, *International Diffusion of Technology: The Case of Semi-Conductors* (Washington, D.C.: Brookings Institution, 1971), p. 23, introduces four different "lags" (including the imitation lag) but none takes into account the question of national ownership and control, although Tilton's book has much of value to say on this matter.

9. Thus, for example, absorption gap (1) would indicate the lapsed time between the first introduction of British-made cotton textiles into India and the efficient production of such machine-made cotton textiles in a plant owned by Indian capital, run by Indian management, and operated in the main by Indian technicians. Absorption gap (2) might indicate the lapsed time between the first introduction of British machine-made cotton textiles into India and the time when say 50 percent of the output of the Indian cotton textiles came from the modern Indian cotton textile industry. I find myself very much in agreement with Stuart Bruchey's statement that "it is not so much the first appearance of new techniques as their spread [within a nation] that matters in economic growth." *The Roots of American Economic Growth* (New York: Harper & Row, 1965), p. 139. Nonetheless, the entry of new techniques in a nation and their initial absorption are clearly a precondition for their spread. Professor Solomon Barkin of the Department of Economics at the University of Massachusetts, Amherst, has been helpful to me in stressing that in considering "absorption" of technological ability—as I have defined it—I should consider separately managerial and technical personnel. I find this idea both stimulating and troubling. For example, in the 1890's, the Royal

Dutch Company in the Dutch East Indies used American drillers in its crude oil producing operations. Royal Dutch had complete ownership and management control. Was the foreign technology absorbed? It seems to me that it was under Dutch corporate control, and one can legitimately refer to true technological diffusion as having taken place. Perhaps the test should be: If the business would fall or be seriously disrupted were foreign technicians removed, the control of technology cannot be said to be in national hands; if, by contrast, the business would remain viable and can find substitutes for the foreign technicians then it may be that despite the presence of foreign technicians in the operations, the technology has been effectively assimilated.

10. In the literature on international technological transfer and diffusion, definitions vary. Sometimes the idea of transfer, diffusion, and adoption are used interchangeably. (See for instance Tilton, *International Diffusion*, pp. 2, 163). Sometimes "transfer" refers to the crossing of borders and "diffusion" to the spread within the borders. See John Joseph Murray's article in Daniel L. Spencer and Alexander Woronick, eds., *The Transfer of Technology to Developing Countries* (New York: Praeger, 1967), p. 9. Rogers, *Diffusion of Innovation*, p. 76, differentiates diffusion from adoption in that diffusion for him involves the spread from source to user or adopter, while adoption is an "individual matter"—"the mental process through which an individual passed from first hearing about an innovation to final adoption." In *Communication of Innovations*, pp. 12, 26, 99ff., Rogers defines diffusion as a special type of communication—"the process by which innovations spread to the members of a social system" and changes his definition of adoption to a "decision to make full use of a new idea." For purposes of this paper, as my reader is now aware, I am distinguishing between mere international transfers and true international diffusion (that is absorption)—the first implying the physical, geographical transfer of an innovation (specifically new technology) over borders, and the second designating the spread of that new technology to nationals of the host country to the extent that they can and do utilize the new technology in production.

11. As Joseph Bower points out in *Managing The Resource Allocation Process* (Boston: Division of Research, Graduate School of Business Administration, Harvard University, 1970), p. 39, "Studies of the research and development process indicate that expenditures rise exponentially as a product moves from the basic and applied research steps to development and production. It is factories, tools, and dies, trained labor, reoriented channels of distribution and promotion which are the truly expensive part of innovation."

12. See Nathan Rosenberg, ed., *The Economics of Technological Change* (London: Penguin Books, 1971), pp. 210, 274–281.

13. Professor Rosenberg has put it, in describing the United States in the nineteenth century, "it required considerable technical expertise to borrow and exploit a foreign industrial technology," *Technology and American Economic Growth* (New York: Harper & Row, 1972), p. 82.

14. See note 54 below for an example of priority barriers. Priority barriers may be erected by governments as well as faced by private companies. Thus, the Soviet government may decide not to manufacture certain consumer goods, not because of demand, capital, natural resource, labor-cost, technological, scale, infrastructure cultural, or language barriers, or even business organization barriers, but because of priority barriers.

15. Effective business organization includes attitudes of management. G. F. Ray, "The Diffusion of New Technology—A Study of Ten Processes in Nine Industries," *National Institute Economic Review* (May 1969), 83, concludes that the attitude of

management has the "greatest impact on the application of new techniques." I am far from alone in talking about the absorptive capabilities of recipient firms. See Jack Baranson, "Technology Transfer Through the International Firm," *American Economic Review*, LX (May 1970), 435–436. Baranson in this article is concerned with factors affecting transfer logistics of the international firm; he barely touches on the problems of transfer as distinct from diffusion but he does recognize the importance of absorptive capabilities. In my general analysis in this paper, I find myself influenced by the body of work that deals specifically with transfers without diffusion, for example, the seminal article by Hans Singer, "Distribution of Gains between Investing and Borrowing Countries" (1950), reprinted in Hans Singer, *International Development* (New York: McGraw-Hill, 1964), pp. 161–172; the concept of "a dual economy" that now appears in most textbooks on less developed countries; and statements such as the one that appeared in a 1956 National Planning Association Study. After noting that U.S. firms had been transferring technology to Latin America for years, this study concluded, "Unfortunately, however, only a low proportion of the many small firms which are still using primitive practices throughout Latin America have as yet been reached by the methods and techniques which are being introduced by U.S. firms and their affiliates." National Planning Association Special Committee on Technical Cooperation, *Technical Cooperation in Latin America—Recommendations for the Future* (Washington, D.C.: National Planning Association, 1956), p. 77. This will henceforth be cited as NPA Technical Cooperation Study. I have a number of reservations about the legitimacy of such views, but find it essential to take their premises into account in a consideration of the history of the international diffusion of technology. These views touch on the basic question of the abilities of recipients of technology to absorb the technology.

16. Details on such British restraints appear in Great Britain, "First Report from Select Committee to Inquire into the Operation of the Existing Laws Affecting the Exportation of Machinery," *Parliamentary Papers*, Vol. 7 (1841).

17. For example the Cockerill firm, using British methods and manufacturing in Belgium and Germany, sold its machines as far east as Poland; new textile enterprises developed, incorporating the new technology. David S. Landes, *The Unbound Prometheus* (Cambridge, Eng.: Cambridge University Press, 1969), pp. 150, 148. Bruchey notes that despite the ban on British machinery exports, a substantial number of British machines reached the United States to be copied and, more important, modified to meet U.S. requirements. Bruchey, *Roots of American Economic Growth*, p. 167.

18. Eugene S. Ferguson, "The Steam Engine Before 1830," in *Technology in Western Civilization*, eds. Melvin Kranzberg and Carroll W. Pursell, Jr. (New York: Oxford University Press, 1967), I, p. 299.

19. Moulton was British, emigrated to the United States, and established his business there. He took the rubber samples to England, hoping to sell "the inventor's secret." William Woodruff, "Origins of An Early English Rubber Manufactory," *Bulletin of the Business Historical Society*, XXV (March 1951), pp. 32–36. Hancock's lawyers denied that the latter had gained technological information directly from Goodyear's samples. Woodruff suggests, "Perhaps his [Hancock's] genius lay in appreciating what Goodyear had done. . . . There can be no doubt that Goodyear's discovery stimulated the English inventory to still further effort."

30. Singer Manufacturing Co. records, State Historical Society of Wisconsin, Madison, Wisconsin.

31. Thus Colt licensed companies on the European continent to make revolvers

under Colt patents in the 1850's. See Mira Wilkins, *The Emergence of Multinational Enterprise: American Business Abroad from the Colonial Era to 1914* (Cambridge, Mass.: Harvard University Press, 1970), p. 30. The predecessor of Aluminum Company of America, The Pittsburgh Reduction Company, that acquired the Hall patents for making aluminum in 1888, granted in 1895 a license under these patents to a small French firm, rights that soon passed to d'Alais et Carmargues, later Cie, Pechiney. See George W. Stocking and Myron W. Watkins, *Cartels in Action* (New York: Twentieth Century Fund, 1946), pp. 220, 227. Annual reports and company prospectuses in the Scudder Collection, Columbia University Library, reveal numerous licensing relationships. Sometimes patents were taken out abroad under the names of individuals on behalf of a company, sometimes by the company itself. U.S. Bureau of Census, *Historical Statistics of the United States* (Washington, D.C.: G.P.O., 1960), pp. 607–608, gives data on the number of patents issued in the United States to residents of foreign countries and foreign corporations. I know of no one who has attempted to use these data in considering problems of international technological transfer.

22. See, for example, Landes, *Unbound Prometheus*, p. 150, on Cockerill exports.

23. Data from company records of exporters of these products.

24. Hufbauer, *Synthetic Materials*, p. 93.

25. All through the twentieth century, American firms have sent technicians to install machinery in plants in Latin America and over time have trained local employees to operate and maintain the machinery. NPA Technical Cooperation Study, pp. 76–77.

26. Wilkins, *Emergence of Multinational Enterprise*, p. 38.

27. See Mira Wilkins, *The Maturing of Multinational Enterprise: American Business Abroad from 1914 to 1970* (Studies in Business History, Cambridge, Mass.: Harvard University Press, forthcoming).

28. *Ibid.*

29. Data obtained in Japan from U.S. and Japanese companies and the Ministry of International Trade and Industry.

30. Herbert Hoover, *Memoirs* (New York: Macmillan, 1952), I, pp. 28ff.

31. P. S. Lokanathan, *Industrial Organization in India* (London: George Allen & Unwin, 1970), pp. 15–16.

32. See Peter Gabriel, *The International Transfer of Corporate Skills* (Boston: Division of Research, Graduate School of Business Administration, Harvard University, 1967).

33. These comments are especially true of the twentieth century as technology became more complex. But even in the nineteenth century, as others have noted, imitation of products and processes and development of patents often required foreign personnel familiar with the techniques. Such men in the nineteenth century were sometimes (and sometimes not) associated with private companies. In recent times, when a company has moved away from specific to "overall technology," it may fail completely. This was the case with Litton Industries' much discussed contract with Greece for the economic development of Crete and the Peloponnesus peninsula.

34. There are numerous instances in the nineteenth century wherein private companies carried technology over borders through direct investments. For the activities of American companies in this respect see Wilkins, *Emergence of Multinational Enterprise*. How many cases of technological transfer through direct investment one can find in the eighteenth century is unknown to the present author, but clearly European companies before 1800 through direct investment appear to

have played a role in technological transfer. Thus, in 1770, a French company operated a coal mine at Hagenbach in Baden and appears to have transferred the more advanced French methods to Germany. See Rondo E. Cameron, *France and the Economic Development of Europe 1800–1914* (Princeton, N.J.: Princeton University Press, 1961), p. 372. Alexander Gerschenkron, *Economic Backwardness in Historical Perspective* (New York: Praeger, 1965), pp. 38–39, suggests such activities by the Fuggers in the fifteenth and sixteenth centuries.

35. See for example Raymond Vernon, *Sovereignty at Bay* (New York: Basic Books, 1971); Wilkins, *Emergence of Multinational Enterprise*; and Wilkins, *Maturing of Multinational Enterprise.*

36. On imitation abroad see Robert B. Stobaugh, "The Product Life Cycle, U.S. Exports and International Investment," DBA dissertation, Graduate School of Business Administration, Harvard University, 1968, and Tilton, *International Diffusion*, p. 164.

37. These two types of diffusion are seldom discussed, yet they are of some significance.

38. Today multinational corporations boast of their contributions in this sphere. It wasn't always so: William Woodruff tells of how in the 1850's American investors in a rubber plant in Scotland imported skilled labor from the United States; part of the reason was the company's fear that skilled British rubber workers "might only stay long enough to make off with the firm's secrets." William Woodruff, "The American Origins of a Scottish Industry," *Scottish Journal of Political Economy*, II (February 1955), 28.

39. A number of governments in recent years have forced multinational enterprises to have local partners in part in order to diffuse technology.

40. There is marvelous, detailed material to illustrate this point that I have uncovered in the files of Ford-Werke, Cologne. When in the early 1930's, Ford began to manufacture in Germany, it needed local suppliers. It made arrangements for German suppliers to learn about U.S. technology so that its German subsidiary could buy quality German-made parts. See Frederick C. Young to E. C. Heine, Dec. 19, 1934; Frederick C. Young, "Report on Cologne," Dec. 22, 1934; and T. F. Gehle to A. M. Wibel, Jan. 31, 1935 and Mar. 14, 1935, Ford-Werke Archives, Cologne. Moving to a totally different area, multinational corporations that are buyers of rubber, cotton, and bananas have given technical assistance to small growers. See NPA Technical Cooperation Study, p. 76.

41. Thus, for example, the Kuwait Oil Company pays taxes to the Kuwait government. That government used part of its revenue to buy technology to build a water desalination plant for Kuwait City. Using tax revenues, the host government becomes the vehicle for technological transfers. Or, as a second example, employees of Kuwait Oil Company have demands. Technologically-advanced goods are imported into Kuwait to meet the new demands.

42. The literature on the multinational corporation and its technological contributions is substantial. The National Planning Association published in the 1950's and early 1960's a series of Case Studies on United States Business Performance Abroad, many of which studies sought to reveal the technological contributions of multinational corporations. James Brian Quinn, "Technology Transfer by Multinational Companies," *Harvard Business Review*, XLVII (Nov.–Dec. 1969), 147–161, provides numerous examples of transfers of technology.

43. Quotation is from Hufbauer, *Synthetic Materials*, p. 68, and applies to his work on the chemical industry; it is also applicable to other industries, although in some industries there is clear evidence that multinational corporations have adapted to foreign conditions—if not too frequently to differences of factor availability at

least to diverse foreign demand. Recent research at the Harvard Business School by Professor Robert B. Stobaugh indicates that often adjustments of technology by multinational corporations occur in *material handling* and *packaging* rather than in the actual production activity.

44. Celso Furtado, *Obstacles to Economic Development* (Garden City, N.Y.: Doubleday & Co., 1970). On the many advocates of some technological adjustment, see Louis T. Wells, Jr., "Economic Man and Engineering Man: Choice of Technology in a Low-Wage Country," *Public Policy,* XXI (Summer 1973), 319, n. 1. This article has fascinating data on the selection of technology in plants in contemporary Indonesia.

45. Such is certainly the thrust of the N.P.A. studies, cited in note 42 above. It is the policy implicitly accepted by Brazilian *government* economists. Gershenkron, *Economic Backwardness in Historical Perspective,* pp. 9, 26, argues that largely by the application of "modern and efficient techniques" can a backward country achieve success and that the advanced technology is the right one. From a different point of view, others agree that techniques to be appropriate should be modified and feel that some international firms are "more willing and able than others to adjust industrial transfers to the specialized needs of developing countries." Baranson, "Technology Transfer through the International Firm," p. 440. For an intelligent, although limited, consideration of the impact of the foreign investor's communication of technology on the Canadian economy, see Report of the Task Force on the Structure of Canadian Industry, *Foreign Ownership and the Structure of Canadian Industry* (Ottawa: Privy Council Office, 1968), pp. 56–60, 66–70.

46. Landes, *Unbound Prometheus,* p. 214.

47. *Ibid.,* p. 221.

48. Rosenberg, *Technology and American Economic Growth,* p. 45n. The British started to import American shoe-making machinery to obtain the appropriate technological processes. See John H. Dunning, *American Investment in British Manufacturing Industry* (London: George Allen & Unwin, 1958), pp. 31–32, and International Management Association, *Case Studies in Foreign Operations* (New York: International Management Association, 1957), pp. 77–78, on United Shoe Machinery's activities in Britain providing American machinery for the "modernized industry."

49. Product cycle theory argues that products are exported, imitated abroad, and that this becomes a basis for direct investment in foreign countries by the exporter. See Raymond Vernon, "International Investment and International Trade in the Product Cycle," *Quarterly Journal of Economics,* LXXX (May 1966), 190–207.

50. The automobile industry is a fine example of this proposition. The mass produced American automobile made with interchangeable parts was exported to Europe. William Richard Morris (later Lord Nuffield) set out to compete with the Model T, producing his first car, the Morris-Oxford in April 1913. Morris borrowed American technology. Mira Wilkins and Frank Ernest Hill, *American Business Abroad: Ford on Six Continents* (Detroit: Wayne State University Press, 1964), p. 51. On the other hand, when in the late 1950's and 1960's Brazil and Argentina determined to substitute domestic car and truck production for imports, it was in the main foreign rather than domestic capital that undertook to manufacture. *Ibid.,* pp. 416–419.

51. Wilkins, *Emergence of Multinational Enterprise,* p. 30.

52. Such data are highly miscellaneous, ranging from annual reports, company records, government hearings and reports, antitrust case materials, to business histories.

53. Wilkins, *Emergence of Multinational Enterprise,* p. 54.

54. Why were Americans so slow to imitate in this case? The reason seems to lie not in business organization, not in capital, natural resource, labor-cost, technological, scale, infrastructure, cultural or language barriers, or even completely in demand factors but rather in priorities. The demand was small; the profit potentials did not seem great; and more important up until World War I the Germans adequately filled the existing demand. With the war, the demand structure changed and the former sources of supply were gone. Working chemical patents became of high priority. Diffusion occurred.

55. James Howard Bridge, *The Inside History of the Carnegie Steel Company* (New York: The Aldine Book Co., 1903), p. 35.

56. *Ibid.*, pp. 75, 86. It is important that Carnegie grasped the potentialities of the new technology. See Robert A. Solo, "Technology Transfer," in Robert A. Solo and Everett M. Rogers, eds., *Inducing Technological Change for Economic Growth and Development* (East Lansing: Michigan State University Press, 1972), p. 18.

57. William S. Dutton, *Du Pont* (New York: Scribners, 1942), p. 31 and *passim.*

58. Interviews in South Africa.

59. Hufbauer, *Synthetic Materials,* pp. 88–89, 131.

60. J. S. Fforde, *An International Trade in Managerial Skills* (Oxford: Basil Blackwell, 1957).

61. Henrietta M. Larson, Evelyn H. Knowlton, and Charles S. Popple, *New Horizons, 1927–1950* (New York: Harper & Row, 1971), pp. 153–159.

62. J. K. Jenney, Foreign Relations Department to J. E. Crane, Dec. 9, 1936, Eleutherian Mills Historical Library, Greenville, Wilmington, Dela., Accession 1231, Box 2.

63. See Terutomo Ozawa, "Should the United States Restrict the Technology Trade," *MSU Business Topics,* XX (Autumn 1972), 35. An excellent pieve on technology transfers to Japan is George Hall and Robert Johnson, "Transfer of U.S. Aerospace Technology to Japan" in *Technology Factor in International Trade,* edited by Raymond Vernon (Special Conference Series No. 22; New York: National Bureau of Economic Research, 1970).

64. The formulation often made is that direct foreign investment takes place after the market for exports is "threatened"—meaning by the existence of imitators or the *potential* for competition.

65. Here the government, which is beyond the subject limits of this paper, may take over the technology.

66. Wilkins, *Maturing of Multinational Enterprise.*

67. *Ibid.* From 1934 to 1958 there had been a steady decline in U.S. influence in the Cuban sugar industry.

68. J.-J. Servan-Schreiber, *The American Challenge* (New York: Atheneum, 1968), p. 4.

69. For example, in 1904 Gordon M. McGregor, a Canadian wagon builder, visited Henry Ford and convinced him operations in Canada were desirable. Ford agreed that he and the American company would furnish the Canadian enterprise with patents, plans, drawings and specifications needed to build Ford cars, and Ford personally would give "such reasonable and sufficient oversight" as was required. In return for the technology, the stockholders in Ford Motor Company obtained a 51 percent interest in the Canadian firm and Ford was paid a fee for his services. (Wilkins and Hill, *American Business Abroad,* pp. 14–18). In the late 1920's and early 1930's, the Japanese wanted to build their own refining industry. One way was through a joint-venture with an American oil company. In this case the Japanese held control, while obtaining U.S. technology. Data from the Archives, Mitsubishi Oil Company, Tokyo, Japan.

70. Based on my own visits to such enterprises in Latin America and the Middle East.

71. William R. Fritsch, *Progress and Profits: The Sears, Roebuck Story in Peru* (Washington, D.C.: Action Committee for International Development, 1962), pp. 22, 50–51.

72. Often in Canada, it was other multinational corporations that met the new demands. Yet, there were cases wherein Canadian private companies took on that role.

# 13

## "Rich beyond the Dreams of Avarice": The Guggenheims in Chile*

Thomas F. O'Brien

*Source: *Business History Review*, 63 (1989), pp. 122–159.

This article focuses on the roles of business-government relations, technology, financing, entrepreneurship, and management in the evolution of multinational corporations. It describes the Guggenheims' successive involvements in Mexican silver, Chilean copper, and Chilean nitrates and stresses the brothers' strategic use of technical innovation and relations with host governments to accomplish these major changes in the focus of their business. The essay's findings suggest the need for a more sophisticated treatment of business-government relations and for the incorporation of entrepreneurship and organizational structure as dynamic variables in theories of the MNE. It also points to the importance of historical conjunctures that shape technology in understanding the emergence of the MNE.

The interaction between theory and history in the study of the multinational enterprise (MNE) has generated a productive but troubled relationship.[1] Theory provides structure and breadth to the work of historians, but theories of the MNE present business historians with widely varying and sometimes conflicting analytical perspectives. International trade, location, and industrial organization theories, grounded in neoclassical economics with its explanatory emphasis on markets, pay little heed to the causal significance of entrepreneurship and management.

Furthermore, theoretical work has focused largely on the postwar realities of developed countries. With their assumptions of a liberal nation-state, theories of the MNE have not adequately explored the relationships of MNEs with peripheral states, which have been characterized by a significant degree of political instability. A similar contemporary bias appears in the theories' conceptualization of management structure, which offers little interpretative insight into alternative forms, such as the extended family or partnerships, in the management process. In other words, "... there is no neat and self contained body of economic theory of the MNE waiting for testing or application by business historians."[2]

At the same time, the record of contributions by business historians to an understanding of the multinational enterprise is not unblemished. Historians have shown only a limited interest in many of the issues raised by theorists. Technology and the ownership advantages that it can provide play a central role in economic theories of the MNE, but they have not been a major focus of historical studies of multinationals, nor has the financing of multinationals been thoroughly investigated.

Given the flawed relationship between theory and history, this essay follows Mark Casson's suggestion that "The best way to further enhance the relevance of the theory [of the MNE] seems to be not to 'purify' or 'generalize' it, but to focus upon specific gaps in it."[3] By exploring the development of a raw materials-based multinational, this examination of the Guggenheims' interests in Chile provides a more sophisticated and complex explanation of business-government relations than that suggested by current theories of the MNE. The essay examines the role of technology and financing in the development of the MNE, demonstrating the influence of time and space on these factors. Finally, it analyzes the entrepreneurship and management variables in the light of evidence that casts them in a more dynamic role than is suggested by current theories. The sectoral and regional concentration of American foreign direct investment in the early decades of the twentieth century offers an opportunity to study the multinational at the firm level and to draw meaningful general conclusions about the evolution of multinational corporations.

As of 1914, Latin America accounted for nearly half of all U.S. direct foreign investment. Mining, which constituted the largest single type of such investments, was concentrated in Mexico and Chile.[4] Leading this multinational expansion were the Guggenheim brothers, who controlled the largest mining operations in both countries.[5] the history of the Guggenheim empire illustrates, perhaps as no other, the forces that shaped the emergence of multinational mining enterprises based in the United States. Within the history of their global empire can be discerned the influence of technological innovation, capital markets, management, and the nation-state in shaping not only the modern multinational, but the modern world economy as well. The interlocking effect of these forces surfaced with the greatest intensity in the Guggenheims' ventures in Chile; investments there would bring both triumph and disaster to this transnational enterprise that dominated the world of mining.

**The Mining Empire**

M. Guggenheim and Sons was the corporate crown of a classic American success story. Meyer Guggenheim, the son of an immigrant Swiss tailor, had grown from his modest beginnings as a street peddler to accumulate a small fortune in the wholesale goods and lace trades. M. Guggenheim and Sons, created in 1875 to oversee his business interests, eventually included all seven of Meyer's sons as equal partners. After their father's death in 1905, the seven brothers were viewed as an inflexible phalanx of capitalists, but it was in fact the second oldest, Daniel, who held the reins of leadership, with his brothers Isaac, Murry, and Solomon serving as his closest working partners.[6] Long before Meyer's death, the family's business interests had shifted from wholesale goods to mining. In 1879, Meyer purchased a part interest in a silver mine in Leadville, Colorado. By 1887, the Guggenheims were earning between one-half and three-quarters of a million dollars annually from their silver-mining ventures.[7] Despite these impressive profits, the mines were using a series of production processes whose techniques had reached a ceiling of efficiency.

The major breakthroughs in deep-metal mining, such as shaft sinking, underground tunneling, and roof support, had been developed since the discovery of the Comstock Lode in Nevada nearly thirty years earlier. These techniques relied on hand operations to extract minerals from the earth and required a labor force of highly skilled craftsmen. Efforts to modify this production system faced the certain opposition of skilled workers, who resisted attempts to reduce wages or to simplify tasks in order to achieve greater profitability. The Guggenheims had already encountered some of these problems in developing their mines in Leadville.[8] In contrast, the related but still separate industry of smelting (the separation of metals from the ore), was undergoing rapid technological change at this time. The first reverberatory furnace was built in the United States in 1879 with a capacity of treating ten tons per day. During the next two decades furnace capacities reached 190 tons. In 1883 the converter method of smelting was introduced, bringing further increases in efficiency.[9]

Meyer Guggenheim was no expert in smelting technology, but he was astute enough to recognize that smelting as a high technology industry offered opportunities for higher profits. In 1888 Meyer built the largest smelter in the world at a cost of $300,000. Located in Pueblo, Colorado, the smelter had a processing capacity of 400 tons per day, and within two years it was generating annual profits of $600,000.[10] With this investment, the Guggenheims shifted their focus from the labor-intensive, highly skilled undertaking of shaft mining to smelting, where most of the innovations were labor-saving devices. In so doing, the brothers became part of a larger phenomenon sweeping the American economy. The industrial sector was entering a new stage of mechanization that introduced simplified production techniques requiring fewer skilled and more semiskilled workers.[11] This simplification of work methods opened the possibility of tapping overseas labor markets that were rich in labor resources but low in skill levels.

The Guggenheims quickly took advantage of foreign investment opportunities created by the process of skill simplification. In 1892 they opened a smelter in Monterrey, Mexico, and another in Aguascalientes in 1894. Subsequently, they built additional smelters and added railroads as well as mines to their Mexican holdings. By 1910 their investments, which exceeded $50 million in value, constituted the largest privately held enterprise in the country.[12]

Mexico was an enticing target for foreign investment given the open door policy of Mexican president Porfirio Diaz. Under an agreement with the accommodating Mexican government, the Guggenheims enjoyed duty-free import of construction materials for their smelters and a minimal tax burden.[13] The most attractive aspect of investment in Mexico, however, was not the country's accommodating government but its low labor costs. Smelter workers in Pueblo received $2.00 in gold per day, whereas Monterrey workers earned daily wages of $.40. Although the smelters employed an equal number of laborers, the weekly payroll in Pueblo was $19,200, in contrast to $3,840 for that of Monterrey. Low wage levels soon became even more important when a stock market crash and the repeal of the Sherman Silver Purchase Act in 1893 drove the price of silver in the United States down from $.92 to $.47 per ounce. The low cost of Mexican labor enabled the Monterrey smelter to continue to produce silver at a profit. Mexico also offered other advantages. The Guggenheims convinced the Mexican government to increase its silver coinage requirements, bringing additional business to their smelters.[14] Operating in Mexico gave the Guggenheims the dual advantages of lower labor costs and an investment climate at times more favorable than that at home. The advantages deriving from their status as a multinational enterprise enabled the Guggenheims to challenge their principal competitor in the U.S. smelting industry.

The American Smelting and Refining Company (ASARCO), a trust formed in 1899, encompassed all the major lead and silver smelters in the United States except those belonging to the Guggenheim brothers. Yet by the summer of 1900, the organizers of ASARCO agreed to bring the Guggenheims into the trust on highly favorable terms. After lengthy negotiations, ASARCO increased its capitalization from $65 million to $100 million, with the Guggenheims receiving $45 million in ASARCO stock. In return, the brothers contributed their three domestic smelters, their refinery in Perth Amboy, New Jersey, and cash and credits with a total value of $20 million. The stock they received had a real market value of $30 million and gave them effective control of the trust.[15]

ASARCO's defeat at the hands of the Guggenheims was due in part to its own inefficient organization, which made it unable to coordinate effectively the operations of the numerous individual smelters that the trust comprised. But equally important was the Guggenheims' ability to turn to their Mexican smelters and flood the world market with cheap silver and lead, delivering a decisive blow to their rival.[16]

Just as the victory over ASARCO was assuring their dominance in smelting and refining, the Guggenheims' mining interests came full circle as they reentered the extractive sector. The brothers' earlier shift from mining to smelting came at a time when the limits of traditional mining methods— including cut-and-fill mining and stoping (or excavating) with square set timbering—as well as craft labor practices had created hindrances to further improvements in mining productivity. Copper mining productivity, for example, was stagnant or declining between 1889 and 1914.[17] This trend, however, underwent a dramatic reversal with the introduction of non-selective mining techniques—the mechanization of functions previously carried out by hand labor.

The use of power shovels to tap the Mesabi iron ore range in 1892 marked the first major step in this direction. The decisive development came in 1904 with Daniel C. Jackling's use of nonselective technology to exploit the Bingham Canyon mine in Utah. Nonselective techniques made possible the profitable extraction of the mine's porphyry (low grade) copper ores.[18] Jackling's efforts went far beyond mechanization of the extraction process. Smelting of minerals such as copper required crushing the ore and submitting it to a process called concentration. At the end of the nineteenth century, techniques for concentration, which relied on differences in specific gravity between the ore components, recovered only two-thirds of the copper. The introduction of the flotation process in 1912, which captured 93 to 94 percent of the copper, radically altered this situation.[19] The linking of mass extraction with the flotation process created at Bingham Canyon "a completely articulated technology of mining and beneficiating."[20] With the development of nonselective techniques, mining now joined smelting in the second industrial revolution characterized by increased mechanization of functions and simplification of tasks. The Guggenheims had begun financing the Bingham Canyon venture in 1906. And as with their smelter operations, they would soon apply the mechanization and task simplification of nonselective mining to overseas operations.

The investment in Bingham Canyon marked several important shifts in the Guggenheims' strategy. These included decisions to return to direct investment in mining operations and to shift their interests away from lead and silver to more promising metals such as copper. To implement this strategy they created a new corporation, American Smelters Security, with most of the common stock held by ASARCO. American Smelters then bought most of the Guggenheims' silver and lead mines, leaving the brothers with the capital to pursue their new mining interests in Utah, Alaska, and The Belgian Congo. The demands of these ventures eventually led them to sell off a large portion of their holdings in ASARCO as well. These maneuvers also indicated that the Guggenheims had become finance capitalists as well as industrialists; they were experts in the flotation of companies and bond issues, able to tap the enormous financial markets of New York and London to harness millions for the development of their mining enterprises. Combining their own fortunes with the resources of the American stock and bond markets, the Guggenheims seemed to have limitless possibilities.[21]

Meanwhile, conditions in Mexico were providing a further incentive for the Guggenheims to diversify their overseas operations. Despite President Díaz's warm welcome to the Guggenheims, their investments were not viewed as an unmixed blessing by all Mexicans. Members of the Mexican elite with mining and smelting interests saw themselves being crushed beneath the Guggenheim juggernaut. Among the powerful families who saw their interests being sacrificed to foreign entrepreneurs was that of Francisco Madero, who challenged Díaz's rule in 1910, setting off a revolutionary upheaval that damaged the Guggenheims' smelting interests.[22] The Guggenheims recognized the need to spread their international risks in the face of growing turmoil in Mexico.

## Chilean Copper

Thus a combination of factors, including the Guggenheims' emergence as finance capitalists, the logic of pursuing the high technology sector of an industry, the opportunity to utilize cheap semiskilled labor, and the encounters with the stirrings of economic nationalism, brought the Guggenheims to the northern deserts of Chile. The Pacific coast nation of Chile was not an entirely new environment for the Guggenheim brothers. They had been involved in silver smelting operations there prior to the turn of the century. But for the Guggenheims, who sought to turn large profits by being at the forefront of technical innovation, Chilean copper mining was now the ideal investment opportunity.

Chile had been the world's leading copper producer in the 1870s, accounting for as much as 43 percent of output, but in subsequent decades the industry stagnated. After the turn of the century, Chilean output fell below the levels reached in the 1870s, and the nation's share of the world market had fallen to less than 5 percent. The decline of copper mining resulted from a number of factors, including the appearance of new competitors in the 1880s, the resulting price declines, and the exhaustion of

Chile's richest ore deposits. Equally significant was the primitive structure of Chilean mining, which remained a labor-intensive, low-capital undertaking that failed to adopt many of the new techniques in shaft mining that had transformed the industry in the United States during the second half of the nineteenth century.[23] Given the moribund state of the copper industry, the Chilean government was willing to allow foreign investors to operate in this sector virtually tax-free.

The Chilean political system constituted another attractive feature for foreign investors. By Latin American standards, Chile had enjoyed a remarkable record of stability. A series of constitutionally elected presidents had succeeded one another since the 1830s, interrupted only by a nine-month civil war in 1891. Chile also offered a cheap labor pool. The country's traditional agrarian sector, which still accounted for the majority of its population and employment, kept wages at subsistence level and set the standard for the rest of the economy. Even when the Guggenheims made their plunge into copper mining and paid wages in excess of other employers in the country, Chilean copper workers still earned only one-third as much as unskilled laborers in the United States.[24] Chile constituted an ideal foreign investment opportunity for the Guggenheims in many ways. Its stagnant mining region provided fertile ground for employing the latest in mining techniques. The new technology's task simplification could maximize the advantages of a cheap supply of semiskilled labor within a notably stable political environment.

The brothers' first major venture in Chile resulted from the efforts of William C. Braden, a former ASARCO employee, who bought the Rancagua copper mine in north central Chile in 1904. Braden began developing the mine on his own but soon turned to the Guggenheims for financial backing. The Guggenheims formed the Braden Copper Company in 1908 with a capitalization of $23 million. However, the key to their Chilean copper ventures lay in the northern desert. In 1900 a Guggenheim employee had identified a large porphyry copper deposit there and recommended its purchase. In the days before Bingham Canyon had proven the effectiveness of profitability of nonselective mining, the suggestion had been quickly rejected, but in 1910 the brothers reversed their earlier decision and purchased a site known as Chuquicamata. What they bought was a mountain with hundreds of millions of tons of porphyry copper ore.[25] The Guggenheims formed the Chile Copper Company with $95 million in stock, $25 million of which went to pay for the mine. An additional $12 million in development funds for a railroad, power plant, and port was raised through a bond issue floated in New York by the brothers' old friend, Bernard Baruch.[26]

The development of the Braden and Chuquicamata mines revolutionized the technology of the antiquated Chilean mining industry. El Teniente, the principal Braden mine, was the first in the world to apply to flotation process in concentrating low-grade ores. Farther north, huge mechanical shovels carved Chuquicamata into the largest open pit mine in the world, while the brothers' engineer, E. A. Cappelen-Smith, developed a new concentration process utilizing sulfuric acid and electrolytic precipitation to treat the mine's ore. By the time they sold Chuquicamata to the Anaconda Corporation in 1923, the Guggenheims were well on their way to dominating and transforming the Chilean copper industry. By 1918 American interests accounted for 87 percent of Chile's copper output. Chilean copper production shot up from 41,000 tons in 1912 to over 200,000 tons in 1926. The advantages of the combination of modern mining technology and cheap labor were strikingly apparent in the New York metals market, where Chilean copper could be delivered for five cents less per pound than the domestic product, prompting fears of a shutdown of U.S. mines. Between 1918 and 1920, the Braden company alone produced profits of $20 million. Despite the gradual imposition of government taxation, the American copper corporations' annual profits ranged between 14 and 40 percent in the late 1920s.[27] Yet at the moment of their greatest success in copper, the Guggenheims shifted their attention to Chile's faltering nitrate industry.

**Chilean Nitrates**

When the Guggenheims entered the Chilean copper sector, the nitrate industry was that nation's principal source of export revenues and government income. Nitrate of soda's uses as a fertilizer and in the manufacture of explosives had given the country an export product with a steadily expanding world market. Since Chile had seized the nitrate-rich northern desert regions from Peru and Bolivia in 1879, European capitalists, particularly the British, had revamped the nitrate industry's technology, thereby expanding its output and improving its productivity. Nitrates then became the keystone in an impressive structure of British investment that included railroads, banking, commercial houses, and government loans.[28] As of 1894 Chile supplied 73 percent of the world nitrate market. In turn, nitrate taxes generated 50 percent or more of the Chilean government's ordinary revenues, which skyrocketed from 49 million gold pesos in 1880 to nearly 249 million in 1918. European capitalists remained dominant into the 1920s, controlling 51 percent of the industry directly and an additional 35 percent in joint enterprises with Chileans; they also dominated the nitrate marketing network.[29] But at the turn of the century, both the efficiency of the Chilean industry and its monopolization of the world fertilizer market were deteriorating.

The rate of worker productivity provides the most obvious indication of the industry's declining efficiency. Output per worker fell by more than 20 percent between 1894 and 1920. The problem stemmed from a lack of technical innovation to cope with the decreasing quality of nitrate ore, or caliche.[30] Specifically, the Shanks process, a steam-heated system for treating caliche introduced in 1878, remained the accepted method for refining nitrate into the 1920s. Modifications were made in the system, such as substituting oil for coal to achieve greater energy efficiency, but the Shanks method remained dominant long after it had been suspended in every comparable industry.[31] Outside the refineries, or *oficinas,* laborers who extracted the caliche relied on hand tools and hand-sorting to accomplish the task. The use of air drills, steam shovels, and other methods of mass extraction remained the exception into the 1920s. One observer concluded: "As a whole there has been less advancement and improvement in the natural nitrate industry than in any other mechanical-chemical process followed on a large scale."[32] The vigor of British capitalists when they first established effective control over the industry had apparently dissipated by the turn of the century. The reasons for that phenomenon lay in the oligopolistic structure of the industry and the condition of Chilean labor.

Chilean nitrates enjoyed a natural monopoly during the last quarter of the nineteenth century. Although a series of oversupply crises struck the industry in this period, the concentration of capital in the industry after 1884 allowed operators to form producers' agreements or combinations to protect prices and profits. The combinations' output reductions consistently succeeded in raising or at least stabilizing prices. Between 1884 and 1909 the industry operated under five such agreements for a total of sixteen years. Pressure for such combinations was renewed after the First World War, when the industry faced increased competition from synthetic producers in Europe. In response, the natural producers formed the Nitrate Producers Association, and until 1925 its price-fixing agreements kept nitrate prices at a higher level than during any similar period in the industry's history (see Table 1). Despite cycles of recession, such price-fixing arrangements made nitrates a profitable endeavor. The more efficient refiners could expect net profits of 29 to 38 percent under these agreements, and even high-cost refiners could manage profits of 12 to 17 percent.[33] Such effective price manipulation deadened competitive incentives to renovate the production process.

Furthermore, the Chilean work force put only feeble pressure on wages, so the industry did not face increasing labor costs that would have encouraged the introduction of labor-saving devices. No single group of Chilean workers was better known for militancy than the nitrate workers. Moreover, nitrate producers down through the decades complained about the scarcity of workers. Despite labor militancy and the apparent undersupply of workers, however, the labor movement proved incapable of significantly improving its position over the decades. A certain degree of

*Table 1*  Chilean nitrate prices 1880–1934 (in U.S. $ per ton)[a]

| Calendar year | Price | Calendar year | Price | Nitrate year (June 30) | Price |
|---|---|---|---|---|---|
| 1880 | $47.05 | 1900 | $25.05 | 1919/20 | $49.66 |
| 1881 | 49.53 | 1901 | 30.07 | 1920/21 | 78.49 |
| 1882 | 37.68 | 1902 | 31.12 | 1921/22 | 51.88 |
| 1883 | 32.27 | 1903 | 31.20 | 1922/23 | 43.91 |
| 1884 | 31.06 | 1904 | 34.60 | 1923/24 | 44.60 |
| 1885 | 33.68 | 1905 | 36.40 | 1924/25 | 44.55 |
| 1886 | 39.25 | 1906 | 40.53 | 1925/26 | 43.12 |
| 1887 | 26.53 | 1907 | 41.40 | 1926/27 | 42.59 |
| 1888 | 28.80 | 1908 | 36.15 | 1927/28 | 37.18 |
| 1889 | 27.35 | 1909 | 32.70 | 1928/29 | 36.78 |
| 1890 | 23.88 | 1910 | 32.93 | 1929/30 | 34.20 |
| 1891 | 26.22 | 1911 | 35.14 | 1930/31 | 28.82 |
| 1892 | 28.32 | 1912 | 38.20 | 1931/32 | 22.32 |
| 1893 | 28.40 | 1913 | 37.55 | 1932/33 | 18.87 |
| 1894 | 28.71 | 1914 | 33.40 | 1933/34 | 18.80 |
| 1895 | 25.92 | 1915 | 33.12 | | |
| 1896 | 26.81 | 1916 | 36.74 | | |
| 1897 | 24.97 | 1917 | 60.13 | | |
| 1898 | 22.34 | 1918 | 58.21 | | |
| 1899 | 23.41 | | | | |

*Source:*  George W. Stocking and Myron W. Watkins, *Cartels in Action: Case Studies in International Business Diplomacy* (New York, 1946), 123.
[a]F.A.S. (free alongside ship) Chilean ports.

tension developed between nitrate producers and agricultural interests as each group attempted to supply their labor-intensive enterprises with low-cost labor. However, *enganches* (gang labor recruitment) by the nitrate producers—run, as one observer noted, with military efficiency—permitted them to keep wages low and to weed out potential agitators.[34]

The cessation of trade with Western Europe in 1914 dealt a severe blow to the nitrate workers' real wages, which fell by 25 percent during the war years. The industry itself rebounded in 1915 and continued to enjoy boom years until the world recession in 1919.[35] It recovered once again in 1921 and enjoyed renewed profits until 1926. Yet in the mid-1920s nitrate workers' real wages still had not returned to their prewar levels. Nitrate producers offered wages that were twice as high as workers could receive elsewhere in the domestic economy, but the difference was a relative one. As with the copper workers, wages remained low compared to wage scales in the developed countries. High levels of underemployment in the domestic economy and the structure of the domestic labor force put downward pressure on the wages of nitrate workers and inhibited the mobilization of the work force.[36]

After the First World War nitrate producers continued to rely on labor-intensive techniques in the extraction and refining processes. Between 1922 and 1925, with real wages still hovering below prewar levels, the industry more than doubled the size of its work force, from 24,000 to 60,000 men. An elaborate division of labor had been introduced into the refineries by the last quarter of the nineteenth century, with workmen divided into a series of gangs working on a piece-rate basis. This organization of labor functioned effectively only when the Shanks process, which treated the caliche in small lots by the boiling method, was employed for refining. The low labor costs that encouraged the preservation of piecework therefore also discouraged a switch to nonboiling refining methods. The reliance on small-lot treatment in the refining plants in turn favored the more selective techniques of hand extraction and sorting over mass extraction, which would require large-lot treatment facilities.[37]

In the nitrate fields, labor intensity was even more acute. There too piecework prevailed, and rarely did more than two men work together in breaking, sorting, and loading the ore. Labor costs were so low that hand-sorted caliche could be delivered for rail transport to the refineries at a cost that compared favorably with that resulting when steam shovels and other methods of power mining were employed. Although it was estimated that technological renovation would cut the industry's costs in half, the low cost of Chilean labor remained a strong disincentive to scrapping existing machinery and methods for more efficient equipment and procedures.[38]

By the beginning of the twentieth century, the nitrate industry's productivity had stalled under oligopolistic controls and low wage levels. Oligopolistic structures precluded competitive pressure for innovation, and the inability of Chilean nitrate workers to achieve advances in real wages ensured the continuation of labor-intensive methods of production. One observer criticizing the high profits of the nitrate companies accurately summarized the condition of the industry in 1926:

> Such profits from an extractive industry most assuredly are excessive, and when in order to maintain same, exorbitant prices have to be sustained, these stimulate competitive industries in other countries, while at the same time it demands a reduced rate of the earnings of the citizens of the land wherein these industries are located. Hence this policy must be esteemed as prejudicial both for controlled labor and for the nation as a whole.[39]

The difficulties created by the stagnation of the Chilean nitrate industry were intensified by developments abroad.

Occasionally during the nineteenth century the European economies had replaced natural products imported from the periphery, such as dyestuffs, with synthetic substitutes.[40] During the twentieth century import substitution became a major trend, and developments in the nitrate industry typified this course. Declining productivity and price-fixing in the industry encouraged the development of synthetic substitutes in Europe.

The figures in Table 2 capture in graphic terms the growing challenge to Chilean nitrates in the world market during the first three decades of the twentieth century. The challenge came from two chemical substitutes, by-product nitrogen and synthetic nitrogen. By-product nitrogen in its most common form, sulphate of ammonia, was derived from coal distillation in the manufacture of coke and artificial gas. Sulphate of ammonia had been produced commercially since 1858, and by 1914 it was a serious competitor in the world nitrogen market. The war encouraged further development and production of the second alternative, synthetic nitrogen. Germany initially relied on synthetics to compensate for the interdiction of Chilean supplies by the Allied blockade and then set up protective barriers for its domestic industry in the postwar years. Synthetics were produced by capturing nitrogen out of the air using one of three methods: the arc, cyanamide, or Haber-Bosch process. The Haber-Bosch process, which produced synthetic ammonia by combining nitrogen and hydrogen at high temperatures, rapidly became the single largest source of non-Chilean nitrogen in the late 1920s and early 1930s.[41]

Initially, growing world demand for nitrates protected the Chilean industry from competition. In 1910 synthetic and by-product output equaled Chilean production figures for 1901, but the natural industry had increased its output by 80 percent in the same period, and the expanding world market still received over 64 percent of its needs from Chile (see Table 2). However, the closing of the German market and competition from synthetics initiated a series of intensifying crises that pushed the Chilean industry to the point of collapse by 1930. It was this declining export industry that attracted the attention of the Guggenheim brothers soon after the First World War.

## The Guggenheim Nitrate Venture

The Guggenheim brothers' interest in the nitrate industry is understandable in light of the factors that had propelled the firm's expansion. First, nitrates represented another product diversification for their mining ventures. Second, Chile still appeared to be a highly stable environment for foreign investment. Third, nitrate production represented a new opportunity to be at the forefront of an industry's technological renovation and to reap the resulting high profits. In nitrates the brothers could see a field of endeavor where both the extractive and the refining industries were capable of

*Table 2* World production of chemical nitrogen 1900–1937 (in thousands of tons)

| Year | Chilean nitrate | By-product nitrogen | Synthetic nitrogen | Total production | World capacity |
|---|---|---|---|---|---|
| 1900 | 220.0 | 110.0 | N/A | 330.0 | 379.5 |
| 1901 | 234.3 | 110.0 | N/A | 344.2 | 385.0 |
| 1902 | 236.5 | 115.5 | N/A | 352.0 | 396.0 |
| 1903 | 253.4 | 124.2 | N/A | 377.6 | 412.5 |
| 1904 | 265.8 | 136.7 | N/A | 402.5 | 456.5 |
| 1905 | 299.2 | 147.3 | N/A | 446.5 | 484.0 |
| 1906 | 310.6 | 164.7 | 0.1 | 475.4 | 577.5 |
| 1907 | 314.8 | 205.8 | .5 | 521.1 | 616.0 |
| 1908 | 337.4 | 197.2 | 1.6 | 536.2 | 671.0 |
| 1909 | 359.9 | 209.0 | 4.3 | 573.2 | 715.0 |
| 1910 | 420.3 | 226.6 | 9.6 | 656.5 | 896.5 |
| 1911 | 429.9 | 246.8 | 20.1 | 696.8 | 902.0 |
| 1912 | 440.8 | 277.2 | 38.1 | 756.1 | 935.0 |
| 1913 | 472.7 | 312.5 | 66.2 | 851.4 | 962.5 |
| 1914 | 420.0 | 283.7 | 75.2 | 778.9 | 1,001.0 |
| 1915 | 299.3 | 301.3 | 94.0 | 694.6 | 1,067.0 |
| 1916 | 496.6 | 336.9 | 164.5 | 998.0 | 1,232.0 |
| 1917 | 511.7 | 365.7 | 219.0 | 1,096.4 | 1,342.0 |
| 1918 | 487.5 | 402.4 | 269.7 | 1,159.6 | 1,507.0 |
| 1919 | 290.4 | 287.9 | 247.6 | 825.9 | 1,562.0 |
| 1920 | 430.2 | 318.3 | 245.3 | 993.8 | 1,551.0 |
| 1921 | 223.3 | 275.3 | 299.2 | 797.8 | 1,540.0 |
| 1922 | 182.6 | 324.3 | 365.0 | 871.9 | 1,523.5 |
| 1923 | 324.5 | 356.9 | 383.1 | 1,064.5 | 1,617.0 |
| 1924 | 412.4 | 352.3 | 476.0 | 1,240.7 | 1,715.0 |
| 1925 | 433.4 | 368.6 | 578.0 | 1,380.0 | 1,900.0 |
| 1926 | 346.1 | 397.6 | 733.9 | 1,477.6 | 2,065.0 |
| 1927 | 277.0 | 440.3 | 911.0 | 1,628.3 | 2,392.0 |
| 1928 | 543.1 | 466.9 | 1,159.4 | 2,169.4 | 2.757.0 |
| 1929 | 554.8 | 496.9 | 1,352.8 | 2.404.2 | 3.278.0 |
| 1930 | 419.7 | 476.5 | 1,274.6 | 2,170.8 | 3,917.0 |
| 1931 | 193.2 | 397.2 | 1,175.6 | 1,766.0 | 4.448.0 |
| 1932 | 120.1 | 345.9 | 1,315.8 | 1,781.8 | 4,788.0 |
| 1933 | 75.6 | 356.6 | 1,462.6 | 1,894.8 | 4,955.0 |
| 1934 | 144.8 | 396.7 | 1,582.7 | 2,124.2 | 5,082.3 |
| 1935 | 205.0 | 434.3 | 1,821.0 | 2,460.3 | N/A |
| 1936 | 219.4 | 498.2 | 2,087.7 | 2,805.3 | N/A |
| 1937 | 237.0 | 519.2 | 2,317.0 | 3,073.2 | N/A |

*Source:* Stocking and Watkins, *Cartels*, 126.

complete renovation simultaneously. Each time the partners embarked on the long train ride from the Chilean coast to their modern facilities in Chuquicamata, they passed a number of old Shanks plants, churning out nitrate in the same way they had for decades. The contrast and the lesson were obvious. The question was how to penetrate the nitrate industry, still alien territory to the Guggenheims.

In the past, the brothers had entered new ventures by working with or employing the best: the best financiers like Baruch, the best mining engineers like Jackling. They pursued much the same strategy in undertaking their nitrate venture. In 1916 the Guggenheims opened a joint nitrate account with J. P. Morgan and Company. By 1922 the Guggenheim-Morgan syndicate had spent $261,000 developing a new nitrate-refining process. The Guggenheims also turned to the London-based firm of Gibbs and Company. The British merchant house had been trading on the west coast of South America for nearly a century and had been producing nitrates since the 1860s. To the end of the nineteenth century, it was among the largest nitrate refiners. The firm had been one of the first to introduce the Shanks system after 1879. By 1900 the house recognized the comparative stagnation in the nitrate production process, and it shifted more of its interests into nitrate marketing, where it controlled one-third of the trade. At the same time the company increased its holdings of undeveloped nitrate lands to $5 million with the intention of floating these properties as joint-stock companies on the London market.[42] With its long experience and substantial holdings in nitrates, Gibbs remained the single most important firm in natural nitrates and the logical target for an approach by the Guggenheims.

Early in 1919, Guggenheim representatives asked Gibbs and Company to prepare a thorough report on the nitrate industry. Although doubting the Guggenheims' assertion that they had no direct interest in nitrates, the Gibbs partners prepared the report hoping to use it to probe the Guggenheims' true intentions. Not much probing was necessary. By June 1919 the Guggenheims had indicated their desire to conduct a joint venture with Gibbs. In the ensuing months, the full dimensions of the brothers' plan emerged. A trust was to be formed, whose stock would be used to purchase the existing nitrate companies and to consolidate the industry's supply system. Inefficient refineries were to be closed and production would focus in a few new plants using the new process being developed by the Guggenheims. The Gibbs house was also informed that the scheme envisioned the full cooperation of the Chilean government.

After much discussion, the Gibbs partners rejected the proposal. They cited a number of reasons: reliance on an unproven process was too risky; a trust would encourage more rapid production by synthetic concerns; closing refineries and consolidating supply lines would antagonise vested interests in Chile.[43] Among the multiplicity of reasons, it is difficult to identify a primary one, but in rejecting the proposal without further investigation the Gibbs house likely was a victim of its long experience in Chile. The Gibbs partners had already observed that in copper, modern methods were "quickly making [copper] a really industrial instead of a mere mining venture...."[44] Yet that comprehension did not extend to nitrates. For Herbert Gibbs, the firm's senior partner, the potential advantage of a trust was to regulate wages.[45] He failed to see that the new technology would radically reduce labor requirements and cause productivity to soar. The cheapness of labor in Chile had not only burdened workers; it had also narrowed the vision of the British entrepreneur. The Gibbs partners would regret that lack of vision and their rejection of the Guggenheim offer.

Undeterred by the Gibbs rejection, the Guggenheims' engineer Cappelen-Smith devoted his attention to designing a new nitrate production system. By 1923 he had settled on a refining process, using refrigeration, that permitted treatment of the material in large lots. This refining method, when linked with mass extraction techniques, far out-performed the Shanks system. The new process could treat ore with an assay of 8 percent, compared to the Shanks minimum of 15 percent. The Guggenheim method also reduced production costs by 20 to 25 percent.[46] Despite the promise of this new production system, the decision to enter the nitrate industry was not made with total unanimity by the Guggenheim family.

The sale of their Chuquicamata copper interests to Anaconda caused bitter conflict among the Guggenheims. Daniel and his brothers could offer strong arguments for the sale of Chuquicamata. First, the Anaconda Company, facing rising costs for its domestic output, was desperate to find a cheaper source of copper. Its proposal of $70 million for 2 million of the Chile Copper Company's 3.8 million shares represented an offer of $35 per share for stock that was then selling for $28. Even with the sale, the brothers would retain $20 million in shares of the company and ownership of the Braden Copper Company, the second largest copper company in Chile. The brothers could also argue that Chuquicamata had been a high-cost, low-return venture. The low world prices for copper had caused the mine to lose $1 million in 1921. The Guggenheims had just completed a $35 million expansion program at the mine that left Chile Copper with a $50 million bonded debt, $15 million of which would fall due in 1924.

Nevertheless, Daniel's son Harry and Murry's son Edmond, now full partners in the firm, bitterly opposed the sale. They had been instrumental in the development of Chuquicamata, and they believed it was foolhardy to surrender control of what was now the lowest-cost copper mine in the world, with ore reserves that could carry into the next century. But the elder partners held sway, and Daniel Guggenheim was soon exulting that "nitrates will make us rich beyond the dreams of avarice!"[47] In 1923 the Guggenheims were poised for the great plunge into nitrates.

The decision to sell Chuquicamata and enter the nitrate industry stemmed in part from the short-term position of the property, which had been costly to develop and yet commanded a high selling price because of the needs of the Anaconda Company. But it also signaled an increasing managerial rigidity in the Guggenheim firm. The management of the firm had been in the hands of Daniel and four of his brothers since two of their siblings had withdrawn from the company in 1901 in an earlier dispute over long-term strategy. Their ranks had been further thinned by the recent demise of Issac. The dispute over Chuquicamata pitted the aging brothers against the youthful and dynamic Harry Guggenheim, who had been the driving force in both the development of Chuquicamata and the exploration of the possibilities in nitrates. Soon after the sale of Chuquicamata was finalized, Harry and Edmond both withdrew from the firm.[48]

The Guggenheims also faced resistance to the nitrate venture from their financial backers. Efforts to induce J. P. Morgan and Company to take a larger share of the nitrate investment were rejected. The Morgan interests were concerned about weak prices for nitrates and the long-term prospects of working closely with a Latin American government. Those concerns led them to cancel their joint account with the Guggenheims in 1924.[49]

Despite these warning signs, the Guggenheim plunge into nitrates should not be perceived as the short-sighted investment strategy or fool-hardy risk-taking of a few old men who managed their company in increasing isolation. Harry Guggenheim, for all his anger over the sale of Chuquicamata, had been and remained an ardent advocate of the nitrate venture. As he had explained on more than one occasion, the Guggenheim nitrate investment was based on two premises: first, that their new process and the consolidation of the industry's production facilities would significantly reduce the cost of production; and second, that the Chilean government could be induced to lower or eliminate the nitrate export duty. The first assumption had been proven out in Cappelen-Smith's laboratory. As for the second premise, calls for reform of the export duty had grown since the turn of the century, and the Chilean government's support of the Nitrate Producers Association made clear its awareness of the need to ensure the industry's survival.[50]

In 1923 the prospect of reducing nitrate production costs by 25 percent was in itself a sufficient inducement to invest. At that time, the Nitrate Producers Association was still maintaining some of the highest price levels for their product in the industry's history. As Table 3 indicates, efficient Shanks producers in 1923 could expect a return of $11.02 per ton as interest on their investment and profit. Profits for such producers were reported to be in the 30 percent range. The Guggenheims could expect a return of $16.22 per ton under their system if 1923 conditions held.

Such projections not only encouraged the Guggenheims to invest; they also set off what has been termed the "nitrogen rush," a scramble by

*Table 3* Nitrate cost/price differentials 1923 (U.S. $ per ton)

| Costs[a] | Shank process | Guggenheim process (projected) |
|---|---|---|
| Refinery stage | $12.96 | $ 7.76[b] |
| Shipping | 6.22 | 6.22 |
| Export duty | 11.19 | 11.19 |
| Port costs | 2.52 | 2.52 |
| Total | 32.89 | 27.69 |
| F.A.S. price | 43.91 | 43.91 |
| Differential | 11.02 | 16.22 |

*Sources:* H. Foster Bain and H.S. Muliken, *Nitrogen Survey Part I, The Cost of Chilean Nitrate*, Bureau of Foreign and Domestic Commerce, Trade Information Bulletin No. 170 (Washington, D.C., 1923), 3–4; Stocking and Watkins, *Cartels*, 133–35; "Report on Compania de Salitre de Chile," prepared by Division of Latin American Affairs, Department of State, 16 Sept. 1932, General Records of the Department of State, Record Group 59, 825.6374/1054, National Archives, Washington, D.C. [cited hereafter as "Cosach Report"], 27–28.
[a]Does not include return on capital.
[b]This figure is based on the estimated 25 percent reduction in production costs achieved by the Guggenheim process. In 1932 the two Guggenheim refineries reported actual production costs of $7.00 and $8.00 per ton.

synthetic producers to expand output that led to a tripling of world productive capacity between 1922 and 1931 (see Table 2). Thus the Guggenheims were neither deluded nor alone in envisioning the possibility of windfall profits in the world nitrogen market of the 1920s. The competitive challenge from synthetic producers was one that they had to weigh carefully in considering their nitrate investments.

It is not clear what figures the Guggenheims used to project their competitive position as they prepared to invest in nitrates in 1923, but Table 4 offers some insight based on actual results. As the table makes clear, the Guggenheim process offered the prospect of windfall returns if the controlled prices of 1923 were maintained. Even decontrol, which in fact occurred in 1927, promised substantial gains. Should prices continue to plummet, relief from the export duty could ensure a profitable return on the order of that achieved by Shanks producers in 1923. The Guggenheim process also appeared competitive with nitrate substitutes in 1923, and it could even deal with significant price reductions for substitutes if the export duty were abolished. If the Guggenheims had projected a worst-case scenario for the industry—and so unwittingly glimpsed the future—they would nevertheless have judged the project salvageable, assuming government cooperation. And government cooperation had been a basic goal in their nitrate plans at least since 1919. It is also highly unlikely that the Guggenheims seriously expected to operate in a free market environment over the long term. Controlled prices had been the norm rather than the

*Table 4*  Guggenheim process estimated cost–competitive position
(U.S. $ per ton)

| Year | F.A.S.[a] price | Guggenheim process F.A.S. cost[ab] with / without export duty | Sulphate of ammonia/ synthetic nitrogen relative price[c] |
|---|---|---|---|
| 1923 | $43.91 | $27.69 / $16.50 | $47.01 / $34.35 |
| 1927 | 42.59 | 27.69 / 16.50 | 40.29 |
| 1928 | 37.18 | 27.69 / 16.50 | 39.78 |
| 1929 | 36.78 | 27.69 / 16.50 | 26.77 |
| 1930 | 34.20 | 27.69 / 16.50 | 29.69 |
| 1931 | 28.82 | 27.69 / 16.50 | 22.28 / 20.17 |

*Sources:* Stocking and Watkins, *Cartels*, 123, 165; R.M. Palmer to T.W. Delahanty, New York, 9 Nov. 1927, Records of Bureau of Foreign And Domestic Commerce, Record Group 151, Chile #235; "Cosach Report," 14–15, 27–28; Bain and Muliken, *Nitrogen Survey*, 3–4.
[a]F.A.S. cost and prices at Chilean ports.
[b]The cost of Guggenheim process nitrate is assumed to be constant. In fact, an annual domestic inflation rate of 3 percent, and a steady exchange rate may have been more than offset by increased economies of scale due to the consolidation of the industry, see for example, the evidence in Table 3, note b.
[c]Direct price comparisons between Chilean nitrate and competing products were not possible since each had a different nitrogen content. Relative price differences expressed as a percentage were applied to the f.a.s. price of the Chilean product to arrive at an artificial price for competing products in order to provide a clear indication of the competitive position of Chilean nitrates.

exception in the industry's history. Control of the industry in Europe was also becoming highly concentrated through ownership or cartelization. With Chile, Germany, and England controlling 88 percent of the world's nitrogen output, the prospects for an international cartel seemed excellent.[51] Decreased production costs in both Chile and Europe would enable such a cartel to lower world nitrogen prices and still enjoy the profits garnered in 1923. Prospects such as these undoubtedly fed Daniel Guggenheim's vision of unlimited wealth.

In September 1924 the brothers bought a 35-square-mile tract of nitrate land and began constructing a refinery named María Elena that incorporated their new technology. The following year they purchased the Anglo-Chilean Nitrate and Railway Company, adding three refineries, a railroad, and port facilities to their holdings. Finally, in June 1929, they acquired the Lautaro Nitrate Company, the most important nitrate producer in Chile. The purchase of the additional properties derived in part from the realization that larger-scale production would be required to achieve the economies of scale envisioned for the Guggenheim process. Cappelen-Smith found that he had to double the size of the María Elena plant to achieve the economies of scale that he had forecast. Additional nitrate lands would be required to feed the giant refinery.[52] The acquisitions also contributed to the longer-term goal of a complete consolidation of the industry. The Guggenheims now controlled approximately one-half of the industry's total output. The power of the New York and London financial markets and the deteriorating condition of the nitrate industry made this rapid expansion possible.

The influence of the financial markets is illustrated by the manner in which the Guggenheims acquired nitrate properties and companies. The purchase of the Anglo-Chilean was financed through two bond issues. The first, a sterling issue equivalent to about $17.5 million, financed the purchase of the company. A second dollar issue for $16.5 million covered the purchase price of the nitrate tract and the initial costs for the construction of the María Elena. Eventually the Guggenheims had to finance advances of an additional $27 million to Anglo-Chilean, over half of which went to cover the unexpectedly high costs of bringing the María Elena on line. Their purchase of the Lautaro Company was handled by Lehman Brothers, and although a complicated swap of Anglo-Chilean for Lautaro stock makes it difficult to determine the exact purchase price of the firm, it was on the order of $40 million. In addition, a $32 million bond issue was floated by the National City Bank to finance the construction of a Guggenheim plant for the Lautaro Company. In sum, capital markets, particularly those in New York, provided $130 million in financing for the Guggenheims' initial nitrate ventures.[53]

At the same time, the deteriorating position of Chilean nitrates in the world market made many producers anxious to sell. It also provided the Guggenheims with a covert ally, the Anglo-South American Bank. Since the turn of the century, this British institution had taken the lead in financing the industry, committing $50 million, or over one-third of all its advances, to nitrates. Desperate to salvage this investment in a disintegrating industry, the bank secretly assisted the Guggenheims in their takeover bid.[54] On the other hand, Chile's president Carlos Ibañez was wary of the Guggenheim colossus.

Ibañez resented what he felt were the high-handed methods of the Guggenheims, particularly their refusal to cooperate with other producers in a government-sponsored marketing agency designed to halt the decline of the natural nitrate industry. To pressure the Guggenheims, Ibañez threatened the U.S. copper companies with an import duty on fuel, while letting it be known that the problem could be solved if the Guggenheims cooperated on the nitrate marketing issue. The Guggenheims, who still held important investments in Chilean copper, got the message and sent Cappelen-Smith and another representative, Edward Savage, to Chile to negotiate a solution.[55] As an American ambassador concluded:

The presence at this time in Santiago of Mr. Savage and Mr. Cappelen

Smith would seem to indicate that the Guggenheims have gotten over the practice of sitting comfortably in New York and endeavoring to tell the Chilean Government by cable what it is to do in nitrates. If they want to do business here they must meet this government as equals and recognize and respect the Chilean point of view.[56]

And in fact Ibañez and the Guggenheim brothers were soon working closely together for several good reasons.

President-elect Herbert Hoover visited Chile in December 1928 and suggested to the Chilean government and the Guggenheims that the nitrate industry be consolidated and converted into a joint enterprise between the government and the Guggenheims with each side controlling 50 percent. Hoover's suggestion was remarkably similar to the industry-wide monopoly with government participation that the Guggenheims had envisioned since 1919. Harry Guggenheim was a friend of Hoover and one of his earliest backers in the race for the presidency. As early as 1921 Hoover had attempted to facilitate the development of harmonious relations between the Chilean government and the Guggenheims. Clearly the president-elect did not make his suggestion to the Chilean government without prior consultation with the Guggenheims. As secretary of commerce, Hoover had pursued a firm policy against monopolies or combinations that controlled raw materials essential to the U.S. economy, particularly when those combinations involved foreign governments. He had energetically sought to dissuade U.S. financial institutions from making loans to such monopolies, including the Nitrate Producers Association. Hoover's change of policy in the case of nitrates was almost certainly related to the fact that under the Guggenheims, nitrates would no longer be a foreign-controlled monopoly. Yet Hoover's earlier actions against the Nitrate Producers Association would have given Ibañez food for thought. With American banks becoming the principal source of Chile's desperately needed government loans, Ibañez was certain to listen attentively to Hoover's suggestions. The dependence on U.S. loans was in turn a reflection of the nitrate industry's disintegration.[57]

As the 1920s came to a close, the natural nitrate industry was being driven to the wall by competition from synthetic products. With the cost of the natural product running 30 percent higher than its principal synthetic rival, the Chilean share of the world market had fallen from a prewar 58 percent to 24 percent. Employment in the industry had fallen to less than 36,000, and nitrates could supply only 15 percent of government revenues. With the natural nitrate industry on the verge of collapse, the Guggenheims' production process and their plans for consolidating the industry appeared to be the government's only solution.[58] For the Guggenheims, government cooperation would thrust aside continuing resistance by British and Chilean producers and middlemen to the creation of their long-dreamed-of monopoly and would make possible the abolition of the nitrate export tax.

This convergence of interests led to the formation of the Compañía de Salitre de Chile (Cosach) in March 1931. Cosach was a joint venture between the Chilean government and private producers, with each side controlling 50 percent of the stock. However, only four of the company's twelve directors were government representatives, giving the Guggenheims effective management control of the company. The corporation would control all production and sales of natural nitrate. In return for the government's elimination of the nitrate export duty, Cosach was committed to make cash payments to the government totaling over $80 million through 1933. After that time, the Chilean treasury would receive 50 percent of the company's profits.[59]

At the time of its creation Cosach appeared to be a monument to the finance capital genius of the Guggenheims. The company issued stock with a face value of $375 million. Most of the stock was distributed to private producers for their refineries and land and to the government for its nitrate tracts. On the private side, Guggenheim and supporting American interests received $92 million in stocks and bonds, British interests $87 million. The Guggenheims opted for common stock, which, though representing a higher risk, gave them real control over the private half of the company. The British settled for preference shares and bonds with a guaranteed return but little power. Whether common or preferred, the shares' nominal value represented a generous return on nitrate investments.

All sides in the bargain—private interests, both foreign and domestic, and the Chilean government—grossly exaggerated the value of their contributions. For example, the purchase price for both private and public nitrate lands was equivalent to prices paid for such tracts between 1901 and 1918 when the industry was at the height of its prosperity.[60] Cosach was an edifice cracking beneath a crushing load of debt imposed by its builders, who received stock and bond values far in excess of the real value of property and services provided.

Even this generous distribution of inflated stock did not satisfy all the parties involved. Since the Cosach stock distribution was limited to companies that owned refineries, firms that held only undeveloped nitrate land stood to lose their entire investment. The once-mighty Gibbs house watched with growing anxiety as the Guggenheims assembled their nitrate juggernaut. If its interest in marketing nitrate and its multimillion-dollar investment in nitrate land were to be salvaged, Gibbs had to reach some agreement with the Guggenheims. In June 1929 Lord Cullen, the head of Gibbs, had an interview in London with Cappelen-Smith, who still held out the prospect of cooperation but expressed regret that Gibbs had not joined them in 1919. As the months passed with no firm offer from the Guggenheim engineer, the Gibbs senior partner made frequent and even desperate attempts to contact him. Cappelen-Smith finally informed Lord Cullen that the Guggenheims had no interest in the Gibbs lands. Cullen hastened to remind the engineer of the favors Gibbs had once done the Guggenheims, particularly the report on the nitrate industry. To this Cappelen-Smith replied that there were innumerable holders of undeveloped nitrate grounds like Gibbs; to bring them into an arrangement would overburden the planned nitrate trust.[61]

As Cosach moved closer to reality, the Gibbs partners tried every weapon at their command to make a forced entry. They appealed to the Foreign Office. However, Foreign Office officials reasoned that, since British nitrate companies would receive stock in Cosach and most of the marketing and insuring of nitrate would still occur in London, general British economic interests were not at risk. Gibbs appealed to leading British bankers, who took their case to the Chilean government, but by then the Ibañez regime was fully committed to the Guggenheims and their plans. Eventually Gibbs, once the dominant power in nitrates, had to write off millions of dollars in nitrate land and settle for a share in the Cosach nitrate insurance business, crumbs from the sumptuous table the Guggenheims were setting.[62]

Despite the burdensome debt represented by inflated stock, Cosach's initial prospects were good. Watered stock was nothing new in the age of financial capital; ASARCO had been built on the same device and had prospered under Guggenheim control. Moreover, the performance of the nitrate industry under the Guggenheims was impressive. Where seventy companies had operated ninety-six refineries in 1925, in 1932 one firm with eleven refineries now stood. The number of workers had been reduced to 8,000 and output per worker increased by 100 percent. Heading a revamped and consolidated natural nitrate industry, the Guggenheims would be in a strong position to bargain with synthetic producers on questions of markets and prices. The announcement of Cosach's formation in May 1930 visibly strengthened the hand of the Chilean government, which was negotiating a cartel agreement with European producers. In August the International Nitrogen Cartel was formed, renewing hopes of stable prices.[63]

Cosach was, however, a corporation without working capital. Its $375 million in stock was payment to the government and private producers for the assets they contributed to Cosach. At its birth, Cosach had only one functioning Guggenheim refinery. Money was needed to complete a second, build a third, and to cover operating expenses.

Table 5 outlines the financial structure of Cosach, which included common and preferred stock issued to producers and to the government, bonds of its constituent companies, which had been guaranteed by Cosach, and authorizations for bond flotations to meet the need for working capital. In 1931 the company had fixed interest-bearing obligations that amounted

*Table 5* Cosach financial structure (in millions)

| | |
|---|---|
| Preferred shares | $ 62.5 |
| Common shares | 213.5 |
| Outstanding bonds | 77.0 |
| Authorized bond issues | 142.0 |
| Total | $594.0 |

*Sources:* Harvey O'Connor, *The Guggenheims: The Making of An American Dynasty* (1937; rpt., New York, 1976), 453; Stocking and Watkins, *Cartels*, 137; "Cosach Report," 34, 40.

to $194 million, carrying an annual interest charge of $12 million. In addition, the corporation was committed to the series of cash payments to the Chilean government, which totaled $22 million in 1931. Projected revenues to cover these payments were based on sales of 2 million tons of nitrate at a price of $35.00 per ton.[64] Table 4 indicates that this price would have left $18.50 per ton as net revenues after allowing for production and transportation costs. On sales of 2 million tons this would have generated $37 million to cover interest obligations and cash payments to the government totaling $34 million. Such a projection was extremely optimistic, since it was based on the selling price of nitrate in May 1930, when nitrate prices had been declining since 1927. Actual sales in 1931 were 1.6 million tons at $25.57, generating approximately $14.5 million in revenues to meet the fixed obligations of the corporation.[65]

The company was also based on the assumption that the Guggenheims could raise $110 million in bond flotations for working capital. The Great Depression gave the lie to this assumption as well, for the Guggenheims could raise only $34 million in 1931. In a desperate effort to stimulate interest in the Cosach bonds, the Chilean government announced a $7.30 per ton tax on nitrates, which would be used to service the bonds. The effect of the announcement was to convince investors that the competitive position of Cosach was being undermined. The Depression ignited bitter disputes in the International Nitrogen Cartel, which failed to renew its agreement in July 1931. During the first month of the ensuing price war, prices for nitrogen fell by 50 percent in some markets.[66] Moreover, the Depression helped topple the Guggenheims' partner Carlos Ibañez in 1931. After a period of internal turmoil, a new civilian government was elected in 1932. The new government's finance minister, Gustavo Ross, soon began grappling with the problem of Cosach's crumbling financial structure.

The policy of the new government toward Cosach was shaped in part by domestic forces. Workers were outraged that the nitrate labor force had been reduced from 36,000 to 8,000, and even this reduced contingent was working less than the customary six-day week. Chilean middlemen had supplied food, tools, and other goods to the industry and speculated in nitrate sales. Cosach effectively circumvented this group when it consolidated supply services and centered them overseas and took total control of nitrate sales as well. These developments also enraged landowners for whom the industry had once provided a prosperous domestic market.[67] The new finance minister thus faced widespread popular demands for a dismantling of Cosach.

In addition to political pressures, the Chilean minister of finance also had to come to grips with the Cosach financial crisis. It was clear that with the collapse of world nitrogen sales and prices, the corporation could do little more than cover production costs and perhaps service its fixed-interest obligations. Payments to the government, dividends, or new bond flotations were out of the question. Gustavo Ross had concluded that if anything was to be salvaged from nitrates, Cosach must be relieved of the enormous debt represented by its capitalization structure. Unfortunately, the two largest groups of stockholders were citizens of the world's two most powerful nations. Nevertheless, on 2 January 1933, Ross issued a government decree liquidating Cosach. A game of divide and conquer had begun.[68]

Ross's plan called for the dissolution of Cosach and the formation of a nitrate sales monopoly controlled jointly by the government and the Guggenheims. Production would fall into the hands of the Anglo-Chilean Consolidated Corporation and the Lautaro Company—the two Guggenheim enterprises. Ross's solution to Cosach's debt structure was to let the unsecured stock and bonds be absorbed by their owners and to abolish the production charge that secured Cosach's bonds. The preferred bonds, about $32 million, would be paid off with profits from the sales monopoly. Since the Guggenheims' holdings were mostly unsecured and those of the British mostly secured, Ross's plan pitted American and British interests against one another. The beleaguered Guggenheim brothers called on the services of Medley Whelpley, the 38-year-old president of the American Express Bank, to protect their interests in what was becoming a bitter struggle over the dismemberment of Cosach.

Despite the acrimonious dispute between the two private interest groups, U.S. and British diplomats maintained coordinated pressure on Ross to ensure at least some return to their investors, including a reimposition of the production charge. As their correspondence indicates, British and American officials were engaged in a joint effort to prevent assaults on their investments by Latin American governments that found themselves in desperate financial circumstances as a result of the Depression. At the same time both public and private interests in the two countries recognized that they could not afford to push Chile to the point of total economic collapse and social upheaval.

Under these conditions, a modified version of the Ross plan was enacted in 1934. Under its terms, the Guggenheims got back their production facilities, while holders of preferred bonds accepted new, lower interest bonds. Those bonds would be paid out of the 75 percent of the sales monopoly's profits that went to the private sector, while the Chilean government received the other 25 percent. Some $44 million in bond values that did not fall into this preferred category were wiped out.[69] Ross's scheme survived because of its divide and conquer strategy, but its success was due to Chile's fragile economic condition. American and British interests could not afford to insist on the reimposition of the production charge and compensation for stocks and bonds at face value with the Chilean government tottering on the brink of financial collapse.

The Guggenheims were not impoverished by the failure of Cosach. They had many other investments, and they still owned the Braden mine and controlled a significant interest in Chuquicamata. Furthermore, most of the bond and stock values that shrank or disappeared were held not by the Guggenheims, but by the American investing public. In 1934 the International Nitrogen Cartel created a new agreement that helped stabilize and even increase prices during the 1930s. The Second World War revived the natural nitrate industry and filled the Guggenheim coffers with profits. After the war, iodine, a derivative product of nitrate, continued to pay them handsome returns.

Cosach neither enriched the Guggenheims beyond the dreams of avarice nor did it destroy them. Rather, its failure removed them from center stage of the financial world. Never again could they command hundreds of millions of dollars to flow forth from the stock and bond markets. The memory of the Cosach debacle would linger.[70]

## Conclusion

Perhaps Daniel Guggenheim—who died in 1930, before the Cosach failure laid waste his dreams of limitless wealth—would have found some moral to the story of the Guggenheims in Chile. But from a historical perspective, the tale is valuable because it crystallizes so many factors that shaped the development of American-based multinationals at the beginning of the twentieth century. It demonstrates several specific ways in which historical investigation can enhance theories of the MNE: by providing more sophisticated analysis of business-government relations and a better understanding of the sensitivity of technology and financing to time and location, and by demonstrating the need for a theory of the MNE based on more dynamic concepts of entrepreneurship and management.

The Guggenheims' experience suggests that business-government relationships play a far more complex and significant role than that suggested by economic theories of multinational enterprise. Business-government relations were a major determinant of foreign investment in both Mexico and Chile. From the outset, the Guggenheims factored in government policy as a critical variable in their nitrate venture. Differing perspectives on state policy influenced investment decisions not only by the Guggenheims, but also by the Gibbs house and the Morgan interests. For its part, the Chilean state welcomed the Guggenheim copper and nitrate investments, which promised to revive vital sectors of the national economy. The Guggenheims welcomed Chile's cheap labor supply and political stability. The realities of underdevelopment dictated that the Chilean government was the subordinate partner, needing the Guggenheims more than the Guggenheims needed Chile's natural resources. Even in its divide and conquer strategy on Cosach, the Chilean government faced a united front from the British and American governments. Yet the Chilean state was not a banana republic. It could and did tax copper, share a partnership in Cosach, and dissolve the corporation as well.

The interactions between the Guggenheims and the Chilean government are suggestive of Mark Casson's conceptualization of the state as a purveyor of services operating in a market situation.[71] Even in that context, however, the state was not an independent actor free to respond to market conditions. Its policies were influenced by pressure groups representing a broad spectrum of Chilean society, whose longstanding relationships with the nitrate industry had been disrupted by the Guggenheims' investments. The state's actions were significantly influenced by social groups who had in part been spawned, and were directly affected, by foreign direct investment. Theories of the MNE must, therefore, incorporate a more dyanamic concept of the nation-state, possibly as an actor within a market place, but an actor that is the target of internal social and political forces that are themselves sensitive to qualitative and quantitative changes in foreign direct investment.

Local conditions had an impact not only on government-business relations, but also on technological development. The Guggenheim ventures fit the pattern of current theoretical explanations of the emergence of the MNE: a firm in an industry with rapidly changing technology seeks to exploit advantages of proprietary technology and knowledge and to avoid market imperfection for such intermediate products. Beyond this confirmation of current theory, the Guggenheims' experience demonstrates the need for historians to explore the time and location sensitivity of technological change. The level of American mining technology and its skill simplification effects had specific applicability to the labor market conditions prevailing in Mexico and Chile, where that technology could be matched with an abundance of semiskilled, low-cost labor. Events in the nitrate industry also indicate that inexpensive labor and oligopoly conditions deterred efforts at technological renovation in established British enterprises.

Financing also proved to be a time-sensitive variable in the Guggenheims' operations. Their initial success abroad illustrates the power of American capital markets; the New York financial market made possible the enormous investments necessary to transform mining in Latin America. Yet the ability to raise capital that gave the Guggenheims competitive advantages over both local and other foreign competitors was also time-sensitive. The Guggenheims' early ventures reflected the spectacular growth in the U.S. industrial securities market during the 1890s. But as their original nitrate syndicate with J. P. Morgan indicates, that market was still dominated by banks, insurance companies, and the wealthy. By the 1920s the emergence of a mass market for securities allowed the Guggenheims to proceed with their nitrate investments despite Morgan's withdrawal.[72] Eventually, their nitrate endeavor was predicated on the assumption that the Guggenheims could tap that market to create Cosach, the ultimate expression of both the strengths and the weaknesses of the entrepreneurial and managerial aspects of the Guggenheim empire.

This study of the Guggenheims provides new evidence that theories in which entrepreneurship and management are reduced to static elements cannot satisfactorily explain the evolution of the multinational enterprise. The Guggenheims in their most dynamic years demonstrated exceptional entrepreneurial skills. Their exploitation of technological breakthroughs and new sources of financing, combined with decisions on where these advantages could be most successfully developed, built a worldwide mining empire at the turn of the century. At the time, those entrepreneurial functions were effectively carried out within a family partnership structure. Later, that management structure showed signs of increasing rigidity, driving out new entrepreneurial talent. Certainly the outcome of the nitrate enterprise—heavy short-term losses with only a gradual long-term trend toward profitability—seems to speak ill of the Guggenheims' managerial system. Management rigidity was an increasing problem as the brothers bickered among themselves and finally drove the two younger partners out of the firm.

Yet if Harry, the most dynamic member of the Guggenheim inner circle, had stayed, he probably would have backed the nitrate venture with the proviso that the firm find a financing mechanism other than the sale of Chuquicamata. Harry had been an ardent advocate of the nitrate investment because its reasoning and projections were sound. The venture was built on a refining process and plans for industry consolidation that could substantially reduce production costs. Significant price declines would leave Chilean nitrate still competitive, and the Guggenheims could call on the government to abolish the nitrate duty—a step that had been part of their master plan from the beginning. The brothers undoubtedly intended to use the revamped nitrate industry to achieve a strong bargaining position in the creation of the international nitrogen cartel that was being formed at the same time as Cosach. The worst possible outcome of a joint nitrate venture with the Chilean government appeared to be modest rather than spectacular returns.

The Guggenheims were eventually undone in the Cosach venture by the enormous debt incurred in buying out private producers and the Chilean government and by the Great Depression. Heavily burdened with debt, Cosach quickly crumbled as the Depression sent nitrate prices into a tailspin, dried up credit sources in New York, and shattered the International Nitrogen Cartel. The Guggenheims' increasingly rigid management failed to anticipate the level of debt that the consolidation scheme would incur, making it a high-risk endeavor, and further increased that risk by overcommitment to a single industry. This flaw in the management process made the Guggenheims vulnerable to a factor that they could not reasonably have anticipated: the ferocity of the Depression, which would destroy their efforts to finance the project.[73] That outcome points to the need for a better understanding of the dynamic between entrepreneurship and organizational structure in the development of the MNE.

The Guggenheims' experience reaffirms the need for theorists to incorporate entrepreneurship and organizational structure into their work as dynamic variables and raises interesting questions about the impact of organizational change on the evolution of the multinational enterprise. Finally, this study of the Guggenheims' ventures in Latin America demonstrates that the relationship between theory and history remains a dynamic and creative one.

## Notes

1. This discussion of theory and history is based largely on Peter Hertner and Geoffrey Jones, "Multinationals: Theory and History," and Mark Casson, "General Theories of the Multinational Enterprise: Their Relevance to Business History," in *Multinationals: Theory and History,* ed. Peter Hertner and Geoffrey Jones (Brookfield, Vt., 1986), 1–18, 42–63. For a concise summary of theories of FDI, see Robert Grosse, "The Theory of Foreign Direct Investment," *University of South Carolina Essays in International Business* 3 (Dec. 1981): 10–27.
2. Hertner and Jones, "Theory and History," 5.
3. Casson, "General Theories," 53.
4. Mira Wilkins, *The Maturing of Multinational Enterprise: American Business Abroad From 1914 to 1970* (Cambridge, Mass., 1974), 4; J. Fred Rippy, *Globe and Hemisphere: Latin America's Place in the Postwar Foreign Relations of the United States* (Chicago, 1958), 36–38.
5. The Guggenheims' empire came to include smelters, mines and refineries for lead, silver, copper, nitrates, and tin in the continental United States, Alaska, British Columbia, Mexico, Peru, Chile, the Belgian Congo, and Southeast Asia, as well as diamond and rubber interests in the Congo. By 1923 their far-flung interests had already created a family fortune that was conservatively estimated at $200 million. See Edwin P. Hoyt, Jr., *The Guggenheims and the American Dream* (New York, 1967), 149–51, 191; and Harvey O'Connor, *The Guggenheims: The Making of an*

*American Dynasty* (1937; rpt., New York, 1976), 422.

6. Hoyt, *American Dream*, 17–37.

7. Ibid., 57.

8. Harold Barger and Sam H. Schurr, *The Mining Industries, 1899–1939: A Study of Output, Employment, and Productivity* (1944; rpt., New York, 1975), 101–6; O'Connor, *Guggenheims*, 56–57.

9. W. H. Dennis, *A Hundred Years of Metallurgy* (Chicago, 1964), 57–133.

10. O'Connor, *Guggenheims*, 71–76; Hoyt, *American Dream*, 64, 68, 76.

11. Thomas R. Navin, *Copper Mining and Management* (Tucson, Ariz., 1978), 52–53; David M. Gordon, Richard Edwards, and Michael Reich, *Segmented Work, Divided Workers: The Historical Transformation of Labor in the United States* (New York, 1982), 12.

12. Marvin D. Bernstein, *The Mexican Mining Industry, 1890–1900: A Study of the Interaction of Politics, Economics, and Technology* (Albany, N.Y., 1965), 50–56; James D. Cockcroft, *Intellectual Precursors of the Mexican Revolution, 1900–1913* (Austin, Texas, 1968), 18–19; John Mason Hart, *Revolutionary Mexico: The Coming and Process of the Mexican Revolution* (Berkeley, Calif., 1987), 142.

13. O'Connor, *Guggenheims*, 93.

14. Hoyt, *American Dream*, 91–92, 103–5; O'Connor, *Guggenheims*, 85–99.

15. O'Connor, *Guggenheims*, 101–17.

16. Hoyt, *American Dream*, 119–22.

17. Barger and Schurr, *Mining*, 110, 224.

18. Porphyry ores are igneous rock formations that contain copper sulfate. The copper content of the ores varies from 1 to 2 percent for mines in Chile and Peru, to 0.4 to 0.8 percent in the southwestern United States and northern Mexico; see Raymond F. Mikesell, *The World Copper Industry: Structure and Economic Analysis* (Baltimore, Md., 1979), 47.

19. Barger and Schurr, *Mining*, 108–9, 137, 152–55.

20. Navin, *Metallurgy*, 45–47.

21. Hoyt, *American Dream*, 143–61, 187–97.

22. The Madero family was the only group of Mexican entrepreneurs who attempted to operate a fully integrated mining operation in direct competition with the Guggenheims and other foreign interests. See Hart, *Revolutionary Mexico*, 142.

23. Clark Winton Reynolds, "The Development Problems of an Export Economy: The Case of Chile and Copper," in Markos Mamalakis and Clark Winton Reynolds, *Essays on The Chilean Economy* (Homewood, Ill., 1965), 210–13; Joanne Fox Przeworski, "The Entrance of North American Capital in the Chilean Copper Industry and the Role of Government, 1904–1916," *Atti del XL Congresso Internazionale degli Americanisti* (Rome, 3–10 Sept., 1972), 398; Markos J. Mamalakis, *The Growth and Structure of the Chilean Economy from Independence to Allende* (New Haven, Conn., 1976), 40–41.

24. Paul H. Douglas, *Real Wages in the United States, 1890–1926* (New York, 1930), 182; U.S. Consul George D. Hopper, "Social and Labor Conditions in the Four Great American Mining Camps in the Antofagasta District," Antofagasta, 24 Sept. 1926, Records of the Foreign Service Posts of the Department of State, Record Group 84, National Archives, Washington, D.C. [cited hereafter as RG 84].

25. At the time the Guggenheims made their investment, it was estimated that Chuquicamata contained 300 million tons of 2.23 percent copper ore; see O'Connor, *Guggenheims*, 347.

26. Ibid., 346–50.

27. C. Van H. Engert, chargé d'affaires to secretary of state, Santiago, 27 Oct. 1926, RG 84, Przeworski, "Chilean Copper," 397–401; Theodore H. Moran,

*Multinational Corporations and the Politics of Dependence: Copper in Chile* (Princeton, N.J., 1974), 22–23; Reynolds, "Chile and Copper," 221; Orris C. Herfindahl, *Copper Costs and Prices: 1870–1957* (Baltimore, Md., 1960), 174; Harry F. Bain and Thomas T. Read, *Ores and Industry in South America* (New York, 1934), 220.

28. On British investment in Chile, see Harold Blakemore, *British Nitrates and Chilean Politics, 1886–1896: Balmaceda and North* (London, 1974); John Mayo, *British Merchants and Chilean Development, 1851–1886* (Boulder, Colo., 1987); Juan Ricardo Couyoumdjian, *Chile y Gran Bretaña durante la Primera Guerra Mundial y la postguerra, 1914–1921* (Santiago, 1986); Michael Monteón, *Chile in the Nitrate Era: The Evolution of Economic Dependence, 1880–1930* (Madison, Wis., 1982).

29. Chile, Ministerio de Hacienda, Sección Salitrera, *Antecedentes sobre la industria salitrera* (Santiago, 1925), 9, 21; Engert to secretary of state, 13 Oct., 1926, RG 84; Ricardo Couyoumdjian, "El mercado del salitre durante la Primera Guerra Mundial y la postguerra, 1914–1921, notas para su estudio," *Historia* 12 (1974): 47–49.

30. The nitrate content of caliche had fallen from 42 percent in 1890 to 20 percent in 1910; see Ministerio de Hacienda, *Industria salitrera*, 8.

31. U.S. Vice-Consul Richard P. Butrick, "Chilean Nitrate Producers Association, a Trust Inimical to American Interests," Iquique, 9 Dec. 1922, RG 84; U.S. Ambassador William Miller Collier to secretary of state, Santiago, 16 Feb. 1925, RG 84; Ministerio de Hacienda, *Industria salitrera*, 57.

32. U.S. Consul Homer Brett, "Nitrate Industry of Tarapaca Province, Chile," Iquique, 11 Jan. 1922, RG 84.

33. R. J. Brown, "Nitrate Crises, Combinations, and the Chilean Government in the Nitrate Age," *Hispanic American Historical Review* 43 (May 1963): 233–43. That twelve of the industry's seventy-three companies accounted for 55 percent of its productive capacity in 1925 is indicative of the degree of concentration in the industry. See U.S. Consul General C. T. Deichman to U.S. military attaché Col. James Hanson, Valparaiso, 23 April 1925, RG 84.

34. Hopper, "The Labor Perspective in Chile," Antofagasta, 3 March 1926, RG 84; U.S. Consul Stewart E. McMillan, "A Brief Review for 1924 of the Nitrate Industry in the Antofagasta Consular District," Antofagasta, 27–28 Jan. 1925, RG 84; Arthur Lawrence Stickell, "Migration and Mining: Labor in Northern Chile in the Nitrate Era, 1880–1930" (Ph.D. diss., Indiana University, 1979), 60.

35. The principal use for sodium nitrate in peacetime was as a fertilizer. Eighty percent of Europe's imports before the war were for that purpose, with only 20 percent going to explosives. The war dramatically increased demands in the explosives industry. In the United States, where 40 percent of prewar nitrate imports went to explosives, the figure jumped to 62 percent with the outbreak of the conflict; see "Latin American Bulletin #1," Records of the War Trade Board, Washington National Records Center, Suitland, Md., Record Group 182.

36. Stickell, "Migration and Mining," 310.

37. H. Foster Bain and H. S. Muliken, *Nitrogen Survey Part I, the Cost of Chilean Nitrate*, Bureau of Foreign and Domestic Commerce, Trade Information Bulletin No. 170 (Washington, D.C., 1923), 20; Stickell, "Migration and Mining," 340; E. Semper and E. Michels, *La industria del salitre en Chile*, trans. and aug. Javier Gandarillas and Orlando Ghigliotto Salas (Santiago, 1908), 69.

38. Bain and Muliken, *Nitrogen Survey*, 12–14; U.S. Consul George A. Makinson, "The Cost of Producing Nitrate in Chile," Valparaiso, 8 Oct. 1923, RG 84.

39. Hopper, "Labor Perspective."

40. William P. Glade, *The Latin American Economics: A Study of Their Institutional Evolution* (New York, 1969), 364.

41. George W. Stocking and Myron W. Watkins, *Cartels in Action: Case Studies in International Business Diplomacy* (New York, 1946), 125–31; Ministerio de Hacienda, *Industria salitrera*, 65.

42. On the Guggenheim-Morgan nitrate syndicate, see O'Connor, *Guggenheims*, 411–13, 417–18; on the history of the Gibbs firm see Wilfred Maude, *Antony Gibbs & Sons Ltd.: Merchants and Bankers, 1808–1958* (London, 1958); on its nineteenth-century nitrate enterprises, see Thomas F. O'Brien, *The Nitrate Industry and Chile's Crucial Transition, 1870–1891* (New York, 1982), passim; on Gibbs's subsequent ventures, see Archives of Antony Gibbs and Sons, Guildhall Library, London, 11,470/23. 11,041/3, 11,115/1, 11,116/1/2 [hereafter cited as GMS].

43. "General Outline Report on the Chilean Nitrate Industry," copy enclosed in David Blair to Earl of Curzon, Santiago, 31 July 1919, Foreign Office Archives, Chile, 132/198, Public Record Office, London [cited hereafter as F.O.]; letter #180, Valparaiso, 25 July 1919, GMS 11,470/22; letter #278, London, 17 Sept. 1919, GMS 11,114/4; Herbert Gibbs to E. C. Grenfell, London, 24 July 1919 and Gibbs to Grenfell, London, 18, 26 Nov. 1919, GMS 11,041/3.

44. Letter #185, Valparaiso, 21 Aug. 1919, GMS 11,470/22.

45. Gibbs to Grenfell, London, 18 Nov. 1919.

46. Stickell, "Migration and Mining," 237; "Report on Compania de Salitre de Chile," prepared by Division of Latin American Affairs, Department of State, 16 Sept. 1932, General Records of the Department of State, Record Group 59,825.6374/1054, National Archives, Washington, D.C. [cited hereafter as "Cosach Report"], 27–28.

47. O'Connor, *Guggenheims*, 413–15; Hoyt, *American Dream*, 261; Reynolds, "Chile and Copper," 215–18.

48. Their presence would be sorely missed. One of their replacements, John K. McGowen, a long-time Guggenheim employee, would be ousted in 1929 in yet another policy dispute. The other, engineer Cappelen-Smith, would be unable to master the financial intricacies that became critical to the Guggenheim nitrate undertaking. O'Connor, *Guggenheims*, 145–46, 412–15, 455.

49. Ibid., 417.

50. Harry Guggenheim to Herbert Hoover, 5 Dec. 1921, Records of the Bureau of Foreign and Domestic Commerce, Record Group 151, National Archives, Washington, D.C. [cited hereafter as RG 151]; O'Connor, *Guggenheims*, 412; Ministerio de Hacienda, *Industria salitrera*, 102. A sign of Harry Guggenheim's continued faith in the nitrate venture was his insistence that he be given a share of the Morgan interests in the nitrate syndicate when Morgan withdrew in 1924; see O'Connor, *Guggenheims*, 417–18.

51. Stocking and Watkins, *Cartels*, 141–43.

52. O'Connor, *Guggenheims*, 418–19.

53. "Cosach Report," 20–27; Hoyt, *American Dream*, 285–86, 316.

54. David Joslin, *A Century of Banking in Latin America* (London, 1963), 266–68; letter #557, Valparaiso, 10 May 1928; letter #572, Valparaiso, 12 Sept. 1928, both GMS 11,470/28; letter #627, Valparaiso, 12 Nov. 1929; letter #657, Valparaiso, 10 July 1930, both GMS 11,470/29; letter #699, Valparaiso, 27 May 1931; letter #668, London, 24 June 1931, both GMS 16,882/31; Blair to Cullen, Valparaiso, 12 Sept. 1928, GMS 16,875/2.

55. U.S. Ambassador William S. Culbertson to secretary of state, Santiago, 12,

19 Dec. 1928; Culbertson to secretary of state, Santiago, 3 Jan. 1929, both RG 84.

56. Culbertson to secretary of state, Santiago, 3 Jan. 1929.

57. Harry Guggenheim to Hoover, 5 Dec. 1921; Hoyt, *American Dream*, 302; Joseph Brandes, *Herbert Hoover and Economic Diplomacy: Department of Commerce Policy, 1921–1928* (Pittsburgh, PA., 1962), 35–147; Rippy, *Globe and Hemisphere*, 54; P. T. Ellsworth, *Chile, an Economy in Transition* (New York, 1945), 9; Hoover to Frank B. Kellogg, Washington, 18 Oct. 1926, RG 84. The U.S. government's interest in a domestically controlled nitrogen source became clear in 1916 when the federal government expended $80 million to construct synthetic nitrogen plans at Muscle Shoals. The plants were not completed until 1919 and were then shut down as wartime demand subsided, only to be subsequently reopened and modernized. See Stocking and Watkins, *Cartels*, 132ff.

58. Ministerio de Hacienda, *Industria salitrera*, 21; "Cosach Report," 14–15, 27–28; Hoyt, *American Dream*, 315–18; Stickell, "Migration and Mining," 340.

59. "Cosach Report," 32–35, 83–84.

60. Ibid., 31–33, 41–42, 48–55.

61. Letter #615, Valparaiso, 6 Aug. 1929; letter #621, Valparaiso, 11 Oct. 1929; letter #627, Valparaiso, 12 Nov. 1929, all GMS 11,470/29; letter #652, Valparaiso, 12 June 1930, GMS 11,370/30; Cullen to Cappelen-Smith, London, 4 July 1929; Cullen to Cappelen-Smith, 23 Aug., 3 Oct. 1929, 12, 15 May 1930, all GMS 11,041/6.

62. David Blair to Walter Gibbs, Valparaiso, 31 March 1930, GMS 16,875/2; letter #652, London, 27 March 1931; letter #657, London, 22 April 1931; letter #662, London, 12 May 1931, letter #633, London, 19 May 1931, all GMS 16,882/30; letter #660, Valparaiso, 6 Aug. 1930, GMS 11,470/30.

63. Stickell, "Migration and Mining," 340; Stocking and Watkins, *Cartels*, 135–44; "Cosach Report," 18.

64. Cosach's $194 million in fixed obligations included $62.5 million of preference shares, $77 million in the bonds of constituent companies, $34 million in bonds raised by the Guggenheims in New York, and $21.4 million in bonds that the Chilean government accepted from Cosach in 1931 in lieu of the cash payment for 1932. The latter measure was one of the desperate efforts to reduce demands on the company's overtaxed revenues. "Cosach Report," 34, 40; Stocking and Watkins, *Cartels*, 137; O'Connor, *Guggenheims*, 453; "Economic and Financial Condition of Chile," by Raul Simon, May 1932, enclosed in Culbertson to secretary of state, Santiago, 6 June 1932, RG 84 [cited hereafter as "Financial Condition of Chile"].

65. "Financial Condition of Chile."

66. "Cosach Report," 33–34; Hoyt, *American Dream*, 316; Stocking and Watkins, *Cartels.* 143–44; C. C. Concannon to Edward B. Almon, Washington, D.C., 13 Feb. 1933, RG 151.

67. "Cosach Report," 42–47. The importance of the nitrate region to agriculturists derived from the fact that the nitrate region had constituted a population of nearly 250,000 people living in a desert region, and entirely dependent on outside sources for foodstuffs. Eighty-five percent of all agricultural products brought into the region came from Chile's Central Valley; see Carman Cariola and Osvaldo Sunkel, "The Growth of the Nitrate Industry and Socioeconomic Change in Chile, 1880–1930," in *The Latin American Economics: Growth and the Export Sector, 1880–1930*, ed. Roberto Cortés Conde and Shane J. Hunt (New York, 1985), 165.

68. Sir Henry Chilton to Sir John Simon, Santiago, 2, 3 Jan. 1933, F.O. 132/406.

69. Foreign Office to ambassador, London, 4 Jan. 1933; Chilton to Simon, Santiago, 19 Jan., 1 Feb. 1933. memorandum by Commercial Secretary A. J. Pack,

Santiago, 2 Feb. 1933; Chilton to Simon, Santiago, 9 Feb. and 1 March 1933; Chilton to Craigie, Santiago, 18 May 1933; Craigie to Chilton, Foreign Office, 6 June 1933, all F.O. 132/406; Culbertson to secretary of state, Santiago, 25 March, 1, 5 April 1933, RG 59, 825.6374/1132/1136/1138; Lawrence Duggan to Edwin C. Wilson, Washington, D.C., 23 May 1933, RG 59, 825.6374/1160; O'Connor, *Guggenheims*, 455.

70. John Hagy Davis, *The Guggenheims: An American Epic* (New York, 1978), 194–95; Stocking and Watkins, *Cartels*, 159–70.

71. Casson, "General Theories," 57–59.

72. Barbara Stallings, *Banker to the Third World: U.S. Portfolio Investment in Latin America, 1900–1986* (Berkeley, Calif., 1987), 198–207; Alfred D. Chandler, Jr., *The Visible Hand: The Managerial Revolution in American Business* (Cambridge, Mass., 1977), 331–33; Harold van B. Cleveland and Thomas F. Huertas, *Citibank, 1812–1970* (Cambridge, Mass., 1985), 135–39.

73. Even if the Guggenheims had chosen to remain exclusively in Chilean copper, the short-term effects of the Depression would have been devastating. The Braden and Chuquicamata mines, which had combined profits of $4.5 million in 1930, reported zero profits in 1931 and 1932; see Reynolds, "Chile and Copper," 383.

# 14

## Mineral Wealth and Economic Development: Foreign Direct Investment in Spain, 1851–1913[*1]

Charles Harvey and Peter Taylor

*Source: *Economic History Review*, XL (1987), pp. 185–207.

One of the more obvious consequences of European industrialization was a large and rapid increase in the demand for raw materials such as iron, lead, sulphur, copper, and mercury. Spain, with its rich reserves of all these minerals, was a natural source of supply for north European industry, and indeed during the latter part of the nineteenth century became one of the world's principal mining nations. Already by mid-century the lead mines and smelters of the southern provinces were of international importance, and over the next decade and a half Spain overhauled Britain to lead the world industry. Production of iron ore and pyrites (valued for its sulphur and copper) remained low until the boom of 1866–78. Thenceforth, the pyrites mines of Andalusia and the haematic iron ore quarries of the northern coast achieved equality, in terms of value of production, with the lead mines of the south. Between 1876 and 1900 Spain, with 23.5 per cent of the world's lead production and 16.8 per cent of its copper,[2] was at the forefront of two major world industries, and over the same period the nation produced more than 86 per cent of the iron ore and 90 per cent of the sulphur sold abroad by European countries.[3] Meanwhile, the fabled mines of Almadén regularly contributed over 40 per cent of world mercury output.[4] Only as the new century dawned was the continued prosperity of the Spanish mineral and metal export industries threatened. The end of the mining investment boom of 1895–1901 marked the beginning of a period of relative decline. Rates of growth of production began to slacken. New competitors emerged around the world, and, after a brief war-time flourish, the Spanish mining sector entered a period of absolute and protracted decline.

The evident prosperity of the mineral industries contrasts starkly with the general pattern of economic development in Spain during the second half of the nineteenth century. The pace of economic change was very slow indeed and only in Catalonia and the Basque provinces was a thorough-going industrial advance achieved.[5] It is not surprising, therefore, that minerals and metals accounted for a progressively higher proportion of Spanish exports. Indeed, an average annual growth rate of 3.8 per cent made mining the most vigorous of Spain's export sectors, to the extent that by the early twentieth century a full third of all exports came from mining.[6] The general pattern of mineral and metal exports is documented in Table 1, which revelas that between 1871 and 1913 the lead, iron and copper-pyrites industries contributed about equally to the Spanish mineral export boom.


# I


A superficial reading of the figures for production, employment, and trade might suggest that Spain was fortunate in having the mineral wealth to sustain a large export sector at a time when there were few other sources of national enrichment. Certainly, few industries could provide employment on a scale equal to that of the mineral extraction and smelting (a total of 135,244 people worked in the sector in 1911—71 per cent of them in the copper, lead, and iron industries).[7] It might also seem that the concomitant effects on the balance of payments and national income must have been great enough to justify designating the mineral industries a leading sector—one of the main sources of the limited economic growth that did occur in Spain.

However, many modern historians reject this view, asserting that the exploitation of Spain's mineral deposits benefited foreign capitalists far more than it did the Spanish economy. They see the mineral export boom as having been sponsored by British, French, and German businessmen who saw in Spain the answer to domestic shortages of metals and minerals, first in lead, then in sulphur and copper, and finally in iron. Foreign penetration of these industries, encouraged by the permissive legislation of successive Spanish governments, was consequently rife as overseas firms rushed in to buy up mineral rights and develop old and new mining properties. Thus, it is argued, the Spanish economy was plundered in true "colonial" fashion. Foreign firms, with the connivance of degenerate political élite, took from Spain precious assets of an irreplaceable nature. In doing so they earned fabulous profits, removing from the country the funds which might have promoted a more broadly based and rapid phase of national economic development. Positive development opportunities resulting from mineral sector growth were further restricted by the absence of substantial backward and forward economic linkages.

This critique of foreign direct investment in the Spanish mineral industries is not new. As early as 1891, the liberal-minded engineer Pablo de Alzola, a director of the pioneering iron and steel enterprise Altos

Table 1  Spanish exports, 1851–1913

| | Metals and minerals | | | | | Average total value of Spanish exports (m. pesetas) | Metal and mineral exports (% of total exports*) |
|---|---|---|---|---|---|---|---|
| | Average annual value (m. pesetas) | Pyrites, copper matte precipitate and bars (% of total) | Iron ore (% of total) | Lead bars (% of total) | Other metals and minerals including mercury (% of total) | | |
| 1851–1860 | 27.9 | n.a. | n.a. | n.a. | n.a. | 237.1 | 11.9 |
| 1861–1870 | 41.9 | n.a. | n.a. | n.a. | n.a. | 312.4 | 13.4 |
| 1871–1880 | 115.6 | 26 | 10 | 39 | 25 | 507.7 | 22.9 |
| 1881–1890 | 152.2 | 29 | 30 | 34 | 7 | 737.9 | 20.4 |
| 1891–1900 | 202.7 | 28 | 31 | 26 | 15 | 806.8 | 25.3 |
| 1901–1910 | 300.1 | 29 | 36 | 25 | 10 | 897.9 | 33.5 |
| 1911–1913 | 283.4 | 32 | 33 | 27 | 8 | 1,033.7 | 27.5 |
| 1871–1913 | 199.0 | 29 | 30 | 29 | 12 | 758.2 | 25.7 |

* Average of annual percentages.
Sources:  Cuadro General del Comercio de España (1851–55); Estadística General del Comercio Exterior de España (1956–1913).

Hornos de Vizcaya, complained that under the direction of "countries provided with capital, spirit of enterprise, and business ability" the Spanish mineral industries had failed to promote "the permanent good of the country", merely creating "a fugitive and ephemeral prosperity".[8] Such opinions found increasing favour amongst leaders of the Spanish business community, especially after defeat by the United States in the war of 1898. Thereafter, many saw the earnings of foreign mining ventures as a legitimate target for higher taxation.[9] Even the labour movement was infected by the rising tide of nationalism. Foreign mining companies were the target of vicious abuse and condemnation. A fairly typical pamphlet, circulating in 1913 in Huelva, declared that "the English burgess has entered this province, and with the cunning of a Carthaginian, the ambition of an American, and the arrogance of the British, threatens to rend it, gouging its flesh, sucking its blood, into slavery".[10]

The contemporary view that foreign interests dominated the mineral industries to the detriment of Spain has found plenty of support in recent times. Juan Muñoz Garciá and his collaborators, for instance, have shown that in 1909 more than 40 per cent of mining concessions were owned by foreigners,[11] whilst Nadal's estimates of mining investment indicate that in 1913 about half of the industry was owned abroad.[12] Many scholars, moreover, have claimed that mining was very profitable and that most of the profits went abroad because of the superior efficiency of foreign firms. González Portilla quotes figures of 40–5 per cent for the annual dividend payments of the British registered Orconera Co.,[13] and calculates that 46.8 per cent of all iron mining profits flowed overseas.[14] He admits that the Basque business community did quite well out of mineral exporting because its members had the sense in the early years to collaborate with foreign capitalists: retaining ownership of some mines whilst leasing others in return for royalty payments, engaging in joint ventures, and sharing transport and other facilities. However, in the case of copper-pyrites, foreign domination was more complete—regular annual dividend payments of 20 per cent for Tharsis and 70 per cent for Rio Tinto are quoted by Nadal.[15] It is argued that lead mining was in a very similar position by the end of the nineteenth century.[16] The upshot, according to Broder, was that, in copper and lead, "exploitations were mainly under foreign control" and "only wages and expenses for the maintenance of installations was returned to Spain—that is, between 20 and 25 per cent of the values accounted for by customs".[17] Harvey has calculated that after about 1897 just one-third of the sales revenue of the Rio Tinto Co. was retained in the country.[18] Thus the general conclusion is that only iron mining formed the basis for a genuine advance in the Spanish economy, and even here Basque industrialization might have proceeded more rapidly if all profits had been retained in Spain.[19]

Much modern scholarship has thus led to the verdict that Spanish policy-makers, unwittingly and unintelligently, made a "cardinal and ineradicable error" in allowing foreigners to exploit the nation's mineral riches directly. In the words of Clive Trebilcock:

> As the *conquistadores* had plundered the Inca cities for gold, the westerners plundered the Spanish interior for pyrites, lead and mercury.... Even if Spain lacked the entrepreneurs and risk capital for native exploitation of endowment, the role played by foreign capital was scarcely an effective substitute. Rather, foreign leverage worked to tip the economy into the lop-sided development produced in the colonial world by the ministrations of economic imperialism. Of all the European economies, Spain's was the most nearly colonized.[20]

The broad intention of this article is to examine critically the current orthodoxy regarding foreign direct investment in the Spanish mineral industries. Fresh evidence is presented from a survey of the general characteristics and financial histories of 174 British registered mining companies formed to operate in Spain between 1851 and 1913. The survey covers nearly all the lead (27), copper-pyrites (44), iron (56), and other (47) companies specifically formed to exploit concessions. Other forms of direct investment—corporate investment without a subsidiary or personal investment—are not covered, but such investments formed only a small part of total British commitments. Britain was by far the biggest investor in the Spanish mineral industries and this allows more general conclusions to be drawn from the results presented.[21] The results are supplemented by a detailed analysis of the 1891 Spanish mining survey which covered both Spanish (423) and foreign (42) iron, copper, and lead concerns with producing mines. Further information is drawn from archival and other primary sources, British, French, and Spanish. The nature, pattern, and extent of foreign direct investment is considered in section II. Profitability and the *modus operandi* of international mining investment are discussed in section III. Issues relating to backward and forward economic linkages are treated in section IV.

## II

British involvement in the Spanish mineral industries began in 1851 when the Linares Lead Mining Co. was formed to work mines at La Carolina in the province of Jaén. Linares was the brainchild of John Taylor & Sons, City-based consulting and managing engineers, who later organized two other companies to take over mines near those of Linares—the Fortuna Co. in 1853 and the Alamillos Co. in 1863. The amounts of capital invested were quite small and the combined maximum capital employed by the

Taylor group was just £175,000.[22] The first really substantial investment followed the formation of the Tharsis Sulphur & Copper Co. in 1866. The company was the first to work the massive pyrites lodes of the province of Huelva. Tharsis invested over £840,000 in the early years and was rewarded by a large output and quick returns.[23] The success of Tharsis inspired such interest that the Spanish government was able to raise £3.7 million when it sold off the ancient *Minas de Riotinto* in 1873.[24] This sale and the coincidental rise in interest in the iron ore deposits of Vizcaya sparked off the first foreign-sponsored mining investment boom in Spanish history.[25] Between 1871 and 1878 British investment in the sector totalled more than £6.5 million and 21 operating companies were formed. The bulk of the cash was sunk in the pyrites mines of Huelva (over £5 million) and most of the remainder went into iron ore mining in the north. A second investment boom, between 1880 and 1884, followed hard on the heels of the first. The greater part of the £3.6 million expended during these years went on increasing capacity at Tharsis and Rio Tinto, although some fair-sized investments were made by the 13 firms registered in the period. The next wave of investment was associated solely with the iron industry. Between 1887 and 1892 £900,000 was invested and 12 iron mining companies were formed. The fourth boom period was in many ways the most spectacular. Between 1895 and 1901 57 new companies were created and £3.5 million invested in Spain. Money flowed into copper (£2.4 million), lead (£160,000), and iron (£900,000) as the price of minerals rose and the leading "Spanish" companies declared record dividends. Finally, there was a more modest expansion phase, again associated with high prices and dividends, between 1905 and 1908. At this time a further £1.1 million was sunk, £900,000 in copper and £200,000 in iron—and 22 new companies were registered.

Table 2 charts the build-up of British mining investment in Spain. One immediately striking feature is the sheer number of British companies involved in the industry by the turn of the century. The figures are consistent with those published by Spanish historians,[26] but it would be a mistake to take the size of the corporate population as showing the true extent of British operations in Spain. In the first place, many of the companies registered never actually entered production. Of the total population of 174 firms, 24 failed to raise the cash needed to survey the properties they had acquired, and a further 66 shut down operations after the proving stage—presumably judging that reserves were insufficient to merit a larger investment. This meant that many companies had very short active lives. In fact 55 per cent of all companies ceased to operate within four years of registration and 75 per cent of firms were active for no more than nine years. Many companies still existed in the legal sense years after they had ceased real activities when they were in fact defunct. Hence the marked difference shown in table 2 between legally existing and genuinely

Table 2  Indicators of activity of British mining companies operating in Spain, 1851–1913 (174 companies)

| | Number of companies* | | | | | Effective share capital + debentures of companies legally in existence (£) | | | | |
|---|---|---|---|---|---|---|---|---|---|---|
| Year | Copper & pyrites | Iron & manganese | Lead & silver | Other | Total | Copper & pyrites | Iron & manganese | Lead & silver | Other | Total |
| 1851 | 0 (0) | 0 (0) | 1 (1) | 0 (0) | 1 (1) | – | – | 45,000 | – | 45,000 |
| 1861 | 0 (0) | 1 (0) | 2 (2) | 0 (0) | 3 (2) | – | 13,350 | 95,000 | – | 108,350 |
| 1871 | 3 (2) | 4 (2) | 4 (4) | 1 (0) | 12 (8) | 939,912 | 226,661 | 185,070 | – | 1,351,643 |
| 1881 | 3 (2) | 12 (4) | 4 (4) | 2 (0) | 21 (10) | 7,885,040 | 1,385,594 | 180,000 | 8,790 | 9,459,424 |
| 1891 | 5 (3) | 18 (9) | 5 (4) | 5 (0) | 33 (16) | 8,976,373 | 2,043,131 | 281,337 | 179,077 | 11,479,918 |
| 1901 | 22 (6) | 32 (12) | 9 (7) | 12 (1) | 75 (26) | 11,137,791 | 3,813,711 | 294,228 | 257,476 | 15,503,206 |
| 1911 | 13 (8) | 25 (13) | 7 (5) | 6 (1) | 51 (27) | 10,346,858 | 4,006,343 | 375,935 | 137,252 | 14,866,388 |

*Companies legally in existence with number of active companies in parentheses.
Sources: see Note on sources and methods, pp. 367–8.

active ventures. On average, the companies had an active life of about 10 years and a legal life of about 15 years. The majority went into voluntary liquidation (76 per cent); others were sold, amalgamated, or reconstructed (12 per cent); and the rest were either compulsorily wound up or struck off the register.

A second important point is that most of the 84 firms that entered production (19 in lead, 22 in copper-pyrites, 27 in iron, and 16 others), operated on a fairly small scale and were not highly capitalized. Mining investment was in fact a highly concentrated affair. In both the iron and lead industries, just three firms provided 45 per cent of British capital sunk in Spain. The corresponding figure for copper-pyrites is 81 per cent, indicating the overwhelming importance in that industry of the Rio Tinto and Tharsis companies. This impression is reinforced when returns on investment are taken into account. Full financial details (capital invested and returns to capital) are available for a subset of 123 firms. Of the cash returned to Britain by these firms—and this certainly represented the bulk of such monies—the top three iron, lead, and copper-pyrites firms accounted for 71 per cent, 83 per cent, and 98 per cent of respective industry returns.

The large size and high capitalization of leading concerns gave the relatively few foreign firms actually producing in Spain a prominent place in the mining sector as a whole. This is clearly shown by the analysis of data extracted from the mining survey conducted in 1891 on behalf of the Spanish government. The accuracy of some of the data contained in the survey may be suspect due to the tendency of companies to underestimate, for tax avoidance purposes, the value of minerals extracted.[27] Nevertheless, some interesting facts are revealed (see table 3). Firstly, foreign firms tended to be much larger than Spanish firms, with on average 10 times as many employees, and 13 times the value of output. Secondly, foreign penetration of Spanish mining was easily greatest in the case of copper-pyrites, but was still very significant in iron and lead, especially if shares in total output are taken as the best guide to foreign participation. Overall, nearly three-fifths of output was attributable to foreigners. Thirdly, the evidence shows that "productivity" was far higher amongst foreign firms; strikingly so in the case of copper-pyrites, substantially in the case of iron, and to a lesser degree in the case of lead. The lead industry was conspicuously less productive and more labour intensive than the copper-pyrites and iron industries.

This account of foreign participation in the Spanish mineral industries distinguishes between the handful of large and successful operating companies that accounted for the greater part of investment and production, and the scores of short-lived enterprises that unsuccessfully scoured the length and breadth of Spain in the hope of striking it rich. Between 1851 and 1913 British firms explored concessions in 34 different

Table 3  Analysis of the Spanish copper, iron and lead mining industries, 1891

| Sector | Aggregates | | | Indicators of corporate size | | Indicators of foreign penetration | | |
|---|---|---|---|---|---|---|---|---|
| | Number | Number employees | Value of production (P'tas) | Average number of employees | Average value of production (P'tas) | % of employees in sector(s) | % of value of production in sector(s) | Value of output per employee (P'tas) |
| (1) Copper & pyrites | | | | | | | | |
| Spanish firms | 11 | 1,591 | 1,096,971 | 145 | 99,725 | 11 | 6 | 689 |
| Foreign firms | 9 | 12,366 | 18,098,141 | 1,374 | 2,010,905 | 89 | 94 | 1,464 |
| All firms | 20 | 13,957 | 19,195,112 | 698 | 959,756 | 100 | 100 | 1,375 |
| (2) Iron & manganese | | | | | | | | |
| Spanish firms | 136 | 9,305 | 14,743,878 | 68 | 108,411 | 65 | 55 | 1,585 |
| Foreign firms | 18 | 5,038 | 11,843,701 | 280 | 657,953 | 35 | 45 | 2,351 |
| All firms | 154 | 14,343 | 26,587,579 | 93 | 172,647 | 100 | 100 | 1,854 |
| (3) Lead & silver | | | | | | | | |
| Spanish firms | 234 | 10,026 | 9,420,391 | 43 | 40,258 | 65 | 62 | 940 |
| Foreign firms | 15 | 5,427 | 5,843,284 | 362 | 389,552 | 35 | 38 | 1,077 |
| All firms | 249 | 15,453 | 15,263,675 | 62 | 61,300 | 100 | 100 | 988 |
| (4) 1–3 combined | | | | | | | | |
| Spanish firms | 381 | 20,922 | 25,261,241 | 55 | 66,302 | 48 | 41 | 1,207 |
| Foreign firms | 42 | 22,831 | 35,785,128 | 544 | 852,027 | 52 | 59 | 1,567 |
| All firms | 423 | 43,753 | 61,046,369 | 103 | 144,318 | 100 | 100 | 1,395 |

Source:  Estadística Minera de España: Catastro de las Minas en Productos Existentes en 30 Junio de 1891 (Ministerio de Fomento, Dirección General de Agricultura, Industria y Comercio, Comisión Ejecutiva de Estadísticas Mineras).

Spanish provinces, grubbing around for silver, gold, tin, mercury, manganese, and many other metals. In the event, very little of worth was found outside the pyrites province of Huelva, the iron provinces of Vizcaya, and Santander, Alermía, and Málaga, or the lead provinces of Jaén and Cuidad Real. Yet the firms which did establish themselves were long-lived and, compared to Spanish firms, very efficient. They achieved a collective importance even greater than that indicated by studies of concessions granted and published capitalizations.

# III

There is no doubt that Spain was a major target for international mining investment after 1851, but it does not follow that fabulous profits were earned. Indeed, the notion that profits were sustained at an extraordinarily high level over a long period runs counter to orthodox economic logic. In competitive conditions (and Spain certainly was an "open" economy) one would expect long-run returns to have been neither higher nor lower than those obtainable elsewhere, after taking account of differing risk factors. Certainly, some companies may well have been super-profitable, but instances of high returns should have attracted fresh investment either on the part of existing firms or through the entry of new firms. Either way, capital mobility ought to have worked to equalize long-run rates of return. Exceptional circumstances might to some degree have prevented the normalization of profit rates, but there is no reason to suppose that they exerted a predominant influence on profitability.[28]

The belief that Spanish minerals were a source of vast and exceptional profits for foreigners is based essentially, as already outlined, on selected dividend payment data relating to leading foreign companies. Such evidence is really of little value as a guide to rates of return on capital employed. An obvious problem is the sort of selectivity which quotes average percentage payments for some periods and fails to consider others when returns were lower. Another difficulty arises from using data taken directly from company financial statements without any attempt to calculate the actual amount of cash raised from shareholders for investment in Spain. To arrive at such figures, premium payments made by shareholders on new issues must be added to balance sheet figures for issued capital (and discounts deducted). Likewise, the value of shares issued to corrupt promoters of highly speculative ventures must be deducted from published figures, since little or no cash flowed to Spain as a result of their activities, which had more to do with the redistribution of assets in Britain than overseas mining. In this way a figure of *effective* share capital employed may be computed. When this is done, and all relevant years of operation are taken into account, average annual dividend payments for leading companies operating in Spain appear rather more modest, as is demonstrated in table 4. Certainly, the figures for Tharsis (16.3 per cent), Rio Tinto (13.8 per cent), and Orconera (44.9 per cent) are impressively large. Even so, for Tharsis and Rio Tinto these averages are much lower than the figures quoted by Nadal.

It may still be contended, however, that accounting-based measures of profitability, like dividends in relation to effective share capital employed, do not provide an accurate measure of return on capital invested. Mining ventures often have fairly long gestation periods, and it may well be several years before any return at all is made on an initial investment. Since ratio measures of performance take no account of the time value of money, their use may in many cases exaggerate the profitability of mining companies. It is for this reason that the internal rate of return (IRR) on capital invested is generally regarded as a truer measure of profitability. Whether the IRR is calculated for individual firms, industries or sectors of industry, it consti-tutes, in simple terms, the rate of compound interest at which an initial investment of cash and all subsequent investments of cash would have to grow in order to provide cash to finance the payments (dividends, interest, and capital repayments) made to investors up to the terminal date for the calculations; thus the IRR axiomatically reflects the time value of money and so can be directly compared with market rates of interest.

Two IRR calculations for each of six leading companies are presented in table 4. The first IRR calculation makes no allowance for the possibility that companies may have continued to make payments to ordinary and preference shareholders after 1913. The second IRR calculation makes such an allowance by adding to the 1913 payment shareholders a terminal payment equal to the stock market valuation of the investment. In this way an allowance is made for both depreciation and capital accumulation through the reinvestment of profits. The second measure gives a fairer reflection of relative profitability, though it is interesting to note just how slight is the difference in most cases between the two calculations. For three of the six companies (Rio Tinto, Bilbao, and Orconera) the results, when compared to the more orthodox indicators of profitability, are as antici-pated by *a priori* reasoning. The sharpest fall in indicated profitability is for the Orconera Co. and is due to the fact that the firm did not consistently pay very large dividends to its shareholders until after 1884. However, two of the six companies (Taylors and Tharsis) paid fairly heavy dividends in their early years with the result that the IRR figures exceed the orthodox indicators of profitability. The French Peñarroya Co. is a rather special case. It pursued a policy of vigorous growth, partly by retaining profits rather than distributing them as dividends, and so by 1913 had a high market valuation. Hence the marked difference between the two IRR computations.

The data presented in table 4 confirm that, by and large, the leading

Table 4 Indicators of effective share capital employed and associated rates of return of leading foreign mining companies operating in Spain, 1851–1913

| Company | Average effective share capital employed £ | Maximum effective share capital employed £ | Total dividends paid £ | Average annual dividend paid (as a % of effective cap. emp.) | IRR computation No. 1* (%) (no TV of assets) | IRR computation No. 2* (%) (with TV of assets) |
|---|---|---|---|---|---|---|
| **Lead** | | | | | | |
| John Taylor Group (1851–1913) | 151,825 | 175,000 | 925,437 | 10.16 | 13.80 | 13.80 |
| Soc. Minière et Métallurgique de Peñarroya (1881–1913) | 777,007 | 2,345,892 | 2,226,580 | 7.74 | negative | 9.81 |
| **Copper & pyrites** | | | | | | |
| Tharsis Sulphur & Copper Co. (1866–1913) | 1,247,236 | 1,513,538 | 10,008,432 | 16.25 | 19.09 | 19.12 |
| Rio Tinto Co. (1873–1913) | 4,276,812 | 7,223,650 | 27,968,438 | 13.79 | 9.89 | 11.01 |
| **Iron ore** | | | | | | |
| Bilbao Iron Ore Co. (1871–1913) | 582,521 | 630,750 | 1,498,375 | 5.57 | 4.47 | 5.04 |
| Orconera Iron Ore Co. (1873–1913) | 187,610 | 200,000 | 3,684,000 | 44.93 | 19.00 | 19.15 |

*TV = terminal valuation of assets

*Sources:* see Note on sources and methods, pp. 367–8.

companies operating in Spain were long-lived and very profitable, though not so fabulously lucrative as sometimes suggested. Leading company data, however, cannot be used to show the profitability of all foreign mining companies. Other firms may have tried to emulate the industry leaders but most failed. Mining investment houses in the City of London and big consumers of raw materials were always on the look-out for new prospects,[29] but many proved unviable and the cash spent on preliminary investigations or mine development was lost forever. Downward price movements, sudden falls in the richness of mineral extracted, and un-expected practical difficulties frequently led to failure. Often mines struggled along for years barely covering production costs. This was the case with the pioneering Luchana mines in which John Brown & Co. and Bolckow Vaughan & Co. had sunk £220,000 by the end of 1876. It was only after 1886 that the steel companies saw any return on their invest-ment.[30] For every big success there were many lesser failures, and it is thus necessary to consider entire industries rather than individual concerns when debating the earning power of foreign capital. Equally, debentures should be treated as equivalent to ordinary and preference shares when calculating values of long-term capital employed.

Tables 5–7 and figure 1 refer to the subset of 123 British companies for which full financial details are available. In devising these, annual series of data were abstracted for each firm: book value of capital (effective share capital plus debentures issued), new investment (yearly additions to book value), new investment to date (cumulative yearly additions to book value), payments (dividends, interest, and capital repayments), and net financial flow (payments less new investment). The individual series were then aggregated across firms to form series for four sub-sectors (copper-pyrites, iron, lead, and other) and the entire mining sector.

In table 5, the figures for average capital employed, average sunk capital and average dividend and interest payments are derived directly from the aggregated book value of capital, new investment to date and payments series respectively. The better of the two ratio measures of profitability is that relating to sunk capital. It is convenient in this context to treat all British investment in Spanish mining as if it were channelled through one giant enterprise—'The British Mining Company of Spain Ltd.' (BMCS)—since no capital is lost, from an accounting point of view, with the failure of particular operations. BMCS managed to secure increasing returns on capital sunk in Spain and an average return of just under 10 per cent. The reason for increasing returns is that some of the biggest operations (like Rio Tinto and Orconera) tended to reinvest heavily during the early years and reap rich harvests later on. The results of this strategy are shown in figure 1, which maps the aggregated net financial flow series. This illustrates that BMCS went through four main phases: an initial phase of modest investment and returns (1851–65), a second phase during which

*Table 5* Annual dividends and interest payments as percentages of capital employed and capital sunk in Spain by 123 British mining companies, 1851–1913

| Period | Average capital* employed (£) | Average sunk** capital (£) | Average dividends + interest payments (£) | Average return on capital employed† (%) | Average return on capital sunk† (%) |
|---|---|---|---|---|---|
| 1851–1860 | 106,900 | 118,100 | 12,898 | 10.80 | 9.85 |
| 1861–1870 | 442,818 | 481,818 | 32,138 | 7.38 | 6.25 |
| 1871–1880 | 5,303,983 | 5,417,102 | 427,395 | 9.73 | 9.53 |
| 1881–1890 | 10,386,614 | 10,706,458 | 972,001 | 9.41 | 9.12 |
| 1891–1900 | 11,890,543 | 12,289,029 | 1,411,681 | 11.67 | 11.30 |
| 1901–1910 | 14,868,309 | 15,893,537 | 2,043,682 | 13.73 | 12.89 |
| 1911–1913 | 13,961,034 | 15,896,722 | 2,100,089 | 15.05 | 13.24 |
| 1851–1913 | 7,490,075 | 7,884,930 | 877,749 | 10.67 | 9.99 |

* Effective share capital + debentures and mortgage bonds.
** Cumulative net capital flows to Spain.
† Average of annual percentage returns.
*Sources:* see Note on sources and methods, pp. 367–8.

new investment greatly exceeded earnings (1866–78), a third phase when earnings began to exceed new investment (1878–84), and a fourth phase in which earnings vastly exceeded new investment (1885–1913). It may well seem from a Spanish standpoint that during this fourth phase British capitalists were draining funds from the country at an increasingly alarming rate. Hence the rising tide of hostility to foreign mining companies after the mid-1880s, and the enduring characterization of these ventures as rapacious.

The sense of outrage felt by Spaniards is quite understandable, but equally it is necessary to recognize that investment precedes profit, and that the time-characteristics of investment and profit flows are critically important to judgements on profitability. The IRR as a prime indicator of performance takes this into account, unlike the ratio measures used above. The results presented in tables 6 and 7 are thus the most important in this study. Both tables are derived from the series for net financial flow; table 6 from the five aggregated series and table 7 from the individual series for 123 individual companies.

In considering table 6, it is again useful to think in terms of BMCS. It can be seen that between 1851 and 1913 our hypothetical company invested £15.7 million in Spain and returned £55.3 million to investors. Copper was by far the biggest subsidiary with iron in second place. Lead was tiny in comparison. All three earned healthy internal rates of return, with or without the inclusion of terminal payments to shareholders. Copper was the most profitable field of investment. The overall IRR on capital

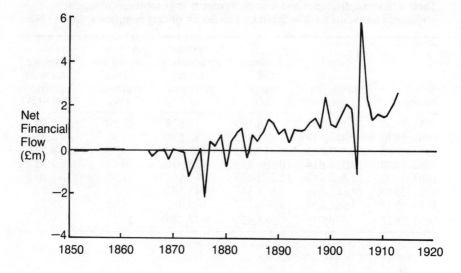

*Figure 1*  Annual net financial flows from Spain to Britain, 1851–1913 (123 companies)

*Table 6*  Internal rates of return on capital employed by 123 British mining companies operating in Spain, 1851–1913

| Sector | Number of companies | Total sunk capital £ | Total return on investment £ | IRR computation no. 1* (%) (with no TV of assets) | IRR computation no. 2* (%) (with TV of assets) |
|---|---|---|---|---|---|
| Copper & pyrites | 33 | 11,709,866 | 43,733,593 | 10.10 | 10.85 |
| Iron & manganese | 42 | 3,219,852 | 10,130,122 | 8.34 | 8.80 |
| Lead & silver | 20 | 504,608 | 1,415,547 | 10.64 | 10.71 |
| Exploration & other | 28 | 242,596 | 22,943 | negative | negative |
| All companies | 123 | 15,676,922 | 55,302,205 | 9.78 | 10.45 |

*TV = terminal valuation of assets.

*Sources:*  see Note on sources and methods, pp. 367–8.

invested was nearly 10.5 per cent, a figure remarkably close to that of 10 per cent for the global average of annual percentage returns on capital sunk in Spain.[31]

Table 7 confirms that mining in Spain was a high-risk business. Only one in five ventures was profitable, and the 98 failed companies together lost nearly £4 million. Of the £11.7 million invested profitably, the bulk of the cash was spent by companies earning internal rates of return in the 5.0–9.9 per cent range, although there was considerable investment in super-profitable concerns. Increasingly, most of the cash lost was invested by companies registered after 1890, whereas most of the cash that yielded a return in excess of 5 per cent was invested by companies registered before 1881. Many of the best prospects were discovered early in the development of the mining sector. When, after about 1890, the major operating companies began to pay high dividends, considerable new investment was drawn to Spain. In the event, most of the new companies failed, consequently reducing industry and sectoral internal rates of return.

From this evidence it is fair to conclude that foreign mining companies, on the whole, did not find Spain a land of rich and easy pickings. The proposition that fabulous profits were earned relative to cash invested is not tenable. However, whilst it is extremely difficult to find data directly comparable with those presented here, industry and sectoral rates of return do appear somewhat higher than normal for the period. In one respect this is quite a predictable outcome. Mining investment was demonstrably risky and the market was bound to demand a substantial premium on money invested in that sector overseas. It is worth noting also that the figures computed effectively represent upper-bound calculations. Firstly, because the investment series have been quite ruthlessly purged of potentially fictitious elements like the share capital issued to corrupt promoters. Secondly, there were 51 companies for which a payments series could not be compiled, and which were omitted from the computations. Although a few were substantial and paid dividends,[32] most were small and unstable, and if data had been available inclusion of these cases would probably have led to a downward adjustment of internal rates of return.

All things considered, aggregate returns on mining investment in Spain were probably super-normal by no more than one or two percentage points. This economic rent is attributable to the unassailable position achieved by the giant copper-pyrites companies early in the development of the industry through control of uniquely rich deposits of ore. Such an advantage may legitimately be seen as the exceptional circumstance which prevented the complete normalization of profit rates. The Spanish experience nonetheless attests to the equalizing power of market forces.

Table 7 Distribution of individual internal rates of return of 123 British mining companies operating in Spain, 1851–1913

| Period when companies established | No dividend or interest payments | | Negative return | | 0–4.99% | | 5.00–9.99% | | 10.00% or higher | |
|---|---|---|---|---|---|---|---|---|---|---|
| | Number of co.s | Capital invested (£) | Number of co.s | Capital invested (£) | Number of co.s | Capital invested (£) | Number of co.s | Capital invested (£) | Number of co.s | Capital invested (£) |
| 1851–1860 | 1 | 10,000 | 2 | 29,000 | – | – | 1 | 55,604 | 1 | 57,675 |
| 1861–1870 | 3 | 136,115 | – | – | – | – | 1 | 70,000 | 1 | 1,513,583 |
| 1871–1880 | 11 | 129,087 | 2 | 20,070 | 1 | 225,000 | 3 | 7,943,532 | 2 | 250,000 |
| 1881–1890 | 21 | 103,035 | 3 | 28,221 | 3 | 83,008 | 2 | 70,270 | 2 | 234,870 |
| 1891–1900 | 27 | 116,155 | 8 | 1,623,811 | 1 | 600,000 | 2 | 161,855 | 2 | 110,762 |
| 1901–1910 | 14 | 1,151,786 | 6 | 572,483 | – | – | – | – | 2 | 345,000 |
| 1911–1913 | – | – | – | – | – | – | – | – | 1 | 36,000 |
| 1851–1913 | 77 | 1,676,178 | 21 | 2,273,585 | 5 | 908,008 | 9 | 8,301,261 | 11 | 2,547,890 |

Sources: see Note on sources and methods, pp. 367–8.

**IV**

It has often been observed that the effects of foreign direct investment in mining may vary quite markedly according to particular conditions prevailing in host economies.[33] For instance, if there is a large enough indigenous business élite prepared to take the chances offered, foreign participation may stimulate economic development in the host country. Equally, if existing impulses to economic change are weak, it is quite possible that foreigners will actually stifle local initiative and exploit natural resources in an "imperialistic" fashion. This is sometimes termed enclave development and in the long run benefits only the foreigner: precious minerals are lost forever and little of substance is left by way of compensation.

A fair case can be made for the proposition that, in the period 1851–1913, Spain had both positive and negative entanglements with foreign mining companies. It can be argued that in the north, where Basque businessmen had the initiative and drive to grasp the business opportunities thrown up by the mineral export boom, regional, industrial and commercial development ensued. In the south, on the other hand, where wealth owners were either decadent or frequently absent in Madrid, it might be argued little that was positive resulted from foreign mining activity. Certainly there is a measure of truth in this representation of regional economic fortunes. There is a danger, however, in adopting such a dichotomous view, of understanding the actual benefits of foreign mining company activities in Spain.

The intimate connexion between the development of iron mining and industrialization of the Basque provinces has been explored in detail by González Portilla.[34] His research shows how leading Basques—like the Ibarra, Chavarri, Zuburía, and Martínez de las Rivas families—made substantial fortunes from iron ore mining, and how simultaneously the export trade created a host of new investment opportunities. Good advantage was taken of these. Most immediately promising was shipping. Freight charges amounted to nearly 50 per cent of the cost per ton of iron ore delivered at British ports, and this slice of value-added was a clear target of Spanish entrepreneurs.[35] Basque vessels carried only 8 per cent of the 2 million tons of iron ore shipped from Spain from 1871–3, rising to 36 per cent of the 25 million tons shipped from 1911–3.[36] Over the years, other demands of the iron ore trade increasingly came to be met from local sources; from explosives and aerial ropeways to insurance and banking services. Banking in particular benefited from the mining boom. Members of the mining community were intimately involved in the affairs of the big banks that began life during these years—the Banco de Vizcaya, the Banco de Bilbao, and the Banco de Crédito Industrial are prominent examples.[37] These proved an important and enduring support to Basque enterprise as industry advanced across a broad front. Iron and steel, shipbuilding, construction, mechanical and electrical engineering all prospered, either directly or indirectly, in consequence of mineral exports and the rising power of the Basque business community.

The prosperity and new-found vitality of Basque entrepreneurs in turn owed much to foreign direct investment in northern Spain. Foreign firms had provided much of the initial capital and direction necessary for the rapid development of the principal mining districts, and they did so at a cost which was by no means extortionate. Through royalty payments and profits from collaborative ventures they swelled the coffers of local businessmen.[38] However, the contribution made by foreigners to Basque industrialization was more than just financial. The technological and economic organization of the northern mining zone was imported.[39] British mining and business methods were adopted generally as local producers emulated their more efficient foreign counterparts. The productivity and profitability of Basque mining ventures rose accordingly. The Basques were thus well aware of what could be gained from collaboration with foreigners, and this led them to encourage foreign involvement in ventures outside mining: in iron and steel,[40] shipbuilding, engineering and elsewhere.[41] In mingling with the top European industrialists and engineers—through sitting as colleagues on boards of directors or in making visits to factories abroad—men like the Ibarra brothers learned the rules and standards of modern business.[42] Knowledge of business management, finance and markets, vital to the long-term health of the Spanish economy, was gained through the mutually rewarding partnership of Basque enterprise and foreign capital. Even before 1913 Basque businessmen were to be found promoting new schemes throughout Spain and beyond.[43]

No such surge in business activity resulted from the arrival of foreign mining companies in southern Spain. Yet this was not simply because conditions on the ground were different in the south. In the lead industry, and to a lesser extent in copper-pyrites, concessions were sold, royalties earned, and Spanish fortunes made, but the general response to new business opportunities was weak. Of the nine million tons of pyrites shipped from Spain from 1911–3, for instance, only 18 per cent went in Spanish vessels.[44] Even then most of the home country ships were Basque owned. Strong alliances between local and foreign firms, like that between Sundheim and Doetsch of Huelva and the Rio Tinto Co., were exceptional. Jordi Nadal's description of the native lead industry as "speculative and pre-capitalist" might well be used to cover the entire business community in the south.[45]

There were few opportunities, moreover, for foreign mining companies to promote economic development directly in southern Spain. Equipment and raw materials (pig iron, explosives, coal, and timber) were needed in large quantities, but plans for local manufacture were mostly shelved at the costing stage.[46] A rare exception is the development of the Belmez coal mines by the Peñarroya Co.[47] Examples of forward integration or diversification are almost equally rare. Faced with a poor regional market, foreign concerns were not moved to think of extending operations, but when obvious opportunities did occur they responded. The Rio Tinto Co. built one of the largest acid and superphosphate plants in Europe at Huelva to meet the rising Spanish demand for artificial manure.[48] The Peñarroya Co. likewise entered the fertilizer business and diversified further into zinc mining and processing.[49]

It is evident that in the south the insularity of foreign mining companies was not a matter of choice but rather due to force of circumstance. With their role as agents of economic development so limited, they stuck to doing what was possible: mining, smelting, and exporting on a large scale and at the lowest possible cost. The result was so-called enclave development. This was most marked in Huelva where the Rio Tinto Co. alone employed 15,000 people in 1913. Many of the major towns of the province—Alonso, Calanas, Nerva, Rio Tinto, and Zalamea—were run as company towns in a distinctly paternalistic fashion. Local politics were managed by the mining companies in typical Spanish style. It is little wonder that local people felt colonized.[50]

But it must not be forgotten that these colonies were islands of wealth-creation in the sea of social distress. In creating comparatively well-paid and secure employment, big foreign mining companies were a force for good. It may be that this was ephemeral wealth, but this would not have troubled the tens of thousands of employees and their families who otherwise would have competed with hundreds of thousands of others to scrape a meagre existence from the land. It may also be true that the expansion of the mineral industries could have been guided exclusively by Spanish capital. If this had been the case, however, much lower levels of productivity, profits and wages would have resulted, and scarce Spanish capital would not have been used to best effect. Foreign capital may have been nominally quite expensive, but considering the activity it generated it was comparatively cheap. This is because capital was imported as part of a bundle of resources: technological, organizational, and financial. The more forward-looking Spaniards mining in the south recognized this and adopted foreign practices. The Taylor group, for instance, was the first to use a whole range of techniques for mining at deeper levels.[51] Without the widespread adoption of these, the subsequent development of the native lead industry would have been severely limited. The Basques were aware of the situation in the south and the possibilities created by the use of foreign methods. Towards the end of the period they joined the French in pursuing consolidation and large scale production in the lead industry. They responded also to the market opportunities created by the development of the copper-pyrites industry, and from the 1890s onwards met an increasing part of the pig iron, explosives, and shipping needs of the foreign companies.[52] There was, then, a positive and progressive side to the activities of foreign mining companies.

## V

Foreign capital did indeed have a major role in promoting the Spanish mineral export boom of 1851–1913. The part played by overseas companies, however, was not an easy one. Mining in Spain was a risky business in which most firms failed. Profits were hard won, and, all in all, were not exceptionally high. In the main, factor mobility worked to normalize the rate of return on capital invested. Only for exceptional reasons did an element of economic rent accrue to capital in the case of investment in the copper-pyrites industry. On balance, the general development effects of foreign direct investment were very beneficial to the economy of Spain. The evidence does not support the textbook view that "foreign capital strayed ... damagingly into the extractive industries" or that the Spanish government made a "cardinal and ineradicable error" in allowing foreigners to participate in developing the nation's mineral resources.[53]

This is not to say that the foreign capitalists and Spanish politicians of the period formed the perfect development team. The politicians acted at times in a desperately short-sighted and sectionally interested manner. They failed most miserably in not recognizing the need for a proper set of policies to capture more fully the benefits of foreign mining activities in Spain. Taxation policies and practices can only be described as woefully inadequate, concentrating as they did on metal values rather than profits. The Villaverde reforms, when they came, were a step in the right direction. An attempt was made thereby to claw back part of the economic rent element of foreign earnings, but even then implementation was so feeble that the Treasury was cheated of its lawful dues.[54] Nor did the big mining companies win any prizes for saintly behaviour. They were content to avoid taxes by any means available. They used the "system" to get strong-arm protection against labour militants, and looked on all claims for higher wages, however modest, as sinister and ill-intended.[55] There was also racial bias, in the way that staff, especially mining engineers, were selected for promotions to the highest position.[56] Without doubt, a government fully committed to economic development could have struck a better bargain with foreign businessmen on things like the division of earnings and the training and employment of key personnel.

Imperfect outcomes, however, do not necessarily indicate foolish choices. In the situation it faced, the Spanish government, as Checkland has remarked, had no real alternative but to take a chance that foreigners could promote economic growth.[57] Spain was a land lacking in knowledge, technology and capital, and also a land desperately in need of relief from poverty. In the event, foreign capital and enterprise did create employment and prosperity where none had existed before, but more importantly, it was the presence of successful foreign firms in their midst that awakened many Spaniards to the requirements, demands, and potential benefits of technological and industrial modernization. The rewards to foreigners may have been quite substantial, but the long-term gain to Spain was very great. That it might have been greater still was the fault of the Spanish government—which was incompetent—rather than of the foreign firms—which were merely predictable.

## Notes

1. The authors would like to thank the Twenty-Seven Foundation and the research committee of Bristol Polytechnic for supporting their research. They are also grateful for the comments of Joseph Harrison, Jon Press, and an anonymous referee. The authors alone are responsible for the arguments and evidence presented, and for any errors contained in the article.
2. Derived from figures for mine production. Schmitz, *World non-ferrous metal*, pp. 64–9, 92–9.
3. For iron, see Mitchell, *European historical statistics*, p. 424. For sulphur, see Harvey, *Rio Tinto*, pp. 53–63 and Haynes, *Brimstone*, pp. 262–93.
4. Schmitz, *World non-ferrous metal*, pp. 128–30.
5. See, for instance, Harrison, *Economic history*.
6. Computed from figures in annual volumes of *Estadística General del Comercio Exterior*.
7. *Estadística Minera de España* (1911).
8. Alzola, 'Iron and steel industry', p. 31.
9. Harrison, 'Heavy industry', pp. 543–5; Harrison, 'Regenerationist movement'.
10. P.R.O. FO371 1754/50106.
11. Muñoz García *et al* 'Minería y capital extranjero', p. 68.
12. Nadal, *El fracaso de la revolución industrial*, pp. 92–3.
13. González Portilla, *La formación de la sociedad capitalista*, vol. I, pp. 55–60.
14. González Portilla, 'El desarrollo industrial de Vizcaya', p. 72.
15. Nadal, *El fracaso de la revolución industrial*, pp. 105–9.
16. Nadal, 'Industrialización y deindustrialización'.
17. Broder, 'Le rôle des intérèts étranger', synopsis, p. 4. See also, Broder 'Les investissements étranger'.
18. Harvey, *Rio Tinto*, p. 119.
19. González Portilla, 'El desarrollo industrial de Vizcaya', pp. 76–83.
20. Trebilcock, *Industrialization*, p. 363.
21. Nadal calculates that the British accounted for 53 per cent of the foreign capital invested in Spain in 1913. Muñoz García *et al.* estimate that British companies accounted for 84 per cent of fixed capital investment held by foreign mining companies in 1923; 'Minería y capital extranjero', p. 88.
22. John Taylor & Sons were active in Spain throughout the period and in 1907

had responsibility for the management of seven Spanish companies. The 1907 edition of the *Mining Manual* shows the firm as managers of 45 companies around the world.

23. Checkland, *Mines of Tharsis*, pp. 104–11.

24. Harvey, *Rio Tinto*, p. 11.

25. Flinn, 'British overseas investment', pp. 38–93; Flinn, 'British steel and Spanish ore'.

26. See, for example, Muñoz García *et al.* 'Minería y capital extranjero', p. 80.

27. Ibid. pp. 61–3.

28. For a useful discussion of these issues, see Frankel, *Investment*, pp. 3–6; also, Edelstein, *Overseas investment*, pp. 111–5.

29. See note 22 on Taylors. There are many examples of big consumers trying to cut their costs by securing their own mineral supplies. The Bede Metal Co. and the United Alkali Co. are good examples in the pyrites industry. The United Alkali records are held at the Cheshire Record Office. See UA15 for entry into Spanish mining. Flinn, 'British overseas investment', gives many examples for the iron industry.

30. British Steel Corporation Northern Regional Records Centre (B.S.C.N.) Bolckow Vaughan & Co. minutes, 21 February 1877; B.S.C.N., Bolckow Vaughan & Co. annual reports 1884–7.

31. The lower than average IRR figures for iron shown in table 6 may be due mainly to transfer pricing on the part of some firms. Orconera, for instance, sold abroad 500,000 tons annually at cost plus £0.08 per ton, and there was also a small amount of transfer pricing within Spain. The effect was to reduce the declared profits of a minority of firms and thence iron mining as a whole. There was little or no transfer pricing in the lead and copper industries.

32. The P.R.O. BT34 319 and BT34 354 files contain winding-up details for the Dicido Iron Co. and the Dicido Pier Co. respectively. Dicido Iron distributed £181,000 between 1912 and 1915 and Dicido Pier £52,000 over the same period. The combined maximum capital employed by the two companies was £132,000.

33. See, for example, O'Faircheallaigh, *Mining and development*; and Bosson and Varon, *The mining industry*, pp. 178–91.

34. González Portilla, *La formación de la sociedad capitalista.*

35. Flinn, 'British overseas investment', pp. 136–60.

36. Computed from figures given in the relevant annual volumes of *Estadística General del Comercio Exterior.*

37. González Portilla, *La formación de la sociedad capitalista*, II, pp. 112–20.

38. See, for instance, B.S.C.N., Orconera Iron Ore Co. Ltd. Memorandum of Association and Contracts. Ibarra Hermanos & Co. received from Orconera an annual railway concession rent of £3,333, a royalty of 8d. per ton mined and other financial benefits.

39. Gill, 'Iron ore district'; Gill, 'Present position'; Barron, 'Works of Bilbao Iron Co.'; Forrest, 'Bilbao iron'.

40. The first two modern iron and steel works built in Spain were of foreign design. Alzola, 'Iron and steel industry', p. 17.

41. For instance, Babcock-Wilcox in engineering and Española de Construcción Naval in shipbuilding.

42. B.S.C.N. Bolckow Vaughan & Co. board minute of 14 March 1872. This, for instance, notes the visit of the Ibarra brothers to Britain and the possibility of joint ventures.

43. For example, Electra del Lima (Portugal), Cooperativa Electro Madrid, Unión Eléctrica de Carthegena and Eléctrica Valenciana.

44. Computed from figures given in the relevant annual volumes of *Estadistica General del Comercio Exterior.*

45. Nadal, 'Industrialización y deindustrialización', p. 60.

46. P.R.O. FO185 694. Equipment and raw materials valued at £670,788 were imported through Huelva in 1884; machinery (£383,000), coal (£106,118), and pig iron (£102,534) were the biggest items.

47. Sociétè Minière et Métallurgique de Peñarroya, typescript history supplied by the company.

48. Harvey, *Rio Tinto*, pp. 159–61.

49. See note 47,

50. Harvey, *Rio Tinto*, pp. 126–43.

51. Heriot, 'Linares lead'; *idem*, 'Lead mining'; *idem*, 'Lead industry'. See also, Ganzález Lana, *El plomo–España*, pp. 15–30.

52. Harvey, *Rio Tinto*, pp. 119–23.

53. Trebilcock, *Industrialization*, pp. 363–5.

54. García-Quintana, 'Evolución histórica del sistima fiscal', pp. 710–4.

55. Harvey, *Rio Tinto*, pp. 126–44.

56. The *Mining Journal* noted in April 1910 that "with the advent of foreign capital and interests, young Spanish graduates are crowded out of the profession in their own country" (p. 547).

57. Checkland, *Mines of Tharsis*, p. 273.

## Note on Sources and Methods

### Sources

(a) British mining activities in Spain

The names of companies operating in Spain were drawn from issues of the *Mining Journal.* The annual lists of new companies registered compiled by Ashmead, for 1877–1908, were especially valuable for this purpose. Other company names were gathered from a range of sources. Most valuable of these was Flinn's thesis, 'British overseas investment'. General and financial data was then gathered, cross-referencing where possible, from the following sources: *Mining Journal* (1851 onwards), *Mining Manual* (1887 onwards), *Mining World* (1851 onwards), *Investor's Monthly Manual, Bradshaw's Railway Manual,* the Flinn thesis, Companies Registration Office files and P.R.O. BT31 files (registration and annual return documents for individual companies), annual reports and accounts for individual companies (when located and available).

(b) Spanish mining survey of 1891

A microfilm of the volume of *Estadística Minera de España,* containing the full survey results, was provided by the British Library.

*Methods*

(a)  British mining activities in Spain

Data were abstracted from available primary sources onto individual company worksheets. At this stage adjustments were made, as necessary, to balance sheet figures for issued share capital to arrive at truer figures for investment in Spanish operations. The first main adjustment was the removal of amounts relating to shares allocated to promoters of second-class or corrupt compannies. This was done because some frauds were on a big scale and had little or nothing to do with mining activities, and no cash flowed to Spain in consequence. If these amounts had been left in rates of return would have been deflated. Whether or not a deduction was made depended on the seriousness and intensity of mining activities subsequent to the promotion of a company. In the case of first class concerns, promotion was a legitimate economic activity and no deduction has been made. The second main adjustment was to add back amounts secured by companies on shares issued at premium prices. If this had not been done, investment figures would have been deflated and rate of return figures inflated. It should also be noted that terminal values based on stock market valuations were only available for the biggest companies (when representative values for 1913 were used). For non-listed companies, terminal values were estimated by discounting a trend cash flow from 1913 to the end of their active lives.

From the company worksheets the data were prepared for computer analysis. Three main data sets were assembled: (1) general characteristics (such as years of registration and dissolution, industry, method of dissolution, and province(s) in which mines were located); (2) leading companies data (on effective share capital employed and returns to equity); (3) financial profile data for all companies (such as effective share capital employed, debentures and mortgage bonds outstanding, dividends paid and interest paid on debentures and mortgage bonds).

The general characteristics data were analysed using the Statistical Package for the Social Sciences (SPSS). The leading company data were analysed on a company-by-company basis using a program for the calculation of the internal rate of return (IRR). The financial profile data were aggregated as necessary using specially developed programs for series addition and manipulation.

(b)  Spanish mining survey of 1891

This was analysed using SPSS.

A paper detailing their statistical and computer methods can be supplied by the authors on request.

## Footnote References

### Official Publications

*Cuadro General del Comercio de España* (Madrid, 1851–5).
*Estadistica General del Comercio Exterior de España* (Madrid, 1856–1913).
*Estadistica Minera de España* (Madrid, 1861, 1891, 1901, 1911).

### Secondary Sources

P. de Alzola, 'The iron and steel industry of Spain', *Journal of the Iron and Steel Institute*, II (1896), pp. 5–32.

F. C. Barron, 'The works of the Bilbao Iron Company', *Proceedings of the Institute of Civil Engineers*, LI (1887–8), pp. 237–60.

R. Bosson and B. Varon, *The mining industry and developing countries* (1977).

A. Broder, 'Les investissements étrangers en Espagne au XIX$^c$ siècle: méthodologie et quantification', *Review d'Histoire Économique et Sociale*, 54 (1976), pp. 29–63.

A. Broder, 'Le rôle des intérèts étrangers dans la croissance de l'Espagne 1768–1920', (unpublished doctoral thesis, Paris, 1981).

S. Checkland, *The mines of Tharsis* (1967).

M. Edelstein, *Overseas investment in the age of high imperialism: the United Kingdom, 1850–1914* (1982).

M. W. Flinn, 'British overseas investment in iron ore mining, 1870–1914' (unpublished M.A. thesis, University of Manchester, 1952).

M. W. Flinn, 'British steel and Spanish ore', *Economic History Review*, 2nd ser. IX (1955–6), pp. 84–90.

B. J. Forrest, 'The Bilbao iron ore district', *Transactions of the North of England Institute of Mining and Mechanical Engineers*, XXXIII (1883–4), pp. 213–34.

S. H. Frankel, *Investment and the return to equity capital in the South African gold mining industry* (Cambridge, Mass. 1967).

C. A. García-Quintana, 'Evolución historica del sistema fiscal Español y lineas idóneas de su reforma', *Boletin de Estudios Económicos*, 99 (1976), pp. 703–43.

W. Gill, 'The iron ore district of Bilbao', *J. of the Iron and Steel Inst.* I (1882), pp. 63–95.

W. Gill, 'The present position of the iron ore industries of Biscay and Santander', *J. of the Iron and Steel Inst.* XI (1896), pp. 36–103.

E. González Llana, *El plomo en España* (Madrid, 1949).

M. González Portilla, 'El desarrollo industrial de Vizcaya y la acumulación de capital en el último tercio del siglo XIX', *Anales de Economia*, 24 (1974), pp. 43–83.

M. González Portilla, *La formación de la sociedad capitalista en el Pais Vasco, 1876–1913*, 2 vols. (San Sebastian, 1981).

J. Harrison, *An economic history of modern Spain* (Manchester, 1978).

J. Harrison, 'The regenerationist movement in Spain after the disaster of 1898', *European Studies Review*, 9 (1979), pp. 1–27.

J. Harrison, 'Heavy industry, the state, and economic development in the Basque region, 1876–1936', *Econ. Hist. Rev.* 2nd ser. XXXVI (1983), pp. 535–51.

C. E. Harvey, *The Rio Tinto Company: an economic history of a leading international mining concern, 1873–1954* (Penzance, 1981).

W. Haynes, *Brimstone: the stone that burns* (New York, 1959).

E. M. Heriot, 'The Linares lead mining industry of Spain', *The Engineering and Mining Journal*, 73 (1902), pp. 68–9.

E. M. Heriot, 'The lead industry in Spain', *Mining Journal*, 80 (1910), pp. 707–8.
E. M. Heriot, 'Lead mining in Spain', *Mining Magazine*, 24 (1914), pp. 358–61.
B. R. Mitchell, *European historical statistics* (1975).
J. Muñoz García *et al.* 'Minería y capital extranjero en la articulación del modelo de desarrollo subordinado y dependiente de la economía española en la segunda mitad del siglo XIX y primeros años del siglo XX', *Información Comercial Española*, no. 514 (1976), pp. 59–89.
J. Nadal, 'Industrialización y deindustrialización del sureste Español, 1817–1913', *Monedo y Crédito*, 120 (1972), pp. 3–80.
J. Nadal, *El fracaso de la revolución industrial en España, 1814–1913* (Barcelona, 1975).
C. O'Faircheallaigh, *Mining and development* (Beckenham, 1984).
C. J. Schmitz, *World non-ferrous metal production and prices, 1700–1976* (1979).
C. Trebilcock, *The industrialization of the continental powers, 1780–1914* (1981).

# 15

# Management Relations in a Multinational Enterprise: The Case of Canadian Industries Limited, 1928–1948*†

Graham D. Taylor

*Source: *Business History Review*, LV (1981) pp. 337–358.

Historians of modern, multinational, diversified industrial economies have learned that to deduce rigid, authoritarian control of subsidiaries, especially those in foreign countries, from the fact of over-all corporate ownership from afar, often leads to very inaccurate conclusions. The case of Canadian Industries, Ltd., a diversified Canadian chemical company jointly owned by the American and British giants, Du Pont and Imperial Chemical Industries, Ltd., reveals that a remarkable degree of independence was retained by the Canadian subsidiary even in such globally important policy matters as diversification, entry into new geographic areas, transfer of technology, and inter-company pricing of materials. Transnational ownership of industrial facilities, in short, produced advantages that were shared by both headquarters and local enterprises, leaving most of the anti-multinational movement to be explained as simpleminded nationalism.

On March 23, 1944, the Hon. M. J. Coldwell, M.P. for Rosetown-Biggar, rose in the Canadian House of Commons to denounce the favoritism allegedly practiced by his government in awarding war contracts to Defense Industries Ltd. Since 1939, he noted, this company had received almost one-third of all Canadian government assistance to business, an expenditure estimated at $600,000,000. Mr. Coldwell's objection was, however, only partially directed toward the issue of favoritism. His main argument was that the recipient of this largesse was the wholly-owned subsidiary of Canadian Industries Ltd., which, he maintained, "is not a Canadian enterprise. It is jointly owned and controlled by the du Pont de Nemours company of the United States, and Imperial Chemical Industries Ltd. of the United Kingdom." Far from being an enterprise devoted to developing Canadian resources for the ultimate benefit of the national economy, he added, Canadian Industries Ltd. was nothing more than a unit in the global operations of a cartel established by these two foreign chemical giants, intended to strangle potential competition in Canada, to prevent the entry of Canadian manufactures into the international chemical and explosives markets, and to exploit the resources of Canada for their exclusive corporate gain.[1]

Mr. Coldwell's observations were based on material presented by the U.S. Justice Department initiating an antitrust suit two months earlier against Du Pont and Imperial Chemical Industries, naming Canadian Industries Ltd. as "co-conspirator." At that time the U.S. antitrust spokesman, Assistant Attorney General Wendell Berge, characterized the corporate structure of which C.I.L. was a part as an Anglo-American "monopoly ... throttling the growth of industry within the dominions of the British Empire ... treating these dominions as economic colonies."[2]

Despite protests by C. D. Howe and other government members in the Canadian Parliament that there were "many Canadian shareholders" in C.I.L. and that its securities "are quoted on Canadian markets every day," the charge that Du Pont and I.C.I. jointly held overwhelming majority control was verified. The two companies admitted later that each held between 46 per cent and 48 per cent of all the voting shares in C.I.L., a total of 92 per cent to 94 per cent of all shares between 1927, when the company was established, and 1951. At that time the U.S. court before which the antitrust case was heard upheld the charges that C.I.L. had suppressed competition in Canada and declined to enter the export market to serve the interests of its British and American corporate parents.[3] Subsequently, Du Pont sold its shares in C.I.L., establishing a new directly owned subsidiary in Canada, while I.C.I. maintained its equity in C.I.L., now holding approximately 74 per cent of the voting shares in the Canadian company.

From one perspective, then, the experience of C.I.L. appears to provide a forceful illustration of the problems raised by the presence of local subsidiaries of foreign companies, in the view of nationalist opponents of multinational enterprise in Canada and other countries in which substantial foreign direct investment has occurred. In such companies, decisions on policy are made by investors not residing in the host country and without reference to or interest in that country's economic needs.[4] Indeed, C.I.L.'s position as an element in an international cartel would seem to strengthen the case made by critics of multinational enterprise. Measures imposed by Du Pont and I.C.I. on C.I.L., such as restrictions on exports and the denial of funds to move into new domestic markets or develop new technology could be seen as detrimental to C.I.L. as a company, and to the growth of the chemical industry in Canada, given the strong position of C.I.L. in that field at the time.

But there is a different perspective from which C.I.L. may be observed, and from which a less clear-cut picture of the relationship between C.I.L. and its corporate parents emerges. To the American judge examining the evidence and to Canadian critics of C.I.L., the demonstration of foreign ownership established a presumption of subordination of the local management to the wishes of these foreign investors. An examination of the internal workings of C.I.L. and the relations between the executives of C.I.L. and those of Du Pont and I.C.I. reveals a more complex pattern that, while it may not alter the ultimate circumstance of subordination, introduces an element of bargaining that is not apparent when the end results, the policy decisions and disposition of company earnings, are treated out of this context. This bargaining element was an essential feature of the parent-subsidiary relationship. The multinational aspect of the companies, moreover, enhanced the bargaining element, and must be taken into account when analyzing the structure of authority in these organizations.

**The Development of C.I.L.**

Canadian Industries Ltd. was the final outgrowth of a process of consolidation and diversification in the Canadian explosives and chemical industries, paralleling in many ways the development of these industries in the United States and Great Britain. The company was also the product of the cartel arrangements that had prevailed in these industries since the middle of the nineteenth century, and provided the particular framework of relations between the leading American and British companies in the field.[5] C.I.L. was more than a paper organization: it owned plants, produced and marketed goods, carried on extensive research and development in new technology, and otherwise behaved like a conventional industrial firm. At the same time, however, C.I.L. was regarded by its owners, Du Pont and I.C.I. as primarily a part of their international arrangements, the instrument through which they would jointly exploit the Canadian market and avoid competition with one another. In this sense, C.I.L. differed from other Canadian subsidiaries of foreign owners.

In 1876, the American powder trust, whose dominant member was E.I. du Pont de Nemours Co., purchased shares in several powder companies in Ontario, which later merged under the name of one of the firms, Hamilton Powder Co., established in 1862. During the next two decades, Hamilton Powder Co. bought other properties in Ontario and Quebec, including a liquid nitroglycerine plant and a heavy chemical company. In 1899, the British company, Nobel Explosives Ltd., bought a large block of shares in the Hamilton company to give it a foothold in the Canadian powder market. Between 1899 and 1908, Nobel also bought three other Canadian firms, Victoria Chemical Co., Acadia Powder Co., and Dominion Cartridge Co. Following the death in 1910 of Thomas Brainerd, the Canadian who had managed Hamilton Powder Co. and held the balance of its shares, Nobel induced Du Pont to join with it in merging the four companies into Canadian Explosives Ltd., with Du Pont taking 45 per cent and Nobel 55 per cent of the shares.[6]

Between 1911 and 1927, Canadian Explosives Ltd. (C.X.L.) took over Canadian branch plants of Du Pont manufacturing paints, nitrocellulose plastics, and an artificial leather called Fabrikoid. C.X.L. also acquired the Canadian properties of other American firms, including those of the Giant Powder Co. of San Francisco, and the Atlas Powder Co. of Wilmington, Delaware, a company in which the Du Pont family had an interest, and which itself had a minority interest in C.X.L. By the end of 1926, C.X.L. had three major explosives plants, substantial investments in acids and heavy chemicals, and a number of smaller properties producing organic chemical-based products. C.X.L. also held a block of 260,000 shares of General Motors. Nobel and Du Pont shared majority control of the company, valued at about $8,000,000 in 1926, with Atlas Powder Co. and a small Canadian interest holding the balance of shares.[7]

In December 1926, Nobel merged with Brunner, Mond and Co., Ltd., the large British fertilizer and heavy chemical producer, and two smaller firms, including British Dyestuffs Corporation Ltd., which specialized in organic chemical products, to form Imperial Chemicals Industries Ltd. This merger gave the new British company an industrial potential parallel in many product lines to those developed by the Du Pont corporation in the United States since 1917. Even before the formation of I.C.I., Nobel and Du Pont had been expanding a relationship that went back to the days of the powder trust and the establishment of C.X.L., to include exclusive patent and license exchange agreements in 1920 and 1925 in explosives and related products, and joint ownership of subsidiary companies to manufacture and sell Duco paints and Fabrikoid in the British Empire outside Canada, participation in the establishment of a company to market tetraethyl gasoline, and the separate purchases of shares in two German competitors in the powder industry, Köln-Rottwiler and Dynamit A.G.[8] The predilection on both sides was thus for an extension of their relationship into the chemicals field, and a pooling of their interests in regions of potentially damaging competition, such as Canada.

As early as June 1919, Lammot du Pont had proposed using C.X.L. as the vehicle for manufacturing and marketing in Canada the new chemical products that the Du Pont company was developing. Later that year, he and Sir Harry McGowan of Nobel agreed to divide C.X.L. common stock on an equal basis and agreed that the partners should provide C.X.L. with patents, licenses, and other technical assistance to enable that company to diversify in selected fields exclusively for the Canadian market. In 1920 the authorized common stock of the company was increased to $22,500,000, and new shares were distributed to permit Du Pont to acquire an equality with Nobel. Five years later, when Du Pont and Nobel renegotiated their general agreements, they arranged that when "exploiting any new products not covered by this agreement," C.X.L. would be given "preference" in acquiring rights to develop these products for the Canadian market.[9] The establishment of C.I.L. in 1927 thus did not represent a major change in policies or corporate relationships, but rather a recognition on both sides, though promoted most strongly by McGowan, of the need to reorganize the Canadian operation to expand its industrial activities following the creation of I.C.I.[10]

Canadian Industries Ltd. was incorporated in June 1927, with a new share issue of which Du Pont and I.C.I. took 46 per cent each, and the understanding that if either party increased its equity in C.I.L. the other would be entitled to acquire an equal amount through a new stock issue. The remainder was held by Atlas Powder Co. and the Canadian investors in C.X.L. The company was initially set up as a holding company with the largest operating subsidiary, Canadian Explosives, being chartered separately. During the next year, C.I.L. bought the Canadian properties of the National Ammonia Co. and the Grasselli Chemical Co. The Grasselli purchase, part of a larger acquisition by Du Pont of Grasselli in the United States, gave C.I.L. a foothold in the synthetic fertilizer field, and C.I.L.'s purchase of Canadian Salt Co. Ltd. in 1928 gave it effective control of the salt industry and its derivatives, chlorine and caustic soda, in Canada. In that same year, C.I.L. was reorganized into an operating company. The various subsidiaries were consolidated into eight divisions, along the lines of the Du Pont corporation, and subsequently reassembled into three broad "groups": the Cellulose Group, including paints and plastics; the Chemical Group, including dyestuffs and alkalis; and the Explosives Group.[11]

Over the next twenty years, C.I.L. continued to expand and diversify its activities within the Canadian chemical industry, largely with technical assistance and some financial help from Du Pont and I.C.I. Despite an overly ambitious move into the fertilizer business at a time when agricultural commodity prices were collapsing, the company weathered the worst of the Depression with only one year of declining sales and earnings, as C.I.L. opened relatively untapped markets for new chemical products through its access to the Canadian rights to many Du Pont patents. In 1933, C.I.L. opened a plant to produce cellophane, and in 1936 began to produce trichlorethylene, a metal solvent. In 1938, C.I.L. was the Canadian sales agent for Du Pont nylon products, and in 1940 established a plant to manufacture nylon yarn. These innovations gave C.I.L. a substantial advantage in exploiting the Canadian market for new chemical products.

Balanced against this advantage were the restrictions placed on C.I.L. in the export market, restrictions of no little consequence in the Depression when the relatively small Canadian market shrank even more in the older fields of fertilizers and explosives. Furthermore, the managers of C.I.L.

later maintained that on at least two occasions in this period the Canadian government pressured the company to venture into the international market to boost Canadian exports. In 1932, the Canadian company sought to export explosives to the British West Indies as the Canadian government was subsidizing steamship operations to that region and was encouraging Canadian manufacturers to use the facilities. Again, in 1935, the government pressed C.I.L. to enter the export market to increase employment, a point of some delicacy since the president of the firm was at that time head of a national commission on unemployment in Canada. In both cases, Du Pont and I.C.I. vetoed any departure from earlier agreements restricting C.I.L. to Canada.[12]

Despite these rebuffs, C.I.L. seems to have been able to develop a profitable mixture of traditional and new markets in Canada between 1928 and 1942. Company assets trebled in value in this period while earnings per share of common stock rose from $.43 in 1927 to $.72 in 1941, and sales and income rose steadily except for the year 1932.[13] To critics of the cartel and C.I.L.'s foreign ownership, the achievement of this growth and generally profitable performance was largely the result of the technical advantages conferred by the Du Pont–I.C.I. connection, and did not involve any substantial transfer of management skills to Canada. But while the managers of C.I.L. did not become "Canadianized" in a conventional sense during this period, they did develop a strong proprietary attitude toward the company, and deployed bargaining skills that helped ensure that C.I.L. would take full advantage of the opportunities provided by its association with Du Pont and I.C.I.

Executives of C.I.L.'s parent corporations in London and Wilmington, Delaware, were at least sporadically aware of the local antagonism that their Canadian operations aroused, although they did little to respond to critics' demands before 1948. Du Pont defense attorneys in the U.S. antitrust suit maintained that one of the underlying factors in the establishment of C.I.L. in 1927 was the "widespread local prejudice among Canadians" against foreign, especially American, companies. Even before this point, there were gestures toward recognizing the nationalist issue. In 1924, when Du Pont and Nobel chiefs met in London to select a new president for C.X.L. to succeed William McMaster, "it was unanimously agreed that the C.X.L. president should be a Canadian if at all possible."[14] The man chosen, however, was Arthur B. Purvis, a Scot who had worked for Nobel in South Africa and South America for twenty years, primarily because of his performance in merging Northern Giant Powder Co. with C.X.L. in 1925. After Purvis left to work for the British government in 1939, the subject recurred when Lord Melchett of I.C.I. noted "dissatisfaction ... expressed by certain representatives of Canadian universities, with C.I.L.'s tendencies to draw its senior staff from England and the United States rather than developing such talent among Canadians."

Nobody else felt strongly enough about this matter to suggest a Canadian successor to Purvis. Instead, the board confirmed George Huggett, an English-born veteran of various I.C.I. subsidiaries, who had served as Purvis's vice-president since 1927. Melchett, however, did propose that C.I.L. should exhibit its interest in developing Canadian talent by "the creation of scientific scholarships at the principal Universities and technical schools."[15] Some Du Pont executives felt that C.I.L. ought to find Canadians qualified to fill top management positions, but Du Pont president Walter S. Carpenter, Jr., in 1942 indicated an equally strong desire to build a C.I.L. staff with an "American background."[16]

The board of directors of C.I.L. included an equal number of Du Pont and I.C.I. directors, with Purvis as president and managing director. Four of the twelve directors were prominent Canadian businessmen: Ross McMaster, son of William McMaster, Purvis's predecessor, and himself a vice-president of the Steel Company of Canada; Lt. Col. Herbert Molson of the Molson brewing company; Sir Charles Gordon, president of Dominion Textile Co. and the Bank of Montreal; and Charles C. Ballantyne, managing director of Sherwin-Williams Co. of Canada. None of these directors held any significant block of shares in C.I.L., and except for McMaster they played only a minor role in the deliberations of the board.[17]

Between 1930 and 1944, virtually all the top management group directly beneath Purvis and the board was composed of Du Pont and Nobel veterans, some of whom moved between C.I.L. and the parent companies.[18] By any objective standards, C.I.L.'s management was extremely inbred during this period; and, despite periodic twinges of regret, the owners took a resolutely indifferent attitude toward demands for greater Canadian participation.

But while the management of C.I.L. was not Canadian, the executives, particularly Purvis, found it advantageous to emphasize the position of C.I.L. as a Canadian enterprise as well as, or instead of, a branch of two foreign corporations. After taking over C.I.L. in 1927, Purvis involved himself in affairs well beyond those of his company. In 1935–36, he served as a member of the national commission on unemployment, and in 1939 became a member, and later head, of the Anglo-French Purchasing Board in the United States until his untimely death in an airplane crash in 1941. Purvis was a director of a number of other Canadian corporations and a governor of McGill University in Montreal. Some business associates felt that Purvis was "aiming to become Prime Minister of Canada," and however improbable that may have been, his view of C.I.L. was suitably expansive.[19] He communicated his viewpoint down the line in his organization. At one point, when Purvis and Du Pont chiefs were at loggerheads, George Huggett wrote to J. Thompson Brown of the Du Pont executive committee that "Purvis was an idol both within the C.I.L. organization and outside in Canada," a factor that the Americans were obliged to take into account in their dealings with him and the Canadian company. As Wendell Swint, a member of the Du Pont foreign relations committee, remarked later, "Mr. Purvis was a pretty tough customer," adding, "We preferred to have C.I.L. a well run company and make money for us rather than continue to press him and probably even then not be successful at it."[20]

Purvis also demonstrated considerable political skill in playing his corporate masters off against one another, alternately posing as a true organization man and as a spokesman for a growing Canadian role in the chemical industry. This attitude proved irritating, especially to Du Pont managers who had to deal with C.I.L. below the policy level. As one exasperated Du Pont official acidly observed, after C.I.L. refused to buy from a key Du Pont supplier: "Mr. Purvis very often talks of the 'family' viewpoint in these matters ... but the trouble with all these C.I.L. discussions is that they generally wind up in one direction."[21]

Although on better terms with his old employers at I.C.I., particularly McGowan, Purvis did irritate with his persistent efforts to circumvent restrictions placed on C.I.L. by a very narrow reading of the clauses of various agreements between the companies, and by his expansion of C.I.L.'s capacity in fields such as fertilizers, where the Canadian market was limited. Purvis's response to criticism in this area was attuned to the conservative, anti-competitive attitude prevalent in I.C.U., arguing that C.I.L. had to develop unprofitable fields to keep out potential rivals who might then proceed to move into more profitable areas.[22] Through variations on these different themes, Purvis successfully promoted C.I.L.'s interests through a decade of constant haggling with Du Pont and I.C.I.

Purvis also figured prominently in a confrontation with Du Pont over the shares held by Atlas Powder Co. in Canadian Explosives and C.I.L. Soon after the formation of C.I.L. the Canadian company sought to have the major shareholders buy out Atlas, but Du Pont objected on the ground that Atlas was asking too high a price for its shares. Writing to McGowan in October 1928, Purvis discerned that the real reason for Du Pont's reluctance was that Atlas was controlled by "certain du Pont individuals through the Christiana Securities Company," giving Du Pont interests a 52 per cent share in the Canadian companies, contrary to the agreements between Du Pont and I.C.I. on stock distribution, not to mention "undesirable ... from the standpoint of a Canadian concern being controlled by U.S. interests." Under this pressure, Lammot Du Pont agreed to pay the Atlas asking price for C.I.L. shares. Although Alfred D. Chandler, Jr., in his biography of Pierre du Pont, has noted that Purvis's view of the Du Pont–Atlas connection was "exaggerated," there seems to be little doubt that Purvis played a pivotal role, characteristically combining appeals to one company head against another with rhetoric about Canadian interests.[23]

In 1939, when Purvis accepted appointment to the Anglo-French Purchasing Board, Du Pont insisted that he resign as president of C.I.L. and sell all his shares in the company to avoid conflict of interest charges. Although Du Pont executives could point to the unfortunate experience of their own company before U.S. congressional investigating committees in 1934–35 as justification for recommending this step, Purvis regarded the proposal as an effort to purge him because of his independence. Typically, he carried the matter to the executive committee of Du Pont, accusing them of bad faith, while other C.I.L. executives warned Du Pont of the wide repercussions Purvis's peremptory removal would have on C.I.L.'s public image in Canada. Ultimately, Purvis called on McGowan to mediate in the dispute, and in the end Du Pont backed down. Purvis remained as president of C.I.L. on extended "leave," retaining his shares in the company as well.[24]

Purvis's successor, George Huggett, proved to be less outspoken and more amenable to the non-Canadian interests, but by this time the parent companies were preoccupied with war production at home and the growing threat of antitrust prosecution, which induced them to undertake substantial changes in intercompany relationships after 1948. Even before that time, C.I.L., prompted by the Canadian government and critics in Parliament and the press, had embarked on an export drive in the Caribbean, and the 1948 agreement simply recognized an accomplished fact, arranging at the same time for C.I.L. to pay for non-exclusive patents and licenses by sharing its royalties on sales for fifteen years.[25]

Symptomatic of C.I.L.'s growing independence was its changing policy toward distribution of profits. Up to 1939 an average of 90 per cent of net earnings was distributed as dividends to shareholders, with the result that C.I.L. was tied to its foreign sponsors for any decisions involving substantial outlays of money. As a Du Pont memorandum noted, the Du Pont interest derived a relatively small gain from this policy after tax deductions and exchange rate differences were taken into account, indicating that the main purpose was control. Wartime demands for capital to expand production and retained earnings to cover increased taxes forced a change in this arrangement as C.I.L. kept more of its net profits for re-investment. The practice continued after the war, the percentage of profits distributed as dividends declining from 78 per cent to 72 per cent between 1945 and 1948.[26]

Another development contributing to its dependent posture was the increase in stock ownership by C.I.L. management, the outgrowth of a policy to provide stock as a bonus incentive to managers initiated in the early 1930s with Du Pont's blessing. By the end of the decade, C.I.L. internal equity had risen to the point that some Du Pont executives feared a dilution of control by the majority shareholders, with the C.I.L. management interest being in a position to play a balancing role between them.[27] Although this situation never developed, the Americans' concern was not misplaced. While the initiative for the changing relations between the companies came from such external pressures as wartime demands on resources and the U.S. antitrust suit, C.I.L. managers proved to be quite prepared to take advantage of the circumstances, just as Purvis had sought to exploit the more limited opportunities available in his tenure.

## Bargaining: Patents and Markets

The essence of the bargaining relationship between C.I.L. and its corporate parents involved a trade-off between the transfer of technology and restrictions on export markets. In principle, Du Pont and I.C.I. had agreed to use C.I.L. as their vehicle for exploiting present and future markets in Canada in all products; in practice, the parent companies, for various reasons, sought to retain Canadian rights over particular products. Under agreements made in 1928 and 1936, C.I.L. was in effect barred from exporting a range of products. Reading the provisions of those agreements as narrowly as possible, the Canadian company continually sought to develop exports in products and regions not specifically identified in the agreements. From these sets of circumstances the bargaining proceeded.

In 1928, the newly established C.I.L. was expected to expand by purchase or merger with Canadian competitors in the chemical industry in Canada, a policy leading to the absorption of such companies as Grasselli and Canadian Salt. The expansionist strategy was stymied, however, by the refusal of Allied Chemical Co., one of Du Pont's major competitors in the United States, to sell a large synthetic ammonia plant at Amherstburg, Ontario, to C.I.L. Imperial Chemical Industries then agreed to provide capital and technical assistance to enable C.I.L. to expand its production in fertilizers and heavy chemicals; but Du Pont objected to C.I.L.'s entering the Canadian dyestuffs market in which the American company was entrenched. As a general principle, Du Pont agreed to give C.I.L. an opportunity to propose to undertake production of any new Du Pont ventures in Canada, but was not bound to do so.[28] Over the next four years, these issues were to reappear in discussions among the companies.

Du Pont had made agreements with American producers of waterproof loading shells not to enter their market. C.I.L., which held its own patents on waterproof shells, announced in October 1928 its intention to enter the American market, as this was not a product scheduled for restriction in the Du Pont–I.C.I. agreements. The proposal naturally aroused resentment among American competitors who regarded the C.I.L. move as a Du Pont maneuver. To head this off, Du Pont agreed to buy the C.I.L. patents. At the same time, Du Pont finally agreed to share the Canadian dyestuffs market with C.I.L., which in effect meant with I.C.I., which supplied most of the C.I.L. product.[29]

In 1931, C.I.L. resurrected the proposal to buy and consolidate Canadian properties of Allied Chemical Co. Du Pont's foreign relations committee was skeptical about this idea since C.I.L. already seemed to have more than sufficient capacity in synthetic ammonia production in a period of agricultural distress. More alarming, however, was the intimation that C.I.L. intended to acquire Sherwin-Williams paint manufacturing and sales properties in Canada, or a share of them. The Du Pont paint division objected to this proposal since it had its own competitive line, and also warned of the possible leaking of technical information to Sherwin-Williams through C.I.L. In the end, C.I.L. backed down on the Sherwin-Williams deal, but Du Pont was obliged to give ground on the Allied Chemical proposal, although ultimately nothing definite came from discussions with Allied because of the stiff terms offered C.I.L.[30]

Although the clear implication of the 1928 Du Pont–I.C.I. agreement was that C.I.L. should keep out of foreign markets altogether, the Canadian company was always probing the outer limits of the provisions, seeking markets that neither of the owners would find objectionable. In 1934, H.J. Mitchell of I.C.I. noted that C.I.L. had been selling sporting equipment and ammunition in South America for more than six years, and the Canadian company argued that this market must be retained by them in order to keep manufacturing operations in the field going. At this same time, C.I.L. was demanding the right to sell ammunition in the West Indies to alleviate pressures from the Canadian government.[31]

By this time, even McGowan of I.C.I., who normally supported Purvis's expansive ambitions, was concerned that C.I.L.'s interpretation of the general patent and process agreements was placing undue strain on Du Pont–I.C.U. relations at a time when the British company was particularly anxious to maintain the cartel. In a confidential letter to Lammot du Pont, he agreed that a complete review of "the whole situation opposite C.I.L." was necessary and that "we shall have to call upon C.I.L. to forgo what may be claimed as existing legal rights if we are to get back to the original ... intention of the parties."[32]

Over the following year and a half, a new agreement was prepared, and after much dickering, it went into effect in December 1936. In the initial drafts of the agreement, Du Pont had introduced certain new restrictions on C.I.L.: the Canadian firm would be bound to pass on any new inventions or patents to Du Pont and I.C.I. even in non-scheduled product lines, while I.C.I. and Du Pont could continue to withhold patents from C.I.L. if they chose. Du Pont and I.C.I. could also establish manufacturing facilities in Canada independent of C.I.L. for the production of items for export from Canada. Purvis naturally opposed these innovations since C.I.L. was now definitely to be excluded from the export business, and I.C.I. backed his position on the issue of surrendering new patents without reciprocation. Purvis also tried to avoid having the new arrangements drawn up formally, but had to concede that point.[33]

Nevertheless, the final agreement did include some important concessions to the C.I.L. viewpoint. All products were itemized, and the right of C.I.L. to participate in, or be excluded from, manufacture of these items was explicitly noted, in place of the vague general statement Du Pont had proposed. Furthermore, C.I.L. was given the right to request disclosure of new patents and processes developed by I.C.I. or Du Pont, and the reasons for exclusion in any given case should be open for discussion among the three parties. Finally, the right of Du Pont and I.C.I. to establish manufacturing facilities in Canada independent of C.I.L. was restricted to the processing of raw materials or semi-finished products for supplying other subdivisions or subsidiaries of Du Pont or I.C.I. in non-scheduled items.[34]

The years 1937–39 were less troubled, as Purvis concentrated on developing C.I.L.'s manufacturing operations and Du Pont arranged for C.I.L. to handle nylon product sales in Canada. But tension persisted beneath the surface. In 1939, C.I.L. proposed to expand its production of synthetic ammonia through a joint undertaking with Shawinigan Chemical Co. Du Pont officials worried that arrangements with a potential rival might result in leaks concerning new Du Pont processes using "water gas" (carbon monoxide and hydrogen), which were applicable to a range of chemical products. Both Du Pont and I.C.I. were also concerned over C.I.L.'s heavy investment in the fertilizer business. Despite Purvis's argument that this move was basically pre-emptive to stymie future competition, the suspicion lingered that C.I.L. was building a case for expanding in product lines and markets when the general agreement came up for renewal in 1940.[35]

The onset of war raised new problems. In 1939, Purvis arranged to take over some of I.C.I.'s South America markets for the duration of the war without consulting Du Pont, and also laid plans for a vast expansion of C.I.L.'s synthetic ammonia and explosives manufacturing capacity through the establishment of a subsidiary, Defense Industries Ltd. After protracted debate, Du Pont vetoed C.I.L.'s entry into South America, where it planned to absorb the entire chemical market hitherto shared with I.C.I. and the German chemical trust, I.G. Farben, at least for the duration of the war. At the same time, Du Pont accepted the plans for Defense Industries Ltd., but made the grudging comment that "C.I.L. had gone a little too far in their proposals for utilizing their own money."[36]

Purvis's departure at the end of the year eased tensions somewhat particularly between C.I.L. and Du Pont, as the new acting president, Huggett, was on close terms with J. Thompson Brown, a Du Pont representative on the C.I.L. board. But the bargaining advantages began to shift more favorably to C.I.L. after 1942. When C.I.L. moved into the West Indies market after the war, it did so on its own initiative after Du

Pont and I.C.I. announced that products manufactured by these companies under patents not licensed to C.I.L. would enter Canada on a competitive basis, a measure probably taken to alleviate antitrust pressures.[37]

## Bargaining: Intercompany Pricing

Another area of contention and maneuvering in the C.I.L.–I.C.I.–Du Pont relationship involved inter-company price arrangements for products sold to the Canadian company by divisions of the parent firms. These arrangements were deceptively simply in principle, but immensely complicated in practice, and produced continuous infighting, primarily between C.I.L. and division heads at Du Pont. Du Pont president Walter S. Carpenter, Jr. noted later: "Mr. Purvis was ... a very astute and aggressive negotiator, and ... he met men of somewhat similar caliber in some of our general managers ... [T]he result of those negotiations ... would be this constant bickering and trading and so on [which produced] a rather unfortunate feeling on the part of both parties."[38] Top management for both Du Pont and I.C.I. at times intervened in these conflicts and sought to work out general formulas to resolve the differences, but their measures were usually only palliatives. In this chronic haggling, C.I.L. often had to give way, particularly if its demands jeopardized the broader I.C.I.–Du Pont arrangements, but C.I.L. negotiators proved no less adept at extracting concessions in this area than they were in discussions concerning patents and markets.

The subject first arose as a matter of controversy between Canadian Explosives Ltd., and Du Pont before the establishment of C.I.L. Under general agreements between Du Pont and Nobel in 1920 and 1925, C.X.L. was to be given prices on raw materials, semi-finished and finished products equivalent to the lowest market price quoted for American and Canadian customers. In 1927 Purvis, as president of C.X.L., complained that Du Pont divisions "had taken something of a trading attitude in dealing with C.X.L.," charging higher prices than those given other Canadian buyers. After some discussion Du Pont agreed to have its divisions treat C.X.L. as if it were an 85 per cent subsidiary of Du Pont, "enjoying as low a price as any other subsidiary ... as would be consistent with Du Pont's costs," except when the product was scarce or difficult to replace.[39]

This agreement did not end the problem, however, since each division had its own special price arrangements with C.X.L., and when C.I.L. was created, the general principle established was that C.I.L. should be supplied "at mill replacement cost (including factory cost and factory overhead) plus 10 per cent, or the best price allowed to any U.S. customers, whichever is lower." This arrangement was not reached without much maneuvering for better terms: Purvis had proposed that Du Pont supply certain products at cost on the ground that in the end the Du Pont corporation would benefit from C.I.L.'s general return on investment. Carpenter of Du Pont countered with a proposal of cost plus 15 per cent on a long-term contract basis that would operate regardless of market price. Mill cost plus 10 per cent thus represented a compromise. I.C.I. subsequently made a similar agreement with C.I.L.[40]

Still matters were not settled. In 1932, Du Pont discovered that C.I.L. in its purchases from one or the other of its parent companies had been "playing the two partners against each other to get a percentage lower than 10 per cent over cost," the difference arising from the fact that some divisions included cost of research in the calculation of "factory overhead" while others did not.[41] Steps were taken to bring about better coordination, if not uniformity, among divisions and companies.

C.I.L. also asserted its right to go outside Du Pont and I.C.I. if the prices quoted seemed unsatisfactory. In 1932, C.I.L. cancelled an order for ethylene glycol, a synthetic glycerine, from British Dyestuffs, an I.C.I. subsidiary, on the ground that the price was too high, and proceeded to build its own equipment for polymerized glycerine rather than accept the price, a decision G.W. White of I.C.I. (New York) characterized as "relatively disastrous."[42]

Du Pont engaged C.I.L. in an extended controversy over the price of isobutanol, a solvent used in producing paints. In 1936, C.I.L. charged that Du Pont was charging it a higher price than Du Pont's own paint division. The general manager of the Du Pont ammonia division countered that the special internal price was given because of the high demand for butanol by the Du Pont paint division, which might otherwise go outside the company to fill its needs, and becasue the Canadian butanol price would be higher in any case, and the price offered was below mill cost plus 10 per cent. H. Greville-Smith of C.I.L. rejected these arguments as specious since the calculation of the Canadian price included duties on imported butanol. At this point Du Pont's foreign relations committee intervened in a vain attempt to demonstrate to C.I.L. that the price offered was the best market price. Rather than accept the Du Pont price, C.I.L. changed its formula for paint solvents from isobutanol to ethyl acetate and pentasol. In 1938, when Canadian duties on isobutanol were lifted temporarily, Du Pont again sought to get C.I.L.'s business, but the Canadian company now argued that it had established relations with Shawinigan Chemical Co. for the supply of ethyl acetate, and did not wish to endanger a growing connection with Shawinigan in other joint endeavors. Despite the fact that Du Pont's ammonia division was now eager to get C.I.L. business, the Canadian company maintained its relations with Shawinigan.[43]

Although Greville-Smith later maintained that his company made no effort to keep track of relative purchases from I.C.I. and Du Pont, documents compiled in 1940 and 1948 indicated that a generally equal division was maintained up to 1939. On balance, however, purchases from Du Pont exceeded those from I.C.I. by about $200,000 per year except in the field of dyestuffs in which I.C.I. actively promoted buying by C.I.L. Outside of this area, C.I.L. seems to have been allowed to follow its own course in seeking the best price between the two parent companies.[44]

The cost plus 10 per cent formula remained in effect until 1946, but in practice it was abandoned after 1940 as individual Du Pont divisions worked out their own sales arrangements with C.I.L.; I.C.I., with its domestic wartime demand, was practically out of the picture. The Canadian company's growth as a major industry during the war gave it a better bargaining position, and its corporate parents were not necessarily shown favoritism. Between 1941 and 1948, Du Pont's share of C.I.L.'s total purchases of raw materials and resale products declined from 25 per cent to 21 per cent and I.C.I.'s from 14 per cent to 3 per cent. By contrast, the share of Canadian suppliers rose from 35 per cent to 55 per cent.[45]

## Conclusion

This study has emphasized the independence exercised by the management of C.I.L. in their relations with the parent companies between 1928 and 1948. The purpose has not been to argue that this situation was typical of management relations in multinational enterprises even during this period when instruments of communication and financial control were less sophisticated and far-reaching than today. Nor could it be said that C.I.L. operated even in its home market with few restraints. On the contrary, the interesting aspect of this case is that C.I.L.'s management possessed any autonomy at all given the preponderance of foreign ownership in the company and the subordinate role that Du Pont and I.C.I. expected it to play in the functioning of the international chemical cartel. Yet from the time of its establishment, the executives of C.I.L. did assert the right to make their own decisions on a range of matters, and continually pressed for a larger role in the international market, while bypassing contractual restrictions placed on them wherever possible. That such a situation should develop within an international corporate system so apparently monolithic to outside observers highlights the need to analyze the actual process of decisionmaking in these organizations as well as the structure of financial control when seeking to determine the distribution of power within multinational enterprises.

There were a number of factors that helped C.I.L. pursue an independent course in its relations with Du Pont and I.C.I. After 1942, of course, the growing criticism in Canada and antitrust prosecution in the United States pressured the parent companies to provide C.I.L. with more freedom to enter export markets. But even before that point, such issues as

C.I.L.'s investment policies, inter-company price policies, and sharing of technology had been settled by bargaining among the companies, not by commands from the parent firms, and in these negotiations C.I.L.'s representatives had taken an active part.

In large measure, C.I.L.'s autonomy derived from the fact that it was a jointly owned enterprise, and that the two major shareholders were sufficiently different that they could be played off against one another. Despite a tradition of cooperation reaching back to the nineteenth century, Du Pont and I.C.I. were companies run by men of different nationalities, with divergent experiences and objectives; and, as William J. Reader, the historian of I.C.I., has noted, their alliance was subject to growing strains even before the American antitrust action forced changes in their relationship.[46] Furthermore, C.I.L. had a natural inclination to rely on I.C.I. for support in many situations, since both were tied to the British imperial system, and since Nobel had been the senior partner in control of C.I.L.'s predecessor companies before the 1920s. Purvis was particularly skilled at manipulating this connection to C.I.L.'s advantage, and the Canadian company fared poorly only when it had managed to antagonize both Du Pont and I.C.I., as was the case in 1934–35 when C.I.L. pressed too hard for export markets. Du Pont does not seem to have regarded C.I.L.'s tactics as evidence of a conspiracy with I.C.I. although Walter Carpenter, Jr. noted the relatively small number of Du Pont men in C.I.L. management. Nevertheless, it is difficult to avoid the conclusion that Purvis and other C.I.L. executives saw I.C.I. as temperamentally the more sympathetic of the two owners and relied on these ties of personal sympathy in their maneuvers.

Another contributing factor was the attitude of both Du Pont and I.C.I. toward management autonomy in principle. Both were large multi-divisional companies that had reorganized their own operations at home in the 1920s to promote decentralization at the operating level.[47] A divisional general manager or head of a domestic subsidiary who performed well and ran a profitable operation would not be likely to meet with much interference from above unless his activities adversely affected broader policies. This attitude was exemplified by Wendell Swint's remark about Purvis that "we preferred to have C.I.L. a well run company and make money" even if this meant tolerating a rather outspoken independence of viewpoint. At the same time, the element of individual personality must be given its due: Purvis was by all accounts a skilled and persuasive negotiator, and he was largely responsible for ensuring that C.I.L.'s interests were advanced in the early years of the company when he had few resources with which to bargain.

One final element contributing to management autonomy was, ironically, Canadian nationalism. While Du Pont and I.C.I. chiefs were generally unresponsive to direct criticisms of their control of C.I.L., they could not disregard the nationalist sentiment altogether. Should they have been tempted to do so, Purvis constantly reminded them that C.I.L. was a Canadian company, subject to the laws and pressures that the government and public opinion of that country could bring to bear upon them, and that C.I.L. by right deserved every opportunity to build up its productive capacity, even though 'n the long run this might require Du Pont and I.C.I. to give it a larger international role than was originally contemplated. In large measure, of course, this kind of argument when made by Purvis was intended to serve his tactical purposes. But the American and British businessmen were made uncomfortably aware that the points he raised had a substantial basis in fact and had to be dealt with diplomatically. To say that concern for Canadian public repercussions conditioned Du Pont's and I.C.I.'s relations with C.I.L. in this period would be an exaggeration; but it was a factor of some consequence, and one that could only be of importance in a multinational enterprise.

## Notes

† Financial assistance for the research in preparing this study was provided by the Dalhousie University Research and Development Fund in 1976, and the Centre for International Business Studies at Dalhousie University, Halifax, Nova Scotia in 1977–78. The author is also indebted to Alfred D. Chandler, Jr. for suggestions relating to research sources and to Richmond Williams and the staff of Eleutherian Mills Historical Library, Greenville, Del., for their assistance.

1. Dominion of Canada, House of Commons, *Debates, 1944 Session*, vol. II, pp. 1763–1769.

2. Statement by Wendell Berge, Assistant Attorney General, U.S. Department of Justice, Wash., D.C., January 10, 1944, in Jasper Crane Papers, Box 1036, Records of E.I. du Pont de Nemours Co., series II, part 2. Eleutherian Mills Historical Library, Greenville, Del. Hereafter referred to as Crane Papers.

3. United States vs. Imperial Chemical Industries, E.I. du Pont de Nemours Co., Inc., et al., 100 *Federal Supplement* 504, 557–564 (1951).

4. Few critical studies of multinational enterprise have dealt specifically with issues of internal management relations in detail, but see Richard J. Barnet and Ronald E. Miller, *Global Reach: The Power of the Multinational Corporations* (New York, 1974), 42–44, and Kari Levitt, *Silent Surrender: The Multinational Corporation in Canada* (Toronto, 1970), 83–89, for representative comments. Detailed studies of the internal management of multinational companies in recent years include J.M. Stopford and L.T. Wells, Jr., *Managing the Multinational Enterprise: Organization of the Firm and Ownership* (New York, 1972); and M.Z. Brooke and H.L. Remmers, *The Strategy of Multinational Enteprise: Organization and Finance* (London, 1970). See also A.E. Safarian, *Foreign Ownership of Canadian Industry* (Toronto, 1973), 50–70.

5. See L.F. Haber, *The Chemical Industry, 1900–1930* (London, 1971), 9–33, 135–149, 173–183, 291–318, on the commercial and technological development of the chemical industry in this period. On the tradition of international cartels in chemicals, see G.W. Stocking and M.W. Watkins, *Cartels in Action: Case Studies in International Business Diplomacy* (New York, 1946), 418–429.

6. "Canadian Industries Ltd. and Predecessor and Associated Companies," in Accession 1460, Box 32, Records of E.I. du Pont de Nemours Co., series II, part 2. See also W.J. Reader, *Imperial Chemical Industries: A History*, vol. I (London, 1970), 196, 211–212.

7. Herbert Marshall, Frank Southard, and Kenneth Taylor, *Canadian-American Industry: A Study in International Investment* (New Haven, 1936), 82–84; A.D. Chandler, Jr. and Stephen Salsbury, *Pierre S. Du Pont and the Making of the Modern Corporation* (New York, 1971), 477, 567–568; W.J. Reader, *Imperial Chemical Industries: A History*, vol. II (London, 1974), 212–213.

8. Stocking and Watkins, *Cartels* 438–450; Chandler and Salsbury, *Pierre S. Du Pont*, 570–571; Reader, *Imperial Chemical*, vol. II, 13–21.

9. United States vs. Imperial Chemical Industries, E.I. du Pont de Nemours Co., Inc., et al., trial records, Govt. Exhibit 15, A.T. 4134; Govt. Exhibit 18, A.T. 4138; Govt Exhibit 21, A.T. 2570-A; Govt. Exhibit 24, A.T. 4206. Hereafter referred to as U.S. v. I.C.I. Records. The trial transcript and records were deposited by the Du Pont corporation at Eleutherian Mills Historical Library.

10. Reader, *Imperial Chemical*, vol. II, 212.

11. "Canadian Industries Ltd. and Predecessor and Associated Companies."

12. Transcript of meeting, Montreal, September 16, 1932. U.S. v. I.C.I. Records, Govt. Exhibit 816, A.T. 4337; testimony of H. Greville-Smith, vice president, Canadian Industries Ltd., May 17, 1950. U.S. v. I.C.I. trial transcript, 2078–2079.

13. Canadian Industries Ltd., Annual Reports, 1928, 1943.

14. Minutes of meeting at Nobel House, London, April 29, 1924. U.S. v. I.C.I. Records, Govt. Exhibit 48, A.T. 4379.

15. Notes on discussion at Walter Carpenter's house, October 3, 1940. Crane Papers, Box 1043.

16. Jasper Crane, Du Pont foreign relations committee, to Walter S. Carpenter, Jr., president, Du Pont, March 2, 1942; Carpenter to Sir Harry McGowan, chairman, Imperial Chemical Industries Ltd., May 15, 1942. Crane Papers, Box 1034.

17. McGowan of Nobel had observed of the Canadian directors of C.I.L.'s predecessor company that "they should clearly understand that their nomination comes from Nobel's," Reader, *Imperial Chemical*, vol. I, 211.

18. In 1934–36, the C.I.L. management committee, which included the president and vice president, Purvis and Huggett, and the heads of the four groups of divisions, consisted of four men from I.C.I. and its subsidiaries, and two from Du Pont. Canadian Industries Ltd., Annual Report, 1935.

19. Reader, *Imperial Chemical*, vol. II, 212–213; *Dictionary of National Biography, 1941–1950* (London, 1959), 700–702.

20. George Huggett, vice president, C.I.L., to J. Thompson Brown, executive committee, Du Pont, November 14, 1939. Crane Papers, Box 1034; testimony of Wendell R. Swint, foreign relations committee, Du Pont, June 6, 1950. U.S. v. I.C.I. trial transcript, 2992.

21. William Richter, Du Pont Fabrics and Finishes Dept. to Jasper Crane, foreign relations committee, Du Pont, November 24, 1930. Crane Papers, Box 1034.

22. Reader, vol. II, 214; minutes of meeting, Wilmington, Del., October 19, 1937. U.S. v. I.C.I. Records, Govt. Exhibit 881, A.T. 3748-A.

23. Arthur B. Purvis, president, C.I.L., to Sir Harry McGowan, October 15, 1928; minutes of meeting, New York, October 23, 1928. U.S. v. I.C.I. Records, Govt. Exhibit 772, ICI(L); Govt. Exhibit 774, ICI(L). Chandler and Salsbury, *Pierre S. Du Pont*, 569.

24. Memorandum on C.I.L. and Arthur B. Purvis, October–November, 1939. Crane Papers, Box 1034.

25. Memorandum regarding Practices and Procedures to be followed with respect to Export Sales, C.I.L. Foreign Relations Committee, February 23, 1948. U.S. v. I.C.I. Records, Defense Exhibit D-673, C.I.L.; Agreement between I.C.I. and C.I.L., August 19, 1948. U.S. v. I.C.I. Records, Defense Exhibit D-743, ICI. These agreements were part of a general restructuring of relations between Du Pont and I.C.I. ending all cross-licensing arrangements and the system of exclusive regional licenses except in certain fields. The final consent decree in the case of U.S. v. I.C.I. et al. in 1952 eliminated these arrangements as well. See Reader, *Imperial Chemical*, vol. II, 437–441.

26. Memorandum: Dividend Policy of Canadian Industries Ltd., April 30, 1941. Crane Papers, Box 1034: U.S. v. I.C.I. Records, Defense Exhibit D-664, CIL. It should be noted that a substantial part of the capital for establishment of Defense Industries Ltd. was provided by the Canadian government.

27. John K. Jenney, assistant director, Foreign Trade Development Division, Du Pont, to Du Pont foreign relations committee, n.d. (1941), Crane Papers, Box 1034. Ironically, I.C.I. had first raised this possibility in 1935, but had been persuaded by Du Pont to endorse the stock bonus program as preferable to cash bonuses. Minutes of meeting, London, June 17, 1935. U.S. v. I.C.I. Records, Govt. Exhibit 846, A.T. 3085-A.

28. Minutes of meeting, Montreal, October 2, 1928. U.S. v. I.C.I. Records, Govt. Exhibit 173, ICI(L); minutes of meeting, Wilmington, Del., October 12, 1928. U.S. v. I.C.I. Records, Govt. Exhibit 174, A.T. 3646.

29. Minutes, Du Pont foreign relations committee meeting, October 6, 1928. U.S. v. I.C.I. Govt. Exhibit 190, A.T. 3641; minutes of meeting. Montreal, December 4, 1930. Crane Papers, Box 1034.

30. Robert Salmon, C.I.L. chemicals group, to Jasper Crane, February 27, 1931; Crane to Purvis, March 6, 1931; Purvis to Crane, March 19, 1931; L.W. Haslett, C.I.L. cellulose group to Crane, April 27, 1931. Crane Papers, Box 1034. I.C.I. held shares in Allied Chemical through an investment by one of its predecessor companies, Brunner, Mond., in Solvay Process Co., which merged with four other firms in 1920 to form Allied. In 1928, I.C.I. sold most of its Allied shares to the French chemical company, Solvay et Cie., but retained a small amount, equal to less than 1 per cent of Allied's issued capital. Despite this participation, relations between I.C.I. and Allied were never very cordial. The initial steps that led to the establishment of I.C.I. in 1926 were the result of a breakdown in merger negotiations between Brunner, Mond, and Allied. See Reader, *Imperial Chemical*, vol. II, 15, 35–37, 49–50.

31. H.J. Mitchell to Lammot du Pont, June 11, 1934. Crane Papers, Box 1039.

32. Sir Harry McGowan to Lammot du Pont, June 11, 1934. Crane Papers, Box 1039.

33. W.R. Swint, foreign relations committee, Du Pont to Lammot du Pont, July 10, 1934. Crane Papers, Box 1034; G.W. White, president, I.C.I. (New York) to L.J. Greenwood, foreign relations department, I.C.I., February 18, 1936. U.S. v. I.C.I. Records, Govt. Exhibit 853, ICI(L); Arthur B. Purvis to Lammot du Pont, September 15, 1936. U.S. v. I.C.I. Records, Govt. Exhibit 858, ICI(L).

34. Agreement between Imperial Chemical Industries, Ltd., E.I. du Pont de Nemours and Co., Canadian Industries Ltd., December 1, 1936. U.S. v. I.C.I. Records, Govt. Exhibit 868, A.T. 1701.

35. F.A. Wardenburg, Du Pont Ammonia Dept. to Jasper Crane, January 25, 1938. Crane Papers, Box 1037; W.R. Swint, foreign relations committee to M.G. Tate, I.C.I. (New York), November 28, 1938. Crane Papers, Box 1034; Minutes of

meeting, Wilmington, Del., October 19, 1937. U.S. v. I.C.I. Records, Govt. Exhibit 881, A.T. 3747-A.

36. E.J. Barnsley, I.C.I. (New York) to Lord Melchett, October 13, 1939. U.S. v. I.C.I. Records, Govt. Exhibit 715, ICI(L).

37. W.R. Swint to George Huggett, president, C.I.L., November 21, 1945; J.H. Wadsworth, I.C.I. Foreign Relations Department, to Huggett, December 11, 1945. U.S. v. I.C.I. Records, Defense Exhibits D-665, D-668, ICI(L); Testimony of Herbert H. Lank, vice president, C.I.L., May 18, 1950. U.S. v. I.C.I. trial transcript, 2122.

38. Testimony of Walter S. Carpenter, Jr., June 8, 1950. U.S. v. I.C.I. trial transcript, 3218.

39. Lammot du Pont to executive committee, Du Pont, June 29, 1927. U.S. v. I.C.I. Records, Defense Exhibit D-755, DP; Walter S. Carpenter, Jr. to Du Pont departments, July 1, 1927. U.S. v. I.C.I. Records, Govt. Exhibit 177, ICI(L).

40. Walter Carpenter, Jr., to Lammot du Pont, August 18, 1927; Carpenter to Arthur B. Purvis, August D-773, DP. See also Reader, *Imperial Chemical*, vol. II, 216.

41. John K. Jenney to W.R. Swint, March 8, 1932. Crane Papers, Box 1034.

42. G.W. White, president, I.C.I. (New York), to H. Greville-Smith, cellulose group, C.I.L., August 11, 1932. U.S. v. I.C.I. Defense Exhibit D-852, ICI.

43. H. Greville-Smith, memorandum: Isobutanol Prices to C.I.L., July 13, 1936; R.W. McClelland, Du Pont Ammonia Dept. to Jasper Crane, July 22, 1936; Greville-Smith to Crane, August 4, 1936; Crane to Greville-Smith, August 7, 1936; Greville-Smith to Crane, January 27, 1938. Crane Papers, Box 1034.

44. J.K. Jenney to W.R. Swint: Data on C.I.L. Purchases from Major Stock-holders, January 8, 1940. Crane Papers, Box 1034; U.S. v. I.C.I. Records, Defense Exhibit D-792, CIL, schedules AS-1, A-2; testimony of H. Greville-Smith, May 17, 1950. U.S. v. I.C.I. trial transcript, 2035–2036.

45. W.R. Swint to George Huggett, November 21, 1945. U.S. v. I.C.I. Records, Defense Exhibit D-782. DP.

46. Reader, *Imperial Chemical*, vol. 416–417.

47. See Alfred D. Chandler, Jr., *Strategy and Structure: Chapters in the History of Industrial Enterprise* (Cambridge, Mass., 1962), 104–111, on Du Pont's decentralization. In the case of I.C.I., decentralization was enhanced by the fact that the two major elements of the company were drawn from quite different industrial and cultural backgrounds. See Reader, *Imperial Chemicals*, vol. II, 71–74.

# 16

## Foreign Direct Investment and Japanese Economic Development, 1899–1931*

Mark Mason[†]

*Source: *Business and Economic History*, 16 (1987), pp. 93–107.

Too often accounts of the economic development of Japan underrate the impact of foreigners. Through statement or omission, for example, much of the literature on modern Japanese economic development attaches little significance to foreign direct investment (FDI) in that country's growth process. William Lockwood, the noted economic historian of Japan, concluded in one study that: "Except in the handling and financing of overseas trade in the early decades, one cannot fail to be impressed with the meager contribution of foreign business in *Japan* to the industrialization process" [11, p. 323]. Few studies have analyzed the development of foreign direct investment in Japan, published data are scarce, and standard economic histories sometimes do not even mention its existence.[1]

Was the role of foreign direct investment in Japan's economic development early in this century really "meager"? This essay examines the roughly three decades between the end of extraterritoriality and the rise of militarism in Japan—the period from 1899 to 1931—to test the validity of this received view of the history of foreign enterprise in Japan. Only from 1899 did changes in international treaties explicitly give foreigners the right to directly invest in Japan outside the so-called Treaty Settlements. The subject here investigated is foreign direct, rather than portfolio or indirect, investment. By foreign direct investment is meant business enterprise based in one country yet operating abroad, with real or potential management participation in a foreign entity—not simple financial flows across boundaries.

Western Electric could hardly wait for treaty revision to establish an operation in Japan. "I am more than ever convinced that there is a large amount of business for us here," wrote Harry Thayer, the manager of the International Department, from Tokyo in 1897. "It will come and continue to come if we give it first class attention, and if we do not it will go to some one, either native or foreign, who does." Conditions called for a direct business presence: "It is too far from home to do it well in any other way than having some technical mechanical and business ability here" [2, Thayer to Welles, 1897].

Yet there were difficulties. For one thing, Japanese law did not yet permit direct investment by foreigners outside the Treaty Settlements. For another, even when the laws would change he worried about a "strong popular and governmental sentiment in favor of home manufacturers" [2, Thayer to Hudson, 1898].

Thayer had a plan. Western Electric would form an alliance with a native concern, Oki Shokai, to manufacture and sell Western Electric telephone equipment in Japan. In Yokohama, the American firm would establish an office to coordinate the importation and supply of necessary parts and knowhow to enable Oki to manufacture. Oki and Western Electric would split profits from sales down the middle. The U.S. company would have the option of a one-half interest in the business "whenever the laws of Japan permit foreign ownership of stock or partnership interests in native enterprise" [2, Thayer to Hudson, 1898]. The talks failed.[2] Western Electric then turned to its Japanese sales agent, Iwadare Kunihiko, and proposed a similar arrangement. On August 31, 1898, Iwadare and an associate formally established Nippon Electric Limited Partnership. It was agreed that, upon treaty revision, the concern would be reorganized into a joint stock company with Western Electric holding a direct interest [14, pp. 5–7].

Western Electric wasted no time entering Japan as a direct investor: the Nippon Electric Company (NEC) was organized under Japanese law, with 54% of the capital supplied by Western Electric, on July 17, 1899—the very day that the revised treaty between Japan and the United States went into effect! As such, it was one of the first joint ventures in Japan proper between foreign and Japanese business in modern history [14, p. 8].

What was the value of foreign direct investment in Japan from 1899 to 1931? Scattered data offer clues.[3] One set of estimates, derived from balance of payment figures of the Ministry of Finance, put total "direct foreign investment in Japanese enterprise" at about $50 million in 1913, $72.5 million between 1919 and 1922, and $122.5 million in 1929 [13, pp. 507–533]. Government figures cited by the Bank of Japan place total foreign investment in Japanese banks and companies at $2.5 million in 1905 and $57 million in 1931 [6, p. 161]. Lockwood figured total foreign direct investment in 1934 at between $75 and $100 million [11, p. 260].

American capital clearly accounted for a greater proportion of foreign direct investment in Japan by the end of this period than did any other single country. Yet the US Department of Commerce estimated all American foreign direct investment in Japan at just $60.7 million in 1929, and manufacturing investment at about $40 million [18, p. 26]. The total capital of the 13 US branch factories in Japan listed in a 1932 report of the

Commerce Department stood at about $27 million [calculated from data in 19].

Whatever the precise figures for world and U.S. foreign direct investment in Japan during this period, in international terms they were small. Foreign direct investment in China, an East Asian neighbor for which there is adequate historical data, far exceeded levels in Japan. According to Remer, total foreign direct investment in China stood at $503 million in 1902, $1.084 billion in 1914 and $2.532 billion in 1931 [16, p. 69]. It therefore appears that, even if we accept the upper end of the range of estimates for Japan, foreign direct investment in China exceeded foreign direct investment in Japan by about a factor of 20 at the time of the Manchurian Incident.[4]

United States direct investment in Japan as compared to all US foreign direct investment similarly suggests the paucity of direct foreign business investment in Japan during this period. It has been estimated that total American direct investment abroad grew from $634.5 million in 1897 to $7.553 billion in 1929. If we accept the 1929 Commerce Department data for Japan cited above, just 0.8% of all US direct investment abroad had found its way to Japan by that year [10, p. 605]. Indeed, even within Asia, the share of US foreign direct investment in Japan accounted for less than 14% of total US FDI for the region in 1929 [10, p. 606].

Yet foreign direct investment in Japan during this period proved highly significant *qualitatively* even if it did not amount to much *quantitatively*. A closer look will bring out numerous aspects of its importance for the developing Japanese economy.

First, of course, foreign enterprise brought with it the manufacture in Japan of a whole range of products using advanced western techniques. Dunlop Rubber, a British firm, established the first modern tire factory in Japan. Libbey-Owens Sheet Glass, an American firm, joined with Japanese interests to modernize the production of window glass. Ford and General Motors assembled automobiles from imported "knocked down" kits using the conveyor belt assembly method. Siemens brought to its joint venture with the Furukawa group new technologies for the production of electrical machinery. As two western economists therefore concluded, "To the rise of manufactures [based upon advanced western technology], after the turn of the century—and still more after the First World War—foreigners made important contributions, sometimes in close partnership with Japanese firms and sometimes alone" [1, p. 228].

A substantial range of foreign companies set up operations in Japan. These included trading firms, commercial banks, shipping concerns, investment houses, life insurance companies, and manufacturing operations. A survey of major foreign capital-affiliated manufacturing firms which had entered Japan by 1932 lists among their output everything from electric lamps to oxygen to bicycle seats [8].

It is additionally interesting to observe the patterns of entry by time between 1899 and the Manchurian Incident. In general it seems clear that there was a shift from foreign direct investment in trading and related activities to FDI in the manufacturing industries.[5] On the industrial field, available studies indicate that a clear majority of foreign direct investors in this period entered between 1917 and 1931. A study of American branch factories in Japan as of 1932 points to a similar pattern. According to this report, at least nine of the reported 13 US direct manufacturing investment entries in Japan during these three decades began operations from 1917. Moreover, five or more of the 13 plants started to operate from 1927, and during these closing years of the period three previously established producers each doubled their capitalization [19]. (See Table 1.)

Japanese and United States Government data reveal the pattern of foreign direct investment by industry. These studies indicate that a plurality of major direct investments took place in the machine tool and electrical machinery industries. Also important were rubber products, automobiles,

*Table 1*  U.S. branch factories in Japan as of 1932

| Japanese firm | U.S. parent | Year operations commenced |
|---|---|---|
| Nippon Electric (NEC) | International Telephone & Telegraph | 1899 |
| Tokyo Electric | International General Electric | 1905 |
| Shibaura Engineering | International General Electric | 1910 |
| Yokohama Rubber | B.F. Goodrich Rubber | 1917 |
| Japan Steel Products | Truscon Steel Products | 1919 |
| Ford Motor Japan | Ford Motor | 1925 |
| Nippon Hanovia Quartz Lamp | Hanovia Chemical | 1926 |
| General Motors Japan | General Motors | 1927 |
| Victor Talking Machine Japan | Victor Talking Machine | 1928 |
| Toyo Carrier Kogyo | Carrier Engineering | 1931 |
| Toyo Otis Elevator | Otis Elevator | 1931 |
| Mitsubishi Oil | Associated Oil | 1932 |
| A.P. Muning & Co. | A.P. Muning & Co. | N/A |

*Source:* [19].

*Notes:* ITT acquired Western Electric's operations in Japan in 1925 through its takeover of International Western Electric. No date given for the commencement of operations by A.P. Muning & Co. Omitted from the above list is Japan Corn Products (U.S. Parent: Corn Products Refining; Year Operations Commenced: 1931), listed as a U.S. branch factory in the Commerce Department data. This branch was located in Korea, a Japanese colony when the Commerce study was written. However, the Commerce Department data fail to include all major instances of U.S. branch factories in Japan in 1932. One clear omission is Libbey-Owens Sheet Glass, which had a direct equity investment in American–Japan Sheet Glass from 1918.

records and miscellaneous mechanical goods based on engineering developments in the West.

Not only did foreign direct investors during this period represent a variety of foreign commercial interests engaged in a broad range of activities, they also included some of that era's great multinational enterprises. There were, among others, major producers of electrical goods such as General Electric, Western Electric and Siemens; the automakers Ford and General Motors; the rubber manufacturers Dunlop Rubber and B. F. Goodrich; and Sweden Match and others.

A second aspect of the importance of foreign direct investment is that foreign capital-related firms provided the Japanese with business knowledge not only of advanced technology but also of western methods of business management—what together might be termed "knowledge transfer." This knowledge the Japanese acquired from the direct investor in two ways: by learning about new business methods and production techniques that the foreign enterprise imported and practiced in Japan, and by participating in training programs and inspection tours of the foreign company's home operations.[6]

The Western Electric-NEC joint venture provides a clear illustration of this knowledge transfer. Even before NEC began to produce telephone equipment, the US firm sent over an advisor to supervise the renovation of the NEC facilities. Western Electric shipped to Japan telephone sets, switchboards, meters, gauges and so forth for sale through NEC to Japanese consumers—thus providing NEC workers with the latest examples of Western Electric engineering and product design [14, p. 7].

At the suggestion of one of the resident American managers of the joint venture, NEC's Managing Director, Iwadare, travelled to the United States in 1905 to observe Western Electric's home operations at first hand. He was impressed with the American firm's "advanced systems of management and production control, and he readily acknowledged the fact that NEC's methods were rather primitive in comparison" [14, p. 9]. As a result, Iwadare directed that the two Japanese NEC trainees at Western Electric concentrate their study on the US firm's accounting and production control systems.

Western Electric's contributions did not stop there. Under the guidance of the American firm, NEC replaced its traditional Japanese *oyakata* system of subcontracting with a system through which NEC itself employed not only supervisors to oversee the completion of individual tasks but also the workers directly responsible for these specific duties. This established "a clear chain of command. At the top of this chain was the plant superintendent and under him came section chiefs, branch chiefs, and foremen, in that order. All work was paid at a set rate for each completed piece. The plant also employed clerks whose tasks included keeping work records of employees and computing the wages to be paid to them" [14, p. 10]. The

US partner also helped organize a production control staff, which "enabled the plant to shed its former inefficiency and emerge into a fully modern manufacturing facility" [14, p. 10].

Western Electric sent to NEC roughly a dozen advisors who offered guidance through their positions in the Engineering, Materials, Accounting, Administration and other Departments. In accounting, for example, Western Electric had:

> ...considerable influence.... Allocation of funds was clearly set down in a budget to which NEC was expected to conform, and the company's staff was taught by WE [Western Electric] how to keep and close books and adjust accounts. Another area on which WE placed emphasis was cost accounting. Modern cost accounting methods were not commonly used by Japanese firms at that time, but through WE's guidance, NEC's accounting practices became as advanced as those of leading foreign enterprises [14, p. 11].

The American firm also sent punch card clocks to NEC, new in Japanese business practice [14, pp. 10–11]. In short,

> ... there can be no doubt that NEC's early success owed much to WE's tutelage and early expertise ... the innovations which NEC introduced [through Western Electric] were quite significant in the history of Japanese industry, contributing greatly to the nation's modernization scheme [14, pp. 11, 12].

Yet instances of knowledge transfer through foreign-affiliated companies extend well beyond that effected through Western Electric's ties to NEC. As a study of the Industrial Bank of Japan noted, "the majority of foreign direct investments were accompanied by technology transfer," and together with the transfer of modern, western methods of management practice, foreign companies made important contributions to Japanese business [7, p. 15]. Another study rightly points out:

> In both the joint enterprises and the wholly-foreign undertakings, of whatever nationality, a prime contribution was the technical knowledge and skill which nowadays are terms "knowhow," but even more important was the sheer impact of innovation. The direct examples, virtually "demonstration projects," of foreign technique and management were a repeated stimulus to Japanese thinking, and helped prevent a premature halt in modernization [17, pp. 177–8].

Third, there is significance in what might be termed the "geography" of foreign direct investment in Japan. That is to say, foreign direct investors did not choose to locate in any single part of Japan—although they clearly preferred certain locales over others—but rather spread their investments among many different regions. Major foreign direct investments were particularly prevalent in Tokyo, Kobe, Yokohama, Osaka and Kawasaki, yet others located in Hyogo and Miyazaki prefectures, in Hokkaido and elsewhere throughout the country [8].

There are indications that this internal dispersion not only influenced the economies of different regions in the short term through the activities of these firms, but that it also had significant long-term effects on the distribution of economic activity in Japan. One Japanese writer noted the example of Dunlop Rubber:

> One of the most famous examples [of an FDI-affiliated firm which established an independent company in Japan] was the purely British firm Dunlop Rubber (Far East), established in Kobe which began operations with the purpose of manufacturing tires and tubes for automobiles and bicycles, medical equipment, industrial products and so forth. Its establishment influenced the development of the Japanese rubber industry in more than one sense. In other words, not only did it encourage the development of [rubber] goods manufacture, it also shifted the center of the rubber industry from Tokyo to the Osaka region [4, pp. 121–2].

Fourth, the entry of many foreign direct investments created or stimulated domestic Japanese industries to supply intermediate goods. The establishment of Ford in Yokohama and General Motors in Osaka illustrate this point well. "The growth of these firms," observed two western scholars, "created a large demand among Japanese producers of tyres, batteries and upholstery" [1, p. 230]. Moreover, the US Trade Commissioner in Tokyo reported that:

> An analysis of the [foreign, and in particular US, branch factories which had begun operations in Japan as of 1932] shows that all of them are using domestic materials to some extent and that ... this is a very important factor. For example ... [t]he two phonograph companies ... use a large proportion of domestic materials ... About the only things which come direct from the United States are some of the component parts of the machines, and of course the Master Records recorded by American artists. These particular companies have been extremely successful in developing local sources of supply ... [19].

Fifth, much of the foreign direct investment during this period took the form of joint partnerships with the great economic combines, or *zaibatsu*. As shown in Table 2, Mitsui, Mitsubishi, Sumitomo and a number of other

*Table 2  Zaibatsu* participation in major prewar FDI joint ventures in Japan

| Zaibatsu investor | Foreign company | Japanese company |
|---|---|---|
| 1. Sumitomo | International Standard Electric | NEC |
| | NEC | Sumitomo Electric |
| | Westinghouse Electric International | Mitsubishi Electric |
| | Eastern Union Investment; Frasar Trust; & Others | Japan Musical Instruments |
| | Libbey–Owens Sheet Glass | American–Japan Sheet Glass |
| | Air Liquids | Imperial Oxygen |
| 2. Mitsui | International General Electric; Eastern Union Investment | Tokyo Electric |
| | Tokyo Electric | Shibaura Electric |
| | Tokyo Electric | United Paper Products |
| | Vicars Armstrong | Japan Steel Products |
| | Babcock & Wilcox | Toyo Babcock |
| 3. Mitsubishi | English Electric | Toyo Electric |
| | Westinghouse Electric International | Mitsubishi Electric |
| | Associated Oil | Mitsubishi Oil |
| 4. Furukawa | Siemens Schuckert; Siemens & Halske | Fuji Electric |
| | Fuji Electric | Fuji Telegraph and Telephone |
| | Westinghouse Electric International | Mitsubishi Electric |
| 5. Yamaguchi | American Linoleum | Tokyo Linoleum |
| 6. Okuragumi | Telefunken Gesellschaft für Drahtlose Telegraphie | Nippon Telephone and Telegraph |
| | Dunlop Rubber | Dunlop Rubber (Far East) |
| 7. Dai Nippon Seito | National Cash Register | Japan National Cash Register |
| 8. Nihon Chisso | Benberg A. G.; I. G. Farben | Asahi-Benberg Rayon |

*Source:* Adapted from [9, pp. 77–8].

*Note:* International Standard Electric was a subsidiary of International Telephone and Telegraph.

*zaibatsu* joined with foreign interests to establish firms in Japan. Through these associations foreign direct investors directly influenced the operations of some of Japan's leading business organizations.

A number of factors explain the high degree of involvement of *zaibatsu* in domestic FDI-affiliated enterprises. Some arose from the needs of the foreign investor. State procurement and other official policies made alliances with domestic firms attractive as a way to sell directly to the Government and to receive various forms of public assistance.[7] In addition, many of the foreign firms lacked adequate knowledge of the Japanese market, and saw in the *zaibatsu* a store of relevant expertise. Also, a number of foreign firms learned that allying with powerful domestic interests could overcome a variety of difficulties associated with the size of their organization in Japan.[8] Finally, some foreign managers sensed a strong economic nationalism in Japan, and believed that a combination with a Japanese concern would shield them from popular prejudice. The *zaibatsu* were a logical choice because they had capital and experience in a variety of business endeavors.

It is equally clear that the *zaibatsu* had their own motivations for tying up with foreign direct investors. Minutes of the 1926 meeting of Mitsui & Co.'s branch managers, for example, show that the firm settled on a policy of establishing joint ventures in Japan with foreign direct investors as a way to compete with domestic manufacturers operating within the newly created tariff walls and receiving other forms of government assistance.[9]

... foreign manufacturers ... sell their goods [in Japan] through representatives. However, as a result of the Government's protectionist policies toward domestic industry together with the development [of this industry], if there is a drop in Japanese domestic demand for these [foreign made] goods, the overseas manufacturer will either construct his own branch factory in Japan or form an association with Japanese to produce domestically ...

In response, Mitsui should either 1) establish factories on its own enabling [the firm] to control the sale of output, or 2) form capital tie-ups with top-flight foreign manufacturers, construct new factories in Japan, and obtain the sales rights [12].

In addition, competition between *zaibatsu* seems to have induced certain joint venture decisions. In 1918, for example, Sumitomo interests joined with the American firm Libbey-Owens Sheet Glass to manufacture window glass domestically. According to one Japanese source, "This [company] was of course established in an attempt to compete with Mitsubishi's Asahi Glass Company" [15, p. 445]. Whatever the motivations, however, it is clear that many of the major foreign direct investors formed joint ventures with the *zaibatsu*—and thereby directly influenced leading Japanese firms in a variety of fields.

Sixth, foreign direct investment in Japan during this period clearly contributed to employment in the modern industrial sector. Evidence shows that the vast majority of the employees of foreign capital-affiliated firms were Japanese—regardless of the relative size of the foreign capital contribution. One official Japanese Government study concluded that, in the manufacturing sector alone, over 24,000 Japanese were employed in firms in which there were substantial direct foreign investments [8].

Japanese employment in US branch factories alone totaled some 10,000 people [19]. (See Table 3)

Moreover, through these jobs Japanese workers were able to develop important skills demanded in the industrializing Japanese economy. In the NEC case cited above, for example, one of the initial impediments to the manufacture of dependable telephones was the inexperience of the firm's Japanese labor force. American advisors helped these workers to turn out a quality product [14, p. 7].

Seventh, foreign direct investment in Japan increased the level of Japanese *exports.* The activity of United States manufacturing plants in Japan clearly illustrates this:

... the fact that local American plants are in a position to manufacture for other Far Eastern markets, is a very important advantage which should receive more detailed consideration. Japan is very favorably located geographically with respect to China and other Oriental markets; it enjoys a stable government and there is a large and steady supply of skilled labor at fairly low wages. Moreover, in many cases it is possible to manufacture in bond for export to other markets, thereby avoiding the payment of import duty on material or parts. *Practically all of the local American plants do some export business with other Oriental markets, and in some cases this accounts for a very substantial percentage*

*Table 3* Employees in U.S. branch factories in Japan as of 1932: Japanese vs. non-Japanese

| Name of company | Japanese employees | Non-Japanese |
| --- | --- | --- |
| NEC | 1,400 | 4 |
| Tokyo Electric | 2,900 | 1 |
| Shibaura Engineering | 2,800 | 1 |
| Yokohama Rubber | N/A | 1 |
| Japan Steel Products | 800 | 4 |
| Ford Motor Japan | 381 | 41 |
| Nippon Hanovia Quartz Lamp | N/A | 2 |
| General Motors Japan | 719 | 12 |
| Victor Talking Machine Japan | 541 | 14 |
| Toyo Carrier Kogyo | 26 | 4 |
| Toyo Otis Elevator | 149 | 2 |
| Mitsubishi Oil | N/A | 3 |
| A.P. Muning & Co. | 15 | 2 |
| TOTALS | 9,731+ | 91 |

*Source:* [19].
*Notes:* No data given for the number of Japanese employees at Mitsubishi Oil, Nippon Hanovia Quartz Lamp and Yokohama Rubber. Japan Corn Products not included; refer to note, Table 1.

*of the total volume. For example, over 15% of the total assemblies during 1931 in one American automobile plant was shipped to China and other markets* [19].[10]

Finally, foreign direct investment in Japan during the first three decades of this century eased pressure on domestic sources of capital and thereby indirectly assisted Japan in itself becoming a base for overseas multinational expansion. As Horie has observed:

> ... after the Russo-Japanese War [1904–05], Japan, upon entering an unprecedented period of foreign capital importation, at the same time began full-scale capital exportation. There was an intimate relationship between the import and export [of capital]. That is to say, precisely because there was a large volume of capital imported, Japan could export capital to Korea and Manchuria and so forth. The imperialistic development of Japanese capitalism was undoubtedly backed up by foreign capital [4, pp. 181–2].[11]

In sum, although the *amount* of foreign capital invested directly in Japan from 1899 to 1931 was not large, the *impact* of this investment on Japan was very great indeed. It is clear that foreign direct investment: first, participated in and stimulated a broad range of business endeavor, often employing advanced methods; second, provided valuable knowledge about western technology and management practice; third, affected the internal economic geography; fourth, encouraged the growth of intermediate industries to supply its needs; fifth, influenced major Japanese business enterprise through direct associations with the *zaibatsu*; sixth, boosted employment and offered training and skill development for workers, particularly in the modern industrial sector; seventh, raised Japanese export levels; and eighth, indirectly supported the advance of Japanese multinational enterprise abroad.

## Notes

†The author wishes to acknowledge in particular the very considerable assistance of Professor Mira Wilkins of Florida International University and Professor Yamazaki Hiroaki of Tokyo University.

1. There are but two comprehensive published accounts of foreign direct investment in prewar Japan, one by the Ministry of Foreign Affairs [9] and the other by the Industrial Bank of Japan [7]. As the economist Kozo Yamamura recently noted, "The full extent of the involvement of Western firms in the Japanese economy during the interwar years is not easily ascertainable, partly because sufficiently detailed information has never been systematically compiled" [22, p. 67].

2. According to a biography of Oki Kibataro, during the course of the negotiations "there emerged a difference of opinion between the two sides with respect to

the basis on which profits would be calculated. Furthermore, [Oki] did not obtain the collaboration of Mr. Iwataro [a close advisor to Oki], because there was a feeling of uneasiness in doing business with foreigners." For these and other reasons, the negotiations ended in failure. [As quoted in 3, p. 118]. All Japanese names in this article are cited by surname first as is the Japanese custom.

3. The following figures have been converted, where necessary, from yen to dollars at the rate of two yen per dollar.

4. Comparing Japan and China in this respect raises, of course, a number of difficulties. The exercise is meant only to offer some sense of relative scale. Interestingly, the proportion of direct to indirect foreign investment in the two countries was roughly opposite: the great preponderance of foreign direct investment in Japan during this period was indirect; in China it was direct [16, pp. 68–9; 13, p. 524].

5. As noted by one Japanese economic historian, "It was during World War One that Japan could restore her commercial right at one stroke, which had long been in the hands of foreign merchants since the opening of the country at the end of the Tokugawa Shogunate. In other words, the exceedingly rapid development of Japanese manufacturing industries, the wonderful growth of her shipping companies and commercial concerns made foreign trade companies [leave] Japan. Foreign investments in Japanese manufacturing industries, however, became more and more active" [5, p. 58].

6. Americans assessed Japanese management practice somewhat differently earlier in this century than they do today. For example, one US official in Japan reported in 1932: "Experience indicates conclusively that there are no serious difficulties in Japanese capital participation [in US manufacturing plants in Japan], provided control is maintained by Americans ... the only factory with a substantial majority of Japanese capital is also the only one which has been operated at a loss for a number of years. This does not necessarily imply that Japanese management is hopelessly bad ... However, Japanese management is notoriously weak in curtailing overhead expenses, reducing expensive personnel and bonuses during hard times, and this accounts for much in this company's loss" [19].

7. According to the 1932 study of the US Department of Commerce, "A company which is organized purely as an American branch factory will not secure the benefits of preferential [Japanese Government] treatment as a domestic plant. However, a company which is organized locally with the participation of Japanese capital and management will very probably secure such preference" [19].

8. As one study explained, "In cases where the foreigner conducted business in Japan [between 1905 and 1914] with insufficient knowledge of the geography and human feelings [*ninjo*], they learned that they would meet with various disadvantages when the scale [of their enterprise] was small. The proof of this is that in later years, when many foreign companies invested in Japanese firms, they gave management rights to *zaibatsu* such as Mitsui, Mitsubishi, Sumitomo and Furukawa" [7, p. 16].

9. Mitsui & Co. was that part of the Mitsui *zaibatsu* principally engaged in trade and related activities.

10. Emphasis is the author's.

11. Horie here makes no distinction between foreign capital directly or indirectly invested in Japan, though it may be presumed that he was referring to both.

## References

1. George C. Allen et al., *Western Enterprise in Far Eastern Economic Development* (NY: Macmillan, 1954).
2. American Telephone and Telegraph Company Corporate Archives.
3. Chokki Toshiaki, "Nihon kigyo keiei no kindaika to gaishi teikei kaisha" (Foreign joint ventures and the modernization of Japanese business management) *Keiei Shirin*, (Vol. 17, No. 4, January 1981), pp. 117–130.
4. Horie Yasuzo, *Gaishi yunyu no kaiko to tenbo* (The Importation of Foreign Capital: Retrospect and Prospect) (Tokyo: Yuhikaku, 1950).
5. ——— , "Foreign Capital and the Japanese Capitalism After the World War 1" [sic] *Kyoto University Economic Review* 2 (1950), pp. 35–59.
6. Japan Bank of Japan, *Hundred-Year Statistics of the Japanese Economy: Supplement* (Tokyo: Bank of Japan, 1966).
7. Japan Industrial Bank of Japan, *Gaikoku kaisha no honpo toshi* (Investments in Japan by Foreign Companies) (Tokyo: Nihon Kogyo Ginko, 1948).
8. Japan Ministry of Finance Archives.
9. Japan Ministry of Foreign Affairs, *Nihon ni okeru gaikoku shihon* (Foreign Capital in Japan) (Tokyo: Sunseisha, 1948).
10. Cleona Lewis, *America's Stake in International Investments* (Washington, DC: Brookings Institution, 1938).
11. William W. Lockwood, *The Economic Development of Japan: Growth and Structural Change, 1868–1938* (Princeton: Princeton University Press, 1954).
12. Mitsui Corporate Archives, "Shitencho Kaigi Gijiroku" (Minutes of the Branch Managers' Meeting), 1926.
13. Harold G. Moulton et al., *Japan: An Economic and Financial Appraisal* (Washington, DC: Brookings Institution, 1931).
14. Nippon Electric Company, *The First 80 Years* (Tokyo: NEC, 1984).
15. Keishi Ohara, ed. and comp., *Japanese Trade & Industry in the Meiji-Taisho Era* in *A History of Japanese-American Cultural Relations (1853–1926)*, Vol. 4 (Tokyo: Obunsha, 1957).
16. Charles F. Remer, *Foreign Investments in China* (NY: Macmillan, 1933).
17. Edward Reubens, "Foreign Capital in Economic Development: The Japanese Exprience, 1868–1913," Ph.D. Dissertation: Columbia University, 1952.
18. United States Department of Commerce Bureau of Foreign and Domestic Commerce, *American Direct Investments in Foreign Countries—1929*, Trade Information Bulletin No. 731 (Washington, DC: GPO, 1930).
19. United States National Archives Record Group 151, Records of the Bureau of Foreign and Domestic Commerce, Department of Commerce.
20. Mira Wilkins, "American-Japanese Direct Investment Relationships, 1930–1952" *Business History Review*, (56:4, Winter 1982), pp. 497–518.
21. ——— , "The Role of US Business" in Dorothy Borg et al. eds., *Pearl Harbor as History: Japanese-American Relations, 1931–1941* (New York: Columbia University Press, 1973), pp. 341–76.
22. Kozo Yamamura, "Japan's Deus ex Machina: Western Technology in the 1920's," *Journal of Japanese Studies* (12: 1, Winter 1986), pp. 65–94.

# 17

## Foreign Multinationals and British Industry before 1945[1]*

Geoffrey Jones

*Source: *Economic History Review*, XLI (1988), pp. 429–453.

Since the late nineteenth century Britain has been the recipient of substantial investment by foreign-owned multinational enterprises. Foreign-owned companies had a significant impact on certain sectors of British industry, and the positions they acquired in those sectors point towards the existence of serious managerial, entrepreneurial, and technological inadequacies within indigenous British business. This article examines the role of foreign multinationals in British manufacturing and utilities before 1945. Section I looks at the dimensions of this investment; section II discusses the reasons which led foreign companies to establish or acquire factories in Britain, and section III examines the impact of these companies on the British economy.

## I

A considerable number of foreign companies established or acquired manufacturing operations in Britain between 1850 and 1945.[2] No full listing of these companies exists, but this study has established 125 such investments, the details of which are given in appendix I. It should be stressed that marketing and sales companies are excluded, although it was usual for foreign firms to establish such companies before they began manufacturing in Britain, and that the analysis is confined to initial investments. Appendix I has been compiled from a wide range of sources, each entry having been checked from at least two different sources. Given that a firm's inclusion in the list depended on the availability of reliable information, the sample cannot claim to have been 'randomly' selected. Nevertheless the data set appears well distributed with respect to industries and dates of foundation, although there is probably a bias towards larger, American, and publicly-quoted firms, about which more information is available. Two earlier estimates give much larger numbers of foreign multinational investments in Britain, but as they do not list the companies concerned it is impossible to verify them. Dunning estimates that around 240 American companies established factories in Britain before 1939. Appendix I lists 67 American investments, or 28 per cent of the Dunning estimate. Law located 162 foreign companies which established plants in Britain between 1918 and 1944. Appendix I lists a total of 71 investments in the same period, or 44 per cent of the Law figure.[3] It would seem safe to conclude that appendix I includes at least one-third of total multinational investments in British industry before 1945; that it contains a high proportion of the larger investments; and that it provides a respectable, if not perfect, sample on which to base inferences about the population of foreign multinationals in Britain as a whole.

Table 1 summarizes the data on the timing and nationality of the 125 multinational investments in appendix I.

From the middle of the nineteenth century a trickle of foreign companies began manufacturing in Britain. The 1900s saw the first large wave of such investment, and there was an even greater number of investments in the 1920s. Although international investment in general slumped in the 1930s, new foreign multinational investment in Britain remained substantial. The United States was the leading multinational investor. Of the sample of 125 investments between 1850 and 1939 54 per cent were American, and the American preponderance grew over time. Between 1850 and 1919, 48 per cent of the 54 investments were American. The other large investors came from Germany (19 per cent), Sweden (11 per cent), and Switzerland (10 per cent). There were also one or two investments by companies from Denmark, the Netherlands, France, and Italy. Between 1920 and 1939, 58 per cent of the 71 investments were

*Table 1* Date of establishment of first factory in Britain by foreign companies, 1850–1939

| Decade | USA | Germany | Sweden | Other | Total |
|--------|-----|---------|--------|-------|-------|
| 1850–9 | 2 | — | — | — | 2 |
| 1860–9 | 2 | 1 | — | — | 3 |
| 1870–9 | — | — | — | 1 | 1 |
| 1880–9 | — | 1 | — | 1 | 2 |
| 1890–9 | 6 | 2 | 1 | — | 9 |
| 1900–9 | 13 | 6 | 1 | 5 | 25 |
| 1910–9 | 3 | — | 4 | 5 | 12 |
| 1920–9 | 24 | 1 | 5 | 10 | 40 |
| 1930–9 | 17 | 6 | 2 | 6 | 31 |
| Total | 67 | 17 | 13 | 28 | 125 |

American. Germany and Sweden followed with 10 per cent each, a smaller number of investments being recorded for companies from Denmark, the Netherlands, France, Italy, Czechoslovakia, Australia, and Canada.

The first 'multinational' manufacturing investments in Britain were probably those of Samuel Colt, the American gun manufacturer, who established a factory in London in 1853, and J. Ford & Co. who established an Edinburgh factory to manufacture vulcanized rubber in 1856. Both companies disinvested within a few years, and the first sustained American investment was that of Singer, which established a sewing machine factory at Glasgow in 1867.[4] Meanwhile, the German electrical firm of Siemens founded a London factory to manufacture sea cables in 1863. Although the British branch of the firm possessed some managerial independence, it can be regarded as a subsidiary of the German parent.[5] In the decades before 1914 a steady stream of American companies established factories in Britain in a wide range of industries. There was a particular emphasis on electrical equipment and telecommunications, but American firms also invested in office machinery, matches, cameras, records, food and—with the establishment of a Ford assembly plant at Manchester in 1911—motor cars.

Although American companies were the most numerous multinational investors, continental firms were also active. By 1914 there were subsidiaries of prominent German firms such as Mannesmann and Hoechst manufacturing in the electrical, chemical, and pharmaceutical sectors in Britain. One Swiss company was an early multinational investor in Britain; in 1872 the Anglo-Swiss Condensed Milk Company, which despite its name was a wholly owned Swiss firm, established a factory. Nestlé, Anglo-Swiss's national rival, established a British factory in 1901 before the two firms merged in 1905.[6] By 1914 Hoffman La Roche, in pharmaceuticals, and the largest Swiss chemicals company, Gesellschaft für chemische Industrie (Ciba), had established or acquired British factories. Swedish companies invested before 1914 in the electrical and telecommunications sector. L.M. Ericsson established a joint venture in 1903 with the British-owned National Telephone Company to manufacture telephone equipment, while Jönköping and Vulcan built a match factory in London in 1910.[7] Among other European investments before 1914 were those undertaken by the Danish margarine manufacturer, Otto Monsted, who established a factory in Manchester in 1888,[8] and Adolphe Clément, a leading French car manufacturer who in 1903 formed a joint venture with British interests known as Clément-Talbot, which assembled and later manufactured 'Talbot' cars in a London factory; another French car manufacturer, Lorraine-Dietrich, established a factory in Birmingham in 1903.[9] In 1914 Pirelli of Italy joined with the British-owned General Electric Company to found the Pirelli General Cable Works, with a factory in Southampton to manufacture cables and electrical equipment.[10]

The First World War did nothing to impede the expansion of foreign multinationals in Britain. After 1919 the numbers of American companies investing in Britain increased. Three leading American tyre manufacturers established British factories. In the motor industry, Ford began the construction of a giant new plant at Dagenham near London in the late 1920s and General Motors acquired a British producer, Vauxhall, in 1925. The 1930s saw some American disinvestment but also new investment in a wide range of sectors, including food, chemicals, and electrical appliances.[11]

Non-American companies also continued to be active investors in Britain, especially in the 1920s. A number of Swedish firms, of which perhaps the most important was Elektrolux (later changed to Electrolux), the manufacturer of domestic electrical equipment, established factories in Britain in this period, while two Dutch viscose yarn companies (Enka and Breda) erected British plants.[12] There was also substantial Dutch investment in margarine manufacture. From 1917 the rival Dutch companies Jurgens and Van den Bergh's established or acquired a large number of margarine factories in Britain.[13] In the late 1920s there was a spate of French direct investments. In 1927 Renault built a British car factory and Michelin established a tyre factory in Britain. In the same year Poulenc Frères (which became Rhône-Poulenc in 1928) secretly acquired May & Baker, the British fine chemicals company.[14] There was also a Czechoslovakian direct investment when Bata, which dominated Czech shoe production in the interwar years, established a footwear factory in East Tilbury. The interwar years also saw the first Australian and Canadian direct investments in Britain.

All German direct investments were sequestrated during the First World War, and there was little significant German direct investment in British industry during the 1920s. The capital-starved German economy had little cash for foreign investments and generally opted for alternative strategies such as licensing and participation in international cartels. German investment in Britain in the 1920s was usually confined to small distribution companies, often joint ventures. Bayer Products Ltd, for example, was established in 1923 to distribute fine chemicals marketed under the Bayer name. It was jointly owned by I.G. Farbenindustrie and Sterling Products Inc. of the United States. There were some unsuccessful attempts by German firms to re-acquire the British subsidiaries which they had lost. German Siemens acquired 15 per cent of the capital of British Siemens in 1929, and the two companies reached a comprehensive technological licensing agreement, but the British company never fell under German control.[15] The 1930s saw more new German direct investment, sometimes in joint ventures with British or American interests.

The nationality of certain multinational investments was obscured by the fact that foreign parents managed their British subsidiaries through companies registered in third countries. Pirelli's British companies, for example, were owned and managed by Société Internationale Pirelli S.A. of Switzerland. A noteworthy variant on this pattern before 1914 was the Nobel-Dynamite Trust, an Anglo-German holding company founded in 1886, which owned the leading British explosives manufacturer, Nobel's Explosives. Although a majority of the share capital was probably German, the Trust was registered in England, had an Anglo-German board of directors, and cannot be accurately counted as a German *direct* investment in British manufacturing.[16] It has been excluded from appendix I.

A number of American and continental companies had multi-plant operations in Britain even before 1914. To the Anglo-Swiss Condensed Milk Company's original Chippenham factory, established in 1872, were added factories in Aylesbury and Middlewich in 1874, and Staverton in the early 1900s. Singer built another factory at Clydebank in 1885. Monsted built a second factory in London in 1895, and Mannesmann a second factory at Newport in 1913.

It is difficult to quantify the amount of capital which foreign companies invested in British industry before 1945. Dunning has estimated total inward direct investment in Britain at US$200 million in 1914 and $700 million in 1938.[17] If half of these totals was in manufacturing, it would suggest that foreign investment in British industry was around £20 million in 1914 and £87.5 million in 1938. These estimates cannot be verified by independent data, but seem about the right order of magnitude. From the late 1920s there is hard evidence on the size of American investment in British manufacturing. In 1929 this was estimated (in book value) by the U.S. Department of Commerce at $268.2 million (£55.2 million). A more thorough survey by the same source in 1932 put the figure at $165 million (£48.5 million), and in 1940 at $275.3 million (£68.3 million).[18] The size of non-American direct investment in British manufacturing is a mystery, but the wartime sequestration of German assets in Britain provides some evidence on German investment. A Board of Trade estimate in the First World War suggested the amount of German equity in identified manufacturing subsidiaries in Britain was just under £1.7 million.[19] During the Second World War the British government took over 130 companies in which German-owned shares had more than 50 per cent of the voting rights, but the total issued capital of these firms was only £676,929.[20] German direct investment in British manufacturing in 1939 is unlikely to have exceeded £0.25 million.

Not only was the amount of foreign direct investment in British industry before 1945 modest, but the place of foreign subsidiaries in Britain's corporate structure was also limited. In 1980, 402 of Britain's 1,000 largest firms were foreign-owned. The available listings of the 50 largest British manufacturing companies (by estimated market value) in 1905, 1919, and 1930 indicate that in terms of corporate size the significance of foreign-owned companies was much less at those dates.[21] In 1905 only the American-owned British Westinghouse (electrical engineering) was included in the largest 50 companies. By 1919 there were no foreign subsidiaries, for in 1918 British Westinghouse had been acquired by British interests. In 1930, 4 of the largest 50 firms—Ford, Associated Electric Industries (AEI), Boots, and Mond Nickel—were under American ownership, while another, the British Match Corporation, was 30 per cent Swedish controlled and 70 per cent British.

The role of foreign companies in certain industries and products was, however, highly significant. Foreign influence was the most extensive in the electrical engineering and other electrical industries. Before 1914 the heavy plant side of British electrical machinery production was dominated by British Siemens and American interests, especially British Thomson Houston (a subsidiary of the General Electric Company of America) and British Westinghouse, a subsidiary of US Westinghouse Electric. In 1918 Vickers and Metropolitan Carriage Wagon and Finance acquired British Westinghouse and it was incorporated in a new British-controlled company, Metropolitan Vickers Electrical Company (Metrovic). However, in 1928 the General Electric Company of America (through its subsidiary formed to control overseas operations, the International General Electric Company) arranged a merger of British electric interests, including Metrovic and British Thomson Houston, to form Associated Electrical Industries (AEI). The whole of Metrovic's assets thereby passed to American control.[22] Elsewhere in the industry, the English Electric Company had been formed in 1919, partly on the basis of the dynamo and electrical engineering parts of the old Siemens business. At the end of the 1920s American interests took control of the company, though this was not disclosed to the public at the time.[23] During the 1930s, therefore, two of the three leading British electrical engineering companies were foreign controlled, although by 1936 a majority of AEI's shares were back in British hands. The manufacture of telephones and telephone equipment was also an area where the subsidiaries of foreign multinationals were very active. In the late 1930s this sector was dominated by the American-owned STC, Swedish-owned Ericsson and British Siemens (which had a minority German shareholding at that stage). In addition, in 1920 the American Theodore Cary group acquired the Automatic Telephone Manufacturing Company, the largest indigenous telephone equipment manufacturer, although in 1935 this company was sold back to British interests.[24]

In the interwar years foreign-owned companies also established a prominent position in the expanding domestic electrical appliances sector. The American-owned Hoover and Swedish-owned Elektrolux were the leading manufacturers in the United Kingdom of vacuum cleaners and refrigerators.[25] Before the merger in 1931 of the Gramophone Company and Columbia Graphophone to form Electrical and Musical Industries (EMI),

American interests also had a prominent role in the gramophone and recording industry. During the interwar years foreign interests were at times important in electrical utilities. In 1928 an American corporation acquired a group of British electricity supply companies, making it 'one of the largest suppliers of electricity in Britain'.[26] In 1936, however, this group was sold back to British interests. Less significant was the purchase in the late 1930s by an Italian group of five British electricity supply companies controlled by a holding company.[27]

The motor car industry was another area where foreign multinationals were active. Ford's construction of a plant at Manchester in 1911 was followed by a period of dominance of the British motor car industry until the early 1920s. After 1923 Ford rapidly lost its position to the British firms of Austin and, especially, Morris, with the American-owned company failing to develop models appropriate to the British market and handicapped by inappropriate selling arrangements. Ford's new Dagenham plant and a managerial re-organization only partially revived the company's British fortunes. By 1939 Ford and Vauxhall (owned by General Motors) controlled about a quarter of British production in the motor industry.[28]

Before the First World War the subsidiaries of foreign multinationals were also significant in the chemical industry. The 1907 Patent Act, which specified that a foreign patent taken out in Britain had to be worked there, led the German and Swiss dyestuffs manufacturers to establish British plants, but the British government did not enforce the requirements of the Act strictly and these ventures remained small. However, Hoechst's Ellesmere Port factory produced almost all of Britain's production of indigo, which amounted to 50 per cent of domestic demand. This factory was also equipped to make certain drugs, especially the anti-syphilic 'Salvarsan', which were made nowhere else in Britain before 1914.[29] The Clayton Aniline Company, one of the few British dyestuffs manufacturers before the First World War, was purchased by the Swiss firm Ciba in 1911.[30] After the War, and particularly after the formation of Imperial Chemical Industries in 1926, the chemical industry in Britain made considerable progress and foreign-owned firms were of importance only in certain limited sectors. In the 1930s, for example, Clayton Aniline still held an important place in dyestuff production, manufacturing 19 per cent of the total value of dyestuffs produced in Britain in 1937.[31] The American firm Monsanto, which established manufacturing operations in Britain in 1920, was a leading producer of new kinds of phenolic and plastic materials.

Foreign companies also acquired strong positions in a wide and diverse range of consumer products. Singer dominated sewing machine production. The British subsidiary of Eastman Kodak shared with the British firm Ilford the domination of the British photographic materials industry.[32] Dutch companies were predominant in margarine manufacture in the second half of the 1920s. By 1939 a Canadian, Garfield Weston, had the largest bakery business in Britain.[33]

The market share of foreign multinationals was never a static phenomenon, and the national ownership of a significant number of firms fluctuated over time. The shifts in ownership in the electrical engineering industry have already been mentioned, but there were many other examples. Boots in the interwar years ceased to be a British company by becoming the subsidiary of an American multinational, but then reverted to being a British company.[34] The Gramophone Company made exactly the same transition in ownership between 1920 and 1931.[35]

'Anglicization' of British subsidiaries of foreign companies was fairly common. In 1901 Diamond Match of the United States acquired a majority shareholding in the leading British match company, Bryant & May, but by 1914 control was back in British hands.[36] When the British-registered British American Tobacco Company (BAT) was formed in 1902 two-thirds of its capital was owned by the American Tobacco Company, but by 1923 British interests had secured both managerial and financial control.[37] In 1927 the Swedish Match Company, whose manufacturing presence in Britain dated back to the Jönköping and Vulcan factory in 1910, merged its British interests with the leading British manufacturer, Bryant & May, to form a new holding company, the British Match Corporation, which was 70 per cent British controlled. Swedish Match hoped that its 30 per cent stake would give it control over this company, but in fact managerial control remained in British hands.[38] A peculiar variant of this pattern was the merger of the Dutch margarine manufacturers with Lever Brothers in 1929 to create Unilever, in which British and Dutch interests both held 50 per cent.[39] The cluster of Dutch margarine factories in Britain thereby passed into Anglo-Dutch ownership.

# II

Modern theories of the multinational enterprise suggest that the explanation for foreign direct investment in British industry before 1945 must be found on several different levels. A firm will invest in a foreign country only if it has an advantage of some kind over domestic competitors. Such 'ownership-specific' advantages can lie in a variety of factors, including superior management structures, better technology or marketing skills, or easier access to finance. A firm can exploit these advantages by exporting to, or licensing in, foreign markets, but under certain conditions it is more beneficial for a firm to internalize its advantages through an extension of its own activities across national boundaries. Generally, the greater the ownership advantages of enterprise the more the incentive they have to exploit these themselves. To explain fully the preference for investing abroad over, say, exporting, another group of 'location-specific' factors also needs to be considered. These factors include market size and growth, and trade barriers in host countries.[40]

The foreign multinationals which invested in British industries can be seen as possessing strong ownership-specific advantages which enabled them to compete successfully with indigenous firms. There were several sources of advantage, but Chandler has argued powerfully that the most important was management structure. In industries such as electrical machinery, and chemicals before the 1920s, British entrepreneurs failed to develop the large integrated enterprises administered by extensive managerial hierarchies which their American counterparts had adopted. In these industries American companies had considerable advantages over their British competitors, enabling them to build factories and prosper in the British market.[41] The reasons why many British entrepreneurs preferred to retain personal family management remain uncertain. However, significant influences included the slower growth of the British market compared to the American; the British education system; the lack of anti-trust legislation; and perhaps a hostility to change among many British industrialists.[42]

Many foreign multinationals also possessed technological advantages over their British competitors. In general terms the success in Britain of continental and American electrical, telecommunication, chemical, and pharmaceutical companies reflected their superior research and development methods, and more generally, the greater scientific and technological strengths of their home economies. The technological advantages of foreign companies were often highly visible: American companies, for example, were frequently more receptive to instrumentation than British companies. H.J. Heinz installed automatic controls in their London factory in 1929 before British food canners introduced any form of control. American multinationals also demonstrated an ability to differentiate between products by brand advertising and selling methods which were often—but not always—superior to those of British competitors.[43] Such advantages were important in explaining the success in Britain of the American quick and instant food manufacturers.

Easier access to capital supplies was a much less important advantage for foreign firms. There is some evidence that foreign companies provided capital to industries which British financial institutions would not fund. In 1890 the dyestuffs manufacturer Levinstein's of Manchester turned to the German firms, Bayer and Agfa, for funds after failing to raise capital in Britain.[44] However, even those historians convinced of institutional failure in the British financial sector can find little evidence that British industry as a whole was short of funds before 1914.[45] Certainly the motor car industry before 1914 experienced little difficulty in raising capital from public issues on the London Stock Exchange, and British firms found it easier to raise capital than their American counterparts, such as Ford, which were excluded from public equity markets until after 1918.

This discussion of the advantages of foreign companies would support a thesis of entrepreneurial and management 'failure' in certain industries at certain times in Britain. There were market opportunities which foreign interests perceived and exploited, but which indigenous entrepreneurs did not. However, this argument does not support a general hypothesis of entrepreneurial failure over all sectors of British industry, for Britain itself was a major home country of multinational investment before 1945, and beyond. From the late nineteenth century British multinationals such as Dunlop, J. & P. Coats, and Courtaulds established worldwide networks of foreign factories which reflected *their* advantages over foreign competitors.[46]

The possession of ownership-specific advantages represents a necessary but not a sufficient condition for multinational investment. A number of location-specific advantages need to be considered. Britain possessed the highest per caput income in Europe, a high population density, and excellent transport, which made it an attractive market for many products. The large British market was particularly attractive to firms based in such countries as Sweden and Switzerland, and most of these companies were large exporters to Britain before they established plants. Some 75 per cent of the production of Anglo-Swiss Condensed Milk was sold in Britain before it established its first British factory in 1872. Similarly, the Swedish telephone manufacturer, L.M. Ericsson, sold 50 per cent of its output in Britain prior to its establishment of a joint venture with the National Telephone Company in 1903.[47]

Why did foreign companies switch from exporting to manufacture in Britain? It is well established that the desire to 'jump' tariff barriers was a major factor which led many British companies to establish factories abroad.[48] Britain before 1914 was still a free trade country, but there were a number of more general trade barriers which prompted foreign investment. Fear of tariffs being imposed at some future date may have influenced some companies, such as Western Electric in the late 1890s.[49] Britain had some import duties designed to encourage domestic manufacture. It was because of a discriminatory duty on manufactured tobacco that the American Tobacco Company acquired a British company in 1901, which led to a brief foray into domestic manufacturing before a wide-ranging cartel agreement was reached with the dominant British firm, Imperial Tobacco.[50] Some foreign companies established British plants in order to take advantage of imperial preference, and thereby penetrate the protected markets of Australia, Canada, and other Dominions. The desire to sell to Australia was also the explicit reason behind Jönköping and Vulcan's decision to establish a match factory in Britain in 1910. Australia levied only 50 per cent of the standard import duty on matches of British origin.[51]

After 1914 the growth of Britain protectionism meant that many factories were established in Britain in order to avoid tariff barriers. The McKenna duties of 1915, which imposed a 33 per cent duty on imported 'non-essentials', such as motor cars, originating outside the Empire, led to a rapid rise in the proportion of local content in Ford vehicles assembled at its Manchester factory, and the continuation of the duties after 1918 eventually led to Ford's decision to construct the huge Dagenham plant in the late 1920s. The same reason prompted General Motors' acquisition of Vauxhall in 1925.[52]

Patent legislation, as already observed, was also an influence prompting British manufacture in some sectors. The 1907 Patent Act not only led the German and Swiss dyestuffs manufacturers to establish British factories but has also been credited with prompting American direct investment in the cinematic film, safety razor, and cash register industries.[53]

A range of other factors prompted individual firms to manufacture in Britain. Sometimes local inputs were important in manufacturing processes. The Swiss condensed milk manufacturers needed access to fresh milk supplies. The peculiarity of British weights and measures was an influence. The decision of SKF, the Swedish ball and roller bearings company, to start manufacture in Britain in 1910 was apparently influenced by the use of the inch system in the United Kingdom.[54] The ability to raise finance in the City of London and London's role in international trade were important. The English language helped to make Britain the first choice for many American companies locating in Europe. According to one estimate, in 1931 almost 40 per cent by number of the American-owned manufacturing plants in Europe and over 40 per cent by value were located in Britain.[55] Lower labour costs do not appear to have been a major location-specific advantage. Singer was initially attracted to Glasgow 'because of the low cost and docile labour as well as the good shipping facilities',[56] but this seems to have been an exception. The fact that most foreign investment was not in labour-intensive industries is significant in this context.

## III

Foreign multinational investment affects a host economy in diverse ways. It can be regarded as transferring 'resources' of various kinds into that economy. It can also influence the corporate structure, the regional distribution of industry, and the balance of payments. This section looks, briefly, at each of these points for the British economy before 1945.

Foreign multinationals can make an important contribution by filling a resource gap in a host economy between desired investment and domestic savings. However, it would appear that the actual transfer of capital into Britain by foreign companies before 1945 was small and it is unlikely that foreign direct investment played an important role in industrial capital formation. Expansion was often financed by ploughed back profits. Singer used re-invested British profits to build a new factory at Clydebank in 1885.[57] It was also common for foreign firms to borrow or sell part of their equity in Britain. The French car manufacturers, Renault and Citroen, borrowed from British banks in the 1920s to finance British subsidiaries.[58] During the 1930s the British subsidiaries of a number of American companies disposed of part of their equity to British investors, including Woolworths, American Radiator Company, and Monsanto.[59] In 1928 Ford offered 40 per cent of the equity of Ford of England to the British public, and subsequently raised more than £4.5 million in the early 1930s to finance the construction of the Dagenham factory.

A more significant 'transfer' may have been of managerial and entrepreneurial skills. Many contemporaries argued that American subsidiaries in Britain were better managed than their indigenous competitors. 'The names Ford, Vauxhall, Singer, Kodak, Hoover, Standard Telephone, are bywords for efficiency [and] good management', observed the city editor of the *News Chronicle* in 1945, going on to contrast these firms with the 'inferiority' of 'inefficient British industries.'[60] American companies can be seen as transferring their managerial advantages into the British economy, and in the process stimulating their indigenous competitors to adopt improved methods. Ford of England in the 1920s was not a well-managed company, but the firm's use of time study experts in the early 1930s helped to diffuse to Britain the benefits of American experience in management.[61]

There are a number of caveats to this argument. Many foreign multinational operations in Britain were not models of superior management. The American-dominated AEI conformed in the 1930s to the typical British management pattern of a loose confederation of subsidiaries with weak central control. Some multinational subsidiaries emitted clear signals of management failure rather than organizational superiority. British Westinghouse, for example, performed poorly before 1914, primarily because of poor management and a failure to adapt American methods to British conditions, and the company could not even make money during the First World War when other electrical companies in Britain made large profits.[62] In 1919 the Swiss firms, Geigy and Sandoz, acquired one-sixth stakes each in Clayton Aniline, formerly wholly owned by Ciba, and over the following decade there were constant disputes between the partners over the running of the British venture.[63]

The number of instances in which foreign companies had their British operations 'anglicized' might also suggest that British managements were sometimes more than competitive with their foreign counterparts, although this may also have reflected the problems of controlling foreign subsidiaries in the pre-1945 period. However, it is clear that in some industries, such as tobacco at the turn of the century, the British response to foreign intruders was so strong that the foreign companies were forced to withdraw or reach a compromise with local interests.[64] In the motor industry British companies overcame an early American lead, although doubts have been raised whether this was indicative of 'superior' British management methods.[65]

One criticism of the impact of multinationals on host countries is that they can reserve managerial and skilled jobs for home country nationals and thereby limit the 'spin-off' benefits of improved managerial techniques. However, many American companies in Britain before 1945 employed British nationals in senior positions. A number of companies, such as Firestone and Gillette, employed entirely British staff, although, as a writer in 1931 noted, 'a portion of it may have had training in the American company'.[66] Ford and General Motors in Britain were both headed by British managers in the 1930s. The willingness of American corporations to appoint British nationals to senior positions can be explained in part by similarities of language and culture, although even some of the continental companies conformed to this pattern. The senior management of Renault's British subsidiary in the interwar years, for example, was British.[67]

Britain may also have benefited because a number of foreign multinationals before 1940 chose to base their international operations in the United Kingdom. Before 1914 the London office of the Nestlé and Anglo-Swiss Condensed Milk Company was responsible for the Swiss firm's sales in Asia, Australia, and Latin America.[68] During the interwar years it was common for American corporations to use their British subsidiaries to control and sometimes to own subsidiaries in other countries, especially but far from exclusively in the British Empire. The most striking example was Ford's decision in 1928 to place all its European and Middle Eastern operations under the control of Ford of England.[69] This phenomenon meant a net gain to Britain in terms of expertise in managing international businesses, as well as in the creation of numerous head office management posts.

Perhaps the most frequently cited transfer associated with multinational enterprise is technology. There are potential benefits to a host country of technology transfer by a multinational, but in practice the size of the gain depends upon such matters as the terms under which the technology is transferred and its suitability. Before 1945 Britain again appears to have been a gainer in this area. In electrical engineering, American and German firms transferred new technologies into Britain, although in some instances—such as that of British Westinghouse before 1919—these were inappropriate to the domestic cost structure.[70] During the interwar years some foreign firms invested in research and development in Britain. In 1928 Kodak's British subsidiary established what may have been the first American industrial research laboratory abroad. By 1939 this laboratory was larger than the entire scientific effort of Kodak's British competitor,

Ilford, and it was also engaged—unlike Ilford—in fundamental research work.[71]

Yet it was far from axiomatic that foreign companies introduced superior technologies. The initial optimism about the beneficial influence of American investment in electrical utilities in the interwar years, for example, soon gave way to alarm about high costs and prices.[72] Nor did the motor car industry provide substantial examples of technology transfer. Ford remained dependent on its American parent in matters of design. Moreover, Ford's Dagenham factory was isolated from the principal centres of British car production, which limited any technological 'spin-off' to domestic firms.[73] Many foreign subsidiaries, such as Clayton Aniline, undertook no serious research and development in Britain. Although imported technology was important for British industry in the interwar years, the major conduits through which this technology was acquired were licensing agreements (as held by ICI and Metal Box) and the acquisition of American machinery (by Austin and Morris, for example) rather than inward direct investment.[74] British companies in the interwar years often demonstrated considerable skill in acquiring and applying foreign technologies acquired in such ways.

Multinationals create employment and can also introduce innovatory labour management practices. Before 1914 foreign multinationals were not large employers. By the eve of the First World War the manufacturing subsidiaries of American companies may have employed 12–15,000 people.[75] A listing of the 100 largest manufacturing employers in 1907 includes only 3 foreign companies: Singer (ranked 31st with 7,000 workers); British Westinghouse (ranked 47th with 5,000 workers); and Siemens (ranked 61st with 4,150 workers).[76] Some of the foreign ventures were very small indeed. Ford in 1914 had a workforce of 1,500, Clayton Aniline employed 300 workers, while the Hoechst and BASF subsidiaries at Liverpool had only 57 and 37 workers respectively. In the interwar years employment by foreign multinationals increased. In 1932 American-owned manufacturing establishments employed over 66,000 people.[77] The continental companies were usually smaller operations, although some were at least medium-sized employers. British Enka and Clayton Aniline, for example, had workforces of 2,600 and 1,200 respectively in the early 1930s. A listing of the 100 largest manufacturing employers in 1935 includes eight American-owned companies; AEI (ranked 11th with 30,000 workers); Singer (43rd, 8,103); National Cash Register (46th, 8,000)' STC (52nd, 7,911); Ford (55th, 7,128); Vauxhall (64th, 6,726); English Electric (67th, 6,091); and Kodak (91st, 4,400). Employing a workforce of 60,000, the Anglo-Dutch Unilever was Britain's largest manufacturing employer.[78]

Foreign multinationals exercised an influence on labour management policies in Britain before 1945, although the paucity of evidence makes generalization difficult. It does seem that American-owned companies may have been more successful than British firms in pursuing the division of labour and simplifying work. The fact that many of their plants and facilities in Britain were new would help to explain this. They also brought with them ideas of scientific management, were quick to introduce work study, and probably tolerated fewer restrictive practices.

In the matter of employment practices, American companies were more sophisticated in some ways than British companies, relying on higher day wages rather than piecework.[79] On the other hand, British companies may have been ahead in terms of providing such fringe benefits as pensions and sick pay.[80] However, it was the appearance in Britain in 1927 of the largest American insurance company, Metropolitan Life of New York, which, responding to the needs of its American clients in Britain such as Kodak and General Motors, introduced American-style group life and pension contracts.[81]

Few American firms in Britain decided to join employers' organizations because this meant recognizing trade unions. Companies such as Ford and Pressed Steel held out against recognition until 1944 when government pressure helped secure recognition. Even after American subsidiaries had accepted unions, they often continued not to join employers' organizations, opting to deal with unions independently within the firm.[82] Their labour policies, on occasions, showed scant regard for conventional practice in Britain. British Westinghouse in the 1900s followed the Pittsburgh practice of employing works police to patrol factories to see that everyone was hard at work. Not surprisingly, the company had a poor labour relations record.[83]

Among other effects of foreign multinationals on Britain was the regional impact of foreign investment. Between 1945 and the 1970s British government policy helped to steer many foreign companies towards the peripheral regions of Scotland, Wales, and the north of England. However, locational distribution of inward direct investment before the Second World War was quite different. Before 1914 the investments shown in appendix I were quite widely dispersed throughout England, although Wales and Scotland never attracted many factories. Between 1850 and 1919, out of the 53 recorded investments only 3 were in Scotland and 1 in Wales. After the First World War, London and the south east became the usual location. This generalization is supported by Law's larger sample of 162 multinational investments in British industry between 1918 and 1944, of which 70.3 per cent were in the south east (mostly London), 11.7 per cent in the north west, and 6.8 per cent in the west midlands. A mere 3.7 per cent were in Scotland, 0.6 per cent in Wales, and none in Northern Ireland.[84] This geographical concentration on the south east must have had a significant impact by introducing new products and methods into that region, and increasing its capacity for innovation in the interwar years.

A second trend was a greater willingness of non-American firms to invest outside the south east. Both before and after the First World War, German companies showed some preference for the north of England. Swedish companies showed interest in areas to the north of London, and the west midlands. Two of the three Canadian multinational investments in the interwar years were initially in Scotland. The different industries in which American and continental companies were engaged was an important factor in explaining variations in geographical distribution.

Foreign multinationals may also have an impact on the market structure of host economies. Multinationals appear most commonly in concentrated industries, and there is some evidence that their presence may increase oligopolistic tendencies in markets. In Britain, however, the impact of foreign companies before 1945 was often to enhance rather than to limit competition. It is true that some product markets, such as that for sewing machines, were totally dominated by a foreign company. However, the merger boom of the 1920s led to certain sectors of British industry being controlled by one or two large British companies. In some of these industries foreign subsidiaries provided the main competition to the local giants, especially as their foreign ownership often made them less vulnerable to takeover by British firms. In the late 1920s, for example, ICI attempted to gain control of Clayton Aniline, 'so as to give ICI a closer approach to monopoly in the British dyestuffs industry', but the Swiss parent company resisted these overtures.[85] Sometimes, however, a foreign threat encouraged British firms to work together—as with the creation of Imperial Tobacco in 1901—and thus increased the degree of oligopoly.

Finally, much attention in post-1945 Britain has focused on the balance of payments effects of foreign multinationals. Before 1945 most foreign subsidiaries in Britain manufactured largely for the home market using local materials, which suggests a neutral impact on the balance of trade. Some foreign-owned companies did have an export business even in this early period. Clayton Aniline exported the bulk of its British production before 1914 to its Swiss parent, and Jönköping and Vulcan's London factory despatched all its matches to Australia before 1915.[86] In the interwar years Ford of England entered the export market. Dagenham manufactured many of the components of Ford cars produced in Germany until the advent of Hitler in 1933, and British-made Ford tractors were sold to many countries, including the United States.[87] Overall, it is impossible to generalize on the balance of payments impact from such scattered anecdotal evidence.

**IV**

The overall significance of foreign multinationals in British industry before the Second World War was limited. Few foreign-owned companies featured in the lists of the largest companies or the largest employers even in the 1930s. Yet the foreign impact on such industries as electrical engineering, telephone equipment, motor cars, domestic electrical appliances, and a range of foodstuffs and consumer products was clearly visible. Many of the fastest growing and/or high technology industries of pre-1945 Britain were sustained by substantial foreign direct investment. Foreign companies invested in Britain because they had a range of managerial, entrepreneurial, and technological advantages over local competitors, sufficiently large to encourage and facilitate their exploitation by direct investment. In industries such as rayon, where British companies possessed appropriate managerial structures and modern technologies, the impact of foreign multinationals on Britain was small, while British-based multinationals were active as direct investors in foreign markets. Location-specific factors such as trade barriers encouraged foreign firms to exploit their advantages by local manufacture in Britain rather than by exporting or licensing.

Given the diversity in the range of multinational activity as well as the data limitations, it would be facile to offer a definitive judgment on the impact of multinational enterprise on the British economy before 1945. Britain avoided the worst problems which can arise from multinational activity, such as technological dependency and threats to sovereignty. Foreign companies introduced new technologies, products, and marketing methods into British industry, and sometimes increased competition in oligopolistic markets. They created employment and probably improved some labour management practices. Capital flows into Britain, on the other hand, do not seem important. Nor did the British subsidiaries of American companies always provide models of managerial perfection for their domestic competitors to emulate. Contemporaries sometimes over-estimated the managerial superiority of the foreign companies in their midst. Overall, however, the evidence suggests more gains than losses to British industry from foreign multinational investment.

The ability of foreign companies to acquire leading positions in parts of British industry indicates inadequate indigenous management structures, enterprise, and technology in those sectors. The continuing attachment to the family firm was possibly an underlying cause of these problems. However, generalizations about British business failure even in these sectors need careful qualification. In chemicals and some other industries British companies proved to be skilled at acquiring superior foreign technologies under licence, keeping foreign enterprises at arm's length. The advantages of foreign companies in Britain were often not sustained. In the motor industry British firms in the interwar years overcame early foreign predominance. British managements on occasion captured the upper hand in joint ventures. Several subsidiaries of foreign companies were 'anglicized'. British entrepreneurs sometimes responded well once challenged. Reluctance to change, to introduce new methods, structures, and products has been a long-term problem for much of British manufacturing industry in the twentieth century. Foreign companies sometimes provided a catalyst which challenged British business to renewed vitality. It was, perhaps, in eliciting such responses that foreign multinationals had their most beneficial impact on British industry before 1945.

### Appendix I: Some Foreign Multinationals in British Manufacturing and Utilities before 1945

This appendix gives details of direct investments by foreign companies in British manufacturing and utilities before 1945. Each entry has been checked from more than one source, but the data on some entries are incomplete and the list cannot be regarded as comprehensive.

There were frequent changes of name by foreign parents and British subsidiaries over the period covered. In general the name of companies at the time of the initial investment has been given. If the name of the British subsidiary has been left blank, it can be assumed to have a title similar to its parent.

The 'start date for manufacturing' column gives the date when a foreign company acquired a British manufacturing company, or established a manufacturing operation in Britain. Occasionally firms made two investments which were entirely separate from one another (e.g. American companies no. 6, 12, 24, 33). These have been counted as *two* investments—for example, the total number of American investments is 67, even though only 63 firms are given. Companies established by foreign individuals are excluded, such as the British office manufacturing company established by the American immigrants, Burroughs and Wellcome in 1896. Purely marketing or sales companies are excluded. It was often difficult to give an exact date when a British company came under foreign 'control'. The U.S. Department of Commerce considers a foreign company 'controls' a domestic company if it holds at least 10 per cent of its equity, but I have preferred to use more subjective measures of when British companies came under, or passed from, foreign ownership and managerial control.

The 'date when manufacture ceased' column gives the date when a foreign company ceased to own and control a British manufacturing operation. If this operation was still in existence in 1945 the column has been left blank. The letters after the dates categorize the fate of the venture. Categories A, S, and W represent a transfer from foreign to British ownership and control; A = acquired by, or control shifted to, a British company, or the British partner in a joint venture; S = sequestrated by the British government; W = foreign company withdrew from British manufacturing, either by liquidating its British company, ceasing manufacturing, or selling the venture to individual (non-corporate) British investors; M = merged with another foreign company.

The 'plant location' column gives the location of the *initial* manufacturing plant in Britain. The location of later factories, and re-locations—such as Ford's move from Manchester to Dagenham—are not recorded. London is used loosely to cover a wide geographical area in and around the capital. The 'product' column gives the main product manufactured by the British subsidiary.

This appendix has been compiled from sources given in the footnotes, supplemented by *Moody's manual of investments*, reports of the Monopolies Commission, the *Stock Exchange year book*, and various British trade directories, especially the *Red book of commerce*.

| Parent | British subsidiary | Start date for manufacturing | Plant location | Date when manufacture ceased | Product |
|---|---|---|---|---|---|
| *1:1  United States companies* | | | | | |
| 1  S. Colt | Colt | 1853 | London | 1857W | firearms |
| 2  J. Ford | North British Rubber Co. | 1856 | Edinburgh | 1868W | rubber |
| 3  Singer | Singer Sewing Machines | 1867 | Glasgow | | sewing machines |
| 4  R. Hoe & Co. | R. Hoe & Co. | 1867 | London | | printing press |
| 5  American Radiator | National Radiator | 1895 | Hull | | radiators |
| 6  Diamond Match | Diamond Match | 1896 | Liverpool | 1901W | matches |
|    Diamond Match | Bryant and May | 1901 | London | 1914W | matches |
| 7  Western Electric | Fowler Waring Cable (STC 1925) | 1898 | London | | telecommunications |
| 8  United Shoe Machinery | British United Shoe Machinery | 1899 | Leicester | | boots and shoes |
| 9  Kodak | Kodak | 1899 | Harrow | | cameras |
| 10  Westinghouse Electric | British Westinghouse | 1899 | Manchester | 1917A | electrical machinery |
| 11  GEC | British Thomson Houston | 1901 | Rugby | 1928M | electrical machinery |
| 12  American Tobacco | Ogdens | 1901 | Liverpool | 1902W | tobacco |
|     American Tobacco | British American Tobacco | 1902 | | 1923A | tobacco |
| 13  Parke, Davis | Parke, Davis & Co. | 1902 | London | | patent medicine |
| 14  Columbia Graphophone | Columbia | 1905 | Surrey | 1923A | record cylinders |
| 15  H.J. Heinz | H.J. Heinz | 1905 | London | | food |
| 16  Horlicks Food Company | Horlicks Malted Milk Co. | 1907 | Slough | | soft drinks |
| 17  Mergenthaler Linotype | Linotype & Machinery | 1909 | Manchester | | typesetting machinery |
| 18  Ford | Ford | 1911 | Manchester | | motor cars |
| 19  American Chicle | | 1900s | London | 1923W | chewing gum |

| Parent | British subsidiary | Start date for manufacturing | Plant location | Date when manufacture ceased | Product |
|---|---|---|---|---|---|
| 20 Chicago Pneumatic Tool | Consolidated Pneumatic Tool | 1900s | Fraserburgh | | pneumatic tools |
| 21 Gillette | Gillette | 1900s | Slough | | safety razors |
| 22 United Drug | | 1912 | Notts | | pharmaceuticals |
| 23 Electric Storage Batteries | Chloride Electric and Storage Company | 1900s | Manchester | | storage batteries |
| 24 National Lead | William Harvey & Co. | 1916 | Liverpool | 1929A | tin smelting |
| National Lead | British Titanium Products | 1933 | Billingham | | titanium |
| 25 Drug Inc. | Boots | 1920 | Nottingham | 1933W | pharmaceuticals |
| 26 Theodore Cary | Automatic Telephone Manufacturing | 1920 | Liverpool | 1935W | telephone equipment |
| 27 Monsanto | Monsanto Chemicals | 1920 | Wales, Sunderland | | chemicals |
| 28 Victor Talking Machine | Gramophone Co. | 1921 | Middlesex | 1931A | records, gramophones |
| 29 Quaker Oats Co. | Quaker Oats Co. | 1920s | London | | food |
| 30 Shredded Wheat Co. | Shredded Wheat Co. | 1920s | Welwyn | | food |
| 31 Otis Elevator | Waywood Otis | 1924 | London | | lifts |
| 32 B.F. Goodrich | British Goodrich | 1924 | Burton | 1934W | rubber goods |
| 33 General Motors | | 1924 | London | | motor cars |
| General Motors | Vauxhall | 1925 | Luton | | motor cars |
| 34 Goodyear | Goodyear Tyre and Rubber | 1927 | Wolverhampton | | tyres |
| 35 Firestone | Firestone Tyre and Rubber | 1928 | London | | tyres |
| 36 American Home Products | W.L. Dodge, St Jacobs Oil, and others | 1926–9 | London | | pharmaceuticals |
| 37 American Tobacco | J. Wix & Sons | 1927 | London | | cigarettes |
| 38 American Timken | British Timken | 1927 | Birmingham, Northampton | | roller bearings |
| 39 Wm Wrigley Jr | Wrigley Products Ltd. | 1927 | London | | chewing gum |
| 40 Chesebrough Manufacturing Company | | 1920s | London | | proprietary medicines |
| 41 Colgate | | 1920s | London | | toiletries and soap |
| 42 Sterling Products | Scott and Turner | 1928 | Newcastle | | pharmaceuticals |
| 43 Utilities Power and Light | Edmundsons | 1929 | various | 1936W | electricity, utilities |
| 44 IBM | International Time Records | 1929 | London | | office equipment |
| 45 International Nickel | Mond Nickel | 1929 | Swansea | | nickel refining |
| 46 Yale and Towne | H. and T. Vaughan | 1929 | Staffs | | locks & keys |
| 47 Chrysler | | 1928 | London | | motor cars |
| 48 American Can | British Can | 1929 | London | 1931A | cans |
| 49 Proctor & Gamble | Thomas Hedley and Sons | 1930 | Newcastle | | soap |
| 50 Hoover | Hoover | 1931 | Middlesex | | domestic electrical applicances |

| Parent | British subsidiary | Start date for manufacturing | Plant location | Date when manufacture ceased | Product |
|---|---|---|---|---|---|
| 51 Standard Brands | Standard Brands | 1932 | Liverpool | | baking powder |
| 52 Bristol's Instruments | | 1932 | Dorset | | industrial instruments |
| 53 General Motors | Frigidaire | 1933 | London | | refrigerators |
| 54 Corn Products | Brown and Polson | 1930s | Paisley | | food |
| 55 N/A | British Laundry Machine Co. Ltd. | 1930s | | | laundry machines |
| 56 York Shippley | York Shippley | 1930s | London | | refrigerators |
| 57 Mars | | 1934 | Slough | | chocolate |
| 58 Du Pont (+ICI) | Nobel Chemical | 1935 | London | | chemicals |
| 59 Dennison Manufacturing | Dennison Manufacturing | 1930s | London | | packaging |
| 60 Champion Spark Plug | Champion Sparking Plugs | 1937 | London | | sparking plugs |
| 61 Armstrong Cork | Armstrong Cork | 1938 | | | cork |
| 62 United States Rubber | North British Rubber Co. | 1938 | Edinburgh | | rubber goods |
| 63 E.W. Bliss | E.W. Bliss (England) | 1939 | Derby | | metal-working machinery |

### 1:2  German companies

| Parent | British subsidiary | Start date for manufacturing | Plant location | Date when manufacture ceased | Product |
|---|---|---|---|---|---|
| 1 Siemens & Halske | Siemens Brothers | 1863 | London | 1916S | electrical machinery |
| 2 Vereinigte Rheinisch-Westphalische Pulverfabriken | Chilworth Gunpowder Co. | 1885 | London | 1915S | explosives |
| 3 Bayer + Agfa | Levinstein Ltd | 1890 | Manchester | 1895A | dyestuffs |
| 4 Mannesmann | British Mannesmann | 1899 | Llandore | 1916S | seamless tubes |
| 5 Bosch | Bosch Magneto | 1907 | London | 1916S | ignitors |
| 6 Hoechst/ Casselle/Kalle | Meiser Lucius & Brüning | 1907 | Liverpool | 1916S | dyestuffs |
| 7 BASF/Dreiband | Mersey Chemical | 1907 | Liverpool | 1916S | dyestuffs |
| 8 V.G.F. | British Glanzstoff | 1908 | Flint | 1916S | cuprammonium yarn |
| 9 Osram (+GEC) | Osram Lamp Works | 1908 | London | 1916A | electrical machinery |
| 10 Bayer | Bayer | 1900s | | 1916S | pharmaceuticals |
| 11 J.P. Bemberg | British Bemberg | 1926 | Doncaster | 1939S | cuprammonium yarn |
| 12 Nitsche and Gunther Optische Werke | Nitsche and Gunther | 1932 | London | 1939S | spectacle frames |
| 13 AEG (+ Westinghouse) | Westinghouse Ticket Machine | 1934 | | 1939S | machinery |
| 14 I.G. Farben (+ ICI) | Trafford Chemical | 1938 | Manchester | 1939S | dyestuffs |
| 15 I.G. Farben (+ Aluminium Corp) | Magnesium Metal Corporation | 1936 | | 1939S | magnesium |
| 16 I.G. Farben (+ Metallgesellschaft) | British Carbo-Union | 1930s | | 1939S | activated carbons |
| 17 Krupps | Tool Metal Manufacturing | 1939 | | 1939S | hard metal |

| Parent | British subsidiary | Start date for manufacturing | Plant location | Date when manufacture ceased | Product |
|--------|-------------------|------------------------------|----------------|-------------------------------|---------|
| *1:3 Swedish companies* | | | | | |
| 1 ASEA | Fuller Weström Manufacturing Co. | 1898 | London | | electrical equipment |
| 2 L.M. Ericsson (+ National Telephone) | L.M. Ericsson Manufacturing | 1903 | | | telephone and office equipment |
| 3 Jönköping & Vulcan | J. John Masters (after 1919) | 1910 | London | 1927A | matches |
| 4 SKF | Skefco Ball Bearing Co. | 1910 | Luton | | ball bearings |
| 5 Landis and Gyr | Landis and Gyr | 1912 | London | | electrical equipment |
| 6 Jungner | Batteries Ltd. | 1918 | Redditch | | accumulators/ mining lamps |
| 7 AGA | Gas Accumulator Co. | 1920s | London | | beacons, railway equipment |
| 8 C.E. Johansson | C.E. Johansson | 1920s | Coventry | 1923M | precision gauges |
| 9 ESAB | Anglo-Swedish Electric Welding | 1920s | | | electric welding |
| 10 Elektrolux | Electrolux | 1926 | Luton | | domestic electrical equipment |
| 11 Separator | Chadburn Ship Telegraph Co. | 1923 | | | machines |
| 12 Wicander | C.A. Greiner | 1937 | Middlesex | | cork, linoleum |
| 13 Altas Diesel | | 1939 | London | | diesel engines |
| *1:4 Danish companies* | | | | | |
| 1 Monsted | | 1888 | Manchester | 1914A | margarine |
| 2 Aahus Oliefabrik | Erith Oil Works | 1900s | London | 1918A | vegetable oils |
| 3 Hellesen's-enke | | interwar | London | | dry cell batteries |
| 4 F.L. Smith | | interwar | Luton | | rotary kilns |
| *1:5 Swiss companies* | | | | | |
| 1 Anglo-Swiss Condensed Milk | | 1872 | Chippenham | | condensed milk |
| 2 Nestlé | | 1901 | Tutbury | | condensed milk |
| 3 Hoffman La Roche | | 1909 | Welwyn | | pharmaceuticals |
| 4 Ciba | Clayton Aniline | 1911 | Manchester | | dyestuffs |
| 5 Sandoz | | 1911 | Bradford | | dyestuffs |
| *1:6 Dutch companies* | | | | | |
| 1 Jurgens | | 1917 | Purfleet | 1929A | margarine |
| 2 Van Den Bergh's | | 1917 | London | 1929A | margarine |
| 3 Enka | British Enka | 1925 | Liverpool | | viscose yarn |
| 4 Breda | Breda Visada | 1928 | Littleborough | | viscose yarn |
| 5 Philips | Mullard Radio Valve | 1924 | London | | domestic electrical equipment |
| *1:7 French companies* | | | | | |
| 1 Clément | Clément-Talbot | 1903 | London | 1919A | motor cars |
| 2 Lorraine-Dietrich | | 1907 | Birmingham | | motor cars |

| Parent | British subsidiary | Start date for manufacturing | Plant location | Date when manufacture ceased | Product |
|---|---|---|---|---|---|
| 3 Renault | Renault | 1927 | London | | motor cars |
| 4 Compagnie Générale des Etablissements Michelin | Michelin Tyre Co. | 1927 | Stoke | | tyres |
| 5 Poulenc Frères | May & Baker | 1927 | London | | fine chemicals |

*1:8  Italian companies*

| | | | | | |
|---|---|---|---|---|---|
| 1 Pirelli (+50% GEC 1918) | Pirelli General Cable Works | 1914 | Southampton | | cables |
| 2 Pirelli | Pirelli Ltd | 1924 | Burnton-on-Trent | | tyres |
| 3 N/A | Lincolnshire and Central Electricity Supply | 1936 | various | 1940S | electrical utility |

*Note* Pirelli's investments were controlled by Société Internationale Pirelli S.A. of Switzerland.

*1:9  Canadian companies*

| | | | | | |
|---|---|---|---|---|---|
| 1 Northern Aluminium | Northern Aluminium | 1928 | Birmingham | | aluminium |
| 2 Massey-Harris | | 1930s | Manchester | | agricultural implements |
| 3 George Weston Ltd | | 1934 | Edinburgh | | biscuits |
| 4 Hiram Walker | | 1937 | Dumbarton | | whisky and spirits distillers |

*1:10  Australian companies*

| | | | | | |
|---|---|---|---|---|---|
| 1 Nicholas | Aspro | 1925 | Slough | | pharmaceuticals |

*1:11  Czech companies*

| | | | | | |
|---|---|---|---|---|---|
| 1 Bata Company | British Shoe Co. (Bata) Ltd. | 1933 | Tilbury | 1939W | footwear |

# Notes

1. I would like to thank John H. Dunning, Howard Gospel, Hans Chr. Johansen, Jonathan Liebenau, Ragnhild Lundström, Mike Robson, Mira Wilkins, the participants in seminars at Cambridge, Edinburgh and Glasgow, and two anonymous referees for their help in preparing this article.

A multinational is defined broadly in this article as an enterprise possessing a controlling interest in income-generating assets or productive activities outside its national boundaries.

2. Dunning, *American investment* was a pioneering study of this subject. Wilkins, *Emergence* and *idem, Maturing* provided valuable new information on American companies in Britain.

3. Dunning, *American investment*, pp. 32–44; Law, *British regional development*, p. 174.

4. Wilkins, *Emergence*, pp. 29, 30, 39–42; Blakemore, 'Colt's London armoury'; Davies, *Peacefully working*, pp. 42–4; Hounshell, *From the American system*, pp. 18–25, 92–6.

5. Scott, *Siemens brothers*, chs. 3 and 4.

6. Heer, *World events*, pp. 57, 67, 79, 89.

7. Lundström, 'Swedish multinational growth', pp. 137, 143; Lindgren, *Corporate growth*, p. 168.

8. H.C. Johansen, 'Danmark pa de multinationale selskabers landkort for 1914' (unpublished paper, 1986).

9. Laux, *In first gear*, pp. 44, 105, 165. Maxcy, *The multinational motor industry*, p. 64.

10. B. Bezza, 'L'activité multinationale de la Pirelli, 1883–1914', paper presented to a conference on 'The early phase of multinational enterprise in Germany, France, and Italy', held at the European University Institute, Florence, 17–19 Oct. 1984.

11. Wilkins, *Maturing*, chs. 4 and 8.

12. Lundström, 'Swedish multinational growth', p. 139; Coleman, *Courtaulds*, II, p. 265.

13. Wilson, *Unilever*, II, pp. 174, 254, 257, 259–60.

14. Slinn, *May & Baker*, pp. 97–9.

15. Scott, *Siemens Brothers*, p. 92. See also Teichova, 'The Mannesmann concern', p. 107.

16. Reader, *ICI*, I, pp. 126–7, 179–82.

17. Dunning, 'Changes in the level and structure of international production', p. 188.

18. Dunning, *American investment*, pp. 32, 44. Wilkins, *Maturing*, p. 185. I have converted dollars into sterling at £1 = $4.86 in 1900 and 1929, $3.40 in 1932 and $4.03 in 1940.

19. P.R.O., Board of Trade files, BT 8/11, Shares etc. held in British companies by alien enemies under Section 3 (ii) Trading with the Enemy Amendment Act 1914.

20. BT/80/12, Departmental meeting, 17 June 1945.

21. Hannah, *Rise of the corporate economy*, pp. 102–3, 187–90, 116.

22. There is a clear account of the corporate structure of the pre-1914 industry in Byatt, *The British electrical industry*, pp. 136–58. For the shifts in ownership see Jones and Marriott, *Anatomy of a merger*, esp. chs. 3 and 5; Davenport-Hines, *Dudley Docker*, pp. 157–8, 178–80.

23. Scott, *Siemens Brothers*, p. 87; Jones and Marriott, *Anatomy of a merger*, ch. 7.

24. Dunning, *American investment*, p. 40.

25. Corley, *Domestic electrical appliances*, pp. 31–5.

26. Hannah, *Electricity before nationalization*, p. 228.

27. Ibid., p. 290. P.R.O., Ministry of Power, POWE 14/15 Memorandum of 16 May 1940.

28. Wilkins and Hill, *American business abroad, passim*; Church and Miller, 'The big three'.

29. Hertner, 'German multinational enterprise', p. 124; Reader, *ICI*, I, p. 266.

30. Haber, *Chemical industry*, pp. 166–7. On the German and Swiss dyestuff companies in Britain see also *Hoechst in England*; Abrahart, *Clayton Aniline Company*; and Hertner, 'Fallstudien zu deutschen multinationalen Unternehmen', p. 27.

31. Gribben (ed.), *Survey of international cartels*, p. 85.
32. Edgerton, 'Industrial research in the British photographic industry'.
33. Hunt, 'Weston', pp. 753–4.
34. Chapman, *Jesse Boot*, ch. 7.
35. Jones, 'The Gramophone Company', pp. 91–8.
36. Hildebrand, *Expansion*, p. 25.
37. Cochran, *Big business in China*, pp. 3, 164.
38. Hildebrand, *Expansion*, p. 85.
39. Wilson, *Unilever*, II, pp. 301–8.
40. Hood and Young, *Economics of multinational enterprise*, ch. 2 provides a good introduction to theories of the multinational enterprise. See also Dunning, *International production*, chs. 2–4.
41. Chandler, 'Emergence of managerial capitalism', pp. 496–7.
42. Colemand and Macleod, 'Attitudes to new techniques'.
43. Dunning, *American investment*, pp. 264–5.
44. Reader, *ICI*, I, pp. 261–2.
45. Elbaum and Lazonick, 'An institutional perspective on British decline', p. 3.
46. Jones, ed., *British multinationals*.
47. Heer, *World events*, p. 56; Lundström, 'Swedish multinational growth', p. 143.
48. Jones, 'Origins, management and performance', pp. 8–9.
49. Young, *Power of speech*, p. 12.
50. Wilkins, *Emergence*, pp. 91–2.
51. Lindgren, *Corporate growth*, pp. 46, 168.
52. Wilkins, *Maturing*, pp. 73–5.
53. Dunning, *American investment*, p. 33.
54. Lundström, 'Swedish multinational growth', p. 148.
55. Southard, *American industry in Europe*, p. 134.
56. Hounshell, *From the American system*, p. 93; Davies, *Peacefully working*, pp. 44–5.
57. Davies, *Peacefully working*, p. 79.
58. Fridenson, 'Growth of multinational activities', p. 161.
59. Wilkins, *Maturing*, pp. 171, 184–5.
60. *News Chronicle*, 7 Sept. 1945.
61. Foreman-Peck, 'American challenge', p. 878.
62. Byatt, *British electrical industry*, pp. 151, 195; Davenport-Hines, *Dudley Docker*, p. 156.
63. I would like to thank Jonathan Liebenau and Mike Robson for allowing me to see the results of their research in the Ciba and Sandoz archives in Switzerland.
64. Alford, *Wills*.
65. Lewchuk, 'Return to capital', p. 18.
66. Southard, *American industry*, p. 146.
67. Fridenson, 'Growth of multinational activities', p. 158.
68. Heer, *World events*, p. 100.
69. Wilkins, *Maturing*, pp. 139–40; Wilkins and Hill, *American business abroad*, pp. 143–4.
70. Byatt, *British electrical industry*, p. 195.
71. Wilkins, *Maturing*, p. 84; Edgerton, 'Industrial research'.
72. Hannah, *Electricity*, pp. 231–3.
73. Wilkins and Hill, *American business abroad*, p. 291; Church, 'Effects of American multinationals', p. 117.
74. Reader, *ICI*, II, pp. 506–13; Reader, *Metal Box*, p. 54; Foreman-Peck,

'American challenge', p. 871. For the pre-1914 period see Saul, 'American impact'.
75. Dunning, *American investment*, p. 36.
76. Shaw, 'Large manufacturing employers of 1907'.
77. Dunning, *American investment*, p. 44.
78. Johnman, 'Large manufacturing companies of 1935'.
79. For the experience of the motor car industry, see Lewchuk, 'Fordism'.
80. I owe this point to Howard Gospel.
81. Hannah, *Inventing retirement*, pp. 34–7.
82. Gospel, 'Employers' organizations'.
83. Byatt, *British electrical industry*, p. 195.
84. Law, *British regional development*, pp. 174–7.
85. Reader, *ICI*, II, pp. 187–8.
86. Haber, *Chemical industry*, p. 149; Lindgren, *Corporate growth*, p. 169.
87. Wilkins and Hill, *American business abroad*, pp. 247, 304.


## Footnote References

Abrahart, E.N., *The Clayton Aniline Company Ltd* (Manchester, 1976)
Alford, B.W.E., *W.D. and H.O. Wills and the development of the U.K. tobacco industry, 1786–1965* (1973).
Blakemore, H.L., 'Colt's London armoury', in S.B. Saul, ed., *Technological change: the United States and Britain in the nineteenth century* (1970), pp. 171–95.
Byatt, I.C., *The British electrical industry, 1875–1914* (Oxford, 1979).
Chandler, A.D., 'The emergence of managerial capitalism', *Bus. Hist. Rev.*, 58 (1984), pp. 473–503.
Chapman, S.D., *Jesse Boot of Boots the chemists* (1974).
Church, R. and Miller, M., 'The big three: competition, management, and marketing in the British motor industry, 1922–1939', in B. Supple, ed., *Essays in British business history* (Oxford, 1977), pp. 163–86.
Church, R., 'The effects of American multinationals on the British motor industry, 1911–83', in A. Teichova, M. Lévy-Leboyer, and H. Nussbaum, eds., *Multinational enterprise in historical perspective* (Cambridge, 1986), pp. 116–30.
Cochran, S., *Big business in China* (Cambridge, Mass., 1980).
Coleman, D.C., *Courtaulds: an economic and social history*, 2 vols. (Oxford, 1969).
Coleman, D.C. and Macleod, C., 'Attitudes to new techniques: British businessmen, 1800–1950', *Econ. Hist. Rev.*, 2nd ser., xxxix (1986), pp. 588–611.
Corley, T.A.B., *Domestic electrical appliances* (1966).
Davenport-Hines, R.P.T., *Dudley Docker* (Cambridge, 1984).
Davies, R.B., *Peacefully working to conquer the world* (New York, 1976).
Dunning, J.H., *American investment in British manufacturing industry* (1958).
Dunning, J.H., *International production and the multinational enterprise* (1981).
Dunning, J.H., 'Changes in the level and structure of international production: the last one hundred years', in M. Casson, ed., *The growth of international business* (1983), pp. 84–139.
Edgerton, D.E.H., 'Industrial research in the British photographic industry, 1879–1939', in J. Liebenau, eds., *The challenge of new technology* (Aldershot, 1988), pp. 106–34.
Elbaum, B. and Lazonick, W., 'An institutional perspective on British decline', in B. Elbaum and W. Lazonick, eds., *The decline of the British economy* (Oxford, 1986), pp. 1–17.

Foreman-Peck, J., 'The American challenge of the twenties: multinationals and the European motor industry', *J. Econ. Hist.*, XLII (1982), pp. 865–81.

Fridenson, P., 'The growth of multinational activities in the French motor industry, 1890–1979', in P. Hertner and G. Jones, eds., *Multinationals: theory and history* (Aldershot, 1986).

Gospel, H.F., 'Employers' organisations: their growth and function in the British system of industrial relations in the period 1918–39' (unpublished Ph.D. thesis, University of London, 1974).

Gribben, J.D., ed., *Survey of international cartels* (1976).

Haber, L., *The chemical industry during the nineteenth century* (Oxford, 1958).

Haber, L., *The chemical industry, 1900–1930* (Oxford, 1971).

Hannah, L., *Electricity before nationalisation* (1979).

Hannah, L., *The rise of the corporate economy* (1983).

Hannah, L., *Inventing retirement* (Cambridge, 1986).

Heer, J., *World events, 1866–1966: the first hundred years of Nestlé* (Rivaz, 1966).

Hertner, P., 'Fallstudien zu deutschen multinationalen Unternehmen vor dem Ersten Weltkrieg', in N. Horn and J. Kocka, eds., *Law and the formation of the big enterprises in the nineteenth and early twentieth centuries* (Göttingen, 1979), pp. 388–419.

Hertner, P., 'German multinational enterprise before 1914: some case studies', in P. Hertner and G. Jones, eds., *Multinationals: theory and history* (Aldershot, 1986), pp. 113–34.

Hildebrand, K.-G., *Expansion, crisis, reconstruction, 1917–1939* (Stockholm, 1985).

*Hoechst in England, 1901–1914* (Frankfurt, 1971).

Hood, N. and Young, S. *The economics of multinational enterprise* (1979).

Hounshell, D.A., *From the American system to mass production, 1800–1932* (Baltimore, 1984).

Hunt, S., 'Williard Garfield Weston', in D.J. Jeremy and C. Shaw, eds., *Dictionary of business biography*, vol. 5 (1986), pp. 752–8.

Johnman, L., 'The large manufacturing companies of 1935', *Bus. Hist.*, XXVIII (1986), pp. 226–45.

Jones, G., ed., *British multinationals: origins, management and performance* (Aldershot, 1986).

Jones, G., 'The Gramophone Company: an Anglo-American multinational, 1898–1931', *Bus. Hist. Rev.*, 59 (1985), pp. 76–100.

Jones, G., 'Origins, management and performance', in *idem.*, ed., *British multinationals: origins, management and performance* (Aldershot, 1986), pp. 1–23.

Jones, R. and Marriott, O., *Anatomy of a merger. A history of G.E.C., A.E.I. and English Electric* (1970).

Laux, J.M., *In first gear: the French automobile industry to 1914* (Liverpool, 1976).

Law, C.M., *British regional development since World War I* (Newton Abbot, 1980).

Lewchuk, W., 'Fordism and British motor car employers, 1896–1932', in H.F. Gospel and C.R. Littler, eds., *Managerial strategies and industrial relations: an historical and comparative study* (1983), pp. 82–110.

Lewchuk, W., 'The return to capital in the British motor vehicle industry, 1896–1939', *Bus. Hist.*, XXVII (1985), pp. 3–25.

Lindgren, H., *Corporate growth. The Swedish match industry in its global setting* (Stockholm, 1979).

Lundström, R., 'Swedish multinational growth before 1930', in P. Hertner and G. Jones, eds., *Multinationals: theory and history* (Aldershot, 1986), pp. 135–56.

Maxcy, G., *The multinational motor industry* (1981)

Reader, W.J., *Imperial Chemical Industries: a history*, 2 vols. (1970, 1975).

Reader, W.J., *Metal Box: a history* (1976).

Saul, S.B., 'The American impact on British industry, 1895–1914', *Bus. Hist.*, III (1960), pp. 19–38.

Scott, J.D., *Siemens Brothers, 1858–1958* (1958).

Shaw, C., 'The large manufacturing employers of 1907', *Bus. Hist.*, XXV (1983), pp. 42–60.

Slinn, J., *A history of May and Baker, 1834–1984* (Cambridge, 1984).

Southard, F.A., *American industry in Europe* (New York, 1931).

Teichova, A., 'The Mannesmann concern in east central Europe in the interwar period', in A. Teichova and P.L. Cottrell, eds., *International business and central Europe, 1918–1939* (Leicester, 1983), pp. 103–37.

Wilkins, M. and Hill, F.E., *American business abroad: Ford on six continents* (Detroit, 1964).

Wilkins, M., *The emergence of multinational enterprise* (Cambridge, Mass., 1970).

Wilkins, M., *The maturing of multinational enterprise* (Cambridge, Mass., 1974).

Wilson, C., *The history of Unilever*, 2 vols. (1954).

Young, P., *Power of speech: a history of Standard Telephone and Cables, 1883–1983* (1983).

# Select Bibliography

Armstrong, Christopher and H.V. Nelles, *Southern Exposure: Canadian Promoters in Latin America and the Carribbean, 1896–1930* (Toronto, University of Toronto Press, 1988).

Brown, Jonathan C., "Why foreign oil companies shifted their production from Mexico to Venezuela during the 1920s", *American Historical Review*, 90 (1985), pp. 362–385.

——— , "Domestic politics and foreign investment: British development of Mexican petroleum, 1899–1911", *Business History Review*, 61 (1987), pp. 387–416.

Brown, S.R. "The transfer of technology to China in the nineteenth century: the role of foreign direct investment", *Journal of Economic History*, XXXIX (1979), pp. 181–197.

Buckley, Peter J. and Brian Roberts, *European Direct Investment in the USA before World War I* (London, Macmillan, 1982).

Carlos, Anne and Stephen Nicholas, "Giants of an earlier capitalism: the chartered trading companies as modern multinationals", *Business History Review*, 62 (1988), pp. 398–419.

Casson, M., ed., *The Growth of International Business* (London, Allen and Unwin, 1983).

Casson, M., "Contractual arrangements for technology transfer: new evidence from business history", *Business History*, XXVIII (1986), pp. 5–35.

Chandler, A.D., *Strategy and Structure* (Cambridge, Mass., Harvard University Press, 1962).

——— , *The Visible Hand* (Cambridge, Mass., Harvard University Press, 1977).

——— , "The growth of the transnational industrial firm in the United States and the United Kingdom: a comparative analysis", *Economic History Review*, XXXIII (1980), pp. 396–410.

——— , "The evolution of modern global competition", in Michael E. Porter, ed., *Competition in Global Industries* (Boston, Mass., Harvard Business School Press, 1986), pp. 405–448.

——— , *Scale and Scope* (Cambridge, Mass., Harvard University Press, 1990).

Chapman, S.D., "British-based investment groups before 1914", *Economic History Review*, XXXVIII (1985), pp. 230–251.

Cheape, Charles, "Not politicians but sound businessmen: Norton Company and the Third Reich", *Business History Review*, 62 (1988), pp. 444–466.

Davenport-Hines, R.P.T., "Vickers' Balkan conscience: aspects of Anglo-Romanian armaments, 1918–1939", *Business History*, XXV (1983), pp. 287–319.

—— and Geoffrey Jones, eds., *British Business in Asia since 1860* (Cambridge, Cambridge University Press, 1989).

Dunning, J.H., *American Investment in British Manufacturing Industry* (London, Allen and Unwin, 1958).

—— , "Changes in the level and structure of international production: the last one hundred years", in Mark Casson, ed., *The Growth of International Business* (London, Allen and Unwin, 1983), pp. 84–139.

—— and Howard Archer, "The eclectic paradigm and the growth of UK multi-national enterprise 1870–1983", *Business and Economic History*, 16 (1987), pp. 19–49.

Eakin, Marshall C. *British Enterprise in Brazil* (Durham, Duke University Press, 1989).

Feinstein, Charles, "Britain's overseas investments in 1913", *Economic History Review*, XLIII (1990), pp. 280–295.

Ferrier, R.W., *The History of the British Petroleum Company* (Cambridge, Cambridge University Press, 1982).

Fieldhouse, D.K., *Unilever Overseas* (Beckenham, Croom Helm, 1978).

Franko, L., *The European Multinationals* (London, Harper and Row, 1976).

—— , "The origins of multinational manufacturing by continental European firms", *Business History Review*, XLVIII (1974), pp. 272–302.

Fridenson, P., "The growth of multinational activities in the French motor industry 1890–1979", in Peter Hertner and G. Jones, eds., *Multinationals: Theory and History* (Aldershot, Gower, 1986), pp. 157–168.

Harvey, Charles and Jon Press, "The City and international mining 1870–1914", *Business History*, XXXII (1990), pp. 98–119.

Harvey, Charles and P. Taylor, "Mineral wealth and economic development: foreign direct investment in Spain, 1851–1913", *Economic History Review*, XL (1987), pp. 185–207.

Hennart, J.F., "Internationalisation in practice: early foreign direct investment in Malaysian tin mining", *Journal of International Business Studies*, 17 (1986), pp. 131–143.

—— , "Transaction costs and the multinational enterprise: the case of tin", *Business and Economic History*, 16 (1987), pp. 147–159.

Hertner, Peter, "Fallstudien zu deutschen multinationalen Unternehmen vor dem ersten Weltkrieg", in N. Horn and J. Kocka, eds., *Law and Formation of the Big Enterprises in the 19th and early 20th Centuries* (Göttingen, Vandenhoeck and Ruprecht, (1979), pp. 388–419.

—— , *Il capitale tedesco in Italia dall'unità alla prima guerra mondiale. Banche miste e sviluppo economico italiano* (Bologna, Il Mulino, 1984).

—— , "German multinational enterprise before 1914: some case studies", in Peter Hertner and G. Jones, eds., *Multinationals: Theory and History* (Aldershot, Gower, 1986), pp. 113–134.

—— and G. Jones, eds. *Multinationals: Theory and History* (Aldershot, Gower, 1986).

—— , ed., *Per la storia dell'imprese multinazionale in Europa* (Milan, Franco Angeli, 1987).

Jones, Charles A., *International Business in the Nineteenth Century* (Brighton, Wheatsheaf, 1987).

Jones, G. *The State and the Emergence of the British Oil Industry* (London, Macmillan, 1981).

——— , "Lombard Street on the Riviera: the British clearing banks and Europe, 1900–1960", *Business History*, XXIV (1982) pp. 186–210.

——— , "The expansion of British multinational manufacturing, 1890–1939", in A. Okochi and T. Inoue, eds., *Overseas Business Activities* (Tokyo, University of Tokyo Press, 1984), pp. 125–153.

——— , "The growth and performance of British multinational firms before 1939: the case of Dunlop", *Economic History Review*, XXXVI (1984), pp. 35–53.

——— , "Multinational chocolate: Cadbury overseas 1918–1939", *Business History*, XXVI (1984), pp. 59–76.

——— , "The Gramophone Company: an Anglo-American multinational, 1898–1931", *Business History Review*, 59 (1985), pp. 76–100.

——— , ed., *British Multinationals: Origins, Management and Performance* (Aldershot, Gower, 1986).

———, *Banking and Empire in Iran* (Cambridge, Cambridge University Press, 1986).

——— , "The performance of British multinational enterprise, 1890–1945", in Peter Hertner and G. Jones, eds., *Multinationals: Theory and History* (Aldershot, Gower, 1986), pp. 96–112.

——— , *Banking and Oil* (Cambridge, Cambridge University Press, 1987).

——— , "The Imperial Bank of Iran and Iranian economic development 1890–1952", *Business and Economic History*, 16 (1987), pp. 69–80.

——— , "Foreign multinationals and British industry before 1945", *Economic History Review*, XLI (1988), pp. 429–453.

——— , "The British Government and foreign multinationals before 1970", in M. Chick, ed., *Governments, Industries and Markets* (Aldershot, Edward Elgar, 1990), pp. 194–214.

——— , ed., *Banks as Multinationals* (London, Routledge, 1990).

——— , ed., *Multinational and International Banking* (Aldershot, Edward Elgar, 1992).

Kawabe, N., "Development of overseas operations by general trading companies 1868–1945", in S. Yonekawa and H. Yoshihara, eds., *Business History of General Trading Companies* (Tokyo, University of Tokyo Press, 1987), pp. 71–103.

——— , "With reservations: prewar Japan as host to Western Electric and ITT", in T. Yuzawa and M. Udgawa, eds., *Foreign Business in Japan before World War II* (Tokyo, University of Tokyo Press, 1990), pp. 175–192.

Mason, Mark, "Foreign direct investment and Japanese economic development, 1899–1931", *Business and Economic History*, 16 (1987), pp. 93–107.

McDowall, Duncan, *The Light: Brazilian Traction, Light and Power Company Limited, 1899–1945* (Toronto, University of Toronto Press, 1988).

Mejcher, Helmut, "Banking and the German oil industry, 1890–1939", in R.W. Ferrier and A. Fursenko, eds., *Oil in the World Economy* (London, Routledge, 1989), pp. 94–106.

Merret, David, *ANZ Bank* (Sydney, Allen and Unwin, 1985).

Nicholas, S., "British multinational investment before 1939", *Journal of European Economic History*, II (1982), pp. 605–630.

——— , "Agency contracts, institutional modes, and the transition to foreign direct investment by British manufacturing multinationals before 1939", *Journal of Economic History*, 43 (1983), pp. 675–686.

——— , "Locational choice, performance and the growth of British multinational firms", *Business History*, XXXI (1989), pp. 122–141.

O'Brien, Thomas F., "Rich beyond the dreams of avarice: the Guggenheims in

Chile", *Business History Review,* 63 (1989), pp. 122–159.

Okochi, A. and T. Inoue, eds., *Overseas Business Activities* (Tokyo, University of Tokyo Press, 1984).

Platt, D.C.M., "British portfolio investment before 1870: some doubts", *Economic History Review,* XXXIII (1980), pp. 1–16.

——— , *Britain's Investment Overseas on the Eve of the First World War* (London, Macmillan, 1986).

Purcell, W.R., "The development of Japan's trading company network in Australia 1890–1941", *Australian Economic History Review,* XXI (1981), pp. 114–132.

Safarian, A.E., *Foreign Ownership of Canadian Industry* (New York, McGraw-Hill, 1966).

Schmitz, C., "The rise of big business in the world copper industry, 1870–1930", *Economic History Review,* XXXIX (1986), pp. 392–410.

Schröter, Harm G. "Risk and control in multinational enterprise: German businesses in Scandinavia, 1918–1939", *Business History Review,* 62 (1988), pp. 420–443.

——— , "Die Auslandsinvestitionen der deutschen chemischen Industrie 1870 bis 1930", *Zeitschrift für Unternehmensgeschichte,* 35 (1990), pp. 1–22.

Sluyterman, Keetie E., "Onderzoek van historici naar multinationale ornderne-mingen", *Orgaan voor de economicsche geschiedenis in Nederland,* 4 (1990), pp. 73–87.

Southard, F.A., *American Industry in Europe* (Boston, Houghton-Mifflin, 1931).

Stanton, J., "Protection, market structure and firm behaviour: inefficiency in the early Australian tyre industry", *Australian Economic History Review,* XXIV (1984), pp. 91–113.

Stopford, J.M., "The origins of British-based multinational manufacturing enterprises", *Business History Review,* XLVIII (1974), pp. 303–345.

Svedberg, P., "The portfolio-direct composition of private foreign investment in 1914 revisited", *Economic Journal,* LXXX (1978), pp. 763–777.

Taylor, Graham D., "Management relations in a multinational enterprise: the case of Canadian Industries Limited, 1928–1948", *Business History Review,* LV (1981), pp. 337–358.

Teichova, Alice and P.L. Cottrell, eds., *International Business and Central Europe 1918–1939* (Leicester, Leicester University Press, 1983).

Teichova, A., M. Levy-Leboyer and H. Nussbaum, eds., *Historical Studies in International Corporate Business* (Cambridge, Cambridge University Press, 1989).

Transnational Corporations and Management Division, *World Investment Report 1992: Transnational Corporations as Engines of Growth* (New York, United Nations, 1992).

Trebilcock, C., "British multinationals in Japan 1900–41: Vickers, Armstrong, Nobel and the defense sector", in T. Yuzawa and M. Udagawa, eds., *Foreign Business in Japan before World War II* (Tokyo, University of Tokyo Press, 1990), pp. 87–111.

Udagawa, M., "Business management and foreign-affiliated companies in Japan before World War II" in T. Yuzawa and M. Udagawa, eds., *Foreign Business in Japan before World War II* (Tokyo, University of Tokyo Press, 1990), pp. 1–30.

UNCTC, *World Investment Report 1991: The Triad in Foreign Direct Investment* (New York, United Nations, 1991).

Wavre, Pierre-Alain, "Swiss investments in Italy from the XVIIIth to the XXth century", *Journal of European Economic History,* 17 (1988), pp. 85–102.

West, Douglas C., "From T-square to T-plan: the London office of the J. Walter

Thompson Advertising Agency, 1919–70", *Business History*, 29 (1987), pp. 199–217.

——— , "Multinational competition in the British advertising agency business, 1936–1987", *Business History Review*, 62 (1988), pp. 467–501.

Wilkins, M., *The Emergence of Multinational Enterprise* (Cambridge, Mass., Harvard University Press, 1970).

——— , *The Maturing of Multinational Enterprise* (Cambridge, Mass., Harvard University Press, 1974).

——— , "The role of private business in the international diffusion of technology", *Journal of Economic History*, 34 (1974), pp. 166–188.

——— , "American–Japanese direct foreign investment relationships, 1930–1952", *Business History Review*, 56 (1982), pp. 497–518.

——— , "Defining a firm: history and theory", in P. Hertner and G. Jones, eds., *Multinationals: Theory and History* (Aldershot, Gower, 1986), pp. 80–95.

——— , "Japanese multinational enterprise before 1914", *Business History Review*, 60 (1986), pp. 199–231.

——— , "The history of European multinationals: a new look", *The Journal of European Economic History*, XV (1986), pp. 483–510.

——— , "The free-standing company, 1870–1914: an important type of British foreign direct investment", *Economic History Review*, XLI (1988), pp. 259–285.

——— , "European and North American multinationals, 1870–1914: comparisons and contrasts", *Business History*, XXX (1988), pp. 8–45.

———, *The History of Foreign Investment in the United States to 1914* (Cambridge, Mass., Harvard University Press, 1989).

———, "Japanese Multinationals in the United States: Continuity and Change, 1879–1990", *Business History Review*, 64 (1990), pp. 585–629.

Yonekawa, S., "The formation of general trading companies: a comparative study", *Japanese Yearbook on Business History* (Tokyo, Japan Business History Institute, 1985), pp. 1–31.

Yuzawa, T. and M. Ugadawa, eds., *Foreign Business in Japan before World War II* (Tokyo, University of Tokyo Press, 1990).

# Name index

# Subject index

absorption gap 287–8, 299–300 (n9)
acquisition 80–1, 92, 98, 101, 103
administration 95, 101, 102, 182, 215
advertising 214, 408
affiliated firms 165
African copperbelt 225, 231, 239
agencies: buying and selling 167–8; commission 168, 195, 196; contracts 196–9; costs 197, 200–1; networks 198; opportunism 195, 198; payments system 198; and sales subsidiaries 113, 191, 193, 194, 197–8
agent-principal theory 194–9
AIV process, fodder 267
Alien Property Custodian 116, 117
alluvial deposits, tin 247, 252
antitrust policies 28, 149, 368, 379
asset-specificity 217, 220 (n33)
Australia 11, 172–3, 231
Austria 40
Austro-Hungarian MNEs 44
automobile assembly 389, 390
automobile industry 4, 116, 402, 406, 408, 412, 413

backwards integration 31, 37
bad debts 198
bakery 407
balance of payments, MNEs 415
banks: Belgium 42; German 27, 36, 37–8, 123–4; Japanese 143, 146–8, 150–1; Swedish 27, 42; Swiss 43; transnational 12; US 37–9

bargaining skills 372, 376–9, 379–81
Basque business community 343, 357–8
bean oil 140
Belgium 3, 42–3
Bolivia, tin 251, 252–4, 255
bonding 195, 196
borax 32–3
branch offices 93, 168, 200; see also sales agencies
brand names 75, 110, 114, 408
brewery mergers 100
Britain: see UK
British Empire 5–6, 71
British Institute of Management 72
British subsidiaries 5, 65, 67, 404–5, 407, 417–22
Bulgaria, MNEs 44
Burma, tin 246
business/government relations 266, 307–8, 331–2

caliche 315, 317
camphor 183
Canada 13, 44, 367–83
capital markets 249
car industry: see automobile industry
cartels: Canada 369; as defence mechanism 270–1; dyestuffs 268; German 39–40, 192, 257, 259, 263, 266–7, 276; international 71, 276, 367, 368, 381, 403; and MNEs 216–17; nitrogen 273–4; political influences 272–4
charcoal 114